Cross-Platform GUI Programming with wxWidgets

BRUCE PERENS' OPEN SOURCE SERIES

www.prenhallprofessional.com/perens

Bruce Perens' Open Source Series is a definitive series of books on Linux and open source technologies, written by many of the world's leading open source professionals. It is also a voice for up-and-coming open source authors. Each book in the series is published under the Open Publication License (www.opencontent.org), an open source compatible book license, which means that electronic versions will be made available at no cost after the books have been in print for six months.

- *Java™ Application Development on Linux®*
  Carl Albing and Michael Schwarz
- *C++ GUI Programming with Qt 3*
  Jasmin Blanchette and Mark Summerfield
- *Managing Linux Systems with Webmin: System Administration and Module Development*
  Jamie Cameron
- *User Mode Linux®*
  Jeff Dike
- *An Introduction to Design Patterns in C++ with Qt 4*
  Alan Ezust and Paul Ezust
- *Understanding the Linux Virtual Memory Manager*
  Mel Gorman
- *PHP 5 Power Programming*
  Andi Gutmans, Stig Bakken, and Derick Rethans
- *Linux® Quick Fix Notebook*
  Peter Harrison
- *Implementing CIFS: The Common Internet File System*
  Christopher Hertel
- *Open Source Security Tools: A Practical Guide to Security Applications*
  Tony Howlett
- *Apache Jakarta Commons: Reusable Java™ Components*
  Will Iverson
- *Linux® Patch Management: Keeping Linux® Systems Up To Date*
  Michael Jang
- *Embedded Software Development with eCos*
  Anthony Massa
- *Rapid Application Development with Mozilla*
  Nigel McFarlane
- *Subversion Version Control: Using the Subversion Version Control System in Development Projects*
  William Nagel
- *Intrusion Detection with SNORT: Advanced IDS Techniques Using SNORT, Apache, MySQL, PHP, and ACID*
  Rafeeq Ur Rehman
- *Cross-Platform GUI Programming with wxWidgets*
  Julian Smart and Kevin Hock with Stefan Csomor
- *Samba-3 by Example, Second Edition: Practical Exercises to Successful Deployment*
  John H. Terpstra
- *The Official Samba-3 HOWTO and Reference Guide, Second Edition*
  John H. Terpstra and Jelmer R. Vernooij, Editors
- *Self-Service Linux®: Mastering the Art of Problem Determination*
  Mark Wilding and Dan Behman
- *AJAX: Creating Web Pages with Asynchronous JavaScript and XML*
  Edmond Woychowsky

Cross-Platform GUI Programming with wxWidgets

Julian Smart and Kevin Hock
with Stefan Csomor

PRENTICE
HALL
PTR

Upper Saddle River, NJ • Boston • Indianapolis • San Francisco
New York • Toronto • Montreal • London • Munich • Paris
Madrid • Capetown • Sydney • Tokyo • Singapore • Mexico City

Many of the designations used by manufacturers and sellers to distinguish their products are claimed as trademarks. Where those designations appear in this book, and the publisher was aware of a trademark claim, the designations have been printed with initial capital letters or in all capitals.

The authors and publisher have taken care in the preparation of this book, but make no expressed or implied warranty of any kind and assume no responsibility for errors or omissions. No liability is assumed for incidental or consequential damages in connection with or arising out of the use of the information or programs contained herein.

The publisher offers excellent discounts on this book when ordered in quantity for bulk purchases or special sales, which may include electronic versions and/or custom covers and content particular to your business, training goals, marketing focus, and branding interests. For more information, please contact:

U. S. Corporate and Government Sales
(800) 382-3419
corpsales@pearsontechgroup.com

For sales outside the U. S., please contact:

International Sales
international@pearsoned.com

 This Book Is Safari Enabled

The Safari Enabled icon on the cover of your favorite technology book means the book is available through Safari Bookshelf. When you buy this book, you get free access to the online edition for 45 days. Safari Bookshelf is an electronic reference library that lets you easily search thousands of technical books, find code samples, download chapters, and access technical information when ever and wherever you need it.

To gain 45-day Safari Enabled access to this book:

- Go to http://www.awprofessional.com/safarienabled
- Complete the brief registration form
- Enter the coupon code 33G2-XGSI-ZFYZ-D7IV-B9HE

If you have difficulty registering on Safari Bookshelf or accessing the online edition, please e-mail customer-service@safaribooksonline.com.

Visit us on the Web: www.phptr.com

Library of Congress Catalog Number: 2005924108

Printed in the United States of America.

ISBN 0131473816

Text printed in the United States on recyled paper at Courier Stoughton in Stoughton, Massachusetts.
6th Printing   September 2009

About Prentice Hall Professional Technical Reference

With origins reaching back to the industry's first computer science publishing program in the 1960s, and formally launched as its own imprint in 1986, Prentice Hall Professional Technical Reference (PH PTR) has developed into the leading provider of technical books in the world today. Our editors now publish over 200 books annually, authored by leaders in the fields of computing, engineering, and business.

Our roots are firmly planted in the soil that gave rise to the technical revolution. Our bookshelf contains many of the industry's computing and engineering classics: Kernighan and Ritchie's *C Programming Language*, Nemeth's *UNIX System Administration Handbook*, Horstmann's *Core Java*, and Johnson's *High-Speed Digital Design*.

PH PTR acknowledges its auspicious beginnings while it looks to the future for inspiration. We continue to evolve and break new ground in publishing by providing today's professionals with tomorrow's solutions.

PRENTICE
HALL
PTR

Contents

Foreword

It's a pleasure to introduce you to *Cross-Platform GUI Programming with wxWidgets*, the first book on wxWidgets since it was originally released more than a decade ago.

wxWidgets is a first-class, open source response to the need for portability in an increasingly heterogeneous computing world. Being tied to specific hardware or a single operating system is often undesirable and sometimes impermissible, hence the well-understood need for cross-platform GUI frameworks. Given the long life of open source products and the often-transient nature of proprietary solutions, developers are wise to base their applications on an infrastructure that is going to survive long-term, as wxWidgets has and will continue to do.

wxWidgets combines countless years' worth of hard-earned wisdom contributed by developers worldwide, abstracting functionality and finding solutions for platform-specific issues. You, the developer, are protected both from shifts in computing trends and from the intricacies and frustrations of each platform's native API.

Becoming a wxWidgets user is an invitation into a community that spans individuals, startups, government organizations, large companies, and open source projects. When you contribute, you are forging a connection between yourself and a community that is broadly representative of the reach of information technology in the 21st century. wxWidgets-based applications may be found not just in the software industry but also in medicine, archaeology, physics, astronomy, processor manufacturing, education, geological exploration, the transport industry, space exploration, and many other fields as well.

"Chandler," the Personal Information Manager now under development at the Open Source Applications Foundation, uses wxWidgets to run under Windows, Mac OS X, and Linux. Some of our developers have become active contributors to the wxWidgets project, following the virtuous circle of open source development.

We look forward to having you join us in the ever-growing community of developers using wxWidgets, and I personally wish you all the best with your wxWidgets projects.

Mitch Kapor, Chair
OSAF
June 2005

Preface

WHO THIS BOOK IS FOR

This book is a guide to using wxWidgets, an open-source construction kit for writing sophisticated C++ applications targeting a variety of platforms, including Windows, Linux, Mac OS X, and Pocket PC. With help from this book, a competent programmer can create multi-platform applications with confidence. Developers already familiar with wxWidgets should also find it useful for brushing up their knowledge.

This book is accessible to developers with a variety of experience and backgrounds. You may come from a Windows or Unix perspective; you may previously have experience in MFC, OWL, Win32, Mac OS, Motif, or console-mode Unix programming. Or perhaps you have come from a different career entirely and are looking for a way to get up to speed on multiple platforms. The book can't specifically cover the details of the C++ language, but it's common for people to successfully learn C++ and wxWidgets at the same time, and the straightforward nature of the wxWidgets API makes this process easier. The reader does not need to know more advanced C++ techniques like templates, streams, and exceptions. However, wxWidgets does not prevent you from using these techniques.

Managers will find the book useful in discovering what wxWidgets can do for them, particularly in Chapter 1, "Introduction." The combination of the book and the resources on the accompanying CD-ROM will give your staff all they need for getting started on cross-platform programming projects. You'll see how wxWidgets puts tools of tremendous power into your hands, with benefits that include:

- ☞ **Cost savings** from writing code once that will compile on Windows, Unix, Mac OS X, and other platforms.
- ☞ **Customer satisfaction** from delivering stable, fast, attractive applications with a native look and feel.

☞ **Increased productivity** from the wide variety of classes that wxWidgets provides, both for creating great GUIs and for general application development.

☞ **Increased market share** due to support for platforms you may not have previously considered, and the ability to internationalize your applications.

☞ **Support** from a large, active wxWidgets community that answers questions helpfully and provides prompt bug fixing. The sample of third-party add-ons listed in Appendix E, "Third-Party Tools for wxWidgets," is evidence of a thriving ecosystem.

☞ **Access to the source** for enhancement and trouble-shooting.

This is a guide to writing wxWidgets application with C++, but you can use a variety of other languages such as Python, Perl, a BASIC variant, Lua, Eiffel, JavaScript, Java, Ruby, Haskell, and C#. Some of these bindings are more advanced than others. For more information, please see Appendix E and the wxWidgets web site at http://www.wxwidgets.org.

We focus on three popular desktop platforms: Microsoft Windows, Linux using GTK+, and Mac OS X. However, most of the book also applies to other platforms supported by wxWidgets. In particular, wxWidgets can be used with most Unix variants.

THE CD-ROM

The CD-ROM contains example code from the book, the wxWidgets 2.6 distribution for Windows, Linux, Mac OS X, and other platforms, and several tools to help you use wxWidgets, including the translation tool poEdit. For Windows users, we supply three free compilers you can use with wxWidgets: MinGW, Digital Mars C++, and OpenWatcom C++.

In addition, we provide you with DialogBlocks Personal Edition, a sophisticated rapid application development (RAD) tool for you to create complex windows with very little manual coding. You can use it to compile and run samples that accompany the book as well as to create your own applications for personal use, and it also provides convenient access to the wxWidgets reference manual.

Updates to the book and CD-ROM can be obtained from this site:
http://www.wxwidgets.org/book

HOW TO USE THIS BOOK

It's advisable to read at least Chapters 1 through 10 in order, but you can skip to other chapters if you need to complete a particular task. If you haven't installed wxWidgets before, you may want to look at Appendix A, "Installing wxWidgets," early on. MFC programmers will find it useful to read Appendix K, "Porting from MFC," as a point of reference.

Because this book is not a complete API reference, you'll find it useful to keep the wxWidgets reference manual open. The reference manual is available in a number of formats, including Windows HTML Help and PDF, and it should be in your wxWidgets distribution; if not, it can be downloaded from the wxWidgets web site. You can also refer to the many samples in the wxWidgets distribution to supplement the examples given in this book.

Note that the book is intended to be used in conjunction with wxWidgets 2.6 or later. The majority of the book will apply to earlier versions, but be aware that some functionality will be missing, and in a small number of cases, the behavior may be different. In particular, sizer behavior changed somewhat between 2.4 and 2.5. For details, please see the topic "Changes Since 2.4.x" in the wxWidgets reference manual.

CONVENTIONS

For code examples, we mostly follow the wxWidgets style guidelines, for example:

- ☞ Words within class names and functions have an initial capital, for example `MyFunkyClass`.
- ☞ The `m_` prefix denotes a member variable, `s_` denotes a static variable, `g_` denotes a global variable; local variables generally start with a lowercase letter, for example `textCtrl`.

You can find more about the wxWidgets style guidelines at `http://www.wxwidgets.org/standard.htm`.

Sometimes we'll also use comments that can be parsed by the documentation tool Doxygen, such as:

```
/*! A class description
 */
```

```
/// A function description
```

Classes, functions, identifiers, variables, and standard wxWidgets objects are marked with a `teletype font` in the text. User interface commands, such as menu and button labels, are marked in italics.

CHAPTER SUMMARY

Chapter 1: Introduction

What is wxWidgets, and why use it? A brief history; the wxWidgets community; the license; wxWidgets ports and architecture explained.

Chapter 2: Getting Started

A small wxWidgets sample: the application class; the main window; the event table; an outline of program flow.

Chapter 3: Event Handling

Event tables and handlers; how a button click is processed; skipping events; pluggable and dynamic event handlers; defining custom events; window identifiers.

Chapter 4: Window Basics

The main features of a window explained; a quick guide to the commonest window classes; base window classes such as wxWindow; top-level windows; container windows; non-static controls; static controls; menus; control bars.

Chapter 5: Drawing and Printing

Device context principles; the main device context classes described; buffered drawing; drawing tools; device context drawing functions; using the printing framework; 3D graphics with wxGLCanvas.

Chapter 6: Handling Input

Handling mouse and mouse wheel events; handling keyboard events; keycodes; modifier key variations; accelerators; handling joystick events.

Chapter 7: Window Layout Using Sizers

Layout basics; sizers introduced; common features of sizers; programming with sizers. Further layout issues: dialog units; platform-adaptive layouts; dynamic layouts.

Chapter 8: Using Standard Dialogs

Informative dialogs such as `wxMessageBox` and `wxProgressDialog`; file and directory dialogs such as `wxFileDialog`; choice and selection dialogs such as `wxColourDialog` and `wxFontDialog`; entry dialogs such as `wxTextEntryDialog` and `wxFindReplaceDialog`; printing dialogs: `wxPageSetupDialog` and `wxPrintDialog`.

Chapter 9: Writing Custom Dialogs

Steps in creating a custom dialog; an example: `PersonalRecordDialog`; deriving a new class; designing data storage; coding the controls and layout; data transfer and validation; handling events; handling UI updates; adding help; adapting dialogs for small devices; further considerations in dialog design; using wxWidgets resource files; loading resources; using binary and embedded resource files; translating resources; the XRC format; writing resource handlers; foreign controls.

Chapter 10: Programming with Images

Image classes in wxWidgets; programming with `wxBitmap`; programming with `wxIcon`; programming with `wxCursor`; programming with `wxImage`; image lists and icon bundles; customizing wxWidgets graphics with `wxArtProvider`.

Chapter 11: Clipboard and Drag and Drop

Data objects; data source duties; data target duties; using the clipboard; implementing drag and drop; implementing a drag source; implementing a drop target; using standard drop targets; creating a custom drop target; more on `wxDataObject`; drag and drop helpers in wxWidgets.

Chapter 12: Advanced Window Classes

`wxTreeCtrl`; `wxListCtrl`; `wxWizard`; `wxHtmlWindow`; `wxGrid`; `wxTaskBarIcon`; writing your own controls; the control declaration; defining a new event class; displaying information; handling input; defining default event handlers; implementing validators; implementing resource handlers; determining control appearance.

Chapter 13: Data Structure Classes

Why not STL? `wxString`; `wxStringTokenizer`; `wxRegEx`; `wxArray`; `wxList`; `wxHashMap`; `wxDateTime`; `wxObject`; `wxLongLong`; `wxPoint` and `wxRealPoint`; `wxRect`; `wxRegion`; `wxSize`; `wxVariant`.

Chapter 14: Files and Streams

`wxFile` and `wxFFile`; `wxTextFile`; `wxTempFile`; `wxDir`; `wxFileName`; file functions; file streams; memory and string streams; data streams; socket streams; filter streams; zip streams; virtual file systems.

Chapter 15: Memory Management, Debugging, and Error Checking

Creating and deleting window objects; creating and copying drawing objects; initializing your application object; cleaning up your application; detecting memory leaks and other errors; facilities for defensive programming; error reporting; providing run-time type information; using `wxModule`; loading dynamic libraries; exception handling; debugging tips.

Chapter 16: Writing International Applications

Introduction to internationalization; providing translations; using message catalogs; using `wxLocale`; character encodings and Unicode; converting data; help files; numbers and dates; other media; an example.

Chapter 17: Writing Multithreaded Applications

When to use threads, and when not to; using `wxThread`; thread creation; starting the thread; how to pause a thread or wait for an external condition; termination; synchronization objects; `wxMutex`; deadlocks; `wxCriticalSection`; `wxCondition`; `wxSemaphore`; the wxWidgets thread sample; alternatives to multithreading: `wxTimer`, idle time processing, and yielding.

Chapter 18: Programming with *wxSocket*

Socket classes and functionality overview; introduction to sockets and basic socket processing; connecting to a server; socket events; socket status and error notifications; sending and receiving socket data; creating a server; socket event recap; socket flags; blocking and non-blocking sockets in wxWidgets; how flags affect socket behavior; using `wxSocket` as a standard socket; using socket streams; alternatives to `wxSocket`.

Chapter 19: Working with Documents and Views

Document/view basics; choosing an interface style; creating and using frame classes; defining your document and view classes; defining your window classes; using `wxDocManager` and `wxDocTemplate`; other document/view capabilities; standard identifiers; printing and previewing; file history; explicit document creation; strategies for implementing undo/redo.

Chapter 20: Perfecting Your Application

Single instance versus multiple instances; modifying event handling; reducing flicker; using a help controller; extended wxWidgets HTML help; authoring help; other ways to provide help; parsing the command line; storing application resources; invoking other applications; launching documents; redirecting process input and output; managing application settings; application installation on Windows, Linux and Mac OS X; following UI design guidelines.

Appendix A: Installing wxWidgets

Downloading and unpacking wxWidgets; configuration/build options; Windows—Microsoft Visual Studio and VC++ command-line; Windows—Borland C++; Windows—MinGW with and without MSYS; Unix/Linux and Mac OS X—GCC; customizing `setup.h`; rebuilding after updating wxWidgets files; using `contrib` libraries.

Appendix B: Building Your Own wxWidgets Applications

Windows—Microsoft Visual Studio; Linux—KDevelop; Mac OS X—Xcode; makefiles; cross-platform builds using Bakefile; wxWidgets symbols and headers; using `wx-config`.

Appendix C: Creating Applications with DialogBlocks

What is DialogBlocks? Installing and upgrading DialogBlocks; the DialogBlocks interface; the sample project; compiling the sample; creating a new project; creating a dialog; creating a frame; creating an application object; debugging your application.

Appendix D: Other Features in wxWidgets

Further window classes; ODBC classes; MIME types manager; network functionality; multimedia classes; embedded web browsers; accessibility; OLE automation; renderer classes; event loops.

Appendix E: Third-Party Tools for wxWidgets

Language bindings such as wxPython and wxPerl; tools such as wxDesigner, DialogBlocks and poEdit; add-on libraries such as wxMozilla, wxCURL, wxPropertyGrid.

Appendix F: wxWidgets Application Showcase

Descriptions of notable wxWidgets applications, such as AOL Communicator and Audacity.

Appendix G: Using the CD-ROM

Browsing the CD-ROM; the CD-ROM contents.

Appendix H: How wxWidgets Processes Events

An illustrated description of how event processing works.

Appendix I: Event Classes and Macros

A summary of the important event classes and macros.

Appendix J: Code Listings

Code listings for the `PersonalRecordDialog` and the `wxWizard` examples.

Appendix K: Porting from MFC

General observations; application initialization; message maps; converting dialogs and other resources; documents and views; printing; string handling and translation; database access; configurable control bars; equivalent functionality by macros and classes.

Acknowledgments

wxWidgets owes its success to the hard work of many talented people. We would like to thank them all, with special consideration for that essential support network: our long-suffering families and partners. wxWidgets supporters and contributors include the following (apologies for any unintentional omissions):

Yiorgos Adamopoulos, Jamshid Afshar, Alejandro Aguilar-Sierra, Patrick Albert, Bruneau Babet, Mitchell Baker, Mattia Barbon, Nerijus Baliunas, Karsten Ballueder, Jonathan Bayer, Michael Bedward, Kai Bendorf, Yura Bidus, Jorgen Bodde, Borland, Keith Gary Boyce, Chris Breeze, Sylvain Bougnoux, Wade Brainerd, Pete Britton, Ian Brown, C. Buckley, Doug Card, Marco Cavallini, Dmitri Chubraev, Robin Corbet, Cecil Coupe, Stefan Csomor, Andrew Davison, Gilles Depeyrot, Duane Doran, Neil Dudman, Robin Dunn, Hermann Dunkel, Jos van Eijndhoven, Chris Elliott, David Elliott, David Falkinder, Rob Farnum, Joel Farley, Tom Felici, Thomas Fettig, Matthew Flatt, Pasquale Foggia, Josep Fortiana, Todd Fries, Dominic Gallagher, Roger Gammans, Guillermo Rodriguez Garcia, Brian Gavin, Wolfram Gloger, Aleksandras Gluchovas, Markus Greither, Norbert Grotz, Stephane Gully, Stefan Gunter, Bill Hale, Patrick Halke, Stefan Hammes, Guillaume Helle, Harco de Hilster, Kevin Hock, Cord Hockemeyer, Klaas Holwerda, Markus Holzem, Ove Kaaven, Mitch Kapor, Matt Kimball, Hajo Kirchoff, Olaf Klein, Jacob Jansen, Leif Jensen, Mark Johnson, Bart Jourquin, John Labenski, Guilhem Lavaux, Ron Lee, Hans Van Leemputten, Peter Lenhard, Jan Lessner, Nicholas Liebmann, Torsten Liermann, Per Lindqvist, Jesse Lovelace, Tatu Männistö, Lindsay Mathieson, Scott Maxwell, Bob Mitchell, Thomas Myers, Oliver Niedung, Stefan Neis, Ryan Norton, Robert O'Connor, Jeffrey Ollie, Kevin Ollivier, William Osborne, Hernan Otero, Ian Perrigo, Timothy Peters, Giordano Pezzoli, Harri Pasanen, Thomaso Paoletti, Garrett Potts, Robert Rae, Marcel Rasche, Mart Raudsepp, Andy Robinson, Robert Roebling, Alec Ross, Gunnar Roth, Thomas Runge, Tom Ryan, Dino Scaringella, Jobst Schmalenbach, Dimitri Schoolwerth, Arthur Seaton, Paul Shirley, Wlodzimierz Skiba, John Skiff, Vaclav Slavik, Brian Smith, Neil

Smith, Stein Somers, Petr Smilauer, Kari Systä, George Tasker, Austin Tate, Arthur Tetzlaff-Deas, Paul Thiessen, Jonathan Tonberg, Jyrki Tuomi, Janos Vegh, Andrea Venturoli, David Webster, Michael Wetherell, Otto Wyss, Vadim Zeitlin, Xiaokun Zhu, Zbigniew Zagórski, Edward Zimmermann. Thanks also to Dotsrc.org and SourceForge for hosting project services.

Thanks are due in particular to Vadim Zeitlin, Vaclav Slavik, Robert Roebling, Stefan Csomor, and Robin Dunn for permission to adapt some of their contributions to the wxWidgets reference manual.

Special thanks go to Stefan Csomor who contributed Chapter 16 and Chapter 17, and to Kevin Ollivier who wrote the Bakefile tutorial in Appendix B. We would also like to thank Mitch Kapor for writing the foreword.

We are very grateful to Mark Taub for his patience and advice throughout. A big thank you goes to Marita Allwood, Harriet Smart, Antonia Smart, Clayton Hock, and Ethel Hock for all their love, support, and encouragement. A debt is also owed to all those who have reviewed and suggested improvements to the book, including: Stefan Csomor, Dimitri Schoolwerth, Robin Dunn, Carl Godkin, Bob Paddock, Chris Elliott, Michalis Kabrianis, Marc-Andre Lureau, Jonas Karlsson, Arnout Engelen, Erik van der Wal, Greg Smith, and Alexander Stigsen.

Finally, we hope that you enjoy reading this book and, most importantly, have fun using wxWidgets to build great-looking, multi-platform applications!

Julian Smart and Kevin Hock
June 2005

About the Authors

Julian Smart has degrees from the University of St. Andrews and the University of Dundee. After working on model-based reasoning at the Scottish Crop Research Institute, he moved to the Artificial Intelligence Applications Institute at the University of Edinburgh, where he founded the wxWidgets project in 1992. Since starting Anthemion Software in 1996, Julian has been helping other companies deploy wxWidgets, and he sells tools for programmers, including DialogBlocks and HelpBlocks. He has worked as a consultant for various companies including Borland and was a member of Red Hat's eCos team, writing GUI tools to support the embedded operating system. In 2004, Julian and his wife Harriet launched a consumer product for fiction writers called Writer's Café, written with wxWidgets. Julian and Harriet live in Edinburgh with their daughter Toni.

Kevin Hock has degrees from Miami University (Oxford, Ohio) in Computer Science and Accounting and has taught courses at Miami in both Java and client-server systems. In 2002, he started work on an instant messaging system and founded BitWise Communications, LLC, in 2003, offering both professional and personal instant messaging. During the course of developing BitWise using wxWidgets, Kevin became a wxWidgets developer and has provided enhancements to all platforms. Kevin lives in Oxford, Ohio.

Stefan Csomor is director and owner of Advanced Concepts AG, a company that specializes in cross-platform development and consulting. In addition to being a qualified medical doctor, he has more than 15 years of experience in object-oriented programming and has been writing software for 25 years. Stefan is the main author of the Mac OS port of wxWidgets.

CHAPTER 1

Introduction

In this chapter, we answer a few basic questions about what wxWidgets is and what sets it apart from other solutions. We outline the project's history, how the wxWidgets community works, how wxWidgets is licensed, and an overview of the architecture and available parts.

WHAT IS WXWIDGETS?

wxWidgets is a programmer's toolkit for writing desktop or mobile applications with graphical user interfaces (GUIs). It's a *framework*, in the sense that it does a lot of the housekeeping work and provides default application behavior. The wxWidgets library contains a large number of classes and methods for the programmer to use and customize. Applications typically show windows containing standard controls, possibly drawing specialized images and graphics and responding to input from the mouse, keyboard, or other sources. They may also communicate with other processes or drive other programs. In other words, wxWidgets makes it relatively easy for the programmer to write an application that does all the usual things modern applications do.

While wxWidgets is often labeled a GUI development toolkit, it is in fact much more than that and has features that are useful for many aspects of application development. This has to be the case because *all* of a wxWidgets application needs to be portable to different platforms, not just the GUI part. wxWidgets provides classes for files and streams, multiple threads, application settings, interprocess communication, online help, database access, and much more.

WHY USE WXWIDGETS?

One area where wxWidgets differs from many other frameworks, such as MFC or OWL, is its *multi-platform* nature. wxWidgets has an Application Programming Interface (API) that is the same, or very nearly the same, on all supported platforms. This means that you can write an application on Windows, for example, and with very few changes (if any) recompile it on Linux or Mac OS X. This has a huge cost benefit compared with completely rewriting an application for each platform, and it also means that you do not need to learn a different API for each platform. Furthermore, it helps to future-proof your applications. As the computing landscape changes, wxWidgets changes with it, allowing your application to be ported to the latest and greatest systems supporting the newest features.

Another distinguishing feature is that wxWidgets provides a *native look and feel*. Some frameworks use the same widget code running on all platforms, perhaps with a theme makeover to simulate each platform's native appearance. By contrast, wxWidgets uses the native widgets wherever possible (and its own widget set in other cases) so that not only does the application *look* native on the major platforms, but it actually *is* native. This is incredibly important for user acceptance because even small, almost imperceptible differences in the way an application behaves, compared with the platform standard, can create an alienating experience for the user. To illustrate, Figure 1-1 shows a wxWidgets application called StoryLines, a tool to help fiction writers plot their stories, running on Windows XP.

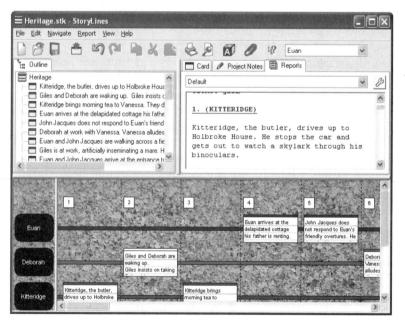

Figure 1-1   StoryLines on Windows

It's recognizably a Windows application, with GUI elements such as tabs, scrollbars, and drop-down lists conforming to the current Windows theme. Similarly, Figure 1-2 shows StoryLines as a Mac OS X application, with the expected Aqua look and feel. There is no menu bar attached to the StoryLines window because it follows the Mac OS convention of showing the current window's menu bar at the top of the screen.

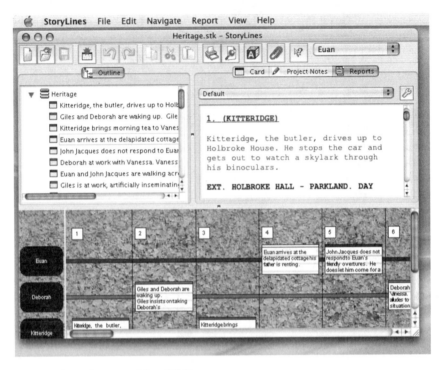

Figure 1-2   StoryLines on Mac OS X

Finally, Figure 1-3 shows StoryLines as a GTK+ application running on Red Hat Linux.

Why not just use Java? While Java is great for web-based applications, it's not always the best choice for the desktop. In general, C++-based applications using wxWidgets are faster, have a more native look and feel, and are easier to install because they don't rely on the presence of the Java virtual machine. C++ also allows greater access to low-level functionality and is easier to integrate with existing C and C++ code. For all these reasons, very few of the popular desktop applications that you use today are built with Java. wxWidgets allows you to deliver the high-performance, native applications that your users expect.

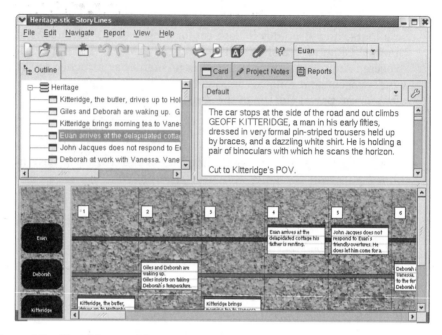

Figure 1-3   StoryLines on Linux

wxWidgets is an *open source* project. Naturally, this means that it costs nothing to use wxWidgets (unless you feel like generously donating to the project!), but it also has important philosophical and strategic significance. Open source software has a habit of outlasting its proprietary equivalents. As a developer using wxWidgets, you know that the code you rely on will never disappear. You can always fix any problems yourself by changing the source code. It can also be a lot more fun to take part in an open source community than trying to get hold of corporate support staff. Participants in open source projects tend to be there because they love what they're doing and can't wait to share their knowledge, whereas corporate support staff members are not always so idealistically motivated. When you use wxWidgets, you tap into an astonishing talent pool, with contributors from a wide range of backgrounds. Many aspects of application development that you might otherwise have to laboriously code yourself have been encapsulated by these developers in easy-to-use classes that you can plug into your code. An active user community will assist you on the mailing lists, and you'll enjoy discussions not only about wxWidgets but often other matters close to the hearts of both experienced and inexperienced developers as well. Perhaps one day you'll join in the success of wxWidgets and become a contributor yourself!

wxWidgets has wide industry support, or to use a popular buzzword, *mindshare*. The list of users includes AOL, AMD, CALTECH, Lockheed Martin, NASA, the Open Source Applications Foundation, Xerox, and many others. wxWidgets encompasses the whole spectrum of users, from single developer software outfits to large corporations, from computer science departments to medical research groups, and from ecological research to the telecommunications industry. It's also used by a myriad of open source projects, such as the Audacity audio editor and the pgAdmin III database design and management system.

People use wxWidgets for many different reasons, whether simply as an elegant MFC replacement on a single platform, or to allow them to move easily from (say) Microsoft Windows to Unix and Mac OS X. wxWidgets is addressing the challenges of mobile platforms, too, with ports for embedded Linux, Microsoft Pocket PC, and (soon) Palm OS.

A BRIEF HISTORY OF WXWIDGETS

The wxWidgets project started life in 1992 when Julian Smart was working at the University of Edinburgh on a diagramming tool called Hardy. He didn't want to choose between deploying it either on Sun workstations or PCs, so he decided to use a cross-platform framework. Because the range of existing cross-platform frameworks was limited, and the department didn't have a budget for it anyway, there was little choice but to write his own. The university gave him permission to upload wxWidgets 1.0 to the department's FTP site in September 1992, and other developers began to use the code. Initially, wxWidgets targeted XView and MFC 1.0; Borland C++ users complained about the requirement for MFC, so it was rewritten to use pure Win32. Because XView was giving way to Motif, a Motif port quickly followed.

Over time, a small but enthusiastic community of wxWidgets users was established and a mailing list created. Contributions and fixes were sent in, including an Xt port by Markus Holzem. wxWidgets gradually picked up more and more users from all over the world: individuals, academics, government departments, and—most gratifying of all—corporate users who found that wxWidgets offered a better product and better support than the commercial products they had looked at or used.

In 1997, a new wxWidgets 2 API was designed with help from Markus Holzem. Wolfram Gloger suggested that wxWidgets should be ported to GTK+, the up-and-coming widget set being adopted for the GNOME desktop environment. Robert Roebling became the lead developer for wxGTK, which is now the main Unix/Linux port of wxWidgets. In 1998, the Windows and GTK+ ports were merged and put under CVS control. Vadim Zeitlin joined the project to contribute huge amounts of design and code, and Stefan Csomor started a Mac OS port, also in 1998.

1999 saw the addition of Vaclav Slavik's impressive wxHTML classes and the HTML-based help viewer. In 2000, SciTech, Inc. sponsored initial development of wxUniversal, wxWidgets's own set of widgets for use on platforms that have no widget set of their own. wxUniversal was first used in SciTech's port to MGL, their low-level graphics layer.

In 2002, Julian Smart and Robert Roebling added the wxX11 port using the wxUniversal widgets. Requiring only Unix and X11, wxX11 is suitable for any Unix environment and can be used in fairly low-spec systems.

In July 2003, wxWidgets started running on Windows CE, and Robert Roebling demonstrated wxGTK applications running on the GPE embedded Linux platform.

In 2004, wxWidgets was renamed from the original moniker "wxWindows," after objections from Microsoft based on its Windows trademark.

Also during 2004, Stefan Csomor and a host of other contributors completely revamped wxMac for OS X, significantly improving the appearance and functionality of OS X applications. A port using Cocoa was also steadily improved, led by David Elliot, and William Osborne won our challenge to deliver an embryonic Palm OS 6 port that supports the wxWidgets "minimal" sample. Version 2.6 was released in April 2005, incorporating major improvements to all ports.

Future plans for wxWidgets include

☞ A package management tool, to make it easier to integrate third-party components

☞ Improved support for embedded applications

☞ Alternative event handling mechanisms

☞ Enhanced controls, such as a combined tree and list control

☞ wxHTML 2, with full web capabilities on all platforms

☞ Further compatibility with standards such as STL

☞ A full Palm OS port

THE wxWIDGETS COMMUNITY

The wxWidgets community is a vibrant one, with two mailing lists: wx-users (for users) and wx-dev (for contributors). The web site has news, articles, and links to releases, and there is also the wxWidgets "Wiki," a set of web pages where everyone can add information. A forum is also available for developers and users alike. Here's a list of the web addresses for these resources:

☞ http://www.wxwidgets.org: the wxWidgets home page

☞ http://lists.wxwidgets.org: the mailing list archives

☞ http://wiki.wxwidgets.org: the wxWidgets Wiki

☞ http://www.wxforum.org: the wxWidgets forum

As with most open source projects, wxWidgets is developed using a CVS repository, a source management system that keeps track of code history. In order to prevent a chaotic free-for-all, a small number of developers have write access to CVS, and others can contribute by posting bug reports and patches (currently handled by SourceForge's trackers). Development occurs on two main branches: the "stable" branch, where only binary-compatible bug fixes are allowed, and the "development" branch (CVS head). So-called stable releases are even-numbered (for example, 2.4.x) and development releases are odd-numbered (for example, 2.5.x). Users can wait for new releases or download the source from the appropriate branch by anonymous CVS.

Decisions about API changes and other technical issues are made by consensus, usually by discussion on the wx-dev list. As well as the main wxWidgets community, many projects have spun off and enjoy their own communities— for example wxPython and wxPerl (see Appendix E, "Third-Party Tools for wxWidgets").

wxWidgets and Object-Oriented Programming

Like all modern GUI frameworks, wxWidgets benefits from heavy use of object-oriented programming concepts. Each window is represented as a C++ object; these objects have well-defined behavior, and can receive and react to events. What the user sees is the visual manifestation of this interacting system of objects. Your job as a developer is to orchestrate these objects' collective behavior, a task made easier by the default behaviors that wxWidgets implements for you.

Of course, it's no coincidence that object-oriented programming and GUIs mesh well—they grew up together. The object-oriented language Smalltalk designed by Alan Kay and others in the 1970s was an important milestone in GUI history, making innovations in user interface technology as well as language design, and although wxWidgets uses a different language and API, the principles employed are broadly the same.

License Considerations

The wxWidgets license (officially, the "wxWindows License" for legal and historical reasons) is L-GPL with an exception clause. You can read the license files in detail on the web site or in the docs directory of the distribution, but in summary, you can use wxWidgets for commercial or free software with no royalty charge. You can link statically or dynamically to the wxWidgets library. If you make changes to the wxWidgets source code, you are obliged to make these freely available. You do *not* have to make your own source code or object files available. Please also consult the licenses for the optional subordinate libraries that are distributed with wxWidgets, such as the PNG and JPEG libraries.

The source code that accompanies this book is provided under the wxWindows License.

THE WXWIDGETS ARCHITECTURE

Table 1-1 shows the four conceptual layers: the wxWidgets public API, each major port, the platform API used by that port, and finally the underlying operating system.

Table 1-1   wxWidgets Ports

wxWidgets API								
wxWidgets Port								
wxMSW	wxGTK	wxX11	wxMotif	wxMac	wxCocoa	wxOS2	wxPalmOS	wxMGL
Platform API								
Win32	GTK+	Xlib	Motif/ Lesstif	Carbon	Cocoa	PM	Palm OS Protein APIs	MGL
Operating System								
Windows/ Windows CE	Unix/Linux			Mac OS 9/ Mac OS X	Mac OS X	OS/2	Palm OS	Unix/ DOS

The following are the main wxWidgets ports that exist at the time of writing.

wxMSW

This port compiles and runs on all 32-bit and 64-bit variants of the Microsoft Windows operating system, including Windows 95, Windows 98, Windows ME, Windows NT, Windows 2000, Windows XP and Windows 2003. It can also be compiled to use Winelib under Linux, and has a configuration that works on Windows CE (see "wxWinCE"). wxMSW can be configured to use the wxUniversal widgets instead of the regular Win32 ones.

wxGTK

wxWidgets for GTK+ can use versions 1.x or 2.x of the GTK+ widget set, on any Unix variant that supports X11 and GTK+ (for example, Linux, Solaris, HP-UX, IRIX, FreeBSD, OpenBSD, AIX, and others). It can also run on embedded platforms with sufficient resources—for example, under the GPE Palmtop Environment (see Figure 1-4). wxGTK is the recommended port for Unix-based systems.

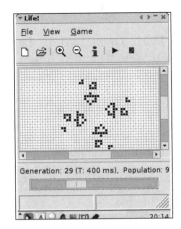

Figure 1-4   The wxWidgets "Life!" demo under GPE on an iPAQ PDA

wxX11

wxWidgets for X11 uses the wxUniversal widget set and runs directly on Xlib with no native widget set. This makes the port suitable for embedded systems, but it can also be used for desktop applications where it is undesirable to link with GTK+. This is supported on any Unix system running X11. wxX11 is not as mature as the wxGTK port. Figure 1-5 shows the Life! demo compiled under wxX11 and running on Familiar Linux / TinyX on an iPAQ PDA.

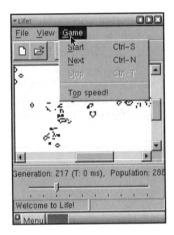

Figure 1-5   The wxWidgets "Life!" demo running on embedded wxX11

wxMotif

This port can use Motif, OpenMotif, or Lesstif on most Unix systems. Sun Microsystems is putting its weight behind GNOME and GTK+, so Motif is no longer an attractive option for most developers and users.

wxMac

wxMac targets Mac OS 9 (from 9.1 upwards) and Mac OS X (from 10.2.8 upwards). For Mac OS 9 builds, you need the Metrowerks CodeWarrior tools, and for Mac OS X, you can use either Metrowerks CodeWarrior or Apple tools. When using Apple's tools, you should use Xcode 1.5 or higher, or—if you are just using command line tools—GCC 3.3 or higher.

wxCocoa

A port in progress, this targets the Cocoa API of Mac OS X. Although the functionality of Carbon and Cocoa is similar, this port has the potential for supporting GNUStep running on platforms other than a Mac.

wxWinCE

The Windows CE port encompasses various SDKs based on the Windows CE platform, including Pocket PC and Smartphone. The bulk of this port consists of the wxMSW Win32 port, with some omissions and additions for the smaller platform. Figure 1-6 shows the wxWidgets Life! demo running on the Pocket PC 2003 emulator. Figure 1-7 shows four screens from the wxWidgets dialog demo running on Smartphone 2003 with a 176×220 pixel display. User interface adaptations done by wxWidgets for this restricted platform include constructing a nested menu in place of the usual menu bar because Smartphone only supports two menu buttons. Some additional application hints are required, such as calling `SetLeftMenu` and `SetRightMenu` instead of adding conventional OK and Cancel buttons to a dialog.

Figure 1-6   The wxWidgets "Life!" demo on Pocket PC 2003

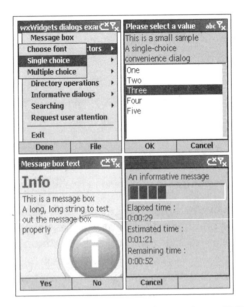

Figure 1-7   The wxWidgets "dialogs" demo on Smartphone 2003

wxPalmOS

This is a port to Palm OS 6 (Cobalt). At the time of writing, the port is in its infancy but can be used to compile and run a simple sample in the Palm OS 6 simulator (see Figure 1-8).

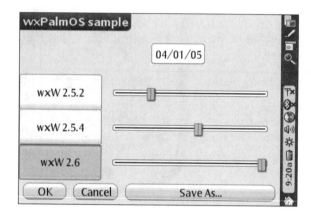

Figure 1-8   A wxWidgets sample under Palm OS 6

wxOS2

wxOS2 is a Presentation Manager port for OS/2 or eComStation.

wxMGL

This port targets the MGL low-level graphics layer from SciTech Software, Inc., and uses the wxUniversal widget set.

Internal Organization

Internally, the wxWidgets code base is broadly separated into six layers:

1. **Common code** is used in all ports. It includes data structure classes, run-time type information, and the base classes, such as wxWindowBase, which are used to factor out code common to all implementations of a class.

2. **Generic code** implements advanced widgets independently of any platform, allowing emulation of controls and other functionality not present on a given platform. wxWizard and wxCalendarCtrl are examples of generic controls.

3. **wxUniversal** is a set of basic widgets for those platforms that do not have their own native widget set, such as bare X11 and MGL.

4. **Platform-specific code** implements classes using native functionality. An example of platform-specific code is the wxMSW implementation of `wxTextCtrl` wrapping the Win32 edit control.

5. **Contributed code** exists in a separate hierarchy named `contrib` and includes non-essential but useful classes such as `wxStyledTextCtrl`.

6. **Third-party code** comprises libraries that were developed independently of wxWidgets but are used to implement important features. Examples of third-party code include the JPEG, Zlib, PNG, and Expat libraries.

Each port takes what it needs from these layers to implement the wxWidgets API.

How does wxWidgets know which classes to use when you're compiling your application? When you include a wxWidgets header file, such as `wx/textctrl.h`, you're actually including a platform-specific file such as `wx/msw/textctrl.h`, due to directives in `wx/textctrl.h` that conditionally include the appropriate declarations. You then link your application against a library that has been compiled with suitable settings for the platform in question. You can have several configurations available at once, in particular Debug and Release versions, and you can normally link either statically or dynamically to the wxWidgets code. If you want, you can disable components in a wxWidgets build, or make choices such as Unicode versus ANSI, by editing the file `setup.h` or using configure options depending on compiler. For more details, please see Appendix A, "Installing wxWidgets."

Note that although wxWidgets is a wrapper around each native API, you are not prevented from writing platform-specific code in that native API if you need to, although this is seldom necessary.

SUMMARY

In this chapter, we've established what wxWidgets is, described a little of its history, summarized the available ports, and taken a brief look at how the library is organized internally.

In the next chapter, "Getting Started," we will look at some sample code and get a feeling for what it's like to write a wxWidgets application.

CHAPTER 2

Getting Started

In this chapter, we'll get a feel for the structure of a simple wxWidgets program, using a tiny sample. We'll look at where and how a wxWidgets application starts and ends, how to show the main window, and how to react to commands from the user. Following the wxWidgets philosophy of keeping things nice and simple, that's all we're going to cover in this chapter. You may also want to refer to Appendix A, "Installing wxWidgets."

A SMALL WXWIDGETS SAMPLE

Figure 2-1 shows what our sample looks like under Windows.

Figure 2-1   Minimal sample under Windows

The minimal wxWidgets application shows a main window (a wxFrame) with a menu bar and status bar. The menus allow you to show an "about box" or quit the program. Not exactly a killer app, but it's enough to show some of the basic principles of wxWidgets—and to reassure you that you can start simple and work your way up to a complete application as your confidence and expertise grow.

THE APPLICATION CLASS

Every wxWidgets application defines an application class deriving from wxApp. There is only one instance of it, and this instance represents the running application. At the very least, your class should define an OnInit function that will be called when wxWidgets is ready to start running your code (equivalent to main or WinMain when writing a C or Win32 application).

Here is the smallest application class declaration you can sensibly write:

```
// Declare the application class
class MyApp : public wxApp
{
public:
    // Called on application startup
    virtual bool OnInit();
};
```

The implementation of OnInit usually creates at least one window, interprets any command-line arguments, sets up data for the application, and performs any other initialization tasks required for the application. If the function returns true, wxWidgets starts the event loop that processes user input and runs event handlers as necessary. If the function returns false, wxWidgets will clean up its internal structures, and the application will terminate.

A simple implementation of OnInit might look like this:

```
bool MyApp::OnInit()
{
    // Create the main application window
    MyFrame *frame = new MyFrame(wxT("Minimal wxWidgets App"));

    // Show it
    frame->Show(true);

    // Start the event loop
    return true;
}
```

This creates an instance of our new class MyFrame (we'll define this class shortly), shows it, and returns true to start the event loop. Unlike child windows, top-level windows such as frames and dialogs need to be shown explicitly after creation.

The frame title is passed to the constructor wrapped in the wxT() macro. You'll see this used a lot in wxWidgets samples and in the library code itself—it converts string and character literals to the appropriate type to allow the application to be compiled in Unicode mode. This macro is also known by the alias _T(). There is no run-time performance penalty for using it. (You'll also see the underscore macro _() used to enclose strings, which tells wxWidgets to translate the string. See Chapter 16, "Writing International Applications," for more details.)

Where is the code that creates the instance of MyApp? wxWidgets does this internally, but you still need to tell wxWidgets what *kind* of object to create. So you need to add a macro in your implementation file:

```
// Give wxWidgets the means to create a MyApp object
IMPLEMENT_APP(MyApp)
```

Without specifying the class, wxWidgets would not know how to create a new application object. This macro also inserts code that checks that the application and library were compiled using the same build configuration, allowing wxWidgets to report accidental mismatches that might later cause a hard-to-debug run-time failure.

When wxWidgets creates a MyApp object, it assigns the result to the global variable wxTheApp. You can use this in your application, but it would be more convenient if you didn't have to cast the wxApp pointer to MyApp. By inserting this macro after your application class declaration:

```
// Implements MyApp& wxGetApp()
DECLARE_APP(MyApp)
```

you can then call the function wxGetApp, which returns a reference to the MyApp object.

Tip

Even if you don't use DECLARE_APP, you can still use the variable wxTheApp to call wxApp functions. This will avoid the need to include your specific application header. It can be useful within code (such as a library) that doesn't know about specific application classes, and to save compilation time.

THE FRAME CLASS

Let's look at the frame class MyFrame. A frame is a top-level window that contains other windows, and usually has a title bar and menu bar. Here's our simple frame class declaration that we will put after the declaration of MyApp:

```
// Declare our main frame class
class MyFrame : public wxFrame
{
public:
    // Constructor
    MyFrame(const wxString& title);

    // Event handlers
```

```
    void OnQuit(wxCommandEvent& event);
    void OnAbout(wxCommandEvent& event);

private:
    // This class handles events
    DECLARE_EVENT_TABLE()
};
```

Our frame class has a constructor, two event handlers to link menu commands to C++ code, and a macro to tell wxWidgets that this class handles events.

THE EVENT HANDLERS

As you may have noticed, the event handler functions in MyFrame are not virtual and should not be virtual. How, then, are they called? The answer lies in the *event table*, as follows.

```
// Event table for MyFrame
BEGIN_EVENT_TABLE(MyFrame, wxFrame)
    EVT_MENU(wxID_ABOUT, MyFrame::OnAbout)
    EVT_MENU(wxID_EXIT,  MyFrame::OnQuit)
END_EVENT_TABLE()
```

An event table, placed in a class's implementation file, tells wxWidgets how events coming from the user or from other sources are routed to member functions.

With the event table shown previously, mouse clicks on menu items with the identifiers wxID_EXIT and wxID_ABOUT are routed to the functions MyFrame::OnQuit and MyFrame::OnAbout, respectively. EVT_MENU is just one of many event table macros you can use to tell wxWidgets what kind of event should be routed to what function. The identifiers used here are predefined by wxWidgets, but you will often define your own identifiers, using enums, consts, or preprocessor defines.

This kind of event table is a *static* way of routing events, and cannot be changed at runtime. In the next chapter, we'll describe how to set up *dynamic* event handlers.

While we're dealing with event tables, let's see the two functions we're using as event handlers.

```
void MyFrame::OnAbout(wxCommandEvent& event)
{
    wxString msg;
    msg.Printf(wxT("Hello and welcome to %s"),
            wxVERSION_STRING);

    wxMessageBox(msg, wxT("About Minimal"),
            wxOK | wxICON_INFORMATION, this);
}
```

```
void MyFrame::OnQuit(wxCommandEvent& event)
{
    // Destroy the frame
    Close();
}
```

`MyFrame::OnAbout` shows a message box when the user clicks on the About menu item. `wxMessageBox` takes a message, a caption, a combination of styles, and a parent window.

`MyFrame::OnQuit` is called when the user clicks on the Quit menu item, thanks to the event table. It calls `Close` to destroy the frame, triggering the shutdown of the application, because there are no other frames. In fact, `Close` doesn't directly destroy the frame—it generates a `wxEVT_CLOSE_WINDOW` event, and the default handler for this event destroys the frame using `wxWindow::Destroy`.

There's another way the frame can be closed and the application shut down—the user can click on the close button on the frame, or select Close from the system (or window manager) menu. How does `OnQuit` get called in this case? Well, it doesn't—instead, wxWidgets sends a `wxEVT_CLOSE_WINDOW` event to the frame via `Close` (as used in `OnQuit`). wxWidgets handles this event by default and destroys the window. Your application can override this behavior and provide its own event handler—for example, if you want to ask the user for confirmation before closing. For more details, please see Chapter 4, "Window Basics."

This sample doesn't need it, but most applications should provide an `OnExit` function in its application class to clean up data structures before quitting. Note that this function is only called if `OnInit` returns `true`.

THE FRAME CONSTRUCTOR

Finally, we have the frame constructor, which implements the frame icon, a menu bar, and a status bar.

```
#include "mondrian.xpm"

MyFrame::MyFrame(const wxString& title)
    : wxFrame(NULL, wxID_ANY, title)
{
    // Set the frame icon
    SetIcon(wxIcon(mondrian_xpm));

    // Create a menu bar
    wxMenu *fileMenu = new wxMenu;

    // The "About" item should be in the help menu
    wxMenu *helpMenu = new wxMenu;
    helpMenu->Append(wxID_ABOUT, wxT("&About...\tF1"),
                     wxT("Show about dialog"));

    fileMenu->Append(wxID_EXIT, wxT("E&xit\tAlt-X"),
                     wxT("Quit this program"));
```

```
// Now append the freshly created menu to the menu bar...
wxMenuBar *menuBar = new wxMenuBar();
menuBar->Append(fileMenu, wxT("&File"));
menuBar->Append(helpMenu, wxT("&Help"));

// ... and attach this menu bar to the frame
SetMenuBar(menuBar);

// Create a status bar just for fun
CreateStatusBar(2);
SetStatusText(wxT("Welcome to wxWidgets!"));
}
```

This constructor calls the base constructor with the parent window (none, hence NULL), window identifier, and title. The identifier argument is wxID_ANY, which tells wxWidgets to generate an identifier itself. The base constructor creates the actual window associated with the C++ instance—another way to achieve this is to call the default constructor of the base class, and then explicitly call wxFrame::Create from within the MyFrame constructor.

Small bitmaps and icons can be implemented using the XPM format on all platforms. XPM files have valid C++ syntax and so can be included as shown previously; the SetIcon line creates an icon on the stack using the C++ variable mondrian_xpm defined in mondrian.xpm, and associates it with the frame.

The menu bar is created next. Menu items are added using the identifier (such as the standard identifier wxID_ABOUT), the label to be displayed, and a help string to be shown on the status bar. Within each label, a mnemonic letter is marked by a preceding ampersand, and an accelerator is preceded by the tab character (\t). A mnemonic is the letter a user presses to highlight a particular item when the menu is displayed. An accelerator is a key combination (such as Alt+X) that can be used to perform that action without showing the menu at all.

The last thing that the constructor does is to create a status bar with two fields at the bottom of the frame and set the first field to the string "Welcome to wxWidgets!"

THE WHOLE PROGRAM

It's worth putting together the bits so you can see what the whole program looks like. Normally, you'd have a separate header file and implementation file, but for such a simple program, we can put it all in the same file.

Listing 2-1 The Complete Example

```
// Name:       minimal.cpp
// Purpose:    Minimal wxWidgets sample
// Author:     Julian Smart

#include "wx/wx.h"
```

```cpp
// Declare the application class
class MyApp : public wxApp
{
public:
    // Called on application startup
    virtual bool OnInit();
};

// Declare our main frame class
class MyFrame : public wxFrame
{
public:
    // Constructor
    MyFrame(const wxString& title);

    // Event handlers
    void OnQuit(wxCommandEvent& event);
    void OnAbout(wxCommandEvent& event);

private:
    // This class handles events
    DECLARE_EVENT_TABLE()
};

// Implements MyApp& GetApp()
DECLARE_APP(MyApp)

// Give wxWidgets the means to create a MyApp object
IMPLEMENT_APP(MyApp)

// Initialize the application
bool MyApp::OnInit()
{
    // Create the main application window
    MyFrame *frame = new MyFrame(wxT("Minimal wxWidgets App"));

    // Show it
    frame->Show(true);

    // Start the event loop
    return true;
}

// Event table for MyFrame
BEGIN_EVENT_TABLE(MyFrame, wxFrame)
    EVT_MENU(wxID_ABOUT, MyFrame::OnAbout)
    EVT_MENU(wxID_EXIT,  MyFrame::OnQuit)
END_EVENT_TABLE()

void MyFrame::OnAbout(wxCommandEvent& event)
{
    wxString msg;
    msg.Printf(wxT("Hello and welcome to %s"),
               wxVERSION_STRING);
```

(continues)

Listing 2-1 (*continued*)

```
    wxMessageBox(msg, wxT("About Minimal"),
                 wxOK | wxICON_INFORMATION, this);
}

void MyFrame::OnQuit(wxCommandEvent& event)
{
    // Destroy the frame
    Close();
}

#include "mondrian.xpm"

MyFrame::MyFrame(const wxString& title)
       : wxFrame(NULL, wxID_ANY, title)
{
    // Set the frame icon
    SetIcon(wxIcon(mondrian_xpm));

    // Create a menu bar
    wxMenu *fileMenu = new wxMenu;

    // The "About" item should be in the help menu
    wxMenu *helpMenu = new wxMenu;
    helpMenu->Append(wxID_ABOUT, wxT("&About...\tF1"),
                     wxT("Show about dialog"));

    fileMenu->Append(wxID_EXIT, wxT("E&xit\tAlt-X"),
                     wxT("Quit this program"));

    // Now append the freshly created menu to the menu bar...
    wxMenuBar *menuBar = new wxMenuBar();
    menuBar->Append(fileMenu, wxT("&File"));
    menuBar->Append(helpMenu, wxT("&Help"));

    // ... and attach this menu bar to the frame
    SetMenuBar(menuBar);

    // Create a status bar just for fun
    CreateStatusBar(2);
    SetStatusText(wxT("Welcome to wxWidgets!"));
}
```

COMPILING AND RUNNING THE PROGRAM

The sample can be found on the accompanying CD-ROM in `examples/chap02`, which you should copy to a folder on your hard drive for compiling. Because it's not possible to provide makefiles that work "out of the box" with every reader's software environment, we provide a DialogBlocks project file with configurations for most platforms and compilers. See Appendix C, "Creating Applications with DialogBlocks," for help with configuring DialogBlocks for your compiler. We also cover compiling wxWidgets applications in detail in Appendix B, "Building Your Own wxWidgets Applications."

Install wxWidgets and DialogBlocks from the accompanying CD-ROM. On Windows, you should install one or more of the compilers provided on the CD-ROM if you do not already own a suitable compiler. After setting your wxWidgets and compiler paths in the DialogBlocks *Paths* settings page, open the file examples/chap02/minimal.pjd. Select a suitable configuration for your compiler and platform such as *MinGW Debug* or *VC++ Debug* (Windows), *GCC Debug GTK+* (Linux), or *GCC Debug Mac* (Mac OS X), and press the green *Build and Run Project* button. You may be prompted to build wxWidgets if you have not already built it for the selected configuration.

You can also find a similar sample in samples/minimal in your wxWidgets distribution. If you do not wish to use DialogBlocks, you can simply compile this sample instead. See Appendix A, "Installing wxWidgets," for instructions on how to build wxWidgets samples.

PROGRAM FLOW

This is how the application starts running:

1. Depending on platform, the main, WinMain, or equivalent function runs (supplied by wxWidgets, not the application). wxWidgets initializes its internal data structures and creates an instance of MyApp.
2. wxWidgets calls MyApp::OnInit, which creates an instance of MyFrame.
3. The MyFrame constructor creates the window via the wxFrame constructor and adds an icon, menu bar, and status bar.
4. MyApp::OnInit shows the frame and returns true.
5. wxWidgets starts the event loop, waiting for events and dispatching them to the appropriate handlers.

As noted here, the application terminates when the frame is closed, when the user either selects the Quit menu item or closes the frame via standard buttons or menus (these will differ from one platform to the next).

SUMMARY

This chapter gave you an idea of how a really simple wxWidgets application works. We've touched on the wxFrame class, event handling, application initialization, and creating a menu bar and status bar. However complicated your own code gets, the basic principles of starting the application will remain the same, as we've shown in this small example. In the next chapter, we'll take a closer look at events and how your application handles them.

CHAPTER 3

Event Handling

This chapter explains the principles behind event-driven programming in wxWidgets, including how events are generated, how an application handles them using event tables, and where window identifiers fit in. We'll also discuss plug-in and dynamic event handlers, and we'll describe how you can create your own event class, types, and macros.

EVENT-DRIVEN PROGRAMMING

When programmers encountered an Apple Macintosh for the first time, they were astonished at how different it was from the conventional computer experience of the period. Moving the pointer from one window to another, playing with scrollbars, menus, text controls and so on, it was hard to imagine how the underlying code sorted out this fabulous complexity. It seemed that many different things were going on in parallel—in reality, a clever illusion. For many people, the Macintosh was their first introduction to the world of event-driven programming.

All GUI applications are event-driven. That is to say, the application sits in a loop waiting for events initiated by the user or from some other source (such as a window needing to be refreshed, or a socket connection), and then dispatches the event to an appropriate function that handles it. Although it may seem that windows are being updated simultaneously, most GUI applications are not multithreaded, so each task is being done in turn—as becomes painfully obvious when something slows your computer to a crawl and you can see each window being repainted, one after the other.

Different frameworks have different ways of exposing event handling to the developer—the primary method in wxWidgets is the use of *event tables*, as explained in the next section.

EVENT TABLES AND HANDLERS

The wxWidgets event processing system is a more flexible mechanism than virtual functions, allowing us to avoid declaring all possible event handlers in a base class, which would be totally impractical as well as inefficient.

Every class that derives from wxEvtHandler, including frames, buttons, menus, and even documents, can contain an event table to tell wxWidgets how events are routed to handler functions. All window classes (derived from wxWindow), and the application class, are derived from wxEvtHandler.

To create a static event table (one that's created at compile time), you need to

1. Declare a new class that is derived directly or indirectly from wxEvtHandler.
2. Add a member function for each event that must be handled.
3. Declare the event table in the class with DECLARE_EVENT_TABLE.
4. Implement the event table in the source file with BEGIN_EVENT_TABLE... END_EVENT_TABLE.
5. Add event table entries to the table (such as EVT_BUTTON), mapping each event to the appropriate member function.

All event handler functions have the same form—their return type is void, they are *not* virtual, and they take a single event object argument. (If you're familiar with MFC, this will come as a relief, because there is no standard signature for message handlers in MFC.) The type of this argument changes according to the type of event being handled; for example, simple control commands and menu commands share the wxCommandEvent class. A size event (caused by a window being resized either by the program or by the user) is represented by the wxSizeEvent class. Each event type has different accessors that you can use to learn about the cause of the event or the resulting UI change, such as a change in the value of a text control. In simple cases (such as a button press), you can often ignore the event object.

Expanding on the example from the previous chapter, let's add a handler for frame sizing, plus an *OK* button. A simple class declaration for an event-handling class looks like this:

```
// Declare our main frame class
class MyFrame : public wxFrame
{
public:
    // Constructor
    MyFrame(const wxString& title);
    // Event handlers
    void OnQuit(wxCommandEvent& event);
    void OnAbout(wxCommandEvent& event);
    void OnSize(wxSizeEvent& event);
    void OnButtonOK(wxCommandEvent& event);
private:
    // This class handles events
    DECLARE_EVENT_TABLE()
};
```

The code to add menu items will be similar to the code in the previous chapter, while code to add an *OK* button might look like this, in the frame constructor:

```
wxButton* button = new wxButton(this, wxID_OK, wxT("OK"),
                                wxPoint(200, 200));
```

Here's the event table, allowing the frame to handle menu, button, and size events.

```
// Event table for MyFrame
BEGIN_EVENT_TABLE(MyFrame, wxFrame)
    EVT_MENU    (wxID_ABOUT,    MyFrame::OnAbout)
    EVT_MENU    (wxID_EXIT,     MyFrame::OnQuit)
    EVT_SIZE    (               MyFrame::OnSize)
    EVT_BUTTON  (wxID_OK,       MyFrame::OnButtonOK)
END_EVENT_TABLE()
```

When the user clicks on the *About* or *Quit* menu items, the event is sent to the frame, and MyFrame's event table tells wxWidgets that a menu event with identifier wxID_ABOUT should be sent to MyFrame::OnAbout, and a menu event with identifier wxID_EXIT should be sent to MyFrame::OnQuit. In other words, these functions will be called with a single argument (in this case, wxCommandEvent) when the event loop processes the events.

The EVT_SIZE macro does not take an identifier argument because a size event can only be handled by the object that generated it.

The EVT_BUTTON entry will cause OnButtonOK to be called when a button in the frame's window hierarchy with identifier wxID_OK is pressed. This example shows that the event can be processed by a window other than the source of the event. Let's assume the button is a child of MyFrame. When the button is pressed, wxWidgets will check the wxButton class for a suitable handler. When one is not found, it checks the parent of the button—in this case, a MyFrame instance. The event matches an entry in the event table, so MyFrame::OnButtonOK is called. This search of the window component hierarchy, as well as the inheritance hierarchy, means that you can choose where you handle events. For example, if you are designing a dialog class that must respond to commands such as wxID_OK, but you need to leave the creation of the actual controls to other programmers using your code, you can still define default behavior for the controls as long as they have the expected identifiers.

The generation of a button click event and its subsequent matching against an appropriate event table entry is illustrated in Figure 3-1. Two class hierarchies are shown, for wxButton and MyFrame. Each class has its own event table that potentially contains the entry that will match the event. When the user clicks on the *OK* button, a new wxCommandEvent object is created that contains the identifier (wxID_OK) and the type of event (wxEVT_COMMAND_BUTTON_CLICKED). Now the event tables are searched using wxEvtHandler::ProcessEvent;

all of the wxButton's event table events are tried, then wxControl's, then wxWindow's. If no appropriate entry is found that matches against the event type and identifier, wxWidgets tries the parent of the button and starts searching its event table. It has a matching entry:

```
EVT_BUTTON(wxID_OK,MyFrame::OnButtonOK)
```

so MyFrame::OnButtonOK is called.

Note that only command events (whose event classes are based directly or indirectly on wxCommandEvent) are recursively applied to the window parent's event handler. As this quite often causes confusion for users, here is a list of system events that will *not* get sent to the parent's event handler: wxActivate Event, wxCloseEvent, wxEraseEvent, wxFocusEvent, wxKeyEvent, wxIdleEvent, wxInitDialogEvent, wxJoystickEvent, wxMenuEvent, wxMouseEvent, wxMoveEvent, wxPaintEvent, wxQueryLayoutInfoEvent, wxSizeEvent, wxScrollWinEvent, and wxSysColourChangedEvent.

These events do not propagate because they are meant for a particular window, and sending a child's paint event to its parent, for example, does not make sense.

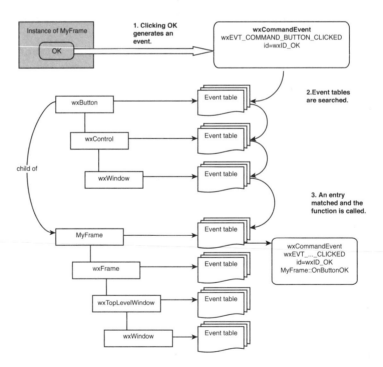

Figure 3-1   Processing a button click event

SKIPPING EVENTS

The wxWidgets event processing system implements something very close to virtual methods in normal C++, which means that it is possible to alter the behavior of a class by overriding its event handling functions. In many cases, this works even for changing the behavior of native controls. For example, it is possible to filter out selected keystroke events sent by the system to a native text control by overriding wxTextCtrl and defining a handler for key events using EVT_KEY_DOWN. This would indeed prevent any key events from being sent to the native control, which might not be what is desired. In this case, the event handler function has to call wxEvent::Skip to indicate that the search for the event handler should continue.

To summarize, instead of explicitly calling the base class version, as you would have done with C++ virtual functions, you should instead call Skip on the event object.

For example, to make the derived text control only accept "a" to "z" and "A" to "Z," we would use this code:

```
void MyTextCtrl::OnChar(wxKeyEvent& event)
{
    if ( wxIsalpha( event.KeyCode() ) )
    {
        // Keycode is within range, so do normal processing.
        event.Skip();
    }
    else
    {
        // Illegal keystroke. We don't call event.Skip() so the
        // event is not processed anywhere else.
        wxBell();
    }
}
```

PLUGGABLE EVENT HANDLERS

You don't have to derive a new class from a window class in order to process events. Instead, you can derive a new class from wxEvtHandler, define the appropriate event table, and then call wxWindow::PushEventHandler to add this object to the window's stack of event handlers. Your new event handler will catch events first; if they are not processed, the next event handler in the stack will be searched, and so on. Use wxWindow::PopEventHandler to pop the topmost event handler off the stack, passing true if you want it to be deleted.

With this method, you can avoid a lot of class derivation and potentially use the same event handler object to handle events from instances of different classes.

Normally, the value returned from `wxWindow::GetEventHandler` is the window itself, but if you have used `PushEventHandler`, this will not be the case. If you ever have to call a window's event handler manually, use the `GetEvent Handler` function to retrieve the window's topmost event handler and use that to call the member function in order to ensure correct processing of the event handler stack.

One use of `PushEventHandler` is to temporarily or permanently change the behavior of the GUI. For example, you might want to invoke a dialog editor in your application. You can grab all the mouse input for an existing dialog box and its controls, processing events for dragging sizing handles and moving controls, before restoring the dialog's normal mouse behavior. This could be a useful technique for online tutorials, where you take a user through a series of steps and don't want them to diverge from the lesson. Here, you can examine the events coming from buttons and windows and, if acceptable, pass them through to the original event handler using `wxEvent::Skip`. Events not handled by your event handler will pass through to the window's event table.

DYNAMIC EVENT HANDLERS

We have discussed event handling mostly in terms of static event tables because this is the most common way to handle events. However, you can also specify the mapping between events and their handlers at runtime. You might use this method because you want to use different event handlers at different times in your program, or because you are using a different language (such as Python) that can't use static event tables, or simply because you prefer it. Event handlers allow greater granularity—you can turn individual event handlers on and off at runtime, whereas `PushEventHandler` and `PopEventHandler` deal with a whole event table. Plus, they allow sharing of event handler functions between different objects.

There are two functions associated with dynamic event tables: `wxEvtHandler::Connect` and `wxEvtHandler::Disconnect`. Often, you won't need to call `wxEvtHandler::Disconnect` because the disconnection will happen when the window object is destroyed.

Let's use our simple frame class with two event handlers as an example.

```
// Declare our main frame class
class MyFrame : public wxFrame
{
public:
    // Constructor
    MyFrame(const wxString& title);

    // Event handlers
    void OnQuit(wxCommandEvent& event);
    void OnAbout(wxCommandEvent& event);

private:
};
```

Notice that this time, we do not use the DECLARE_EVENT_TABLE macro. To specify event handling dynamically, we add a couple of lines to our application class's OnInit function:

```
frame->Connect( wxID_EXIT,
    wxEVT_COMMAND_MENU_SELECTED,
    wxCommandEventHandler(MyFrame::OnQuit) );

frame->Connect( wxID_ABOUT,
    wxEVT_COMMAND_MENU_SELECTED,
    wxCommandEventHandler(MyFrame::OnAbout) );
```

We pass to Connect the window identifier, the event identifier, and finally a pointer to the event handler function. Note that the event identifier (wxEVT_COMMAND_MENU_SELECTED) is different from the event table macro (EVT_MENU); the event table macro makes use of the event identifier internally. The wxCommandEventHandler macro around the function name is necessary to appease the compiler—casts are done by static event table macros automatically. In general, if you have a handler that takes an event called wxXYZEvent, then in your Connect call, you will wrap the function name in the macro wxXYZEventHandler.

If we want to remove the mapping between event and handler function, we can use the wxEvtHandler::Disconnect function, as follows:

```
frame->Disconnect( wxID_EXIT,
    wxEVT_COMMAND_MENU_SELECTED,
    wxCommandEventHandler(MyFrame::OnQuit) );

frame->Disconnect( wxID_ABOUT,
    wxEVT_COMMAND_MENU_SELECTED,
    wxCommandEventFunction(MyFrame::OnAbout) );
```

WINDOW IDENTIFIERS

Window identifiers are integers, and are used to uniquely determine window identity in the event system. In fact, identifiers do not need to be unique across your entire application, just unique within a particular context, such as a frame and its children. You may use the wxID_OK identifier, for example, on any number of dialogs as long as you don't have several within the same dialog.

If you pass wxID_ANY to a window constructor, an identifier will be generated for you automatically by wxWidgets. This is useful when you don't care about the exact identifier, either because you're not going to process the events from the control being created at all, or because you process the events from all controls in one place. In this case, you should specify wxID_ANY in the event table or wxEvtHandler::Connect call as well. The generated identifiers are always negative, so they will never conflict with the user-specified identifiers, which must always be positive.

wxWidgets supplies the standard identifiers listed in Table 3-1. Use the standard identifiers wherever possible: some systems can use the information to provide standard graphics (such as the *OK* and *Cancel* buttons on GTK+) or default behavior (such as responding to the Escape key by emulating a wxID_CANCEL event). On Mac OS X, wxID_ABOUT, wxID_PREFERENCES and wxID_EXIT menu items are interpreted specially and transferred to the application menu. Some wxWidgets components, such as wxTextCtrl, know how to handle menu items or buttons with identifiers such as wxID_COPY, wxID_PASTE, wxID_UNDO.

You can use wxID_HIGHEST to determine the number above which it is safe to define your own identifiers, or you can use identifiers below wxID_LOWEST.

Table 3-1   Standard Window Identifiers

Identifier Name	Description
wxID_ANY	This may be passed to a window constructor as an identifier, and wxWidgets will generate an appropriate identifier
wxID_LOWEST	The lowest standard identifier value (4999)
wxID_HIGHEST	The highest standard identifier value (5999)
wxID_OPEN	File open
wxID_CLOSE	Window close
wxID_NEW	New window, file or document
wxID_SAVE	File save
wxID_SAVEAS	File save as (prompts for a save dialog)
wxID_REVERT	Revert (revert to file on disk)
wxID_EXIT	Exit application
wxID_UNDO	Undo the last operation
wxID_REDO	Redo the last undo
wxID_HELP	General help (for example, for dialog Help buttons)
wxID_PRINT	Print
wxID_PRINT_SETUP	Print setup dialog
wxID_PREVIEW	Print preview
wxID_ABOUT	Show a dialog describing the application
wxID_HELP_CONTENTS	Show the help contents
wxID_HELP_COMMANDS	Show the application commands
wxID_HELP_PROCEDURES	Show the application procedures

Identifier Name	Description
wxID_HELP_CONTEXT	Unused
wxID_CUT	Cut
wxID_COPY	Copy
wxID_PASTE	Paste
wxID_CLEAR	Clear
wxID_FIND	Find
wxID_DUPLICATE	Duplicate
wxID_SELECTALL	Select all
wxID_DELETE	Delete (cut without copying)
wxID_REPLACE	Replace
wxID_REPLACE_ALL	Replace all
wxID_PROPERTIES	Show properties for the selection
wxID_VIEW_DETAILS	View details in a list control
wxID_VIEW_LARGEICONS	View as large icons in a list control
wxID_VIEW_SMALLICONS	View as small icons in a list control
wxID_VIEW_LIST	View as a list in a list control
wxID_VIEW_SORTDATE	Sort by date
wxID_VIEW_SORTNAME	Sort by name
wxID_VIEW_SORTSIZE	Sort by size
wxID_VIEW_SORTTYPE	Sort by type
wxID_FILE1 to wxID_FILE9	View recent file
wxID_OK	Confirms dialog selections
wxID_CANCEL	Vetoes dialog selections
wxID_APPLY	Applies selections to data
wxID_YES	Identifier for a *Yes* button
wxID_NO	Identifier for a *No* button
wxID_STATIC	Identifier for static text or bitmap control
wxID_FORWARD	Navigate forward
wxID_BACKWARD	Navigate backward
wxID_DEFAULT	Restore default settings
wxID_MORE	View more settings
wxID_SETUP	View a setup dialog
wxID_RESET	Reset settings

(continues)

Table 3-1   Standard Window Identifiers (*Continued*)

Identifier Name	Description
wxID_CONTEXT_HELP	Show context-sensitive help
wxID_YESTOALL	Reply yes to all prompts
wxID_NOTOALL	Reply no to all prompts
wxID_ABORT	Abort the current operation
wxID_RETRY	Retry the operation
wxID_IGNORE	Ignore an error condition
wxID_UP	Navigate up
wxID_DOWN	Navigate down
wxID_HOME	Navigate home
wxID_REFRESH	Refresh
wxID_STOP	Stop the current operation
wxID_INDEX	Show an index
wxID_BOLD	Highlight in bold
wxID_ITALIC	Highlight in italic
wxID_JUSTIFY_CENTER	Center
wxID_JUSTIFY_FILL	Format
wxID_JUSTIFY_RIGHT	Right align
wxID_JUSTIFY_LEFT	Left align
wxID_UNDERLINE	Underline
wxID_INDENT	Indent
wxID_UNINDENT	Unindent
wxID_ZOOM_100	Zoom to 100%
wxID_ZOOM_FIT	Fit to page
wxID_ZOOM_IN	Zoom in
wxID_ZOOM_OUT	Zoom out
wxID_UNDELETE	Undelete
wxID_REVERT_TO_SAVED	Revert to saved state

DEFINING CUSTOM EVENTS

If you want to define your own event class and macros, you need to follow these steps:

1. Derive your class from a suitable class, declaring dynamic type information and including a Clone function. You may or may not want to add data members and accessors. Derive from wxCommandEvent if you want the event

to propagate up the window hierarchy, and from wxNotifyEvent if you also want handlers to be able to call Veto.

2. Define a typedef for the event handler function.

3. Define a table of event types for the individual events your event class supports. The event table is defined in your header with BEGIN_DECLARE_EVENT_TYPES()... END_DECLARE_EVENT_TYPES() and each type is declared with DECLARE_EVENT_TABLE(name, integer). Then in your implementation file, write DEFINE_EVENT_TYPE(name).

4. Define an event table macro for each event type.

Let's make this clearer with an example. Say we want to implement a new control class, wxFontSelectorCtrl, which displays a font preview; the user can click on the preview to pop up a font selector dialog to change the font. The application may want to intercept the font selection event, so we'll send a custom command event from within our low-level mouse handling code.

We will need to define a new event class wxFontSelectorCtrlEvent. An application will be able to route font change events to an event handler with the macro EVT_FONT_SELECTION_CHANGED(id, func), which uses the single event type wxEVT_COMMAND_FONT_SELECTION_CHANGED. Here's what we need in our new control header file, as well as the control declaration itself (not shown):

```
/*!
 * Font selector event class
 */
class wxFontSelectorCtrlEvent : public wxNotifyEvent
{
public:
    wxFontSelectorCtrlEvent(wxEventType commandType = wxEVT_NULL,
       int id = 0): wxNotifyEvent(commandType, id)
    {}

    wxFontSelectorCtrlEvent(const wxFontSelectorCtrlEvent& event):
wxNotifyEvent(event)
    {}

    virtual wxEvent *Clone() const
                    { return new wxFontSelectorCtrlEvent(*this); }

DECLARE_DYNAMIC_CLASS(wxFontSelectorCtrlEvent);
};

typedef void (wxEvtHandler::*wxFontSelectorCtrlEventFunction)
                                        (wxFontSelectorCtrlEvent&);

/*!
 * Font selector control events and macros for handling them
 */
```

```
BEGIN_DECLARE_EVENT_TYPES()
    DECLARE_EVENT_TYPE(wxEVT_COMMAND_FONT_SELECTION_CHANGED, 801)
END_DECLARE_EVENT_TYPES()

#define EVT_FONT_SELECTION_CHANGED(id, fn) DECLARE_EVENT_TABLE_ENTRY(
wxEVT_COMMAND_FONT_SELECTION_CHANGED, id, -1, (wxObjectEventFunction)
(wxEventFunction) (wxFontSelectorCtrlEventFunction) & fn,
(wxObject *) NULL ),
```

In our implementation file, we write

```
DEFINE_EVENT_TYPE(wxEVT_COMMAND_FONT_SELECTION_CHANGED)
IMPLEMENT_DYNAMIC_CLASS(wxFontSelectorCtrlEvent, wxNotifyEvent)
```

To send the custom event, the font selector control can call ProcessEvent when a selection is detected from within the mouse handling code:

```
wxFontSelectorCtrlEvent event(
                   wxEVT_COMMAND_FONT_SELECTION_CHANGED, GetId());
event.SetEventObject(this);
GetEventHandler()->ProcessEvent(event);
```

Now an application can write a font selection event handler, for example:

```
BEGIN_EVENT_TABLE(MyDialog, wxDialog)
   EVT_FONT_SELECTION_CHANGED(ID_FONTSEL, MyDialog::OnChangeFont)
END_EVENT_TABLE()

void MyDialog::OnChangeFont(wxFontSelectorCtrlEvent& event)
{
    // Take appropriate action when the font selection changed
    ...
}
```

The event identifier value (801) is not used in recent versions of wxWidgets and is only included for compatibility with wxWidgets 2.4.

Let's take another look at the event macro definition:

```
#define EVT_FONT_SELECTION_CHANGED(id, fn) DECLARE_EVENT_TABLE_ENTRY(
wxEVT_COMMAND_FONT_SELECTION_CHANGED, id, -1, (wxObjectEventFunction)
(wxEventFunction) (wxFontSelectorCtrlEventFunction) & fn,
(wxObject *) NULL ),
```

The macro places information into an array that forms the event table, which is why the syntax looks rather strange. The five entries in the event table record are as follows:

1. The event type. One event class can handle several types, but in our example, we only define one event type, and therefore there is only one event table macro. This type must match the type of the event being processed for the event handler to be called.

2. The identifier value passed to the macro. The event handler function will only be called if the value in the table matches the value in the event being processed.

3. A second identifier value, used when specifying a range of values. -1 indicates that there is no second value.

4. The event handler function. The sequence of casts is needed for some compilers, and this is where the member function typedef is used.

5. User data, normally NULL.

The full custom event example can be found in examples/chap03, and it includes a font selection control implementation and handy validator class that you can use in your own applications. You can also look at include/wx/event.h in your wxWidgets distribution for more inspiration.

SUMMARY

In this chapter, we've discussed how events are propagated through inheritance and window hierarchies, introduced pluggable and dynamic event handlers, talked about window identifiers, and described how you can write your own custom event classes and macros. For more on the mechanics of event handling, please refer to Appendix H, "How wxWidgets Processes Events." Appendix I, "Event Classes and Macros," lists commonly used event classes and macros. You can also look at a number of the wxWidgets samples for examples of event usage, notably samples/event. Next, we'll discuss a range of important GUI components that you can start putting to use in your applications.

CHAPTER 4

Window Basics

In this chapter, we'll first look at the main elements of a window before describing the window classes that are most commonly used in applications. These elements will almost certainly be familiar from other programming you've done or from applications you've used. Despite the differences between systems, the available controls are surprisingly similar in functionality, with wxWidgets handling nearly all of the differences. Remaining differences are usually handled using optional platform-specific window styles.

ANATOMY OF A WINDOW

Naturally, you know what a window is, but for a full understanding of how to use the wxWidgets API, it's good to have a grasp of the *window model* that wxWidgets uses. This differs in small respects from the window model used on each individual platform. Figure 4-1 shows the basic elements of a window.

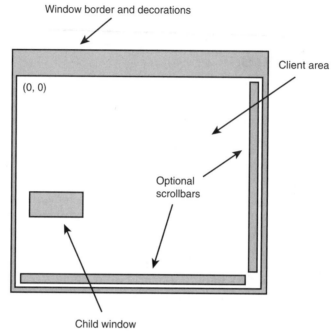

Figure 4-1   The elements of a window

The Concept of a Window

A window is any rectangular area with a common set of properties: it can be resized, it can paint itself, it can be shown and hidden, and so on. It may contain other windows (such as a frame with menu bar, toolbar, and status bar), or no child windows (such as a static text control). Normally, a window that you see on the screen in a wxWidgets application has a corresponding object of the wxWindow class or derived class, but this is not always the case: for example, the drop-down list in a native wxComboBox is not usually modeled with a separate wxWindow.

Client and Non-Client Areas

When we refer to the size of a *window*, we normally include the outer dimensions, including decorations such as the border and title bar. When we refer to the size of the *client area* of a window, we mean the area inside the window that can be drawn upon or into which child windows may be placed. A frame's client area excludes any space taken by the menu bar, status bar, and toolbar.

Scrollbars

Most windows are capable of showing scrollbars, managed by the window rather than added explicitly by the application. The client area is then reduced by the space used by the scrollbars. For optimization, only windows that have the wxHSCROLL and wxVSCROLL style are guaranteed to own their own scrollbars. More information on scrolling can be found later in this chapter when we discuss wxScrolledWindow.

Caret and Cursor

A window can have a wxCaret (for displaying the current text position) and a wxCursor (for displaying the current mouse position). When the mouse enters a window, wxWidgets automatically displays the cursor that has been set for the window. When a window receives the focus, the caret (if any) will be shown at its current position, or at the mouse position if the focus was a result of a mouse button click.

Top-Level Windows

Windows are broadly divided into top-level windows (wxFrame, wxDialog, wxPopup) and other windows. Only top-level windows may be created with a NULL parent, and only top-level windows have delayed destruction (they are not deleted until idle time, when all other events have been processed). Except for pop-up windows, top-level windows can have decorations such as title bars and close buttons and can normally be dragged around the screen and resized, if the application allows it.

Coordinate System

The coordinate system always has (0, 0) at the top-left corner, and window dimensions are in pixels. The origin and scale can be changed for a *device context* that is used to paint on the window. For more on device contexts, see Chapter 5, "Drawing and Printing."

Painting

When a window needs to be painted, it receives two events, wxEVT_ERASE_BACKGROUND to paint the background, and wxEVT_PAINT to paint the foreground. Ready-to-use classes such as wxButton paint themselves, but to create your own special window class, you will need to handle these events. You can optimize painting by getting the *update region* (the part that needs refreshing) from the window.

Color and Font

Every window has background and foreground color settings that can be used
to determine the background color and (less commonly) foreground color. The
default background erase handler uses the window's background color, or if
none has been set, the appropriate color or texture for the current color
scheme or theme. A window also has a font setting, which may or may not be
used depending on the kind of window.

Window Variant

On Mac OS X, a window has the concept of *window variant*, whereby it can be
shown in a selection of sizes: wxWINDOW_VARIANT_NORMAL (the default), wxWINDOW_
VARIANT_SMALL, wxWINDOW_VARIANT_MINI, or wxWINDOW_VARIANT_LARGE. Changing to
a smaller variant is useful when you have a lot of information to convey and
limited space, but it should be used in moderation. Some applications use the
small variant throughout.

Sizing

When a window is resized, either by the application or by the user, it receives
a wxEVT_SIZE event. If the window has children, they will need to be positioned
and sized appropriately, and the recommended way is to use *sizers,* as discussed in Chapter 7, "Window Layout Using Sizers." Most stock windows have
a notion of a default size and position if you pass them wxDefaultSize or
wxDefaultPosition (or -1 as an individual size or position value). To this end,
each control implements DoGetBestSize, which returns a reasonable default
size based on the control content, current font, and other factors.

Input

Any window can receive input from the mouse at any time, unless another
window has temporarily *captured* the mouse or the window is *disabled*. Only
the window with the current *focus* can receive keyboard input. An application
can set the window focus itself; wxWidgets also sets the focus to a window
when the user clicks on it. The wxEVT_SET_FOCUS event is sent to a window that
is receiving the focus; wxEVT_KILL_FOCUS is sent when the focus is moving to a
different window. See Chapter 6, "Handling Input," for more details on handling input.

Idle Time Processing and UI Updates

All windows are (unless otherwise specified) recipients of *idle* events
(wxEVT_IDLE), which are sent when all other events have been processed, specified with the EVT_IDLE(func) macro. For more information, see "Idle Time
Processing" in Chapter 17, "Writing Multithreaded Applications."

A special kind of idle time processing is *user interface updating*, in which all windows can specify a function that updates the window's state. This function is called periodically in idle time. In the descriptions of events that follow, EVT_UPDATE_UI(id, func) is usually omitted for brevity. User interface updating is covered in Chapter 9, "Creating Custom Dialogs."

Window Creation and Deletion

In general, windows are created on the heap with new, but see Chapter 15, "Memory Management, Debugging, and Error Checking," for details and exceptions. Most window classes allow creation either in one or two steps. wxButton has typical constructor signatures:

```
wxButton();
wxButton(wxWindow* parent,
    wxWindowID id,
    const wxString& label = wxEmptyString,
    const wxPoint& pos = wxDefaultPosition,
    const wxSize& size = wxDefaultSize,
    long style = 0,
    const wxValidator& validator = wxDefaultValidator,
    const wxString& name = wxT("button"));
```

The following example of one-step construction takes advantage of all the constructor's default values:

```
wxButton* button  = new wxButton(parent, wxID_OK);
```

Unless the window is a frame or dialog, you must pass a non-NULL parent window to the constructor. This will automatically add the child window to the parent, and when the parent is destroyed, the children will also be destroyed. As we've seen previously, you pass a standard or user-defined identifier to the window for the purposes of uniquely identifying it. You can also pass wxID_ANY, and wxWidgets will generate a suitable identifier (a negative value, to differentiate it from user-defined or standard identifiers). You can pass a position and size to the window, a validator, if appropriate (see Chapter 9), a style (see the following), and a string name. You can pass an arbitrary string to the name parameter, or ignore it; it is rarely used now but was introduced to allow window customization under Xt and Motif, which require controls to be identified by name.

With two-step construction, you use the default constructor and then call Create, which has the same signature as the full constructor. For example, to create a button in two steps:

```
wxButton* button  = new wxButton;
button->Create(parent, wxID_OK);
```

Only when you call Create is the underlying window created, and a wxEVT_ CREATE event sent to the window in case it needs to do further processing at this point.

Why would you want to use two-step construction? One reason is that you may want to delay full creation of the window until it's really required. Another is to set some properties of the window before Create is called, especially if those properties are used within the Create call. For example, you may want to set the wxWS_EX_VALIDATE_RECURSIVELY extra style (which must be set with SetExtraStyle). In the case of a dialog, this style is used from within its Create function when initial validation takes place, so if you need it, it's important to set it before the dialog is created.

When you create a wxWindow, or any non-top-level derived window class, it is always in a visible state—so if the parent is visible at the time of creation, the window will also be visible. You can then use Show(false) to hide it if required. This is different from wxDialog and wxFrame, which are initially created in a hidden state to enable the application to lay out the controls without initial flicker, before showing with Show or (for modal dialogs) ShowModal.

Windows are deleted by calling Destroy (for top-level windows) or delete (for child windows), and the wxEVT_DESTROY event is sent just before the actual window is destroyed. In fact, child windows are deleted automatically, so it is rare to delete them explicitly.

Window Styles

A window has a *style* and an *extra style*. Window styles are a concise way to specify alternative behavior and appearances for windows when they are created. The symbols are defined in such as way that they can be combined in a "bit-list" using the C++ bitwise-or operator. For example:

```
wxCAPTION ¦ wxMINIMIZE_BOX ¦ wxMAXIMIZE_BOX ¦ wxTHICK_FRAME
```

The wxWindow class has a basic set of styles, such as border styles, and each derived class may add further styles. The "extra" style accommodates values that cannot fit into the style value.

A QUICK GUIDE TO THE WINDOW CLASSES

The rest of this chapter provides you with enough detailed information about the most commonly used window classes for you to apply them to your own applications. However, if you are reading this book for the first time, you may want to skip ahead to Chapter 5 and browse the window descriptions later.

Here's a summary of the classes we cover, to help you navigate this chapter. For other window classes, see Chapter 12, "Advanced Window Classes," and Appendix E, "Third-Party Tools for wxWidgets."

Base Window Classes

These base classes implement functionality for derived concrete classes.

☞ wxWindow. The base class for all windows.

☞ wxControl. The base class for controls, such as wxButton.

☞ wxControlWithItems. The base class for multi-item controls.

Top-Level Windows

Top-level windows usually exist independently on the desktop.

☞ wxFrame. A resizable window containing other windows.

☞ wxMDIParentFrame. A frame that manages other frames.

☞ wxMDIChildFrame. A frame managed by a parent frame.

☞ wxDialog. A resizable window for presenting choices.

☞ wxPopupWindow. A transient window with minimal decoration.

Container Windows

Container windows manage child windows.

☞ wxPanel. A window for laying out controls.

☞ wxNotebook. A window for switching pages using tabs.

☞ wxScrolledWindow. A window that scrolls children and graphics.

☞ wxSplitterWindow. A window that manages two child windows.

Non-Static Controls

These controls can be edited by the user.

☞ wxButton. A push-button control with a text label.

☞ wxBitmapButton. A push-button control with a bitmap label.

☞ wxChoice. A drop-down list of choices.

☞ wxComboBox. An editable field with a list of choices.

☞ wxCheckBox. A control representing a check box, on or off.

☞ wxListBox. A list of selectable string items.

☞ wxRadioBox. A grid of radio buttons.

☞ wxRadioButton. A control resembling a radio button, on or off.

☞ wxScrollBar. A scrollbar control.

☞ wxSpinButton. Arrows for incrementing/decrementing values.

☞ wxSpinCtrl. A text field and spin button for editing integers.

☞ wxSlider. A control for changing a value within a given range.

☞ wxTextCtrl. A single- or multiple-line text entry field.

☞ wxToggleButton. A button that can be toggled on and off.

Static Controls

These controls present information and cannot be edited by the user.

☞ wxGauge. A control showing a quantity.

☞ wxStaticText. A control that shows a text label.

☞ wxStaticBitmap. A control that shows a bitmap label.

☞ wxStaticLine. A control displaying a line.

☞ wxStaticBox. A control displaying a box around other controls.

Menus

Menus are transient windows containing lists of commands.

☞ wxMenu. A menu that can be used as a popup or in a menu bar.

Control Bars

Control bars present concise access to commands and information, usually within a wxFrame.

☞ wxMenuBar. A menu bar that presents commands in a wxFrame.

☞ wxToolBar. A toolbar that provides quick access to commands.

☞ wxStatusBar. A status bar that shows information in multiple fields.

BASE WINDOW CLASSES

It's worth mentioning base classes that you may or may not be able use directly but that implement a lot of functionality for derived classes. Use the API reference for these (and other) base classes as well as the reference for the derived classes to get a full understanding of what's available.

wxWindow

wxWindow is both an important base class and a concrete window class that you can instantiate. However, it's more likely that you will derive classes from it (or use pre-existing derived classes) than use it on its own.

As we've seen, a wxWindow may be created either in one step, using a non-default constructor, or two steps, using the default constructor followed by Create. For one-step construction, you use this constructor:

```
wxWindow(wxWindow* parent,
    wxWindowID id,
    const wxPoint& pos = wxDefaultPosition,
    const wxSize& size = wxDefaultSize,
    long style = 0,
    const wxString& name = wxT("panel"));
```

For example:

```
wxWindow* win  = new wxWindow(parent, wxID_ANY,
    wxPoint(100, 100), wxSize(200, 200));
```

wxWindow Styles

Each window class may add to the basic styles defined for wxWindow, listed in Table 4-1. Not all native controls support all border styles, and if no border is specified, a default style appropriate to that class will be used. For example, on Windows, most wxControl-derived classes use wxSUNKEN_BORDER by default, which will be interpreted as the border style for the current theme. An application may suppress the default border by using a style such as wxNO_BORDER.

Table 4-1   Basic Window Styles

wxSIMPLE_BORDER	Displays a thin border around the window.
wxDOUBLE_BORDER	Displays a double border.
wxSUNKEN_BORDER	Displays a sunken border, or control border consistent with the current theme.
wxRAISED_BORDER	Displays a raised border.
wxSTATIC_BORDER	Displays a border suitable for a static control. Windows only.
wxNO_BORDER	Displays no border. This overrides any attempt wxWidgets makes to add a suitable border.
wxTRANSPARENT_WINDOW	Specifies a transparent window (one that doesn't receive paint events). Windows only.

(continues)

Table 4-1   Basic Window Styles (*Continued*)

wxTAB_TRAVERSAL	Use this to enable tab traversal for non-dialog windows.
wxWANTS_CHARS	Use this to indicate that the window wants to get all char/key events—even for keys like Tab or Enter, which are used for dialog navigation and which wouldn't be generated without this style.
wxFULL_REPAINT_ON_RESIZE	By default on Windows, wxWidgets won't repaint the entire client area during a resize. This style ensures that the whole client area will be invalidated during a resize.
wxVSCROLL	Enables a vertical scrollbar.
wxHSCROLL	Enables a horizontal scrollbar.
wxALWAYS_SHOW_SB	If a window has scrollbars, disables them instead of hiding them when they are not needed (when the size of the window is big enough to not require the scrollbars to navigate it). This style is currently only implemented for Windows and wxUniversal.
wxCLIP_CHILDREN	On Windows only, used to eliminate flicker caused by a window erasing the background of its children.

Table 4-2 lists extra styles that cannot be accommodated in the regular style and that are set using wxWindow::SetExtraStyle.

Table 4-2   Basic Extra Window Styles

wxWS_EX_VALIDATE_RECURSIVELY	By default, Validate, TransferDataToWindow, and TransferDataFromWindow only work on direct children of the window. Set this style to make them recursively descend into all subwindows.
wxWS_EX_BLOCK_EVENTS	wxCommandEvents and the objects of derived classes are forwarded to the parent window and so on recursively by default. Using this style for the given window enables you to block this propagation at this window to prevent the events from being propagated further upwards. Dialogs have this style on by default, but note that if SetExtraStyle is called by the application, it may be reset.
wxWS_EX_TRANSIENT	Don't use this window as an implicit parent for other windows. This must be used with transient windows; otherwise, there is the risk of creating a dialog or frame with this window as a parent, which would lead to a crash if the parent were destroyed before the child.

| wxWS_EX_PROCESS_IDLE | This window should always process idle events, even if the mode set by wxIdleEvent::SetMode is wxIDLE_PROCESS_SPECIFIED. |
| wxWS_EX_PROCESS_UI_UPDATES | This window should always process UI update events, even if the mode set by wxUpdateUIEvent:: SetMode is wxUPDATE_UI_PROCESS_SPECIFIED. See Chapter 9 for more information on UI update events. |

wxWindow Events

wxWindow and all its derived classes generate the events listed in Table 4-3. Events generated by mouse, keyboard, or joystick input are covered in Chapter 6.

Table 4-3   wxWindow Events

EVT_WINDOW_CREATE(func)	Processes a wxEVT_CREATE propagating event, generated when the underlying window has just been created. Handlers take a wxWindowCreateEvent object.
EVT_WINDOW_DESTROY(func)	Processes a wxEVT_DELETE propagating event, generated when the window is about to be destroyed. Handlers take a wxWindowDestroyEvent object.
EVT_PAINT(func)	Processes a wxEVT_PAINT event, generated when the window needs updating. Handlers take a wxPaintEvent object.
EVT_ERASE_BACKGROUND(func)	Processes a wxEVT_ERASE_BACKGROUND event, generated when the window background needs updating. Handlers take a wxEraseEvent object.
EVT_MOVE(func)	Processes a wxEVT_MOVE event, generated when the window moves. Handlers take a wxMoveEvent object.
EVT_SIZE(func)	Processes a wxEVT_SIZE event, generated when the window is resized. Handlers take a wxSizeEvent object.
EVT_SET_FOCUS(func) EVT_KILL_FOCUS(func)	Processes wxEVT_SET_FOCUS and wxEVT_KILL_FOCUS events, generated when the keyboard focus is gained or lost for this window. Handlers take a wxFocusEvent object.
EVT_SYS_COLOUR_CHANGED(func)	Processes a wxEVT_SYS_COLOUR_CHANGED event, generated when the user changed a color in the control panel (Windows only). Handlers take a wxSysColourChangedEvent object.
EVT_IDLE(func)	Processes a wxEVT_IDLE event, generated in idle time. Handlers take a wxIdleEvent object.
EVT_UPDATE_UI(func)	Processes a wxEVT_UPDATE_UI event, generated in idle time to give the window a chance to update itself.

wxWindow Member Functions

Because wxWindow is the base class for all other window classes, it has the largest number of member functions. We can't describe them all here in detail, so instead we present a summary of some of the most important functions. Browsing them should give you a good idea of the general capabilities of windows, and you can refer to the reference manual for details of parameters and usage.

CaptureMouse captures all mouse input, and ReleaseMouse releases the capture. This is useful in a drawing program, for example, so that moving to the edge of the canvas scrolls it rather than causing another window to be activated. Use the static function GetCapture to retrieve the window with the current capture (if it's within the current application), and HasCapture to determine if this window is capturing input.

Centre (Center), CentreOnParent (CenterOnParent), and CentreOnScreen (CenterOnScreen) center the window relative to the screen or the parent window.

ClearBackground clears the window by filling it with the current background color.

ClientToScreen and ScreenToClient convert between coordinates relative to the top-left corner of this window, and coordinates relative to the top-left corner of the screen.

Close generates a wxCloseEvent whose handler usually tries to close the window. Although the default close event handler will destroy the window, calling Close may not actually close the window if a close event handler has been provided that *doesn't* destroy the window.

ConvertDialogToPixels and ConvertPixelsToDialog convert between dialog and pixel units, which is useful when basing size or position on font size in order to give more portable results.

Destroy destroys the window safely. Use this function instead of the delete operator because different window classes can be destroyed differently. Frames and dialogs are not destroyed immediately when this function is called but are added to a list of windows to be deleted on idle time, when all pending events have been processed. This prevents problems with events being sent to non-existent windows.

Enable enables or disables the window and its children for input. Some controls display themselves in a different color when disabled. Disable can be used instead of passing false to Enable.

FindFocus is a static function that can be used to find the window that currently has the keyboard focus.

FindWindow can be used with an identifier or a name to find a window in this window's hierarchy. It can return a descendant or the parent window itself. If you know the type of the window, you can use wxDynamicCast to safely cast to the correct type, returning either a pointer to that type or NULL:

```
MyWindow* window = wxDynamicCast(FindWindow(ID_MYWINDOW), MyWindow);
```

Fit resizes the window to fit its children. This should be used with sizer-based layout. FitInside is similar, but it uses the virtual size (useful when the window has scrollbars and contains further windows).

Freeze and Thaw are hints to wxWidgets that display updates between these two function calls should be optimized. For example, you could use this when adding a lot of lines to a text control separately. Implemented for wxTextCtrl on GTK+, and all windows on Windows and Mac OS X.

GetAcceleratorTable and SetAcceleratorTable get and set the accelerator table for this window.

GetBackgroundColour and SetBackgroundColour are accessors for the window background color, used by the default wxEVT_ERASE_BACKGROUND event. After setting the color, you will need to call Refresh or ClearBackground to show the window with the new color. SetOwnBackgroundColour is the same as SetBackgroundColour but the color is not inherited by the window's children.

GetBackgroundStyle and SetBackgroundStyle are accessors for the window background style. By default, the background style is wxBG_STYLE_SYSTEM, which tells wxWidgets to draw the window background with whatever style is appropriate, whether a texture drawn according to the current theme (for example, wxDialog), or a solid color (for example, wxListBox). If you set the style to wxBG_STYLE_COLOUR, wxWidgets will use a solid color for this window. If you set it to wxBG_STYLE_CUSTOM, wxWidgets will suppress the default background drawing, and the application can paint it from its erase or paint event handler. If you want to draw your own textured background, then setting the style to wxBG_STYLE_CUSTOM is recommended for flicker-free refreshes.

GetBestSize returns the minimal size for the window in pixels (as implemented for each window by DoGetBestSize). This is a hint to the sizer system not to resize the window so small that it cannot be viewed or used properly. For example, for a static control, it will be the minimum size such that the control label is not truncated. For windows containing subwindows (typically wxPanel), the size returned by this function will be the same as the size the window would have had after calling Fit.

GetCaret and SetCaret are accessors for the wxCaret object associated with the window.

GetClientSize and SetClientSize are accessors for the size of the client area in pixels. The client area is the region within any borders and window decorations, inside which you can draw or place child windows.

GetCursor and SetCursor are accessors for the cursor associated with the window.

GetDefaultItem returns a pointer to the child button that is the default for this window, or NULL. The default button is the one activated by pressing the Enter key. Use wxButton::SetDefault to set the default button.

GetDropTarget and SetDropTarget are accessors for the wxDropTarget object which handles dropped data objects for this window. Drag and drop is covered in Chapter 11, "Clipboard and Drag and Drop."

GetEventHandler and SetEventHandler are accessors for the first event handler for the window. By default, the event handler is the window itself, but you can interpose a different event handler. You can also use PushEventHandler and PopEventHandler to set up a handler chain, with different handlers dealing with different events. wxWidgets will search along the chain for handlers that match incoming events (see Chapter 3, "Event Handling").

GetExtraStyle and SetExtraStyle are accessors for the "extra" style bits. Extra styles normally start with wxWS_EX_.

GetFont and SetFont are accessors for the font associated with this window. SetOwnFont is the same as SetFont, except that the font is not inherited by the window's children.

GetForegroundColour and SetForegroundColour are accessors for the window foreground color, whose meaning differs according to the type of window. SetOwnForegroundColour is the same as SetForegroundColour but the color is not inherited by the window's children.

GetHelpText and SetHelpText are accessors for the context-sensitive help string associated with the window. The text is actually stored by the current wxHelpProvider implementation, and not in the window.

GetId and SetId are accessors for the window identifier.

GetLabel returns the label associated with the window. The interpretation of this value depends on the particular window class.

GetName and SetName are accessors for the window name, which does not have to be unique. The window name has no special significance to wxWidgets, except under Motif where it is the resource name for the window.

GetParent returns a pointer to the parent window.

GetPosition returns the position of the top-left corner of the window in pixels, relative to its parent.

GetRect returns a wxRect object (see Chapter 13, "Data Structure Classes") representing the size and position of the window in pixels.

GetSize and SetSize retrieve and set the outer window dimensions in pixels.

GetSizer and SetSizer are accessors for the top-level sizer used for arranging child windows on this window.

GetTextExtent gets the dimensions of the string in pixels, as it would be drawn on the window with the currently selected font.

GetToolTip and SetToolTip are accessors for the window tooltip object.

GetUpdateRegion returns the portion of the window that currently needs refreshing (since the last paint event was handled).

GetValidator and SetValidator are accessors for the optional wxValidator object associated with the window, to handle transfer and validation of data. See Chapter 9 for more about validators.

GetVirtualSize returns the virtual size of the window in pixels, as determined by setting the scrollbar dimensions.

GetWindowStyle and SetWindowStyle are accessors for the window style.

InitDialog sends a wxEVT_INIT_DIALOG event to initiate transfer of data to the window.

IsEnabled indicates whether the window is enabled or disabled.

IsExposed indicates whether a point or a part of the rectangle is in the update region.

IsShown indicates whether the window is shown.

IsTopLevel indicates whether the window is top-level (a wxFrame or a wxDialog).

Layout invokes the sizer-based layout system if there is a sizer associated with the window. See Chapter 7 for more about sizers.

Lower sends a window to the bottom of the window hierarchy, while Raise raises the window above all other windows. This works for top-level windows and child windows.

MakeModal disables all the other top-level windows in the application so that the user can only interact with this window.

Move moves the window to a new position.

MoveAfterInTabOrder moves the tab order of this window to a position just after the window passed as argument, and MoveBeforeInTabOrder is the same but moves the tab order in front of the window argument.

PushEventHandler pushes an event handler onto the event stack for this window, and PopEventHandler removes and returns the top-most event handler on the event handler stack. RemoveEventHandler finds a handler in the event handler stack and removes it.

PopupMenu shows a menu at the specified position.

Refresh and RefreshRect causes a paint event (and optionally an erase event) to be sent to the window.

SetFocus gives the window the current keyboard focus.

SetScrollbar sets the properties for a built-in scrollbar.

SetSizeHints allows specification of the minimum and maximum window sizes, and window size increments, in pixels. This is applicable to top-level windows only.

Show shows or hides the window; Hide is equivalent to passing false to Show.

TransferDataFromWindow and TransferDataToWindow transfer data from and to the window. By default, these call validator functions, but they can be overridden by the application.

Update immediately repaints the invalidated area of the window.

UpdateWindowUI sends wxUpdateUIEvents to the window to give the window (and application) a chance to update window elements, such as toolbars as menu items.

Validate validates the current values of the child controls using their validators.

wxControl

wxControl derives from wxWindow and is the abstract base class for controls: windows that display items of data and usually respond to mouse clicks or keyboard input by sending command events.

wxControlWithItems

wxControlWithItems is an abstract base class for some wxWidgets controls that contain several items, such as wxListBox, wxCheckListBox, wxChoice, and wxComboBox. The use of this intermediate class ensures that a consistent API is used across several controls that have similar functionality.

The items in a wxControlWithItems have string labels and, optionally, *client data* associated with them. Client data comes in two different flavors: either simple untyped (void*) pointers, which are stored by the control but not used in any way by it, or typed pointers (wxClientData*). These typed pointers are owned by the control, meaning that the typed client data will be deleted when an item is deleted or when the entire control is cleared (for example, when it is destroyed). All items in the same control must have client data of the same type: either all typed or all untyped (if it has any at all). The client data type is determined by the first call to Append, SetClientData, or SetClientObject. To work with typed client data, you should derive a class from wxClientData containing the data you want to store, and pass it to Append or SetClientObject.

wxControlWithItems Member Functions

Append adds a single item or an array of items to the control. When adding a single item, you can also associate typed or untyped data with the item by passing a second argument. For example:

```
wxArrayString strArr;
strArr.Add(wxT("First string"));
strArr.Add(wxT("Second string"));
controlA->Append(strArr);
controlA->Append(wxT("Third string"));
controlB->Append(wxT("First string"), (void *) myPtr);
controlC->Append(wxT("First string"), new MyTypedData(1));
```

Clear clears all items from the controls (deleting all typed client data).

Delete removes an item (and its typed client data) using a zero-based position.

FindString returns the zero-based index to the item matching a string, or wxNOT_FOUND if no item was found.

GetClientData and GetClientObject return a pointer to the client data associated with the specified item (if any). SetClientData and SetClientObject can be used to set the data for a specified item.

GetCount returns the number of items in the control.

GetSelection returns the index of the selected item, or wxNOT_FOUND if none was selected. SetSelection sets the index of the selected item.

GetString returns the item label at the given position; SetString sets an item's label.

GetStringSelection returns the label of the selected item or an empty string if no item is selected; SetStringSelection sets the selection. To avoid an assertion, first check that the string is available in the control using FindString.

Insert inserts an item (with or without client data) at a specified position in the control.

IsEmpty returns true if the control has no items, and false otherwise.

TOP-LEVEL WINDOWS

Top-level windows are placed directly on the desktop and are not contained within other windows. They can be moved around the screen, and resized if the application permits it. There are three basic kinds of top-level window: wxFrame and wxDialog, both derived from an abstract base class called wxTopLevelWindow, and wxPopupWindow, which has less functionality and is derived directly from wxWindow. A dialog can be either modal or modeless, whereas a frame is almost always modeless. Modal means that flow through the application effectively halts until the user dismisses the dialog. This is very handy for getting a response before continuing, but it's always good to see whether an alternative user interface can be used (for example, a font control on the toolbar rather than in a properties window) to keep the interaction more fluid.

Top-level windows normally have a title bar and can have decorations for closing, minimizing, or restoring the window. A frame often has a menu bar, toolbar, and status bar, but a dialog generally does not. On Mac OS X, a frame's menu bar is not shown at the top of the frame, but at the top of the screen.

Don't confuse this usage of "top-level window" with the window returned by wxApp::GetTopWindow, by which wxWidgets or your application can get hold of the "main window," most often the first frame or dialog you create.

If needed, you can access all current top-level windows using the global variable wxTopLevelWindows, which is a wxWindowList.

wxFrame

wxFrame is a popular choice for the main application window. Figure 4-2 shows the elements that compose a frame. A frame may optionally have a title bar (with decorations such as a button for closing the window), a wxMenuBar, a wxToolBar, and a wxStatusBar. The area that is left for child windows is called the client area, and it is up to the application to arrange the children's size and position if there is more than one child. You should use sizers for this purpose, described in Chapter 7, or perhaps a splitter window (covered later in this chapter) if you need a couple of child windows.

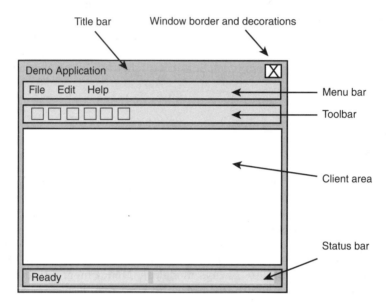

Figure 4-2   The elements of a frame

Because some platforms do not allow direct painting on a frame, and to support keyboard navigation between child controls, you should create an intermediate wxPanel (see later).

A frame can have more than one toolbar, but it will only do sizing and positioning for one toolbar. You must implement explicit layout for multiple toolbars.

It is highly likely that you will derive a new class from wxFrame rather than using it directly, so that you can handle events such as wxEVT_CLOSE (see the following) and command events. Often you will create child windows and a menu bar within your frame constructor.

You can assign an icon to the frame to be shown by the system, such as on the taskbar or in the file manager. On Windows, it's best to use a compound icon at 16×16 and 32×32 pixels and perhaps several color depths. On Linux, the same icons as for Windows usually suffices. On Mac OS X, you'll need a variety of icons in different colors and depths. For more details on icons and icon bundles, see Chapter 10, "Programming with Images."

wxFrame has the following constructor in addition to the default constructor:

```
wxFrame(wxWindow* parent, wxWindowID id, const wxString& title,
    const wxPoint& pos = wxDefaultPosition,
    const wxSize& size = wxDefaultSize,
    long style = wxDEFAULT_FRAME_STYLE,
    const wxString& name = wxT("frame"));
```

For example:

```
wxFrame* frame = new wxFrame(NULL, ID_MYFRAME,
    wxT("Hello wxWidgets"), wxDefaultPosition,
    wxSize(500, 300));
frame->Show(true);
```

Note that the frame won't be shown until Show(true) is called, to give the application the chance to do child window layout invisibly.

You don't have to pass a parent window to the new frame, but if you do, the new window will be displayed on top of the parent window if the wxFRAME_FLOAT_ON_PARENT style is specified.

To destroy a frame, do not use delete, but instead use Destroy or Close to tell wxWidgets to clean up the frame in idle time when all its events have been processed. When you call Close, you send a wxEVT_CLOSE event to the window. The default handler for this event calls Destroy. When a frame is deleted, its children are automatically deleted, as long as they are not themselves top-level windows.

When the last top-level window has been destroyed, the application exits (although you can change this behavior by calling wxApp::SetExitOnFrame Delete). Your main window's wxEVT_CLOSE handler may need to destroy other top-level windows that might be open—for example, a Find dialog—otherwise the application will not close when the main window is closed.

A frame does not have the equivalent of wxDialog::ShowModal to enter an event loop and disable other top-level windows. However, you can get similar behavior by creating a wxWindowDisabler object when you require other top-level windows to be disabled. Or, you can use a wxModalEventLoop object, passing the frame pointer, calling Run to start a local event loop and calling Exit (usually from an event handler) to quit the loop.

Figure 4-3 shows the frame of a consumer application running on Windows. The frame has a title bar at the top, a menu bar, a colorful toolbar, a splitter window in the frame's client area, and a status bar at the bottom, giving help on toolbar buttons and menu items as the user drags the mouse over them.

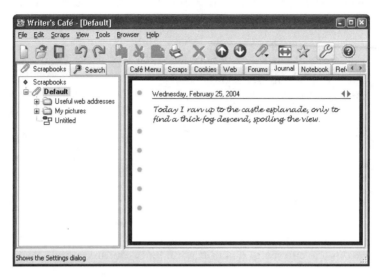

Figure 4-3   A typical wxFrame

wxFrame Styles

wxFrame can have the window styles listed in Table 4-4, in addition to those described for wxWindow.

Table 4-4   wxFrame Styles

wxDEFAULT_FRAME_STYLE	Defined as wxMINIMIZE_BOX ¦ wxMAXIMIZE_BOX ¦ wxRESIZE_BORDER ¦ wxSYSTEM_MENU ¦ wxCAPTION ¦ wxCLOSE_BOX.
wxICONIZE	Displays the frame iconized (minimized). Windows only.
wxCAPTION	Puts a caption on the frame.
wxMINIMIZE	Identical to wxICONIZE. Windows only.
wxMINIMIZE_BOX	Displays a minimize box on the frame.
wxMAXIMIZE	Displays the frame maximized. Windows only.
wxMAXIMIZE_BOX	Displays a maximize box on the frame.
wxCLOSE_BOX	Displays a close box on the frame.
wxSTAY_ON_TOP	The frame stays on top of all other windows. Windows only.
wxSYSTEM_MENU	Displays a system menu.
wxRESIZE_BORDER	Displays a resizable border around the window.
wxFRAME_TOOL_WINDOW	Causes a frame with a small title bar to be created; the frame does not appear in the taskbar under Windows.

wxFRAME_NO_TASKBAR	Creates an otherwise normal frame, but it does not appear in the taskbar under Windows or Linux (note that on Windows it will minimize to the desktop window, which may seem strange to users and thus it might be better to use this style without the wxMINIMIZE_BOX style). Has no effect under other platforms.
wxFRAME_FLOAT_ON_PARENT	The frame will always be on top of its parent. A frame created with this style must have a non-NULL parent.
wxFRAME_SHAPED	Windows with this style are allowed to have their shape changed with the SetShape method.

Table 4-5 shows the extra styles that couldn't be accommodated in the regular style and that are set using wxWindow::SetExtraStyle.

Table 4-5   wxFrame Extra Styles

wxFRAME_EX_CONTEXTHELP	Under Windows, puts a query button on the caption. When pressed, Windows will go into a context-sensitive help mode and wxWidgets will send a wxEVT_HELP event if the user clicked on an application window. You cannot use this style together with wxMAXIMIZE_BOX or wxMINIMIZE_BOX.
wxFRAME_EX_METAL	Under Mac OS X, this style will give the frame a metallic appearance. This should be used sparingly and is intended for consumer applications that emulate a physical device such as an audio player.

wxFrame Events

wxFrame and its derived classes generate the events listed in Table 4-6, in addition to those mentioned for wxWindow.

Table 4-6   wxFrame Events

EVT_ACTIVATE(func)	Processes a wxEVT_ACTIVATE event, generated when the frame is about to be activated or deactivated. Handlers take a wxActivateEvent object.
EVT_CLOSE(func)	Processes a wxEVT_CLOSE event, generated when the program or windowing system is trying to close the frame. Handlers take a wxCloseEvent object and can veto the close by calling Veto on the object.

(continues)

Table 4-6   wxFrame Events (*Continued*)

EVT_ICONIZE(func)	Processes a wxEVT_ICONIZE event, generated when the frame is being iconized (minimized) or restored. Handlers take a wxIconizeEvent object. Call IsIconized to check if this is an iconize or restore event.
EVT_MAXIMIZE(func)	Processes a wxEVT_MAXIMIZE event, generated when the frame is being maximized or restored. Handlers take a wxMaximizeEvent object. Call IsMaximized to check if this is a maximize or restore event.

wxFrame Member Functions

These are the major wxFrame functions. Because wxFrame derives from wxTopLevelWindow and wxWindow, please also refer also to the member functions for these classes.

CreateStatusBar creates one or more status fields at the bottom of the frame. Use SetStatusText to set the text for a particular field, and SetStatusWidths to customize the widths of the fields (see also wxStatusBar later in this chapter). For example:

```
frame->CreateStatusBar(2, wxST_SIZEGRIP);
int widths[3] = { 100, 100, -1 };
frame->SetStatusWidths(3, widths);
frame->SetStatusText(wxT("Ready"), 0);
```

CreateToolBar creates a toolbar under the menu bar and associates it with the frame. Alternatively, you can create a toolbar by using the wxToolBar constructor, but to allow it to be managed by the frame, you need to call wxFrame::SetToolBar.

GetMenuBar and SetMenuBar are accessors for the frame's wxMenuBar. There is only one menu bar per frame. You can replace an existing one with a new menu bar, and the old menu bar will be deleted.

GetTitle and SetTitle are accessors for the title that appears on the frame's title bar.

Iconize iconizes or restores the frame. You can test the frame's iconic state by calling IsIconized.

Maximize resizes the frame to fit the desktop, or restores it to the previous state if it is currently maximized. Call IsMaximized to test whether the frame is maximized.

SetIcon sets the icon displayed when the frame is minimized. It's also used for other purposes by the window manager, such as displaying the program's icon in Windows Explorer or on the taskbar. You can also use SetIcons to set an icon bundle (multiple icons with a variety of resolutions and depths).

SetShape sets a region specifying the shape of the frame on some platforms (currently Windows, Mac OS X, and GTK+, and X11 if the appropriate X11 extension is available).

ShowFullScreen hides as many decorations as possible and shows the client window at the maximum size of the display. It can also restore the frame to its former size and state. Use IsFullScreen to determine whether the frame is currently being shown full-screen.

Non-Rectangular Frames

If you want to write a more unusual-looking consumer application, such as a clock or media player, you can set a non-rectangular region for the frame, and only that region will be displayed. In Figure 4-4, the frame has no decorations (such as caption, border, or menu bar), and its paint handler is displaying a penguin bitmap. There is a region associated with the frame that acts as a mask that lets only the penguin show through.

Figure 4-4 A shaped wxFrame

The principles are demonstrated by the code in samples/shaped, although it uses a different image from the one shown here. When the frame is created, a bitmap is loaded, and a region is created out of it. On GTK+, setting the window shape must be delayed until the window creation event is sent, so you will need a __WXGTK__ test in your code. The following code demonstrates the required event table, frame constructor, and window creation event handler:

```
BEGIN_EVENT_TABLE(ShapedFrame, wxFrame)
    EVT_MOTION(ShapedFrame::OnMouseMove)
    EVT_PAINT(ShapedFrame::OnPaint)
```

```
#ifdef __WXGTK__
    EVT_WINDOW_CREATE(ShapedFrame::OnWindowCreate)
#endif
END_EVENT_TABLE()

ShapedFrame::ShapedFrame()
       : wxFrame((wxFrame *)NULL, wxID_ANY, wxEmptyString,
                   wxDefaultPosition, wxSize(250, 300),
                   ┊ wxFRAME_SHAPED
                   ┊ wxSIMPLE_BORDER
                   ┊ wxFRAME_NO_TASKBAR
                   ┊ wxSTAY_ON_TOP
              )
{
    m_hasShape = false;
    m_bmp = wxBitmap(wxT("penguin.png"), wxBITMAP_TYPE_PNG);
    SetSize(wxSize(m_bmp.GetWidth(), m_bmp.GetHeight()));

#ifndef __WXGTK__
    // On wxGTK we can't do this yet because the window hasn't
    // been created yet so we wait until the EVT_WINDOW_CREATE
    // event happens. On wxMSW and wxMac the window has been created
    // at this point so we go ahead and set the shape now.
    SetWindowShape();
#endif
}

// Used on GTK+ only
void ShapedFrame::OnWindowCreate(wxWindowCreateEvent& WXUNUSED(evt))
{
    SetWindowShape();
}
```

To set the shape, we create a region from the bitmap and the color to be used
as the transparent color, and call SetShape.

```
void ShapedFrame::SetWindowShape()
{
    wxRegion region(m_bmp, *wxWHITE);
    m_hasShape = SetShape(region);
}
```

In order to allow the window to be moved around the screen, there is a mouse
handler that explicitly moves the window.

```
void ShapedFrame::OnMouseMove(wxMouseEvent& evt)
{
    wxPoint pt = evt.GetPosition();
    if (evt.Dragging() && evt.LeftIsDown())
    {
        wxPoint pos = ClientToScreen(pt);
        Move(wxPoint(pos.x - m_delta.x, pos.y - m_delta.y));
    }
}
```

The paint handler is very simple, but of course in a real application, you will have other windows or graphics displayed inside the frame.

```
void ShapedFrame::OnPaint(wxPaintEvent& evt)
{
    wxPaintDC dc(this);
    dc.DrawBitmap(m_bmp, 0, 0, true);
}
```

For more details, see samples/shaped in the wxWidgets distribution.

Mini-Frames

On Windows and GTK+, you can use wxMiniFrame for frames that must have a small caption—for example, if implementing tool palettes. Figure 4-5 shows a wxMiniFrame on Windows. This class is implemented as a normal frame on Mac OS X. There are no special styles or member functions for this class.

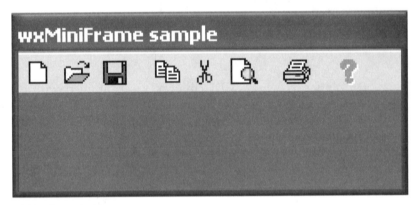

Figure 4-5   A wxMiniFrame

wxMDIParentFrame

This frame class, derived from wxFrame, is part of wxWidgets' Multiple Document Interface (MDI) support, whereby a parent frame manages zero or more wxMDIChildFrame windows. How it does so depends on platform; the main visual differences are illustrated in Figure 4-6. On Windows, the child windows are clipped to the boundary of the main window. These windows can be tiled, overlapped, or maximized within the main frame so that only one shows at a time, and a *Window* menu (automatically added by wxWidgets) is available for controlling the child windows. The MDI style has the advantage of keeping a desktop relatively uncluttered, grouping together all the windows in the application. Also, because the main frame's menu bar is replaced by the active child frame's menu bar, the clutter of multiple menu bars is also reduced.

Under GTK+, wxWidgets emulates the MDI style using tabbed windows; only one window is shown at a time, but the user can switch between windows quickly using the tabs. On Mac OS, wxMDIParentFrame and wxMDIChildFrame windows look like normal frames, reflecting the fact that documents always open in a new window on Mac OS.

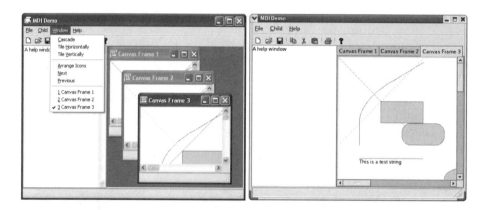

Figure 4-6   wxMDIParentFrame on Windows and GTK+

On platforms where MDI children are contained within the parent, a wxMDIParentFrame arranges its children on a wxMDIClientWindow, which can coexist with other windows in the frame. In Figure 4-6, the parent frame's size event handler sets the sizes and positions of a text control and the client window. For details, see samples/mdi in your wxWidgets distribution.

Each child frame can have its own menu bar, in addition to the parent frame's menu bar. When a child frame is activated, its menu bar is shown. When there are no child frames, the parent frame's menu bar is shown. You need to construct your child frame menu bar carefully to include the same commands as the parent's menu bar, adding others that are specific to the child. The parent frame and child frames can have their own toolbars and status bars, but they are not swapped like menu bars.

wxMDIParentFrame has the same constructor as wxFrame.

wxMDIParentFrame Styles

wxMDIParentFrame can have the window styles listed in Table 4-7, in addition to those described for wxFrame.

Table 4-7   wxMDIParentFrame Styles

wxFRAME_NO_WINDOW_MENU	Under Windows, removes the Window menu that is normally added automatically.

wxMDIParentFrame Member Functions

These are the major `wxMDIParentFrame` functions, in addition to those defined for `wxFrame`.

`ActivateNext` and `ActivatePrevious` activate the next or previous child frame.

`Cascade` and `Tile` provide two methods to arrange the child frames: overlapping and tiling them, respectively. `ArrangeIcons` lays out any minimized frames within the client window. These three functions only apply on Windows.

`GetActiveChild` provides the application with a pointer to the currently active child (if any).

`GetClientWindow` returns a pointer to the client window (a container for the child frames). You can provide a different client window from the default by overriding `OnCreateClient` and returning an instance of your own `wxMDIClientWindow`-derived class, but you must then use two-step parent frame construction.

wxMDIChildFrame

`wxMDIChildFrame` should always be created as a child of a `wxMDIParentFrame` window. As explained in the previous section, its appearance depends on the platform and will either be free-floating or constrained to the boundary of its parent.

Its constructor is the same as a regular frame; despite the fact that its true parent is a `wxMDIClientWindow`, you should pass the frame parent to the constructor.

For example:

```
#include "wx/mdi.h"

wxMDIParentFrame* parentFrame = new wxMDIParentFrame(
    NULL, ID_MYFRAME, wxT("Hello wxWidgets"));

wxMDIChildFrame* childFrame = new wxMDIChildFrame(
    parentFrame, ID_MYCHILD, wxT("Child 1"));

childFrame->Show(true);
parentFrame->Show(true);
```

wxMDIChildFrame Styles

`wxMDIChildFrame` takes the same styles as `wxFrame`, although depending on platform, not all of them will take effect.

wxMDIChildFrame Member Functions

These are the major wxMDIChildFrame functions. See also the base class, wxFrame.

Activate activates this frame, bringing it to the front and displaying its menu bar.

Maximize resizes the frame to fit the parent (Windows only).

Restore sets the frame to the size it was before it was maximized (Windows only).

wxDialog

A dialog is a top-level window used for presenting information, options, or selections. It can optionally have a title bar with decorations such as the close window button and minimize button, and as with wxFrame, you can assign an icon to the dialog to be shown in the taskbar or equivalent. A dialog can contain any combination of non-top level windows and control—for example, a wxNotebook with *OK* and *Cancel* buttons underneath. As its name suggests, you use this class to initiate a dialog with a user, presenting specific information and choices, compared with the frame's usual role as the main window of an application.

There are two kinds of dialog—modal and modeless. A modal dialog blocks program flow and user input on other windows until it is dismissed (EndModal is called), whereas a modeless dialog behaves more like a frame in that program flow continues, and input in other windows is still possible. To show a modal dialog, you should use the ShowModal method, whereas to show a dialog modelessly, you simply use Show, as with frames.

Note that the modal dialog is one of the very few examples of wxWindow-derived objects that may be created on the stack and not on the heap. In other words, you can use the heap method as follows:

```
void AskUser()
{
    MyAskDialog *dlg = new MyAskDialog(...);
    if ( dlg->ShowModal() == wxID_OK )
        ...
    //else: dialog was cancelled or some another button pressed

    dlg->Destroy();
}
```

You can also achieve the same result by using the stack:

```
void AskUser()
{
    MyAskDialog dlg(...);
    if ( dlg.ShowModal() == wxID_OK )
        ...

    // no need to call Destroy() here
}
```

Normally you will derive a new class from wxDialog rather than using it directly so that you can handle events such as wxEVT_CLOSE (see the following) and command events. Often you will create your dialog's controls within the constructor.

Just as with wxFrame, wxWidgets will resize a single child window to fill the dialog, but for more than one child, the application is responsible for sizing and positioning the controls using sizers (see Chapter 7).

When you call Show, wxWidgets calls InitDialog to send a wxInitDialog Event to the dialog, transferring data to the dialog via validators or other means.

wxDialog has the following constructor in addition to the default constructor:

```
wxDialog(wxWindow* parent, wxWindowID id, const wxString& title,
    const wxPoint& pos = wxDefaultPosition,
    const wxSize& size = wxDefaultSize,
    long style = wxDEFAULT_DIALOG_STYLE,
    const wxString& name = wxT("dialog"));
```

For example:

```
wxDialog* dialog = new wxDialog(NULL, ID_MYDIALOG,
    wxT("Hello wxWidgets"), wxDefaultPosition,
    wxSize(500, 300));
dialog->Show(true);
```

The dialog won't be shown until Show(true) or ShowModal is called to give the application the chance to do child window layout invisibly.

By default, a dialog created with a NULL parent window will be given the application's top-level window as parent. Use the wxDIALOG_NO_PARENT style to prevent this from happening and create an orphan dialog. This is not recommended for modal dialogs.

As with wxFrame, do not use delete to destroy a dialog, but instead use Destroy or Close to delay deletion until all the object's events have been processed. When you call Close, the default wxEVT_CLOSE handler for this function usually calls Destroy.

Note that before a *modal* dialog is destroyed, an event handler should have called EndModal, passing the identifier of the command that closed it (for example, wxID_OK or wxID_CANCEL). This will exit the dialog's event loop so that the dialog object can be destroyed by the code that called ShowModal. The identifier passed to EndModal will be returned by ShowModal. To clarify, the OnCancel function in the following example will be called while ShowModal is in its event loop:

```
// Event handler for wxID_CANCEL
void MyDialog::OnCancel(wxCommandEvent& event)
{
    EndModal(wxID_CANCEL);
}

// Show a dialog
void ShowDialog()
{
    // Show the dialog
    MyDialog dialog;

    // OnCancel or other function is called from within ShowModal
    if (dialog.ShowModal() == wxID_CANCEL)
    {
        ...
    }
}
```

Figure 4-7 shows a typical simple dialog, which we'll create in Chapter 9. Dialogs can, of course, get more complicated, such as the settings dialog shown in Figure 4-8. This one has a splitter window, a tree control to navigate between multiple panels, and a grid control acting as a property editor.

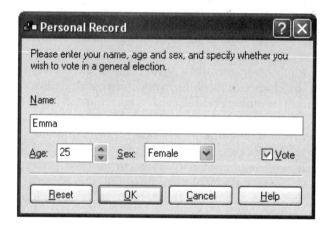

Figure 4-7   A typical simple dialog

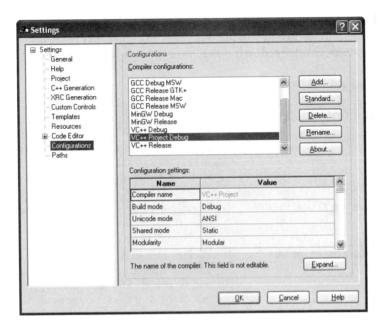

Figure 4-8   A more complex dialog

wxDialog Styles

`wxDialog` can have the window styles listed in Table 4-8 in addition to those described for `wxWindow`.

Table 4-8   `wxDialog` Styles

`wxDEFAULT_DIALOG_STYLE`	Defined as `wxSYSTEM_MENU` ¦ `wxCAPTION` ¦ `wxCLOSE_BOX`.
`wxCAPTION`	Puts a caption on the dialog.
`wxMINIMIZE_BOX`	Displays a minimize box on the dialog.
`wxMAXIMIZE_BOX`	Displays a maximize box on the dialog.
`wxCLOSE_BOX`	Displays a close box on the dialog.
`wxSTAY_ON_TOP`	The dialog stays on top of all other windows. Windows only.
`wxSYSTEM_MENU`	Displays a system menu.
`wxRESIZE_BORDER`	Displays a resizable border around the window.
`wxDIALOG_NO_PARENT`	A dialog created with a `NULL` parent window will be given the application's top-level window as parent. Use this style to create an "orphan" dialog. This is not recommended for modal dialogs.

Table 4-9 describes extra styles that couldn't be accommodated in the regular style, and so are set using wxWindow::SetExtraStyle. Although wxWS_EX_BLOCK_ EVENTS is valid for all windows, we repeat it here because it is set by default.

Table 4-9 wxDialog Extra Styles

wxDIALOG_EX_CONTEXTHELP	Under Windows, puts a query button on the caption. When pressed, Windows will go into a context-sensitive help mode and wxWidgets will send a wxEVT_HELP event if the user clicked on an application window. You cannot use this style together with wxMAXIMIZE_BOX or wxMINIMIZE_BOX.
wxWS_EX_BLOCK_EVENTS	Blocks command event propagation above this window (the default). Be aware that calling SetExtra Style may reset the style.
wxDIALOG_EX_METAL	Under Mac OS X, this style will give the dialog a metallic appearance. This should be used sparingly and is intended for consumer applications that emulate a physical device such as an audio player.

wxDialog Events

wxDialog generates the events listed in Table 4-10, in addition to those mentioned for wxWindow.

Table 4-10 wxDialog Events

EVT_ACTIVATE(func)	Processes a wxEVT_ACTIVATE event, generated when the dialog is about to be activated or deactivated. Handlers take a wxActivateEvent object.
EVT_CLOSE(func)	Processes a wxEVT_CLOSE event, generated when the program or windowing system is trying to close the dialog. Handlers take a wxCloseEvent object and can veto the close by calling Veto on the object.
EVT_ICONIZE(func)	Processes a wxEVT_ICONIZE event, generated when the dialog is being iconized (minimized) or restored. Handlers take a wxIconizeEvent object. Call IsIconized to check if this is an iconize or restore event.
EVT_MAXIMIZE(func)	Processes a wxEVT_MAXIMIZE event, generated when the dialog is being maximized or restored. Handlers take a wxMaximizeEvent object. Call IsMaximized to check if this is a maximize or restore event.
EVT_INIT_DIALOG(func)	Processes a wxEVT_INIT_DIALOG event, generated to enable the dialog to initialize itself. Handlers take a wxInit DialogEvent object. This event is also generated for wxPanel. The default handler calls TransferDataToWindow.

wxDialog Member Functions

These are the major `wxDialog` functions. Please refer also to the member functions for `wxWindow` and `wxTopLevelWindow`, from which `wxDialog` is derived.

`GetTitle` and `SetTitle` are accessors for the title that appears on the dialog's title bar.

`Iconize` iconizes or restores the dialog. You can test the dialog's iconic state by calling `IsIconized`.

`Maximize` maximizes the dialog (makes it as large as the desktop) or restores it to the previous state. Call `IsMaximized` to test whether the dialog is maximized. Windows only.

`SetIcon` sets the icon displayed when the dialog is minimized. It's also used for other purposes by the window manager, such as displaying the program's icon in Windows Explorer or on the taskbar. You can also use `SetIcons` to set an icon bundle (multiple icons with a variety of resolutions and depths).

`ShowModal` is used when showing a modal dialog. It returns the value of the identifier passed to `EndModal`—normally this is the identifier of the control that the user clicked on to dismiss the dialog. By default (implemented in the dialog's `wxEVT_CLOSE` handler), closing the dialog sends a simulated `wxID_CANCEL` to the dialog. The default handler for `wxID_CANCEL` calls `EndModal` with `wxID_CANCEL`. Therefore, if you provide a button with the identifier `wxID_CANCEL`, the logic for canceling the dialog is handled for you, unless you need extra functionality.

`SetLeftMenu` and `SetRightMenu` are only available on Microsoft Smartphone, and they set the commands allocated to the left and right menu buttons. They take a command identifier, such as `wxID_OK`, a label, and an optional pointer to a `wxMenu` to show.

wxPopupWindow

Pop-up windows are not implemented on all platforms (in particular, they are missing from Mac OS X), and so we will only briefly mention them.

`wxPopupWindow` is a top-level window that normally has minimal decoration and is used to implement windows that are shown briefly, such as a menu or a tooltip. Create it by passing a parent window and optional style to the constructor (defaulting to `wxNO_BORDER`). Move it into position with `Position`, which takes a screen position and size and makes sure that the popup is visible on the display.

`wxPopupTransientWindow` is a special kind of `wxPopupWindow` that dismisses itself (hides) when it loses the focus or the mouse is clicked outside of the window. It can also be hidden with `Dismiss`.

CONTAINER WINDOWS

Container windows are designed to hold further visual elements, either child windows or graphics drawn on the window.

wxPanel

wxPanel is essentially a wxWindow with some dialog-like properties. This is usually the class to use when you want to arrange controls on a window that's not a wxDialog, such as a wxFrame. It's often used for pages of a wxNotebook. wxPanel normally takes the system dialog color.

As with wxDialog, you can use InitDialog to send a wxInitDialogEvent to the panel, transferring data to the panel via validators or other means. wxPanel also handles navigation keys such as the Tab key to provide automatic traversal between controls, if the wxTAB_TRAVERSAL style is provided.

wxPanel has the following constructor in addition to the default constructor:

```
wxPanel(wxWindow* parent, wxWindowID id,
    const wxPoint& pos = wxDefaultPosition,
    const wxSize& size = wxDefaultSize,
    long style = wxTAB_TRAVERSAL|wxNO_BORDER,
    const wxString& name = wxT("panel"));
```

For example:

```
wxPanel* panel = new wxPanel(frame, wxID_ANY,
    wxDefaultPosition, wxSize(500, 300));
```

wxPanel Styles

There are no specific styles for wxPanel, but see the styles for wxWindow.

wxPanel Member Functions

There are no distinct wxPanel functions; please refer to the wxWindow member functions, inherited by wxPanel.

wxNotebook

This class represents a control with several pages, switched by clicking on tabs along an edge of the control. A page is normally a wxPanel or a class derived from it, although you may use other window classes.

Notebook tabs may have images as well as, or instead of, text labels. The images are supplied via a wxImageList (see Chapter 10), and specified by position in the list.

To use a notebook, create a wxNotebook object and call AddPage or InsertPage, passing a window to be used as the page. Do not explicitly destroy the window for a page that is currently managed by wxNotebook; use DeletePage instead, or let the notebook destroy the pages when it is itself destroyed.

Here's an example of creating a notebook with three panels, and a text label and icon for each tab:

```
#include "wx/notebook.h"

#include "copy.xpm"
#include "cut.xpm"
#include "paste.xpm"

// Create the notebook
wxImageList* imageList = new wxImageList(16,16,true, 3);
  imageList->Add(wxIcon(copy_xpm));

// Create the image list
wxImageList* imageList = new wxImageList(16,16,true, 3);
imageList->Add(wxIcon(cut_xpm));
imageList->Add(wxIcon(paste_xpm));
notebook->SetimageList(imageList);

// Create and add the pages
wxPanel* window1 = new wxPanel(notebook, wxID_ANY);
wxPanel* window2 = new wxPanel(notebook, wxID_ANY);
wxPanel* window3 = new wxPanel(notebook, wxID_ANY);

notebook->AddPage(window1, wxT("Tab one"), true, 0);
notebook->AddPage(window2, wxT("Tab two"), false, 1);
notebook->AddPage(window3, wxT("Tab three"), false, 2);
```

Figure 4-9 shows the result on Windows.

Figure 4-9 A wxNotebook

On most platforms, there are scroll buttons to view tabs that cannot all be displayed on the window at once. However, on Mac OS, the tabs do not scroll, so the number you can display is limited by the window and tab label size.

If you use sizers to lay out controls on individual pages, and pass wxDefaultSize to the notebook constructor, wxNotebook will adjust its size to fit the sizes of its pages.

Notebook Theme Management

On Windows XP, the default theme paints a gradient on the notebook's pages. Although this is the expected native behavior, it can slow down performance, and you may prefer a solid background for aesthetic reasons, especially when the notebook is not being used in a dialog. If you want to suppress themed drawing, there are three ways of doing it. You can use the wxNB_NOPAGETHEME style to disable themed drawing for a particular notebook, you can call wxSystemOptions::SetOption to disable it for the whole application, or you can disable it for individual pages by using SetBackgroundColour. To disable themed pages globally, do this:

```
wxSystemOptions::SetOption(wxT("msw.notebook.themed-background"), 0);
```

Set the value to 1 to enable it again. To give a single page a solid background that matches the current theme, use

```
wxColour col = notebook->GetThemeBackgroundColour();
if (col.Ok())
{
    page->SetBackgroundColour(col);
}
```

On platforms other than Windows, or if the application is not using Windows themes, GetThemeBackgroundColour will return an uninitialized color object, and this code will therefore work on all platforms. Please note that this syntax and behavior is subject to change, so refer to the wxNotebook documentation in your wxWidgets distribution for the latest information.

wxNotebook Styles

wxNotebook can have the window styles listed in Table 4-11, in addition to those described for wxWindow.

Table 4-11 wxNotebook Styles

wxNB_TOP	Place tabs on the top side.
wxNB_LEFT	Place tabs on the left side. Not supported under Windows XP for all themes.
wxNB_RIGHT	Place tabs on the right side. Not supported under Windows XP for all themes.
wxNB_BOTTOM	Place tabs under instead of above the notebook pages. Not supported under Windows XP for all themes.
wxNB_FIXEDWIDTH	All tabs will have same width. Windows only.
wxNB_MULTILINE	There can be several rows of tabs. Windows only.
wxNB_NOPAGETHEME	On Windows, suppresses the textured theme painting for the notebook's pages, drawing a solid color to match the current theme instead. This can improve performance in addition to giving an aesthetic choice.

wxNotebook Events

wxNotebook generates wxNotebookEvent propagating events (events that can be handled by the notebook or its ancestors) specified in Table 4-12.

Table 4-12 wxNotebook Events

EVT_NOTEBOOK_PAGE_CHANGED(id, func)	The page selection has changed.
EVT_NOTEBOOK_PAGE_CHANGING(id, func)	The page selection is about to change. You can veto the selection change with Veto.

wxNotebook Member Functions

These are the major wxNotebook functions.

AddPage adds a page, and InsertPage inserts a page at the given position. You can use a text label for the tab, or an image (specified by index into an image list), or both. For example:

```
// Adds an unselected page with a label and an image
// (index 2 in the associated image list).
notebook->AddPage(page, wxT("My tab"), false, 2);
```

DeletePage removes and destroys the specified page, while RemovePage just removes the page without deleting the page. Call DeleteAllPages to delete all the pages. When the wxNotebook is deleted, it will delete all its pages.

AdvanceSelection cycles through the pages, and SetSelection sets the specified page by zero-based index. Use GetSelection to get the index of the selected page, or wxNOT_FOUND if none was selected.

SetImageList sets a wxImageList to be used by the notebook but does not take ownership of it. Call AssignImageList if you want the notebook to delete the image list when it is destroyed. GetImageList returns the associated image list. An image list stores images to be shown on each page tab, if required. wxImageList is described in Chapter 10.

Use GetPage to return the page window for a given index, and use GetPageCount to return the number of pages in the notebook.

SetPageText and GetPageText are accessors for the label for a given page (by index).

SetPageImage and GetPageImage are accessors for the index of a page's image index in the notebook's image list.

Alternatives to *wxNotebook*

wxNotebook is derived from a base class wxBookCtrlBase, which abstracts the concept of a control that manages pages. There are two API-compatible variations of the wxNotebook concept, wxListbook and wxChoicebook, and you can implement your own, such as wxTreebook.

wxListbook uses a wxListCtrl to change pages; the list control displays icons with text labels underneath them, and can be on any of the four sides, defaulting to the left side. This is an attractive alternative to wxNotebook, and it has the advantage of being able to cope with an arbitrary number of pages even on Mac OS X because the list control can scroll.

wxChoicebook uses a choice control (a drop-down list) and is particularly handy for small devices with restricted screen space, such as smartphones. It does not display images, and by default, it will display the choice control at the top.

The include files for these classes are wx/listbook.h and wx/choicebk.h. Event handlers for these two classes take a wxListbookEvent or wxChoicebookEvent argument, respectively, and you can use the event macros EVT_XXX_PAGE_CHANGED(id, func) and EVT_XXX_PAGE_CHANGING(id, func) where XXX is LISTBOOK or CHOICEBOOK.

You can use the same window styles as wxNotebook, or you can use the equivalents, such as wxCHB_TOP or wxLB_TOP instead of wxNB_TOP.

wxScrolledWindow

All windows can have scrollbars, but extra code is required to make scrolling work. This gives the flexibility to define appropriate scrolling behaviors for different kinds of windows. wxScrolledWindow implements commonly required scrolling behavior by assuming that scrolling happens in consistent units, not different-sized jumps, and that page size (the amount scrolled when "paging" up, down, left, or right) is represented by the visible portion of the window. It is suited to drawing applications but is not so suitable for a sophisticated editor in which the amount scrolled may vary according to the size of text on a given line. For this, you would derive from wxWindow and implement scrolling yourself. wxGrid is an example of a class that implements its own scrolling, largely because columns and rows can vary in size.

To use a scrolled window, you need to define the number of pixels per logical scroll unit (how much the window is scrolled for a line up or down scroll event) and provide the virtual size in logical units. wxScrolledWindow will then take care of showing the scrollbars with appropriately sized "thumbs" (the parts you can drag) and will show or hide scrollbars as appropriate, according to the actual size of the window.

The following fragment shows how to create a scrolled window:

```
#include "wx/scrolwin.h"

wxScrolledWindow* scrolledWindow = new wxScrolledWindow(
    this, wxID_ANY, wxPoint(0, 0), wxSize(400, 400),
    wxVSCROLL|wxHSCROLL);

// Set up virtual window dimensions. It will be 1000x1000
// and will scroll 10 pixels at a time
int pixelsPerUnitX = 10;
int pixelsPerUnitY = 10;
int noUnitsX = 1000;
int noUnitsY = 1000;

scrolledWindow->SetScrollbars(pixelsPerUnitX, pixelsPerUnitY,
    noUnitsX, noUnitsY);
```

A second way to specify the virtual size is to use SetVirtualSize, which takes the virtual size in pixels, plus a call to SetScrollRate to set the horizontal and vertical scrolling increments. A third way is to set a sizer for the window, and the scrolled window will calculate the required scrollbar dimensions from the space taken up by the child windows. You will still need to call SetScrollRate to specify the scrolling increments.

You can provide a paint event handler as normal, but in order to draw the graphics at the appropriate position for the current positions of the scrollbars, call DoPrepareDC before drawing. This sets the device context's device origin. For example:

```
void MyScrolledWindow::OnPaint(wxPaintEvent& event)
{
    wxPaintDC dc(this);
    DoPrepareDC(dc);

    dc.SetPen(*wxBLACK_PEN);
    dc.DrawLine(0, 0, 100, 100);
}
```

Alternatively, you can override the OnDraw virtual function; wxScrolledWindow creates a paint device context and calls DoPrepareDC for you before calling your OnDraw function, so the code simplifies to the following:

```
void MyScrolledWindow::OnDraw(wxDC& dc)
{
    dc.SetPen(*wxBLACK_PEN);
    dc.DrawLine(0, 0, 100, 100);
}
```

Note that you will need to call DoPrepareDC if you draw on the window from outside the paint event, such as within a mouse event handler.

You can provide your own DoPrepareDC function. The default function simply shifts the device origin according to the current scroll positions so that subsequent drawing will appear at the right place:

```
void wxScrolledWindow::DoPrepareDC(wxDC& dc)
{
    int ppuX, ppuY, startX, startY;

    GetScrollPixelsPerUnit(& ppuX, & ppuY);
    GetViewStart(& startX, & startY);

    dc.SetDeviceOrigin( - startX * ppuX, - startY * ppuY );
}
```

For more on painting on a wxScrolledWindow, including using buffered drawing, please see the section on wxPaintDC in Chapter 5, "Drawing and Printing."

wxScrolledWindow Styles

There are no special styles for wxScrolledWindow, but usually you will supply wxVSCROLL¦wxHSCROLL (the default style for wxScrolledWindow). On some platforms, if these styles are not present, no scrollbars will be provided for efficiency reasons.

wxScrolledWindow Events

wxScrolledWindow generates wxScrollWinEvent events (see Table 4-13). These events do not propagate up the window parent-child hierarchy, so if you want to intercept these events, you must derive a new class or plug an event handler object into the window object. Normally you will not need to override the existing handlers for these events.

Table 4-13 wxScrolledWindow Events

EVT_SCROLLWIN(func)	Handles all scroll events.
EVT_SCROLLWIN_TOP(func)	Handles wxEVT_SCROLLWIN_TOP scroll-to-top events.
EVT_SCROLLWIN_BOTTOM(func)	Handles wxEVT_SCROLLWIN_TOP scroll-to-bottom events.
EVT_SCROLLWIN_LINEUP(func)	Handles wxEVT_SCROLLWIN_LINEUP line up events.
EVT_SCROLLWIN_LINEDOWN(func)	Handles wxEVT_SCROLLWIN_LINEDOWN line down events.
EVT_SCROLLWIN_PAGEUP(func)	Handles wxEVT_SCROLLWIN_PAGEUP page up events.
EVT_SCROLLWIN_PAGEDOWN(func)	Handles wxEVT_SCROLLWIN_PAGEDOWN page down events.

wxScrolledWindow Member Functions

These are the major wxScrolledWindow functions.

CalcScrolledPosition and CalcUnscrolledPosition both take four arguments: two integers for the position input in pixels, and two pointers to integers for the transformed position output, also in pixels. CalcScrolledPosition calculates the device position from the logical position. For example, if the window is scrolled 10 pixels down from the top, the *logical* first visible position is 0, but the *device* position is -10. CalcUnscrolledPosition does the inverse, calculating the logical position from the device position.

EnableScrolling enables or disables physical scrolling in horizontal and vertical directions independently. Physical scrolling is the physical transfer of bits up or down the screen when a scroll event occurs. If the application scrolls by a variable amount (for example, if there are different font sizes), then physical scrolling will not work, and you should switch it off. If physical scrolling is disabled, you will have to reposition child windows yourself. Physical scrolling may not be available on all platforms, but it is enabled by default where it is available.

GetScrollPixelsPerUnit returns the horizontal and vertical scroll unit sizes in two pointers to integers. A value of zero indicates that there is no scrolling in that direction.

GetViewStart returns the position of the first visible position on the window, in logical units. Pass two pointers to integers to receive the values. You will need to multiply by the values returned by GetScrollPixelsPerUnit to get pixel values.

GetVirtualSize returns the size in device units (pixels) of the scrollable window area. Pass two pointers to integers to receive the virtual width and height.

DoPrepareDC prepares the device context by setting the device origin according to the current scrollbar positions.

Scroll scrolls a window so that the view is at the given point in scroll units (not pixels), passed as two integers. If either parameter is -1, that position will be unchanged.

SetScrollbars sets the pixels per unit in each direction, the number of units for the virtual window in each direction, the horizontal and vertical position to scroll to (optional), and a boolean to indicate whether the window should be refreshed (false by default).

SetScrollRate sets the horizontal and increment scroll rate (the same as the pixels per unit parameters in SetScrollbars).

SetTargetWindow can be used to scroll a window other than the wxScrolledWindow.

Scrolling Without Using *wxScrolledWindow*

If you want to implement your own scrolling behavior, you can derive a class from wxWindow and use wxWindow::SetScrollbar to set scrollbar properties.

SetScrollbar takes the arguments listed in Table 4-14.

Table 4-14   SetScrollbar Arguments

int orientation	The scrollbar to set: wxVERTICAL or wxHORIZONTAL.
int position	The position of the scrollbar "thumb" in scroll units.
int visible	The size of the visible portion of the scrollbar, in scroll units. Normally, a scrollbar is capable of indicating the visible portion visually by showing a different length of thumb.
int range	The maximum value of the scrollbar, where zero is the start position. You choose the units that suit you, so if you wanted to display text that has 100 lines, you would set this to 100. Note that this doesn't have to correspond to the number of pixels scrolled—it is up to you how you actually show the contents of the window.
bool refresh	true if the scrollbar should be repainted immediately.

Let's say you want to display 50 lines of text, using the same font. The window is sized so that you can only see 16 lines at a time.

You would use

```
SetScrollbar(wxVERTICAL, 0, 16, 50)
```

Note that with the window at this size, the thumb position can never go above 50 minus 16, or 34.

You can determine how many lines are currently visible by dividing the current view size by the character height in pixels.

When defining your own scrollbar behavior, you will always need to recalculate the scrollbar settings when the window size changes. You could therefore introduce a new function AdjustScrollbars into which you place your scrollbar calculations and SetScrollbar call. AdjustScrollbars can be called initially, and also from your wxSizeEvent handler function.

It's instructive to look at the implementations of wxScrolledWindow and wxGrid if you're thinking of implementing your own scrolling behavior.

You may want to look at wxVScrolledWindow in the wxWidgets reference manual; this can be used to build a scrolled window class that can scroll by lines of unequal height in the vertical direction.

wxSplitterWindow

This class manages up to two subwindows (use nested splitter windows if you need more splits). The current view can be split into two by the application, for example, from a menu command. It can be unsplit either by the application or via the splitter window user interface by double-clicking on the sash or dragging the sash until one of the panes has zero size (override the latter behavior with SetMinimumPaneSize).

On most platforms, when the sash is dragged, a reverse-video line will be drawn to show where the sash will end up. You can pass wxSP_LIVE_UPDATE to let the sash move in "real time" instead, resizing the child windows. This is the default (and only) mode on Mac OS X.

The following fragment shows how to create a splitter window, creating two subwindows and hiding one of them.

```
#include "wx/splitter.h"

wxSplitterWindow* splitter = new wxSplitterWindow(this, wxID_ANY,
    wxPoint(0, 0), wxSize(400, 400), wxSP_3D);

leftWindow = new MyWindow(splitter);
leftWindow->SetScrollbars(20, 20, 50, 50);

rightWindow = new MyWindow(splitter);
  rightWindow->SetScrollbars(20, 20, 50, 50);
  rightWindow->Show(false);

splitter->Initialize(leftWindow);

// Unncomment this to prevent unsplitting
//    splitter->SetMinimumPaneSize(20);
```

This fragment shows how the splitter window can be manipulated after creation:

```
void MyFrame::OnSplitVertical(wxCommandEvent& event)
{
    if ( splitter->IsSplit() )
        splitter->Unsplit();
    leftWindow->Show(true);
    rightWindow->Show(true);
    splitter->SplitVertically( leftWindow, rightWindow );
}

void MyFrame::OnSplitHorizontal(wxCommandEvent& event)
{
    if ( splitter->IsSplit() )
        splitter->Unsplit();
    leftWindow->Show(true);
    rightWindow->Show(true);
    splitter->SplitHorizontally( leftWindow, rightWindow );
}

void MyFrame::OnUnsplit(wxCommandEvent& event)
{
    if ( splitter->IsSplit() )
        splitter->Unsplit();
}
```

Figure 4-10 shows how the wxWidgets splitter sample looks on Windows without the wxSP_NO_XP_THEME style. If you use this style, the splitter will take on a more traditional look with a sunken border and 3D sash.

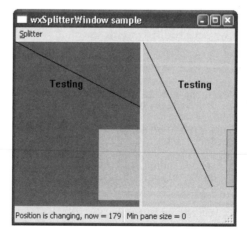

Figure 4-10   A wxSplitterWindow

wxSplitterWindow Styles

wxSplitterWindow can have the window styles shown in Table 4-15 in addition to those described for wxWindow.

Table 4-15 wxSplitterWindow Styles

wxSP_3D	Draws a 3D-effect border and sash.
wxSP_3DSASH	Draws a 3D-effect sash.
wxSP_3DBORDER	Synonym for wxSP_BORDER.
wxSP_BORDER	Draws a standard border.
wxSP_NOBORDER	No border (the default).
wxSP_NO_XP_THEME	Add a sunken border and 3D sash on Windows, if you don't like the minimal (but more native) look.
wxSP_PERMIT_UNSPLIT	Always enable the window to unsplit, even with the minimum pane size other than zero.
wxSP_LIVE_UPDATE	Resize the child windows immediately as the splitter is being moved.

wxSplitterWindow Events

wxSplitterWindow generates wxSplitterEvent propagating events, as listed in Table 4-16.

Table 4-16 wxSplitterWindow Events

EVT_SPLITTER_SASH_POS_CHANGING(id, func)	Processes a wxEVT_COMMAND_SPLITTER_SASH_POS_CHANGING event, generated when the sash position is in the process of being changed. Call Veto to stop the sash position changing, or call the event's SetSashPosition function to change the sash position.
EVT_SPLITTER_SASH(id, func)	Processes a wxEVT_COMMAND_SPLITTER_SASH_POS_CHANGED event, generated when the sash position is changed. May be used to modify the sash position before it is set, or to prevent the change from taking place, by calling the event's SetSashPosition function.
EVT_SPLITTER_UNSPLIT(id, func)	Processes a wxEVT_COMMAND_SPLITTER_UNSPLIT event, generated when the splitter is unsplit.
EVT_SPLITTER_DCLICK(id, func)	Processes a wxEVT_COMMAND_SPLITTER_DOUBLECLICKED event, generated when the sash is double-clicked.

wxSplitterWindow Member Functions

These are the major wxSplitterWindow functions.

GetMinimumPaneSize and SetMinimumPaneSize are accessors for the minimum pane size. The default minimum pane size is zero, which means that either pane can be reduced to zero by dragging the sash, thus removing one of the panes. To prevent this behavior (and veto out-of-range sash dragging), set a minimum size, for example 20 pixels. However, if the wxSP_PERMIT_UNSPLIT style is used when a splitter window is created, the window may be unsplit even if the minimum size is non-zero.

GetSashPosition and SetSashPosition are accessors for the sash position. Passing true to SetSashPosition resizes the pane and redraws the sash and border.

GetSplitMode and SetSplitMode are accessors for the split orientation, which can be wxSPLIT_VERTICAL or wxSPLIT_HORIZONTAL.

GetWindow1 and GetWindow2 get the pointers to the two panes.

Initialize can be called with a pointer to a window if you only want to have one pane initially.

IsSplit tests whether the window is split.

ReplaceWindow replaces one of the windows managed by the wxSplitter Window with another one. Generally, it's better to use this function instead of calling Unsplit and then resplitting the window.

SetSashGravity takes a floating-point argument, which determines the position of the sash as the window is resized. A value of 0.0 (the default) means that only the bottom or right child window will be resized, and a value of 1.0 means that only the top or left child window will be resized. Values inbetween indicate that the change in size should be distributed between both child windows (a value of 0.5 distributes the size evenly). Use GetSashGravity to return the current setting.

SplitHorizontally and SplitVertically initialize the splitter window with two panes and optionally an initial sash size.

Unsplit removes the specified pane.

UpdateSize causes the splitter to update its sash position immediately (normally, this is done in idle time).

Sizing Issues with *wxSplitterWindow*

There are subtleties to be aware of when using a splitter window as part of a sizer hierarchy. If you don't need the sash to be moveable, you can create both child windows with absolute sizes. This will fix the minimum size of both child windows, and the sash will therefore not be free to move. If you need the sash to be moveable, as is normally the case, pass default values to the child windows and specify an initial minimum size in the splitter window constructor. Then add the splitter window to its sizer, passing the wxFIXED_MINSIZE flag to Add, which tells wxWidgets to treat the specified size as the minimum size.

Another issue is that a splitter does not set its sash position (and therefore the sizes of its child windows) until idle time, when it can be sure that sizing has been finalized and the sash position won't be set prematurely. This can result in a sash that visibly repositions itself just after the window has been shown. To fix this, call wxSplitterWindow::UpdateSize as soon as you have done your layout, for example after a wxSizer::Fit call. The splitter will update its sash and child window sizes immediately.

By default, when the user or application resizes the splitter, only the bottom (or right) window is adjusted to take into account the new size. If you need different behavior, use SetSashGravity as documented in the previous section.

Alternatives to *wxSplitterWindow*

If you have a lot of "split" windows in your application, consider using wxSashWindow. This is a window that allows any of its edges to have a sash (as specified by the application) that can be dragged to resize the window. The actual content window is normally created by the application as a child of wxSashWindow.

When a sash is dragged, it notifies the application with a wxSashEvent so the handler can change the window size accordingly before laying out the windows. Layout is achieved via a class called wxLayoutAlgorithm, which provides LayoutWindow, LayoutFrame, and LayoutMDIFrame methods for arranging the sash windows on different kinds of parent windows.

You can also use the class wxSashLayoutWindow, which responds to events of type wxQueryLayoutInfoEvent to provide orientation and size information to wxLayoutAlgorithm.

Please see the reference manual for further details. wxSashWindow doesn't permit moving or undocking windows, and it's likely that these classes will be superceded by a general docking and layout framework in the near future.

Figure 4-11 shows a view of the wxSashWindow sample provided in samples/sashtest.

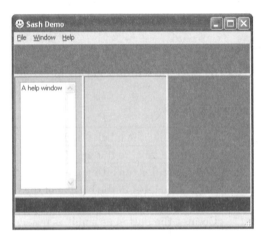

Figure 4-11   The wxSashWindow demo

NON-STATIC CONTROLS

Non-static controls, such as wxButton and wxListBox, respond to mouse and keyboard input. We'll describe the basic ones here; more advanced controls are described in Chapter 12. You can also download others (see Appendix E) or create your own.

wxButton

A wxButton is a control that looks like a physical push button with a text label, and it is one of the most common elements of a user interface. It may be placed on a dialog box or panel, or almost any other window. A command event is generated when the user clicks on the button.

Here's a simple example of creating a button:

```
#include "wx/button.h"

wxButton* button = new wxButton(panel, wxID_OK, wxT("OK"),
    wxPoint(10, 10), wxDefaultSize);
```

Figure 4-12 shows how a button with the default size looks on Windows XP.

Figure 4-12   A wxButton

wxWidgets obtains the default button size by calling the static function wxButton::GetDefaultSize, calculated appropriately for each platform, but you can let wxWidgets size the button to just fit the label by passing the style wxBU_EXACTFIT.

wxButton Styles

Table 4-17 lists the specific window styles for wxButton.

Table 4-17   wxButton Styles

wxBU_LEFT	Left-justifies the label. Windows and GTK+ only.
wxBU_TOP	Aligns the label to the top of the button. Windows and GTK+ only.
wxBU_RIGHT	Right-justifies the bitmap label. Windows and GTK+ only.
wxBU_BOTTOM	Aligns the label to the bottom of the button. Windows and GTK+ only.
wxBU_EXACTFIT	Creates the button as small as possible instead of making it the standard size.
wxNO_BORDER	Creates a flat button. Windows and GTK+ only.

wxButton Events

`wxButton` generates a `wxCommandEvent` propagating event, as shown in Table 4-18.

Table 4-18 wxButton Events

`EVT_BUTTON(id, func)`	Processes a `wxEVT_COMMAND_BUTTON_CLICKED` event, generated when the user left-clicks on a `wxButton`.

wxButton Member Functions

These are the major `wxButton` functions.

`SetLabel` and `GetLabel` are accessors for the button label. You can use an ampersand to indicate that the following letter is a mnemonic on Windows and GTK+.

`SetDefault` sets this button to be the default button on the parent window, so pressing the Enter key activates this button.

wxButton Labels

You can use an ampersand in the button label to indicate that the next letter is an underlined mnemonic (or "access key"), so that the user can press that key instead of clicking on the button. The mnemonic only works on Windows and GTK+; on other platforms, the ampersand will simply be stripped from the label and ignored.

On some systems, notably GTK+, standard buttons such as *OK* and *New* are displayed with special graphics in line with the native look and feel for that platform. wxWidgets maps some of its standard window identifiers to these stock buttons, but it also permits the application to substitute a custom label should the need arise.

The recommended usage is as follows. When using a stock button identifier, and you want wxWidgets to supply the label, just supply the identifier and not the label (or an empty string for the label). For example:

```
wxButton* button = new wxButton(this, wxID_OK);
```

wxWidgets will substitute the correct standard label on all platforms. For example, on Windows and Mac OS X, the string `"&OK"` will be used. On GTK+, the stock *OK* button will be used. However, if you supply a label that is different from the stock label, wxWidgets will use that label. For example:

```
wxButton* button = new wxButton(this, wxID_OK, wxT("&Apply"));
```

This will result in the "Apply" label being displayed on all platforms, overriding the standard identifier.

You can get the stock button label for a given identifier with `wxGetStockLabel` (include `wx/stockitem.h`), passing the identifier, `true` (if you want menu codes to be included), and an optional accelerator string to append.

Table 4-19 shows the stock button identifiers and their corresponding labels.

Table 4-19   Stock Button Identifiers

Stock Button Identifier	Stock Button Label
wxID_ADD	"Add"
wxID_APPLY	"&Apply"
wxID_BOLD	"&Bold"
wxID_CANCEL	"&Cancel"
wxID_CLEAR	"&Clear"
wxID_CLOSE	"&Close"
wxID_COPY	"&Copy"
wxID_CUT	"Cu&t"
wxID_DELETE	"&Delete"
wxID_FIND	"&Find"
wxID_REPLACE	"Rep&lace"
wxID_BACKWARD	"&Back"
wxID_DOWN	"&Down"
wxID_FORWARD	"&Forward"
wxID_UP	"&Up"
wxID_HELP	"&Help"
wxID_HOME	"&Home"
wxID_INDENT	"Indent"
wxID_INDEX	"&Index"
wxID_ITALIC	"&Italic"
wxID_JUSTIFY_CENTER	"Centered"
wxID_JUSTIFY_FILL	"Justified"
wxID_JUSTIFY_LEFT	"Align Left"
wxID_JUSTIFY_RIGHT	"Align Right"
wxID_NEW	"&New"
wxID_NO	"&No"
wxID_OK	"&OK"
wxID_OPEN	"&Open"
wxID_PASTE	"&Paste"

wxID_PREFERENCES	"&Preferences"
wxID_PRINT	"&Print"
wxID_PREVIEW	"Print previe&w"
wxID_PROPERTIES	"&Properties"
wxID_EXIT	"&Quit"
wxID_REDO	"&Redo"
wxID_REFRESH	"Refresh"
wxID_REMOVE	"Remove"
wxID_REVERT_TO_SAVED	"Revert to Saved"
wxID_SAVE	"&Save"
wxID_SAVEAS	"Save &As..."
wxID_STOP	"&Stop"
wxID_UNDELETE	"Undelete"
wxID_UNDERLINE	"&Underline"
wxID_UNDO	"&Undo"
wxID_UNINDENT	"&Unindent"
wxID_YES	"&Yes"
wxID_ZOOM_100	"&Actual Size"
wxID_ZOOM_FIT	"Zoom to &Fit"
wxID_ZOOM_IN	"Zoom &In"
wxID_ZOOM_OUT	"Zoom &Out"

wxBitmapButton

A bitmap button is like a normal text button, but it shows a bitmap instead of text. A command event is generated when the user clicks on the button.

Here's a simple example of creating a bitmap button:

```
#include "wx/bmpbuttn.h"

wxBitmap bitmap(wxT("print.xpm"), wxBITMAP_TYPE_XPM);
wxBitmapButton* button = new wxBitmapButton(panel, wxID_OK,
    bitmap, wxDefaultPosition, wxDefaultSize, wxBU_AUTODRAW);
```

Figure 4-13 shows the result under Windows.

Figure 4-13 A wxBitmapButton

A bitmap button can be supplied with a single bitmap (optionally with transparency information), and wxWidgets will draw all button states using this bitmap. If the application needs more control, additional bitmaps for the selected state, unpressed focused state, and grayed-out state may be supplied.

XPM is a good choice of bitmap format for buttons because it supports transparency and can be included into C++ code, but you can load them from other formats too, such as JPEG, PNG, GIF, and BMP.

wxBitmapButton Styles

Table 4-20 lists the specific window styles for wxBitmapButton.

Table 4-20   wxBitmapButton Styles

wxBU_AUTODRAW	If this is specified, the button will be drawn automatically using the label bitmap only, providing a 3D-look border. If this style is not specified, the button will be drawn without borders and using all provided bitmaps. Windows and Mac OS only.
wxBU_LEFT	Left-justifies the bitmap label. Ignored on Mac OS.
wxBU_TOP	Aligns the bitmap label to the top of the button. Ignored on Mac OS.
wxBU_RIGHT	Right-justifies the bitmap label. Ignored on Mac OS.
wxBU_BOTTOM	Aligns the bitmap label to the bottom of the button. Ignored on Mac OS.

wxBitmapButton Events

wxBitmapButton generates wxCommandEvent propagating events, identical to wxButton.

wxBitmapButton Member Functions

These are the major wxBitmapButton functions.

SetBitmapLabel and GetBitmapLabel are accessors for the main button label bitmap. You can also use SetBitmapFocus, SetBitmapSelected, and SetBitmapDisabled and their corresponding getters for more precise control of the button in different states.

SetDefault sets this button to be the default button on the parent window, so pressing the Enter key will activate the button.

wxChoice

The choice control consists of a read-only text area that reflects the selection of a drop-down list box. The list box is hidden until the user presses a button on the control to reveal the list of strings.

To create a choice control, pass the usual parent window, identifier, position, size, and style parameters, plus an array of strings to populate the list. For example:

```
#include "wx/choice.h"

wxArrayString strings;
strings.Add(wxT("One"));
strings.Add(wxT("Two"));
strings.Add(wxT("Three"));

wxChoice* choice = new wxChoice(panel, ID_COMBOBOX,
    wxDefaultPosition, wxDefaultSize, strings);
```

On most platforms, the look is similar to wxComboBox (see Figure 4-14), except that the user cannot edit the text. On GTK+, wxChoice is a button with a drop-down menu. You may like to use a read-only wxComboBox to get the benefit of the scrolling drop-down list.

wxChoice Styles

There are no special styles for wxChoice.

wxChoice Events

wxChoice generates wxCommandEvent propagating events, as shown in Table 4-21.

Table 4-21   wxChoice Events

EVT_CHOICE(id, func)	Processes a wxEVT_COMMAND_CHOICE_SELECTED event, generated by a wxChoice control when the user selects an item in the list.

wxChoice Member Functions

All wxChoice functions are described by wxControlWithItems: Clear, Delete, FindString, GetClientData, GetClientObject, SetClientData, SetClientObject, GetCount, GetSelection, SetSelection, GetString, SetString, GetStringSelection, SetStringSelection, Insert, and IsEmpty.

wxComboBox

The combo box is a combination of a list box and a single-line text field, and it allows you to set and get the text of the text field independently of the list box. The text field can be read-only, in which case it behaves very much like wxChoice. Normally, the list box is hidden until the user presses a button on the control to reveal the list of strings. This makes for a very compact way of allowing the user to enter text and also to choose from a list of existing options.

To create a combo box, pass the usual parent window, identifier, position, size, and style parameters, plus the initial text and an array of strings to populate the list. For example:

```
#include "wx/combobox.h"

wxArrayString strings;
strings.Add(wxT("Apple"));
strings.Add(wxT("Orange"));
strings.Add(wxT("Pear"));
strings.Add(wxT("Grapefruit"));

wxComboBox* combo = new wxComboBox(panel, ID_COMBOBOX,
    wxT("Apple"), wxDefaultPosition, wxDefaultSize,
    strings, wxCB_DROPDOWN);
```

The result on Windows is shown in Figure 4-14 with the drop-down list activated.

Figure 4-14   A wxComboBox

wxComboBox Styles

Table 4-22 lists the specific window styles for wxComboBox.

Table 4-22   wxComboBox Styles

wxCB_SIMPLE	Creates a combo box with a permanently displayed list. Windows only.
wxCB_DROPDOWN	Creates a combo box with a drop-down list.
wxCB_READONLY	Same as wxCB_DROPDOWN but only the strings specified as the combo box choices can be selected, and it is impossible to select a string that is not in the choices list, even from application code.
wxCB_SORT	Creates a combo box whose items are always sorted alphabetically.

wxComboBox Events

wxComboBox generates wxCommandEvent propagating events, described in Table 4-23.

Table 4-23   wxComboBox Events

EVT_TEXT(id, func)	Processes a wxEVT_COMMAND_TEXT_UPDATED event, generated by the wxComboBox control when its text is edited.
EVT_COMBOBOX(id, func)	Processes a wxEVT_COMMAND_COMBOBOX_SELECTED event, generated by a wxComboBox control when the user selects an item in the list.

wxComboBox Member Functions

These are the major wxComboBox functions. Please refer also to the wxControlWithItems member functions from earlier in this chapter.

Copy copies the selected text onto the clipboard from the text field. Cut does the same, and it also deletes the selected text. Paste copies text from the clipboard into the text field.

GetInsertionPoint returns the insertion point for the combo box's text field (a long integer representing the position), and SetInsertionPoint sets it. Use SetInsertionPointEnd to set the insertion point at the end of the text field.

GetLastPosition returns the last position in the text field.

GetValue returns the value of the text field, and SetValue sets it. For a combo box with the wxCB_READONLY style, the string must be in the combo box choices list; otherwise, the call is ignored in release mode, and it displays an alert in debug mode.

SetSelection with two arguments selects the text in the combo box text field between two given positions. Replace replaces the text between two given positions with specified text. Remove removes the text between two given positions.

See also the following functions from wxControlWithItems: Clear, Delete, FindString, GetClientData, GetClientObject, SetClientData, SetClientObject, GetCount, GetSelection, SetSelection, GetString, SetString, GetStringSelection, SetStringSelection, Insert, and IsEmpty.

wxCheckBox

A check box is a control that normally has two states: on or off. It is represented by a box containing a cross or tick if checked, with a label to the left or right of the check box. Optionally, it can have a third state, called the mixed or undetermined state, which can be used to indicate that the item does not apply (for example, a component in an installer that is always installed and therefore cannot be selected or deselected).

Here's a simple example of creating a check box:

```
#include "wx/checkbox.h"

wxCheckBox* checkbox = new wxCheckBox(panel, ID_CHECKBOX,
    wxT("&Check me"), wxDefaultPosition, wxDefaultSize);
checkBox->SetValue(true);
```

Figure 4-15 shows how this looks on Windows.

☑ Check me

Figure 4-15   A wxCheckBox

A check box with the wxCHK_3STATE style looks like Figure 4-16 on Windows.

■ Indeterminate

Figure 4-16   A three-state wxCheckBox

wxCheckBox Styles

Table 4-24 lists the specific window styles for wxCheckBox.

Table 4-24   wxCheckBox Styles

wxCHK_2STATE	Create a two-state check box. This is the default.
wxCHK_3STATE	Create a three-state check box.
wxCHK_ALLOW_3RD_STATE_FOR_USER	By default, a user can't set a three-state check box to the third state. It can only be done from code. Using this style enables the user to set the check box to the third state by clicking.
wxALIGN_RIGHT	Makes the check box appear to the right of the label.

wxCheckBox Events

wxCheckBox generates wxCommandEvent propagating events, described in Table 4-25.

Table 4-25 wxCheckBox Events

EVT_CHECKBOX(id, func)	Processes a wxEVT_COMMAND_CHECKBOX_ CLICKED event, generated when the user checks or unchecks a wxCheckBox control.

wxCheckBox Member Functions

These are the major wxCheckBox functions.

SetLabel and GetLabel are accessors for the check box label. You can use an ampersand to indicate that the following letter is the mnemonic (or "access key") on Windows and GTK+.

GetValue and SetValue get and set the boolean state. Use Get3StateValue or Set3StateValue to get and set one of wxCHK_UNCHECKED, wxCHK_CHECKED, or wxCHK_UNDETERMINED.

Is3State can be used to determine whether the check box is a three-state check box.

IsChecked returns true if the check box is checked.

wxListBox and *wxCheckListBox*

A wxListBox is used to select one or more of a list of strings, numbered from zero. The strings are displayed in a scrolling box, with the selected strings marked in reverse video. A list box can be single-selection: if an item is selected, the previous selection is removed. In a multiple-selection list box, clicking an item toggles the item on or off independently of other selections.

Here's an example of creating a single-selection list box:

```
#include "wx/listbox.h"

wxArrayString strings;
strings.Add(wxT("First string"));
strings.Add(wxT("Second string"));
strings.Add(wxT("Third string"));
strings.Add(wxT("Fourth string"));
strings.Add(wxT("Fifth string"));
strings.Add(wxT("Sixth string"));

wxListBox* listBox = new wxListBox(panel, ID_LISTBOX,
    wxDefaultPosition, wxSize(180, 80), strings, wxLB_SINGLE);
```

Figure 4-17 shows what this looks like under Windows.

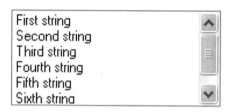

Figure 4-17   A wxListBox

wxCheckListBox is derived from wxListBox and inherits its functionality, but in addition, it can display a check box next to each item label. Include wx/checklst.h to use this class. Figure 4-18 shows a wxCheckListBox on Windows.

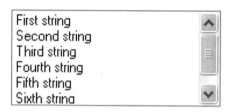

Figure 4-18   A wxCheckListBox

If you have a lot of items to display, consider using wxVListBox. This is a virtual list box that displays data directly from a source that you specify by deriving a new class and implementing the functions OnDrawItem and OnMeasureItem. Its event macros are the same as for wxListBox.

wxHtmlListBox is derived from wxVListBox and offers an easy way to display complex items. wxHtmlListBox obtains HTML fragments from the OnGetItem function, which your derived class must override. Figure 4-19 shows the wxWidgets wxHtmlListBox sample (in samples/htlbox), with custom separators drawn by an overridden OnDrawSeparator function.

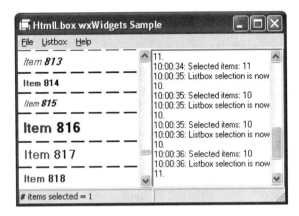

Figure 4-19   The wxHtmlListBox sample

wxListBox and *wxCheckListBox* Styles

Table 4-26 lists the specific window styles for wxListBox and wxCheckListBox.

Table 4-26   wxListBox and wxCheckListBox Styles

wxLB_SINGLE	Single-selection list.
wxLB_MULTIPLE	Multiple-selection list: the user can toggle multiple items on and off.
wxLB_EXTENDED	Extended-selection list: the user can select multiple items using the Shift key and the mouse or special key combinations.
wxLB_HSCROLL	Create a horizontal scrollbar if contents are too wide. Windows only.
wxLB_ALWAYS_SB	Always show a vertical scrollbar.
wxLB_NEEDED_SB	Only create a vertical scrollbar if needed.
wxLB_SORT	The list box contents are sorted in alphabetical order.

wxListBox and *wxCheckListBox* Events

wxListBox and wxCheckListBox generate wxCommandEvent propagating events, described in Table 4-27.

Table 4-27 wxListBox Events

EVT_LISTBOX(id, func)	Processes a wxEVT_COMMAND_LISTBOX_SELECTED event, generated by a wxListBox control when the user selects an item in the list.
EVT_LISTBOX_DCLICK(id, func)	Processes a wxEVT_COMMAND_LISTBOX_ DOUBLECLICKED event, generated by a wxListBox control when the user double-clicks on an item in the list.
EVT_CHECKLISTBOX (id, func)	Processes a wxEVT_COMMAND_CHECKLISTBOX_ TOGGLED event, generated by a wxCheckListBox control when the user checks or unchecks an item.

wxListBox Member Functions

These are the major wxListBox functions.

Deselect deselects an item in the list box.

GetSelections fills a wxArrayInt array with the positions of the currently selected items and returns it.

InsertItems inserts the given number of strings before the specified position. Pass either the number of items, a C++ array of wxStrings, and the insertion position, or a wxArrayString object and the insertion position.

Selected returns true if the given item is selected.

Set clears the list box and adds the given strings to it. Pass either the number of items, a C++ array of wxStrings, and an optional array of void* client data, or a wxArrayString object and an optional array of void* client data.

SetFirstItem sets the specified item to be the first visible item.

SetSelection and SetStringSelection take an integer or string item and an optional boolean for the selection state, defaulting to true.

See also the wxControlWithItems functions: Clear, Delete, FindString, GetClientData, GetClientObject, SetClientData, SetClientObject, GetCount, GetSelection, GetString, SetString, GetStringSelection, Insert, and IsEmpty.

wxCheckListBox Member Functions

In addition to wxListBox's functions, wxCheckListBox has the following functions.

Check takes an item index and boolean and checks or unchecks the item.

IsChecked returns true if the given item is checked, and false otherwise.

wxRadioBox

A radio box is used to select an item from a number of mutually exclusive buttons. It is displayed as a vertical column or horizontal row of labeled buttons, within a static box, which may have a label.

The way that the buttons are laid out depends on two constructor parameters: the major dimension, and the orientation style, which can be wxRA_
SPECIFY_COLS (the default) or wxRA_SPECIFY_ROWS. The major dimension is the
number of rows or columns. For example, eight buttons laid out with a major
dimension of two and the wxRA_SPECIFY_COLS style will have two columns and
four rows. Changing to wxRA_SPECIFY_ROWS will give the radio box two rows and
four columns.

Here's an example of creating a radio box with three columns:

```
#include "wx/radiobox.h"

wxArrayString strings;
strings.Add(wxT("&One"));
strings.Add(wxT("&Two"));
strings.Add(wxT("T&hree"));
strings.Add(wxT("&Four "));
strings.Add(wxT("F&ive "));
strings.Add(wxT("&Six "));

wxRadioBox* radioBox = new wxRadioBox(panel, ID_RADIOBOX,
    wxT("Radiobox"), wxDefaultPosition, wxDefaultSize,
    strings, 3, wxRA_SPECIFY_COLS);
```

The constructor specifies that the buttons should be laid out in three columns.
On Windows, this produces the result shown in Figure 4-20.

Figure 4-20 A wxRadioBox

wxRadioBox Styles

wxRadioBox can have the window styles listed in Table 4-28 in addition to those
described for wxWindow. Specifying a different major dimension changes the button ordering.

Table 4-28 wxRadioBox Styles

wxRA_SPECIFY_ROWS	The major dimension parameter refers to the maximum number of rows.
wxRA_SPECIFIY_COLS	The major dimension parameter refers to the maximum number of columns.

wxRadioBox Events

wxRadioBox generates wxCommandEvent propagating events, as shown in Table 4-29.

Table 4-29   wxRadioBox Events

EVT_RADIOBOX(id, func)	Processes a wxEVT_COMMAND_RADIOBOX_ SELECTED event, generated by a wxRadioBox control when the user clicks on a radio button.

wxRadioBox Member Functions

These are the major wxRadioBox functions.

Enable with an index and a boolean enables or disables a specified button.

FindString returns the index of a button matching the given string, or wxNOT_FOUND if no match was found.

GetCount returns the number of buttons in the radio box.

GetString and SetString are accessors for the label of the specified button. GetLabel and SetLabel set the radio box label.

GetSelection returns the zero-based index of the selected radio button. GetStringSelection returns the label of the selected button. SetSelection and SetStringSelection set the selection without generating a command event.

Show shows or hides an individual button or the whole radio box.

wxRadioButton

A radio button usually denotes one of several mutually exclusive options. It has a text label next to a button, which is normally round in appearance.
It has two states: on or off. You can create a group of mutually exclusive radio buttons by specifying wxRB_GROUP for the first in the group. The group ends when another radio button group is created, or when there are no more controls. You can also create other types of control within a group.

You might use a group of radio buttons instead of a radio box when the layout is slightly more complex: for example, you may have an extra description or other control next to each radio button. Or you may use radio buttons simply to avoid the static box that wxRadioBox provides.

Figure 4-21   A pair of radio buttons

Here's a simple example of a group of two radio buttons.

```
#include "wx/radiobut.h"

wxRadioButton* radioButton1 = new wxRadioButton (panel,
    ID_RADIOBUTTON1, wxT("&Male"), wxDefaultPosition,
    wxDefaultSize, wxRB_GROUP);
radioButton1->SetValue(true);
wxRadioButton* radioButton2 = new wxRadioButton (panel,
    ID_RADIOBUTTON2, wxT("&Female"));

// Sizer code to group the buttons horizontally
wxBoxSizer* sizer = new wxBoxSizer(wxHORIZONTAL);
sizer->Add(radioButton1, 0, wxALIGN_CENTER_VERTICAL¦wxALL, 5);
sizer->Add(radioButton2, 0, wxALIGN_CENTER_VERTICAL¦wxALL, 5);
parentSizer->Add(sizer, 0, wxALIGN_CENTER_VERTICAL¦wxALL, 5);
```

On Windows, this will create the controls shown in Figure 4-21.

wxRadioButton Styles

Table 4-30 lists the specific window styles for wxRadioButton.

Table 4-30   wxRadioButton Styles

wxRB_GROUP	Marks the beginning of a new group of radio buttons.
wxRB_USE_CHECKBOX	Displays a check box button instead of a radio button (Palm OS only).

wxRadioButton Events

wxRadioButton generates wxCommandEvent propagating events, which are described in Table 4-31.

Table 4-31   wxRadioButton Events

EVT_RADIOBUTTON(id, func)	Processes a wxEVT_COMMAND_ RADIOBUTTON_ SELECTED event, generated by a wxRadioButton control when a user clicks on it.

wxRadioButton Member Functions

GetValue and SetValue get and set the boolean state.

wxScrollBar

A wxScrollBar is a control that represents a horizontal or vertical scrollbar. It is distinct from the two scrollbars that some windows provide automatically, but the two types of scrollbar share the way events are received. A scrollbar has the following main attributes: range, thumb size, page size, and position.

The range is the total number of units associated with the view represented by the scrollbar. For a table with 15 columns, the range would be 15.

The thumb size is the number of units that are currently visible. For the table example, the window might be sized so that only 5 columns are currently visible, in which case the application would set the thumb size to 5. When the thumb size becomes the same as or greater than the range, the scrollbar will automatically be hidden on most platforms.

The page size is the number of units that the scrollbar should scroll when paging through the data.

The scrollbar position is the current thumb position.

To create a scrollbar control, pass the usual parent window, identifier, position, size, and style parameters. For example:

```
#include "wx/scrolbar.h"

wxScrollBar* scrollBar = new wxScrollBar(panel, ID_SCROLLBAR,
    wxDefaultPosition, wxSize(200, 20), wxSB_HORIZONTAL);
```

Under Windows, this will look like the control in Figure 4-22.

Figure 4-22 A wxScrollBar

After creation, call SetScrollbar to set its properties. For more information on using this function, see the description of wxScrolledWindow earlier in this chapter.

wxScrollBar Styles

Table 4-32 lists the specific window styles for wxScrollBar.

Table 4-32   wxScrollBar Styles

wxSB_HORIZONTAL	Specifies a horizontal scrollbar.
wxSB_VERTICAL	Specifies a vertical scrollbar.

wxScrollBar Events

wxScrollBar generates wxScrollEvent propagating events. You can use EVT_ COMMAND_SCROLL... macros with window identifiers when intercepting scroll events from controls, or EVT_SCROLL... macros without window identifiers for intercepting scroll events from the receiving window—except for this, the macros behave exactly the same. Use EVT_SCROLL(func) to respond to all scroll events. For a comprehensive list of scroll event macros, please see Table I-1 in Appendix I, "Event Classes and Macros," and also see the reference manual.

wxScrollBar Member Functions

These are the major wxScrollBar functions.

GetRange returns the length of the scrollbar.

GetPageSize returns the number of scroll units that will be scrolled when the user pages up or down. Often it is the same as the thumb size.

GetThumbPosition and SetThumbPosition are accessors for the current position of the scrollbar thumb.

GetThumbLength returns the thumb or "view" size.

SetScrollbar sets the scrollbar properties. It takes the position in scroll units, thumb size, range, page size, and optional boolean to specify whether the control will be refreshed.

wxSpinButton

wxSpinButton has two small up and down (or left and right) arrow buttons. It is often used next to a text control for incrementing and decrementing a value. Portable programs should try to use wxSpinCtrl instead as wxSpinButton is not implemented for all platforms.

The range supported by this control (and wxSpinCtrl) depends on the platform but is at least -32768 to 32767.

To create a wxSpinButton control, pass the usual parent window, identifier, position, size, and style parameters. For example:

```
#include "wx/spinbutt.h"

wxSpinButton* spinButton = new wxSpinButton(panel, ID_SPINBUTTON,
    wxDefaultPosition, wxDefaultSize, wxSP_VERTICAL);
```

On Windows, the result is the control shown in Figure 4-23.

Figure 4-23   A wxSpinButton

wxSpinButton Styles

Table 4-33 lists the specific window styles for wxSpinButton.

Table 4-33   wxSpinButton Styles

wxSP_HORIZONTAL	Specifies a horizontal spin button. This style is not supported in wxGTK.
wxSP_VERTICAL	Specifies a vertical spin button.
wxSP_ARROW_KEYS	The user can use arrow keys to change the value.
wxSP_WRAP	The value wraps at the minimum and maximum.

wxSpinButton Events

wxSpinButton generates wxSpinEvent propagating events, as shown in Table 4-34.

Table 4-34   wxSpinButton Events

EVT_SPIN(id, func)	Handles a wxEVT_SCROLL_THUMBTRACK event, generated whenever the up or down arrows are clicked.
EVT_SPIN_UP(id, func)	Handles a wxEVT_SCROLL_LINEUP event, generated when the up arrow is clicked.
EVT_SPIN_DOWN(id, func)	Handles a wxEVT_SCROLL_LINEDOWN event, generated when the down arrow is clicked.

wxSpinButton Member Functions

These are the major wxSpinButton functions.

GetMax returns the maximum permissible value.

GetMin returns the minimum permissible value.

GetValue returns the current spin button value, and SetValue sets the current spin value.

SetRange sets the minimum and maximum values.

wxSpinCtrl

wxSpinCtrl combines a wxTextCtrl and a wxSpinButton into one control. When you click on the up and down arrow buttons, the value displayed in the text control will be incremented or decremented, and you can also type integers directly into the text control.

To create a `wxSpinCtrl` control, pass the usual parent window, identifier, position, size, and style parameters. The following code creates a spin control with a range of zero to 100 and an initial value of 5.

```
#include "wx/spinctrl.h"

wxSpinCtrl* spinCtrl = new wxSpinCtrl(panel, ID_SPINCTRL,
    wxT("5"), wxDefaultPosition, wxDefaultSize, wxSP_ARROW_KEYS,
    0, 100, 5);
```

On Windows, this will look like the control in Figure 4-24.

Figure 4-24   A `wxSpinCtrl`

wxSpinCtrl Styles

Table 4-35 lists the specific window styles for `wxSpinCtrl`.

Table 4-35   `wxSpinCtrl` Styles

`wxSP_ARROW_KEYS`	The user can use arrow keys to change the value.
`wxSP_WRAP`	The value wraps at the minimum and maximum.

wxSpinCtrl Events

`wxSpinCtrl` generates `wxSpinEvent` propagating events as shown in Table 4-36. You can also use `EVT_TEXT` to intercept text updates with a `wxCommandEvent` handler.

Table 4-36   `wxSpinCtrl` Events

`EVT_SPIN(id, func)`	Handles a `wxEVT_SCROLL_THUMBTRACK` event, generated whenever the up or down arrow is clicked.
`EVT_SPIN_UP(id, func)`	Handles a `wxEVT_SCROLL_LINEUP` event, generated when the up arrow is clicked.
`EVT_SPIN_DOWN(id, func)`	Handles a `wxEVT_SCROLL_LINEDOWN` event, generated when the down arrow is clicked.
`EVT_SPINCTRL(id, func)`	Handles all events generated for the `wxSpinCtrl`.

wxSpinCtrl Member Functions

These are the major `wxSpinCtrl` functions.

GetMax returns the maximum permissible value.

GetMin returns the minimum permissible value.

GetValue returns the current integer spin button value, and SetValue sets the current spin value.

SetRange sets the minimum and maximum values.

wxSlider

A slider is a control with a handle that can be moved back and forth to change the value.

To create a `wxSlider` control, pass the usual parent window, identifier, position, size, and style parameters. The following code creates a slider control with a range of zero to 40 and an initial position of 16.

```
#include "wx/slider.h"

wxSlider* slider = new wxSlider(panel, ID_SLIDER, 16, 0, 40,
    wxDefaultPosition, wxSize(200, -1),
    wxSL_HORIZONTAL|wxSL_AUTOTICKS|wxSL_LABELS);
```

On Windows, this creates the control shown in Figure 4-25.

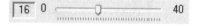

Figure 4-25   A wxSlider

wxSlider Styles

Table 4-37 lists the specific window styles for `wxSlider`.

Table 4-37   wxSlider Styles

wxSL_HORIZONTAL	Displays the slider horizontally.
wxSL_VERTICAL	Displays the slider vertically.
wxSL_AUTOTICKS	Displays tick marks.
wxSL_LABELS	Displays minimum, maximum, and value labels.
wxSL_LEFT	Displays ticks on the left if it's a vertical slider.
wxSL_RIGHT	Displays ticks on the right if it's a vertical slider.
wxSL_TOP	Displays ticks on the top if it's a horizontal slider. The default is to display them along the bottom.
wxSL_SELRANGE	Enables the user to select a range on the slider. Windows only.

wxSlider Events

`wxSlider` generates `wxCommandEvent` propagating events, as shown in Table 4-38, but if you need finer control, you can use `EVT_COMMAND_SCROLL_...` with `wxScrollEvent` handlers; see Table I-1 in Appendix I.

Table 4-38   `wxSlider` Events

`EVT_SLIDER(id, func)`	Processes a `wxEVT_COMMAND_SLIDER_UPDATED` event, generated by a `wxSlider` control when the user moves the slider.

wxSlider Member Functions

These are the major `wxSlider` functions.

`ClearSel` clears the selection for a slider with `wxSL_SELRANGE` on Windows. `ClearTicks` clears the ticks on Windows.

`GetLineSize` and `SetLineSize` are accessors for the number of units incremented or decremented when the arrow buttons are clicked. `GetPageSize` and `SetPageSize` are accessors for the number of units paged when clicking either side of the thumb.

`GetMax` returns the maximum permissible value.

`GetMin` returns the minimum permissible value.

`GetSelEnd` and `GetSelStart` return the selection end and start points; use `SetSelection` to set the selection. These functions are only implemented on Windows.

`GetThumbLength` and `SetThumbLength` are accessors for the slider thumb size.

`GetTickFreq` and `SetTickFreq` are accessors for the tick frequency on Windows. Use `SetTick` to set a tick position on Windows.

`GetValue` returns the current slider value, and `SetValue` sets the slider value.

`SetRange` sets the minimum and maximum values.

wxTextCtrl

The text control enables text to be displayed and edited, either as a single-line or a multi-line control. Some simple styling and formatting is supported on some platforms (Windows, GTK+, and Mac OS X via setting and getting text attributes using the `wxTextAttr` class.

To create a text control, pass the usual parent window, identifier, position, size, and style parameters, plus the initial text. For example, to create a multi-line text control:

```
#include "wx/textctrl.h"

wxTextCtrl* textCtrl = new wxTextCtrl(panel, ID_TEXTCTRL,
    wxEmptyString, wxDefaultPosition, wxSize(240, 100),
    wxTE_MULTILINE);
```

On Windows, this will create the control shown in Figure 4-26.

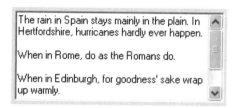

Figure 4-26   A multiline `wxTextCtrl`

Multi-line text controls always store text as a sequence of lines separated by \n characters, using Unix newlines even on non-Unix platforms. As a result, you can ignore the differences between platforms, but at a price: indices such as those returned by `GetInsertionPoint` or `GetSelection` cannot be used as indices into the string returned by `GetValue` as they're going to be slightly off for platforms using \r\n as the separator as Windows does.

Instead, if you need to obtain a substring between the two indices obtained from the control with the help of the functions mentioned previously, you should use `GetRange`. The indices themselves can only be passed to other methods, such as `SetInsertionPoint` or `SetSelection`. Never use the indices returned by multi-line text controls as indices into the string it contains, but only as arguments to be passed back to other `wxTextCtrl` methods.

Multi-line text controls support setting styles: you can set colors and fonts for individual characters. Note that under Windows, the `wxTE_RICH` style is required for style support. To use the styles, you can either call `SetDefaultStyle` before inserting the text or call `SetStyle` later to change the style of the text already in the control. The first method is much more efficient.

In either case, if the style doesn't specify some of the attributes, the values of the default style will be used. If there is no default style, the attributes of the text control itself are used.

In the following code, the second call to SetDefaultStyle doesn't change the text foreground color (which stays red), while the last one doesn't change the background color (which stays gray):

```
text->SetDefaultStyle(wxTextAttr(*wxRED));
text->AppendText(wxT("Red text\n"));
text->SetDefaultStyle(wxTextAttr(wxNullColour, *wxLIGHT_GREY));
text->AppendText(wxT("Red on gray text\n"));
text->SetDefaultStyle(wxTextAttr(*wxBLUE);
text->AppendText(wxT("Blue on gray text\n"));
```

wxTextCtrl Styles

Table 4-39 lists the specific window styles for wxTextCtrl.

Table 4-39 wxTextCtrl Styles

wxTE_PROCESS_ENTER	The control will generate the event wxEVT_COMMAND_TEXT_ENTER. Otherwise, pressing the Enter key is either processed internally by the control or used for navigation between dialog controls.
wxTE_PROCESS_TAB	The control will receive wxEVT_CHAR events when Tab is pressed—normally, the Tab key is used for passing to the next control in a dialog instead.
wxTE_MULTILINE	The text control supports multiple lines.
wxTE_PASSWORD	Text will be echoed as asterisks.
wxTE_READONLY	The text will not be user-editable.
wxTE_RICH	Uses a rich text control under Windows. This enables the control to store more than 64KB of text in the control; the vertical scrollbar is only shown when needed. This style is ignored under other platforms.
wxTE_RICH2	Uses a rich text control version 2.0 or 3.0 under Windows; the vertical scrollbar is always shown. This style is ignored on other platforms.
wxTE_AUTO_URL	Highlight URLs and generate wxTextUrlEvents when mouse events occur over them. On Windows this requires wxTE_RICH. Windows and GTK+ only.
wxTE_NOHIDESEL	By default, the Windows text control doesn't show the selection when it doesn't have focus—use this style to force it to always show the selection. Ignored under other platforms.
wxHSCROLL	A horizontal scrollbar will be created and used so that text won't be wrapped. No effect under GTK+.
wxTE_LEFT	The text in the control will be left justified (the default).
wxTE_CENTRE	The text in the control will be centered.
wxTE_RIGHT	The text in the control will be right justified.

(continues)

Table 4-39   wxTextCtrl Styles *(Continued)*

wxTE_DONTWRAP	Same as the wxHSCROLL style.
wxTE_LINEWRAP	Wrap lines that are too long to be shown entirely at any position. Currently only supported under wxUniversal.
wxTE_WORDWRAP	Wrap lines that are too long to be shown entirely at word boundaries only. Currently only supported under wxUniversal.
wxTE_NO_VSCROLL	Removes the vertical scrollbar. No effect on GTK+.

wxTextCtrl Events

wxTextCtrl generates wxCommandEvent propagating events, as described in Table 4-40.

Table 4-40   wxTextCtrl Events

EVT_TEXT(id, func)	Processes a wxEVT_COMMAND_TEXT_UPDATED event, generated when the text is changed.
EVT_TEXT_ENTER(id, func)	Processes a wxEVT_COMMAND_TEXT_ENTER event, generated when the user presses the Enter key. Note that you must use wxTE_PROCESS_ENTER style when creating the control if you want it to generate such events.
EVT_TEXT_MAXLEN(id, func)	Processes a wxEVT_COMMAND_TEXT_MAXLEN event, generated when the user tries to enter more characters into it than the limit previously set with SetMaxLength. Windows and GTK+ only.

wxTextCtrl Member Functions

These are the major wxTextCtrl functions.

AppendText appends the given text to the end of the text control, and WriteText writes the text at the current insertion point. SetValue clears and then sets the value, after which IsModified returns false. You can pass strings with newlines for a multi-line text control. Be aware that these functions send text update events.

GetValue returns the entire contents of the control, possibly with newlines for a multi-line control. GetLineText gets just one line from a multi-line control. GetRange gets the text between two positions.

Copy copies the selected text onto the clipboard from the text field. Cut does the same, and it also deletes the selected text. Paste copies text from the clipboard into the text field. You can use CanCopy, CanCut, and CanPaste in UI update event handlers.

Clear clears the text in the control. Note that this will generate a text update event.

DiscardEdits resets the internal "modified" flag as if the current edits had been saved.

EmulateKeyPress inserts the character that would have been inserted if the given key event had occurred in the text control.

GetDefaultStyle and SetDefaultStyle are accessors for the font currently used for new text. GetStyle returns the style at the given position in the text, and SetStyle sets the style for the given range.

GetInsertionPoint and SetInsertionPoint get and set the current insertion point for new text. GetLastPosition returns the last position in the control, and SetInsertionPointEnd sets the insertion point at the end of the text.

GetLineLength returns the length of the specified line in characters.

GetNumberOfLines returns the number of lines of text in the control.

GetStringSelection returns the text currently selected in the control, or an empty string if there is no selection. GetSelection returns the current selection span in two pointers to long integers. SetSelection selects the text range indicated by two long integers representing positions in the text.

IsEditable returns true if the contents may be edited. Call SetEditable to make the control read-only or writeable. IsModified returns true if the user has modified the text. IsMultiline returns true if the control is multi-line.

LoadFile loads text from a file into the control, and SaveFile saves the contents as a file.

PositionToXY converts a pixel position to character position and line number, whereas XYToPosition goes the other way.

Remove removes the text in the given span. Replace replaces the text in the given span.

ShowPosition makes the line containing the given position visible.

Undo undoes the last edit, and Redo redoes the last edit. This may do nothing on some platforms. You can use CanUndo and CanRedo to test whether these operations can be applied to the control's text (but not whether the platform supports undo/redo).

wxToggleButton

wxToggleButton is a button that stays pressed when clicked. In other words, it is similar to wxCheckBox in functionality but looks like a wxButton.

Here's a simple example of creating a toggle button:

```
#include "wx/tglbtn.h"

wxToggleButton* toggleButton = new wxToggleButton(panel, ID_TOGGLE,
    wxT("&Toggle label"), wxDefaultPosition, wxDefaultSize);
toggleButton->SetValue(true);
```

Figure 4-27 shows how a toggle button looks on Windows in the toggled state.

Figure 4-27   A wxToggleButton

wxToggleButton Styles

There are no specific wxToggleButton styles.

wxToggleButton Events

wxToggleButton generates wxCommandEvent propagating events, described in Table 4-41.

Table 4-41   wxToggleButton Events

EVT_TOGGLEBUTTON(id, func)	Processes a wxEVT_COMMAND_TOGGLEBUTTON_CLICKED event, generated when the user clicks the button.

wxToggleButton Member Functions

These are the major wxToggleButton functions.

SetLabel and GetLabel are accessors for the button label. You can use an ampersand to indicate that the following letter is the mnemonic (or "access key"), used on Windows and GTK+.

GetValue and SetValue get and set the boolean state.

STATIC CONTROLS

Static controls do not take any input and are used to display information or to enhance the application's aesthetics.

wxGauge

This is a horizontal or vertical bar that shows a quantity (often time) from zero to the specified range. No command events are generated for the gauge. Here's a simple example of creating a gauge:

```
#include "wx/gauge.h"

wxGauge* gauge = new wxGauge(panel, ID_GAUGE,
  200, wxDefaultPosition, wxDefaultSize, wxGA_HORIZONTAL);
gauge->SetValue(50);
```

Under Windows, this is displayed as shown in Figure 4-28.

Figure 4-28   A wxGauge

wxGauge Styles

Table 4-42 lists the specific window styles for wxGauge.

Table 4-42   wxGauge Styles

wxGA_HORIZONTAL	Creates a horizontal gauge.
wxGA_VERTICAL	Creates a vertical gauge.
wxGA_SMOOTH	Creates a smooth progress bar with no spaces between steps. This is only supported on Windows.

wxGauge Events

Because it only displays information, wxGauge does not generate events.

wxGauge Member Functions

These are the major wxGauge functions.

GetRange and SetRange are accessors for the gauge range (the maximum integer value).

GetValue and SetValue get and set the integer value of the gauge.

IsVertical returns true if the gauge is vertical, and false if horizontal.

wxStaticText

A static text control displays one or more lines of read-only text.

To create a wxStaticText control, pass a parent window, identifier, label, position, size, and style. For example:

```
#include "wx/stattext.h"

wxStaticText* staticText = new wxStaticText(panel, wxID_STATIC,
    wxT("This is my &static label"),
    wxDefaultPosition, wxDefaultSize, wxALIGN_LEFT);
```

Under Windows, this creates the control shown in Figure 4-29.

This is my static label

Figure 4-29   A wxStaticText

An ampersand in the label (as shown here) indicates to some platforms—currently Windows and GTK+—that the following letter should be under-scored and used as a shortcut key for navigating to the next non-static control.

wxStaticText Styles

Table 4-43 lists the specific window styles for wxStaticText.

Table 4-43   wxStaticText Styles

wxALIGN_LEFT	Aligns the text to the left.
wxALIGN_RIGHT	Aligns the text to the right.
wxALIGN_CENTRE wxALIGN_CENTER	Centers the text horizontally.
wxST_NO_AUTORESIZE	By default, the control will adjust its size to exactly fit the size of the text when SetLabel is called. If this style is given, the control will not change its size. This style is especially useful with controls that also have wxALIGN_RIGHT or wxALIGN_CENTER because otherwise they won't make sense any longer after a call to SetLabel.

wxStaticText Member Functions

GetLabel and SetLabel are accessors for the text label.

wxStaticBitmap

A static bitmap control displays an image.

To create a wxStaticBitmap control, pass a parent window, identifier, bitmap, position, size and style. For example:

```
#include "wx/statbmp.h"
#include "print.xpm"

wxBitmap bitmap(print_xpm);
wxStaticBitmap* staticBitmap = new wxStaticBitmap(panel, wxID_STATIC,
  bitmap);
```

This produces a simple image on the panel or dialog as shown in Figure 4-30.

Figure 4-30   A wxStaticBitmap

wxStaticBitmap Styles

There are no special styles for wxStaticBitmap.

wxStaticBitmap Member Functions

GetBitmap and SetBitmap are accessors for the bitmap label.

wxStaticLine

This control displays a horizontal or vertical line, to be used as a separator in dialogs.

Here's an example of creating a wxStaticLine control:

```
#include "wx/statline.h"

wxStaticLine* staticLine = new wxStaticLine(panel, wxID_STATIC,
    wxDefaultPosition, wxSize(150, -1), wxLI_HORIZONTAL);
```

Figure 4-31 shows what a horizontal static line looks like under Windows.

Figure 4-31   A wxStaticLine

wxStaticLine Styles

Table 4-44 lists the specific window styles for wxStaticLine.

Table 4-44   wxStaticLine Styles

wxLI_HORIZONTAL	Creates a horizontal line.
wxLI_VERTICAL	Creates a vertical line.

wxStaticLine Member Functions

IsVertical returns true if the line is vertical, false otherwise.

wxStaticBox

This control is a rectangle drawn around other controls to denote a logical grouping of items, with an optional text label. At present, the control should not be used as a parent for further controls; the controls that it surrounds are actually siblings of the box and should be created after it but with the same parent as the box. Future versions of wxWidgets may allow contained controls to be either siblings or children.

Here's an example of creating a wxStaticBox control:

```
#include "wx/statbox.h"

wxStaticBox* staticBox = new wxStaticBox(panel, wxID_STATIC,
  wxT("&Static box"), wxDefaultPosition, wxSize(100, 100));
```

This will look like the control in Figure 4-32 under Windows.

Figure 4-32   A wxStaticBox

wxStaticBox Styles

There are no special styles for wxStaticBox.

wxStaticBox Member Functions

Use GetLabel and SetLabel to get and set the static box text.

MENUS

In this section, we'll describe programming with wxMenu, a simple way to present commands without taking up a lot of display space. In the next section, we'll look at how menus are used in menu bars.

wxMenu

A menu is a list of commands that pops up either from a menu bar or on an arbitrary window, often as a "context menu" invoked by clicking the right mouse button (or equivalent). A menu item can be a normal command, or it can have a check or radio button next to the label. A menu item in a disabled state won't respond to commands. A special kind of menu item can display a visual indication of a further pull-right menu, and this can be nested to an arbitrary level. Another kind of menu item is the separator, which simply displays a line or space to indicate separation between two groups of items.

Figure 4-33 shows a typical menu with normal, check, and radio items and a submenu.

Figure 4-33   A typical menu

The example shows the use of both mnemonics and shortcuts. A mnemonic is a highlighted key in a label (such as the "N" in "New") that can be pressed when the menu is shown to execute that command. Specify a mnemonic by preceding the letter with an ampersand ("&"). A shortcut (or accelerator) is a key combination that can be used when the menu is not shown, and it is indicated in a menu item by a key combination following a tab character. For example, the *New* menu item in the example was created with this code:

```
menu->Append(wxID_NEW, wxT("&New...\tCtrl+N"));
```

For more on creating accelerators via menu items or by programming with wxAcceleratorTable, please see Chapter 6.

Check and radio items automatically update their state; that is, when the user toggles a check item, it will be shown in the reverse state when the menu is next popped up. Similarly, consecutive radio items form a group and when one item is checked, the other items in the group are unchecked. You can also set these states yourself, for example from a user interface update event handler (see Chapter 9).

You can create a menu and show it at a particular point in a window using wxWindow::PopupMenu, for example:

```
void wxWindow::OnRightClick(wxMouseEvent& event)
{
    if (!m_menu)
    {
        m_menu = new wxMenu;
        m_menu->Append(wxID_OPEN, wxT("&Open"));
        m_menu->AppendSeparator();
        m_menu->Append(wxID_EXIT, wxT("E&xit"));
    }

    PopupMenu(m_menu, event.GetPosition());
}
```

Events are sent to the menu itself before travelling up the hierarchy of windows starting from the window the popup menu was shown on. PopupMenu will cause program flow to "block" at this point, resuming when the user has dismissed the menu. If you want, you can delete and re-create the menu every time it needs to be shown, or you can reuse the same menu.

Where possible, use standard wxWidgets identifiers in menus, such as wxID_OPEN, wxID_ABOUT, wxID_PRINT, and so on. You can find a full list of these in Chapter 3. In particular, wxID_ABOUT, wxID_PREFERENCES and wxID_EXIT are interpreted specially on Mac OS X. When used in a menu bar, these menu items are not shown in the menus to which they are appended, but are shown instead in the standard application menu. Thus wxWidgets adapts your menus automatically to Mac OS X conventions, but beware of side effects such as a *Help* menu with no menu items, or two separators together.

See samples/menu in the wxWidgets distribution for a test of most menu functionality, and also see samples/ownerdrw for a demonstration of the use of custom fonts and bitmaps in menu items.

wxMenu Events

There are four different kinds of event associated with wxMenu: wxCommandEvent, wxUpdateUIEvent, wxMenuEvent, and wxContextMenuEvent.

Table 4-45 lists the command events, whose handlers take a wxCommandEvent argument. Use these for processing menu commands, either from a pop-up menu or a menu bar on a frame. These are interchangeable with the equivalent toolbar event macros so that events generated from both menus and toolbar buttons can be processed by the same handler.

Table 4-45 wxMenu Command Events

EVT_MENU(id, func)	Processes a wxEVT_COMMAND_MENU_SELECTED event, generated by a menu item.
EVT_MENU_RANGE(id1, id2, func)	Processes a wxEVT_COMMAND_MENU_RANGE event, generated by a range of menu items.

Table 4-46 lists the event macros for update events—events generated by the framework in idle time to give the application a chance to update elements of the UI—for example, enabling or disabling menu items. Although wxUpdateUIEvent applies to all windows, menu event handlers can use them slightly differently than other event handlers: they can call Check and SetText as well as Enable. Check checks or unchecks the menu item, while SetText sets the menu item label, which is useful if the label changes dynamically according to some condition. For example:

```
BEGIN_EVENT_TABLE(MyFrame, wxFrame)
    EVT_UPDATE_UI(ID_TOGGLE_TOOLBAR, MyFrame::OnUpdateToggleToolbar)
END_EVENT_TABLE()

void MyFrame::OnUpdateToggleToolbar(wxUpdateUIEvent& event)
{
    event.Enable(true);
    event.Check(m_showToolBar);
    event.SetText(m_showToolBar ?
                  wxT("Show &Toolbar (shown)") :
                  wxT("Show &Toolbar (hidden)"));
}
```

For more on UI update events, please see Chapter 9.

Table 4-46 wxMenu Update Events

EVT_UPDATE_UI(id, func)	Processes a wxEVT_UPDATE_UI event. The handler can call Enable, Check, and SetText among other functions.
EVT_UPDATE_UI_RANGE(id1, id2, func)	Processes a wxEVT_UPDATE_UI event for a range of identifiers.

Table 4-47 lists the other menu-related events. EVT_CONTEXT_MENU handlers take a wxContextMenuEvent, which is derived from wxCommandEvent and therefore propagates up the parent-child window hierarchy. Use this in preference to intercepting a right mouse button click when you want to show a context menu, and call the event object's GetPosition function to find out where to show the menu.

The remaining macros process wxMenuEvent objects, and these are only sent from a menu bar to its frame. They tell the application when a menu has been opened and closed, and when the user has highlighted a menu item. The default EVT_MENU_HIGHLIGHT handler shows a menu item's help string in the status bar, but you can provide your own handler to do something different.

Table 4-47   Other wxMenu Events

EVT_CONTEXT_MENU(func)	Processes the event generated when the user has requested a popup menu to appear by pressing a special key (under Windows) or by right-clicking the mouse. The handler takes a wxContextMenuEvent.
EVT_COMMAND_CONTEXT_MENU(id, func)	The same as EVT_CONTEXT_MENU, but it takes a window identifier.
EVT_MENU_OPEN(func)	Handles a wxEVT_MENU_OPEN event, sent when a menu is about to be opened. On Windows, this is only sent once for each navigation of the menu bar.
EVT_MENU_CLOSE(func)	Handles a wxEVT_MENU_CLOSE event, sent when a menu has just been closed.
EVT_MENU_HIGHLIGHT(id, func)	Handles a wxEVT_MENU_HIGHLIGHT event, sent when the menu item with the specified id has been highlighted. This is used to show help prompts in a frame's status bar.
EVT_MENU_HIGHLIGHT_ALL(func)	Handles a wxEVT_MENU_HIGHLIGHT event for any menu identifier.

wxMenu Member Functions

These are the major wxMenu functions.

Append adds a menu item: specify an identifier, a label, a help string, and the kind of item (wxITEM_NORMAL, wxITEM_SEPARATOR, wxITEM_CHECK or wxITEM_RADIO). You can also use AppendCheckItem and AppendRadioItem to avoid specifying wxITEM_CHECK or wxITEM_RADIO. For example:

```
// Append a normal item
menu->Append(wxID_NEW, wxT("&New...\tCtrl+N"));

// Append a check item
menu->AppendCheckItem(ID_SHOW_STATUS, wxT("&Show Status"));

// Append a radio item
menu->AppendRadioItem(ID_PAGE_MODE, wxT("&Page Mode"));
```

Another overload of Append enables you to append a submenu, for example:

```
// Append a submenu
menu->Append(ID_SUBMENU, wxT("&More options..."), subMenu);
```

Yet another overload of Append enables you to use a wxMenuItem object directly to append an item, and this is the only way to show bitmaps on menus or to set special fonts. For example:

```
// Initialization of bitmaps and font not shown
wxBitmap bmpEnabled, bmpDisabled;
wxFont fontLarge;

// Create a menu item
wxMenuItem* pItem = new wxMenuItem(menu, wxID_OPEN, wxT("&Open…"));

// Set bitmaps and font
pItem->SetBitmaps(bmpEnabled, bmpDisabled);
pItem->SetFont(fontLarge);

// Finally append it to the menu
menu->Append(pItem);
```

Use Insert to insert a menu at a particular position. There are also the functions Prepend, PrependCheckItem, PrependRadioItem, and PrependSeparator for inserting items at the start of the menu.

AppendSeparator adds a separator, and InsertSeparator inserts a separator in a given position. For example:

```
// Append a separator
menu->AppendSeparator();
```

Break inserts a break in a menu, causing the next appended item to appear in a new column.

Use Check to toggle a check or radio item on or off, passing the menu item identifier and a boolean value. Use IsChecked to get the checked status.

Delete deletes a menu item specified by identifier or by wxMenuItem pointer. If the item is a menu, the submenu will not be deleted. Use Destroy if you want to remove and delete a submenu. Remove removes the menu item from a menu without deleting the returned wxMenuItem object.

Use Enable to enable or disable a menu item, but rather than doing this explicitly, you may want to use UI update events (see Chapter 9). IsEnabled returns the enabled status.

Use FindItem to find an item by label or identifier. Use FindItemByPosition to find an item by position in the menu.

GetHelpString and SetHelpString are accessors for the help string associated with a menu item. When the menu is part of a menu bar, wxFrame shows this string in the status bar (if available), as the user highlights each menu item.

GetLabel and SetLabel get or set the menu item label, given its identifier.

GetMenuCount returns the number of items in the menu.

GetMenuItems returns a reference to the list of menu items, a wxMenuItemList object.

GetTitle and SetTitle are accessors for the optional title of a menu and are only used for pop-up menus.

UpdateUI sends UI update events to the event handler argument or to the owning window if NULL is passed. This is called just before the menu is popped up, but the application may call it at other times if required.

CONTROL BARS

A control bar provides a convenient way to contain and arrange multiple controls. There are currently three kinds of control bars: wxMenuBar, wxToolBar, and wxStatusBar. wxMenuBar can only belong to a wxFrame. wxToolBar and wxStatusBar are most commonly used with wxFrame, but they can also be children of other windows.

wxMenuBar

A menu bar contains a series of menus accessible from the top of a frame under the title bar. You can replace a frame's current menu bar by calling SetMenuBar. To create a menu bar, use the default constructor and append wxMenu objects. For example:

```
wxMenuBar* menuBar = new wxMenuBar;
wxMenu* fileMenu = new wxMenu;
fileMenu->Append(wxID_OPEN, wxT("&Open..."), wxT("Opens a file"));
fileMenu->AppendSeparator();
fileMenu->Append(wxID_EXIT, wxT("E&xit"), wxT("Quits the program"));
menuBar->Append(fileMenu);
frame->SetMenuBar(menuBar, wxT("&File"));
```

This code creates a one-menu menu bar, as shown in Figure 4-34.

Figure 4-34   A wxMenuBar

You can append submenus to a wxMenu, and you can create check and radio menu items (refer to the "Menus" section earlier in this chapter). As in the previous example, an ampersand in a label indicates that the following character should be used as a mnemonic (pressing that key when the menu is shown executes the associated command).

If you provide a help string, it will be shown in the frame's status bar (if any) by virtue of the default EVT_MENU_HIGHLIGHT handler.

wxMenuBar Styles

wxMenuBar takes the wxMB_DOCKABLE style, used under GTK+ to allow the menu bar to be detached from the frame.

wxMenuBar Events

Menu bars use the events already covered in the description of wxMenu.

wxMenuBar Member Functions

These are the major wxMenuBar functions.

Append adds a menu to the end of the menu bar, which will then own the menu and will destroy it when the menu bar is destroyed (usually by the owning frame). Pass the menu and a label. Insert inserts a menu at the given position.

Enable enables or disables the given menu item, given its identifier. Use IsEnabled to check its enabled status.

Check checks or unchecks a check or radio menu item. Use IsChecked to test its checked status.

EnableTop enables or disables a whole menu, by zero-based position.

FindMenu returns the index of a menu whose label matches the given string, with or without mnemonic characters. It returns wxNOT_FOUND if there was no match.

FindMenuItem returns the index of a menu item given a menu name and a menu item.

FindItem returns the wxMenuItem object given a menu item identifier, and if it is a submenu, its wxMenu pointer will be returned in the second argument.

GetHelpString and SetHelpString are accessors for the help string for a given menu item.

GetLabel and SetLabel are accessors for a menu item's label.

GetLabelTop and SetLabelTop are accessors for a menu's label in the menu bar, given the zero-based menu position.

GetMenu returns a pointer to the wxMenu at the given zero-based position.

GetMenuCount returns the number of menus in the menu bar.

Refresh redraws the menu bar.

Remove removes a menu and returns the wxMenu object, which the application is then responsible for deleting.

Replace replaces a menu at the given position with another one. The old menu is returned, and the application is responsible for deleting it.

wxToolBar

A toolbar contains a number of buttons and controls. It can be horizontal or vertical, and the buttons can be push, check, or radio buttons. The buttons can show labels as well as bitmaps. If you use wxFrame::CreateToolBar to create the toolbar, or wxFrame::SetToolBar to associate it with a frame, the frame will manage the toolbar, and it will not be counted as part of the client area. If you use it in any other way, then your code will have to manage the toolbar size and position using sizers or some other method.

Here's an example of creating a toolbar and associating it with a frame:

```
#include "wx/toolbar.h"

#include "open.xpm"
#include "save.xpm"

wxToolBar* toolBar = new wxToolBar(frame, wxID_ANY,
    wxDefaultPosition, wxDefaultSize, wxTB_HORIZONTAL|wxNO_BORDER);
wxBitmap bmpOpen(open_xpm);
wxBitmap bmpSave(save_xpm);
toolBar->AddTool(wxID_OPEN, bmpOpen, wxT("Open"));
toolBar->AddTool(wxID_SAVE, bmpSave, wxT("Save"));
toolBar->AddSeparator();
wxComboBox* comboBox = new wxComboBox(toolBar, ID_COMBOBOX);
toolBar->AddControl(comboBox);
toolBar->Realize();
frame->SetToolBar(toolBar);
```

Under Windows, this will create a toolbar, as shown in Figure 4-35.

Figure 4-35   A wxToolBar

Note the call to `Realize`, which must be performed after all buttons and controls have been added to the toolbar; otherwise, nothing will appear in the toolbar.

Check out the wxWidgets sample in `samples/toolbar` for a demonstration of changing orientation, showing labels on buttons, changing the button size, and other aspects of `wxToolBar`.

Tool Bitmap Colors Under Windows

Under Windows, wxWidgets will attempt to map colors in the tool bitmaps that are close to "standard" colors to equivalents used by the current theme. In particular, light gray is used to indicate transparency within the bitmap. Table 4-48 lists these colors. In fact, colors in the bitmap only have to be close to the indicated color (each RGB element can be within 10 units of the standard value) for the substitution to take place.

Table 4-48 Standard Bitmap Colors

Color Value	Color Name	Used For
`wxColour(0, 0, 0)`	Black	Dark shadows
`wxColour(128, 128, 128)`	Dark gray	Shadows for 3D edges facing away from the light source
`wxColour(192, 192, 192)`	Light gray	3D face (button background), indicates transparent area
`wxColour(255, 255, 255)`	White	Highlights for 3D edges facing the light source

This is fine for 16-color tool bitmaps, but if you use more colors, the mapping can be undesirable because it leads to a grainy effect. In this case, add the following line to your code before the creation of the toolbar to switch off the mapping:

```
wxSystemOptions::SetOption(wxT("msw.remap"), 0);
```

You will need to include `wx/sysopt.h` in your source file.

wxToolBar Styles

Table 4-49 lists the specific window styles for `wxToolBar`.

Table 4-49   wxToolBar Styles

wxTB_HORIZONTAL	Creates a horizontal toolbar.
wxTB_VERTICAL	Creates a vertical toolbar.
wxTB_FLAT	Gives the toolbar a flat look. Windows and GTK+ only.
wxTB_DOCKABLE	Makes the toolbar floatable and dockable. GTK+ only.
wxTB_TEXT	Shows the text in the toolbar buttons; by default, only icons are shown.
wxTB_NOICONS	Specifies no icons in the toolbar buttons; by default, they are shown.
wxTB_NODIVIDER	Specifies no divider above the toolbar. Windows only.
wxTB_HORZ_LAYOUT	Shows the text and the icons alongside, not vertically stacked. Windows and GTK+ only. This style must be used with wxTB_TEXT.
wxTB_HORZ_TEXT	Combination of wxTB_HORZ_LAYOUT and wxTB_TEXT.

wxToolBar Events

Toolbar event macros are listed in Table 4-50. The toolbar class emits menu commands in the same way that a frame's menu bar does, so you can use one `EVT_MENU` or `EVT_TOOL` macro for both a menu item and a toolbar button. The event handler functions take a `wxCommandEvent` argument. For most of the event macros, the identifier of the tool is passed, but for `EVT_TOOL_ENTER`, the toolbar window identifier is passed, and the tool identifier is retrieved from the `wxCommandEvent`. This is because the identifier may be -1 when the mouse moves off a tool, and -1 is not allowed as an identifier in the event system.

Table 4-50   wxToolBar Events

EVT_TOOL(id, func)	Processes a wxEVT_COMMAND_TOOL_CLICKED event (a synonym for wxEVT_COMMAND_MENU_SELECTED), generated when the user clicks on a toolbar tool. Pass the identifier of the tool.
EVT_TOOL_RANGE(id1, id2, func)	Processes a wxEVT_COMMAND_TOOL_CLICKED event for a range of identifiers. Pass the identifier of the tools.
EVT_TOOL_RCLICKED(id, func)	Processes a wxEVT_COMMAND_TOOL_RCLICKED event, generated when the user right-clicks on a control. Pass the identifier of the tool.
EVT_TOOL_RCLICKED_RANGE (id1, id2, func)	Processes a wxEVT_COMMAND_TOOL_RCLICKED event for a range of identifiers. Pass the identifiers of the tools.

EVT_TOOL_ENTER(id, func)	Processes a wxEVT_COMMAND_TOOL_ENTER event, generated when the mouse pointer moves into or out of a tool. Pass the identifier of the toolbar itself. The value of wxCommandEvent::GetSelection is the tool identifier, or -1 if the pointer has moved off a tool.

wxToolBar Member Functions

These are the major wxToolBar functions.

AddTool adds a tool: specify the identifier, an optional label, a bitmap, a help string, and the kind of tool (wxITEM_NORMAL, wxITEM_CHECK, or wxITEM_RADIO). Use InsertTool to insert the tool at a particular position. You can also use AddCheckTool and AddRadioTool to avoid specifying wxITEM_CHECK or wxITEM_RADIO. AddSeparator adds a separator, which is a line or a space depending on implementation. Use InsertSeparator to insert a separator in a given position. For example, the following line adds a checkable tool with a caption ("Save"), a bitmap, and a help string ("Toggle button 1"):

```
toolBar->AddTool(wxID_SAVE, wxT("Save"), bitmap,
                 wxT("Toggle button 1"), wxITEM_CHECK);
```

AddControl adds a control, such as a combo box. InsertControl inserts a control at a given position.

DeleteTool deletes a tool specified by identifier. DeleteToolByPos deletes a tool by position. RemoveTool removes a tool from the toolbar but doesn't delete the wxToolBarTool object, which is returned from the function.

Use EnableTool to enable or disable a tool, but rather than doing this explicitly, you may want to use UI update events (see Chapter 9). GetToolEnabled returns the enabled status.

Use FindById and FindControl to find a tool or control by identifier.

If you need to add bitmaps with a size other than the default 16×15, call SetToolBitmapSize. GetToolBitmapSize returns the current bitmap size. GetToolSize returns the size including decorations around the tool.

GetMargins and SetMargins are accessors for the left/right and top/bottom margins.

GetToolClientData and SetToolClientData can be used to return or associate an arbitrary wxObject for a tool, given the tool identifier.

GetToolLongHelp and SetToolLongHelp are accessors for the long help string associated with a tool. This is a line of help that could be shown in a status bar, for example. GetToolShortHelp and SetToolShortHelp are accessors for the short help string (tooltip) associated with a tool.

GetToolPacking and SetToolPacking are accessors for the tool spacing in the vertical direction if the toolbar is horizontal, and for spacing in the horizontal direction if the toolbar is vertical.

GetToolPosition returns the position in the toolbar given a tool identifier.

GetToolSeparation and SetToolSeparation are accessors for the tool separator size.

GetToolState and SetToolState are accessors for a check or radio tool on/off state.

Realize must always be called after tools have been added.

ToggleTool toggles the given radio or check tool on or off.

wxStatusBar

A status bar is a narrow window that can be placed along the bottom of a frame to give small amounts of status information. It can contain one or more fields, which can have fixed or variable width. If you use wxFrame::CreateStatusBar to create the status bar, or wxFrame::SetStatusBar to associate it with a frame, the frame will manage the status bar, and it will not be counted as part of the client area. If you use it in any other way, then your code will have to manage the status bar size and position using sizers or some other method.

Here's an example of creating a status bar with three fields, two that are 60 pixels wide and a third that expands to fill the rest of the status bar.

```
#include "wx/statusbr.h"

wxStatusBar* statusBar = new wxStatusBar(frame, wxID_ANY,
    wxST_SIZEGRIP);
frame->SetStatusBar(statusBar);
int widths[] = { 60, 60, -1 };
statusBar->SetFieldWidths(WXSIZEOF(widths), widths);
statusBar->SetStatusText(wxT("Ready"), 0);
```

The resulting status bar is shown in Figure 4-36.

Figure 4-36   A wxStatusBar

If you want, you can create small controls inside status bar fields. You will have to manage their size and position yourself—for example, from within the size event handler of a class derived from wxStatusBar.

wxStatusBar Styles

Table 4-51 shows the specific window style for wxStatusBar. You can also determine the appearance of the individual field borders using SetStatusStyles.

Table 4-51   wxStatusBar Style

wxST_SIZEGRIP	Displays a gripper at the right side of the status bar.

wxStatusBar Events

There are no special events for wxStatusBar.

wxStatusBar Member Functions

These are the major wxStatusBar functions.

GetFieldRect returns the size and position of a field's internal bounding rectangle.

GetFieldsCount returns the number of fields in the status bar. Use SetFieldsCount to set the number of fields.

GetStatusText gets the status text for a field, and SetStatusText sets the text for a field.

PushStatusText saves the current field text in a stack and sets the field text to the string passed as an argument. PopStatusText sets the field text to the top of the stack and pops the stack of saved strings.

SetMinHeight sets the minimal possible height for the status bar.

SetStatusWidths takes the number of fields and an array of integers that represent each field's width, or a negative number to specify a proportion of the status bar to fill. For example, to create one field of fixed width 100 in the right part of the status bar and two more fields that get 66% and 33% of the remaining space respectively, you should specify an array containing -2, -1, and 100. The negative numbers are used to distinguish absolute pixel values from proportions.

SetStatusStyles takes the number of fields and an array of integer styles that determine the appearance of the fields. Use wxSB_NORMAL for a sunken field with a 3D border, wxSB_FLAT for a flat field with no border, and wxSB_RAISED for a field with a raised 3D border.

Summary

This chapter has given you enough information about the capabilities of essential window and control classes to know how to start building useful applications. For more details on these and other window classes, please refer to the reference manual. For further window classes, and how to create your own controls, see Chapter 12. You'll also find it useful to look at the samples in your wxWidgets distribution, such as `samples/widgets`, `samples/toolbar`, `samples/text`, and `samples/listbox`.

Next, we'll look at how how your application can draw on a variety of surfaces, including windows, bitmaps, and the printed page.

Drawing and Printing

This chapter introduces the idea of the *device context*, generalizing the concept of a drawing surface such as a window or a printed page. We will discuss the available device context classes and the set of "drawing tools" that wxWidgets provides for handling fonts, color, line drawing, and filling. Next we describe a device context's drawing functions and how to use the wxWidgets printing framework. We end the chapter by briefly discussing wxGLCanvas, which provides a way for you to draw 3D graphics on your windows using OpenGL.

UNDERSTANDING DEVICE CONTEXTS

All drawing in wxWidgets is done on a device context, using an instance of a class derived from wxDC. There is no such thing as drawing directly to a window; instead, you create a device context for the window and then draw on the device context. There are also device context classes that work with bitmaps and printers, or you can design your own. A happy consequence of this abstraction is that you can define drawing code that will work on a number of different device contexts: just parameterize it with wxDC, and if necessary, take into account the device's resolution by scaling appropriately. Let's describe the major properties of a device context.

A device context has a coordinate system with its origin at the top-left of the surface. This position can be changed with SetDeviceOrigin so that graphics subsequently drawn on the device context are shifted—this is used when painting with wxScrolledWindow. You can also use SetAxisOrientation if you prefer, say, the *y*-axis to go from bottom to top.

There is a distinction between *logical units* and *device units*. Device units are the units native to the particular device—for a screen, a device unit is a pixel. For a printer, the device unit is defined by the resolution of the printer, which can be queried using GetSize (for a page size in device units) or GetSizeMM (for a page size in millimeters).

The *mapping mode* of the device context defines the unit of measurement used to convert logical units to device units. Note that some device contexts, in particular wxPostScriptDC, do not support mapping modes other than wxMM_TEXT. Table 5-1 lists the available mapping modes.

Table 5-1   Mapping Modes

wxMM_TWIPS	Each logical unit is 1/20 of a point, or 1/1440 of an inch.
wxMM_POINTS	Each logical unit is a point, or 1/72 of an inch.
wxMM_METRIC	Each logical unit is 1 millimeter.
wxMM_LOMETRIC	Each logical unit is 1/10 of a millimeter.
wxMM_TEXT	Each logical unit is 1 pixel. This is the default mode.

You can impose a further scale on your logical units by calling SetUser Scale, which multiplies with the scale implied by the mapping mode. For example, in wxMM_TEXT mode, a user scale value of (1.0, 1.0) makes logical and device units identical. By default, the mapping mode is wxMM_TEXT, and the scale is (1.0, 1.0).

A device context has a clipping region, which can be set with SetClipping Region and cleared with DestroyClippingRegion. Graphics will not be shown outside the clipping region. One use of this is to draw a string so that it appears only inside a particular rectangle, even though the string might extend beyond the rectangle boundary. You can set the clipping region to be the same size and location as the rectangle, draw the text, and then destroy the clipping region, and the text will be truncated to fit inside the rectangle.

Just as with real artistry, in order to draw, you must first select some tools. Any operation that involves drawing an outline uses the currently selected pen, and filled areas use the current brush. The current font, together with the foreground and background text color, determines how text will appear. We will discuss these tools in detail later, but first we'll look at the types of device context that are available to us.

Available Device Contexts

These are the device context classes you can use:

☞ wxClientDC. For drawing on the client area of a window.
☞ wxBufferedDC. A replacement for wxClientDC for double-buffered painting.

☞ `wxWindowDC`. For drawing on the client and non-client (decorated) area of a window. This is rarely used and not fully implemented on all platforms.

☞ `wxPaintDC`. For drawing on the client area of a window during a paint event handler.

☞ `wxBufferedPaintDC`. A replacement for `wxPaintDC` for double-buffered painting.

☞ `wxScreenDC`. For drawing on or copying from the screen.

☞ `wxMemoryDC`. For drawing into or copying from a bitmap.

☞ `wxMetafileDC`. For creating a metafile (Windows and Mac OS X).

☞ `wxPrinterDC`. For drawing to a printer.

☞ `wxPostScriptDC`. For drawing to a PostScript file or printer.

The following sections describe how to create and work with these device contexts. Working with printer device contexts is discussed in more detail later in the chapter in "Using the Printing Framework."

Drawing on Windows with *wxClientDC*

Use `wxClientDC` objects to draw on the client area of windows outside of paint events. For example, to implement a doodling application, you might create a `wxClientDC` object within your mouse event handler. It can also be used within background erase events.

Here's a code fragment that demonstrates how to paint on a window using the mouse:

```
BEGIN_EVENT_TABLE(MyWindow, wxWindow)
    EVT_MOTION(MyWindow::OnMotion)
END_EVENT_TABLE()

void MyWindow::OnMotion(wxMouseEvent& event)
{
    if (event.Dragging())
    {
        wxClientDC dc(this);
        wxPen pen(*wxRED, 1); // red pen of width 1
        dc.SetPen(pen);
        dc.DrawPoint(event.GetPosition());
        dc.SetPen(wxNullPen);
    }
}
```

For more realistic doodling code, see Chapter 19, "Working with Documents and Views." The "Doodle" example uses line segments instead of points and implements undo/redo. It also stores the line segments, so that when the window is repainted, the graphic is redrawn; using the previous code, the graphic will only linger on the window until the next paint event is received. You may also want to use CaptureMouse and ReleaseMouse to direct all mouse events to your window while the mouse button is down.

An alternative to using wxClientDC directly is to use wxBufferedDC, which stores your drawing in a memory device context and transfers it to the window in one step when the device context is about to be deleted. This can result in smoother updates—for example, if you don't want the user to see a complex graphic being updated bit by bit. Use the class exactly as you would use wxClientDC. For efficiency, you can pass a stored bitmap to the constructor to avoid the object re-creating a bitmap each time.

Erasing Window Backgrounds

A window receives two kinds of paint event: wxPaintEvent for drawing the main graphic, and wxEraseEvent for painting the background. If you just handle wxPaintEvent, the default wxEraseEvent handler will clear the background to the color previously specified by wxWindow::SetBackgroundColour, or a suitable default.

This may seem rather convoluted, but this separation of background and foreground painting enables maximum control on platforms that follow this model, such as Windows. For example, suppose you want to draw a textured background on a window. If you tile your texture bitmap in OnPaint, you will see a brief flicker as the background is cleared prior to painting the texture. To avoid this, handle wxEraseEvent and do nothing in the handler. Alternatively, you can do the background tiling in the erase handler, and paint the foreground in the paint handler (however, this defeats buffered drawing as described in the next section).

On some platforms, intercepting wxEraseEvent still isn't enough to suppress default background clearing. The safest thing to do if you want to have a background other than a plain color is to call wxWindow::SetBackgroundStyle passing wxBG_STYLE_CUSTOM. This tells wxWidgets to leave all background painting to the application.

If you do decide to implement an erase handler, call wxEraseEvent::GetDC and use the returned device context if it exists. If it's NULL, you can use a wxClientDC instead. This allows for wxWidgets implementations that don't pass a device context to the erase handler, which can be an unnecessary expense if it's not used. This is demonstrated in the following code for drawing a bitmap as a background texture:

```
BEGIN_EVENT_TABLE(MyWindow, wxWindow)
  EVT_ERASE_BACKGROUND(MyWindow::OnErase)
```

```
END_EVENT_TABLE()

void MyWindow::OnErase(wxEraseEvent& event)
{
    wxClientDC* clientDC = NULL;
    if (!event.GetDC())
        clientDC = new wxClientDC(this);

    wxDC* dc = clientDC ? clientDC : event.GetDC() ;

    wxSize sz = GetClientSize();
    wxEffects effects;
    effects.TileBitmap(wxRect(0, 0, sz.x, sz.y), *dc, m_bitmap);

    if (clientDC)
        delete clientDC;
}
```

As with paint events, the device context will be clipped to the area that needs to be repaired, if using the object returned from wxEraseEvent::GetDC.

Drawing on Windows with *wxPaintDC*

If you define a paint event handler, you must always create a wxPaintDC object, even if you don't use it. Creating this object will tell wxWidgets that the invalid regions in the window have been repainted so that the windowing system won't keep sending paint events *ad infinitum*. In a paint event, you can call wxWindow::GetUpdateRegion to get the region that is invalid, or wxWindow::IsExposed to determine if the given point or rectangle is in the update region. If possible, just repaint this region. The device context will automatically be clipped to this region anyway during the paint event, but you can speed up redraws by only drawing what is necessary.

Paint events are generated when user interaction causes regions to need repainting, but they can also be generated as a result of wxWindow::Refresh or wxWindow::RefreshRect calls. If you know exactly which area of the window needs to be repainted, you can invalidate that region and cause as little flicker as possible. One problem with refreshing the window this way is that you can't guarantee exactly when the window will be updated. If you really need to have the paint handler called immediately—for example, if you're doing time-consuming calculations—you can call wxWindow::Update after calling Refresh or RefreshRect.

The following code draws a red rectangle with a black outline in the center of a window, if the rectangle was in the update region:

```
BEGIN_EVENT_TABLE(MyWindow, wxWindow)
  EVT_PAINT(MyWindow::OnPaint)
END_EVENT_TABLE()

void MyWindow::OnPaint(wxPaintEvent& event)
{
```

```
    wxPaintDC dc(this);

    dc.SetPen(*wxBLACK_PEN);
    dc.SetBrush(*wxRED_BRUSH);

    // Get window dimensions
    wxSize sz = GetClientSize();

    // Our rectangle dimensions
    wxCoord w = 100, h = 50;

    // Center the rectangle on the window, but never
    // draw at a negative position.
    int x = wxMax(0, (sz.x—w)/2);
    int y = wxMax(0, (sz.y—h)/2);

    wxRect rectToDraw(x, y, w, h);

    // For efficiency, do not draw if not exposed
    if (IsExposed(rectToDraw))
        dc.DrawRectangle(rectToDraw);
}
```

Note that by default, when a window is resized, only the newly exposed areas are included in the update region. Use the wxFULL_REPAINT_ON_RESIZE window style to have the entire window included in the update region when the window is resized. In our example, we need this style because resizing the window changes the position of the graphic, and we need to make sure that no odd bits of the rectangle are left behind.

wxBufferedPaintDC is a buffered version of wxPaintDC. Simply replace wxPaintDC with wxBufferedPaintDC in your paint event handler, and the graphics will be drawn to a bitmap before being drawn all at once on the window, reducing flicker.

As we mentioned in the previous topic, another thing you can do to make drawing smoother (particularly when resizing) is to paint the background in your paint handler, and not in an erase background handler. All the painting will then be done in your buffered paint handler, so you don't see the background being erased before the paint handler is called. Add an empty erase background handler, and call SetBackgroundStyle with wxBG_STYLE_CUSTOM to hint to some systems not to clear the background automatically. In a scrolling window, where the device origin is moved to shift the graphic for the current scroll position, you will need to calculate the position of the window client area for the current origin. The following code snippet illustrates how to achieve smooth painting and scrolling for a class derived from wxScrolledWindow:

```
#include "wx/dcbuffer.h"

BEGIN_EVENT_TABLE(MyCustomCtrl, wxScrolledWindow)
```

```
      EVT_PAINT(MyCustomCtrl::OnPaint)
      EVT_ERASE_BACKGROUND(MyCustomCtrl::OnEraseBackground)
END_EVENT_TABLE()

/// Painting
void MyCustomCtrl::OnPaint(wxPaintEvent& event)
{
    wxBufferedPaintDC dc(this);

    // Shifts the device origin so we don't have to worry
    // about the current scroll position ourselves
    PrepareDC(dc);

    // Paint the background
    PaintBackground(dc);

    // Paint the graphic
    ...
}

/// Paint the background
void MyCustomCtrl::PaintBackground(wxDC& dc)
{
    wxColour backgroundColour = GetBackgroundColour();
    if (!backgroundColour.Ok())
        backgroundColour =
            wxSystemSettings::GetColour(wxSYS_COLOUR_3DFACE);

    dc.SetBrush(wxBrush(backgroundColour));
    dc.SetPen(wxPen(backgroundColour, 1));

    wxRect windowRect(wxPoint(0, 0), GetClientSize());

    // We need to shift the client rectangle to take into account
    // scrolling, converting device to logical coordinates
    CalcUnscrolledPosition(windowRect.x, windowRect.y,
                            & windowRect.x, & windowRect.y);
    dc.DrawRectangle(windowRect);
}

// Empty implementation, to prevent flicker
void MyCustomCtrl::OnEraseBackground(wxEraseEvent& event)
{
}
```

To increase efficiency when using wxBufferedPaintDC, you can maintain a bitmap large enough to cope with all window sizes (for example, the screen size) and pass it to the wxBufferedPaintDC constructor as its second argument. Then the device context doesn't have to keep creating and destroying its bitmap for every paint event.

The area that wxBufferedPaintDC copies from its buffer is normally the size of the window client area (the part that the user can see). The actual paint context that is internally created by the class is *not* transformed by the window's PrepareDC to reflect the current scroll position. However, you can specify that both the paint context and your buffered paint context use the same transformations by passing wxBUFFER_VIRTUAL_AREA to the wxBufferedPaintDC constructor, rather than the default wxBUFFER_CLIENT_AREA. Your window's PrepareDC function will be called on the actual paint context so the transformations on both device contexts match. In this case, you will need to supply a bitmap that is the same size as the virtual area in your scrolled window. This is inefficient and should normally be avoided. Note that at the time of writing, using buffering with wxBUFFER_CLIENT_AREA does not work with scaling (SetUserScale).

For a full example of using wxBufferedPaintDC, you might like to look at the wxThumbnailCtrl control in examples/chap12/thumbnail on the CD-ROM.

Drawing on Bitmaps with *wxMemoryDC*

A memory device context has a bitmap associated with it, so that drawing into the device context draws on the bitmap. First create a wxMemoryDC object with the default constructor, and then use SelectObject to associate a bitmap with the device context. When you have finished with the device context, you should call SelectObject with wxNullBitmap to remove the association.

The following example creates a bitmap and draws a red rectangle outline on it:

```
wxBitmap CreateRedOutlineBitmap()
{
    wxMemoryDC memDC;
    wxBitmap bitmap(200, 200);
    memDC.SelectObject(bitmap);
    memDC.SetBackground(*wxWHITE_BRUSH);
    memDC.Clear();
    memDC.SetPen(*wxRED_PEN);
    memDC.SetBrush(*wxTRANSPARENT_BRUSH);
    memDC.DrawRectangle(wxRect(10, 10, 100, 100));
    memDC.SelectObject(wxNullBitmap);
    return bitmap;
}
```

You can also copy areas from a memory device context to another device context with the Blit function, described later in the chapter.

Creating Metafiles with *wxMetafileDC*

wxMetafileDC is available on Windows and Mac OS X, where it models a drawing surface for a Windows metafile or a Mac PICT, respectively. It allows you to draw into a wxMetafile object, which consists of a list of drawing instructions that can be interpreted by an application or rendered into a device context with wxMetafile::Play.

Accessing the Screen with *wxScreenDC*

Use wxScreenDC for drawing on areas of the whole screen. This is useful when giving feedback for dragging operations, such as the sash on a splitter window. For efficiency, you can limit the screen area to be drawn on to a specific region (often the dimensions of the window in question). As well as drawing with this class, you can copy areas to other device contexts and use it for capturing screenshots. Because it is not possible to control where other applications are drawing, use of wxScreenDC to draw on the screen usually works best when restricted to windows in the current application.

Here's example code that snaps the current screen and returns it in a bitmap:

```
wxBitmap GetScreenShot()
{
    wxSize screenSize = wxGetDisplaySize();
    wxBitmap bitmap(screenSize.x, screenSize.y);
    wxScreenDC dc;
    wxMemoryDC memDC;
    memDC.SelectObject(bitmap);
    memDC.Blit(0, 0, screenSize.x, screenSize.y, & dc, 0, 0);
    memDC.SelectObject(wxNullBitmap);
    return bitmap;
}
```

Printing with *wxPrinterDC* and *wxPostScriptDC*

wxPrinterDC represents the printing surface. On Windows and Mac, it maps to the respective printing system for the application. On other Unix-based systems where there is no standard printing model, a wxPostScriptDC is used instead, unless GNOME printing support is available (see the later section, "Printing Under Unix with GTK+").

There are several ways to construct a wxPrinterDC object. You can pass it a wxPrintData after setting paper type, landscape or portrait, number of copies, and so on. An easier way is to show a wxPrintDialog and then call wxPrintDialog::GetPrintDC to retrieve an appropriate wxPrinterDC for the settings chosen by the user. At a higher level, you can derive a class from wxPrintout to specify behavior for printing and print previewing, passing it to an instance of wxPrinter (see the later section on printing).

If your printout is mainly text, consider using the wxHtmlEasyPrinting class to bypass the need to deal with wxPrinterDC or wxPrintout altogether: just write an HTML file (using wxWidgets' subset of HTML syntax) and create a wxHtmlEasyPrinting object to print or preview it. This could save you days or even weeks of programming to format your text, tables, and images. See Chapter 12, "Advanced Window Classes," for more on this.

wxPostScriptDC is a device context specifically for creating PostScript files for sending to a printer. Although mainly for Unix-based systems, it can be used on other systems too, where PostScript files need to be generated and you can't guarantee the presence of a PostScript printer driver.

You can create a wxPostScriptDC either by passing a wxPrintData object, or by passing a file name, a boolean to specify whether a print dialog should be shown, and a parent window for the dialog. For example:

```
#include "wx/dcps.h"

wxPostScriptDC dc(wxT("output.ps"), true, wxGetApp().GetTopWindow());

if (dc.Ok())
{
    // Tell it where to find the AFM files
    dc.GetPrintData().SetFontMetricPath(wxGetApp().GetFontPath());

    // Set the resolution in points per inch (the default is 720)
    dc.SetResolution(1440);

    // Draw on the device context
    ...
}
```

One of the quirks of wxPostScriptDC is that it can't directly return text size information from GetTextExtent. You will need to provide AFM (Adobe Font Metric) files with your application and use wxPrintData::SetFontMetricPath to specify where wxWidgets will find them, as in this example. You can get a selection of GhostScript AFM files from ftp://biolpc22.york.ac.uk/pub/support/gs_afm.tar.gz.

DRAWING TOOLS

Drawing code in wxWidgets operates like a very fast artist, rapidly selecting colors and drawing tools, drawing a little part of the scene, then selecting different tools, drawing another part of the scene, and so on. Here we describe the wxColour, wxPen, wxBrush, wxFont and wxPalette classes. You will also find it useful to refer to the descriptions of other classes relevant to drawing—wxRect, wxRegion, wxPoint, and wxSize, which are described in Chapter 13, "Data Structure Classes."

Note that these classes use "reference-counting," efficiently copying only internal pointers rather than chunks of memory. In most circumstances, you can create color, pen, brush, and font objects on the stack as they are needed without worrying about speed implications. If your application does have performance problems, you can take steps to improve efficiency, such as storing some objects as data members.

wxColour

You use wxColour to define various aspects of color when drawing. (Because wxWidgets started life in Edinburgh, the API uses British spelling. However, to cater for the spelling sensibilities of the New World, wxWidgets defines wxColor as an alias for wxColour.)

You can specify the text foreground and background color for a device context using a device context's SetTextForeground and SetTextBackground functions, and you also use wxColour to create pens and brushes.

A wxColour object can be constructed in a number of different ways. You can pass red, green, and blue values (each 0 to 255), or a standard color string such as WHITE or CYAN, or you can create it from another wxColour object. Alternatively, you can use the stock color objects, which are pointers: wxBLACK, wxWHITE, wxRED, wxBLUE, wxGREEN, wxCYAN, and wxLIGHT_GREY. The stock object wxNullColour is an uninitialized color for which the Ok function always returns false.

Using the wxSystemSettings class, you can retrieve some standard, system-wide colors, such as the standard 3D surface color, the default window background color, menu text color, and so on. Please refer to the documentation for wxSystemSettings::GetColour for the identifiers you can pass.

Here are some different ways to create a wxColour object:

```
wxColour color(0, 255, 0); // green
wxColour color(wxT("RED")); // red

// The color used for 3D faces and panels
wxColour color(wxSystemSettings::GetColour(wxSYS_COLOUR_3DFACE));
```

You can also use the wxTheColourDatabase pointer to add a new color, find a wxColour object for a given name, or find the name corresponding to the given color:

```
wxTheColourDatabase->Add(wxT("PINKISH"), wxColour(234, 184, 184));
wxString name = wxTheColourDatabase->FindName(
                                    wxColour(234, 184, 184));
wxString color = wxTheColourDatabase->Find(name);
```

These are the available standard colors: aquamarine, black, blue, blue violet, brown, cadet blue, coral, cornflower blue, cyan, dark gray, dark green, dark olive green, dark orchid, dark slate blue, dark slate gray dark turquoise, dim gray, firebrick, forest green, gold, goldenrod, gray, green, green yellow, indian red, khaki, light blue, light gray, light steel blue, lime green, magenta, maroon, medium aquamarine, medium blue, medium forest green, medium goldenrod, medium orchid, medium sea green, medium slate blue, medium spring green, medium turquoise, medium violet red, midnight blue, navy, orange, orange red, orchid, pale green, pink, plum, purple, red, salmon, sea green, sienna, sky blue, slate blue, spring green, steel blue, tan, thistle, turquoise, violet, violet red, wheat, white, yellow, and yellow green.

wxPen

You define the current pen for the device context by passing a wxPen object to SetPen. The current pen defines the outline color, width, and style for subsequent drawing operations. wxPen has a low overhead, so you can create instances on the stack within your drawing code rather than storing them.

As well as a color and a width, a pen has a style, as described in Table 5-2. Hatch and stipple styles are not supported by the GTK+ port.

Table 5-2   *wxPen* Styles

Style	Example	Description
wxSOLID	———————————	Lines are drawn solid.
wxTRANSPARENT		Used when no pen drawing is desired.
wxDOT	- - - - - - - - - - - - -	The line is drawn dotted.
wxLONG_DASH	—— —— ——	Draws with a long dashed style.
wxSHORT_DASH	▬ ▬ ▬ ▬ ▬	Draws with a short dashed style. On Windows, this is the same as wxLONG_SASH.
wxDOT_DASH	— - — - — -	Draws with a dot and a dash.
wxSTIPPLE	★ ★ ★	Uses a stipple bitmap, which is passed as the first constructor argument.
wxUSER_DASH	——————————————	Uses user-specified dashes. See the reference manual for further information.
wxBDIAGONAL_HATCH	/////////////	Draws with a backward-diagonal hatch.
wxCROSSDIAG_HATCH	××××××××××	Draws with a cross-diagonal hatch.
wxFDIAGONAL_HATCH	\\\\\\\\\\\\\	Draws with a forward-diagonal hatch.
wxCROSS_HATCH	┼┼┼┼┼┼┼┼┼┼	Draws with a cross hatch.
wxHORIZONTAL_HATCH	≣	Draws with a horizontal hatch.
wxVERTICAL_HATCH	I I I I I I I I I I I I	Draws with a vertical hatch.

Call SetCap if you need to specify how the ends of thick lines should look: wxCAP_ROUND (the default) specifies rounded ends, wxCAP_PROJECTING specifies a square projection on either end, and wxCAP_BUTT specifies that the ends should be square and should not project.

You can call SetJoin to set the appearance where lines join. The default is wxJOIN_ROUND, where the corners are rounded. Other values are wxJOIN_BEVEL and wxJOIN_MITER.

There are some stock pens that you can use: wxRED_PEN, wxCYAN_PEN, wxGREEN_PEN, wxBLACK_PEN, wxWHITE_PEN, wxTRANSPARENT_PEN, wxBLACK_DASHED_PEN, wxGREY_PEN, wxMEDIUM_GREY_PEN, and wxLIGHT_GREY_PEN. These are pointers, so you'll need to dereference them when passing them to SetPen. There is also the object wxNullPen (an object, not a pointer), an uninitialized pen object that can be used to reset the pen in a device context.

Here are some examples of creating pens:

```
// A solid red pen
wxPen pen(wxColour(255, 0, 0), 1, wxSOLID);
wxPen pen(wxT("RED"), 1, wxSOLID);
wxPen pen = (*wxRED_PEN);
wxPen pen(*wxRED_PEN);
```

The last two examples use reference counting, so pen's internal data points to wxRED_PEN's data. Reference counting is used for all drawing objects, and it makes the assignment operator and copy constructor cheap operations, but it does mean that sometimes changes in one object affect the properties of another.

One way to reduce the amount of construction and destruction of pen objects without storing pen objects in your own classes is to use the global pointer wxThePenList to create and store the pens you need, for example:

```
wxPen* pen = wxThePenList->FindOrCreatePen(*wxRED, 1, wxSOLID);
```

The pen object will be stored in wxThePenList and cleaned up on application exit. Obviously, you should take care not to use this indiscriminately to avoid filling up memory with pen objects, and you also need to be aware of the reference counting issue mentioned previously. You can remove a pen from the list without deleting it by using RemovePen.

wxBrush

The current brush, specified with SetBrush, defines the fill color and style for drawing operations. You also specify the device context background color using a wxBrush, rather than with just a color. As with wxPen, wxBrush has a low overhead and can be created on the stack.

Pass a color and a style to the brush constructor. The style can be one of the values listed in Table 5-3.

Table 5-3 *wxBrush* Styles

Style	Example	Description
wxSOLID	�	Solid color is used.
wxTRANSPARENT		Used when no filling is desired.
wxBDIAGONAL_HATCH	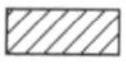 ▨	Draws with a backward-diagonal hatch.
wxCROSSDIAG_HATCH	 ▨	Draws with a cross-diagonal hatch.
wxFDIAGONAL_HATCH	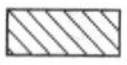 ▧	Draws with a forward-diagonal hatch.
wxCROSS_HATCH	 ▦	Draws with a cross hatch.
wxHORIZONTAL_HATCH	 ▤	Draws with a horizontal hatch.
wxVERTICAL_HATCH	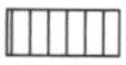 ▥	Draws with a vertical hatch.
wxSTIPPLE	 ★ ★ ★	Uses a stipple bitmap, which is passed as the first constructor argument.

You can use the following stock brushes: wxBLUE_BRUSH, wxGREEN_BRUSH, wxWHITE_BRUSH, wxBLACK_BRUSH, wxGREY_BRUSH, wxMEDIUM_GREY_BRUSH, wxLIGHT_GREY_BRUSH, wxTRANSPARENT_BRUSH, wxCYAN_BRUSH, and wxRED_BRUSH. These are pointers. You can also use the wxNullBrush object (an uninitialized brush object).

Here are some examples of creating brushes:

```
// A solid red brush
wxBrush brush(wxColour(255, 0, 0), wxSOLID);
wxBrush brush(wxT("RED"), wxSOLID);
wxBrush brush = (*wxRED_BRUSH); // a cheap operation
wxBrush brush(*wxRED_BRUSH);
```

As with wxPen, wxBrush also has an associated list, wxTheBrushList, which you can use to cache brush objects:

```
wxBrush* brush = wxTheBrushList->FindOrCreateBrush(*wxBLUE, wxSOLID);
```

Use this with care to avoid proliferation of brush objects and side effects from reference counting. You can remove a brush from the list without deleting it by using RemoveBrush.

wxFont

You use font objects for specifying how text will appear when drawn on a device context. A font has the following properties:

The *point size* specifies the maximum height of the text in points (1/72 of an inch). wxWidgets will choose the closest match it can if the platform is not using scalable fonts.

The *font family* specifies one of a small number of family names, as described in Table 5-4. Specifying a family instead of an actual face name makes applications be more portable because you can't usually rely on a particular typeface being available on all platforms.

The *style* can be wxNORMAL, wxSLANT, or wxITALIC. wxSLANT may not be implemented for all platforms and fonts.

The *weight* is one of wxNORMAL, wxLIGHT, or wxBOLD.

A font's *underline* can be on (true) or off (false).

The *face name* is optional and specifies a particular typeface. If empty, a default typeface will be chosen from the family specification.

The optional *encoding* specifies the mapping between the character codes used in the program and the letters that are drawn onto the device context. Please see Chapter 16, "Writing International Applications," for more on this topic.

Table 5-4   Font Family Identifiers

Identifier	Example	Description
wxFONTFAMILY_SWISS	ABCDEFGabcdefg12345	A sans-serif font—often Helvetica or Arial depending on platform.
wxFONTFAMILY_ROMAN	ABCDEFGabcdefg12345	A formal, serif font.
wxFONTFAMILY_SCRIPT	ABCDEFGabcdefg12345	A handwriting font.
wxFONTFAMILY_MODERN	ABCDEFGabcdefg12345	A fixed pitch font, often Courier.
wxFONTFAMILY_DECORATIVE	ABCDEFGabcdefg12345	A decorative font.
wxFONTFAMILY_DEFAULT		wxWidgets chooses a default family.

You can create a font with the default constructor or by specifying the properties listed in Table 5-4.

There are some stock font objects that you can use: wxNORMAL_FONT, wxSMALL_FONT, wxITALIC_FONT, and wxSWISS_FONT. These have the size of the standard system font (wxSYS_DEFAULT_GUI_FONT), apart from wxSMALL_FONT, which is two points smaller. You can also use wxSystemSettings::GetFont to retrieve standard fonts.

To use a font object, pass it to `wxDC::SetFont` before performing text operations, in particular `DrawText` and `GetTextExtent`.

Here are some examples of font creation.

```
wxFont font(12, wxFONTFAMILY_ROMAN, wxITALIC, wxBOLD, false);
wxFont font(10, wxFONTFAMILY_SWISS, wxNORMAL, wxBOLD, true,
            wxT("Arial"), wxFONTENCODING_ISO8859_1));
wxFont font(wxSystemSettings::GetFont(wxSYS_DEFAULT_GUI_FONT));
```

`wxFont` has an associated list, `wxTheFontList`, which you can use to find a previously created font or add a new one:

```
wxFont* font = wxTheFontList->FindOrCreateFont(12, wxSWISS,
                                          wxNORMAL, wxNORMAL);
```

As with the pen and brush lists, use this with moderation because the fonts will be deleted only when the application exits. You can remove a font from the list without deleting it by using `RemoveFont`.

We'll see some examples of working with text and fonts later in the chapter. Also, you may like to play with the font demo in `samples/font` (see Figure 5-1). It lets you set a font to see how some text will appear, and you can change the font size and other properties.

Figure 5-1   wxWidgets font demo

wxPalette

A palette is a table, often with a size of 256, that maps index values to the red, green, and blue values of the display colors. It's normally used when the display has a very limited number of colors that need to be shared between applications. By setting a palette for a client device context, an application's color needs can be balanced with the needs of other applications. It is also used to map the colors of a low-depth bitmap to the available colors, and so wxBitmap has an optional associated wxPalette object.

Because most computers now have full-color displays, palettes are rarely needed. RGB colors specified in an application are mapped to the nearest display color with no need for a palette.

A wxPalette can be created by passing a size and three arrays (unsigned char*) for each of the red, green, and blue components. You can query the number of colors with GetColoursCount. To find the red, green, and blue values for a given index, use GetRGB, and you can find an index value for given red, green, and blue values with GetPixel.

Set the palette into a client, window, or memory device context with wxDC::SetPalette. For example, you can set the palette obtained from a low-depth wxBitmap you are about to draw, so the system knows how to map the index values to device colors. When using drawing functions that use wxColour with a device context that has a palette set, the RGB color will be mapped automatically to the palette index by the system, so choose a palette that closely matches the colors you will be using.

Another use for wxPalette is to query a wxImage or wxBitmap for the colors in a low-color image that was loaded from a file, such as a GIF. If there is an associated wxPalette object, it will give you a quick way to identify the unique colors in the original file, even though the image will have been converted to an RGB representation. Similarly, you can create and associate a palette with a wxImage that is to be saved in a reduced-color format. For example, the following fragment loads a PNG file and saves it as an 8-bit Windows bitmap file:

```
// Load the PNG
wxImage image(wxT("image.png"), wxBITMAP_TYPE_PNG);

// Make a palette
unsigned char* red = new unsigned char[256];
unsigned char* green = new unsigned char[256];
unsigned char* blue = new unsigned char[256];
for (size_t i = 0; i < 256; i ++)
{
    red[i] = green[i] = blue[i] = i;
}
wxPalette palette(256, red, green, blue);

// Set the palette and the BMP depth
image.SetPalette(palette);
```

```
image.SetOption(wxIMAGE_OPTION_BMP_FORMAT, wxBMP_8BPP_PALETTE);

// Save the file
image.SaveFile(wxT("image.bmp"), wxBITMAP_TYPE_BMP);
```

More realistic code would "quantize" the image to reduce the number of colors; see "Color Reduction" in Chapter 10, "Programming with Images," for use of the wxQuantize class to do this.

wxWidgets defines a null palette object, wxNullPalette.

DEVICE CONTEXT DRAWING FUNCTIONS

In this section, we'll take a closer look at how we draw on device contexts. The major functions are summarized in Table 5-5. We cover most of them in the following sections, and you can also find more details in the reference manual.

Table 5-5   Device Context Functions

Blit	Copies from one device context to another. You can specify how much of the original to draw, where drawing should start, the logical function to use, and whether to use a mask if the source is a memory device context.
Clear	Fills the device context with the current background brush.
SetClippingRegion DestroyClippingRegion GetClippingBox	Sets and destroys the clipping region, which restricts drawing to a specified area. The clipping region can be specified as a rectangle or a wxRegion. Use GetClippingBox to get the rectangle surrounding the current clipping region.
DrawArc DrawEllipticArc	Draws an arc or elliptic arc using the current pen and brush.
DrawBitmap DrawIcon	Draws a wxBitmap or wxIcon at the specified location. The bitmap may have a mask to specify transparency.
DrawCircle	Draws a circle using the current pen and brush.
DrawEllipse	Draws an ellipse using the current pen and brush.
DrawLine DrawLines	Draws a line or number of lines using the current pen. The last point of the line is not drawn.
DrawPoint	Draws a point using the current pen.
DrawPolygon DrawPolyPolygon	DrawPolygon draws a filled polygon using an array of points or list of pointers to points, adding an optional offset coordinate. wxWidgets automatically closes the first and last points. DrawPolyPolygon draws one or more polygons at once, which can be a more efficient operation on some platforms.

`DrawRectangle` `DrawRoundedRectangle`	Draws a rectangle or rounded rectangle using the current pen and brush.
`DrawText` `DrawRotatedText`	Draws a text string, or rotated text string, at the specified point using the current text font and the current text foreground and background colors.
`DrawSpline`	Draws a spline between all given control points, using the current pen.
`FloodFill`	Flood fills the device context starting from the given point, using the current brush color.
`Ok`	Returns `true` if the device context is OK to use.
`SetBackground` `GetBackground`	Sets and gets the background brush used in `Clear` and in functions that use a complex logical function. The default is `wxTRANSPARENT_BRUSH`.
`SetBackgroundMode` `GetBackgroundMode`	Sets and gets the background mode for drawing text: `wxSOLID` or `wxTRANSPARENT`. Normally, you will want to set the mode to `wxTRANSPARENT` (the default) so the existing background will be kept when drawing text.
`SetBrush` `GetBrush`	Sets and gets the brush to be used to fill shapes in subsequent drawing operations. The initial value of the brush is undefined.
`SetPen` `GetPen`	Sets and gets the pen to be used to draw the outline of shapes in subsequent drawing operations. The initial value of the pen is undefined.
`SetFont` `GetFont`	Sets and gets the font to be used in `DrawText`, `DrawRotatedText`, and `GetTextExtent` calls. The initial value of the font is undefined.
`SetPalette` `GetPalette`	Sets and gets `wxPalette` object mapping index values to RGB colors.

`SetTextForeground`
`GetTextForeground`
`SetTextBackground`
`GetTextBackground`
	Sets and gets the color to be used for text foreground and background. The defaults are black and white, respectively.

`SetLogicalFunction` `GetLogicalFunction`	The logical function determines how a source pixel from a pen or brush color, or source device context if using `Blit`, combines with a destination pixel in the current device context. The default is `wxCOPY`, which simply draws with the current color.
`GetPixel`	Returns the color at the given point. This is not implemented for `wxPostScriptDC` and `wxMetafileDC`.
`GetTextExtent` `GetPartialTextExtents`	Returns metrics for a given text string.
`GetSize` `GetSizeMM`	Returns the dimensions of the device in device units or millimeters.

(continues)

Table 5-5   Device Context Functions   (*Continued*)

`StartDoc` `EndDoc`	Starts and ends a document. This is only applicable to printer device contexts. When `StartDoc` is called, a message will be shown as the document is printed, and `EndDoc` will hide the message box.
`StartPage` `EndPage`	Starts and ends a page. This is only applicable to printer device contexts.

`DeviceToLogicalX`
`DeviceToLogicalXRel`
`DeviceToLogicalY`
`DeviceToLogicalYRel`
	Converts device coordinates to logical coordinates, either absolute (for positions) or relative (for widths and heights).

`LogicalToDeviceX`
`LogicalToDeviceXRel`
`LogicalToDeviceY`
`LogicalToDeviceYRel`
	Converts logical coordinates to device coordinates, either absolute (for positions) or relative (for widths and heights).

`SetMapMode` `GetMapMode`	As described earlier, this determines (along with `SetUserScale`) how logical units are converted to device units.
`SetAxisOrientation`	Sets the x- and y-axis orientation: the direction from lowest to highest values on the axis. The default orientation is to have the x-axis from left to right (`true`) and the y-axis from top to bottom (`false`).
`SetDeviceOrigin` `GetDeviceOrigin`	Sets and gets the device origin. You can use this to place a graphic in a particular place on a page, for example.
`SetUserScale` `GetUserScale`	Sets and gets the scale to be applied when converting from logical units to device units.

Drawing Text

The way text is drawn on a device context with `DrawText` is determined by the current font, the background mode (transparent or solid drawing), and the text foreground and background colors. If the background mode is `wxSOLID`, the area behind the text will be drawn in the current background color, and if `wxTRANSPARENT`, the text will be drawn without disturbing the background.

Pass a string and either two integers or a `wxPoint` to `DrawText`. The text will be drawn with the given location at the very top-left of the string. Here's a simple example of drawing a text string:

```
// Draw a text string on a window at the given point
void DrawTextString(wxDC& dc, const wxString& text,
                    const wxPoint& pt)
{
    wxFont font(12, wxFONTFAMILY_SWISS, wxNORMAL, wxBOLD);
    dc.SetFont(font);
    dc.SetBackgroundMode(wxTRANSPARENT);
```

```
        dc.SetTextForeground(*wxBLACK);
        dc.SetTextBackground(*wxWHITE);
        dc.DrawText(text, pt);
}
```

You can also use the device context function `DrawRotatedText` to draw text at an angle by specifying the angle in degrees as the last parameter. The following code draws text at 45-degree increments, and the result is illustrated in Figure 5-2.

```
wxFont font(20, wxFONTFAMILY_SWISS, wxNORMAL, wxNORMAL);

dc.SetFont(font);
dc.SetTextForeground(*wxBLACK);
dc.SetBackgroundMode(wxTRANSPARENT);

for (int angle = 0; angle < 360; angle += 45)
    dc.DrawRotatedText(wxT("Rotated text..."), 300, 300, angle);
```

Figure 5-2   Drawing rotated text

On Windows, only TrueType fonts can be drawn rotated. Be aware that the stock object `wxNORMAL_FONT` is not TrueType.

Often, you'll need to find out how much space text will take on a device context, which you can do by passing `wxCoord` (integer) pointers to the function `GetTextExtent`. Its prototype is

```
void GetTextExtent(const wxString& string,
    wxCoord* width, wxCoord* height,
    wxCoord* descent = NULL, wxCoord* externalLeading = NULL,
    wxFont* font = NULL);
```

The default arguments mean that you can call it just to find the overall width and height the string occupies, or you can pass extra arguments to get further text dimensions. If you imagine the bottoms of the characters sitting on a baseline, the *descent* is how far below the baseline the characters extend. The letter "g," for example, extends below the baseline. *External leading* is the space between the descent of one line and the top of the line below. Finally, you can provide a font to be used in place of the current device context font.

Here's code that uses GetTextExtent to center a string on a window:

```
void CenterText(const wxString& text, wxDC& dc, wxWindow* win)
{
    // Set font, background mode for drawing text,
    // and text color
    dc.SetFont(*wxNORMAL_FONT);
    dc.SetBackgroundMode(wxTRANSPARENT);
    dc.SetTextForeground(*wxRED);

    // Get window and text dimensions
    wxSize sz = win->GetClientSize();
    wxCoord w, h;
    dc.GetTextExtent(text, & w, & h);

    // Center the text on the window, but never
    // draw at a negative position.
    int x = wxMax(0, (sz.x - w)/2);
    int y = wxMax(0, (sz.y - h)/2);

    dc.DrawText(msg, x, y);
}
```

You can also use GetPartialTextExtents to retrieve the width of each character, passing a wxString and a wxArrayInt reference to receive the character width values. If you need accurate information about individual character widths, this can be quicker on some platforms than calling GetTextExtent for each character.

Drawing Lines and Shapes

The simpler drawing primitives include points, lines, rectangles, circles, and ellipses. The current pen determines the line or outline color, and the brush determines the fill color. For example:

```
void DrawSimpleShapes(wxDC& dc)
{
    // Set line color to black, fill color to green
    dc.SetPen(wxPen(*wxBLACK, 2, wxSOLID));
    dc.SetBrush(wxBrush(*wxGREEN, wxSOLID));

    // Draw a point
    dc.DrawPoint(5, 5);
```

```
    // Draw a line
    dc.DrawLine(10, 10, 100, 100);

    // Draw a rectangle at (50, 50) with size (150, 100)
    // and hatched brush
    dc.SetBrush(wxBrush(*wxBLACK, wxCROSS_HATCH));
    dc.DrawRectangle(50, 50, 150, 100);

    // Set a red brush
    dc.SetBrush(*wxRED_BRUSH);

    // Draw a rounded rectangle at (150, 20) with size (100, 50)
    // and corner radius 10
    dc.DrawRoundedRectangle(150, 20, 100, 50, 10);

    // Draw another rounded rectangle with no border
    dc.SetPen(*wxTRANSPARENT_PEN);
    dc.SetBrush(wxBrush(*wxBLUE));
    dc.DrawRoundedRectangle(250, 80, 100, 50, 10);

    // Set a black pen and black brush
    dc.SetPen(wxPen(*wxBLACK, 2, wxSOLID));
    dc.SetBrush(*wxBLACK);

    // Draw a circle at (100, 150) with radius 60
    dc.DrawCircle(100, 150, 60);

    // Set a white brush
    dc.SetBrush(*wxWHITE);

    // Draw an ellipse that fills the given rectangle
    dc.DrawEllipse(wxRect(120, 120, 150, 50));
}
```

This produces the graphic in Figure 5-3.

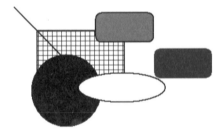

Figure 5-3   Drawing simple shapes

Note that by convention, the last point of a line is not drawn.

To draw a circular arc, use DrawArc, taking a starting point, end point, and center point. The arc is drawn counterclockwise from the starting point to the end. For example:

```
// Draw a cup-shaped arc
int x = 10, y = 200, radius = 20;
dc.DrawArc(x-radius, y, x + radius, y, x, y);
```

This produces the arc shown in Figure 5-4.

Figure 5-4   A circular arc

For an elliptic arc, DrawEllipticArc takes the position and size of a rectangle that contains the arc, plus the start and end of the arc in degrees specified from the three o'clock position from the center of the rectangle. If the start and end points are the same, a complete ellipse will be drawn. The following code draws the arc shown in Figure 5-5.

```
// Draws an elliptical arc within a rectangle at (10, 100),
// size 200x40. Arc extends from 270 to 420 degrees.
dc.DrawEllipticArc(10, 100, 200, 40, 270, 420);
```

Figure 5-5   An elliptical arc

If you need to draw a lot of lines quickly, DrawLines can be more efficient than using DrawLine multiple times. The following example draws lines between ten points, at an offset of (100, 100).

```
wxPoint points[10];
for (size_t i = 0; i < 10; i++)
{
  pt.x = i*10; pt.y = i*20;
}
```

```
int offsetX = 100;
int offsetY = 100;

dc.DrawLines(10, points, offsetX, offsetY);
```

DrawLines does not fill the area surrounded by the lines. You can draw a filled shape with an arbitrary number of sides using DrawPolygon, and several of them with DrawPolyPolygon. DrawPolygon takes a point count, an array of points, optional offsets to add to the points, and an optional fill style: wxODDEVEN_RULE, the default, or wxWINDING_RULE. DrawPolygonPolygon additionally takes an array of integers that specifies the number of points to be used for each polygon.

The following code demonstrates how to draw polygons and poly-polygons, with the result shown in Figure 5-6.

```
void DrawPolygons(wxDC& dc)
{
    wxBrush brushHatch(*wxRED, wxFDIAGONAL_HATCH);
    dc.SetBrush(brushHatch);

    wxPoint star[5];
    star[0] = wxPoint(100, 60);
    star[1] = wxPoint(60, 150);
    star[2] = wxPoint(160, 100);
    star[3] = wxPoint(40, 100);
    star[4] = wxPoint(140, 150);

    dc.DrawPolygon(WXSIZEOF(star), star, 0, 30);
    dc.DrawPolygon(WXSIZEOF(star), star, 160, 30, wxWINDING_RULE);

    wxPoint star2[10];
    star2[0] = wxPoint(0, 100);
    star2[1] = wxPoint(-59, -81);
    star2[2] = wxPoint(95, 31);
    star2[3] = wxPoint(-95, 31);
    star2[4] = wxPoint(59, -81);
    star2[5] = wxPoint(0, 80);
    star2[6] = wxPoint(-47, -64);
    star2[7] = wxPoint(76, 24);
    star2[8] = wxPoint(-76, 24);
    star2[9] = wxPoint(47, -64);
    int count[2] = {5, 5};

    dc.DrawPolyPolygon(WXSIZEOF(count), count, star2, 450, 150);
}
```

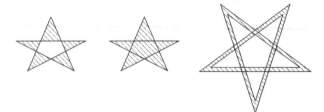

Figure 5-6   Drawing polygons

Drawing Splines

DrawSpline lets you draw a curve known as a "spline" between multiple points. There is a version for three points, and a version for an arbitrary number of points, both illustrated in this example code:

```
// Draw 3-point spline
dc.DrawSpline(10, 100, 200, 200, 50, 230);

// Draw 5-point spline
wxPoint star[5];
star[0] = wxPoint(100, 60);
star[1] = wxPoint(60, 150);
star[2] = wxPoint(160, 100);
star[3] = wxPoint(40, 100);
star[4] = wxPoint(140, 150);
dc.DrawSpline(WXSIZEOF(star), star);
```

This produces the two splines illustrated in Figure 5-7.

Figure 5-7   Drawing splines

Drawing Bitmaps

There are two main ways of drawing bitmaps on a device context: DrawBitmap and Blit. DrawBitmap is a simplified form of Blit, and it takes a bitmap, a position, and a boolean flag specifying transparent drawing. The transparency can be either a simple mask or an alpha channel (which offers translucency), depending on how the bitmap was loaded or created. The following code loads an image with an alpha channel and draws it over lines of text.

```
wxString msg = wxT("Some text will appear mixed in the image's
shadow...");
int y = 75;
for (size_t i = 0; i < 10; i++)
{
    y += dc.GetCharHeight() + 5;
    dc.DrawText(msg, 200, y);
}

wxBitmap bmp(wxT("toucan.png"), wxBITMAP_TYPE_PNG);
dc.DrawBitmap(bmp, 250, 100, true);
```

This produces the drawing in Figure 5-8, where the shadows in the bitmap appear to partially obscure the text underneath.

Figure 5-8   Drawing with transparency

The Blit function is more flexible and enables you to copy a specific portion of a source device context onto a destination device context. This is its prototype:

```
bool Blit(wxCoord destX, wxCoord destY,
          wxCoord width, wxCoord height, wxDC* dcSource,
          wxCoord srcX, wxCoord srcY,
          int logicalFunc = wxCOPY,
          bool useMask = false,
          wxCoord srcMaskX = -1, wxCoord srcMaskY = -1);
```

This code copies an area from a source device context dcSource to the destination (the object that the function is operating on). An area of specified width and height is drawn starting at the position (destX, destY) on the destination surface, taken from the position (srcX, srcY) on the source. The logical function logicalFunc is usually wxCOPY, which means the bits are transferred from source to destination with no transformation. Not all platforms support a logical function other than wxCOPY. For more information, please see "Logical Functions" later in this chapter.

The last three parameters are used only when the source device context is a wxMemoryDC with a transparent bitmap selected into it. useMask specifies whether transparent drawing is used, and srcMaskX and srcMaskY enable the bitmap's mask to start from a different position than the main bitmap start position.

The following example loads a small pattern into a bitmap and uses Blit to fill a larger destination bitmap, with transparency if available.

```
wxMemoryDC dcDest;
wxMemoryDC dcSource;

int destWidth = 200, destHeight = 200;

// Create the destination bitmap
wxBitmap bitmapDest(destWidth, destHeight);

// Load the pattern bitmap
wxBitmap bitmapSource(wxT("pattern.png"), wxBITMAP_TYPE_PNG);

int sourceWidth = bitmapSource.GetWidth();
int sourceHeight = bitmapSource.GetHeight();

// Clear the destination background to white
dcDest.SelectObject(bitmapDest);
dcDest.SetBackground(*wxWHITE_BRUSH);
dcDest.Clear();

dcSource.SelectObject(bitmapSource);

// Tile the smaller bitmap onto the larger bitmap
for (int i = 0; i < destWidth; i += sourceWidth)
    for (int j = 0; j < destHeight; j += sourceHeight)
    {
        dcDest.Blit(i, j, sourceWidth, sourceHeight,
                    & dcSource, 0, 0, wxCOPY, true);
    }

// Tidy up
dcDest.SelectBitmap(wxNullBitmap);
dcSource.SelectBitmap(wxNullBitmap);
```

You can also draw icons directly, with DrawIcon. This operation always takes transparency into account. For example:

```
#include "file.xpm"

wxIcon icon(file_xpm);
dc.DrawIcon(icon, 20, 30);
```

Filling Arbitrary Areas

FloodFill can be used to fill an arbitrary area of a device context up to a color boundary. Pass a starting point, a color for finding the flood area boundary, and a style to indicate how the color parameter should be used. The device context will be filled with the current brush color.

The following example draws a green rectangle with a red border and fills it with black, followed by blue.

```
// Draw a green rectangle outlines in red
dc.SetPen(*wxRED_PEN);
dc.SetBrush(*wxGREEN_BRUSH);

dc.DrawRectangle(10, 10, 100, 100);
dc.SetBrush(*wxBLACK_BRUSH);

// Now fill the green area with black (while green is found)
dc.FloodFill(50, 50, *wxGREEN, wxFLOOD_SURFACE);
dc.SetBrush(*wxBLUE_BRUSH);

// Then fill with blue (until red is encountered)
dc.FloodFill(50, 50, *wxRED, wxFLOOD_BORDER);
```

The function may fail if it cannot find the color specified, or the point is outside the clipping region. FloodFill won't work with printer device contexts, or with wxMetafileDC.

Logical Functions

The current *logical function* determines how a source pixel (from a pen or brush color, or source device context if using Blit) combines with a destination pixel in the current device context. The default is wxCOPY, which simply draws with the current color. The others combine the current color and the background using a logical operation. wxINVERT is commonly used for drawing rubber bands or moving outlines because with this operation drawing a shape the second time erases the shape.

The following example draws a dotted line using wxINVERT and then erases it before restoring the normal logical function.

```
wxPen pen(*wxBLACK, 1, wxDOT);
dc.SetPen(pen);

// Invert pixels
dc.SetLogicalFunction(wxINVERT);
```

```
dc.DrawLine(10, 10, 100, 100);

// Invert again, rubbing it out
dc.DrawLine(10, 10, 100, 100);

// Restore to normal drawing
dc.SetLogicalFunction(wxCOPY);
```

Another use for logical functions is to combine images to create new images. For example, here's one method for creating transparent jigsaw puzzle pieces out of an image. First, draw a black outline of each shape on a white bitmap, using a grid of standard (but randomized) puzzle edges. Then, for each piece, flood-fill the outline to create a black puzzle shape on a white background. Blit the corresponding area of the puzzle image onto this template bitmap with the wxAND_REVERSE function to mask out the unwanted parts of the puzzle, leaving the "stamped out" puzzle piece on a black background. This can be made into a transparent wxBitmap by converting to a wxImage, setting black as the image mask color, and converting back to a transparent wxBitmap, which can be drawn appropriately. (Note that this technique depends on there being no black in the puzzle image, or else holes will appear in the puzzle pieces.)

Table 5-6 shows the logical function values and their meanings.

Table 5-6   Logical Functions

Logical Function	Meaning (*src* = source, *dst* = destination)
wxAND	src AND dst
wxAND_INVERT	(NOT src) AND dst
wxAND_REVERSE	src AND (NOT dst)
wxCLEAR	0
wxCOPY	src
wxEQUIV	(NOT src) XOR dst
wxINVERT	NOT dst
wxNAND	(NOT src) OR (NOT dst)
wxNOR	(NOT src) AND (NOT dst)
wxNO_OP	dst
wxOR	src OR dst
wxOR_INVERT	(NOT src) OR dst
wxOR_REVERSE	src OR (NOT dst)
wxSET	1
wxSRC_INVERT	NOT src
wxXOR	src XOR dst

USING THE PRINTING FRAMEWORK

As we've seen, wxPrinterDC can be created and used directly. However, a more flexible method is to use the wxWidgets printing framework to "drive" printing. The main task for the developer is to derive a new class from wxPrintout, overriding functions that specify how to print a page (OnPrintPage), how many pages there are (GetPageInfo), document setup (OnPreparePrinting), and so on. The wxWidgets printing framework will show the print dialog, create the printer device context, and call appropriate wxPrintout functions when appropriate. The same printout class can be used for both printing and preview.

To start printing, a wxPrintout object is passed to a wxPrinter object, and Print is called to kick off the printing process, showing a print dialog before printing the pages specified by the layout object and the user. For example:

```
// A global object storing print settings
wxPrintDialogData g_printDialogData;

// Handler for Print menu item
void MyFrame::OnPrint(wxCommandEvent& event)
{
    wxPrinter printer(& g_printDialogData);
    MyPrintout printout(wxT("My printout"));

    if (!printer.Print(this, &printout, true))
    {
        if (wxPrinter::GetLastError() == wxPRINTER_ERROR)
            wxMessageBox(wxT("There was a problem printing.\nPerhaps your
current printer is not set correctly?"), wxT("Printing"), wxOK);
        else
            wxMessageBox(wxT("You cancelled printing"),
                         wxT("Printing"), wxOK);
    }
    else
    {
        (*g_printDialogData) = printer.GetPrintDialogData();
    }
}
```

Because the Print function returns only after all pages have been rendered and sent to the printer, the printout object can be created on the stack.

The wxPrintDialogData class stores data related to the print dialog, such as the pages the user selected for printing and the number of copies to be printed. It's a good idea to keep a global wxPrintDialogData object in your application to store the last settings selected by the user. You can pass a pointer to this data to wxPrinter to be used in the print dialog, and then if printing is successful, copy the settings back from wxPrinter to your global object, as in the previous example. (In a real application, g_printDialogData would probably be a data member of your application class.) See Chapter 8, "Using Standard Dialogs," for more about print and page dialogs and how to use them.

To preview the document, create a wxPrintPreview object, passing two printout objects to it: one for the preview and one to use for printing if the user requests it. You can also pass a wxPrintDialogData object so that the preview picks up settings that the user chose earlier. Then pass the preview object to wxPreviewFrame, call the frame's Initialize function, and show the frame. For example:

```
// Handler for Preview menu item
void MyFrame::OnPreview(wxCommandEvent& event)
{
    wxPrintPreview *preview = new wxPrintPreview(
                             new MyPrintout, new MyPrintout,
                             & g_printDialogData);
    if (!preview->Ok())
    {
        delete preview;
        wxMessageBox(wxT("There was a problem previewing.\nPerhaps your
current printer is not set correctly?"),
                     wxT("Previewing"), wxOK);
        return;
    }

    wxPreviewFrame *frame = new wxPreviewFrame(preview, this,
                            wxT("Demo Print Preview"));
    frame->Centre(wxBOTH);
    frame->Initialize();
    frame->Show(true);
}
```

When the preview frame is initialized, it disables all other top-level windows in order to avoid actions that might cause the document to be edited after the print or preview process has started. Closing the frame automatically destroys the two printout objects. Figure 5-9 shows the print preview window, with a control bar along the top providing page navigation, printing, and zoom control.

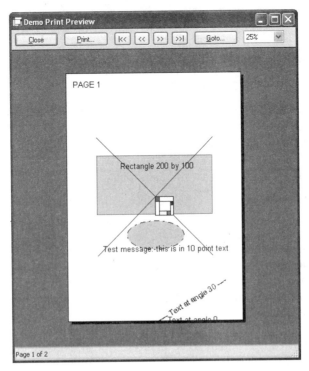

Figure 5-9   Print preview window

More on *wxPrintout*

When creating a printout object, the application can pass an optional title that will appear in the print manager under some operating systems. You will need to provide at least GetPageInfo, HasPage, and OnPrintPage, but you can override any of the other methods below as well.

GetPageInfo should be overridden to return minPage, maxPage, pageFrom, and pageTo. The first two integers represent the range supported by this printout object for the current document, and the second two integers represent a user selection (not currently used by wxWidgets). The default values for minPage and maxPage are 1 and 32,000, respectively. However, the printout will stop printing if HasPage returns false. Typically, your OnPreparePrinting function will calculate the values returned by GetPageInfo and will look something like this:

```
void MyPrintout::GetPageInfo(int *minPage, int *maxPage,
                             int *pageFrom, int *pageTo)
{
    *minPage = 1; *maxPage = m_numPages;
    *pageFrom = 1; *pageTo = m_numPages;
}
```

HasPage must return false if the argument is outside the current page range. Often its implementation will look like this, where m_numPages has been calculated in OnPreparePrinting:

```
bool MyPrintout::HasPage(int pageNum)
{
    return (pageNum >= 1 && pageNum <= m_numPages);
}
```

OnPreparePrinting is called before the print or preview process commences, and overriding it enables the application to do various setup tasks, including calculating the number of pages in the document. OnPreparePrinting can call wxPrintout functions such as GetDC, GetPageSizeMM, IsPreview, and so on to get the information it needs.

OnBeginDocument is called with the start and end page numbers when each document copy is about to be printed, and if overridden, it must call the base wxPrintout::OnBeginDocument function. Similarly, wxPrintout::OnEndDocument must be called if overridden.

OnBeginPrinting is called once for the printing cycle, regardless of the number of copies, and OnEndPrinting is called at the end.

OnPrintPage is passed a page number, and the application should override it to return true if the page was successfully printed (returning false cancels the print job). This function will use wxPrintout::GetDC to get the device context to draw on.

The following are the utility functions you can use in your overridden functions, and they do not need to be overridden.

IsPreview can be called to determine whether this is a real print task or a preview.

GetDC returns a suitable device context for the current task. When printing, a wxPrinterDC will be returned, and when previewing, a wxMemoryDC will be returned because a preview is rendered into a bitmap via a memory device context.

GetPageSizeMM returns the size of the printer page in millimeters, whereas GetPageSizePixels returns the size in pixels (the maximum resolution of the printer). For a preview, this will not be the same as the size returned by wxDC::GetSize, which will return the preview bitmap size.

`GetPPIPrinter` returns the number of pixels per logical inch for the current device context, and `GetPPIScreen` returns the number of pixels per logical inch of the screen.

Scaling for Printing and Previewing

When drawing on a window, you probably don't concern yourself about scaling your graphics because displays tend to have similar resolutions. However, there are several factors to take into account when drawing to a printer:

☞ You need to scale and position graphics to fit the width of the page, and break the graphics into pages if necessary.

☞ Fonts are based on screen resolution, so when drawing text, you need to set a scale so that the printer device context matches the screen resolution. Dividing the printer resolution (`GetPPIPrinter`) by the screen resolution (`GetPPIScreen`) can give a suitable scaling factor for drawing text.

☞ When rendering the preview, wxWidgets uses a `wxMemoryDC` to draw into a bitmap. The size of the bitmap (returned by `wxDC::GetSize`) depends on the zoom scale, and an extra scale factor must be calculated to deal with this. Divide the size returned by `GetSize` by the actual page size returned by `GetPageSizePixels` to get this scale factor. This value should be multiplied by any other scale you calculated.

You can use `wxDC::SetUserScale` to let the device context perform the scaling for subsequent graphics operations and `wxDC::SetDeviceOrigin` to set the origin (for example, to center a graphic on a page). You can keep calling these scaling and device origin functions for different parts of your graphics, on the same page if necessary.

The wxWidgets sample in `samples/printing` shows how to do scaling. The following example shows a function adapted from the printing sample, which scales and positions a 200×200 pixel graphic on a printer or preview device context.

```
void MyPrintout::DrawPageOne(wxDC *dc)
{
    // You might use THIS code if you were scaling
    // graphics of known size to fit on the page.

    // We know the graphic is 200x200. If we didn't know this,
    // we'd need to calculate it.
    float maxX = 200;
    float maxY = 200;

    // Let's have at least 50 device units margin
    float marginX = 50;
    float marginY = 50;
```

```
      // Add the margin to the graphic size
      maxX += (2*marginX);
      maxY += (2*marginY);

      // Get the size of the DC in pixels
      int w, h;
      dc->GetSize(&w, &h);

      // Calculate a suitable scaling factor
      float scaleX=(float)(w/maxX);
      float scaleY=(float)(h/maxY);

      // Use x or y scaling factor, whichever fits on the DC
      float actualScale = wxMin(scaleX,scaleY);

      // Calculate the position on the DC for centring the graphic
      float posX = (float)((w - (200*actualScale))/2.0);
      float posY = (float)((h - (200*actualScale))/2.0);

      // Set the scale and origin
      dc->SetUserScale(actualScale, actualScale);
      dc->SetDeviceOrigin( (long)posX, (long)posY );

      // Now do the actual drawing
      dc.SetBackground(*wxWHITE_BRUSH);
      dc.Clear();
      dc.SetFont(wxGetApp().m_testFont);

      dc.SetBackgroundMode(wxTRANSPARENT);

      dc.SetBrush(*wxCYAN_BRUSH);
      dc.SetPen(*wxRED_PEN);

      dc.DrawRectangle(0, 30, 200, 100);

      dc.DrawText( wxT("Rectangle 200 by 100"), 40, 40);

      dc.SetPen( wxPen(*wxBLACK,0,wxDOT_DASH) );
      dc.DrawEllipse(50, 140, 100, 50);
      dc.SetPen(*wxRED_PEN);

      dc.DrawText( wxT("Test message: this is in 10 point text"),
                   10, 180);
}
```

In this code, we simply use wxDC::GetSize to get the preview or printer resolution so we can fit the graphic on the page. In this example, we're not interested in the points-per-inch printer resolution, as we might be if we were drawing text or lines of a specific length in millimeters, because the graphic doesn't have to be a precise size: it's just scaled to fit the available space.

Next, we'll show code that prints text at a size to match how it appears on the screen and that also draws lines that have a precise length, rather than simply being scaled to fit.

```
void MyPrintout::DrawPageTwo(wxDC *dc)
{
    // You might use THIS code to set the printer DC to roughly
```

```
// reflect the screen text size. This page also draws lines of
// actual length 5cm on the page.

// Get the logical pixels per inch of screen and printer
int ppiScreenX, ppiScreenY;
GetPPIScreen(&ppiScreenX, &ppiScreenY);
int ppiPrinterX, ppiPrinterY;
GetPPIPrinter(&ppiPrinterX, &ppiPrinterY);

// This scales the DC so that the printout roughly represents the
// the screen scaling.
float scale = (float)((float)ppiPrinterX/(float)ppiScreenX);

// Now we have to check in case our real page size is reduced
// (e.g. because we're drawing to a print preview memory DC)
int pageWidth, pageHeight;
int w, h;
dc->GetSize(&w, &h);
GetPageSizePixels(&pageWidth, &pageHeight);

// If printer pageWidth == current DC width, then this doesn't
// change. But w might be the preview bitmap width,
// so scale down.
float overallScale = scale * (float)(w/(float)pageWidth);
dc->SetUserScale(overallScale, overallScale);

// Calculate conversion factor for converting millimetres into
// logical units.
// There are approx. 25.4 mm to the inch. There are ppi
// device units to the inch. Therefore 1 mm corresponds to
// ppi/25.4 device units. We also divide by the
// screen-to-printer scaling factor, because we need to
// unscale to pass logical units to DrawLine.

// Draw 50 mm by 50 mm L shape
float logUnitsFactor = (float)(ppiPrinterX/(scale*25.4));
float logUnits = (float)(50*logUnitsFactor);
dc->SetPen(* wxBLACK_PEN);
dc->DrawLine(50, 250, (long)(50.0 + logUnits), 250);
dc->DrawLine(50, 250, 50, (long)(250.0 + logUnits));

dc->SetBackgroundMode(wxTRANSPARENT);
dc->SetBrush(*wxTRANSPARENT_BRUSH);

dc->SetFont(wxGetApp().m_testFont);

dc->DrawText(wxT("Some test text"), 200, 300 );
}
```

Printing Under Unix with GTK+

Unlike Mac OS X and Windows, Unix does not provide a standard way to display text and graphics onscreen and print it using the same API. Instead, screen display is done via the X11 library (via GTK+ and wxWidgets), whereas printing has to be done by sending a file of PostScript commands to the printer. Fonts are particularly tricky to handle; until recently, only a small number of applications have offered WYSIWYG (What You See Is What You

Get) under Unix. In the past, wxWidgets offered its own printing implementation using PostScript that never fully matched the screen display.

From version 2.8, the GNOME Free Software Desktop Project provides printing support through the libgnomeprint and libgnomeprintui libraries by which most printing problems are solved. Beginning with version 2.5.4, the GTK+ port of wxWidgets can make use of these libraries if wxWidgets is configured accordingly and if the libraries are present. You need to configure wxWidgets with the --with-gnomeprint switch, which will cause your application to search for the GNOME print libraries at runtime. If they are found, printing will be done through these; otherwise, the application will fall back to the old PostScript printing code. Note that the application will not require the GNOME print libraries to be installed in order to run (there is no dependency on these libraries).

3D GRAPHICS WITH *wxGLCANVAS*

It's worth mentioning that wxWidgets comes with the capability of drawing 3D graphics, thanks to OpenGL and wxGLCanvas. You can use it with the OpenGL clone Mesa if your platform doesn't support OpenGL.

To enable wxGLCanvas support under Windows, edit include/wx/msw/setup.h, set wxUSE_GLCANVAS to 1, and compile with USE_OPENGL=1 on the command line. You may also need to add opengl32.lib to the list of libraries your program is linked with. On Unix and Mac OS X, pass --with-opengl to the configure script to compile using OpenGL or Mesa.

If you're already an OpenGL programmer, using wxGLCanvas is very simple. You create a wxGLCanvas object within a frame or other container window, call wxGLCanvas::SetCurrent to direct regular OpenGL commands to the window, issue normal OpenGL commands, and then call wxGLCanvas::SwapBuffers to show the OpenGL buffer on the window.

The following paint handler shows the principles of rendering 3D graphics and draws a cube. The full sample can be compiled and run from samples/opengl/cube in your wxWidgets distribution.

```
void TestGLCanvas::OnPaint(wxPaintEvent& event)
{
    wxPaintDC dc(this);

    SetCurrent();

    glMatrixMode(GL_PROJECTION);
    glLoadIdentity();
    glFrustum(-0.5f, 0.5f, -0.5f, 0.5f, 1.0f, 3.0f);
    glMatrixMode(GL_MODELVIEW);

    /* clear color and depth buffers */
    glClear(GL_COLOR_BUFFER_BIT | GL_DEPTH_BUFFER_BIT);

    /* draw six faces of a cube */
    glBegin(GL_QUADS);
```

```
    glNormal3f( 0.0f, 0.0f, 1.0f);
    glVertex3f( 0.5f, 0.5f, 0.5f); glVertex3f(-0.5f, 0.5f, 0.5f);
    glVertex3f(-0.5f,-0.5f, 0.5f); glVertex3f( 0.5f,-0.5f, 0.5f);

    glNormal3f( 0.0f, 0.0f,-1.0f);
    glVertex3f(-0.5f,-0.5f,-0.5f); glVertex3f(-0.5f, 0.5f,-0.5f);
    glVertex3f( 0.5f, 0.5f,-0.5f); glVertex3f( 0.5f,-0.5f,-0.5f);

    glNormal3f( 0.0f, 1.0f, 0.0f);
    glVertex3f( 0.5f, 0.5f, 0.5f); glVertex3f( 0.5f, 0.5f,-0.5f);
    glVertex3f(-0.5f, 0.5f,-0.5f); glVertex3f(-0.5f, 0.5f, 0.5f);

    glNormal3f( 0.0f,-1.0f, 0.0f);
    glVertex3f(-0.5f,-0.5f,-0.5f); glVertex3f( 0.5f,-0.5f,-0.5f);
    glVertex3f( 0.5f,-0.5f, 0.5f); glVertex3f(-0.5f,-0.5f, 0.5f);

    glNormal3f( 1.0f, 0.0f, 0.0f);
    glVertex3f( 0.5f, 0.5f, 0.5f); glVertex3f( 0.5f,-0.5f, 0.5f);
    glVertex3f( 0.5f,-0.5f,-0.5f); glVertex3f( 0.5f, 0.5f,-0.5f);

    glNormal3f(-1.0f, 0.0f, 0.0f);
    glVertex3f(-0.5f,-0.5f,-0.5f); glVertex3f(-0.5f,-0.5f, 0.5f);
    glVertex3f(-0.5f, 0.5f, 0.5f); glVertex3f(-0.5f, 0.5f,-0.5f);
    glEnd();

    glFlush();
    SwapBuffers();
}
```

Figure 5-10 shows another OpenGL sample, a cute (if angular) penguin that can be rotated using the mouse. You can find this sample in `samples/opengl/penguin`.

Figure 5-10   OpenGL "penguin" sample

SUMMARY

In this chapter, you have learned how to draw on device contexts and use the wxWidgets printing framework, and you received a quick introduction to wxGLCanvas. You can look at the following source code in your wxWidgets distribution for examples of drawing and printing code:

- ☞ samples/drawing
- ☞ samples/font
- ☞ samples/erase
- ☞ samples/image
- ☞ samples/scroll
- ☞ samples/printing
- ☞ src/html/htmprint.cpp
- ☞ demos/bombs
- ☞ demos/fractal
- ☞ demos/life

For advanced 2D drawing applications, you might want to consider the wxArt2D library, which offers loading and saving of graphical objects using SVG files (Scalable Vector Graphics), flicker-free updating, gradients, vector paths, and more. See Appendix E, " Third-Party Tools for wxWidgets," for where to get wxArt2D.

Next, we'll look at how your application can respond to mouse, keyboard, and joystick input.

CHAPTER 6

Handling Input

All GUI applications must respond to input in some way. This chapter shows how you can respond to user input from the mouse, keyboard, and joystick.

MOUSE INPUT

Broadly speaking, there are two categories of mouse input. Basic mouse events are sent using wxMouseEvent and are passed uninterpreted to your handler function. Commands associated with controls, on the other hand, are often the result of interpreting a mouse (or other) event as a particular command.

For example, when you add EVT_BUTTON to an event table, you are intercepting a wxCommandEvent that was generated by the wxButton. Internally, the button is intercepting EVT_LEFT_DOWN and generating the command event as a result. (Of course, on most platforms, wxButton is implemented natively and doesn't use low-level wxWidgets event handling, but it's true of custom classes.)

Because we've already seen examples of handling command events, we will concentrate on basic mouse events.

You can intercept button up, button down, and double-click events for left, middle, and right mouse buttons. You can intercept motion events, whether the mouse is moving with or without buttons pressed. You can intercept events telling you that the mouse is entering or leaving the window. Finally, you can intercept scroll wheel events if the hardware provides a scroll wheel.

When you receive a mouse event, you can also check the state of the mouse buttons, and the pressed state of the modifier keys (Shift, Alt, Control, and Meta). You can also retrieve the current mouse position relative to the top-left corner of the window's client area.

Table 6-1 lists the event table macros you can use. wxMouseEvent does not propagate to parents of the originating window, so to handle these events, you must derive from a window class or derive from wxEvtHandler and plug the object into the window with SetEventHandler or PushEventHandler. Alternatively, you can use dynamic event handling with Connect.

Table 6-1   Mouse Event Table Macros

EVT_LEFT_DOWN(func)	Handles a wxEVT_LEFT_DOWN event, generated when the left mouse button changes to the "down" state.
EVT_LEFT_UP(func)	Handles a wxEVT_LEFT_UP event, generated when the left mouse button changes to the "up" state.
EVT_LEFT_DCLICK(func)	Handles a wxEVT_LEFT_DCLICK event, generated when the left mouse button is double-clicked.
EVT_MIDDLE_DOWN(func)	Handles a wxEVT_MIDDLE_DOWN event, generated when the middle mouse button changes to the "down" state.
EVT_MIDDLE_UP(func)	Handles a wxEVT_MIDDLE_UP event, generated when the middle mouse button changes to the "up" state.
EVT_MIDDLE_DCLICK(func)	Handles a wxEVT_MIDDLE_DCLICK event, generated when the middle mouse button is double-clicked.
EVT_RIGHT_DOWN(func)	Handles a wxEVT_RIGHT_DOWN event, generated when the right mouse button changes to the "down" state.
EVT_RIGHT_UP(func)	Handles a wxEVT_RIGHT_UP event, generated when the right mouse button changes to the "up" state.
EVT_RIGHT_DCLICK(func)	Handles a wxEVT_RIGHT_DCLICK event, generated when the right mouse button is double-clicked.
EVT_MOTION(func)	Handles a wxEVT_MOTION event, generated when the mouse moves.
EVT_ENTER_WINDOW(func)	Handles a wxEVT_ENTER_WINDOW event, generated when the mouse enters the window.
EVT_LEAVE_WINDOW(func)	Handles a wxEVT_LEAVE_WINDOW event, generated when the mouse leaves the window.
EVT_MOUSEWHEEL(func)	Handles a wxEVT_MOUSEWHEEL event, generated when the mouse wheel moves.
EVT_MOUSE_EVENTS(func)	Handles all mouse events.

Handling Button and Motion Events

These are the main mouse event functions that you can use within your event handler when handling mouse button and motion events.

To test whether a modifier key is down at the time of generating the event, use AltDown, MetaDown, ControlDown, or ShiftDown. Use CmdDown if you want to test for either the Meta key (on Mac OS X) or the Control key (other platforms). See "Modifier Key Variations" later in the chapter for more on this.

To determine which mouse button is currently pressed, use LeftIsDown, MiddleIsDown, and RightIsDown. You can also test whether a button is pressed by passing wxMOUSE_BTN_LEFT, wxMOUSE_BTN_MIDDLE, wxMOUSE_BTN_RIGHT or wxMOUSE_BTN_ANY to Button. Note that these test whether a button is down at the time of the mouse event, rather than whether the button changed state.

On Mac OS X, the Command key translates to Meta, and the Option key is Alt. Because the Mac is often configured with only one mouse button, the user holds down the Control key while clicking to generate a right-click event. This means that there is no such thing as Control-Right Click on Mac unless you have an external mouse with two or three buttons.

You can test for the type of mouse event with Dragging (the mouse is moving with a button pressed down), Moving (no button is currently pressed), Entering, Leaving, ButtonDown, ButtonUp, ButtonDClick, LeftClick, LeftDClick, LeftUp, RightClick, RightDClick, RightUp, ButtonUp, and IsButton.

Retrieve the mouse position in device units (relative to the client window's top-left corner) with GetPosition or GetX and GetY. You can get the position in logical units by passing a device context to GetLogicalPosition.

Here's an example of mouse handling for a simple doodling application.

```
BEGIN_EVENT_TABLE(DoodleCanvas, wxWindow)
    EVT_MOUSE_EVENTS(DoodleCanvas::OnMouseEvent)
END_EVENT_TABLE()

void DoodleCanvas::OnMouseEvent(wxMouseEvent& event)
{
    static DoodleSegment *s_currentSegment = NULL;

    wxPoint pt(event.GetPosition());

    if (s_currentSegment && event.LeftUp())
    {
        // End the segment on mouse left up
        if (s_currentSegment->GetLines().GetCount() == 0)
        {
            // Empty segment: delete it
            delete s_currentSegment;
            s_currentSegment = (DoodleSegment *) NULL;
        }
        else
        {
            // We've got a valid segment, so store it
            DrawingDocument *doc = GetDocument();

            doc->GetCommandProcessor()->Submit(
```

```
                      new DrawingCommand(wxT("Add Segment"), DOODLE_ADD,
                                         doc, s_currentSegment));
                doc->Modify(true);
                s_currentSegment = NULL;
            }
        }
        else if (m_lastX > -1 && m_lastY > -1 && event.Dragging())
        {
            // We're dragging: append a line to the current segment
            if (!s_currentSegment)
                s_currentSegment = new DoodleSegment;

            DoodleLine *newLine = new DoodleLine(m_lastX, m_lastY, pt.x,
pt.y);
            s_currentSegment->GetLines().Append(newLine);

            wxClientDC dc(this);
            DoPrepareDC(dc);

            dc.SetPen(*wxBLACK_PEN);
            dc.DrawLine( m_lastX, m_lastY, pt.x, pt.y);
        }
        m_lastX = pt.x;
        m_lastY = pt.y;
}
```

In this application, line segments are stored in a document. While the user
drags using the left button, the function adds lines to the current segment and
also draws the lines. When the user releases the left mouse button, the current
segment is submitted to the document using the command processor (part of
the document-view framework), which allows undo/redo to be implemented. In
the application's OnPaint handler (not shown), all the document's line segments are drawn. For a complete doodling program with undo/redo, see
Chapter 19, "Working with Documents and Views."

A more realistic application would capture the mouse on left button
down and release it on left button up so that when dragging outside the window, the window would still receive events.

Handling Mouse Wheel Events

When you get a mouse wheel event, you retrieve the positive or negative rotation amount with GetWheelRotation. Divide this value by the value returned by
GetWheelDelta to get the number of lines that this rotation represents. Most
devices generate one event per delta, but future devices may send events more
frequently, so you need to be able to accumulate the amount of rotation and
only take action when rotation equivalent to a full line has been received.
Alternatively, you may be able to scroll by a fraction of a line. You should take
into account the value returned by GetLinesPerAction, as configured by the
user via the system control panel, and multiply by this amount to scroll the
desired number of actual lines.

In fact, the mouse may be configured to scroll by a page at a time. In this case, you need to call IsPageScroll, and if this returns true, scroll by a page.

To illustrate, here's how wxScrolledWindow implements default scroll wheel processing. The variable m_wheelRotation accumulates the rotation, and action is only taken if the number of lines is non-zero.

```cpp
void wxScrollHelper::HandleOnMouseWheel(wxMouseEvent& event)
{
    m_wheelRotation += event.GetWheelRotation();
    int lines = m_wheelRotation / event.GetWheelDelta();
    m_wheelRotation -= lines * event.GetWheelDelta();

    if (lines != 0)
    {
        wxScrollWinEvent newEvent;

        newEvent.SetPosition(0);
        newEvent.SetOrientation(wxVERTICAL);
        newEvent.m_eventObject = m_win;

        if (event.IsPageScroll())
        {
            if (lines > 0)
                newEvent.m_eventType = wxEVT_SCROLLWIN_PAGEUP;
            else
                newEvent.m_eventType = wxEVT_SCROLLWIN_PAGEDOWN;

            m_win->GetEventHandler()->ProcessEvent(newEvent);
        }
        else
        {
            lines *= event.GetLinesPerAction();
            if (lines > 0)
                newEvent.m_eventType = wxEVT_SCROLLWIN_LINEUP;
            else
                newEvent.m_eventType = wxEVT_SCROLLWIN_LINEDOWN;

            int times = abs(lines);
            for (; times > 0; times--)
                m_win->GetEventHandler()->ProcessEvent(newEvent);
        }
    }
}
```

HANDLING KEYBOARD EVENTS

Keyboard events are represented by the class wxKeyEvent. There are three different kinds of keyboard events in wxWidgets: key down, key up, and character. Key down and up events are *untranslated* events, whereas character events are *translated*, which we'll explain shortly. If the key is held down, you will typically get many down events but only one up event, so don't assume that one up event corresponds to each down event.

To receive key events, your window needs to have the keyboard focus, which you can achieve by calling `wxWindow::SetFocus`—for example, when a mouse button is pressed.

Table 6-2 lists the three keyboard event table macros.

Table 6-2   Keyboard Event Table Macros

`EVT_KEY_DOWN(func)`	Handles a `wxEVT_KEY_DOWN` event (untranslated key press).
`EVT_KEY_UP(func)`	Handles a `wxEVT_KEY_UP` event (untranslated key release).
`EVT_CHAR(func)`	Handles a `wxEVT_CHAR` event (translated key press).

These are the main `wxKeyEvent` functions that you can use within your key event handler when handling keyboard events.

To get the keycode, call `GetKeyCode` (in Unicode builds, you can also call `GetUnicodeKeyCode`). All valid key codes are listed in Table 6-3.

Table 6-3   Key Code Identifiers

`WXK_BACK`	`WXK_RIGHT`
`WXK_TAB`	`WXK_DOWN`
`WXK_RETURN`	`WXK_SELECT`
`WXK_ESCAPE`	`WXK_PRINT`
`WXK_SPACE`	`WXK_EXECUTE`
`WXK_DELETE`	`WXK_SNAPSHOT`
	`WXK_INSERT`
`WXK_START`	`WXK_HELP`
`WXK_LBUTTON`	
`WXK_RBUTTON`	`WXK_NUMPAD0`
`WXK_CANCEL`	`WXK_NUMPAD1`
`WXK_MBUTTON`	`WXK_NUMPAD2`
`WXK_CLEAR`	`WXK_NUMPAD3`
`WXK_SHIFT`	`WXK_NUMPAD4`
`WXK_CONTROL`	`WXK_NUMPAD5`
`WXK_MENU`	`WXK_NUMPAD6`
`WXK_PAUSE`	`WXK_NUMPAD7`
`WXK_CAPITAL`	`WXK_NUMPAD8`
`WXK_PRIOR`	`WXK_NUMPAD9`
`WXK_NEXT`	
`WXK_END`	`WXK_MULTIPLY`
`WXK_HOME`	`WXK_ADD`
`WXK_LEFT`	`WXK_SEPARATOR`
`WXK_UP`	`WXK_SUBTRACT`

WXK_DECIMAL	WXK_PAGEDOWN
WXK_DIVIDE	
	WXK_NUMPAD_SPACE
WXK_F1	WXK_NUMPAD_TAB
WXK_F2	WXK_NUMPAD_ENTER
WXK_F3 WXK_F4	WXK_NUMPAD_F1
WXK_F5	WXK_NUMPAD_F2
WXK_F6	WXK_NUMPAD_F3
WXK_F7	WXK_NUMPAD_F4
WXK_F8	WXK_NUMPAD_HOME
WXK_F9	WXK_NUMPAD_LEFT
WXK_F10	WXK_NUMPAD_UP
WXK_F11	WXK_NUMPAD_RIGHT
WXK_F12	WXK_NUMPAD_DOWN
WXK_F13	WXK_NUMPAD_PRIOR
WXK_F14	WXK_NUMPAD_PAGEUP
WXK_F15	WXK_NUMPAD_NEXT
WXK_F16	WXK_NUMPAD_PAGEDOWN
WXK_F17	WXK_NUMPAD_END
WXK_F18	WXK_NUMPAD_BEGIN
WXK_F19	WXK_NUMPAD_INSERT
WXK_F20	WXK_NUMPAD_DELETE
WXK_F21	WXK_NUMPAD_EQUAL
WXK_F22	WXK_NUMPAD_MULTIPLY
WXK_F23	WXK_NUMPAD_ADD
WXK_F24	WXK_NUMPAD_SEPARATOR
	WXK_NUMPAD_SUBTRACT
WXK_NUMLOCK	WXK_NUMPAD_DECIMAL
WXK_SCROLL	WXK_NUMPAD_DIVIDE
WXK_PAGEUP	

To test whether a modifier key is pressed down at the time of generating the event, use AltDown, MetaDown, ControlDown, or ShiftDown. HasModifiers returns true if either Control or Alt was down at the time of the key event (but not the Shift or Meta key states).

Instead of using ControlDown or MetaDown, you may want to use the higher-level CmdDown function that calls MetaDown on Mac OS X and ControlDown on other platforms. See also "Modifier Key Variations" in the following section for further explanation.

GetPosition returns the position of the mouse pointer in client coordinates at the time the event was received.

> **Tip**
>
> If a key down event is caught and the event handler does not call
> `event.Skip()`, then the corresponding character event will not happen. If
> you don't call `event.Skip()` for events that you don't process in key event
> function, shortcuts may cease to work on some platforms.

An Example Character Event Handler

Here's the key handler from the `wxThumbnailCtrl` sample that you can find in
`examples/chap12/thumbnail` on the CD-ROM:

```
BEGIN_EVENT_TABLE( wxThumbnailCtrl, wxScrolledWindow )
    EVT_CHAR(wxThumbnailCtrl::OnChar)
END_EVENT_TABLE()

void wxThumbnailCtrl::OnChar(wxKeyEvent& event)
{
    int flags = 0;
    if (event.ControlDown())
        flags |= wxTHUMBNAIL_CTRL_DOWN;
    if (event.ShiftDown())
        flags |= wxTHUMBNAIL_SHIFT_DOWN;
    if (event.AltDown())
        flags |= wxTHUMBNAIL_ALT_DOWN;

    if (event.GetKeyCode() == WXK_LEFT ||
        event.GetKeyCode() == WXK_RIGHT ||
        event.GetKeyCode() == WXK_UP ||
        event.GetKeyCode() == WXK_DOWN ||
        event.GetKeyCode() == WXK_HOME ||
        event.GetKeyCode() == WXK_PAGEUP ||
        event.GetKeyCode() == WXK_PAGEDOWN ||
        event.GetKeyCode() == WXK_PRIOR ||
        event.GetKeyCode() == WXK_NEXT ||
        event.GetKeyCode() == WXK_END)
    {
        Navigate(event.GetKeyCode(), flags);
    }
    else if (event.GetKeyCode() == WXK_RETURN)
    {
        wxThumbnailEvent cmdEvent(
            wxEVT_COMMAND_THUMBNAIL_RETURN,
            GetId());
        cmdEvent.SetEventObject(this);
        cmdEvent.SetFlags(flags);
        GetEventHandler()->ProcessEvent(cmdEvent);
    }
    else
        event.Skip();
}
```

For clarity, the navigation key handling is delegated to a separate function,
`Navigate`. Pressing the Return or Enter key generates a higher-level command

event that an application using the control can catch; for all other key presses, Skip is called to enable other parts of the application to process unused key events.

Key Code Translation

Key events provide untranslated key codes, whereas the character event provides a translated key code. The untranslated code for alphanumeric keys is always an uppercase value. For the other keys, it is one of the WXK_XXX values from the keycodes table. The translated key is, in general, the character the user expects to appear as the result of the key combination when typing text into a text entry field.

Here are a few examples to clarify this. When the A key is pressed, the key down event key code is equal to ASCII "A" (65), but the character event key code is ASCII "a" (97). On the other hand, if you press both the Shift and A keys simultaneously, the key code in the key down event will still be A, while the character event key code will now be A as well.

In this simple case, it is clear that the ASCII code could be found in the key down event handler by checking both the untranslated key code and the value returned by ShiftDown. But in general, if you want the ASCII key code, you should use the character event (with EVT_CHAR) because for non-alphanumeric keys, the translation is dependent on keyboard layout and can only be done properly by the system itself.

Another kind of translation is done when the Control key is pressed: for example, for Ctrl+A, the key down event still passes the same key code A as usual, but the character event will have a key code of 1, which is the ASCII value of this key combination.

You may discover how the other keys on your system behave interactively by running the keyboard sample (samples/keyboard) and pressing keys.

Modifier Key Variations

On Windows, there are Control and Alt modifier keys, and the special Windows key acts as the Meta key. On Unix, the key that acts as Meta is configurable (run xmodmap to see how your system is configured). The Numlock key is sometimes configured as a Meta key, and this is the reason HasModifiers does not return true if the Meta key is down—this allows key presses to be processed normally when Numlock is on.

On Mac OS X, the Command key (with the apple symbol) translates to Meta, while the Option key translates to Alt.

These differences are shown in Table 6-4, with the wxWidgets modifier name shown in the first column, and the key used for this modifier on each of the three major platforms. The Mac's Option and Command keys are illustrated for clarification.

Table 6-4   Modifier Keys Under Windows, Unix, and Mac OS X

Modifier	Key on Windows	Key on Unix	Key on Mac	
Shift	Shift	Shift	Shift	
Control	Control	Control	Control	
Alt	Alt	Alt	Option	alt / option
Meta	Windows	(Configurable)	Command	⌘

Because Mac OS X uses the Command key as a modifier where Control is used on other platforms, you may use wxKeyEvent's CmdDown function instead of ControlDown or MetaDown to catch the appropriate command modifier on each platform.

Note that as well as testing for a modifier key from within an event handler function, you can pass a key code to wxGetKeyState to test whether that key is down.

Accelerators

An accelerator implements a keyboard shortcut for a menu command, enabling the user to execute that command quickly. These shortcuts take precedence over other keyboard processing, such as EVT_CHAR handlers. Standard shortcuts include Ctrl+O to open a file and Ctrl+V to paste data into the application. The easiest way to implement accelerators is to specify them in menu items. For example:

```
menu->Append(wxID_COPY, wxT("Copy\tCtrl+C"));
```

wxWidgets interprets the text after the "tab" character as an accelerator and adds it to the menu's accelerator table. In this example, when the user presses Ctrl+C the wxID_COPY command is sent, just as though the menu item was selected.

You can use Ctrl, Alt, or Shift in various combinations, followed by a + or - and a character or function key. The following are all valid accelerator specifications: Ctrl+B, G, Shift-Alt-K, F9, Ctrl+F3, Esc, and Del. You can use the following special key names: Del, Back, Ins, Insert, Enter, Return, PgUp, PgDn, Left, Right, Up, Down, Home, End, Space, Tab, Esc, and Escape. Case is not significant when interpreting the names (any combination of uppercase and lowercase will work).

Note that on Mac OS X, a shortcut specification involving Ctrl will actually use the Command key.

Another way to provide accelerators is to populate an wxAccelerator Table with wxAcceleratorEntry objects and associate it with a window using wxWindow::SetAcceleratorTable. Each wxAcceleratorEntry is initialized with a bit-list of modifiers (one or more of wxACCEL_ALT, wxACCEL_CTRL, wxACCEL_SHIFT, and wxACCEL_NORMAL), a key code (see Table 6-3), and an identifier. For example:

```
wxAcceleratorEntry entries[4];
entries[0].Set(wxACCEL_CTRL,   (int) 'N',    wxID_NEW);
entries[1].Set(wxACCEL_CTRL,   (int) 'X',    wxID_EXIT);
entries[2].Set(wxACCEL_SHIFT,  (int) 'A',    wxID_ABOUT);
entries[3].Set(wxACCEL_NORMAL, WXK_DELETE,   wxID_CUT);

wxAcceleratorTable accel(4, entries);
frame->SetAcceleratorTable(accel);
```

You can use several accelerator tables in a window hierarchy, and you can combine menu string accelerator specifications with an explicit wxAcceleratorTable. This is useful if you have alternative accelerators for a single command, which you cannot entirely specify in the menu item label.

HANDLING JOYSTICK EVENTS

The wxJoystick class gives your application control over one or two joysticks on Windows or Linux. Typically, you'll create a wxJoystick object passing wxJOYSTICK1 or wxJOYSTICK2 and keep the object on the heap while it's needed. When you need input, call SetCapture passing a window pointer for receiving the joystick events, and then call ReleaseCapture when you no longer need the events. You might set the capture for the lifetime of the application instance (that is, calling SetCapture on initialization and ReleaseCapture on exit).

Before describing the events and functions in more detail, let's take a look at samples/joystick from the wxWidgets distribution. The user can control the joystick to draw a sequence of lines on a canvas by clicking on one of the joystick's buttons. Pressing the button also plays a sound.

The following is a snippet of the initialization code. First, the application checks whether a joystick is installed by creating a temporary joystick object, terminating if a joystick isn't found. The buttonpress.wav sound file is loaded into the wxSound object stored in the application object, and the minimum and maximum joystick positions are stored to permit scaling input to the size of the drawing window.

```
#include "wx/wx.h"
#include "wx/sound.h"
#include "wx/joystick.h"

bool MyApp::OnInit()
{
    wxJoystick stick(wxJOYSTICK1);
    if (!stick.IsOk())
    {
```

```
        wxMessageBox(wxT("No joystick detected!"));
        return false;
    }

    m_fire.Create(wxT("buttonpress.wav"));

    m_minX = stick.GetXMin();
    m_minY = stick.GetYMin();
    m_maxX = stick.GetXMax();
    m_maxY = stick.GetYMax();

    // Create the main frame window
    ...

    return true;
}
```

MyCanvas is a window that stores the joystick object and also receives the joystick events. Here's the implementation of MyCanvas.

```
BEGIN_EVENT_TABLE(MyCanvas, wxScrolledWindow)
    EVT_JOYSTICK_EVENTS(MyCanvas::OnJoystickEvent)
END_EVENT_TABLE()

MyCanvas::MyCanvas(wxWindow *parent, const wxPoint& pos,
    const wxSize& size):
    wxScrolledWindow(parent, wxID_ANY, pos, size, wxSUNKEN_BORDER)
{
    m_stick = new wxJoystick(wxJOYSTICK1);
    m_stick->SetCapture(this, 10);
}

MyCanvas::~MyCanvas()
{
    m_stick->ReleaseCapture();
    delete m_stick;
}

void MyCanvas::OnJoystickEvent(wxJoystickEvent& event)
{
    static long xpos = -1;
    static long ypos = -1;

    wxClientDC dc(this);

    wxPoint pt(event.GetPosition());

    // if negative positions are possible then shift everything up
    int xmin = wxGetApp().m_minX;
    int xmax = wxGetApp().m_maxX;
    int ymin = wxGetApp().m_minY;
    int ymax = wxGetApp().m_maxY;

    if (xmin < 0) {
        xmax += abs(xmin);
        pt.x += abs(xmin);
    }
```

```
    if (ymin < 0) {
        ymax += abs(ymin);
        pt.y += abs(ymin);
    }

    // Scale to canvas size
    int cw, ch;
    GetSize(&cw, &ch);

    pt.x = (long) (((double)pt.x/(double)xmax) * cw);
    pt.y = (long) (((double)pt.y/(double)ymax) * ch);

    if (xpos > -1 && ypos > -1 && event.IsMove() && event.ButtonIsDown())
    {
        dc.SetPen(*wxBLACK_PEN);
        dc.DrawLine(xpos, ypos, pt.x, pt.y);
    }

    xpos = pt.x;
    ypos = pt.y;

    wxString buf;
    if (event.ButtonDown())
        buf.Printf(wxT("Joystick (%d, %d) Fire!"), pt.x, pt.y);
    else
        buf.Printf(wxT("Joystick (%d, %d)"), pt.x, pt.y);

    frame->SetStatusText(buf);

    if (event.ButtonDown() && wxGetApp().m_fire.IsOk())
    {
        wxGetApp().m_fire.Play();
    }
}
```

wxJoystick Events

wxJoystick generates events of type wxJoystickEvent, and the relevant event table macros are listed in Table 6-5. Each event table macro takes a single argument: the event handler function.

Table 6-5 Joystick Event Table Macros

EVT_JOY_BUTTON(func)	Handles a wxEVT_JOY_BUTTON_DOWN event, generated when a button is pressed.
EVT_JOY_BUTTON(func)	Handles a wxEVT_JOY_BUTTON_UP event, generated when a button is released.
EVT_JOY_MOVE(func)	Handles a wxEVT_JOY_MOVE event, generated when the joystick is moved in the X-Y plane.
EVT_JOY_ZMOVE(func)	Handles a wxEVT_JOY_ZMOVE event, generated when the joystick is moved in the z-axis.
EVT_JOYSTICK_EVENTS(func)	Handles all joystick events.

wxJoystickEvent Member Functions

These are the wxJoystickEvent functions you can call to retrieve more information about the event. As usual, you can call GetEventType to get the type, which is useful if you are using EVT_JOYSTICK_EVENTS to catch all joystick events.

Call ButtonDown to check if the event was a button press event; you can optionally pass a button identifier wxJOY_BUTTON*n* (where *n* is 1, 2, 3, or 4) to test which button was pressed, or wxJOY_BUTTON_ANY if you don't care which button was pressed. ButtonUp is similar but tests for a button up event. The function IsButton is equivalent to ButtonDown() ¦¦ ButtonUp().

To test whether a button is down at the time of an event (not whether the event itself was a button press), call ButtonIsDown with the same arguments as for ButtonDown. Alternatively, use GetButtonState with the same arguments to return a bit-list of wxJOY_BUTTON*n* identifiers.

Call IsMove to test whether the event was a move event in the X-Y plane and IsZMove for a move in the z-axis.

GetPosition returns a wxPoint for the current joystick position in the X-Y plane, while GetZPosition returns an integer representing the Z position, if supported.

Finally, you can determine which joystick controller generated the event (wxJOYSTICK1 or wxJOYSTICK2) by calling GetJoystick.

wxJoystick Member Functions

We won't list the joystick functions exhaustively—you can refer to the wxJoystick class reference for that—but the following are the more interesting ones.

As we've seen in the example, SetCapture needs to be called to direct joystick input to a specified window, with a matching ReleaseCapture to release it and enable other applications to take control of the joystick. In case another application has captured the joystick, or the joystick is not functioning, call IsOK before trying to capture input. You can also determine the capabilities of the joystick with GetNumberButtons, GetNumberJoysticks, GetNumberAxes, HasRudder, and other functions.

You can get the state of the joystick from outside an event handler with functions such as GetPosition and GetButtonState.

Your application will almost always need to call GetXMin, GetXMax, and similar functions in order to determine the range supported by the joystick.

SUMMARY

In this chapter, you have learned about mouse, keyboard, and joystick input, and you can now add sophisticated interaction to your applications. For more insight, see wxWidgets samples such as `samples/keyboard`, `samples/joytest`, and `samples/dragimag`, and also the `wxThumbnailCtrl` class in `examples/chap12` on the CD-ROM.

The next chapter describes how you can achieve window layouts that are resizable, portable, translation-friendly, and above all attractive by using our flexible friend, the *sizer*.

CHAPTER 7

Window Layout Using Sizers

As graphic designers will testify, people are very sensitive to the way that visual objects are arranged. A GUI framework must allow the creation of a visually appealing layout, but unlike with print layout, an application's windows must often dynamically adapt to changes in size, font preferences, and even language. For platform-independent programming, the layout must also take into account the different sizes of individual controls from one platform to the next. All this means that a näive approach using absolute positions and sizes for controls simply won't work. This chapter describes wxWidgets' system of *sizers,* which gives you all the flexibility you need for even the most complex layouts. If it seems a bit daunting at first, remember that there are tools that will help you create sizer-based layouts—such as DialogBlocks, included on the accompanying CD-ROM—and you will rarely need to create entire layouts by hand.

LAYOUT BASICS

Before taking the plunge into the world of sizers, let's review where you might need to program layout behavior and what options you have.

A simple case is where you have a frame with a single window inside the client area. This is so simple that wxWidgets does the layout itself, fitting the child window to the size of the frame client area. For each frame, wxWidgets also manages the menu bar, one toolbar, and one status bar if they have been associated with the frame. If you need two toolbars, then you have to manage at least one of them yourself. If you have more than one child window in the client area, then wxWidgets expects you to manage them explicitly. You can do this with an OnSize event handler and calculate the position and size for each window and then set them. Or, you can use sizers. Similarly, if you create a custom control that consists of several child windows, you need to arrange for the child windows to resize appropriately when the overall control is resized.

Most applications have custom dialogs, sometimes dozens of them. The dialogs may be resizable, in which case the layout should look sensible even when the dialog is much larger than the initial size. The language may be changed, making some elements much larger or smaller than in the default language. If you had to program a hundred resize-friendly dialogs by hand, even with sizers, it would be almost impossibly daunting, so it's fortunate that editors are available to make this task simple—even a pleasure.

If (and when!) you choose to use sizers, you need to decide how you will create and deploy them. You or your dialog editor can create code in C++ or another language, or you can use XRC files, which are a declarative XML specification of the sizer layout. XRC files can be loaded dynamically or embedded in the executable by compiling them into C++ files with the utility wxrc. Most dialog editors can generate both code and XRC files. Your choice of code or XRC may be a matter of taste; perhaps you prefer to separate the layout from the class, or maybe you prefer the additional flexibility of tweaking the C++ code and the immediacy of having it in the same file as the class.

The next section describes the principles behind sizers, and the following sections describe how to program with individual sizer classes.

SIZERS

The layout algorithm used by sizers in wxWidgets is closely related to layout systems in other GUI toolkits, such as Java's AWT, the GTK+ toolkit, or the Qt toolkit. It is based upon the idea of individual windows reporting their minimal required size and their ability to be stretched if the size of the parent window has changed. This will most often mean that the programmer does not set the initial size of a dialog; instead, the dialog will be assigned a sizer, which will be queried about the recommended size. This sizer in turn will query its children (which can be windows, empty space, or other sizers) and further descendants. Note that wxSizer does not derive from wxWindow and thus does not interfere with tab ordering and requires very few resources compared to a real window. Sizers form a containment hierarchy parallel to the actual window hierarchy: the sizer hierarchy for a complex dialog may be many deep, but the controls themselves will probably all be siblings with the dialog as their parent.

This sizer hierarchy is depicted graphically in wxWidgets dialog editors. Figure 7-1 shows Anthemion Software's DialogBlocks editing the Personal Record dialog that we will use as an example in Chapter 9, "Creating Custom Dialogs." A red border in the editor pane surrounds the currently selected element, and its immediate parent is shown with a blue border. The tree you see on the left represents the sizer view of the hierarchy, but all controls are still parented directly on the dialog as far as the window hierarchy is concerned.

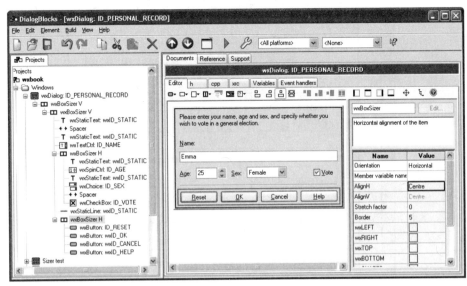

Figure 7-1   Viewing a sizer hierarchy in a dialog editor

To get a mental picture of how nested sizers work, consider Figure 7-2, a schematic view of the dialog being edited in Figure 7-1. The shaded areas represent actual windows, while the white boxes represent sizers. There are two vertical sizers inside the dialog (to give extra space around the edge of the dialog), and two horizontal sizers within the inner vertical sizer. A spacer is employed inside a horizontal sizer to keep one control away from another group of controls. As you can see, creating a sizer-based layout is really like sorting through a collection of different-sized cardboard boxes, placing smaller boxes in bigger boxes, and adding objects and packing material inside some of them. Of course, the analogy is imperfect because cardboard doesn't stretch!

There are currently five basic sizer classes available in wxWidgets. Each either represents a specific way to lay out windows or fulfills a special task such as wrapping a static box around another element. These sizers will be discussed in the following sections.

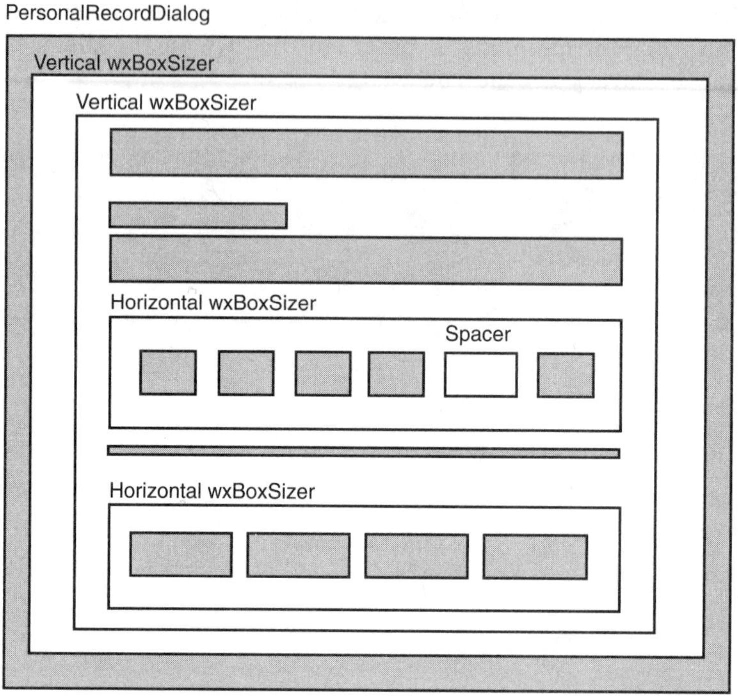

PersonalRecordDialog

Figure 7-2   A schematic view of the sizers for PersonalRecordDialog

Common Features of Sizers

All sizers are containers—that is, they are used to lay out one or more elements, which they contain. No matter how the individual sizers lay out their children, all children have certain features in common.

A minimal size: The minimal size of a control is calculated from the control's notion of its "best size" (supplied by implementing DoGetBestSize for each control). This is the control's natural size. For example, the best size of a check box comprises the space taken up by the check box graphic and the label. However, if you want the initial window size (as passed to the window's constructor) to be used as the minimal size instead, you can use the wxFIXED_MINSIZE style when adding the control to a sizer. Note that only some windows can calculate their size (such as a check box), whereas others (such as a list box) don't have any natural width or height and thus require an explicit size. Some windows can calculate their height, but not their width—for example, a single-line text control. Figure 7-3 shows three controls on their own in a dialog, showing how they expand the dialog to fit their own minimal size.

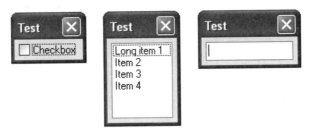

Figure 7-3   Windows reporting their minimal size

A border: The border is just empty space that is used to separate elements. This border can be all around, or it can be at any combination of sides, such as only above and below the control. The thickness of this border must be set explicitly, typically 5 pixels. Figure 7-4 shows dialogs with only one control (a button) and a border of 0, 5, and 10 pixels around the button, respectively.

Figure 7-4   Different border sizes

An alignment: An element can be moved to the center of the available space, or to either side of the space. Figure 7-5 shows a horizontal box sizer containing a list box and three buttons. One button is centered, one is aligned at the top, and one is aligned at the bottom. Alignment can be specified in horizontal or vertical orientations, but for most sizers, only one of these will have an effect. For example, in Figure 7-5, we have specified alignment in the vertical orientation, but horizontal alignment isn't possible because of the way space is distributed among children of the sizer. (To achieve the effect of horizontal alignment, we would need to insert a stretching spacer, which we will look at shortly.)

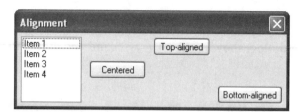

Figure 7-5   Sizer alignment

A stretch factor: If a sizer contains more than one child and is offered more space than its children and their borders need, the surplus space needs to be distributed among the children. For this purpose, a stretch factor may be assigned to each child, where the default value of zero indicates that the child will not get more space than its requested minimal size. A value of more than zero is interpreted in relation to the sum of all stretch factors in the children of the respective sizer, so if two children get a stretch factor of 1, they will each get half the extra space, independent of their minimal size. Figure 7-6 shows a dialog with three buttons, at the initial size and after resizing. The first button has a stretch factor of 1 and thus gets stretched, whereas the other two buttons have a stretch factor of zero and keep their initial width.

Note that the term "proportion" is sometimes used instead of stretch factor in the wxWidgets reference manual.

Figure 7-6   Stretch factor

PROGRAMMING WITH SIZERS

To create a sizer-based layout, create a top-level sizer (any kind of sizer may be used) and associate it with the parent window with wxWindow::SetSizer. Now you can hang your hierarchy of windows and further sizers from the top-level sizer. If you want the top-level window to fit itself around the contents, you call wxSizer::Fit passing the top-level window. If the window should never be resized smaller than the initial size, call wxSizer::SetSizeHints passing the top-level window. This will call wxWindow::SetSizeHints with the appropriate values.

Instead of the three functions described in the previous paragraph, you can simply call the function wxWindow::SetSizerAndFit, which sets the sizer, calls Fit, and also calls SetSizeHints.

If you have a panel inside a frame, you may be wondering which window gets the top-level sizer. Assuming you only have one panel in the frame, the frame already knows how to size the panel to fill the frame's client area when the frame size is changed. Therefore, you should set the sizer for the *panel* to manage the panel's children. If you had more than one panel in the frame, you might set a top-level sizer for the frame, which would manage the frame's children. However, you would still need a top-level sizer for each child panel that had its own children to lay out.

The following sections describe each kind of sizer and how to use it.

Programming with *wxBoxSizer*

wxBoxSizer can lay out its children either vertically or horizontally, depending on the style passed to its constructor. When using a vertical sizer, each child can be centered, aligned to the right, or aligned to the left. Correspondingly, when using a horizontal sizer, each child can be centered, aligned at the bottom, or aligned at the top. The stretch factor described previously is used for the main orientation, so when using a horizontal box sizer, the stretch factor determines how much the child can be stretched horizontally. Figure 7-7 shows the same dialog as in Figure 7-6, except that the sizer is a vertical box sizer.

Figure 7-7 A verical wxBoxSizer

You add child elements to a box sizer with Add:

```
// Add a window
void Add(wxWindow* window, int stretch = 0, int flags = 0,
        int border = 0);

// Add a sizer
void Add(wxSizer* window, int stretch = 0, int flags = 0,
        int border = 0);
```

The first parameter is a window or sizer.

The second is the proportion or stretch factor.

The third parameter is a bit-list specifying alignment behavior and borders. The alignment flags specify what happens when a vertical sizer changes its width, or when a horizontal sizer changes its height. The allowed values for specifying alignment and borders are shown in Table 7-1. The default alignment is wxALIGN_LEFT ¦ wxALIGN_TOP.

Table 7-1   Sizer Flags

0	Indicates that the window will preserve its original size.
wxGROW	Forces the window to grow with the sizer. wxEXPAND is a synonym for wxGROW.
wxSHAPED	Tells the window to change its size proportionally, preserving the original aspect ratio.
wxALIGN_LEFT	Aligns to the left edge of the sizer.
wxALIGN_RIGHT	Aligns to the right edge of the sizer.
wxALIGN_TOP	Aligns to the top edge of the sizer.
wxALIGN_BOTTOM	Aligns to the bottom edge of the sizer.
wxALIGN_CENTER_HORIZONTAL	Centers horizontally.
wxALIGN_CENTER_VERTICAL	Centers vertically.
wxALIGN_CENTER	Centers both horizontally and vertically. Defined as wxALIGN_CENTER_HORIZONTAL | wxALIGN_CENTER_VERTICAL.
wxLEFT	Specifies a border on the left edge of the element.
wxRIGHT	Specifies a border on the right edge of the element.
wxTOP	Specifies a border on the top edge of the element.
wxBOTTOM	Specifies a border on the bottom edge of the element.
wxALL	Specifies a border on all edges of the element. Defined as wxLEFT | wxRIGHT | wxTOP | wxBOTTOM.

The fourth parameter specifies the size of the border (on the edges that have been specified in the `flags` parameter).

You can also add a spacer. There are three ways to do this:

```
// Add a spacer (old method)
void Add(int width, int height, int stretch = 0, int flags = 0,
        int border = 0);

// Add a fixed-size spacer
void AddSpacer(int size);

// Add a stretching spacer
void AddStretchSpacer(int stretch = 1);
```

The second method is the equivalent of calling `Add(size, size, 0)`, and the third method is equivalent to calling `Add(0, 0, stretch)`.

As an example, we will construct a dialog that will contain a text field at the top and two buttons at the bottom. This can be seen at the top level as a column with the text at the top and buttons at the bottom, and at the second level as a row with an *OK* button to the left and a *Cancel* button to the right. In many cases, the main window will be resizable by the user, and this change of size will have to be propagated to its children. Here, we want the text area to grow with the dialog, whereas the buttons should have a fixed size. In addition, the buttons will be centered as the width of the dialog changes. Figure 7-8 shows how it will look.

Figure 7-8   A simple dialog using sizers

Here's the code that produces this dialog:

```
// A dialog with a stretching text control

MyDialog::MyDialog(wxWindow *parent, wxWindowID id,
                  const wxString &title )
        : wxDialog(parent, id, title,
                  wxDefaultPosition, wxDefaultSize,
                  wxDEFAULT_DIALOG_STYLE ¦ wxRESIZE_BORDER)
{
    wxBoxSizer *topSizer = new wxBoxSizer( wxVERTICAL );

    // Create text ctrl with minimal size 100x60
    topSizer->Add(
        new wxTextCtrl( this, wxID_ANY, "My text.",
            wxDefaultPosition, wxSize(100,60), wxTE_MULTILINE),
        1,            // make vertically stretchable
        wxEXPAND¦     // make horizontally stretchable
        wxALL,        // and make border all around
        10 );         // set border width to 10


    wxBoxSizer *buttonSizer = new wxBoxSizer( wxHORIZONTAL );
    buttonSizer->Add(
        new wxButton( this, wxID_OK, "OK" ),
        0,            // make horizontally unstretchable
```

```
        wxALL,      // make border all around: implicit top alignment
        10 );       // set border width to 10

    buttonSizer->Add(
      new wxButton( this, wxID_CANCEL, "Cancel" ),
      0,            // make horizontally unstretchable
      wxALL,        // make border all around (implicit top alignment)
      10 );         // set border width to 10

    topSizer->Add(
      buttonSizer,
      0,                    // make vertically unstretchable
      wxALIGN_CENTER );  // no border and centre horizontally

    SetSizer( topSizer ); // use the sizer for layout

    topSizer->Fit( this );           // fit the dialog to the contents
    topSizer->SetSizeHints( this ); // set hints to honor min size
}
```

Programming with *wxStaticBoxSizer*

wxStaticBoxSizer is a sizer derived from wxBoxSizer that manages a static box around the sizer. Note that this static box has to be created separately. Create wxStaticBoxSizer by passing a pointer to the static box and the orientation (wxHORIZONTAL or wxVERTICAL). The Add function is the same as for wxBoxSizer.

Figure 7-9 shows an example of a dialog with a static box containing a check box control.

Figure 7-9   A wxStaticBoxSizer

Here's the corresponding code:

```
MyDialog::MyDialog(wxWindow *parent, wxWindowID id,
                   const wxString &title )
       : wxDialog(parent, id, title,
                  wxDefaultPosition, wxDefaultSize,
                  wxDEFAULT_DIALOG_STYLE | wxRESIZE_BORDER)
{
    // Create top-level sizer
    wxBoxSizer* topLevel = new wxBoxSizer(wxVERTICAL);
```

```
// Create static box and static box sizer
wxStaticBox* staticBox = new wxStaticBox(this,
    wxID_ANY, wxT("General settings"));
wxStaticBoxSizer* staticSizer = new wxStaticBoxSizer(staticBox,
    wxVERTICAL);
topLevel->Add(staticSizer, 0,
    wxALIGN_CENTER_HORIZONTAL¦wxALL, 5);

// Create a check box inside the static box sizer
wxCheckBox* checkBox = new wxCheckBox( this, ID_CHECKBOX,
    wxT("&Show splash screen"), wxDefaultPosition, wxDefaultSize);
staticSizer->Add(checkBox, 0, wxALIGN_LEFT ¦wxALL, 5);

SetSizer(topLevel);
topLevel->Fit(this);
topLevel->SetSizeHints(this);
}
```

Programming with *wxGridSizer*

wxGridSizer is a sizer that lays out its children in a two-dimensional table with all table fields having the same size; that is, the width of each field is the width of the widest child, and the height of each field is the height of the tallest child. Create a wxGridSizer by passing the number of rows, number of columns, extra vertical gap between children, and extra horizontal gap between children. Add is the same as for wxBoxSizer.

Figure 7-10 shows a grid sizer with three columns and two rows. The extra size of the second button has caused the space occupied by all the buttons to increase because all the cells of a wxGridSizer are the same size.

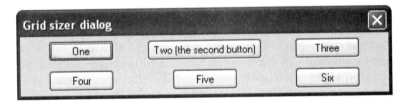

Figure 7-10   A wxGridSizer

Here's the code:

```
MyDialog::MyDialog(wxWindow *parent, wxWindowID id,
                const wxString &title )
      : wxDialog(parent, id, title,
                wxDefaultPosition, wxDefaultSize,
                wxDEFAULT_DIALOG_STYLE ¦ wxRESIZE_BORDER)
{
    // Create top-level grid sizer
    wxGridSizer* gridSizer = new wxGridSizer(2, 3, 0, 0);
```

```
        SetSizer(gridSizer);

        wxButton* button1 = new wxButton(this, ID_BUTTON1, wxT("One"));
        gridSizer->Add(button1, 0, wxALIGN_CENTER_HORIZONTAL|
                                    wxALIGN_CENTER_VERTICAL|wxALL, 5);

        wxButton* button2 = new wxButton(this, ID_BUTTON2, wxT("Two (the
    second button)"));
        gridSizer->Add(button2, 0, wxALIGN_CENTER_HORIZONTAL|
                                    wxALIGN_CENTER_VERTICAL|wxALL, 5);

        wxButton* button3 = new wxButton(this, ID_BUTTON3, wxT("Three"));
        gridSizer->Add(button3, 0, wxALIGN_CENTER_HORIZONTAL|
                                    wxALIGN_CENTER_VERTICAL|wxALL, 5);

        wxButton* button4 = new wxButton(this, ID_BUTTON4, wxT("Four"));
        gridSizer->Add(button4, 0, wxALIGN_CENTER_HORIZONTAL|
                                    wxALIGN_CENTER_VERTICAL|wxALL, 5);

        wxButton* button5 = new wxButton(this, ID_BUTTON5, wxT("Five"));
        gridSizer->Add(button5, 0, wxALIGN_CENTER_HORIZONTAL|
                                    wxALIGN_CENTER_VERTICAL|wxALL, 5);

        wxButton* button6 = new wxButton(this, ID_BUTTON6, wxT("Six"));
        gridSizer->Add(button6, 0, wxALIGN_CENTER_HORIZONTAL|
                                    wxALIGN_CENTER_VERTICAL|wxALL, 5);

        gridSizer->Fit(this);
        gridSizer->SetSizeHints(this);
    }
```

Programming with *wxFlexGridSizer*

wxFlexGridSizer is a sizer that lays out its children in a two-dimensional table
with all table fields in one row having the same height and all fields in one
column having the same width. However, unlike wxGridSizer, all rows or all
columns are not necessarily the same height or width: this will depend on the
size of elements in a row or column. Additionally, columns and rows can be
declared to be stretchable, which means that as the sizer is expanded, these
columns or rows will be allocated extra space.

Create a wxFlexGridSizer by passing the number of rows, number of
columns, extra vertical gap between children, and extra horizontal gap
between children. Add is the same as for wxBoxSizer.

Figure 7-11 shows a flex grid sizer at its initial size, where the first column has been made stretchable. It's essentially the same as the wxGridSizer
example, but as you can see, the layout is more compact because the size of the
middle column is not reflected in the other columns.

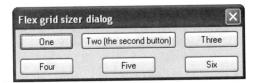

Figure 7-11   A wxFlexGridSizer at its initial size

Initially, we don't see the effect of making the first column stretchable, but if we stretch it horizontally, as in Figure 7-12, we can see this column (containing buttons One and Four) taking up the extra space, with the buttons centered in the column.

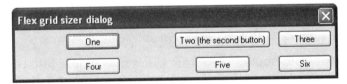

Figure 7-12   A resized wxFlexGridSizer

Here's the code that creates the dialogs we've shown:

```
MyDialog::MyDialog(wxWindow *parent, wxWindowID id,
                   const wxString &title )
       : wxDialog(parent, id, title,
                  wxDefaultPosition, wxDefaultSize,
                  wxDEFAULT_DIALOG_STYLE | wxRESIZE_BORDER)
{
    // Create top-level flex grid sizer
    wxFlexGridSizer* flexGridSizer = new wxFlexGridSizer(2, 3, 0, 0);
    this->SetSizer(flexGridSizer);

    // Make the 1st row growable
    flexGridSizer->AddGrowableCol(0);

    wxButton* button1 = new wxButton(this, ID_BUTTON1, wxT("One"));
    flexGridSizer->Add(button1, 0, wxALIGN_CENTER_HORIZONTAL|
                              wxALIGN_CENTER_VERTICAL|wxALL, 5);

    wxButton* button2 = new wxButton(this, ID_BUTTON2, wxT("Two (the
second button)"));
    flexGridSizer->Add(button2, 0, wxALIGN_CENTER_HORIZONTAL|
                              wxALIGN_CENTER_VERTICAL|wxALL, 5);

    wxButton* button3 = new wxButton(this, ID_BUTTON3, wxT("Three"));
    flexGridSizer->Add(button3, 0, wxALIGN_CENTER_HORIZONTAL|
```

```
                                        wxALIGN_CENTER_VERTICAL¦wxALL, 5);

    wxButton* button4 = new wxButton(this, ID_BUTTON4, wxT("Four"));
    flexGridSizer->Add(button4, 0, wxALIGN_CENTER_HORIZONTAL¦
                                        wxALIGN_CENTER_VERTICAL¦wxALL, 5);

    wxButton* button5 = new wxButton(this, ID_BUTTON5, wxT("Five"));
    flexGridSizer->Add(button5, 0, wxALIGN_CENTER_HORIZONTAL¦
                                        wxALIGN_CENTER_VERTICAL¦wxALL, 5);

    wxButton* button6 = new wxButton(this, ID_BUTTON6, wxT("Six"));
    flexGridSizer->Add(button6, 0, wxALIGN_CENTER_HORIZONTAL¦
                                        wxALIGN_CENTER_VERTICAL¦wxALL, 5);

    flexGridSizer->Fit(this);
    flexGridSizer->SetSizeHints(this);
}
```

Programming with *wxGridBagSizer*

This sizer attempts to reconcile the worlds of absolute positioning and sizer-based layout. It can lay out elements in a virtual grid, like a flex grid sizer, but in this case item row and column positions are specified using wxGBPosition, and items can optionally span more than one row and/or column using wxGBSpan.

When creating a wxGridBagSizer, optionally pass sizers for vertical and horizontal gaps between rows and columns (defaulting to zero). Use the Add function to add windows or sizers, passing the position and optional span, plus optional flags and border size as for wxBoxSizer.

Figure 7-13 shows a simple grid bag sizer example with four buttons, one of them spanning two columns (button Two). We also specify that the second row and third column are growable so that when we resize the dialog, we get the effect shown in Figure 7-14.

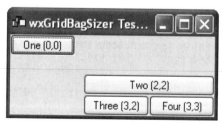

Figure 7-13   A wxGridBagSizer at its original size

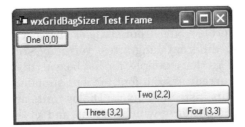

Figure 7-14 A wxGridBagSizer after resizing

Here's the code that produces this layout:

```
MyDialog::MyDialog(wxWindow *parent, wxWindowID id,
                   const wxString &title )
        : wxDialog(parent, id, title,
                   wxDefaultPosition, wxDefaultSize,
                   wxDEFAULT_DIALOG_STYLE | wxRESIZE_BORDER)
{
    wxGridBagSizer* gridBagSizer = new wxGridBagSizer();
    SetTopSizer(gridBagSizer);

    wxButton* b1 = new wxButton(this, wxID_ANY, wxT("One (0,0)"));
    gridBagSizer->Add(b1, wxGBPosition(0, 0));

    wxButton* b2 = new wxButton(this, wxID_ANY, wxT("Two (2,2)"));
    gridBagSizer->Add(b2, wxGBPosition(2, 2), wxGBSpan(1, 2),
                      wxGROW);

    wxButton* b3 = new wxButton(this, wxID_ANY, wxT("Three (3,2)"));
    gridBagSizer->Add(b3, wxGBPosition(3, 2));

    wxButton* b4 = new wxButton(this, wxID_ANY, wxT("Four (3,3)"));
    gridBagSizer->Add(b4, wxGBPosition(3, 3));

    gridBagSizer->AddGrowableRow(3);
    gridBagSizer->AddGrowableCol(2);

    gridBagSizer->Fit(this);
    gridBagSizer->SetSizeHints(this);
}
```

FURTHER LAYOUT ISSUES

In this section, we'll discuss some further topics to bear in mind when you're working with sizers.

Dialog Units

Although sizers protect you from changes in basic control size on different platforms and in different languages, you may still have some hard-coded sizes in your dialogs (for example, for list boxes). If you would like these sizes to adjust to the current system font (or font supplied by the application), you can use *dialog units* instead of pixels. Dialog units are based on average character width and height for a window's font, and so the actual pixel dimension for a given dialog unit value will vary according to the current font. wxWindow has functions ConvertDialogToPixels and ConvertPixelsToDialog, and a convenience macro wxDLG_UNIT(window, ptOrSz) that can be used with both wxPoint and wxSize objects. So instead of passing a pixel size to your control, use the wxDLG_UNIT macro, for example:

```
wxListBox* listBox = new wxListBox(parent, wxID_ANY,
    wxDefaultPosition, wxDLG_UNIT(parent, wxSize(60, 20)));
```

Dialog units can be specified in an XRC file by appending "d" to dimension values.

Platform-Adaptive Layouts

Although dialogs on different platforms are largely similar, sometimes the style guides are incompatible. For example, on Windows and Linux, it's acceptable to have right-justified or centered *OK*, *Cancel*, and *Help* buttons, in that order. On Mac OS X, the *Help* should be on the left, and *Cancel* and *OK* buttons are right aligned, in that order.

To help with this issue, wxStdDialogButtonSizer is provided. It's derived from wxBoxSizer, so it can be used in a similar way, but its orientation will depend on platform.

This sizer's constructor has no arguments. There are two ways of adding buttons: pass the button pointer to AddButton, or (if you're not using standard identifiers) call SetAffirmativeButton, SetNegativeButton, and SetCancelButton. If using AddButton, you should use identifiers from this list: wxID_OK, wxID_YES, wxID_CANCEL, wxID_NO, wxID_SAVE, wxID_APPLY, wxID_HELP, and wxID_CONTEXT_HELP.

Then, after the buttons have been added, call Realize so that the sizer can add the buttons in the appropriate order with the appropriate spacing (which it can only do when it knows about all the buttons in the sizer). The following code creates a standard button sizer with *OK*, *Cancel*, and *Help* buttons:

```
wxBoxSizer* topSizer = new wxBoxSizer(wxVERTICAL);
dialog->SetSizer(topSizer);

wxButton* ok = new wxButton(dialog, wxID_OK);
wxButton* cancel = new wxButton(dialog, wxID_CANCEL);
```

```
wxButton* help = new wxButton(dialog, wxID_HELP);

wxStdDialogButtonSizer* buttonSizer = new wxStdDialogButtonSizer;
topSizer->Add(buttonSizer, 0, wxEXPAND¦wxALL, 10);

buttonSizer->AddButton(ok);
buttonSizer->AddButton(cancel);
buttonSizer->AddButton(help);

buttonSizer->Realize();
```

As a convenience, wxDialog::CreateButtonSizer can be used, indirectly creating a wxStdDialogButtonSizer with buttons based on a flag list. If you look at the dialog implementations in src/generic, you will see that CreateButtonSizer is used for many of them. The flags in Table 7-2 can be passed to this function.

Table 7-2   Flags for CreateButtonSizer

wxYES_NO	Add *Yes* and *No* buttons to the panel.
wxYES	Add *Yes* button to the panel, with identifier wxID_YES.
wxNO	Add *No* button to the panel, with identifier wxID_NO.
wxNO_DEFAULT	Make the *No* button the default, otherwise *Yes* or *OK* will be the default.
wxOK	Add an *OK* button to the panel, with identifier wxID_OK.
wxCANCEL	Add a *Cancel* button to the panel, with identifier wxID_CANCEL.
wxAPPLY	Add an *Apply* button to the panel, with identifier wxID_APPLY.
wxHELP	Add a *Help* button to the panel, with identifier wxID_HELP.

Using CreateButtonSizer simplifies the example code shown previously to the following:

```
wxBoxSizer* topSizer = new wxBoxSizer(wxVERTICAL);
dialog->SetSizer(topSizer);

topSizer->Add(CreateButtonSizer(wxOK¦wxCANCEL¦wxHELP), 0,
              wxEXPAND¦wxALL, 10);
```

There is another way to specify variations in UI on different platforms. XRC allows a *platform* parameter to be associated with each object; this parameter's value can be a combination of unix, win, mac, and os2 separated by the pipe character ("|"). XRC will only create the element if the platform value matches the actual platform the program is running on. DialogBlocks supports this property and can generate conditional C++ code if XRC is not being used.

Alternatively, you can load a different XRC file for each platform, but this is harder to maintain than having the differences contained within a single dialog design.

Dynamic Layouts

Sometimes you'd like the layout to change dynamically; for example, clicking on a *Details* button might expand the dialog and show further controls. You can hide controls contained in sizers the same way you would hide any control, using the `wxWindow::Show` method. However, `wxSizer` also offers a separate method, which can tell the sizer not to consider a window in its size calculations. To hide a window using the sizer, pass `false` to `wxSizer::Show`. You must then call `wxSizer::Layout` to force an update.

SUMMARY

Sizers takes some getting used to, so don't worry if you found this chapter a bit heavy going. The best way of getting to grips with them is to play with a dialog editor such as DialogBlocks (included on the CD-ROM), experimenting with different layouts and examining the generated code. You can also look at `samples/layout` in your wxWidgets distribution. After you've tamed them, you'll find sizers a very powerful tool, and their ability to adapt to different platforms and languages will prove to be a huge productivity benefit.

Next, we'll look at the standard dialogs provided by wxWidgets.

CHAPTER 8

Using Standard Dialogs

This chapter describes the set of standard dialogs that wxWidgets provides for displaying information or getting data from users with just a few lines of code. Becoming familiar with the available standard dialogs is going to save you a lot of coding time, and it will help give your applications a professional feel. Where possible, wxWidgets uses the native dialogs implemented by each windowing system, but some, such as `wxTextEntryDialog`, are implemented in wxWidgets itself, and these are referred to as "generic" dialogs. In this chapter, we will show pictures of dialogs on more than one platform where there are significant visual differences.

We will divide the dialogs into the categories *Informative Dialogs*, *File and Directory Dialogs*, *Choice and Selection Dialogs*, and *Entry Dialogs*.

INFORMATIVE DIALOGS

In this section, we'll look at dialogs that present information: `wxMessageDialog`, `wxProgressDialog`, `wxBusyInfo`, and `wxShowTip`.

wxMessageDialog

This dialog shows a message plus buttons that can be chosen from *OK*, *Cancel*, *Yes*, and *No*. An optional icon can be shown, such as an exclamation mark or question mark. The message text can contain newlines ("\n").

The return value of `wxMessageDialog::ShowModal` indicates which button the user pressed.

Figure 8-1 shows how the dialog looks under Windows, Figure 8-2 shows it under GTK+, and Figure 8-3 is the same dialog on Mac OS X.

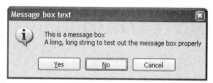

Figure 8-1   wxMessageDialog under Windows

Figure 8-2   wxMessageDialog under GTK+

Figure 8-3   wxMessageDialog under Mac OS X

To create this dialog, pass a parent window, message, and optional caption, style, and position. Then call ShowModal to display the window, and test the returned value.

The style is a bit-list of the values shown in Table 8-1.

Table 8-1   wxMessageDialog Styles

wxOK	Shows an OK button.
wxCANCEL	Shows a Cancel button.
wxYES_NO	Shows Yes and No buttons.
wxYES_DEFAULT	Sets Yes as the default. Use with wxYES_NO. This is the default behavior for wxYES_NO.
wxNO_DEFAULT	Sets No as the default. Use with wxYES_NO.
wxICON_EXCLAMATION	Shows an exclamation mark.

wxICON_ERROR	Shows an error icon.
wxICON_HAND	Shows an error icon. The same as wxICON_ERROR.
wxICON_QUESTION	Shows a question mark.
wxICON_INFORMATION	Shows an information icon.
wxSTAY_ON_TOP	On Windows, the message box will stay on top of all other windows, even those of other applications.

wxMessageDialog Example

Here's an example of using wxMessageDialog:

```
#include "wx/msgdlg.h"

wxMessageDialog dialog( NULL, wxT("Message box caption"),
    wxT("Message box text"),
    wxNO_DEFAULT|wxYES_NO|wxCANCEL|wxICON_INFORMATION);

switch ( dialog.ShowModal() )
{
  case wxID_YES:
      wxLogStatus(wxT("You pressed \"Yes\""));
      break;

  case wxID_NO:
      wxLogStatus(wxT("You pressed \"No\""));
      break;

  case wxID_CANCEL:
      wxLogStatus(wxT("You pressed \"Cancel\""));
      break;

  default:
      wxLogError(wxT("Unexpected wxMessageDialog return code!"));
}
```

wxMessageBox

You can also use the convenience function wxMessageBox, which takes a message string, caption string, style, and parent window. For example:

```
if (wxYES == wxMessageBox(wxT("Message box text"),
    wxT("Message box caption"),
    wxNO_DEFAULT|wxYES_NO|wxCANCEL|wxICON_INFORMATION,
    parent))
{
    return true;
}
```

Be aware that wxMessageBox returns values that are different from those returned by wxMessageDialog::ShowModal. wxMessageBox returns wxOK, wxCANCEL, wxYES, and wxNO, whereas wxMessageDialog::ShowModal returns wxID_OK, wxID_CANCEL, wxID_YES, and wxID_NO.

wxProgressDialog

wxProgressDialog shows a short message and a progress bar representing how long the user has to wait. It can display a Cancel button to abort the task in progress, and it can also display elapsed time, estimated total time, and remaining time. This dialog is implemented by wxWidgets on all platforms. Figure 8-4 shows wxProgressDialog under Windows.

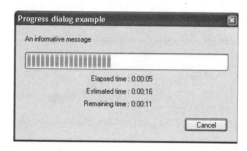

Figure 8-4   wxProgressDialog under Windows

You can create the dialog object on the stack or dynamically. Pass the following parameters: a caption string, a message string to be displayed above the progress bar, the maximum value for the progress bar, a parent window, and a style.

The style is a bit-list of the values listed in Table 8-2.

Table 8-2   wxProgressDialog Styles

wxPD_APP_MODAL	Makes the progress dialog modal. If this style is not given, it is only "locally" modal—that is, the input to the parent window is disabled, but not to the other ones.
wxPD_AUTO_HIDE	Causes the progress dialog to disappear from the screen as soon as the maximum value of the progress meter has been reached.
wxPD_CAN_ABORT	Tells the dialog that it should have a Cancel button that the user may press. If this happens, the next call to Update will return false.
wxPD_ELAPSED_TIME	Tells the dialog that it should show the elapsed time since creating the dialog.
wxPD_ESTIMATED_TIME	Tells the dialog that it should show the estimated time.
wxPD_REMAINING_TIME	Tells the dialog that it should show the remaining time.

After dialog creation, the program flow continues, but the parent window is disabled for input. If wxPD_APP_MODAL is specified, then all other windows in the application are disabled as well. The application should call Update with a value (between zero and the maximum specified in the constructor) and, optionally, a new message to display in the dialog. If specified, the elapsed, estimated, and remaining times are all calculated automatically by the dialog.

If wxPD_AUTO_HIDE is specified, the progress dialog will be hidden (but not destroyed) as soon as the maximum value has been passed to Update. The application should destroy the dialog. You can call Resume if you need to resume an aborted progress dialog.

wxProgressDialog Example

Here's an example of using the progress dialog:

```
#include "wx/progdlg.h"

void MyFrame::ShowProgress()
{
    static const int max = 10;

    wxProgressDialog dialog(wxT("Progress dialog example"),
                            wxT("An informative message"),
                            max,     // range
                            this,    // parent
                            wxPD_CAN_ABORT |
                            wxPD_APP_MODAL |
                            wxPD_ELAPSED_TIME |
                            wxPD_ESTIMATED_TIME |
                            wxPD_REMAINING_TIME);

    bool cont = true;
    for ( int i = 0; i <= max; i++ )
    {
        wxSleep(1);
        if ( i == max )
            cont = dialog.Update(i, wxT("That's all, folks!"));
        else if ( i == max / 2 )
            cont = dialog.Update(i, wxT("Only a half left (very
        ➥long message)!"));
        else
            cont = dialog.Update(i);

        if ( !cont )
        {
            if ( wxMessageBox(wxT("Do you really want to cancel?"),
                              wxT("Progress dialog question"),
                              wxYES_NO | wxICON_QUESTION) == wxYES )
                break;

            dialog.Resume();
        }
    }

    if ( !cont )
        wxLogStatus(wxT("Progress dialog aborted!"));
    else
        wxLogStatus(wxT("Countdown from %d finished"), max);
}
```

wxBusyInfo

wxBusyInfo isn't actually a dialog—it's derived from wxObject—but it behaves in a similar way. It shows a window displaying a message for as long as the object exists, and it is useful for asking the user to wait while the application is working on something. On Windows, it looks like the window in Figure 8-5.

Create a wxBusyInfo object on the stack or dynamically, passing a message and a window parent.

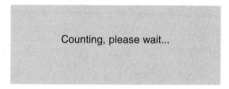

Counting, please wait...

Figure 8-5   wxBusyInfo dialog under Windows

wxBusyInfo Example

Here's an example of using wxBusyInfo, first using wxWindowDisabler to disable all windows currently open in the application.

```
#include "wx/busyinfo.h"

wxWindowDisabler disableAll;

wxBusyInfo info(wxT("Counting, please wait..."), parent);
for (int i = 0; i < 1000; i++)
{
    DoCalculation();
}
```

wxShowTip

Many applications show a tip on startup to give you extra insights into using the application. Tips can be a good way to learn an application in small, easily digested doses, especially for users who find it tedious to read documentation.

The startup tip dialog under Windows is shown in Figure 8-6.

Figure 8-6   Tip dialog under Windows

Unlike most of the standard dialogs, startup tips are shown by calling a function: wxShowTip. Pass a parent window, a pointer to a wxTipProvider object, and optionally a boolean value specifying whether to show the Show Tips at Startup check box. The return value is the value of this check box.

You must derive a new class from wxTipProvider and override the GetTip function to return a wxString containing the tip. Fortunately, wxWidgets provides an implementation already: wxCreateFileTipProvider, which takes the name of a file of tips (one per line) and an index into the tips.

The application is responsible for deleting the wxTipProvider object when it is no longer needed.

wxShowTip Example

Here's a function that shows a startup tip using the standard tip provider:

```
#include "wx/tipdlg.h"

void MyFrame::ShowTip()
{
    static size_t s_index = (size_t)-1;

    if ( s_index == (size_t)-1 )
    {
        // randomize...
        srand(time(NULL));

        // ...and pick a new tip
        s_index = rand() % 5;
    }
```

```
// pass a tips file and tip index
wxTipProvider *tipProvider =
    wxCreateFileTipProvider(wxT("tips.txt"), s_index);

m_showAtStartup = wxShowTip(this, tipProvider, true);
delete tipProvider;
}
```

FILE AND DIRECTORY DIALOGS

There are two dialogs you can use to get file and directory information from
the user: wxFileDialog and wxDirDialog.

wxFileDialog

wxFileDialog can handle the selection of one file or several files, and it has
variants for opening and saving files.

Figure 8-7 shows the file dialog under Windows.

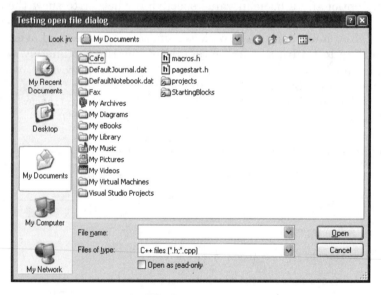

Figure 8-7   wxFileDialog under Windows

Figure 8-8 and Figure 8-9 show the file dialog under Linux using GTK+ versions 1 and 2, respectively.

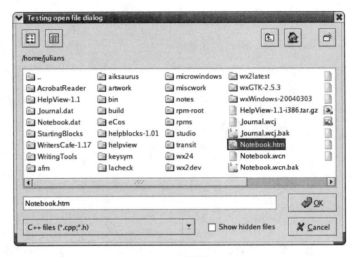

Figure 8-8   Generic `wxFileDialog` under GTK+

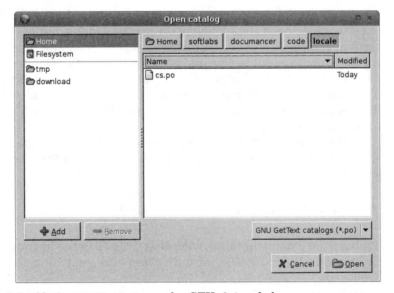

Figure 8-9   Native `wxFileDialog` under GTK+2.4 and above

The file dialog appearance under Mac OS X is shown in Figure 8-10.

Figure 8-10   wxFileDialog under Mac OS X

To create a wxFileDialog, pass a parent window, a message to display in the dialog caption, a default directory, a default file name, a wildcard, the dialog style, and a position (ignored on some platforms). Call ShowModal and test for a wxID_OK return value, which is returned if the user confirms a selection.

Directory and file name are distinct elements of a full path name. If the directory is empty, the current directory will be used. If the file name is empty, no default file name will be supplied.

The wildcard determines what files are displayed in the file selector. The wildcard may be a specification for multiple types of file with a description for each, such as

```
"BMP files (*.bmp)¦*.bmp¦GIF files (*.gif)¦*.gif"
```

Typing a file name containing wildcards ("*", "?") in the file name text item and clicking on OK will result in only those files matching the pattern being displayed.

wxFileDialog Styles

The file dialog has the styles shown in Table 8-3.

Table 8-3 wxFileDialog Styles

wxSAVE	Specifies a "save" dialog.
wxOPEN	Specifies an "open" dialog (the default).
wxOVERWRITE_PROMPT	For a "save" dialog, the user will be prompted if the chosen file already exists.
wxFILE_MUST_EXIT	The user is forced to select an existing file.
wxMULTIPLE	The user can select multiple files.

wxFileDialog Functions

The wxFileDialog functions are as follows.

GetDirectory returns the default directory or the directory component of the selected file for a single-selection file dialog. Use SetDirectory to specify the default directory.

GetFilename returns the default file name (without the directory) or the selected file name for a single-selection file dialog. Use SetFilename to set the default file name.

GetFilenames returns a wxArrayString of the file names of all selections in a multiple-selection dialog. Generally, these file names do not include the directory, but under Windows, if any shortcuts are selected, the file names *do* include directories. This is because the application cannot determine the full path of each referenced file by appending the file name to the selected directory. Use GetPaths if you want to get an array of the selections including their directories.

GetFilterIndex returns a zero-based index of the default or selected filter. Filters are usually displayed in a drop-down list under the list of files. Use SetFilterIndex to set the default index to be displayed when the dialog is shown.

GetMessage returns the dialog caption. Use SetMessage to set the caption.

GetPath returns the full path (directory and file name) of the file selected by the user or the default path. Use SetPath to set the default path. For a multiple-selection dialog, use GetPaths to get a wxArrayString of all selections including their directories.

GetWildcard returns the wildcard specification, and SetWildcard sets it.

wxFileDialog Example

Here's an example of using wxFileDialog to open a single BMP or GIF file:

```
#include "wx/filedlg.h"

wxString caption = wxT("Choose a file");
wxString wildcard =
    wxT("BMP files (*.bmp)¦*.bmp¦GIF files (*.gif)¦*.gif");
```

```
wxString defaultDir = wxT("c:\\temp"));
wxString defaultFilename = wxEmptyString;

wxFileDialog dialog(parent, caption, defaultDir, defaultFilename,
    wildcard, wxOPEN);
if (dialog.ShowModal() == wxID_OK)
{
    wxString path = dialog.GetPath();
    int filterIndex = dialog.GetFilterIndex();
}
```

wxDirDialog

wxDirDialog allows the user to choose a local or network directory (folder). Optionally, it can allow the user to create a new directory if the wxDD_NEW_DIR_BUTTON style is passed to the constructor.

Figure 8-11 shows wxDirDialog under Windows, where Windows supplies the dialog. The generic version of wxDirDialog is used for GTK+ on Linux, as Figure 8-12 shows.

Figure 8-11   wxDirDialog under Windows

Figure 8-12   wxDirDialog under GTK+

wxDirDialog on Mac OS X (Figure 8-13) looks very much like the file dialog.

Figure 8-13   wxDirDialog under Mac OS X

To create the directory dialog, pass a parent window, a message to show on the dialog, a default directory, a window style, a position, and a size (these last two may be ignored, depending on implementation). Call ShowModal and test for a wxID_OK return value, which indicates that the user confirmed a directory selection.

wxDirDialog Functions

The functions for this dialog are described in the following.

SetPath and GetPath are accessors for the default or user-selected directory.

SetMessage sets the message that appears on the dialog, and GetMessage returns the current value.

wxDirDialog Example

Using wxDirDialog is easy, as this example shows:

```
#include "wx/dirdlg.h"

wxString defaultPath = wxT("/");

wxDirDialog dialog(parent,
    wxT("Testing directory picker"),
    defaultPath, wxDD_NEW_DIR_BUTTON);

if (dialog.ShowModal() == wxID_OK)
{
    wxString path = dialog.GetPath();
    wxMessageBox(path);
}
```

CHOICE AND SELECTION DIALOGS

In this section, we look at dialogs for getting choices and selections from the user: wxColourDialog, wxFontDialog, wxSingleChoiceDialog, and wxMultiChoiceDialog.

wxColourDialog

This dialog allows the user to pick from a standard set or a full range of colors.

Under Windows, the native color selector dialog is used. This dialog contains three main regions: at the top left, a palette of 48 commonly used colors is shown. Below this, there is a palette of 16 custom colors, which can be set by the application. Additionally, the user may add to the custom color palette by expanding the dialog box and choosing a precise color from the color selector panel on the right. Figure 8-14 shows the color selector under Windows in full selection mode.

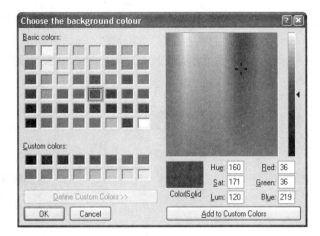

Figure 8-14   wxColourDialog under Windows

The generic color dialog, shown in Figure 8-15 under GTK+ 1 and X11, shows palettes of 48 standard and 16 custom colors, with the area on the right containing three sliders for the user to select a color from red, green, and blue components. This color may be added to the custom color palette, and it will replace either the currently selected custom color or the first one in the palette if none is selected. The RGB color sliders are not optional in the generic color selector. The generic color selector is also available under Windows and other platforms; use the name wxGenericColourDialog.

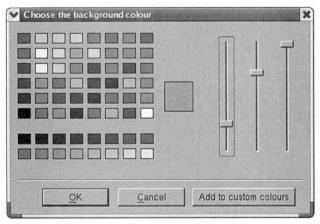

Figure 8-15   Generic wxColourDialog under X11

Figure 8-16 shows the native color dialog under GTK+.

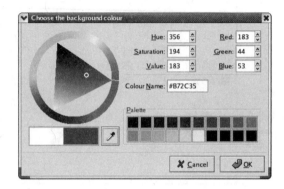

Figure 8-16   wxColourDialog under GTK+

Figure 8-17 shows Mac OS X's color dialog, which offers yet another way of getting a color from the user.

Figure 8-17   wxColourDialog under Mac OS X

To use this dialog, create a wxColourDialog object (dynamically allocated or on the stack) and pass it a parent window and a pointer to a wxColourData object. The information in wxColourData will be copied to the dialog to set some defaults. Call ShowModal to enter the modal loop, and when control is returned to your code, you can retrieve the user-modified data by calling GetColourData.

wxColourData Functions

wxColourData has the following functions.

SetChooseFull specifies that the color dialog should show the full selection of colors; otherwise only a subset will be shown. This currently works only under Windows. GetChooseFull retrieves the value of this boolean.

SetColour sets the default color to show in the color selector, and GetColour retrieves the color that the user has chosen.

SetCustomColour takes a zero-based index (maximum 15) and a wxColour object and sets one of the 16 custom colors. Use GetCustomColour to retrieve the custom colors, which may have changed if the user has added to the custom colors from within the color selector.

wxColourDialog Example

Here is an example of using wxColourDialog. The code sets various parameters of a wxColourData object, including a gray scale for the custom colors. If the user did not cancel the dialog, the application retrieves the selected color and uses it to set the background of a window.

```
#include "wx/colordlg.h"

wxColourData data;
data.SetChooseFull(true);
for (int i = 0; i < 16; i++)
{
    wxColour color(i*16, i*16, i*16);
    data.SetCustomColour(i, color);
}

wxColourDialog dialog(this, &data);
if (dialog.ShowModal() == wxID_OK)
{
    wxColourData retData = dialog.GetColourData();
    wxColour col = retData.GetColour();
    myWindow->SetBackgroundColour(col);
    myWindow->Refresh();
}
```

wxFontDialog

wxFontDialog allows the user to provide font and, on some platforms, font color selections.

Under Windows, the native font selector standard dialog is used. This presents a dialog box with controls for font name, point size, style, weight, underlining, strikeout, and text foreground color. A sample of the font is shown on a white area of the dialog box. Note that in the translation from full Windows fonts to wxWidgets font conventions, strikeout is ignored, and a font family (such as Swiss or Modern) is deduced from the actual font name (such as Arial or Courier). Under GTK+, the GTK+ standard font selector is used, which does not allow color selection.

Figure 8-18 shows how the font dialog looks under Windows.

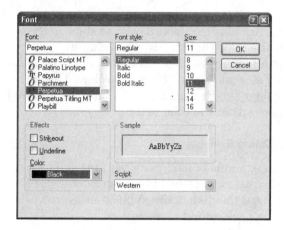

Figure 8-18   wxFontDialog under Windows

Figure 8-19 shows the native font dialog under GTK+.

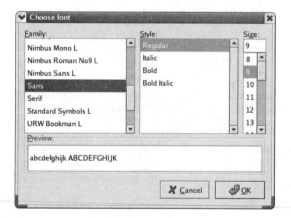

Figure 8-19   wxFontDialog under GTK+

Under platforms other than Windows and GTK+, the font selector is simpler: see Figure 8-20 for a view of the generic dialog on Mac OS X. Controls for font family, point size, style, weight, underlining, and text foreground color are provided, and a sample is shown upon a white background. The generic font selector is available on all platforms; use the name wxGenericFontDialog.

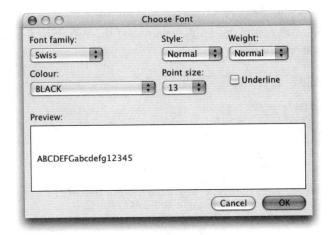

Figure 8-20   Generic wxFontDialog under Mac OS X

To use wxFontDialog, create an object dynamically or on the stack and pass a parent window and a wxFontData object. Call ShowModal and test for a wxID_OK return value. Then retrieve the wxFontData from the dialog and call GetChosenFont and GetChosenColour as required.

wxFontData Functions

wxFontData has the following functions.

EnableEffects enables controls for manipulating color and underline properties under Windows or on the generic dialog (no effect on GTK+). GetEnableEffects returns the current boolean value of this setting. Note that even if effects are disabled, the font color will be preserved.

SetAllowSymbols allows the selection of symbol fonts (Windows only), and GetAllowSymbols returns the current boolean value of this setting.

SetColour sets the default font color, and GetColour retrieves the font color selected by the user.

SetInitialFont sets the default font that will be selected when the dialog is first opened. GetChosenFont retrieves the wxFont selected by the user.

SetShowHelp can be called to indicate that the help button should be displayed (under Windows only). Use GetShowHelp to return the value of this setting.

Call SetRange with the minimum and maximum point size that the user can select; the default (0, 0) indicates that any point size can be selected. This has an effect on Windows only.

Font Selector Example

In this fragment, the application uses the returned font and color for drawing text on a window.

```
#include "wx/fontdlg.h"

wxFontData data;
data.SetInitialFont(m_font);
data.SetColour(m_textColor);

wxFontDialog dialog(this, &data);
if (dialog.ShowModal() == wxID_OK)
{
    wxFontData retData = dialog.GetFontData();
    m_font = retData.GetChosenFont();
    m_textColor = retData.GetColour();

    // Update the window to reflect the new font and color
    myWindow->Refresh();
}
```

wxSingleChoiceDialog

wxSingleChoiceDialog presents the user with a list of strings and allows the user to select one. It looks like the dialog in Figure 8-21.

Figure 8-21   wxSingleChoiceDialog under Windows

Pass to the dialog constructor the parent window, a message to show on the dialog, the dialog caption, and a wxArrayString for the strings to appear in the list. You can also pass an array size and a C array of strings (wxChar**) instead of passing a wxArrayString.

You can use SetSelection to set the default selection before showing the dialog; after the dialog has been dismissed, query the user's choice with GetSelection (to return the index) or GetStringSelection (to return the string).

You also can pass an array of char* client data to the dialog's constructor; when the dialog is dismissed, GetSelectionClientData will return the char* client data corresponding to the user selection.

wxSingleChoiceDialog Example

Here's some code to show how wxSingleChoiceDialog is used.

```
#include "wx/choicdlg.h"

const wxArrayString choices;
choices.Add(wxT("One"));
choices.Add(wxT("Two"));
choices.Add(wxT("Three"));
choices.Add(wxT("Four"));
choices.Add(wxT("Five"));

wxSingleChoiceDialog dialog(this,
                    wxT("This is a small sample\nA single-
              ➥choice convenience dialog"),
                    wxT("Please select a value"),
                    choices);

dialog.SetSelection(2);

if (dialog.ShowModal() == wxID_OK)
    wxMessageBox(dialog.GetStringSelection(), wxT("Got string"));
```

wxMultiChoiceDialog

wxMultiChoiceDialog is similar to wxSingleChoiceDialog, presenting the user with a list of strings, but it allows the user to select zero or more. This dialog is illustrated in Figure 8-22.

Figure 8-22 wxMultiChoiceDialog under Windows

Pass to the dialog constructor the parent window, a message to show on the dialog, the dialog caption, and a wxArrayString array of strings. As with wxSingleChoiceDialog, you may pass an array size and wxChar** array instead of the wxArrayString argument. Unlike wxSingleChoiceDialog, no client data may be passed to the constructor.

To set the default selections, call SetSelections passing a wxArrayInt where each element specifies an index in the passed array of strings. Query the user's choice with GetSelections to return a wxArrayInt of indices specifying the user's selections.

wxMultiChoiceDialog Example

Here's how you use a wxMultiChoiceDialog.

```
#include "wx/choicdlg.h"

const wxArrayString choices;
choices.Add(wxT("One"));
choices.Add(wxT("Two"));
choices.Add(wxT("Three"));
choices.Add(wxT("Four"));
choices.Add(wxT("Five"));

wxMultiChoiceDialog dialog(this,
                      wxT("A multi-choice convenience
                           ➥dialog"),
                      wxT("Please select several values"),
                      choices);

if (dialog.ShowModal() == wxID_OK)
{
    wxArrayInt selections = dialog.GetSelections();
    wxString msg;
    msg.Printf(wxT("You selected %u items:\n"),
        selections.GetCount());

    for ( size_t n = 0; n < selections.GetCount(); n++ )
    {
        msg += wxString::Format(wxT("\t%d: %d (%s)\n"),
                           n, selections[n],
                           choices[selections[n]].c_str());
    }

    wxMessageBox(msg, wxT("Got selections"));
}
```

ENTRY DIALOGS

These dialogs ask you to type in information. They include wxNumberEntryDialog, wxTextEntryDialog, wxPasswordEntryDialog, and wxFindReplaceDialog.

wxNumberEntryDialog

wxNumberEntryDialog prompts the user for an integer within a given range. The dialog shows a spin control so that the number can be entered directly or by clicking on the up and down arrows. This dialog is implemented by wxWidgets, so it has the same functionality on all platforms.

Create a wxNumberEntryDialog passing a parent window, message text, prompt text (that will precede the spin control), caption, default value, minimum value, maximum value, and position. Then call ShowDialog and, if wxID_OK is returned, retrieve the number using GetValue.

Figure 8-23 shows what the dialog looks like under Windows.

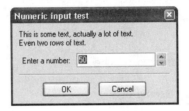

Figure 8-23   wxNumberEntryDialog under Windows

wxNumberEntryDialog Example

Figure 8-23 was created using the following code:

```
#include "wx/numdlg.h"

wxNumberEntryDialog dialog(parent,
  wxT("This is some text, actually a lot of text\nEven two rows of
➥text"),
  wxT("Enter a number:"), wxT("Numeric input test"), 50, 0, 100);
if (dialog.ShowModal() == wxID_OK)
{
  long value = dialog.GetValue();

}
```

wxTextEntryDialog and wxPasswordEntryDialog

wxTextEntryDialog and wxPasswordEntryDialog present the user with a single-line text control and a message. They function identically except that the letters typed into a wxPasswordEntryDialog are masked so that they cannot be read. Figure 8-24 shows a wxTextEntryDialog under Windows.

Figure 8-24   wxTextEntryDialog under Windows

Pass a parent window, message, caption, default value, and style to the constructor. The style can be a bit-list of wxOK, wxCANCEL, and wxCENTRE (or wxCENTER), and you can also pass wxTextCtrl styles such as wxTE_CENTRE (or wxTE_CENTER).

You can set the default string separately with SetValue, and GetValue returns the text entered by the user.

wxTextEntryDialog Example

Figure 8-24 was created using this code:

```
#include "wx/textdlg.h"

wxTextEntryDialog dialog(this,
                         wxT("This is a small sample\n")
                         wxT("A long, long string to test out the
                             ➥text entrybox"),
                         wxT("Please enter a string"),
                         wxT("Default value"),
                         wxOK | wxCANCEL);

if (dialog.ShowModal() == wxID_OK)
    wxMessageBox(dialog.GetValue(), wxT("Got string"));
```

wxFindReplaceDialog

wxFindReplaceDialog is a modeless dialog that allows the user to search for some text and replace it with something else, if desired. The actual searching must be done in a derived class or a parent window, responding to events generated by the dialog's buttons. Unlike most standard dialogs, this one must have a parent window. This dialog cannot be used modally; it is always, by design and implementation, modeless.

The Windows Find and Replace dialog is shown in Figure 8-25.

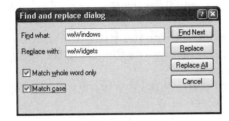

Figure 8-25 `wxFindReplaceDialog` under Windows

On other platforms, such as GTK+ and Mac OS X, wxWidgets uses the generic version of the dialog, as shown in Figure 8-26.

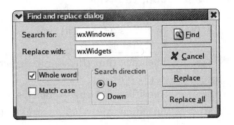

Figure 8-26 `wxFindReplaceDialog` under GTK+

Handling Events from the Dialog

`wxFindReplaceDialog` sends command events when the user clicks on controls in the dialog. Event handlers take a `wxFindDialogEvent` argument, and the event table macros take the dialog identifier and handler function, as listed in Table 8-4.

Table 8-4 `wxFindReplaceDialog` Events

`EVT_FIND(id, func)`	Handles Find button clicks.
`EVT_FIND_NEXT(id, func)`	Handles Next button clicks.
`EVT_FIND_REPLACE(id, func)`	Handles Replace button clicks.
`EVT_FIND_REPLACE_ALL(id, func)`	Handles Replace All button clicks.
`EVT_FIND_CLOSE(id, func)`	Handles a close event, generated when the user closes the dialog via Cancel or other means.

wxFindDialogEvent Functions

wxFindDialogEvent has the following functions.

GetFlags returns flags for the current selections on the dialog. The value is a bit-list of wxFR_DOWN, wxFR_WHOLEWORD, and wxFR_MATCHCASE.

GetFindString returns the string the user entered as the text to find.

GetReplaceString returns the string the user entered as the text to use as the replacement.

GetDialog returns a pointer to the wxFindReplaceDialog that generated the event.

Passing Data to the Dialog

To create a wxFindReplaceDialog, pass a window parent, a pointer to a wxFindReplaceData object, a dialog caption, and a style, which is a bit-list of values shown in Table 8-5.

Table 8-5   wxFindReplaceData Style

wxFR_REPLACEDIALOG	Specifies a find and replace dialog; otherwise, it will be a find dialog.
wxFR_NOUPDOWN	Specifies that the search direction should not be adjustable.
wxFR_NOMATCHCASE	Specifies that case-sensitive searching is not allowable.
wxFR_NOWHOLEWORD	Specifies that whole-word searching is not allowable.

wxFindReplaceData holds the data for wxFindReplaceDialog. It is used to initialize the dialog with the default values and will keep the last values from the dialog when it is closed. It is also updated each time a wxFindDialogEvent is generated, so instead of using the wxFindDialogEvent methods, you can also directly query this object. Use the dialog's GetData function to return a pointer to the data you passed to the dialog constructor.

wxFindReplaceData Functions

These are the functions for setting and accessing data in wxFindReplaceData. Note that the setters may only be called before showing the dialog, and calling them has no effect later.

GetFindString and SetFindString are accessors for the search string, provided by the application or entered by the user.

GetFlags and SetFlags are accessors for the flags specifying the state of the find dialog (refer to Table 8-5).

GetReplaceString and SetReplaceString are accessors for the replace string, provided by the application or entered by the user.

Find and Replace Example

The following shows an example fragment of wxFindReplaceDialog usage, employing hypothetical DoFind and DoReplace functions to do the actual search and replace for the application. These functions would maintain application-dependent variables in the dialog class, storing the last position that was searched, so that each time the functions are called, the next match can be found. The functions will also change the document view and highlight the match.

```cpp
#include "wx/fdrepdlg.h"

BEGIN_EVENT_TABLE(MyFrame, wxFrame)
    EVT_MENU(ID_REPLACE, MyFrame::ShowReplaceDialog)
    EVT_FIND(wxID_ANY, MyFrame::OnFind)
    EVT_FIND_NEXT(wxID_ANY, MyFrame::OnFind)
    EVT_FIND_REPLACE(wxID_ANY, MyFrame::OnReplace)
    EVT_FIND_REPLACE_ALL(wxID_ANY, MyFrame::OnReplaceAll)
    EVT_FIND_CLOSE(wxID_ANY, MyFrame::OnFindClose)
END_EVENT_TABLE()

void MyFrame::ShowReplaceDialog( wxCommandEvent& event )
{
    if ( m_dlgReplace )
    {
        delete m_dlgReplace;
        m_dlgReplace = NULL;
    }
    else
    {
        m_dlgReplace = new wxFindReplaceDialog
                            (
                             this,
                             &m_findData,
                             wxT("Find and replace dialog"),
                             wxFR_REPLACEDIALOG
                            );

        m_dlgReplace->Show(true);
    }
}

void MyFrame::OnFind(wxFindDialogEvent& event)
{
    if (!DoFind(event.GetFindString(), event.GetFlags()))
    {
        wxMessageBox(wxT("No more matches."));
    }
}

void MyFrame::OnReplace(wxFindDialogEvent& event)
{
    if (!DoReplace(event.GetFindString(), event.GetReplaceString(),
        event.GetFlags(), REPLACE_THIS))
```

```
        {
            wxMessageBox(wxT("No more matches."));
        }
    }

    void MyFrame::OnReplaceAll(wxFindDialogEvent& event)
    {
        if (DoReplace(event.GetFindString(), event.GetReplaceString(),
            event.GetFlags(), REPLACE_ALL))
        {
            wxMessageBox(wxT("Replacements made."));
        }
        else
        {
            wxMessageBox(wxT("No replacements made."));
        }

    }

    void MyFrame::OnFindClose(wxFindDialogEvent& event)
    {
        m_dlgReplace->Destroy();
        m_dlgReplace = NULL;
    }
```

PRINTING DIALOGS

You use wxPageSetupDialog and wxPrintDialog in applications that print documents. If you use the printing framework (including wxPrintout, wxPrinter, and
other classes), you won't need to invoke these dialogs explicitly in your code.
For more on printing, refer to Chapter 5, "Drawing and Printing."

wxPageSetupDialog

wxPageSetupDialog contains controls for paper size such as A4 and letter, orientation (landscape or portrait), and controls for setting left, top, right, and bottom margin sizes in millimeters. The user can also set printer-specific options
by invoking a further dialog from this one.

Figure 8-27 shows the wxPageSetupDialog dialog under Windows.

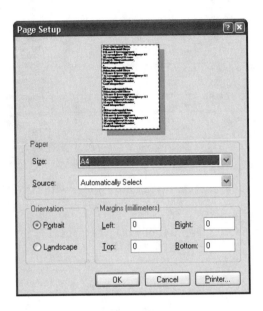

Figure 8-27   wxPageSetupDialog under Windows

Figure 8-28 shows wxPageSetupDialog using the generic implementation under GTK+. If the GNOME printing libraries are installed, wxWidgets will instead use a native GNOME page setup dialog, as shown in Figure 8-29.

Figure 8-28   wxPageSetupDialog under GTK+ without GNOME printing

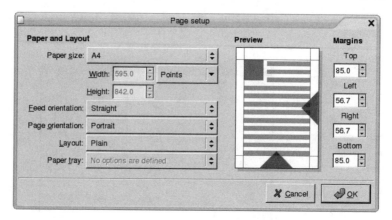

Figure 8-29   wxPageSetupDialog under GTK+ with GNOME printing

The Mac OS X version of wxPageSetupDialog is shown in Figure 8-30.

Figure 8-30   wxPageSetupDialog under Mac OS X

To use this dialog, pass to the constructor a parent window and a pointer to a wxPageSetupDialogData object, which contains settings to pass to and retrieve from the dialog. You can create the dialog on the stack or dynamically. The page setup data will be copied to the dialog's own data; use GetPageSetupData to return a reference to the dialog's data.

wxPageSetupData Functions

`wxPageSetupDialogData` has the following functions.

`Ok` returns `true` if the print data associated with the object is valid. This can return `false` on Windows if the current printer is not set, for example. On all other platforms, it returns `true`.

`SetMarginTopLeft` takes a `wxPoint` object and sets the left and top margins in millimeters. Call `GetMarginTopLeft` to retrieve this value.

`SetMarginBottomRight` takes a `wxPoint` object and sets the bottom and right margins in millimeters. Call `GetMarginBottomRight` to retrieve this value.

`SetPaperId` sets the paper identifier to select the current paper size, instead of using `SetPaperSize`. See the documentation for this function for the symbols that are available. `GetPaperId` retrieves the paper identifier.

`SetPaperSize` takes a `wxSize` object and sets the paper size in millimeters. Use `GetPaperSize` to retrieve the current paper size.

`EnableMargins` enables or disables the margin controls (Windows only). Call `GetEnableMargins` to test the value of this setting.

`EnableOrientation` enables or disables the orientation control (Windows only). Call `GetEnableOrientation` to test the value of this setting.

`EnablePaper` enables or disables the paper size control (Windows only). Call `GetEnablePaper` to test the value of this setting.

`EnablePrinter` enables or disables the Printer button, which invokes a print setup dialog. Call `GetEnablePrinter` to test the value of this setting.

wxPageSetupDialog Example

Here's an example of using `wxPageSetupDialog`:

```
#include "wx/printdlg.h"

void MyFrame::OnPageSetup(wxCommandEvent& event)
{
    wxPageSetupDialog pageSetupDialog(this, & m_pageSetupData);
    if (pageSetupDialog.ShowModal() == wxID_OK)
        m_pageSetupData = pageSetupDialog.GetPageSetupData();
}
```

wxPrintDialog

This class represents the print and print setup standard dialogs. You may obtain a `wxPrinterDC` device context from a successfully dismissed print dialog.

Figure 8-31 shows wxPrintDialog under Windows.

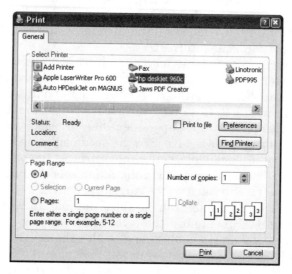

Figure 8-31   wxPrintDialog under Windows

Figure 8-32 shows wxPrintDialog under GTK+ without the GNOME printing libraries, and Figure 8-33 shows the dialog shown when the GNOME printing libraries are installed.

Figure 8-32   wxPrintDialog under GTK+ without GNOME printing

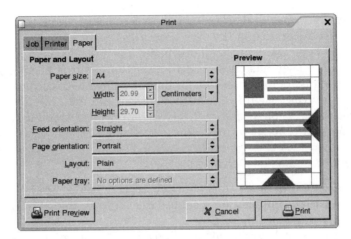

Figure 8-33 wxPrintDialog under GTK+ with GNOME printing

Figure 8-34 shows wxPrintDialog under Mac OS X. As you can see from the buttons along the bottom, Mac OS X gives you the added advantage of saving your document as a PDF file, and you can use the Mac OS X previewer as an alternative to the application's preview window.

Figure 8-34 wxPrintDialog under Mac OS X

To use wxPrintDialog, create it on the stack or dynamically and pass the parent window and a pointer to a wxPrintDialogData object, whose contents will be copied to internal data in the dialog object. Call wxPrintDialogData:: SetSetupDialog with true before passing the data to the dialog if you want to show the print setup dialog instead of the print dialog. Following Microsoft's conventions, the print setup dialog has been replaced by the wxPageSetupDialog, but for compatibility, some applications may still need to use the setup dialog.

When the dialog returns successfully, you can retrieve the wxPrintDialogData using the GetPrintDialogData function.

Call GetPrintDC on the dialog to get a printer device context based on the settings the user has chosen. If the function returns a non-null pointer, the application is then responsible for deleting the device context.

Ok returns true if the print data associated with the dialog is valid. This can return false on Windows if the current printer is not set, for example. On all other platforms, it returns true.

wxPrintDialogData Functions

These are the functions you can use with wxPrintDialogData.

EnableHelp enables or disables the Help button. Use GetEnableHelp to return the value of this setting.

EnablePageNumbers enables or disables the page number controls, and GetEnablePageNumbers returns the value of this setting.

EnablePrintToFile enables or disables the Print to File check box. Use GetEnablePrintToFile to return the value of this setting.

EnableSelection enables or disables the Selection radio button that lets the user specify that the current selection should be printed. Use GetEnableSelection to return the value of this setting.

SetCollate sets the Collate check box to be true or false. Use GetCollate to return the value of this setting.

SetFromPage and SetToPage set the page range to print. Use GetFromPage and GetToPage to return this range.

SetMinPage and SetMaxPage set the minimum and maximum page numbers that can be printed. Use GetMinPage and GetMaxPage to return these values.

SetNoCopies sets the default number of copies that will be printed. Use GetNoCopies to return the value of this setting.

SetPrintToFile sets the *Print to File* check box to true or false. Use GetPrintToFile to return the value of this setting.

SetSelection sets the *Selection* radio button. Use GetSelection to return the value of this setting.

SetSetupDialog determines whether the print setup dialog is shown (true) or the normal print dialog is shown (false). Use GetSetupDialog to return the value of this setting.

SetPrintData sets the internal wxPrintData object. GetPrintData returns a reference to the internal wxPrintData object.

wxPrintDialog Example

The following example shows wxPrintDialog being used to return a suitable printer device context:

```
#include "wx/printdlg.h"

void MyFrame::OnPrint(wxCommandEvent& event)
{
```

```
wxPrintDialogData dialogData;
dialogData.SetFromPage(0);
dialogData.SetToPage(10);

wxPrintDialog printDialog(this, & m_dialogData);
if (printDialog.ShowModal() == wxID_OK)
{
    // After calling GetPrintDC(), the application
    // owns the DC
    wxDC* dc = printDialog.GetPrintDC();

    // Draw on the device context
    ...

    // Destroy it
    delete dc;
}
}
```

However, usually you can avoid invoking the print dialog directly. Instead, use the higher-level printing framework (refer to Chapter 5). The print dialog will be shown as a side effect of calling wxPrinter::Print.

SUMMARY

In this chapter, you have learned about the standard dialogs that you can use to present information and retrieve user choices with very little code. For further examples of using standard dialogs, see samples/dialogs in your wxWidgets distribution. Next, we'll show you how to write your own dialogs.

Writing Custom Dialogs

Sooner or later, you will have to create your own dialogs, whether simple ones with only a few buttons and some text or highly complex dialogs with notebook controls, multiple panels, custom controls, context-sensitive help, and so on. In this chapter, we cover the principles of creating custom dialogs and transferring data between C++ variables and the controls. We also describe the wxWidgets resource system, which enables you to load dialogs and other user interface elements from XML files.

STEPS IN CREATING A CUSTOM DIALOG

When you start writing your own specialized dialogs, the fun really starts. Here are the steps you'll typically need to take:

1. Derive a new class from `wxDialog`.
2. Decide where the data is stored and how the application accesses user choices.
3. Write code to create and lay out the controls.
4. Add code that transfers data between C++ variables and the controls.
5. Add functions and their event table entries to handle events from controls.
6. Add user interface (UI) update handlers to set controls to the correct state.
7. Add help, in particular tooltips, context-sensitive help (not implemented on Mac OS X), and a way of showing an explanation of the dialog in your application's user manual.
8. Invoke the dialog from a suitable place in your application code.

Let's illustrate these steps with a concrete example.

AN EXAMPLE: *PERSONALRECORDDIALOG*

As we saw in the previous chapter, dialogs come in two flavors: modal and modeless. We'll illustrate custom dialog creation with a modal dialog because it's the more common kind and has fewer complications. The application will invoke the dialog with ShowModal and then query the dialog for user selections. Until ShowModal returns, all user interactions with the application will be contained within the little world of your custom dialog (and any further modal dialogs that your dialog may invoke).

Many of the steps involved in creating a custom dialog can be accomplished very easily by using a dialog editor, such as wxDesigner or DialogBlocks. The amount of coding left to do depends on the complexity of your dialog. Here, we will assume handcrafting of all the code in order to demonstrate the principles, but it's highly recommended that you use a tool to help you because it will save you many hours of repetitive work.

We'll illustrate the steps involved in creating a custom dialog with a simple example where the user is required to enter his or her name, age, sex, and whether the user wants to vote. This dialog is called PersonalRecordDialog, as shown in Figure 9-1.

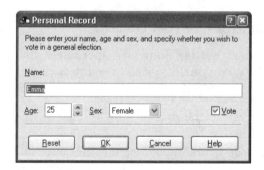

Figure 9-1   Personal record dialog under Windows

The *Reset* button restores all controls to their default values. The *OK* button dismisses the dialog and returns wxID_OK from ShowModal. The *Cancel* button returns wxID_CANCEL and does not update the dialog's variables from the values shown in the controls. The *Help* button invokes a few lines of text describing the dialog (although in a real application, this button should invoke a nicely formatted help file).

A good user interface should not allow the user to enter data that has no meaning in the current context. In this example, the user should not be able to use the *Vote* control if *Age* is less than the voting age (18 in the U.S. or U.K.). So, we will ensure that when the age entered is less than 18, the *Vote* check box is disabled.

Deriving a New Class

Here's the declaration for our `PersonalRecordDialog`. We provide run-time type information by using `DECLARE_CLASS`, and we add an event table with `DECLARE_EVENT_TABLE`.

```
/*!
 * PersonalRecordDialog class declaration
 */

class PersonalRecordDialog: public wxDialog
{
    DECLARE_CLASS( PersonalRecordDialog )
    DECLARE_EVENT_TABLE()

public:
    // Constructors
    PersonalRecordDialog( );
    PersonalRecordDialog( wxWindow* parent,
        wxWindowID id = wxID_ANY,
        const wxString& caption = wxT("Personal Record"),
        const wxPoint& pos = wxDefaultPosition,
        const wxSize& size = wxDefaultSize,
        long style = wxCAPTION|wxRESIZE_BORDER|wxSYSTEM_MENU );

    // Initialize our variables
    void Init();

    // Creation
    bool Create( wxWindow* parent,
        wxWindowID id = wxID_ANY,
        const wxString& caption = wxT("Personal Record"),
        const wxPoint& pos = wxDefaultPosition,
        const wxSize& size = wxDefaultSize,
        long style = wxCAPTION|wxRESIZE_BORDER|wxSYSTEM_MENU );

    // Creates the controls and sizers
    void CreateControls();
};
```

Note that we follow wxWidgets convention by allowing both one-step and two-step construction—we provide a default constructor and `Create` function as well as a more verbose constructor.

Designing Data Storage

We have four pieces of data to store: name (string), age (integer), sex (boolean), and voting preference (boolean). To make it easier to use a wxChoice control with the data, we're going to use an integer to store the boolean value for sex, but the class interface can present it as boolean: `true` for female and `false` for male. Let's add these data members and accessors to the `PersonalRecordDialog` class:

```
// Data members
wxString      m_name;
int           m_age;
int           m_sex;
bool          m_vote;

// Name accessors
void SetName(const wxString& name) { m_name = name; }
wxString GetName() const { return m_name; }

// Age accessors
void SetAge(int age) { m_age = age; }
int GetAge() const { return m_age; }

// Sex accessors (male = false, female = true)
void SetSex(bool sex) { sex ? m_sex = 1 : m_sex = 0; }
bool GetSex() const { return m_sex == 1; }

// Does the person vote?
void SetVote(bool vote) { m_vote = vote; }
bool GetVote() const { return m_vote; }
```

Coding the Controls and Layout

Now let's add a `CreateControls` function to be called from `Create`. `CreateControls` adds `wxStaticText` controls, `wxButton` controls, a `wxSpinCtrl`, a `wxTextCtrl`, a `wxChoice`, and a `wxCheckBox`. Refer to Figure 9-1 earlier in the chapter to see the resulting dialog.

We're using sizer-based layout for this dialog, which is why it looks a bit more involved than you might expect for a small number of controls. (We described sizers in Chapter 7, "Window Layout Using Sizers"—briefly, they enable you to create dialogs that look good on any platform and that easily adapt to translation and resizing.) You can use a different method if you want, such as loading the dialog from a wxWidgets resource file (XRC file).

The basic principle of sizer-based layout is to put controls into nested boxes (sizers), which can distribute space among the controls or stretch just enough to contain its controls. The sizers aren't windows—they form a separate hierarchy, and the controls remain children of their parent, regardless of the complexity of the hierarchy of sizers. You might like to refresh your memory by looking at the schematic view of a sizer layout that we showed in Figure 7-2 in Chapter 7.

In `CreateControls`, we're using a vertical box sizer (`boxSizer`) nested in another vertical box sizer (`topSizer`) to give a decent amount of space around the dialog's controls. A horizontal box sizer is used for the `wxSpinCtrl`, `wxChoice`, and `wxCheckBox`, and a second horizontal box sizer (`okCancelSizer`) is used for the *Reset*, *OK*, *Cancel*, and *Help* buttons.

```
/*!
 * Control creation for PersonalRecordDialog
 */
```

```
void PersonalRecordDialog::CreateControls()
{
    // A top-level sizer

    wxBoxSizer* topSizer = new wxBoxSizer(wxVERTICAL);
    this->SetSizer(topSizer);

    // A second box sizer to give more space around the controls

    wxBoxSizer* boxSizer = new wxBoxSizer(wxVERTICAL);
    topSizer->Add(boxSizer, 0, wxALIGN_CENTER_HORIZONTAL|wxALL, 5);

    // A friendly message

    wxStaticText* descr = new wxStaticText( this, wxID_STATIC,
        wxT("Please enter your name, age and sex, and specify whether
you wish to\nvote in a general election."), wxDefaultPosition,
wxDefaultSize, 0 );
    boxSizer->Add(descr, 0, wxALIGN_LEFT|wxALL, 5);

    // Spacer

    boxSizer->Add(5, 5, 0, wxALIGN_CENTER_HORIZONTAL|wxALL, 5);

    // Label for the name text control

    wxStaticText* nameLabel = new wxStaticText ( this, wxID_STATIC,
        wxT("&Name:"), wxDefaultPosition, wxDefaultSize, 0 );
    boxSizer->Add(nameLabel, 0, wxALIGN_LEFT|wxALL, 5);

    // A text control for the user's name

    wxTextCtrl* nameCtrl = new wxTextCtrl ( this, ID_NAME, wxT("Emma"),
wxDefaultPosition, wxDefaultSize, 0 );
    boxSizer->Add(nameCtrl, 0, wxGROW|wxALL, 5);

    // A horizontal box sizer to contain age, sex and vote

    wxBoxSizer* ageSexVoteBox = new wxBoxSizer(wxHORIZONTAL);
    boxSizer->Add(ageSexVoteBox, 0, wxGROW|wxALL, 5);

    // Label for the age control

    wxStaticText* ageLabel = new wxStaticText ( this, wxID_STATIC,
        wxT("&Age:"), wxDefaultPosition, wxDefaultSize, 0 );
    ageSexVoteBox->Add(ageLabel, 0, wxALIGN_CENTER_VERTICAL|wxALL, 5);

    // A spin control for the user's age

    wxSpinCtrl* ageSpin = new wxSpinCtrl ( this, ID_AGE,
        wxEmptyString, wxDefaultPosition, wxSize(60, -1),
        wxSP_ARROW_KEYS, 0, 120, 25 );
    ageSexVoteBox->Add(ageSpin, 0, wxALIGN_CENTER_VERTICAL|wxALL, 5);

    // Label for the sex control

    wxStaticText* sexLabel = new wxStaticText ( this, wxID_STATIC,
        wxT("&Sex:"), wxDefaultPosition, wxDefaultSize, 0 );
    ageSexVoteBox->Add(sexLabel, 0, wxALIGN_CENTER_VERTICAL|wxALL, 5);

    // Create the sex choice control
```

```
wxString sexStrings[] = {
    wxT("Male"),
    wxT("Female")
};

wxChoice* sexChoice = new wxChoice ( this, ID_SEX,
    wxDefaultPosition, wxSize(80, -1), WXSIZEOF(sexStrings),
        sexStrings, 0 );
sexChoice->SetStringSelection(wxT("Female"));
ageSexVoteBox->Add(sexChoice, 0, wxALIGN_CENTER_VERTICAL¦wxALL, 5);

// Add a spacer that stretches to push the Vote control
// to the right

ageSexVoteBox->Add(5, 5, 1, wxALIGN_CENTER_VERTICAL¦wxALL, 5);

wxCheckBox* voteCheckBox = new wxCheckBox( this, ID_VOTE,
    wxT("&Vote"), wxDefaultPosition, wxDefaultSize, 0 );
voteCheckBox ->SetValue(true);
ageSexVoteBox->Add(voteCheckBox, 0,
    wxALIGN_CENTER_VERTICAL¦wxALL, 5);

// A dividing line before the OK and Cancel buttons

wxStaticLine* line = new wxStaticLine ( this, wxID_STATIC,
    wxDefaultPosition, wxDefaultSize, wxLI_HORIZONTAL );
boxSizer->Add(line, 0, wxGROW¦wxALL, 5);

// A horizontal box sizer to contain Reset, OK, Cancel and Help

wxBoxSizer* okCancelBox = new wxBoxSizer(wxHORIZONTAL);
boxSizer->Add(okCancelBox, 0, wxALIGN_CENTER_HORIZONTAL¦wxALL, 5);

// The Reset button

wxButton* reset = new wxButton( this, ID_RESET, wxT("&Reset"),
    wxDefaultPosition, wxDefaultSize, 0 );
okCancelBox->Add(reset, 0, wxALIGN_CENTER_VERTICAL¦wxALL, 5);

// The OK button

wxButton* ok = new wxButton ( this, wxID_OK, wxT("&OK"),
    wxDefaultPosition, wxDefaultSize, 0 );
okCancelBox->Add(ok, 0, wxALIGN_CENTER_VERTICAL¦wxALL, 5);

// The Cancel button

wxButton* cancel = new wxButton ( this, wxID_CANCEL,
    wxT("&Cancel"), wxDefaultPosition, wxDefaultSize, 0 );
okCancelBox->Add(cancel, 0, wxALIGN_CENTER_VERTICAL¦wxALL, 5);

// The Help button

wxButton* help = new wxButton( this, wxID_HELP, wxT("&Help"),
    wxDefaultPosition, wxDefaultSize, 0 );
okCancelBox->Add(help, 0, wxALIGN_CENTER_VERTICAL¦wxALL, 5);
}
```

Data Transfer and Validation

Now we have the bare controls of the dialog, but the controls and the dialog's data are not connected. How do we make that connection?

When a dialog is first shown, wxWidgets calls InitDialog, which in turn sends a wxEVT_INIT_DIALOG event. The default handler for this event calls TransferDataToWindow on the dialog. To transfer data from the controls back to the variables, you can call TransferDataFromWindow when the user confirms his or her input. Again, wxWidgets does this for you by defining a default handler for wxID_OK command events, which calls TransferDataFromWindow before calling EndModal to dismiss the dialog.

So, you can override TransferDataToWindow and TransferDataFromWindow to transfer your data. For our dialog, the code might look like this:

```
/*!
 * Transfer data to the window
 */

bool PersonalRecordDialog::TransferDataToWindow()
{
    wxTextCtrl* nameCtrl = (wxTextCtrl*) FindWindow(ID_NAME);
    wxSpinCtrl* ageCtrl = (wxSpinCtrl*) FindWindow(ID_AGE);
    wxChoice* sexCtrl = (wxChoice*) FindWindow(ID_SEX);
    wxCheckBox* voteCtrl = (wxCheckBox*) FindWindow(ID_VOTE);

    nameCtrl->SetValue(m_name);
    ageCtrl->SetValue(m_age);
    sexCtrl->SetSelection(m_sex);
    voteCtrl->SetValue(m_vote);

    return true;
}

/*!
 * Transfer data from the window
 */

bool PersonalRecordDialog::TransferDataFromWindow()
{
    wxTextCtrl* nameCtrl = (wxTextCtrl*) FindWindow(ID_NAME);
    wxSpinCtrl* ageCtrl = (wxSpinCtrl*) FindWindow(ID_AGE);
    wxChoice* sexCtrl = (wxChoice*) FindWindow(ID_SEX);
    wxCheckBox* voteCtrl = (wxCheckBox*) FindWindow(ID_VOTE);

    m_name = nameCtrl->GetValue();
    m_age = ageCtrl->GetValue();
    m_sex = sexCtrl->GetSelection();
    m_vote = voteCtrl->GetValue();

    return true;
}
```

However, there's an easier way of transferring data. wxWidgets supports *validators*, which are objects that link data variables and their corresponding

controls. Although not always applicable, the use of validators where possible
will save you a lot of time and can make it unnecessary to write `TransferData`
`ToWindow` and `TransferDataFromWindow` functions. In our `PersonalRecordDialog`
example, we can use the following code instead of the previous two functions:

```
FindWindow(ID_NAME)->SetValidator(
      wxTextValidator(wxFILTER_ALPHA, & m_name));
FindWindow(ID_AGE)->SetValidator(
      wxGenericValidator(& m_age));
FindWindow(ID_SEX)->SetValidator(
      wxGenericValidator(& m_sex);
FindWindow(ID_VOTE)->SetValidator(
      wxGenericValidator(& m_vote);
```

These few lines of code at the end of `CreateControls` replace the two overridden functions. As a bonus, the user will be prevented from accidentally entering
numbers in the *Name* field.

Validators can perform two jobs—as well as data transfer, they can
validate the data and show error messages if the data doesn't conform to a
particular specification. In this example, no actual validation of the input is
done, other than for the name. `wxGenericValidator` is a relatively simple class,
only doing data transfer. However, it works with the basic control classes. The
other validator provided as standard, `wxTextValidator`, has more sophisticated
behavior and can even intercept keystrokes to veto invalid characters. In the
example, we just use the standard style `wxFILTER_ALPHA`, but we could also
specify which characters should or should not be regarded as valid by using
the validator's `SetIncludes` and `SetExcludes` functions.

We need to dig a bit deeper into how wxWidgets handles validators in
order to understand what's going on here. As we've seen, the default `OnOK` handler calls `TransferDataFromWindow`, but before it does so, it calls `Validate`, vetoing the calls to `TransferDataFromWindow` and `EndModal` if validation fails. This is
the default implementation of `OnOK`:

```
void wxDialog::OnOK(wxCommandEvent& event)
{
    if ( Validate() && TransferDataFromWindow() )
    {
        if ( IsModal() )
            EndModal(wxID_OK); // If modal
        else
        {
            SetReturnCode(wxID_OK);
            this->Show(false); // If modeless
        }
    }
}
```

The default implementation of `Validate` iterates through all the children of
the dialog (and their descendants, if you specified the extra window style
`wxWS_EX_VALIDATE_RECURSIVELY`), calling `Validate` for each control's `wxValidator`

object. If any of these calls fails, then validation for the dialog fails, and the dialog is not dismissed. The validator is expected to show a suitable error message from within its `Validate` function if it fails the validation.

Similarly, `TransferDataToWindow` and `TransferDataFromWindow` will be called automatically for the validators of a dialog's controls. A validator must do data transfer, but validation is optional.

A validator is an event handler, and the event processing mechanism will route events to the validator, if present, before passing the events on to the control. This enables validators to intercept user input—for example, to veto characters that are not permitted in a control. Such vetoing should normally be accompanied by a beep to inform the user that the key was pressed but not accepted.

Because the two provided validator classes may not be sufficient for your needs, especially if you write your own custom controls, you can derive new validator classes from `wxValidator`. This class should have a copy constructor and a `Clone` function that returns a copy of the validator object, as well as implementations for data transfer and validation. A validator will typically store a pointer to a C++ variable, and the constructor may take flags to specify modes of use. You can look at the files `include/wx/valtext.h` and `src/common/valtext.cpp` in wxWidgets to see how a validator can be implemented; see also "Writing Your Own Controls" in Chapter 12, "Advanced Window Classes."

Handling Events

In this example, wxWidgets' default processing for *OK* and *Cancel* are sufficient without any extra coding on our part, as long as we use the standard `wxID_OK` and `wxID_CANCEL` identifiers for the controls. However, for non-trivial dialogs, you probably will have to intercept and handle events from controls. In our example, we have a *Reset* button, which can be clicked at any time to reset the dialog back to its default values. We add an `OnResetClick` event handler and a suitable entry in our event table. Implementing `OnResetClick` turns out to be very easy; first we reset the data variables by calling the `Init` function we added to centralize data member initialization. Then we call `TransferDataToWindow` to display that data.

```
BEGIN_EVENT_TABLE( PersonalRecordDialog, wxDialog )
    ...
    EVT_BUTTON( ID_RESET, PersonalRecordDialog::OnResetClick)
    ...
END_EVENT_TABLE()

void PersonalRecordDialog::OnResetClick( wxCommandEvent& event )
{
    Init();
    TransferDataToWindow();
}
```

Handling UI Updates

One of the challenges faced by the application developer is making sure that the user can't click on controls and menus that are not currently applicable. A sure sign of sloppy programming is the appearance of messages that say, "This option is not currently available." If an option isn't available, then it should not *look* available, and clicking on the control or menu should do nothing. As time-consuming as it can be, the programmer should update the elements of the interface to reflect the context at every instant.

In our example, we must disable the *Vote* check box when the user's age is less than 18 because in that case, the decision is not available to the user. Your first thought might be to add an event handler for the *Age* spin control and enable or disable the *Vote* check box according to the spin control's value. Although this may be fine for simple user interfaces, imagine what happens when many factors are influencing the availability of controls. Even worse, there are some cases where the approach doesn't work at all because you cannot be notified when the change occurs. An example of this situation is when you need to enable a *Paste* button or menu item when data becomes available on the clipboard. This event is outside your power to intercept because the data may become available from another program.

To solve these problems, wxWidgets provides an event class called wxUpdateUIEvent that it sends to all windows in idle time—that is, when the event loop has finished processing all other input. You can add EVT_UPDATE_UI event table entries to your dialog, one for each control whose state you need to maintain. Each UI update event handler evaluates the current state of the world and calls functions in the event object (not the control) to enable, disable, check, or uncheck the control. This technique puts the logic for updating each control in *one* place, calling the event handler even when no real event has been handled in the application. You can breathe a sigh of relief because you don't have to remember to update the user interface after any change that might happen to be relevant!

Here's our UI update handler for the Vote control. Note that we can't use the m_age variable because transfer from the controls to the variables doesn't happen until the user clicks *OK*.

```
BEGIN_EVENT_TABLE( PersonalRecordDialog, wxDialog )
    ...
    EVT_UPDATE_UI( ID_VOTE, PersonalRecordDialog::OnVoteUpdate )
    ...
END_EVENT_TABLE()

void PersonalRecordDialog::OnVoteUpdate( wxUpdateUIEvent& event )
{
    wxSpinCtrl* ageCtrl = (wxSpinCtrl*) FindWindow(ID_AGE);
    if (ageCtrl->GetValue() < 18)
    {
```

```
            event.Enable(false);
            event.Check(false);
    }
    else
            event.Enable(true);
}
```

Don't worry unduly about efficiency considerations; plenty of spare cycles are available for processing these handlers. However, if you have a very complex application and run into performance problems, see the wxUpdateUIEvent documentation for the functions SetMode and SetUpdateInterval that can be used to decrease the time wxWidgets spends processing these events.

Adding Help

There are at least three kinds of help you can provide for your dialog:

☞ Tooltips
☞ Context-sensitive help
☞ Online help

You can probably think of further techniques not explicitly supported by wxWidgets. We already have some descriptive text on the dialog described here. For a more complex dialog, you could create a wxHtmlWindow instead of a wxStaticText and load an HTML file containing further details. Alternatively, a small help button could be placed next to each control to show a description when clicked.

The three main types of help supported by wxWidgets are described in the following sections.

Tooltips

Tooltips are little windows that pop up when the pointer is hovering over a control, containing a short description of the control's purpose. You call SetToolTip to set the tooltip text for a control. Because this can get annoying for experienced users, you should provide an application setting to switch this off (that is, SetToolTip will not be called when dialogs are created and displayed).

Context-Sensitive Help

Context-sensitive help provides a short pop-up description similar to a tooltip. The user must first click on a special button and then on a control to get the help or press F1 to get help for the focused control (on Windows). On Windows, you can specify the extra window style wxDIALOG_EX_CONTEXTHELP to create the little question mark button on the dialog title. On other platforms, you can create a wxContextHelpButton on the dialog (usually next to the *OK* and *Cancel* buttons). In your application initialization, you should call

```
#include "wx/cshelp.h"

    wxHelpProvider::Set(new wxSimpleHelpProvider);
```

This tells wxWidgets how to provide the strings for context-sensitive help. You call SetHelpText to set the help text for a control. Here's a function to add context-sensitive help and tooltips to our dialog:

```
// Sets the help text for the dialog controls
void PersonalRecordDialog::SetDialogHelp()
{
    wxString nameHelp = wxT("Enter your full name.");
    wxString ageHelp = wxT("Specify your age.");
    wxString sexHelp = wxT("Specify your gender, male or female.");
    wxString voteHelp = wxT("Check this if you wish to vote.");

    FindWindow(ID_NAME)->SetHelpText(nameHelp);
    FindWindow(ID_NAME)->SetToolTip(nameHelp);

    FindWindow(ID_AGE)->SetHelpText(ageHelp);
    FindWindow(ID_AGE)->SetToolTip(ageHelp);

    FindWindow(ID_SEX)->SetHelpText(sexHelp);
    FindWindow(ID_SEX)->SetToolTip(sexHelp);

    FindWindow(ID_VOTE)->SetHelpText(voteHelp);
    FindWindow(ID_VOTE)->SetToolTip(voteHelp);
}
```

If you want to invoke context-sensitive help yourself, as opposed to letting the dialog or wxContextHelpButton handle it, you can simply put this in an event handler:

```
wxContextHelp contextHelp(window);
```

This will put wxWidgets in a loop that detects a left-click on a control, after which it will send a wxEVT_HELP event to the control to initiate popping up a help window.

You don't have to limit yourself to the way wxWidgets implements the storage and display of help text, though. You can create your own class derived from wxHelpProvider, overriding GetHelp, SetHelp, AddHelp, RemoveHelp, and ShowHelp.

Online Help

Most applications come with a help file that provides detailed instructions for use. wxWidgets provides the means to control several kinds of help windows through different derivations of the wxHelpControllerBase class. See Chapter 20, "Perfecting Your Application," for more information about providing online help.

For the purposes of this example, we'll just use a wxMessageBox to display some help when the user clicks on the *Help* button.

```
BEGIN_EVENT_TABLE( PersonalRecordDialog, wxDialog )
    ...
    EVT_BUTTON( wxID_HELP, PersonalRecordDialog::OnHelpClick )
    ...
END_EVENT_TABLE()

void PersonalRecordDialog::OnHelpClick( wxCommandEvent& event )
{
    // Normally we would wish to display proper online help.
    /*
    wxGetApp().GetHelpController().DisplaySection(wxT("Personal record
dialog"));
    */

    // For this example, we're just using a message box.
    wxString helpText =
      wxT("Please enter your full name, age and gender.\n")
      wxT("Also indicate your willingness to vote in general
elections.\n\n")
      wxT("No non-alphabetical characters are allowed in the name
field.\n")
      wxT("Try to be honest about your age.");

    wxMessageBox(helpText,
        wxT("Personal Record Dialog Help"),
        wxOK|wxICON_INFORMATION, this);
}
```

The Complete Class

The complete implementation of the dialog is listed in Appendix J, "Code Listings," and can also be found in examples/chap09 on the CD-ROM.

Invoking the Dialog

Now that we have the dialog completely coded, we can invoke it:

```
PersonalRecordDialog dialog(NULL, ID_PERSONAL_RECORD,
    wxT("Personal Record"));
dialog.SetName(wxEmptyString);
dialog.SetAge(30);
dialog.SetSex(0);
dialog.SetVote(true);
if (dialog.ShowModal() == wxID_OK)
{
    wxString name = dialog.GetName();
    int age = dialog.GetAge();
    bool sex = dialog.GetSex();
    bool vote = dialog.GetVote();
}
```

ADAPTING DIALOGS FOR SMALL DEVICES

wxWidgets can be used on mobile and other embedded devices, using GTK+, X11, and Windows CE ports (and others in the future). The most obvious limitation associated with many of these devices is the size of the display, which for a smartphone may be as little as 176×220 pixels.

Many dialogs will need an alternative dialog layout for small displays; some controls may be omitted altogether, especially as the functionality of the application may be reduced compared with a desktop application. You can detect the size of the device with wxSystemSettings::GetScreenType, for example:

```
#include "wx/settings.h"
bool isPda = (wxSystemSettings::GetScreenType() <= wxSYS_SCREEN_PDA);
```

GetScreenType returns one of the values listed in Table 9-1. Because the types increase in value as the screen size increases, you can use integer comparison operators to deal with classes of devices with screens below a certain size, as in the example we've just seen.

Table 9-1   Screen Types

wxSYS_SCREEN_NONE	Undefined screen type
wxSYS_SCREEN_TINY	Tiny screen, less than 320×240
wxSYS_SCREEN_PDA	PDA screen, 320×240 or more but less than 640×480
wxSYS_SCREEN_SMALL	Small screen, 640×480 or more but less than 800×600
wxSYS_SCREEN_DESKTOP	Desktop screen, 800×600 or more

If you need more detail about the display size, there are three ways to get it:

1. Use wxSystemSettings::GetMetric, passing wxSYS_SCREEN_X or wxSYS_SCREEN_Y.
2. Call wxGetDisplaySize, which returns a wxSize object.
3. Create a wxDisplay object and call GetGeometry, which returns a wxRect containing the bounding rectangle of the display.

When you know you may have a stunted display to run on, what can you do with this information? Here are some strategies you can use:

1. Replace the whole layout by loading a different XRC file or executing different control creation code. If the controls don't change type, you may not need to change the event handling code at all.
2. Reduce the number of controls and space.

3. Change the type of some controls to take less space (for example, from wxListBox to wxComboBox). This will need some modification of the associated event handler.

4. Change the orientation of one or several sizers. Some small devices have a lot more space in one direction than in another.

Occasionally you will need to use API enhancements for particular platforms. Microsoft Smartphone has two special buttons that you can assign labels, such as "OK" and "Cancel". On this platform, instead of creating two wxButton objects, you should call wxDialog::SetLeftMenu and wxDialog::SetRightMenu with an identifier, label, and optional submenu to show. Because these functions only exist on the Smartphone port, you need to conditionally compile your code. For example:

```
#ifdef __SMARTPHONE__
    SetLeftMenu(wxID_OK, wxT("OK"));
    SetRightMenu(wxID_OK, wxT("Cancel"));
#else
    wxBoxSizer* buttonSizer = new wxBoxSizer(wxHORIZONTAL);
    GetTopSizer()->Add(buttonSizer, 0, wxALL|wxGROW, 0);
    buttonSizer->Add(new wxButton(this, wxID_OK), 0, wxALL, 5);
    buttonSizer->Add(new wxButton(this, wxID_CANCEL), 0, wxALL, 5);
#endif
```

FURTHER CONSIDERATIONS IN DIALOG DESIGN

Here are a few tips to help you create professional-looking dialogs.

Keyboard Navigation

Provide mnemonics in static text labels and other labeled controls by inserting ampersands in front of characters. On some platforms (notably Windows and GTK+), this will help the user navigate between controls.

Always provide a means for the user to cancel the dialog, preferably with the option of using the Escape key. If a dialog has a button with the identifier wxID_CANCEL, its handler will automatically be called when the user presses the Escape key. So, if you have a Close button, consider giving it the wxID_CANCEL identifier.

Provide a default button (often *OK*)—for example, by calling wxButton::SetDefault. The command for this button will be invoked when the user presses the Enter key.

Data and UI Separation

To simplify the example, the data variables that `PersonalRecordDialog` uses are stored in the class itself. However, a better design would be to provide a data class separate from the dialog class, with a copy constructor and assignment operator, so that you can pass a copy of the data to the dialog and retrieve the modified data from the dialog only if the user confirms any changes. This is the approach adopted for some of the standard dialogs. As an exercise, you can rewrite the `PersonalRecordDialog` using a `PersonalRecordData` class. The dialog constructor will take a `PersonalRecordData` reference, and there will be a `GetData` function so that the calling application can retrieve the data.

In general, always consider how you can separate out the UI functionality from non-UI functionality. The result will usually be code that is more compact and easier to understand and debug. Don't be afraid to introduce new classes to make the design more elegant, and make use of copy constructors and assignment operators so that objects can easily be copied and assigned without the application having to repeat lots of low-level code.

Unless you provide an *Apply* button that commits your changes to the underlying data, canceling the dialog should leave the application data in the same state as it was before the dialog was opened. The use of a separate data class makes this easier to achieve because the dialog isn't editing "live" data but rather a copy.

Layout

If your dialog looks claustrophobic or somehow odd, it may be due to a lack of space. Try adding a bigger border around the edge of the dialog by using an additional sizer (as in our `PersonalRecordDialog` example) and adding space between groups of controls. Use `wxStaticBoxSizer` and `wxStaticLine` to logically group or separate controls. Use `wxGridSizer` and `wxFlexGridSizer` to align controls and their labels so that they don't appear as a random jumble. In sizer-based layouts, use expanding spacers to align a group of controls. For example, often *OK*, *Cancel,* and *Help* buttons are in a right-aligned group, which can be achieved by placing a spacer and the buttons in a horizontal `wxBoxSizer` and setting the spacer to expand horizontally (give it a positive stretch factor).

If possible and appropriate, make your dialog resizable. Traditionally, Windows dialog boxes haven't often been resizable, but there is no reason why this should be the case, and fiddling with tiny controls on a large display can be a frustrating experience for the user. wxWidgets makes it easy to create resizable dialogs with sizers, and you should be using sizers anyway to allow for font and control size differences and changes in language. Choose carefully which elements should grow; for example, there may be a multi-line text control that is a good candidate for growing and giving the user more elbow room. Again, you can put expanding spacers to good use to preserve alignment in a resized dialog. Note that we're not resizing controls in the sense of zooming in and out, making text bigger or smaller—we're simply giving more or less space for items in the control. See Chapter 7 for more about sizers.

If you find that your dialog is becoming too large, split it up into a number of panels and use a wxNotebook, wxListbook, or wxChoicebook to enable selection of one page at a time. Using lots of independent dialogs is annoying to the user and clutters up your menus, whereas browsing through pages is perfectly acceptable. Scrolling panels should be avoided unless there's a very good reason to use them. The ability to scroll controls is not supported on all platforms, and use of scrolling can be a sign that the user interface has not been adequately planned. If you have many properties to edit, consider using a property editor based on wxGrid or a third-party class (see wxPropertyGrid, which is mentioned in Appendix E, "Third-Party Tools for wxWidgets").

Aesthetics

Be consistent with label capitalization. Don't be tempted to use custom colors or fonts in your dialog; this can be distracting and can look out of place in the context of the current theme and other dialogs in the application. For best results across platforms, leave control fonts and colors to wxWidgets. Instead, consider providing some impact through judicious use of wxStaticBitmap controls.

Alternatives to Dialogs

Finally, consider whether you should be creating an independent dialog box at all—a modeless solution, such as a tab in the main application window, might be better. Most of the principles of dialog design and implementation apply to modeless dialogs and panels, but there are added challenges of layout (the window has less control of its size) and synchronization (the window may no longer have exclusive use of the data it is showing).

USING WXWIDGETS RESOURCE FILES

You can load specifications of dialogs, frames, menu bars, toolbars, and so on from XML files with extension xrc instead of creating these elements explicitly in C++ code. This enables better separation of code and user interface, such as enabling an application's dialog design to be changed at runtime. XRC files can be exported by a range of UI design tools, including wxDesigner, DialogBlocks, XRCed, and wxGlade.

Loading Resources

To use XRC files in your application, you need to include `wx/xrc/xmlres.h` in your application code.

If you will be converting your XRC files to binary XRS files, as we will describe shortly, install the zip file system handler by placing an `AddHandler` call in your `OnInit` function:

```
#include "wx/filesys.h"
#include "wx/fs_zip.h"

wxFileSystem::AddHandler(new wxZipFSHandler);
```

Initialize the XRC system by adding this to your `OnInit`:

```
wxXmlResource::Get()->InitAllHandlers();
```

Load the XRC file with code like this:

```
wxXmlResource::Get()->Load(wxT("resources.xrc"));
```

This makes wxWidgets aware of the resources in the file; to create a real UI element, we need another call. For example, the following fragment creates a dialog whose resource name is `dialog1`:

```
MyDialog dlg;
wxXmlResource::Get()->LoadDialog(& dlg, parent, wxT("dialog1"));
dlg.ShowModal();
```

The following code shows how to load menu bars, menus, toolbars, bitmaps, icons, and panels.

```
MyFrame::MyFrame(const wxString& title): wxFrame(NULL, -1, title)
{
    SetMenuBar(wxXmlResource::Get()->LoadMenuBar(wxT("mainmenu")));
    SetToolBar(wxXmlResource::Get()->LoadToolBar(this,
                                          wxT("toolbar")));

    wxMenu* menu = wxXmlResource::Get()->LoadMenu(wxT("popupmenu"));

    wxIcon icon = wxXmlResource::Get()->LoadIcon(wxT("appicon"));
    SetIcon(icon);

    wxBitmap bitmap = wxXmlResource::Get()->LoadBitmap(wxT("bmp1"));

    // Finish creating panelA after making an instance of it
```

```
        MyPanel* panelA = new MyPanel;
        panelA = wxXmlResource::Get()->LoadPanel(panelA, this,
                                                      wxT("panelA"));

        // A second method: get XRC to both create and load panelB
        wxPanel* panelB = wxXmlResource::Get()->LoadPanel(this,
                                                      wxT("panelB"));
}
```

wxWidgets maintains a single wxXmlResource object that you can use, but alternatively, you can create a wxXmlResource object, load resources, and then destroy it. You can also use wxXmlResource::Set to set the current global resource object, destroying the old one.

To define event tables for windows loaded from a resource file, you can't use integer identifiers because resources have string names. Instead, use the XRCID macro, which takes a resource name and returns an integer identifier associated with the name. XRCID is an alias for the function wxXmlResource::GetXRCID. Here's an example of XRCID usage:

```
BEGIN_EVENT_TABLE(MyFrame, wxFrame)
    EVT_MENU(XRCID("menu_quit"),  MyFrame::OnQuit)
    EVT_MENU(XRCID("menu_about"), MyFrame::OnAbout)
END_EVENT_TABLE()
```

Using Binary and Embedded Resource Files

It can be convenient to combine a number of resource files into one binary file (extension xrs). To compile XRC files into a zip file that the resource system can load, use the utility wxrc located in the utils/wxrc directory in your wxWidgets distribution:

```
wxrc resource1.xrc resource2.xrc -o resource.xrs
```

Use wxXmlResource::Load to load a binary resource file in just the same way as with a plain XML file.

Tip

Instead of creating a separate zip file for your XRC files, you can include them in a single zip file that includes other files your applications needs, such as HTML files, images, and so on. wxXmlResource::Load accepts virtual file system specifications, as described in Chapter 14, "Files and Streams," so you can write

```
wxXmlResource::Get()->Load(wxT("resources.bin#zip:dialogs.xrc"));
```

You can also compile your XRC files into C++ code that may be embedded in your application, thereby eliminating a separate resource file. Here's the wxrc command to do this:

```
wxrc resource1.xrc resource2.xrc -c -o resource.cpp
```

Compile this C++ file as normal and link it with your application. The file includes a function InitXmlResource, which you have to call, for example:

```
extern void InitXmlResource(); // defined in generated file

wxXmlResource::Get()->InitAllHandlers();
InitXmlResource();
```

Table 9-2 lists the command-line options and arguments that wxrc accepts.

Table 9-2   *wxrc* Commands

Short Command	Long Command	Description
-h	—help	Shows a help message.
-v	—verbose	Shows verbose logging information.
-c	—cpp-code	Writes C++ source rather than an XRS file.
-p	—python-code	Writes Python source rather than an XRS file.
-e	—extra-cpp-code	If used together with -c, generates a C++ header file containing class definitions for the windows defined by the XRC file.
-u	—uncompressed	Do not compress XML files (C++ only).
-g	—gettext	Outputs underscore-wrapped strings that poEdit or gettext can scan. Outputs to stdout, or a file if -o is used.
-n	—function <name>	Specifies a C++ initialization function name (use with -c).
-o <filename>	—output <filename>	Specifies the output file, such as resource.xrs or resource.cpp.
-l <filename>	—list-of-handlers <filename>	Outputs a list of resource handlers that are needed for the specified resources.

Translating Resources

If the wxXmlResource object has been created with the wxXRC_USE_LOCALE flag (the default behavior), all displayable strings will be subject to translation, as detailed in Chapter 16, "Writing International Applications." However, poEdit cannot scan XRC files for strings to translate as it can for C++ code, so you can create a file of such strings using wxrc with the -g option. For example:

```
wxrc -g resources.xrc -o resource_strings.cpp
```

Then you can run poEdit to scan the strings in this and other files.

The XRC Format

There isn't space to describe the XRC format in detail, but here is an example showing a simple dialog with sizers:

```xml
<?xml version="1.0"?>
<resource version="2.3.0.1">
<object class="wxDialog" name="simpledlg">
    <title>A simple dialog</title>
    <object class="wxBoxSizer">
      <orient>wxVERTICAL</orient>
      <object class="sizeritem">
        <object class="wxTextCtrl">
          <size>200,200d</size>
          <style>wxTE_MULTILINE|wxSUNKEN_BORDER</style>
          <value>Hello, this is an ordinary multiline\n
textctrl....</value>
        </object>
        <option>1</option>
        <flag>wxEXPAND|wxALL</flag>
        <border>10</border>
      </object>
      <object class="sizeritem">
        <object class="wxBoxSizer">
          <object class="sizeritem">
            <object class="wxButton" name="wxID_OK">
              <label>Ok</label>
              <default>1</default>
            </object>
          </object>
          <object class="sizeritem">
            <object class="wxButton" name="wxID_CANCEL">
              <label>Cancel</label>
            </object>
            <border>10</border>
            <flag>wxLEFT</flag>
          </object>
        </object>
        <flag>wxLEFT|wxRIGHT|wxBOTTOM|wxALIGN_RIGHT</flag>
```

```
        <border>10</border>
      </object>
    </object>
  </object>
</resource>
```

A detailed specification of the XRC format can be found in the technical note docs/tech/tn0014.txt in your wxWidgets distribution. If you use an editor to create your user interfaces, you won't need to know about XRC's format.

You may be wondering how a text XRC file can be used to specify binary bitmaps and icons. These resources may be specified as URLs, and wxWidgets' virtual file system will extract them from sources such as a zip file. For example:

```
<object class="wxBitmapButton" name="wxID_OK">
  <bitmap>resources.bin#zip:okimage.png</bitmap>
</object>
```

See Chapter 10, "Programming with Images," and Chapter 14, "Files and Streams," for more information on using virtual file systems to load resources such as images.

Writing Resource Handlers

The XRC system uses a *resource handler* to recognize the XML specification of each type of resource. If you write your own custom control, you may want to write a resource handler so that applications can use the custom control with XRC.

As an illustration, the declaration for wxButton's handler looks like this:

```
#include "wx/xrc/xmlres.h"

class wxButtonXmlHandler : public wxXmlResourceHandler
{
DECLARE_DYNAMIC_CLASS(wxButtonXmlHandler)
public:
    wxButtonXmlHandler();
    virtual wxObject *DoCreateResource();
    virtual bool CanHandle(wxXmlNode *node);
};
```

The handler implementation is quite simple. In the handler's constructor, the XRC_ADD_STYLE macro is used to make the handler aware of specific button styles, and AddWindowStyles is called to add common window styles. In DoCreateResource, the button object is created in two steps, using XRC_MAKE_INSTANCE and then Create, extracting parameters such as the label, position, and size. Finally, `CanHandle` tests whether this handler can handle the node in question. It's permissible for a single handler class to handle more than one kind of resource.

```
IMPLEMENT_DYNAMIC_CLASS(wxButtonXmlHandler, wxXmlResourceHandler)

wxButtonXmlHandler::wxButtonXmlHandler()
: wxXmlResourceHandler()
{
    XRC_ADD_STYLE(wxBU_LEFT);
    XRC_ADD_STYLE(wxBU_RIGHT);
    XRC_ADD_STYLE(wxBU_TOP);
    XRC_ADD_STYLE(wxBU_BOTTOM);
    XRC_ADD_STYLE(wxBU_EXACTFIT);
    AddWindowStyles();
}

wxObject *wxButtonXmlHandler::DoCreateResource()
{
    XRC_MAKE_INSTANCE(button, wxButton)

    button->Create(m_parentAsWindow,
                        GetID(),
                        GetText(wxT("label")),
                        GetPosition(), GetSize(),
                        GetStyle(),
                        wxDefaultValidator,
                        GetName());

    if (GetBool(wxT("default"), 0))
        button->SetDefault();
    SetupWindow(button);

    return button;
}

bool wxButtonXmlHandler::CanHandle(wxXmlNode *node)
{
    return IsOfClass(node, wxT("wxButton"));
}
```

To use a handler, an application needs to include the header and register the handler, as follows:

```
#include "wx/xrc/xh_bttn.h"
wxXmlResource::AddHandler(new wxBitmapXmlHandler);
```

Foreign Controls

An XRC file can specify a foreign, or "unknown" control, by specifying `class="unknown"` in the object definition. This can stand in for a control that is actually created in the C++ code, after the parent is loaded from XRC. When

XRC loads the unknown object, a placeholder window is created. Then the application calls `AttachUnknownControl` to superimpose the real window onto the placeholder window, with the correct position and size. For example:

```
wxDialog dlg;

// Load the dialog
wxXmlResource::Get()->LoadDialog(&dlg, this, wxT("mydialog"));

// Make an instance of our new custom class.
MyCtrl* myCtrl = new MyCtrl(&dlg, wxID_ANY);

// Attach it to the dialog
wxXmlResource::Get()->AttachUnknownControl(wxT("custctrl"), myCtrl);

// Show the dialog
dlg.ShowModal();
```

The custom control definition can look like this:

```
<object class="unknown" name="custctrl">
  <size>100,100</size>
</object>
```

Using this technique, you can lay out interfaces in tools that don't know about your custom controls, and you also avoid the need to write a resource handler.

SUMMARY

In this chapter, you have learned the fundamentals of custom dialog design and implementation, including a quick look at sizers, the use of validators, and the advantages of using UI update events. For examples of creating custom dialogs, see `samples/dialogs` in your wxWidgets distribution. Also see `samples/validate` for use of the generic and text validator classes. Next, we'll look at how to handle images.

CHAPTER 10

Programming with Images

This chapter shows what you can do with bitmapped images. Images are great for introducing "design values" into your application, and they can be used with controls such as toolbars, tree controls, notebooks, buttons, HTML windows, or in custom drawing code. Sometimes they can be used invisibly in an application, for example to achieve flicker-free drawing. In this chapter, we cover the different image classes and how to override standard icons and bitmaps used with wxWidgets.

IMAGE CLASSES IN WXWIDGETS

wxWidgets supports four kinds of bitmap images: wxBitmap, wxIcon, wxCursor, and wxImage.

wxBitmap represents a platform-dependent bitmap, with an optional wxMask to support drawing with transparency. On Windows, wxBitmap is implemented using device-independent bitmaps (DIBs). On GTK+ and X11, each wxBitmap contains the pixmap object of GDK and X11, respectively. On Mac, a PICT is used. A wxBitmap can be converted to and from a wxImage.

wxIcon represents the platform's concept of an icon, a small image with transparency that can be used for giving frames and dialogs a recognizable visual cue, among other things. On GTK+, X11, and Mac, an icon is simply a bitmap that always has a wxMask. On Windows, an icon is represented by an HICON object.

wxCursor represents the mouse pointer image; this is a GdkCursor on GTK+, a Cursor on X11, an HCURSOR in Windows, and a Cursor on Mac. It has the notion of a hotspot (the pixel in the cursor image that is considered to be the exact mouse pointer location) and a mask.

wxImage is the only class of the four with a platform-independent implementation, supporting 24-bit images with an optional alpha channel. A wxImage can be created from data or by using wxBitmap::ConvertToImage. A wxImage can be loaded from a file in a variety of formats, and it is extensible to new formats via image format handlers. Functions are available to set and get image bits, so it can be used for basic image manipulation. Unlike a wxBitmap, a wxImage cannot be drawn directly to a wxDC. Instead, a wxBitmap object must be created from the wxImage. This bitmap can then be drawn in a device context by using wxDC:: DrawBitmap. wxImage supports a mask color indicating transparent areas, and it also supports alpha channel data to allow for more sophisticated transparency effects.

You can convert between these bitmap objects, though there are platform dependencies on some conversion operations.

Note that all image classes are reference-counted, so assignment and copying are very cheap operations because the image data itself is not copied. However, you need to be aware that if you change an image, other image objects that refer to the same image data will also be changed.

All image classes use standard wxBitmapType identifiers for loading and saving bitmap data, as described in Table 10-1.

Table 10-1   Bitmap Types

wxBITMAP_TYPE_BMP	A Windows bitmap file (BMP).
wxBITMAP_TYPE_BMP_RESOURCE	A Windows bitmap to be loaded from the resource part of the executable.
wxBITMAP_TYPE_ICO	A Windows icon file (ICO).
wxBITMAP_TYPE_ICO_RESOURCE	A Windows icon to be loaded from the resource part of the executable.
wxBITMAP_TYPE_CUR	A Windows cursor (CUR).
wxBITMAP_TYPE_CUR_RESOURCE	A Windows cursor to be loaded from the resource part of the executable.
wxBITMAP_TYPE_XBM	An XBM monochrome bitmap file, used on Unix.
wxBITMAP_TYPE_XBM_DATA	An XBM monochrome bitmap, to be constructed from C++ data.
wxBITMAP_TYPE_XPM	An XPM color bitmap file, a good cross-platform format for small images that can be compiled into the application.
wxBITMAP_TYPE_XPM_DATA	An XPM color bitmap, to be constructed from C++ data.
wxBITMAP_TYPE_TIF	A TIFF bitmap file, popular for large images.
wxBITMAP_TYPE_GIF	A GIF bitmap file, with a maximum 256 colors and optional transparency information.
wxBITMAP_TYPE_PNG	A PNG bitmap file, a popular file format with optional transparency and alpha channel, and free of patent problems.
wxBITMAP_TYPE_JPEG	A JPEG bitmap file, a popular compressed format for large images, but it uses lossy compression, so it's not suitable for multiple saving/loading cycles.
wxBITMAP_TYPE_PCX	PCX bitmap file.
wxBITMAP_TYPE_PICT	Mac PICT bitmap file.

wxBITMAP_TYPE_PICT_RESOURCE	Mac PICT bitmap file to be loaded from the resource part of the executable.
wxBITMAP_TYPE_ICON_RESOURCE	On Mac OS X only, loads a standard icon (such as wxICON_INFORMATION) or an icon resource.
wxBITMAP_TYPE_ANI	Windows animated icon file (ANI).
wxBITMAP_TYPE_IFF	IFF bitmap file.
wxBITMAP_TYPE_MACCURSOR	Mac cursor file.
wxBITMAP_TYPE_MACCURSOR_RESOURCE	Mac cursor, to be loaded from the resource part of the executable.
wxBITMAP_TYPE_ANY	Tells the image loading code to figure out the type itself.

PROGRAMMING WITH *WXBITMAP*

These are some of the things you can do with a wxBitmap:

☞ Draw it on a window via a device context.

☞ Use it as a bitmap label for classes such as wxBitmapButton, wxStaticBitmap, and wxToolBar.

☞ Use it to implement double buffering (drawing into an off-screen wxMemoryDC before drawing to a window).

On some platforms (in particular, Windows), the bitmap is a limited resource, so if you have many images to store in memory, you may prefer to work mainly with wxImage objects and convert to a temporary wxBitmap when drawing on a device context.

Before discussing how to create wxBitmap and draw with it, let's summarize the main functions (Table 10-2).

Table 10-2   wxBitmap Functions

wxBitmap	A bitmap can be created given a width and height, another bitmap, a wxImage, XPM data (char**), raw data (char[]), or a file name and type.
ConvertToImage	Converts to a wxImage, preserving transparency.
CopyFromIcon	Creates the bitmap from a wxIcon.
Create	Creates the bitmap from data or a given size.
GetWidth, GetHeight	Returns the bitmap's size.
GetDepth	Returns the bitmap's color depth.
GetMask, SetMask	Returns the wxMask object or NULL.
GetSubBitmap	Returns an area of the bitmap as a new bitmap.
LoadFile, SaveFile	Files can be loaded and (for some formats) saved.
Ok	Returns true if the bitmap's data is present.

Creating a *wxBitmap*

There are several ways to create a wxBitmap object.

You can create the object in an uninitialized state (no bitmap data) by using the default constructor. You will need to call Create or LoadFile or assign another bitmap to it to do anything useful with the object.

You can create a wxBitmap with a given size and depth. The bitmap will be filled with random data, so for this object to be useful, you will need to draw on it. The following code creates a 200×100 pixel bitmap and gives it a white background.

```
// Create a 200x100 bitmap with the current display depth
wxBitmap bitmap(200, 100,  -1);

// Create a memory device context
wxMemoryDC dc;

// Select the bitmap into the DC
dc.SelectObject(bitmap);

// Set the background
dc.SetBackground(*wxWHITE_BRUSH);

// Color the bitmap white
dc.Clear();

// Select the bitmap out of the DC
dc.SelectObject(wxNullBitmap);
```

You can create a bitmap from an image object, preserving any mask or alpha channel in the original image:

```
// Load an image
wxImage image(wxT("image.png"), wxBITMAP_TYPE_PNG);

// Convert it to a bitmap
wxBitmap bitmap(image);
```

A bitmap can also be constructed from an icon by using CopyFromIcon:

```
// Load an icon
wxIcon icon(wxT("image.xpm"), wxBITMAP_TYPE_XPM);

// Convert it to a bitmap
wxBitmap bitmap;
bitmap.CopyFromIcon(icon);
```

Or you can load a bitmap from a file:

```
// Load from a file
wxBitmap bitmap(wxT("picture.png", wxBITMAP_TYPE_PNG);
if (!bitmap.Ok())
{
    wxMessageBox(wxT("Sorry, could not load file."));
}
```

wxBitmap can load all the file types that wxImage can (see Table 10-7), by using either wxImage or a more efficient platform-specific implementation for certain file types. Some of the most popular formats are PNG, JPEG, TIFF, BMP, and XPM, which are available on all platforms for both loading and saving, assuming that wxWidgets support for these formats has been enabled.

On Mac OS X, a PICT resource can also be loaded by specifying wxBITMAP_TYPE_PICT_RESOURCE.

If you want to load a bitmap from a platform-dependent source, you can use the wxBITMAP macro. For example:

```
#if !defined(__WXMSW__) && !defined(__WXPM__)
#include "picture.xpm"
#endif

wxBitmap bitmap(wxBITMAP(picture));
```

This will load the resource named picture from the executable on Windows and OS/2, and on all other platforms, it will load an XPM from the picture_xpm variable. However, the XPM format is supported on all platforms, so use of this macro is not usually necessary.

Setting a *wxMask*

Each wxBitmap object can contain a wxMask, a monochrome bitmap that indicates the transparent areas of the main bitmap. This will be created automatically when you load a transparent image, for example using XPM, PNG, or GIF, but you can also create it programmatically and assign it to a bitmap with SetMask. You can create a wxMask object from a wxBitmap, or a wxBitmap plus a color to indicate the transparent area.

The following example creates a monochrome transparent image called mainBitmap, 32 pixels wide by 32 pixels high, from bitmap data (imageBits) and a mask (maskBits) where 1 is black and 0 is white for the bits, and 1 is opaque and 0 is transparent for the mask.

```
static char imageBits[] = { 255, 255, 255, 255, 31,
    255, 255, 255, 31, 255, 255, 255, 31, 255, 255, 255,
    31, 255, 255, 255, 31, 255, 255, 255, 31, 255, 255,
    255, 31, 255, 255, 255, 31, 255, 255, 255, 25, 243,
```

```
    255, 255, 19, 249, 255, 255, 7, 252, 255, 255, 15, 254,
    255, 255, 31, 255, 255, 255, 191, 255, 255, 255, 255,
    255, 255, 255, 255, 255, 255, 255, 255, 255, 255, 255,
    255, 255, 255, 255, 255, 255, 255, 255, 255, 255, 255,
    255, 255, 255, 255, 255, 255, 255, 255, 255, 255, 255,
    255, 255, 255, 255, 255, 255, 255, 255, 255, 255, 255,
    255, 255, 255, 255, 255, 255, 255, 255, 255, 255, 255,
    255, 255, 255, 255, 255, 255, 255, 255, 255, 255,
    255 };

static char maskBits[] = { 240, 1, 0, 0, 240, 1,
    0, 0, 240, 1, 0, 0, 240, 1, 0, 0, 240, 1,
    0, 0, 240, 1, 0, 0, 240, 1, 0, 0, 255, 31, 0, 0, 255,
    31, 0, 0, 254, 15, 0, 0, 252, 7, 0, 0, 248, 3, 0, 0,
    240, 1, 0, 0, 224, 0, 0, 0, 64, 0, 0, 0, 0, 0, 0, 0, 0,
    0, 0, 0, 0, 0, 0, 0, 0, 0, 0, 0, 0, 0, 0, 0, 0, 0, 0, 0,
    0, 0, 0, 0, 0, 0, 0, 0, 0, 0, 0, 0, 0, 0, 0, 0, 0, 0, 0,
    0, 0, 0, 0, 0, 0, 0, 0, 0, 0, 0, 0, 0, 0, 0, 0, 0, 0, 0,
    0, 0, 0, 0, 0 };

wxBitmap mainBitmap(imageBits, 32, 32);
wxBitmap maskBitmap(maskBits, 32, 32);
mainBitmap.SetMask(new wxMask(maskBitmap));
```

The XPM Format

Where small bitmaps with transparency are needed, for example as toolbar
buttons or bitmaps in notebooks and tree controls, wxWidgets programmers
often use XPM. One advantage of this format is that it uses C/C++ syntax, and
it can either be loaded dynamically or compiled into your program. Here's an
example.

```
// You can also use #include "open.xpm"

static char *open_xpm[] = {
/* columns rows colors chars-per-pixel */
"16 15 5 1",
"   c None",
".  c Black",
"X c Yellow",
"o c Gray100",
"O c #bfbf00",
/* pixels */
"                ",
"          ...   ",
"        .   . .  ",
"             .. ",
"  ...        ... ",
" .XoX.......    ",
" .oXoXoXoXo.    ",
" .XoXoXoXoX.    ",
" .oXoX..........",
```

```
"  .XoX.000000000.  ",
"  .oo.000000000.  ",
"  .X.000000000.   ",
"  ..000000000.    ",
"  ..........      "
"                  "
};

wxBitmap bitmap(open_xpm);
```

As you can see, XPMs are encoded using character data. Before the image data, there is a palette section that maps each character to its color, either as an identifier or as a hash-prefixed six-digit hexadecimal string. Using the identifier None causes this character to represent the transparent area in the bitmap. Although XPM support is uncommon among Windows image manipulation programs, you can create images as PNGs and convert to XPM using a tool such as ImageBlocks (bundled with DialogBlocks), or you can simply write your own converter using wxWidgets.

Drawing with Bitmaps

You can draw with a bitmap in a couple different ways. You can associate it with a memory device context (wxMemoryDC) and then use wxDC::Blit to transfer the contents of the bitmap to another device context. Or, you can use the simpler wxDC::DrawBitmap. In either case, if the bitmap is transparent or has an alpha channel, you can specify transparent drawing by passing true to the function.

The two methods are illustrated in the following.

```
// Draw a bitmap using a wxMemoryDC
wxMemoryDC memDC;
memDC.SelectObject(bitmap);

// Draw the bitmap at 100, 100 on the destination DC
destDC.Blit(100, 100,                                    // Draw at (100, 100)
    bitmap.GetWidth(), bitmap.GetHeight(),               // Draw full bitmap
    & memDC,                                             // Draw from memDC
    0, 0,                                                // Draw from bitmap origin
    wxCOPY,                                              // Logical operation
    true);                                               // Take mask into account
memDC.SelectObject(wxNullBitmap);

// Alternative method: use DrawBitmap
destDC.DrawBitmap(bitmap, 100, 100, true);
```

Chapter 5, "Drawing and Printing," discusses drawing with bitmaps in more detail.

Packaging Bitmap Resources

If you come from a Windows programming background, you are accustomed to loading bitmaps from the resource section of the executable. You can still do this by passing a resource name and the wxBITMAP_TYPE_BMP_RESOURCE type to the constructor, but you are likely to want a less platform-specific method.

A portable way to package resources, whether they are bitmaps, HTML files, or other files required by an application, is to store them in a single zip file alongside the executable or in a separate data folder. Then you can use the virtual file system functionality in wxWidgets to load the image directly from the zip file, as the following fragment shows.

```
// Create a new file system object
wxFileSystem*fileSystem = new wxFileSystem;

wxString archiveURL(wxT("myapp.bin"));
wxString filename(wxT("myimage.png"));
wxBitmapType bitmapType = wxBITMAP_TYPE_PNG;

// Create a URL
wxString combinedURL(archiveURL + wxString(wxT("#zip:")) + filename);
wxImage image;
wxBitmap bitmap;

// Open the file in the archive
wxFSFile* file = fileSystem->OpenFile(combinedURL);
if (file)
{
    wxInputStream* stream = file->GetStream();

    // Load and convert to a bitmap
    if (image.LoadFile(* stream, bitmapType))
        bitmap = wxBitmap(image);

    delete file;
}
delete fileSystem;

if (bitmap.Ok())
{
    ...
}
```

For more information about virtual file systems, please see Chapter 14, "Files and Streams."

PROGRAMMING WITH *wxIcon*

A wxIcon is a small bitmap that always has a mask. Its uses include

☞ Setting the icon for a frame or dialog

☞ Adding icons to a `wxTreeCtrl`, `wxListCtrl`, or `wxNotebook` via the `wxImageList` class (see more information later in this chapter)

☞ Drawing an icon on a device context with `wxDC::DrawIcon`

Table 10-3 summarizes the major icon functions.

Table 10-3   `wxIcon` Functions

`wxIcon`	An icon can be created given another icon, XPM data (`char**`), raw data (`char[]`), or a file name and type.
`CopyFromBitmap`	Creates the icon from a `wxBitmap`.
`GetWidth`, `GetHeight`	Returns the icon's size.
`GetDepth`	Returns the icon's depth.
`LoadFile`	Files can be loaded.
`Ok`	Returns `true` if the icon's data is present.

Creating a *wxIcon*

A `wxIcon` object can be created from XPM data included in the application, from a `wxBitmap` object, from raw data, or by loading the icon from a file, such as a transparent XPM file. wxWidgets provides the `wxICON` macro, which is similar to the `wxBITMAP` macro described earlier; the icon is loaded either from a platform-specific resource or from XPM data.

On Windows, `LoadFile` and the equivalent constructor will work for Windows bitmap (BMP) and icon (ICO) resources and files. If you want to load other formats, load the file into a `wxBitmap` and convert it to an icon.

On Mac OS X and Unix/Linux with GTK+, `wxIcon` has the same file loading capabilities as `wxBitmap`.

The following code fragment shows four different ways to create a `wxIcon` object.

```
// Method 1: load from XPM data
#include "icon1.xpm"
wxIcon icon1(icon1_xpm);

// Method 2: load from an ICO resource (Windows and OS/2 only)
wxIcon icon2(wxT("icon2"));

// Method 3: load from an ICO file (Windows and OS/2 only)
// You can specify the desired width since an icon may
// contain multiple images.
wxIcon icon3(wxT("icon3.ico"), wxBITMAP_TYPE_ICO, 16, 16);

// Method 4: create from a bitmap
wxIcon icon4;
wxBitmap bitmap(wxT("icon4.png"), wxBITMAP_TYPE_PNG);
icon4.CopyFromBitmap(bitmap);
```

Using *wxIcon*

The following code shows three different ways to use wxIcon: setting a frame icon, adding an icon to an image list, and drawing an icon on a device context.

```
#include "myicon.xpm"
wxIcon icon(myicon_xpm);

// 1: Set a frame icon
frame->SetIcon(icon);

// 2: Add an icon to a wxImageList
wxImageList* imageList = new wxImageList(16, 16);
imageList->Add(icon);

// 3: Draw the icon at (10, 10)
wxClientDC dc(window);
dc.DrawIcon(icon, 10, 10);
```

Associating an Icon with an Application

Associating an icon with an application (so the operating system can present a clickable graphic to the user) cannot be done from within the wxWidgets toolkit, and this is one of the few areas where you need to use a different technique for each platform.

On Windows, you need to add a resource script (extension .rc) to your makefile or project file and add an ICON statement to the .rc file—for example:

```
aardvarkpro ICON aardvarkpro.ico
#include "wx/msw/wx.rc"
```

Here, aardvarkpro.ico is the name of a Windows icon file with multiple resolutions and depths (typically at 48×48, 32×32 and 16×16 resolutions). When showing the icon in Windows Explorer, Windows looks alphabetically for the first resource, so you may want to prepend a few *a*'s to your chosen resource, just to make sure it'll be found first; otherwise, you'll see an unexpected icon on the desktop or in a folder.

On the Mac, you need to prepare an application bundle containing some ICNS files. See the installation section in Chapter 20, "Perfecting Your Application," for more on bundles; the relevant sections of a bundle's Info.plist file might look like this:

```
        <key>CFBundleDocumentTypes</key>
        <array>
              <dict>
                    <key>CFBundleTypeExtensions</key>
                    <array>
```

```
                    <string>pjd</string>
                </array>
                <key>CFBundleTypeIconFile</key>
                <string>dialogblocks-doc.icns</string>
                <key>CFBundleTypeName</key>
                <string>pjdfile</string>
                <key>CFBundleTypeRole</key>
                <string>Editor</string>
            </dict>
        </array>
        <key>CFBundleIconFile</key>
        <string>dialogblocks-app.icns</string>
    ...
```

The icons for the application and its document types are specified with the
CFBundleIconFile and CFBundleTypeIconFile properties. You can create ICNS
files with the icon editor that Apple provides. If you predominantly work on
another platform, you might want to create a number of different icons in
16×16, 32×32, 48×48, and 128×128 resolutions, save them as PNGs, copy them
to the Mac, and then open each file and copy and paste its contents into the
appropriate icon editor location. Make sure that each PNG file has a mask that
the editor can use to construct the icon.

On Linux, the GNOME and KDE environments have their own methods
for providing an icon to use with the application, described briefly in Chapter 20.

PROGRAMMING WITH *WXCURSOR*

A cursor is used to give feedback on the mouse pointer position. You can
change the cursor for a given window—using different cursors gives a cue to
the user to expect specific mouse behavior. Like icons, cursors are small, transparent images that can be created using platform-specific as well as generic
constructors. Some of these constructors take a hotspot position relative to the
top-left corner of the cursor image, with which you specify the location of the
actual pointer "tip."

Table 10-4 shows the cursor functions.

Table 10-4   wxCursor Functions

wxCursor	A cursor can be created from a wxImage, raw data (char[]), a stock cursor identifier, or a file name and type.
Ok	Returns true if the cursor's data is present.

Creating a *wxCursor*

The easiest way to create a cursor is to pass a stock cursor identifier to the cursor constructor, as the following example shows.

```
// Create a cursor from a stock identifier
wxCursor cursor(wxCURSOR_WAIT);
```

Table 10-5 lists the available identifiers and their appearances (subject to some variation between platforms).

You can also use the predefined cursor pointers wxSTANDARD_CURSOR, wxHOURGLASS_CURSOR, and wxCROSS_CURSOR.

Table 10-5   Stock Cursor Identifiers

wxCURSOR_ARROW	▷	Standard arrow cursor.
wxCURSOR_RIGHT_ARROW	◁	Standard arrow cursor pointing to the right.
wxCURSOR_BLANK		Transparent cursor.
wxCURSOR_BULLSEYE	⊙	Bullseye cursor.
wxCURSOR_CROSS	+	Cross cursor.
wxCURSOR_HAND	☝	Hand cursor.
wxCURSOR_IBEAM	I	I-beam cursor (vertical line).
wxCURSOR_LEFT_BUTTON	▣	Represents a mouse with the left button depressed (GTK+ only).
wxCURSOR_MAGNIFIER	⚲	Magnifier cursor.
wxCURSOR_MIDDLE_BUTTON	▣	Represents a mouse with the middle button depressed (GTK+ only).
wxCURSOR_NO_ENTRY	⊘	No-entry sign cursor.
wxCURSOR_PAINT_BRUSH	⛏	Paintbrush cursor.
wxCURSOR_PENCIL	✎	Pencil cursor.
wxCURSOR_POINT_LEFT	☜	A cursor that points left.

wxCURSOR_POINT_RIGHT	☞	A cursor that points right.
wxCURSOR_QUESTION_ARROW	▷?	An arrow and question mark.
wxCURSOR_RIGHT_BUTTON	▥	Represents a mouse with the right button depressed (GTK+ only).
wxCURSOR_SIZENESW	↗	Sizing cursor pointing NE-SW.
wxCURSOR_SIZENS	↕	Sizing cursor pointing N-S.
wxCURSOR_SIZENWSE	↖	Sizing cursor pointing NW-SE.
wxCURSOR_SIZEWE	↔	Sizing cursor pointing W-E.
wxCURSOR_SIZING	✛	General sizing cursor.
wxCURSOR_SPRAYCAN	⛏	Spraycan cursor.
wxCURSOR_WAIT	⧗	Wait cursor.
wxCURSOR_WATCH	◔	Watch cursor.
wxCURSOR_ARROWWAIT	▷⧗	Cursor with both an arrow and an hourglass.

wxCursor can load a Windows cursor resource on Windows or a Mac OS X cursor resource on Mac OS X:

```
// Cursor from a Windows resource
wxCursor cursor(wxT("cursor_resource"), wxBITMAP_TYPE_CUR_RESOURCE,
                hotSpotX, hotSpotY);
```

```
// Cursor from a Mac OS cursor resource
wxCursor cursor(wxT("cursor_resource"), wxBITMAP_TYPE_MACCUR_RESOURCE);
```

You can create a custom cursor by specifying a wxImage object. The "hotspot" position needs to be specified using wxImage::SetOptionInt because the actual mouse pointer position may not correspond to the top-left corner of the cursor image. For example, a cross-hair cursor would have the hotspot in the center of the image. Here's some code that loads a PNG image and makes a cursor out of it:

```
// Create a cursor from a wxImage
wxImage image(wxT("cursor.png"), wxBITMAP_TYPE_PNG);
image.SetOptionInt(wxIMAGE_OPTION_CUR_HOTSPOT_X, 5);
image.SetOptionInt(wxIMAGE_OPTION_CUR_HOTSPOT_Y, 5);
wxCursor cursor(image);
```

Using *wxCursor*

Each window can have an associated cursor, which will be shown when the mouse pointer moves into the window. If there is no associated cursor, the cursor for an ancestor window will be shown, and if there is no ancestor with a cursor set, the standard cursor will be shown.

Set the cursor for a window like this:

```
window->SetCursor(wxCursor(wxCURSOR_WAIT));
```

Using *wxSetCursorEvent*

On Windows and Mac OS X, there is a little wrinkle that you may need to be aware of, particularly if you implement your own container windows. Say you implement your own splitter window that arranges its children such that only a small part of the splitter window is visible; this is used as the draggable divider or "sash." You then set an appropriate cursor for the splitter (say, wxCURSOR_WE) so the sash indicates that it can be dragged. If the children of the splitter window don't have cursors specified, they may inappropriately show the parent's cursor that is intended only for the sash.

To indicate that the cursor should only be used when the mouse pointer is over the sash and that no cursor should be set otherwise, you need to define an event handler for wxSetCursorEvent. This event is generated on Windows and Mac OS X when the cursor should be set (normally as the mouse pointer moves over the window). Your event handler should call wxSetCursorEvent::SetCursor if you want to indicate a particular cursor for this window, as follows:

```
BEGIN_EVENT_TABLE(wxSplitterWindow, wxWindow)
    EVT_SET_CURSOR(wxSplitterWindow::OnSetCursor)
END_EVENT_TABLE()

// Indicate that the cursor should only be set for the sash
void wxSplitterWindow::OnSetCursor(wxSetCursorEvent& event)
{
    // If we don't do this, the resizing cursor might be set for
```

```
    // child windows. Here, we explicitly say that our cursor
    // should not be used for child windows that overlap us.

    if ( SashHitTest(event.GetX(), event.GetY(), 0) )
    {
        // Use default processing
        event.Skip();
    }
    //else: Do nothing, in particular, don't call Skip()
}
```

In this example, if the mouse pointer is over the sash, SashHitTest returns true, and Skip is called, which makes the event handler "fail." This is equivalent to defining no cursor event handler at all, and it causes wxWidgets to display the window's cursor (wxCURSOR_WE) as normal. If SashHitTest returns false, however, it means the cursor is over a child window, and the cursor for the splitter window should *not* be used. Allowing the handler to "succeed" (by not calling Skip) without setting a cursor indicates to wxWidgets that we should treat the splitter window as having no cursor. As a result, the child window will correctly *not* inherit the parent's cursor, even if it has no known cursor of its own. (If the child window is a wxTextCtrl, for example, the native implementation will provide its own cursor, but wxWidgets has no knowledge of it.)

PROGRAMMING WITH *WXIMAGE*

Use wxImage when you need to manipulate images in a platform-independent manner, or as an intermediate step for loading or saving image files. Images are stored using a byte per pixel for each of the red, green, and blue channels, plus a further byte per pixel if an alpha channel is present.

The major wxImage functions are listed in Table 10-6.

Table 10-6   wxImage Functions

wxImage	An image can be created given a width and height, another image, XPM data, raw data (char[]) and optional alpha data, a file name and type, or an input stream.
ConvertAlphaToMask	Converts the alpha channel (if any) to a mask.
ConvertToMono	Converts to a new monochrome image.
Copy	Returns an identical copy without using reference counting.
Create	Creates an image of a given size, optionally initializing it from data.
Destroy	Destroys the internal data if no other object is using it.
GetData, SetData	Gets and sets its pointer to internal data (unsigned char*).

(continues)

Table 10-6   wxImage Functions (*Continued*)

GetImageCount	Returns the number of images in a file or stream.
GetOption, GetOptionInt, SetOption, HasOption	Gets, sets, and tests for the presence of options.
GetSubImage	Returns an area of the image as a new image.
GetWidth, GetHeight	Returns the image size.
GetRed, GetGreen, GetBlue, SetRGB, GetAlpha, SetAlpha	Gets and sets the red, blue, green, and alpha value for a pixel.
HasMask, GetMaskRed, GetMaskGreen, GetMaskBlue, SetMaskColour	Functions for testing for the presence of a mask and setting and getting the mask color.
LoadFile, SaveFile	Files can be loaded and saved using various formats.
Mirror	Mirrors the image in either orientation, returning a new image.
Ok	Returns true if the image is initialized.
Paste	Pastes an image into this image at a given position.
Rotate, Rotate90	Rotates the image, returning a new image.
SetMaskFromImage	Sets a mask, specifying an image and color to use for the transparent area.
Scale, Rescale	Scales to a new image or scales in place.

Loading and Saving Images

wxImage can load and save in a variety of formats, using image handlers that plug into wxImage and provide extensibility. The wxImage file-handling capabilities are used as a fallback for the other bitmap classes for when they don't provide appropriate native implementations.

Table 10-7 shows the image handlers available on all platforms supported by wxWidgets. wxBMPHandler is always installed by default. To use other image formats, install the appropriate handler with wxImage::AddHandler or wxInitAllImageHandlers.

Table 10-7   Available Image Handlers

wxBMPHandler	For loading and saving Windows bitmap files.
wxPNGHandler	For loading and saving PNG files. Images with transparency or an alpha channel are supported.
wxJPEGHandler	For loading and saving JPEG files.
wxGIFHandler	GIF files: only for loading, due to legal issues.
wxPCXHandler	For loading and saving PCX files. wxPCXHandler will count the number of different colors in the image; if there are 256 or fewer colors, it will save as 8-bit; otherwise it will save as 24-bit.

wxPNMHandler	For loading and saving PNM files. Loading PNMs only works for ASCII or raw RGB images. When saving in PNM format, wxPNMHandler will always save as raw RGB.
wxTIFFHandler	For loading and saving TIFF files.
wxIFFHandler	For loading IFF files.
wxXPMHandler	For loading and saving XPM files.
wxICOHandler	For loading and saving Windows icon files.
wxCURHandler	For loading and saving Windows cursor files.
wxANIHandler	For loading Windows animated cursor files.

If you will be using a specific set of formats, you might typically have these in your wxApp::OnInit function:

```
#include "wx/image.h"

wxImage::AddHandler( new wxPNGHandler );
wxImage::AddHandler( new wxJPEGHandler );
wxImage::AddHandler( new wxGIFHandler );
wxImage::AddHandler( new wxXPMHandler );
```

Alternatively, you can just call:

```
wxInitAllImageHandlers();
```

Here are some different ways of loading and saving images from files and streams. Note that when loading files, you should normally use absolute paths instead of depending on the setting of the current directory.

```
// Load image using constructor and specific type
wxImage image(wxT("image.png"), wxBITMAP_TYPE_PNG);
if (image.Ok())
{
    ...
}

// Leave wxImage to work out the image type
wxImage image(wxT("image.png"));

// Two-step loading
wxImage image;
if (image.LoadFile(wxT("image.png")))
{
    ...
}

// Two-step loading with an index into a multi-image file:
// load image number 2 if available
wxImage image;
int imageCount = wxImage::GetImageCount(wxT("image.tif"));
if (imageCount > 2)
    image.LoadFile(wxT("image.tif"), wxBITMAP_TYPE_TIFF, 2);
```

```
// Load from a stream
wxFileInputStream stream(wxT("image.tif"));
wxImage image;
image.LoadFile(stream, wxBITMAP_TYPE_TIF);

// Save to a file
image.SaveFile(wxT("image.png")), wxBITMAP_TYPE_PNG);

// Save to a stream
wxFileOutputStream stream(wxT("image.tif"));
image.SaveFile(stream, wxBITMAP_TYPE_TIF);
```

Images will be saved as 24-bit files, with the exception of XPM and PCX formats, whose handlers will count the number of colors and save with the appropriate depth. JPEG has a quality setting that you can set before saving the file. The setting is a number between 0 and 100, where 0 is poor quality and high compression, and 100 is high quality and poor compression.

```
// Save with reasonable quality and compression
image.SetOption(wxIMAGE_OPTION_QUALITY, 80);
image.SaveFile(wxT("picture.jpg"), wxBITMAP_TYPE_JPEG);
```

You also might want to use wxImage::SetOption when saving an XPM to a stream—because no file name is passed, the handler won't know what name to use for the C variable that is part of the XPM data. For example:

```
// Save XPM to a stream
image.SetOption(wxIMAGE_OPTION_FILENAME, wxT("myimage"));
image.SaveFile(stream, wxBITMAP_TYPE_XPM);
```

Note that it will append _xpm to the file name that you specify.

Transparency

There are two ways of using transparency with wxImage: masks and alpha channels. One color value of the image may be used as a mask color, which will lead to the automatic creation of a wxMask object when converted to a wxBitmap.

wxImage also supports alpha channel data. In addition to a byte for the red, green, and blue color components for each pixel, it also stores a byte representing the pixel opacity. The alpha value of 0 corresponds to a transparent pixel (zero opacity), and the value of 255 means that the pixel is 100% opaque.

Not all images have an alpha channel, and before using GetAlpha, you should determine whether this image contains alpha values with HasAlpha. Currently, only images loaded from PNG files or assigned an alpha channel with SetAlpha can have an alpha channel. Saving images with an alpha channel is not yet supported. Drawing with the alpha channel is supported by converting the image to a wxBitmap and calling wxDC::DrawBitmap or wxDC::Blit.

The following code shows how to create a wxImage with a mask. The image will be blue, containing a transparent rectangle.

```
// Create masked image
// First, draw on a wxBitmap
wxBitmap bitmap(400, 400);
wxMemoryDC dc;
dc.SelectObject(bitmap);
dc.SetBackground(*wxBLUE_BRUSH);
dc.Clear();
dc.SetPen(*wxRED_PEN);
dc.SetBrush(*wxRED_BRUSH);
dc.DrawRectangle(50, 50, 200, 200);
dc.SelectObject(wxNullBitmap);

// Convert the bitmap to an image
wxImage image = bitmap.ConvertToImage();

// Set the mask color to red
image.SetMaskColour(255, 0, 0);
```

Another method is to create the mask from another image. In the following example, image.bmp contains the main image, and mask.bmp has black pixels where the transparent area should be.

```
// Load image and its mask
wxImage image(wxT("image.bmp"), wxBITMAP_TYPE_BMP);
wxImage maskImage(wxT("mask.bmp"), wxBITMAP_TYPE_BMP);

// Specify black for the transparent area
image.SetMaskFromImage(maskImage, 0, 0, 0);
```

If you have loaded a transparent image from disk, you can check for transparency and retrieve the mask color:

```
// Load transparent image
wxImage image(wxT("image.png"), wxBITMAP_TYPE_PNG);

// Retrieve the mask
if (image.HasMask())
{
    wxColour maskColour(image.GetMaskRed(),
    image.GetMaskGreen(),
    image.GetMaskBlue());
}
```

Transformations

wxImage supports scaling, rotating, and mirroring transformations. Here are some examples:

```
// Scale an image to 200x200 and assign to another image.
// image1 remains unmodified.
wxImage image2 = image1.Scale(200, 200);

// Rescale an image to 200x200
image1.Rescale(200, 200);

// Rotate by a specified number of radians.
// image1 remains unmodified.
wxImage image2 = image1.Rotate(0.5, wxPoint(100, 100));

// Rotate by 90 degrees in the clockwise direction.
// image1 remains unmodified.
wxImage image2 = image1.Rotate90(true);

// Mirror the image horizontally.
// image1 remains unmodified.
wxImage image2 = image1.Mirror(true);
```

Color Reduction

If you need to reduce the number of colors in an image, you can use the static functions of the wxQuantize class. The main function of interest, Quantize, takes an input image, an output image, an optional wxPalette** to get a new palette containing the reduced colors, and the desired number of colors. You can also pass an unsigned char** variable to retrieve an 8-bit representation of the output image and a style for further control of what is returned; see the reference manual for more on these.

The following code shows how to reduce an image to a maximum of 256 colors:

```
#include "wx/image.h"
#include "wx/quantize.h"

wxImage image(wxT("image.png"));

int maxColorCount = 256;
int colors = image.CountColours();
wxPalette* palette = NULL;
if (colors > maxColorCount )
{
    wxImage reducedImage;
    if (wxQuantize::Quantize(image, reducedImage,
                             & palette, maxColorCount))
    {
        colors = reducedImage.CountColours();
        image = reducedImage;
    }
}
```

An image can have a wxPalette associated with it, for example when the image has been loaded from a GIF file. However, the image is still in RGB format, and the palette merely indicates the original mapping between index values and RGB values. wxPalette can also be set for a wxImage so that SaveFile can save it in a format that has a limited number of colors. For example, the Windows BMP handler determines whether the wxBMP_8BPP_PALETTE image option is set and, if so, uses the image's palette; if the wxBMP_8BPP option is set, it does its own quantization. Some handlers always do their own color reduction, such as PCX, unless they find that the number of unique colors is already low enough.

For more on wxPalette, please see "wxPalette" in Chapter 5.

Manipulating *wxImage* Data Directly

You can access image data with GetData for faster manipulation than using GetRed, GetBlue, GetGreen, and SetRGB. Here's an example of converting a color image to a grayscale:

```
void wxImage::ConvertToGrayScale(wxImage& image)
{
    double red2Gray   = 0.297;
    double green2Gray = 0.589;
    double blue2Gray  = 0.114;
    int w = image.GetWidth(), h = image.GetHeight();
    unsigned char *data = image.GetData();

    int x,y;
    for (y = 0; y < h; y++)
        for (x = 0; x < w; x++)
        {
            long pos = (y * w + x) * 3;

            char g = (char) (data[pos]*red2Gray +
                             data[pos+1]*green2Gray +
                             data[pos+2]*blue2Gray);
            data[pos] = data[pos+1] = data[pos+2] = g;
        }
}
```

IMAGE LISTS AND ICON BUNDLES

Sometimes it's useful to aggregate a number of images. You can use wxImageList directly in your application or in conjunction with some of the wxWidgets controls that require image lists when setting icons. wxNotebook, wxTreeCtrl, and wxListCtrl all support wxImageList to identify the icons used in the controls. You can also draw an individual image in a wxImageList on a device context.

Create a wxImageList with the width and height of each image, a boolean to specify whether a mask will be used, and the initial size of the list (purely for internal optimization purposes). Then add one or more wxBitmap or wxIcon images. You can't add a wxImage directly, but you can pass one to wxBitmap's constructor. wxImageList::Add returns an integer index you can use to identify that image; after you have added an image, the original image can be destroyed because wxImageList makes a copy of it.

Here are some examples of creating a wxImageList and adding images to it.

```
// Create a wxImageList
wxImageList *imageList = new wxImageList(16, 16, true, 1);

// Add a bitmap with transparency from a PNG
wxBitmap bitmap1(wxT("image.png"), wxBITMAP_TYPE_PNG);
imageList->Add(bitmap1);

// Add a bitmap with transparency from another bitmap
wxBitmap bitmap2(wxT("image.bmp"), wxBITMAP_TYPE_BMP);
wxBitmap maskBitmap(wxT("mask.bmp"), wxBITMAP_TYPE_BMP);
imageList->Add(bitmap2, maskBitmap);

// Add a bitmap with transparency specified with a color
wxBitmap bitmap3(wxT("image.bmp"), wxBITMAP_TYPE_BMP);
imageList->Add(bitmap3, *wxRED);

// Add an icon
#include "folder.xpm"
wxIcon icon(folder_xpm);
imageList->Add(icon);
```

You can draw an image to a device context, passing flags that determine how the image will be drawn. Pass wxIMAGELIST_DRAW_TRANSPARENT to draw with transparency, and also one of these values to indicate the state that should be drawn: wxIMAGELIST_DRAW_NORMAL, wxIMAGELIST_DRAW_SELECTED, or wxIMAGELIST_DRAW_FOCUSED.

```
// Draw all the images in the list
wxClientDC dc(window);
size_t i;
for (i = 0; i < imageList->GetImageCount(); i++)
{
    imageList->Draw(i, dc, i*16, 0, wxIMAGELIST_DRAW_NORMAL|
                            wxIMAGELIST_DRAW_TRANSPARENT);
}
```

To associate icons with notebook tabs, create an image list containing 16×16 icons, and call wxNotebook::SetImageList or wxNotebook::AssignImageList. If you use the first form, the notebook doesn't delete the image list when it is destroyed; with the second form, the notebook takes over management of the list, and you don't have to worry about destroying it yourself. Now when you add pages, you can specify the index of an icon to use as the image next to the text label (or instead of it, if the text label is empty). The following code creates a notebook and adds two pages with icons on the tabs.

```
// Create a wxImageList
wxImageList *imageList = new wxImageList(16, 16, true, 1);

// Add some icons
wxBitmap bitmap1(wxT("folder.png"), wxBITMAP_TYPE_PNG);
wxBitmap bitmap2(wxT("file.png"), wxBITMAP_TYPE_PNG);
int folderIndex = imageList->Add(bitmap1);
int fileIndex = imageList->Add(bitmap2);

// Create a notebook and two pages
wxNotebook* notebook = new wxNotebook(parent, wxID_ANY);
wxPanel* page1 = new wxPanel(notebook, wxID_ANY);
wxPanel* page2 = new wxPanel(notebook, wxID_ANY);

// Assign the image list
notebook->AssignImageList(imageList);

// Add the pages, with icons
notebook->AddPage(page1, wxT("Folder options"), true, folderIndex);
notebook->AddPage(page2, wxT("File options"), false, fileIndex);
```

wxTreeCtrl and wxListCtrl work in a similar way, with the option to assign or set the image list.

If you have a lot of icons and find it hard to keep track of icons by integer index, you might want to write a class that maps string names to the image list index. A simple implementation might look like this:

```
#include "wx/hashmap.h"

WX_DECLARE_STRING_HASH_MAP(int, IconNameToIndexHashMap);

// Class to refer to image indices by name
class IconNameToIndex
{
public:
    IconNameToIndex() {}

    // Add a named bitmap to the image list
    void Add(wxImageList* list, const wxBitmap& bitmap,
        const wxString& name) {
        m_hashMap[name] = list->Add(bitmap);
    }

    // Add a named icon to the image list
    void Add(wxImageList* list, const wxIcon& icon,
        const wxString& name) {
        m_hashMap[name] = list->Add(icon);
    }

    // Find the index from the name
    int Find(const wxString& name) { return m_hashMap[name]; }

private:
    IconNameToIndexHashMap m_hashMap;
};
```

The `wxIconBundle` class also aggregates images, but its purpose is to store an icon in multiple resolutions rather than multiple different images. This enables the system to choose the appropriate resolution for a given purpose. For example, the icon shown in the title bar of a frame may be smaller than the icon shown in a file or task manager. Here are some examples of creating and using an icon bundle.

```
// Create a bundle with a single icon
#include "file16x16.xpm"
wxIconBundle iconBundle(wxIcon(file16x16_xpm));

// Add a further icon from a file
iconBundle.Add(wxIcon(wxT("file32x32.png"), wxBITMAP_TYPE_PNG));

// Creates an icon bundle from several images in one file
wxIconBundle iconBundle2(wxT("multi-icons.tif"), wxBITMAP_TYPE_TIF);

// Gets the icon with the given size, or if not found, one with size
// wxSYS_ICON_X, wxSYS_ICON_Y
wxIcon icon = iconBundle.GetIcon(wxSize(16,16));

// Associates the icon bundle with a frame
wxFrame* frame = new wxFrame(parent, wxID_ANY);
frame->SetIcons(iconBundle);
```

Under Windows, `SetIcons` extracts 16×16 and 32×32 icons from the icon bundle.

CUSTOMIZING ART IN WXWIDGETS

`wxArtProvider` is a class that allows you to customize the built-in graphics ("art") in a wxWidgets application. For example, you might want to replace the standard icons used by the wxWidgets HTML Help viewer or the icons used by the generic dialogs such as the log dialog.

wxWidgets provides a standard `wxArtProvider` object, and parts of the framework that need icons and bitmaps call `wxArtProvider::GetBitmap` and `wxArtProvider::GetIcon` to retrieve a graphic.

Art is specified by two identifiers: the art identifier (`wxArtID`) and client identifier (`wxArtClient`). The client identifier is only a hint in case different windows need different graphics for the same art identifier. As an example, the wxHTML help window uses this code to get a bitmap for the *Back* toolbar button:

```
wxBitmap bmp = wxArtProvider::GetBitmap(wxART_GO_BACK,wxART_TOOLBAR);
```

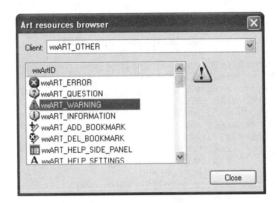

Figure 10-1 Art resources browser

You can browse the identifiers and graphics that are built into wxWidgets by compiling and running `samples/artprov` in your wxWidgets distribution. Figure 10-1 shows the browser in action.

To provide your own replacements for wxWidgets art, simply derive a new class from `wxArtProvider`, override `CreateBitmap`, and call `wxArtProvider::PushProvider` from your application's `OnInit` function to make it known to wxWidgets. Here's an example that replaces most of the wxHTML help window artwork.

```
// XPMs with the art
#include "bitmaps/helpbook.xpm"
#include "bitmaps/helppage.xpm"
#include "bitmaps/helpback.xpm"
#include "bitmaps/helpdown.xpm"
#include "bitmaps/helpforward.xpm"
#include "bitmaps/helpoptions.xpm"
#include "bitmaps/helpsidepanel.xpm"
#include "bitmaps/helpup.xpm"
#include "bitmaps/helpuplevel.xpm"
#include "bitmaps/helpicon.xpm"

#include "wx/artprov.h"

// The art provider class
class MyArtProvider : public wxArtProvider
{
protected:
    virtual wxBitmap CreateBitmap(const wxArtID& id,
                                  const wxArtClient& client,
                                  const wxSize& size);
};

// CreateBitmap function
wxBitmap MyArtProvider::CreateBitmap(const wxArtID& id,
                                     const wxArtClient& client,
                                     const wxSize& size)
```

```
{
    if (id == wxART_HELP_SIDE_PANEL)
        return wxBitmap(helpsidepanel_xpm);
    if (id == wxART_HELP_SETTINGS)
        return wxBitmap(helpoptions_xpm);
    if (id == wxART_HELP_BOOK)
        return wxBitmap(helpbook_xpm);
    if (id == wxART_HELP_FOLDER)
        return wxBitmap(helpbook_xpm);
    if (id == wxART_HELP_PAGE)
        return wxBitmap(helppage_xpm);
    if (id == wxART_GO_BACK)
        return wxBitmap(helpback_xpm);
    if (id == wxART_GO_FORWARD)
        return wxBitmap(helpforward_xpm);
    if (id == wxART_GO_UP)
        return wxBitmap(helpup_xpm);
    if (id == wxART_GO_DOWN)
        return wxBitmap(helpdown_xpm);
    if (id == wxART_GO_TO_PARENT)
        return wxBitmap(helpuplevel_xpm);
    if (id == wxART_FRAME_ICON)
        return wxBitmap(helpicon_xpm);
    if (id == wxART_HELP)
        return wxBitmap(helpicon_xpm);

    // Any wxWidgets icons not implemented here
    // will be provided by the default art provider.
    return wxNullBitmap;
}

// Initialization
bool MyApp::OnInit()
{
    ...

    wxArtProvider::PushProvider(new MyArtProvider);

    ...
    return true;
}
```

SUMMARY

In this chapter, we've seen how to use the four major image classes—wxBitmap, wxIcon, wxCursor, and wxImage—and two classes for aggregating images— wxImageList and wxIconBundle. We've also looked at how you can replace the standard wxWidgets icons and bitmaps with your own images. For examples of using image classes, see samples/image, samples/listctrl, and samples/ dragimag in your wxWidgets distribution.

Next, we'll tackle the classes that you use to implement the transfer of data objects via the clipboard or drag and drop.

CHAPTER 11

Clipboard and Drag and Drop

Most applications offer transfer of data to and from the clipboard via copy, cut, and paste. It's a basic way of implementing interoperation between your application and others. More sophisticated applications also allow the user to drag objects between windows, either within a single application or between two applications. For example, dragging a file from a file browser to an application window causes the data to fill the window, be added to a list, or some other behavior. This can be a much faster way to associate data with the application than using menus and dialogs to achieve the same thing, and your users will appreciate having it as an option.

Clipboard and drag and drop operations share some classes in wxWidgets, reflecting the fact that they both deal with data transfer, and so this chapter deals with both topics together. We'll see how to use the standard data objects that wxWidgets provides, as well as how to implement our own.

DATA OBJECTS

The `wxDataObject` class is at the heart of both clipboard and drag and drop. Instances of classes derived from `wxDataObject` represent the data that is being dragged by the mouse during a drag and drop operation or copied to or pasted from the clipboard. `wxDataObject` is a "smart" piece of data because it knows which formats it supports (via `GetFormatCount` and `GetAllFormats`) and knows how to render itself in any of them (via `GetDataHere`). It can also receive its value from outside the application in a format it supports if it implements the `SetData` method. We'll see how to do that later in the chapter.

Standard data formats such as `wxDF_TEXT` are identified by integers, and custom data formats are identified by a text string. The `wxDataFormat` class represents both of these kinds of identifiers by virtue of a constructor for each. Table 11-1 lists the standard data formats.

Table 11-1   Standard Data Formats

wxDF_INVALID	An invalid format, used as default argument for functions taking a wxDataFormat argument.
wxDF_TEXT	Text format. Standard data object: wxTextDataObject.
wxDF_BITMAP	Bitmap format. Standard data object: wxBitmapDataObject.
wxDF_METAFILE	Metafile (Windows only). Standard data object: wxMetafileData Object.
wxDF_FILENAME	A list of file names. Standard data object: wxFileDataObject.

You can also create a custom data format by passing an arbitrary string to the wxDataFormat constructor. The format will be registered the first time it is referenced.

Both clipboard and drag and drop deal with a source (data provider) and a target (data receiver). These may be in the same application and even the same window when, for example, you drag some text from one position to another in a word processor. Let's describe what each should do.

Data Source Duties

The data source is responsible for creating a wxDataObject containing the data to be transferred. Then the data source should either pass the wxDataObject to the clipboard using the SetData function or pass it to a wxDropSource object when dragging starts and call the DoDragDrop function.

The main difference from a clipboard operation is that the object for clipboard transfer must always be created on the heap using new and will be freed by the clipboard when it is no longer needed. Indeed, it is not known in advance when, if ever, the data will be pasted from the clipboard. On the other hand, the object for the drag and drop operation must exist only while DoDragDrop executes and may be safely deleted afterwards, so it can be created either on the heap or on the stack (that is, as a local variable).

Another small difference is that in the case of a clipboard operation, the application usually knows in advance whether it copies or cuts data. In a clipboard cut, the data is copied and then removed from the object being edited. This usually depends on which menu item the user chose. But for drag and drop, the application can only know this information after DoDragDrop returns.

Data Target Duties

To receive data from the clipboard (that is, a paste operation), you should create a wxDataObject derived class that supports the data formats you need and pass it to wxClipboard::GetData. If it returns false, no data in any of the supported formats is available. If it returns true, the data has been successfully transferred to wxDataObject.

For the drag and drop case, the wxDropTarget::OnData virtual function will be called when a data object is dropped, from which the data itself may be requested by calling the wxDropTarget::GetData method.

USING THE CLIPBOARD

To use the clipboard, you call member functions of the global pointer wxTheClipboard.

Before copying or pasting, you must take temporary ownership of the clipboard by calling wxClipboard::Open. If this operation returns true, you now own the clipboard. Call wxClipboard::SetData to put data on the clipboard or wxClipboard::GetData to retrieve data from the clipboard. Call wxClipboard::Close to close the clipboard and relinquish ownership. You should keep the clipboard open only as long as you are using it.

wxClipboardLocker is a helpful class that will open the clipboard (if possible) in its constructor and close it in its destructor, so you can write

```
wxClipboardLocker locker;
if (!locker)
{
    ... report an error and return ...
}
... use the clipboard ...
```

The following code shows how to write text to and read text from the clipboard:

```
// Write some text to the clipboard
if (wxTheClipboard->Open())
{
    // Data objects are held by the clipboard,
    // so do not delete them in the app.
    wxTheClipboard->SetData(new wxTextDataObject(wxT("Some text")));
    wxTheClipboard->Close();
}

// Read some text
if (wxTheClipboard->Open())
{
    if (wxTheClipboard->IsSupported(wxDF_TEXT))
    {
        wxTextDataObject data;
        wxTheClipboard->GetData(data);
        wxMessageBox(data.GetText());
    }
    wxTheClipboard->Close();
}
```

Here's the same thing, but with bitmaps:

```
// Write a bitmap to the clipboard
wxImage image(wxT("splash.png"), wxBITMAP_TYPE_PNG);
wxBitmap bitmap(image.ConvertToBitmap());
if (wxTheClipboard->Open())
{
    // Data objects are held by the clipboard,
    // so do not delete them in the app.
    wxTheClipboard->SetData(new wxBitmapDataObject(bitmap));
    wxTheClipboard->Close();
}

// Read a bitmap
if (wxTheClipboard->Open())
{
    if (wxTheClipboard->IsSupported(wxDF_BITMAP))
    {
        wxBitmapDataObject data;
        wxTheClipboard->GetData( data );
        bitmap = data.GetBitmap();
    }
    wxTheClipboard->Close();
}
```

If you implement clipboard operations, you will have to update the user interface to enable or disable clipboard commands, whether they are menu items,
toolbar buttons, or ordinary buttons. This is a job for the wxWidgets user interface update mechanism, which sends wxUpdateUIEvent events to your application in idle time; refer to Chapter 9, "Creating Custom Dialogs," for details.
The idle time updating allows your interface to be updated even when data is
copied to the clipboard without your application's knowledge.

Some controls, such as wxTextCtrl, already implement user interface
update events. If you use the standard identifiers wxID_CUT, wxID_COPY, and
wxID_PASTE for your menus and toolbars and arrange for command events from
the focused control to be processed first, the interface will be updated as the
user expects. Chapter 20, "Perfecting Your Application," shows how to direct
command events to the focused control by overriding wxFrame::ProcessEvent.

IMPLEMENTING DRAG AND DROP

You may implement drag sources, drag targets, or both in your application.

Implementing a Drag Source

To implement a drag source—that is, to provide the data that may be dragged
by the user to a target—you use an instance of the wxDropSource class. Note
that the following describes what happens after your application has decided
that a drag is starting—the logic to detect the mouse motion that indicates the
start of a drag is left entirely up to the application. Some controls help you by

generating an event when dragging is starting, so you don't have to code the logic yourself (which could potentially interfere with the native mouse behavior for the control). This chapter provides a summary of when wxWidgets notifies you of the start of a drag.

The following steps are involved, as seen from the perspective of the drop source.

1. Preparation

First of all, a data object must be created and initialized with the data you want to drag. For example:

```
wxTextDataObject myData(wxT("This text will be dragged."));
```

2. Drag Start

To start the dragging process, typically in response to a mouse click, you must create a wxDropSource object and call wxDropSource::DoDragDrop, like this:

```
wxDropSource dragSource(this);
dragSource.SetData(myData);
wxDragResult result = dragSource.DoDragDrop(wxDrag_AllowMove);
```

The flags you can pass to DoDragDrop are listed in Table 11-2.

Table 11-2   Flags for DoDragDrop

wxDrag_CopyOnly	Only allow copying.
wxDrag_AllowMove	Allow moving.
wxDrag_DefaultMove	The default operation is to move the data.

When creating the wxDropSource object, you have the option of also specifying the window that initiates the drag, and three cursors for Copy, Move, and Can't Drop feedback. These are actually icons in GTK+ and cursors on other platforms, so the macro wxDROP_ICON can be used to hide this difference, as we'll see in our text drop example shortly.

3. Dragging

The call to DoDragDrop blocks the program until the user releases the mouse button (unless you override the GiveFeedback function to do something special). When the mouse moves in a window of a program that understands the same drag and drop protocol, the corresponding wxDropTarget methods are called—see the following section, "Implementing a Drop Target."

4. Processing the Result

DoDragDrop returns an effect code, which is one of the values of the wxDragResult type, as listed in Table 11-3.

Table 11-3   *wxDragResult* Return Types from *DoDragDrop*

wxDragError	An error prevented the drag and drop operation from completing.
wxDragNone	The drop target didn't accept the data.
wxDragCopy	The data was successfully copied.
wxDragMove	The data was successfully moved (Windows only).
wxDragLink	This was a link operation.
wxDragCancel	The user canceled the operation.

Respond to the result of DoDragDrop appropriately in your application. If the return value was wxDragMove, it's normal to delete the data associated with the drop source and update the display. A return value of wxDragNone means that the drag was cancelled. For example:

```
switch (result)
{
    case wxDragCopy: /* Data was copied or linked:
                          do nothing special */
    case wxDragLink:
        break;

    case wxDragMove: /* Data was moved: delete original */
        DeleteMyDraggedData();
        break;

    default:          /* Drag was cancelled, or the data was
                          not accepted, or there was an error:
                          do nothing */
        break;
}
```

Here's an example showing how to implement a text drop source. DnDWindow contains a member variable m_strText—when the left mouse button is clicked, a drag operation is started using the value of m_strText. The result of the drag operation is reported in a message box. In practice, the drag operation wouldn't be started until the pointer has been dragged a minimum distance so that simple left-click actions can be distinguished from a drag.

```
void DnDWindow::OnLeftDown(wxMouseEvent& event )
{
    if ( !m_strText.IsEmpty() )
    {
        // start drag operation
        wxTextDataObject textData(m_strText);
        wxDropSource source(textData, this,
```

```
                         wxDROP_ICON(dnd_copy),
                         wxDROP_ICON(dnd_move),
                         wxDROP_ICON(dnd_none));

        int flags = 0;
        if ( m_moveByDefault )
            flags |= wxDrag_DefaultMove;
        else if ( m_moveAllow )
            flags |= wxDrag_AllowMove;

        wxDragResult result = source.DoDragDrop(flags);

        const wxChar *pc;
        switch ( result )
        {
            case wxDragError:    pc = wxT("Error!");      break;
            case wxDragNone:     pc = wxT("Nothing");     break;
            case wxDragCopy:     pc = wxT("Copied");      break;
            case wxDragMove:     pc = wxT("Moved");       break;
            case wxDragCancel:   pc = wxT("Cancelled");   break;
            default:             pc = wxT("Huh?");        break;
        }

        wxMessageBox(wxString(wxT("Drag result: ")) + pc);
    }
}
```

Implementing a Drop Target

To implement a drop target—that is, to receive the data dropped by the user—you associate a wxDropTarget object with a window using wxWindow::SetDrop Target. You must derive your own class from wxDropTarget and override its pure virtual methods. In particular, override OnDragOver to return a wxDragResult code indicating how the cursor should change when it's over the given point in the window, and override OnData to react to the drop. Alternatively, you may derive from wxTextDropTarget or wxFileDropTarget and override their OnDropText or OnDropFiles method.

The following steps happen in a drag and drop operation from the perspective of a drop target.

1. Initialization

wxWindow::SetDropTarget is called during window creation to associate the drop target with the window. At creation, or during subsequent program execution, a data object is associated with the drop target using wxDropTarget:: SetDataObject. This data object will be responsible for the format negotiation between the drag source and the drop target.

2. Dragging

As the mouse moves over the target during a drag operation, wxDropTarget::
OnEnter, wxDropTarget::OnDragOver and wxDropTarget::OnLeave are called as
appropriate, each returning a suitable wxDragResult so that the drag implementation can give suitable visual feedback.

3. Drop

When the user releases the mouse button over a window, wxWidgets asks
the associated wxDropTarget object if it accepts the data by calling
wxDataObject::GetAllFormats. If the data type is accepted, then wxDrop
Target::OnData will be called, and the wxDataObject belonging to the drop target can be filled with data. wxDropTarget::OnData returns a wxDragResult, which
is then returned from wxDropSource::DoDragDrop.

Using Standard Drop Targets

wxWidgets provides classes derived from wxDropTarget so that you don't have
to program everything yourself for commonly used cases. You just derive from
the class and override a virtual function to get notification of the drop.

wxTextDropTarget receives dropped text—just override OnDropText to do
something with the dropped text. The following example implements a drop
target that appends dropped text to a list box.

```
// A drop target that adds text to a listbox
class DnDText : public wxTextDropTarget
{
public:
    DnDText(wxListBox *owner) { m_owner = owner; }

    virtual bool OnDropText(wxCoord x, wxCoord y,
                                     const wxString& text)
    {
        m_owner->Append(text);
        return true;
    }

private:
    wxListBox *m_owner;
};

// Set the drop target
wxListBox* listBox = new wxListBox(parent, wxID_ANY);
listBox->SetDropTarget(new DnDText(listBox));
```

The next example shows how to use wxFileDropTarget, which accepts files
dropped from the system's file manager (such as Explorer on Windows) and
reports the number of files dropped and their names.

```
// A drop target that adds filenames to a list box
class DnDFile : public wxFileDropTarget
{
public:
    DnDFile(wxListBox *owner) { m_owner = owner; }

    virtual bool OnDropFiles(wxCoord x, wxCoord y,
                                  const wxArrayString& filenames)
    {
        size_t nFiles = filenames.GetCount();
        wxString str;
        str.Printf( wxT("%d files dropped"), (int) nFiles);
        m_owner->Append(str);
        for ( size_t n = 0; n < nFiles; n++ ) {
            m_owner->Append(filenames[n]);
        }

        return true;
    }

private:
    wxListBox *m_owner;
};

// Set the drop target
wxListBox* listBox = new wxListBox(parent, wxID_ANY);
listBox->SetDropTarget(new DnDFile(listBox));
```

Creating a Custom Drop Target

Now we'll create a custom drop target that can accept URLs (web addresses). This time we need to override OnData and OnDragOver, and we introduce a virtual function OnDropURL that derived classes can override.

```
// A custom drop target that accepts URL objects
class URLDropTarget : public wxDropTarget
{
public:
    URLDropTarget() { SetDataObject(new wxURLDataObject); }

    void OnDropURL(wxCoord x, wxCoord y, const wxString& text)
    {
        // Of course, a real program would do something more
        // useful here...
        wxMessageBox(text, wxT("URLDropTarget: got URL"),
                         wxICON_INFORMATION | wxOK);
    }

    // URLs can't be moved, only copied
    virtual wxDragResult OnDragOver(wxCoord x, wxCoord y,
                                         wxDragResult def)
    {
        return wxDragLink;
    }
```

```
        // translate this to calls to OnDropURL() just for convenience
        virtual wxDragResult OnData(wxCoord x, wxCoord y,
                                    wxDragResult def)
        {
            if ( !GetData() )
                return wxDragNone;

            OnDropURL(x, y, ((wxURLDataObject *)m_dataObject)->GetURL());

            return def;
        }
    };

    // Set the drop target
    wxListBox* listBox = new wxListBox(parent, wxID_ANY);
    listBox->SetDropTarget(new URLDropTarget);
```

More on *wxDataObject*

As we've seen, a wxDataObject represents data that can be copied to or from the clipboard or dragged and dropped. The important thing about wxDataObject is that it is a "smart" piece of data, unlike the usual dumb data containers such as memory buffers or files. Being "smart" means that the data object itself should know what data formats it supports and how to render itself in each of its supported formats.

A supported format is the format in which the data can be requested from a data object or from which the data object may be set. In the general case, an object may support different formats on input and output, so it may be able to render itself in a given format but not be created from data in this format, or *vice versa*.

Several solutions are available to you when you need to use a wxDataObject class:

1. Use one of the built-in classes. You may use wxTextDataObject, wxBitmap DataObject, or wxFileDataObject in the simplest cases when you only need to support one format and your data is text, a bitmap, or a list of files.

2. Use wxDataObjectSimple. Deriving from wxDataObjectSimple is the simplest solution for custom data—you will only support one format, and so you probably won't be able to communicate with other programs, but data transfer will work in your program (or between different copies of it).

3. Derive from wxCustomDataObject (a subclass of wxDataObjectSimple) for user-defined formats.

4. Use wxDataObjectComposite. This is a simple but powerful solution that allows you to support any number of formats (either standard or custom if you combine it with the previous solutions).

5. Use wxDataObject directly. This is the solution for maximum flexibility and efficiency, but it is also the most difficult to implement.

The easiest way to use drag and drop and the clipboard with multiple formats is by using wxDataObjectComposite, but it is not the most efficient one because each wxDataObjectSimple contains all the data in its specific format. Imagine that you want to paste to the clipboard 200 pages of text in your proprietary format, as well as Word, RTF, HTML, Unicode, and plain text. Even today's computers would struggle to support this task. For efficiency, you will have to derive from wxDataObject directly, make it enumerate its formats, and provide the data in the requested format on demand.

The underlying data transfer mechanisms for clipboard and drag and drop don't copy any data until another application actually requests it. So although a user may think that the data resides in the clipboard after pressing the application's Copy command, in reality it may only have been declared to be available.

Deriving from *wxDataObject*

Let's look at what's needed to derive a new class from wxDataObject. Deriving from the other classes mentioned earlier is similar but easier, so we won't cover them all here.

Each class derived directly from wxDataObject must override and implement all of its functions that are pure virtual in the base class. Data objects that only render their data or only set it (that is, work in only one direction) should return 0 from GetFormatCount for the unsupported direction.

GetAllFormats takes an array of wxDataFormat values and a Direction (Get or Set). Copy all the supported formats in the given direction to the formats array. GetFormatCount determines the number of elements in the array.

GetDataHere takes a wxDataFormat and a void* buffer, returning true on success and false otherwise. It must write the data for the given format into the buffer. This can be arbitrary binary or text data that need only be recognized by SetData.

GetDataSize takes a wxDataFormat and returns the data size for the given format.

GetFormatCount returns the number of available formats for rendering or setting the data.

GetPreferredFormat takes a Direction and returns the preferred wxDataFormat for this direction.

SetData takes a wxDataFormat, integer buffer length, and void* buffer. You interpret the data in the buffer in the required way for this object, such as copying it to an internal structure. This function should return true on success and false on failure.

The wxWidgets Drag and Drop Sample

We'll use the wxWidgets drag and drop sample in `samples/dnd` to demonstrate how to write a custom `wxDataObject` with a user-defined data format. The sample shows a simple shape—a triangle, rectangle, or ellipse—and allows you to edit it, drag it to a new position, and copy it to and paste it back from the clipboard. You can show the shape frame with the New Frame command on the File menu. This window is illustrated in Figure 11-1.

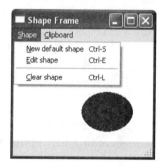

Figure 11-1   The `wxWidgets` drag and drop sample

The shapes are modeled with classes derived from `DnDShape`, and the data object is called `DnDShapeDataObject`. Before examining the implementation of `DndShapeDataObject`, let's see how the application will use them.

When a clipboard copy operation is invoked, a `DnDShapeDataObject` will be added to the clipboard, taking a copy of the current shape in case it's deleted while the object is still on the clipboard. Here's the code to do it:

```
void DnDShapeFrame::OnCopyShape(wxCommandEvent& event)
{
    if ( m_shape )
    {
        wxClipboardLocker clipLocker;
        if ( !clipLocker )
        {
            wxLogError(wxT("Can't open the clipboard"));
            return;
        }

        wxTheClipboard->AddData(new DnDShapeDataObject(m_shape));
    }
}
```

A clipboard paste is also straightforward, calling `wxClipboard::GetData` to try to get shape data from the clipboard and then retrieving the shape data from the data object. We also show the UI update handler that will enable the Paste menu command only if there is shape data on the clipboard. shapeFormatId is a global variable containing the shape format name, wxShape.

```
void DnDShapeFrame::OnPasteShape(wxCommandEvent& event)
{
    wxClipboardLocker clipLocker;
    if ( !clipLocker )
    {
        wxLogError(wxT("Can't open the clipboard"));
        return;
    }

    DnDShapeDataObject shapeDataObject(NULL);
    if ( wxTheClipboard->GetData(shapeDataObject) )
    {
        SetShape(shapeDataObject.GetShape());
    }
    else
    {
        wxLogStatus(wxT("No shape on the clipboard"));
    }
}

void DnDShapeFrame::OnUpdateUIPaste(wxUpdateUIEvent& event)
{
    event.Enable( wxTheClipboard->
                        IsSupported(wxDataFormat(shapeFormatId)) );
}
```

To implement drag and drop, a drop target class is required that will notify the application when data is dropped. Objects of class DnDShapeDropTarget contain a DnDShapeDataObject that is ready to receive data when its OnData member is called. Here's the declaration (and implementation) of DnDShapeDropTarget:

```
class DnDShapeDropTarget : public wxDropTarget
{
public:
    DnDShapeDropTarget(DnDShapeFrame *frame)
        : wxDropTarget(new DnDShapeDataObject)
    {
        m_frame = frame;
    }

    // override base class (pure) virtuals
    virtual wxDragResult OnEnter(wxCoord x, wxCoord y, wxDragResult def)
    {
        m_frame->SetStatusText(_T("Mouse entered the frame"));
        return OnDragOver(x, y, def);
    }

    virtual void OnLeave()
    {
        m_frame->SetStatusText(_T("Mouse left the frame"));
    }

    virtual wxDragResult OnData(wxCoord x, wxCoord y, wxDragResult def)
```

```
    {
        if ( !GetData() )
        {
            wxLogError(wxT("Failed to get drag and drop data"));

          · return wxDragNone;
        }

        // Notify the frame of the drop
        m_frame->OnDrop(x, y,
                ((DnDShapeDataObject *)GetDataObject())->GetShape());

        return def;
    }

private:
    DnDShapeFrame *m_frame;
};
```

The target is set when the shape frame is created during application initialization:

```
DnDShapeFrame::DnDShapeFrame(wxFrame *parent)
            : wxFrame(parent, wxID_ANY, _T("Shape Frame"))
{
    ...
    SetDropTarget(new DnDShapeDropTarget(this));
    ...
}
```

A drag starts when a left mouse button click is detected, and the event handler creates a wxDropSource passing a DnDShapeDataObject before calling DoDragDrop to initiate the drag operation. DndShapeFrame::OnDrag looks like this:

```
void DnDShapeFrame::OnDrag(wxMouseEvent& event)
{
    if ( !m_shape )
    {
        event.Skip();
        return;
    }

    // start drag operation
    DnDShapeDataObject shapeData(m_shape);
    wxDropSource source(shapeData, this);

    const wxChar *pc = NULL;
    switch ( source.DoDragDrop(true) )
    {
        default:
        case wxDragError:
            wxLogError(wxT("An error occured during drag and drop"));
            break;

        case wxDragNone:
```

```
                SetStatusText(_T("Nothing happened"));
                break;

        case wxDragCopy:
                pc = _T("copied");
                break;

        case wxDragMove:
                pc = _T("moved");
                if ( ms_lastDropTarget != this )
                {
                    // don't delete the shape if we dropped it
                    // on ourselves!
                    SetShape(NULL);
                }
                break;

        case wxDragCancel:
                SetStatusText(_T("Drag and drop operation cancelled"));
                break;
    }

    if ( pc )
    {
        SetStatusText(wxString(_T("Shape successfully ")) + pc);
    }
    //else: status text already set
}
```

When the drop is signaled by the user releasing the mouse button, wxWidgets calls DnDShapeDropTarget::OnData, which in turn calls DndShapeFrame::OnDrop with a new DndShape to set at the drop position. This completes the drag and drop operation.

```
void DnDShapeFrame::OnDrop(wxCoord x, wxCoord y, DnDShape *shape)
{
    ms_lastDropTarget = this;

    wxPoint pt(x, y);

    wxString s;
    s.Printf(wxT("Shape dropped at (%d, %d)"), pt.x, pt.y);
    SetStatusText(s);

    shape->Move(pt);
    SetShape(shape);
}
```

The only remaining tricky bit is to implement the custom wxDataObject. We'll show the implementation in parts for clarity. First, we'll see the custom format identifier declaration, the DndShapeDataObject class declaration, its constructor and destructor, and its data members.

The format identifier is shapeFormatId, and it is a global variable used throughout the sample. The constructor takes a new copy of the shape (if one is passed) by using GetDataHere; the copy could also have been implemented by using a DndShape::Clone function, had one been provided. The DnDShapeData Object destructor will delete this shape object.

DndShapeDataObject can provide bitmap and (on supported platforms) metafile renderings of its shape, so it also has wxBitmapDataObject and wxMetaFileDataObject members (and associated flags to indicate whether they're valid) to cache these formats when asked for them.

```
// Custom format identifier
static const wxChar *shapeFormatId = wxT("wxShape");

class DnDShapeDataObject : public wxDataObject
{
public:
    // ctor doesn't copy the pointer, so it shouldn't go away
    // while this object is alive
    DnDShapeDataObject(DnDShape *shape = (DnDShape *)NULL)
    {
        if ( shape )
        {
            // we need to copy the shape because the one
            // we've handled may be deleted while it's still on
            // the clipboard (for example) - and we reuse the
            // serialisation methods here to copy it
            void *buf = malloc(shape->DnDShape::GetDataSize());
            shape->GetDataHere(buf);
            m_shape = DnDShape::New(buf);

            free(buf);
        }
        else
        {
            // nothing to copy
            m_shape = NULL;
        }

        // this string should uniquely identify our format, but
        // is otherwise arbitrary
        m_formatShape.SetId(shapeFormatId);

        // we don't draw the shape to a bitmap until it's really
        // needed (i.e. we're asked to do so)
        m_hasBitmap = false;
        m_hasMetaFile = false;
    }

    virtual ~DnDShapeDataObject() { delete m_shape; }

    // after a call to this function, the shape is owned by the
    // caller and it is responsible for deleting it
    DnDShape *GetShape()
    {
        DnDShape *shape = m_shape;
```

```
            m_shape = (DnDShape *)NULL;
            m_hasBitmap = false;
            m_hasMetaFile = false;

            return shape;
        }

    // The other member functions omitted
    ...

    // The data members
private:
        wxDataFormat        m_formatShape; // our custom format
        wxBitmapDataObject  m_dobjBitmap;  // it handles bitmaps
        bool                m_hasBitmap;   // true if m_dobjBitmap valid
        wxMetaFileDataObject m_dobjMetaFile;// handles metafiles
        bool                m_hasMetaFile;// true if MF valid
        DnDShape            *m_shape;       // our data
};
```

Next, let's look at the functions that need to be provided to answer questions
about the data that the object provides. GetPreferredFormat simply returns the
"native" format for this object, m_formatShape, which we initialized with wxShape
in the constructor. GetFormatCount determines whether the custom format can
be used for setting and getting data—bitmap and metafile formats can only be
handled when getting data. GetDataSize returns a suitable size depending on
what kind of data is requested, if necessary creating the data in bitmap or
metafile format in order to find out its size.

```
    virtual wxDataFormat GetPreferredFormat(Direction dir) const
    {
        return m_formatShape;
    }

    virtual size_t GetFormatCount(Direction dir) const
    {
        // our custom format is supported by both GetData()
        // and SetData()
        size_t nFormats = 1;
        if ( dir == Get )
        {
            // but the bitmap format(s) are only supported for output
            nFormats += m_dobjBitmap.GetFormatCount(dir);
            nFormats += m_dobjMetaFile.GetFormatCount(dir);
        }

        return nFormats;
    }

    virtual void GetAllFormats(wxDataFormat *formats, Direction dir)
const
    {
        formats[0] = m_formatShape;
        if ( dir == Get )
        {
```

```
                         // in Get direction we additionally support bitmaps and
metafiles
                         //under Windows
                         m_dobjBitmap.GetAllFormats(&formats[1], dir);

                         // don't assume that m_dobjBitmap has only 1 format
                         m_dobjMetaFile.GetAllFormats(&formats[1 +
                                 m_dobjBitmap.GetFormatCount(dir)], dir);
                 }
         }

         virtual size_t GetDataSize(const wxDataFormat& format) const
         {
             if ( format == m_formatShape )
             {
                 return m_shape->GetDataSize();
             }
             else if ( m_dobjMetaFile.IsSupported(format) )
             {
                 if ( !m_hasMetaFile )
                     CreateMetaFile();

                 return m_dobjMetaFile.GetDataSize(format);
             }
             else
             {
                 wxASSERT_MSG( m_dobjBitmap.IsSupported(format),
                               wxT("unexpected format") );

                 if ( !m_hasBitmap )
                     CreateBitmap();

                 return m_dobjBitmap.GetDataSize();
             }
         }
```

GetDataHere copies data into a void* buffer, again depending on what format is
requested, as follows:

```
     virtual bool GetDataHere(const wxDataFormat& format, void
➥*pBuf) const
     {
         if ( format == m_formatShape )
         {
             // Uses a ShapeDump struct to stream itself to void*
             m_shape->GetDataHere(pBuf);

             return true;
         }
         else if ( m_dobjMetaFile.IsSupported(format) )
         {
             if ( !m_hasMetaFile )
                 CreateMetaFile();

             return m_dobjMetaFile.GetDataHere(format, pBuf);
         }
         else
         {
```

```
                wxASSERT_MSG( m_dobjBitmap.IsSupported(format),
                              wxT("unexpected format") );

                if ( !m_hasBitmap )
                    CreateBitmap();

                return m_dobjBitmap.GetDataHere(pBuf);
            }
    }
```

SetData only deals with the native format, so all it has to do is call DndShape::New to make a shape out of the supplied buffer:

```
    virtual bool SetData(const wxDataFormat& format,
                         size_t len, const void *buf)
    {
        wxCHECK_MSG( format == m_formatShape, false,
                     wxT( "unsupported format") );

        delete m_shape;
        m_shape = DnDShape::New(buf);

        // the shape has changed
        m_hasBitmap = false;
        m_hasMetaFile = false;

        return true;
    }
```

The way that DndShape serializes itself in and out of a void* buffer is quite straightforward: it uses a ShapeDump structure that stores the shape's details. Here's how:

```
// Static function that creates a shape from a void* buffer
DnDShape *DnDShape::New(const void *buf)
{
    const ShapeDump& dump = *(const ShapeDump *)buf;
    switch ( dump.k )
    {
        case Triangle:
            return new DnDTriangularShape(
                            wxPoint(dump.x, dump.y),
                            wxSize(dump.w, dump.h),
                            wxColour(dump.r, dump.g, dump.b));

        case Rectangle:
            return new DnDRectangularShape(
                            wxPoint(dump.x, dump.y),
                            wxSize(dump.w, dump.h),
                            wxColour(dump.r, dump.g, dump.b));

        case Ellipse:
            return new DnDEllipticShape(
                            wxPoint(dump.x, dump.y),
                            wxSize(dump.w, dump.h),
                            wxColour(dump.r, dump.g, dump.b));
```

```
            default:
                wxFAIL_MSG(wxT("invalid shape!"));
                return NULL;
        }
}

// Gets the data size
size_t DndShape::GetDataSize() const
{
    return sizeof(ShapeDump);
}

// Serialises into a void* buffer
void DndShape::GetDataHere(void *buf) const
{
    ShapeDump& dump = *(ShapeDump *)buf;
    dump.x = m_pos.x;
    dump.y = m_pos.y;
    dump.w = m_size.x;
    dump.h = m_size.y;
    dump.r = m_col.Red();
    dump.g = m_col.Green();
    dump.b = m_col.Blue();
    dump.k = GetKind();
}
```

Finally, going back to the DnDShapeDataObject class, the functions that create data in metafile and bitmap formats when required look like this:

```
void DnDShapeDataObject::CreateMetaFile() const
{
    wxPoint pos = m_shape->GetPosition();
    wxSize size = m_shape->GetSize();

    wxMetaFileDC dcMF(wxEmptyString, pos.x + size.x, pos.y + size.y);

    m_shape->Draw(dcMF);

    wxMetafile *mf = dcMF.Close();

    DnDShapeDataObject *self = (DnDShapeDataObject *)this;
    self->m_dobjMetaFile.SetMetafile(*mf);
    self->m_hasMetaFile = true;

    delete mf;
}

void DnDShapeDataObject::CreateBitmap() const
{
    wxPoint pos = m_shape->GetPosition();
    wxSize size = m_shape->GetSize();
    int x = pos.x + size.x,
        y = pos.y + size.y;
    wxBitmap bitmap(x, y);
    wxMemoryDC dc;
    dc.SelectObject(bitmap);
    dc.SetBrush(wxBrush(wxT("white"), wxSOLID));
```

```
        dc.Clear();
        m_shape->Draw(dc);
        dc.SelectObject(wxNullBitmap);

        DnDShapeDataObject *self = (DnDShapeDataObject *)this;
        self->m_dobjBitmap.SetBitmap(bitmap);
        self->m_hasBitmap = true;
}
```

Our custom data object implementation is now complete, apart from the details of how shapes draw themselves and the code to create GUI. For these details, please see the drag and drop sample source in samples/dnd in your wxWidgets distribution.

Drag and Drop Helpers in wxWidgets

Here are some of the controls that give you a helping hand when implementing drag and drop.

wxTreeCtrl

You can use the EVT_TREE_BEGIN_DRAG or EVT_TREE_BEGIN_RDRAG event table macros to intercept the start of left or right dragging, as determined by the internal tree control mouse-handling code. In your handler for the start of the drag, call wxTreeEvent::Allow if you want wxTreeCtrl to use its own drag implementation and send an EVT_TREE_END_DRAG event. If you elect to use the tree control's implementation for dragging, a drag image will be created and moved as the mouse is dragged around the tree control. The drop behavior is determined entirely by application code in the "end drag" handler.

The following example shows how to use the tree control's drag and drop events. When the user drags and drops an item onto another item, a copy will be appended after the second item.

```
BEGIN_EVENT_TABLE(MyTreeCtrl, wxTreeCtrl)
    EVT_TREE_BEGIN_DRAG(TreeTest_Ctrl, MyTreeCtrl::OnBeginDrag)
    EVT_TREE_END_DRAG(TreeTest_Ctrl, MyTreeCtrl::OnEndDrag)
END_EVENT_TABLE()

void MyTreeCtrl::OnBeginDrag(wxTreeEvent& event)
{
    // need to explicitly allow drag
    if ( event.GetItem() != GetRootItem() )
    {
        m_draggedItem = event.GetItem();

        wxLogMessage(wxT("OnBeginDrag: started dragging %s"),
                    GetItemText(m_draggedItem).c_str());
```

```
            event.Allow();
    }
    else
    {
        wxLogMessage(wxT("OnBeginDrag: this item can't be
➥dragged."));
    }
}

void MyTreeCtrl::OnEndDrag(wxTreeEvent& event)
{
    wxTreeItemId itemSrc = m_draggedItem,
                 itemDst = event.GetItem();
    m_draggedItem = (wxTreeItemId)0l;

    // where to copy the item?
    if ( itemDst.IsOk() && !ItemHasChildren(itemDst) )
    {
        // copy to the parent then
        itemDst = GetItemParent(itemDst);
    }

    if ( !itemDst.IsOk() )
    {
        wxLogMessage(wxT("OnEndDrag: can't drop here."));
        return;
    }

    wxString text = GetItemText(itemSrc);
    wxLogMessage(wxT("OnEndDrag: '%s' copied to '%s'."),
                 text.c_str(), GetItemText(itemDst).c_str());

    // append the item here
    int image = wxGetApp().ShowImages() ? TreeCtrlIcon_File : -1;
    AppendItem(itemDst, text, image);
}
```

If you want to handle a drag operation your own way, for example using wxDropSource, you can omit the wxTreeEvent::Allow call in the drag start handler and start the drag operation using your chosen method. The tree drag end event will not be sent because it's up to your code to decide how the drag ends (if using wxDropSource::DoDragDrop, the drag end detection is handled for you).

wxListCtrl

This class doesn't provide any default drag image or an end of drag notification, but it does let you know when to start a drag operation for an item; use the EVT_LIST_BEGIN_DRAG or EVT_LIST_BEGIN_RDRAG event table macros and implement your own drag and drop code. You can also detect when column dividers are being dragged by using EVT_LIST_COL_BEGIN_DRAG, EVT_LIST_COL_DRAGGING and EVT_LIST_COL_END_DRAG.

wxDragImage

wxDragImage is a handy class to use when implementing your own drag and drop; it draws an image on top of a window, and it provides methods to move the image without damaging the window underneath. The generic implementation does this by saving a copy of the underlying window and repainting it along with the image when necessary.

Figure 11-2 shows the main window of the wxDragImage sample, which you can find in samples/dragimag in your wxWidgets distribution. When the three puzzle shapes are dragged, a different drag image is used for each: the shape itself, an icon, and an image dynamically created out of a text string. If you check *Use Whole Screen for Dragging*, then the shape may be dragged outside of the window. On Windows, the sample may be compiled using either the generic wxDragImage implementation (the default), or the native class by setting the value of wxUSE_GENERIC_DRAGIMAGE to 1 in dragimag.cpp.

Figure 11-2   The wxDragImage sample

When the start of a drag operation is detected, create a wxDragImage object and store it somewhere that you can access it as the drag progresses. Call BeginDrag to start and EndDrag to stop the drag. To move the image, initially call Show and then Move. If you want to update the screen contents during the drag (for example, highlight an item as in the dragimag sample), call Hide, update the window, call Move, and then call Show.

You can drag within one window, or you can use full-screen dragging either across the whole screen or across just one area of it to save resources. If you want the user to drag between two windows with different top-level parents, then you will need to use full-screen dragging. Full-screen dragging is not ideal because it takes a snapshot of the screen at the start of the drag and doesn't take into account changes that are happening in other applications during the drag.

In the following example, based on the sample illustrated in Figure 11-2, MyCanvas displays a number of shapes of class DragShape, each of which has a bitmap associated with it. When dragging starts, a new wxDragImage is created using the shape's bitmap, and BeginDrag is called. When mouse motion is detected, wxDragImage::Move is called to render the shape at the appropriate position on the window. Finally, when the left mouse button is released, the drag image is destroyed, and the dragged shape is redrawn in its new position.

```cpp
void MyCanvas::OnMouseEvent(wxMouseEvent& event)
{
    if (event.LeftDown())
    {
        DragShape* shape = FindShape(event.GetPosition());
        if (shape)
        {
            // We tentatively start dragging, but wait for
            // mouse movement before dragging properly.
            m_dragMode = TEST_DRAG_START;
            m_dragStartPos = event.GetPosition();
            m_draggedShape = shape;
        }
    }
    else if (event.LeftUp() && m_dragMode != TEST_DRAG_NONE)
    {
        // Finish dragging
        m_dragMode = TEST_DRAG_NONE;

        if (!m_draggedShape || !m_dragImage)
            return;

        m_draggedShape->SetPosition(m_draggedShape->GetPosition()
                        + event.GetPosition() - m_dragStartPos);

        m_dragImage->Hide();
        m_dragImage->EndDrag();
        delete m_dragImage;
        m_dragImage = NULL;

        m_draggedShape->SetShow(true);
        m_draggedShape->Draw(dc);
        m_draggedShape = NULL;
    }
    else if (event.Dragging() && m_dragMode != TEST_DRAG_NONE)
    {
        if (m_dragMode == TEST_DRAG_START)
        {
            // We will start dragging if we've moved beyond a
            // couple of pixels
            int tolerance = 2;
            int dx = abs(event.GetPosition().x - m_dragStartPos.x);
            int dy = abs(event.GetPosition().y - m_dragStartPos.y);
            if (dx <= tolerance && dy <= tolerance)
                return;

            // Start the drag.
            m_dragMode = TEST_DRAG_DRAGGING;
```

```
        if (m_dragImage)
            delete m_dragImage;

        // Erase the dragged shape from the canvas
        m_draggedShape->SetShow(false);

        wxClientDC dc(this);
        EraseShape(m_draggedShape, dc);
        DrawShapes(dc);

        m_dragImage = new wxDragImage(
                                m_draggedShape-
                                //>GetBitmap());

        // The offset between the top-left of the shape image and
        // the current shape position
        wxPoint beginDragHotSpot = m_dragStartPos -
                                m_draggedShape-
                                //>GetPosition();

        // Always assume coordinates relative to the capture
        // window (client coordinates)
        if (!m_dragImage->BeginDrag(beginDragHotSpot, this))
        {
            delete m_dragImage;
            m_dragImage = NULL;
            m_dragMode = TEST_DRAG_NONE;

        } else
        {
            m_dragImage->Move(event.GetPosition());
            m_dragImage->Show();
        }
    }
    else if (m_dragMode == TEST_DRAG_DRAGGING)
    {
        // Move the image
        m_dragImage->Move(event.GetPosition());
    }
  }
}
```

If you want to draw the image yourself during the drag, instead of just passing a bitmap as the dragged image, use wxGenericDragImage and override wxDragImage::DoDrawImage and wxDragImage::GetImageRect. wxDragImage is an alias for wxGenericDragImage on non-Windows platforms. The Windows implementation doesn't support DoDrawImage and is also limited to drawing rather ghostly translucent images, so you will probably want to use wxGenericDragImage on all platforms.

When you start a drag, just before calling wxDragImage::Show, you normally need to first erase the object you're about to drag so that wxDragImage can maintain a backing bitmap consisting of the window *without* the dragged object, and so that the object can be superimposed onto this snapshot as it is dragged. This will cause a slight flicker at the start of the drag. To eliminate

this (for `wxGenericDragImage` only), override the function `UpdateBacking`
`FromWindow` and on the memory device context passed to you, draw the window
contents minus the object about to be dragged. Now you don't have to erase the
object before the drag image is shown, and the next time the image is moved,
the correct window contents will be drawn, resulting in a completely smooth
drag operation.

Summary

In this chapter, we've seen how to transfer data to and from the clipboard.
We've also seen how to implement drag and drop from the point of view of both
the data being dropped and the window that's receiving the data, and
we've covered other areas of wxWidgets related to drag and drop. Check
out `samples/dnd`, `samples/dragimag`, and `samples/treectrl` in your wxWidgets
distribution for further insight.

In the next chapter, we will be returning to the topic of windows and
describing some advanced classes that will help you take your application to
new levels of sophistication.

CHAPTER 12

Advanced Window Classes

Although this book can't cover all the classes in wxWidgets in detail, it's worth looking at a few of the more advanced GUI classes that can contribute to the creation of a more interesting application. This chapter covers the following topics:

☞ wxTreeCtrl; a control that helps you model hierarchical data.

☞ wxListCtrl; a flexible control for showing lists of text labels and icons in several styles.

☞ wxWizard; a special dialog to guide your user through a specific task using a sequence of pages.

☞ wxHtmlWindow; a highly versatile, lightweight HTML control for use in anything from "About" boxes to report windows.

☞ wxGrid; a feature-rich control for displaying tabular data.

☞ wxTaskBarIcon; a quick way for your users to access features in your application from the system tray or equivalent.

☞ Writing your own controls. The necessary steps to build a well-behaved "custom control."

WXTREECTRL

A tree control presents information as a hierarchy, with items that may be expanded or collapsed. Figure 12-1 shows the wxWidgets tree control sample, displaying different font styles and colors. Each item is referenced by the wxTreeItemId type and has text and an optional icon that can be changed dynamically. A tree control can be created in single-selection or multiple-selection mode. To associate data with tree items, derive a class from wxTree ItemData and use wxTreeCtrl::SetItemData and wxTreeCtrl::GetItemData. The tree data will be destroyed when the item or tree is destroyed, so you may want to store only a pointer to the actual data within your tree item data objects.

Figure 12-1 `wxTreeCtrl`

Because clicks on tree item images can be detected by the application, you can simulate controls within the tree by swapping the images according to the state you want to show for that item. For example, you can easily add simulated check boxes to your tree.

The following fragment shows how to create a tree window with custom tree item data and an image list.

```cpp
#include "wx/treectrl.h"

// Declare a class to hold tree item data
class MyTreeItemData : public wxTreeItemData
{
public:
    MyTreeItemData(const wxString& desc) : m_desc(desc) { }

    const wxString& GetDesc() const { return m_desc; }

private:
    wxString m_desc;
};

// Images for tree items
#include "file.xpm"
```

```
#include "folder.xpm"

// Create the tree
wxTreeCtrl* treeCtrl = new wxTreeCtrl(
    this, wxID_ANY, wxPoint(0, 0), wxSize(400, 400),
    wxTR_HAS_BUTTONS¦wxTR_SINGLE);


wxImageList* imageList = new wxImageList(16, 16);
imageList->Add(wxIcon(folder_xpm));
imageList->Add(wxIcon(file_xpm));
treeCtrl->AssignImageList(imageList);

// Create a root showing the folder icon, and two items showing
// the file icon
wxTreeItemId rootId = treeCtrl->AddRoot(wxT("Root"), 0, 0,
                            new MyTreeItemData(wxT("Root item")));
wxTreeItemId itemId1 = treeCtrl->AppendItem(rootId,
                        wxT("File 1"), 1, 1,
                        new MyTreeItemData(wxT("File item 1")));
wxTreeItemId itemId2 = treeCtrl->AppendItem(rootId,
                        wxT("File 2"), 1, 1,
                        new MyTreeItemData(wxT("File item 2")));
```

wxTreeCtrl Styles

Table 12-1 lists the styles you can pass to the `wxTreeCtrl` constructor or `Create` function; also refer to the available styles for `wxWindow` in Table 4-1.

Table 12-1 `wxTreeCtrl` Window Styles

`wxTR_DEFAULT_STYLE`	The styles that are closest to the defaults for the native control for a particular toolkit.
`wxTR_EDIT_LABELS`	Use this style if you want the user to be able to edit labels in the tree control.
`wxTR_NO_BUTTONS`	Specifies that no buttons should be drawn.
`wxTR_HAS_BUTTONS`	Use this style to show plus and minus buttons to the left of parent items.
`wxTR_NO_LINES`	Use this style to hide vertical level connectors.
`wxTR_FULL_ROW_HIGHLIGHT`	Use this style to make the background color and the selection highlight extend over the entire horizontal row of the tree control window. (This style is ignored under Windows unless you specify `wxTR_NO_LINES` as well.)

(continues)

Table 12-1   wxTreeCtrl Window Styles *(Continued)*

wxTR_LINES_AT_ROOT	Use this style to show lines between root nodes. Only applicable if wxTR_HIDE_ROOT is set and wxTR_NO_LINES is not set.
wxTR_HIDE_ROOT	Use this style to suppress the display of the root node, effectively causing the first-level nodes to appear as a series of root nodes.
wxTR_ROW_LINES	Use this style to draw a contrasting border between displayed rows.
wxTR_HAS_VARIABLE_ROW_HEIGHT	Use this style to cause row heights to be just big enough to fit the content. If not set, all rows use the largest row height. The default is that this style is unset. Generic implementation only.
wxTR_SINGLE	Specifies that only one item may be selected at a time. Selecting another item causes the current selection, if any, to be deselected. This is the default.
wxTR_MULTIPLE	Use this style to enable a range of items to be selected. If a second range is selected, the current range, if any, is deselected.
wxTR_EXTENDED	Use this style to enable disjoint items to be selected. (Only partially implemented.)

wxTreeCtrl Events

wxTreeCtrl generates wxTreeEvent events, listed in Table 12-2. These events propagate up the window parent-child hierarchy.

Table 12-2   wxTreeCtrl Events

EVT_TREE_BEGIN_DRAG(id, func) EVT_TREE_BEGIN_RDRAG(id, func)	Generated when a left or right drag is starting. For details on handling these events, see Chapter 11, "Clipboard and Drag and Drop."
EVT_TREE_BEGIN_LABEL_EDIT(id, func) EVT_TREE_END_LABEL_EDIT(id, func)	Generated when the user starts or finishes editing an item label.
EVT_TREE_DELETE_ITEM(id, func)	Generated when an item is deleted.
EVT_TREE_GET_INFO(id, func)	Generated when an item's data is requested.
EVT_TREE_SET_INFO(id, func)	Generated when an item's data is set.

EVT_TREE_ITEM_ACTIVATED(id, func)	Generated when an item has been activated, that is, chosen by double-clicking or via the keyboard. For example, if the tree represents a file hierarchy, you might display a preview of the activated file.
EVT_TREE_ITEM_COLLAPSED(id, func)	Generated when the given item has been collapsed (all its children are hidden).
EVT_TREE_ITEM_COLLAPSING(id, func)	Generated when the given item is about to be collapsed. This event can be vetoed to prevent the collapse from taking place.
EVT_TREE_ITEM_EXPANDED(id, func)	Generated when the given item has been expanded (all its children are exposed).
EVT_TREE_ITEM_EXPANDING(id, func)	Generated when the given item is about to be expanded. This event can be vetoed to prevent the item from being expanded.
EVT_TREE_SEL_CHANGED(id, func)	Generated when a selection has changed.
EVT_TREE_SEL_CHANGING(id, func)	Generated when a selection is about to change. This event can be vetoed to prevent the item from being selected.
EVT_TREE_KEY_DOWN(id, func)	Used to detect whether a key has been pressed.
EVT_TREE_ITEM_GET_TOOLTIP(id, func)	Enables you to set a tooltip for a particular item; this is only available on Windows.

wxTreeCtrl Member Functions

These are the important wxTreeCtrl functions.

Use AddRoot to create the first item and then AppendItem, InsertItem, or PrependItem to add subsequent items. Remove an item with Delete, clear all items with DeleteAllItems, or remove all of an item's immediate descendants with DeleteChildren.

Set an item's label with SetItemText; you can change the label's appearance with SetItemTextColour, SetItemBackgroundColour, SetItemBold, and SetItemFont.

If you show images in your tree items, use SetImageList or AssignImage List to associate a wxImageList with the tree control. Each item can show an image for each of the possible item states: wxTreeItemIcon_Normal, wxTreeItemIcon_Selected, wxTreeItemIcon_Expanded, and wxTreeItemIcon_Selected Expanded. Use SetItemImage to pass an index into the tree control's image list and an optional state. If only the image for the normal state is specified, it will be used for the other states, too.

Scroll an item into view with ScrollTo, or use EnsureVisible if items may need to be expanded to show the desired item. Expand shows the children of an item. Collapse an item that has children with Collapse or CollapseAndReset: the latter also removes the children. This is useful if you're implementing a tree control with a very large number of items. You may want to add items only when they are visible—that is, when you process an EVT_TREE_ITEM_EXPANDING event. In this case, you will need to use SetItemHasChildren to provide visual feedback that an unexpanded item has children, even when it doesn't.

You can select or deselect an item with SelectItem. For a single-selection tree, you can get the currently selected item with GetSelection. If there is no selection, it returns an invalid wxTreeItemId, such that a call to wxTree ItemId::IsOk returns false. For a multiple-selection tree, retrieve all the selections with GetSelections by passing a wxArrayTreeItemItemIds reference to the function. Unselect removes the current selection for a single-selection tree, whereas UnselectAll removes all selections from a multiple-selection tree. UnselectItem can be used in a multiple-selection tree to deselect a specific item.

There are several ways to traverse the tree: you can start at the top with GetRootItem and iterate through the children of an item with GetFirstChild and GetNextChild. Find the next and previous siblings of an item with GetNextSibling and GetPrevSibling, determine whether an item has children with ItemHasChildren, and get the parent of an item with GetParent. GetCount returns the total number of items in the tree, and GetChildrenCount counts the number of descendants for the given item.

HitTest is a useful function if you're implementing drag and drop—it enables you to find the item under the mouse position, together with the part of the item. See the reference manual for the flags returned by HitTest. You can find the bounding rectangle for an item with GetBoundingRect.

For more information on these functions, see the reference manual and the wxTreeCtrl sample in samples/treectrl.

wxLISTCTRL

The list control displays items in one of four views: a multi-column list view, a multi-column report view with optional icons, a large icon view, and a small icon view. See Figure 12-2 for examples of these views from the wxListCtrl sample. Each item in a list control is identified by a long integer index representing its zero-based position in the list, which will change as items are added and deleted or as the content is sorted. Unlike the tree control, the default is to allow multiple selections, and single-selection can be specified with a window style. You can supply a sort function if you need the items to be sorted. The report view can display an optional header, whose columns respond to mouse clicks—useful for sorting the contents of the column, for example. The widths of a report view's columns can be changed either by the application or by dragging on the column dividers.

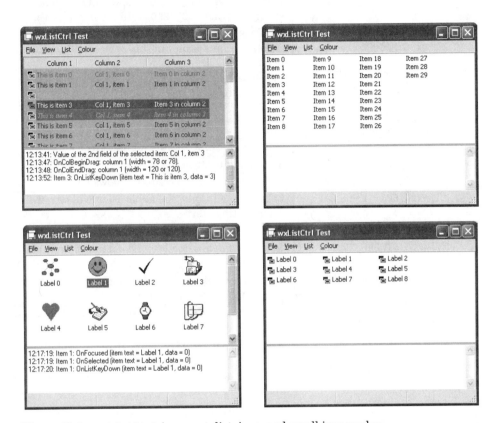

Figure 12-2   wxListCtrl in report, list, icon, and small icon modes

Client data can be associated with items, but it works differently from wxTreeCtrl. Each item has a long integer available for client data, so if you have objects to associate with items, this must be done by the application—for example, with a mapping from long integer to object pointer—and you must free this data yourself.

wxListCtrl Styles

Table 12-3 lists the styles you can pass to the wxListCtrl constructor or Create function. Also refer to the available styles for wxWindow in Table 4-1.

Table 12-3   wxListCtrl Window Styles

wxLC_LIST	A multicolumn list view with optional small icons. Columns are computed automatically—you don't set columns as in wxLC_REPORT. In other words, the list wraps, unlike a wxListBox.
wxLC_REPORT	A single or multicolumn report view with optional header.
wxLC_VIRTUAL	Specifies that the application provides text on demand; may only be used with wxLC_REPORT.
wxLC_ICON	Large icon view with optional labels.
wxLC_SMALL_ICON	Small icon view with optional labels.
wxLC_ALIGN_TOP	Icons align to the top. Windows only.
wxLC_ALIGN_LEFT	Icons align to the left.
wxLC_AUTO_ARRANGE	Icons arrange themselves. Windows only.
wxLC_EDIT_LABELS	Labels are editable; the application will be notified when editing starts.
wxLC_NO_HEADER	No header will be shown in report mode.
wxLC_SINGLE_SEL	Specifies single-selection; the default is multiple-selection.
wxLC_SORT_ASCENDING	Sorts in ascending order. The application must still supply a comparison callback in SortItems.
wxLC_SORT_DESCENDING	Sorts in descending order. The application must still supply a comparison callback in SortItems.
wxLC_HRULES	Draws light horizontal rules between rows in report mode.
wxLC_VRULES	Draws light horizontal rules between columns in report mode.

wxListCtrl Events

wxListCtrl generates wxListEvent events, described in Table 12-4. These events propagate up the window parent-child hierarchy. Events dealing with a single item return the item index with wxListEvent::GetIndex.

Table 12-4   wxListCtrl Events

EVT_LIST_BEGIN_DRAG(id, func) EVT_LIST_BEGIN_RDRAG(id, func)	Use these events to detect a drag start event; you need to supply code to implement the rest of the drag behavior. Call wxListEvent::GetPoint to get the position of the mouse pointer.

EVT_LIST_BEGIN_LABEL_EDIT(id, func) EVT_LIST_END_LABEL_EDIT(id, func)	Use these events to detect when the user has started or finished editing a label. The edit can be vetoed by calling the event object's Veto function. wxListEvent::GetText returns the label.
EVT_LIST_DELETE_ITEM(id, func) EVT_LIST_DELETE_ALL_ITEMS(id, func)	These events tell you when an item was deleted or when all items were deleted.
EVT_LIST_ITEM_SELECTED(id, func) EVT_LIST_ITEM_DESELECTED(id, func)	Used to detect a selection or deselection event.
EVT_LIST_ITEM_ACTIVATED(id, func)	Detect an activation with the Enter key or a double-click.
EVT_LIST_ITEM_FOCUSED(id, func)	Use to be notified when the focus has changed to a different item.
EVT_LIST_ITEM_MIDDLE_CLICK(id, func) EVT_LIST_ITEM_RIGHT_CLICK(id, func)	Use to detect when the middle or right mouse button has been clicked.
EVT_LIST_KEY_DOWN(id, func)	Use to detect when a key has been pressed. Use wxListEvent::GetKeyCode to find the key pressed.
EVT_LIST_INSERT_ITEM(id, func)	Use to detect the insertion of an item.
EVT_LIST_COL_CLICK(id, func) EVT_LIST_COL_RIGHT_CLICK(id, func)	Use to detect a left or right mouse click on a column. Use wxListEvent::Get Column in conjunction with these events.
EVT_LIST_COL_BEGIN_DRAG(id, func) EVT_LIST_COL_DRAGGING(id, func) EVT_LIST_COL_END_DRAG(id, func)	Generated when a column is being resized; you can veto the begin drag event. Use wxListEvent::GetColumn in conjunction with these events.
EVT_LIST_CACHE_HINT(id, func)	If you are implementing a virtual list control, you may want to update internal data structures before a range of items is drawn. Use this event to do the updating at the right time, calling wxListEvent::GetCacheFrom and wxListEvent::GetCacheTo to find the items that need updating.

wxListItem

wxListItem is a class you can use to insert an item, set an item's properties, or retrieve information from an item.

Use SetMask to indicate which properties you want to be taken into account, as described in Table 12-5.

Table 12-5 wxListItem Mask Flags

wxLIST_MASK_STATE	The state property is valid.
wxLIST_MASK_TEXT	The text property is valid.
wxLIST_MASK_IMAGE	The image property is valid.
wxLIST_MASK_DATA	The data property is valid.
wxLIST_MASK_WIDTH	The width property is valid.
wxLIST_MASK_FORMAT	The format property is valid.

Call SetId to set the zero-based item position, and call SetColumn to set the zero-based column position if the control is in report mode.

Call SetState to set the item state, as listed in Table 12-6.

Table 12-6 wxListItem State Styles

wxLIST_STATE_DONTCARE	We don't care what the state is.
wxLIST_STATE_DROPHILITED	The item is highlighted to receive a drop event (Windows only).
wxLIST_STATE_FOCUSED	The item has the focus.
wxLIST_STATE_SELECTED	The item is selected.
wxLIST_STATE_CUT	The item is in the cut state (Windows only).

Call SetStateMask to indicate which states you are modifying. This method uses the same symbols as for SetState.

Call SetText to set the label or header text, and call SetImage to set the zero-based index into an image list.

Call SetData with a long integer argument to associate data with the item.

For columns only, call SetFormat with wxLIST_FORMAT_LEFT, wxLIST_FORMAT_RIGHT, or wxLIST_FORMAT_CENTRE (identical to wxLIST_FORMAT_CENTER). Also for columns only, call SetColumnWidth to set the column's width.

Other functions set various additional visual properties: SetAlign, SetBackgroundColour, SetTextColour, and SetFont. These don't require a mask flag to be specified. All wxListItem functions have equivalent accessors prefixed by Get for retrieving information about an item.

Here's an example of using wxListItem to select the second item, set its text label, and color it red:

```
wxListItem item;
item.SetId(1);
item.SetMask(wxLIST_MASK_STATE|wxLIST_MASK_TEXT);
item.SetStateMask(wxLIST_STATE_SELECTED);
item.SetState(wxLIST_STATE_SELECTED);
item.SetTextColour(*wxRED);
item.SetText(wxT("Red thing"));

listCtrl->SetItem(item);
```

As an alternative to using wxListItem, you can set and get properties for an item with wxListCtrl convenience functions such as SetItemText, SetItemImage, SetItemState, GetItemText, GetItemImage, GetItemState, and so on as described in the following.

wxListCtrl Member Functions

These are the important wxListCtrl functions.

Call Arrange to arrange the items in icon or small icon view, on Windows only.

Use AssignImageList to associate an image list and have wxListCtrl handle its deletion; use SetImageList if you don't want wxListCtrl to delete it. Pass wxIMAGE_LIST_NORMAL or wxIMAGE_LIST_SMALL to tell wxListCtrl what set of icons this image list will be used for. GetImageList retrieves a pointer to either list.

InsertItem inserts an item at the specified position in the control. You can pass a wxListItem object having set its member variables. Alternatively, you can pass an item index and a string label, or an item index and an image index, or an item index, a label, and an image index. InsertColumn inserts a column in report view.

ClearAll deletes all items and (in report view) columns, and it generates an all-items deletion event. DeleteAllItems deletes all items but not columns and generates an all-items deletion event. DeleteItem deletes a single item and generates an item deletion event. DeleteColumn deletes a column in report view.

Use SetItem to set information about an item: you can pass a wxListItem object as explained previously, or you can pass an index, column, label, and image index. GetItem can be used to get information about the index specified with wxListItem::SetId.

Call SetItemData with an index and a long data value to associate application-defined data with the item. For most platforms, you can store a pointer in this integer value, but on some platforms, a pointer will not fit into an integer. In these cases, you can use a hashmap to map from integer to object pointer, for example. GetItemData retrieves the item for the given index. Note that if the position of an item moves due to sorting, insertion, or removal, the index of the item may change, but its item data will remain the same, so this is a way of identifying an item.

Use SetItemImage to change the image associated with an item; it takes an item index and an index into the image list.

SetItemState sets the state for the given item; you must supply a state mask to specify which state flags are being changed. See the description for wxListItem in the previous section for more details. GetItemState is used to retrieve the state for a given item.

Use SetItemText to set the item's label and GetItemText to retrieve the label.

SetTextColour sets the text color for all items, and SetBackgroundColour sets the background color for the control. SetItemTextColour and SetItemBackgroundColour set an individual item's text and background colors, in report view only. The usual getters are available to retrieve text and background colors.

EditLabel starts editing a label and sends a wxEVT_LIST_BEGIN_LABEL_EDIT event. You can get the current text control used for editing with GetEditControl (Windows only).

Use EnsureVisible if you need a particular item to be visible. ScrollList scrolls by a given number of pixels in each orientation (Windows only). Use RefreshItem or RefreshItems to refresh the appearance of an item or a range of items, particularly when using a virtual list control when the underlying data has changed. GetTopItem returns the index of the topmost visible item when in list or report view.

FindItem is a versatile overloaded function that can be used to search for items with a given label, data, or position. GetNextItem is used to search for an item with the given state (for example, to find all selected items). Use HitTest to find an item at a given point. GetItemPosition returns the position of an item in icon or small icon view in client coordinates, and GetItemRect returns an item's size and position in client coordinates.

You can change the style of a wxListCtrl dynamically, without having to destroy and re-create it: use SetSingleStyle to set a style such as wxLC_REPORT. Pass false to this function to remove the style.

Use SetColumn in report mode to set information about a column, such as header label and width: see wxListItem in the previous section. Use SetColumnWidth to set a column's width, as a simpler alternative to SetColumn. You can get column information with GetColumn and GetColumnWidth. Get the number of columns with GetColumnCount (report view only).

Get the number of items in a list control with GetItemCount and the number of selected items with GetSelectedItemCount. GetCountPerPage returns the number of items that can fit vertically in the visible area of the control (in list or report view) or the total number of items in the control (icon or small icon view).

Finally, SortItems can be used to sort the items in a list control. Pass the address of a wxListCtrlCompare function that takes two item data values and a further data integer, and returns an integer representing the ordering of the two items. This integer should be zero for identity, negative if the first is less than the second, and positive if the first is greater than the second. For sorting to work, you must associate a long integer value with each item (via wxListItem::SetData, for example). These values will be passed to the comparison function.

Using *wxListCtrl*

The following fragment shows how to create and populate a report list control. The list has three columns and ten items, each with a 16×16 file icon at the start of the row.

```cpp
#include "wx/listctrl.h"

// Images for report items
#include "file.xpm"
#include "folder.xpm"

// Create a list in report mode
wxListCtrl* listCtrlReport = new wxListCtrl(
    this, wxID_ANY, wxDefaultPosition, wxSize(400, 400),
    wxLC_REPORT|wxLC_SINGLE_SEL);

// Assign an image list to the control
wxImageList* imageList = new wxImageList(16, 16);
imageList->Add(wxIcon(folder_xpm));
imageList->Add(wxIcon(file_xpm));
listCtrlReport->AssignImageList(imageList, wxIMAGE_LIST_SMALL);

// Insert three columns
wxListItem itemCol;
itemCol.SetText(wxT("Column 1"));
itemCol.SetImage(-1);
listCtrlReport->InsertColumn(0, itemCol);
listCtrlReport->SetColumnWidth(0, wxLIST_AUTOSIZE );

itemCol.SetText(wxT("Column 2"));
itemCol.SetAlign(wxLIST_FORMAT_CENTRE);
listCtrlReport->InsertColumn(1, itemCol);
listCtrlReport->SetColumnWidth(1, wxLIST_AUTOSIZE );

itemCol.SetText(wxT("Column 3"));
itemCol.SetAlign(wxLIST_FORMAT_RIGHT);
listCtrlReport->InsertColumn(2, itemCol);
listCtrlReport->SetColumnWidth(2, wxLIST_AUTOSIZE );

// Insert ten items
for ( int i = 0; i < 10; i++ )
{
    int imageIndex = 0;
    wxString buf;

    // Insert an item, with a string for column 0,
    // and image index 0
    buf.Printf(wxT("This is item %d"), i);
    listCtrlReport->InsertItem(i, buf, imageIndex);

    // The item may change position due to e.g. sorting,
    // so store the original index in the item's data
    listCtrlReport->SetItemData(i, i);

    // Set a string for column 1
    buf.Printf(wxT("Col 1, item %d"), i);
    listCtrlReport->SetItem(i, 1, buf);
```

```
        // Set a string for column 2
        buf.Printf(wxT("Item %d in column 2"), i);
        listCtrlReport->SetItem(i, 2, buf);
}
```

Virtual List Controls

Normally, wxListCtrl stores the label, image, and visual attributes for each
item. This is fine for a modest amount of data, but if you have thousands of
items, you may want to consider implementing a virtual list control. You supply the virtual functions OnGetItemLabel, OnGetItemImage, and OnGetItemAttr for
the control to call when it needs the information. You must call SetItemCount to
indicate how many items there are in the list control because you won't be
appending any items in the usual way. You can optionally use
EVT_LIST_CACHE_HINT to update your internal structures for a given range of
items, just before painting is about to happen. Here are trivial examples of the
three overridden functions:

```
wxString MyListCtrl::OnGetItemText(long item, long column) const
{
    return wxString::Format(wxT("Column %ld of item %ld"), column, item);
}

int MyListCtrl::OnGetItemImage(long WXUNUSED(item)) const
{
    // Return the zeroth image for all items
    return 0;
}

wxListItemAttr *MyListCtrl::OnGetItemAttr(long item) const
{
    // Use internally stored attributes for every other items
    return item % 2 ? NULL : (wxListItemAttr *)&m_attr;
}
```

To create and populate the virtual list, we don't append any items; we simply
set the item count to a ridiculously large number:

```
virtualListCtrl = new MyListCtrl(parent, wxID_ANY,
        wxDefaultPosition, wxDefaultSize, wxLC_REPORT|wxLC_VIRTUAL);
virtualListCtrl->SetImageList(imageListSmall, wxIMAGE_LIST_SMALL);

virtualListCtrl->InsertColumn(0, wxT("First Column"));
virtualListCtrl->InsertColumn(1, wxT("Second Column"));
virtualListCtrl->SetColumnWidth(0, 150);
virtualListCtrl->SetColumnWidth(1, 150);

virtualListCtrl->SetItemCount(1000000);
```

When the underlying data changes in the control, set the item count if it has changed and call `wxListCtrl::RefreshItem` or `wxListCtrl::RefreshItems`.

For a full sample, please see `samples/listctrl`.

wxWIZARD

The wizard is a great way to break a complex set of choices and settings down into a sequence of simple dialogs. It can be presented to novice users to help them get started with a particular feature in an application, such as gathering information for a new project, exporting data, and so on. Often the settings presented in a wizard can be altered elsewhere in the application's user interface, but presenting them in a wizard focuses the user on the essentials for getting a specific task completed.

A wizard comprises a series of dialog-like pages set inside a window that normally has an image on the left (the same for all pages, or different for each page), and a row of buttons along the bottom for navigating between pages and getting help. As the user progresses through the wizard, the old page is hidden and a new one is shown. The path through a wizard can be determined by choices the user makes, so not all available pages are necessarily shown each time a wizard is presented.

When the standard wizard buttons are pressed, events are sent to the pages (and to the `wxWizard` object). You can catch events either in the page class or in a class derived from `wxWizard`.

To show a wizard, create an instance of `wxWizard` (or a derived class) and create the pages as children of the wizard. You can use `wxWizardPageSimple` (or a derived class) and chain the pages together with `wxWizardPageSimple::Chain`. Or, if you need to determine the path through the wizard dynamically according to user selections, you can derive from `wxWizardPage` and override `GetPrev` and `GetNext`. Add each page to the sizer returned by `GetPageAreaSizer` so that the wizard can adapt its size to the largest page.

`wxWizard`'s only special window style is `wxWIZARD_EX_HELPBUTTON`, which adds a *Help* button to the wizard's row of standard buttons. This is an "extra" style, which must be set with `SetExtraStyle` before `Create` is called.

wxWizard Events

`wxWizard` generates `wxWizardEvent` events, which are described in Table 12-7. These events are sent first to the page, and if not processed, to the wizard itself. Except for `EVT_WIZARD_FINISHED`, event handlers can call `wxWizard Event::GetPage` to determine the currently active page.

Table 12-7 wxWizard Events

EVT_WIZARD_PAGE_CHANGED(id, func)	Use this event to detect when a page has been changed. The event handler function can call wxWizardEvent:: GetDirection (true if going forward).
EVT_WIZARD_PAGE_CHANGING(id, func)	Use to detect when a page is about to be changed (including when the *Finish* button was clicked); the event can be vetoed. The event handler function can call wxWizardEvent::GetDirection (true if going forward).
EVT_WIZARD_CANCEL(id, func)	Used to detect when the user has clicked the *Cancel* button; this can be vetoed.
EVT_WIZARD_HELP(id, func)	Use to show help when the user clicks on the *Help* button.
EVT_WIZARD_FINISHED(id, func)	Use to react to the user clicking on the *Finish* button. This event is generated just after the dialog has been closed.

wxWizard Member Functions

These are the main member functions for wxWizard.

GetPageAreaSizer returns the sizer that manages the page area. Add all pages to this sizer, or one page from which the others can be reached with GetNext, to make the wizard size itself according to the maximum page size. If you don't do this, you should call FitToPage for the first page before running the wizard, or for all pages if calling wxWizardPage::GetNext might not visit all pages.

GetCurrentPage returns the current active page, or NULL if RunWizard is not executing.

GetPageSize returns the size available for all pages. You can use SetPageSize to set the page size used by all pages, but this is deprecated in favor of adding pages to the sizer returned by GetPageAreaSizer.

Call RunWizard to set the wizard running, passing the first page to be shown. RunWizard returns true if the user successfully finished the wizard, or false if the user cancelled it.

To specify the border around the page area, call SetBorder. The default is zero.

wxWizard Example

Let's examine the wxWizard sample from the wxWidgets distribution. It consists of four pages, illustrated in Figure 12-3 (the numbers are for clarity and are not on the actual dialogs).

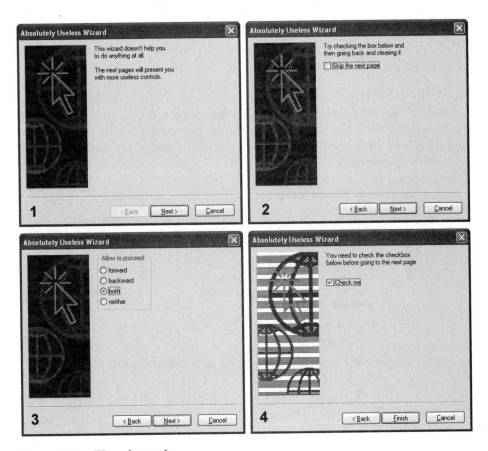

Figure 12-3   Wizard sample

The first page is so simple that it doesn't have its own derived class—the driving function `MyFrame::OnRunWizard` simply creates an instance of `wxWizardPageSimple` and adds a static text control to it, like this:

```
#include "wx/wizard.h"

wxWizard *wizard = new wxWizard(this, wxID_ANY,
                wxT("Absolutely Useless Wizard"),
                wxBitmap(wiztest_xpm),
                wxDefaultPosition,
                wxDEFAULT_DIALOG_STYLE | wxRESIZE_BORDER);
// PAGE 1
wxWizardPageSimple *page1 = new wxWizardPageSimple(wizard);
wxStaticText *text = new wxStaticText(page1, wxID_ANY,
```

```
        wxT("This wizard doesn't help you\nto do anything at all.\n")
        wxT("\n")
        wxT("The next pages will present you\nwith more useless controls."),
            wxPoint(5,5));
```

The second page, wxCheckboxPage, is derived from wxWizardPage and implements
GetPrev and GetNext. GetPrev always returns the first page, but GetNext can
return either the next page or the last page, depending on whether the user
checked *Skip the Next Page*. Here's the declaration and implementation of
wxCheckBoxPage:

```
// this shows how to dynamically (i.e. during run-time) arrange
// the page order
// PAGE 2
class wxCheckboxPage : public wxWizardPage
{
public:
    wxCheckboxPage(wxWizard *parent,
                   wxWizardPage *prev,
                   wxWizardPage *next)
        : wxWizardPage(parent)
    {
        m_prev = prev;
        m_next = next;

        wxBoxSizer *mainSizer = new wxBoxSizer(wxVERTICAL);

        mainSizer->Add(
            new wxStaticText(this, wxID_ANY, wxT("Try checking the box
below and\n")
                                         wxT("then going back and clearing it")),
            0, // No vertical stretching
            wxALL,
            5 // Border width
        );

        m_checkbox = new wxCheckBox(this, wxID_ANY,
                        wxT("&Skip the next page"));
        mainSizer->Add(
            m_checkbox,
            0, // No vertical stretching
            wxALL,
            5 // Border width
        );

        SetSizer(mainSizer);
        mainSizer->Fit(this);
    }

    // implement wxWizardPage functions
    virtual wxWizardPage *GetPrev() const { return m_prev; }
    virtual wxWizardPage *GetNext() const
    {
        return m_checkbox->GetValue() ? m_next->GetNext() : m_next;
```

```
    }

private:
    wxWizardPage *m_prev,
                 *m_next;

    wxCheckBox *m_checkbox;
};
```

The third page, wxRadioboxPage, intercepts cancel and page changing events. If
you try to cancel at this point, you will be asked to confirm the cancel: if you
click on *No*, wxWizardEvent::Veto will be called and the wizard will not be cancelled. OnWizardPageChanging vetoes any attempt to go forwards or backwards
that hasn't first been specified using the radio buttons. In a realistic application, you might use the page changing event to ensure that the user has filled
out all mandatory fields in this page before proceeding. Or you may want to
prevent the user from going back one page for some reason. This is the code for
wxRadioboxPage:

```
// This is a more complicated example of validity checking:
// using events we may allow the user to return to the previous
// page, but not to proceed. It also demonstrates how to
// intercept a Cancel button press.
// PAGE 3
class wxRadioboxPage : public wxWizardPageSimple
{
public:
    // directions in which we allow the user to proceed from this
    // page
    enum
    {
        Forward, Backward, Both, Neither
    };

    wxRadioboxPage(wxWizard *parent) : wxWizardPageSimple(parent)
    {
        // should correspond to the enum above
        static wxString choices[] = { wxT("forward"), wxT("backward"),
wxT("both"), wxT("neither") };

        m_radio = new wxRadioBox(this, wxID_ANY, wxT("Allow to proceed:"),
                                 wxDefaultPosition, wxDefaultSize,
                                 WXSIZEOF(choices), choices,
                                 1, wxRA_SPECIFY_COLS);
        m_radio->SetSelection(Both);

        wxBoxSizer *mainSizer = new wxBoxSizer(wxVERTICAL);
        mainSizer->Add(
            m_radio,
            0, // No stretching
            wxALL,
            5 // Border
        );
        SetSizer(mainSizer);
```

```
        mainSizer->Fit(this);
    }

    // wizard event handlers
    void OnWizardCancel(wxWizardEvent& event)
    {
        if ( wxMessageBox(wxT("Do you really want to cancel?"),
                          wxT("Question"),
                          wxICON_QUESTION | wxYES_NO, this) != wxYES )
        {
            // not confirmed
            event.Veto();
        }
    }

    void OnWizardPageChanging(wxWizardEvent& event)
    {
        int sel = m_radio->GetSelection();

        if ( sel == Both )
            return;

        if ( event.GetDirection() && sel == Forward )
            return;

        if ( !event.GetDirection() && sel == Backward )
            return;

        wxMessageBox(wxT("You can't go there"), wxT("Not allowed"),
                     wxICON_WARNING | wxOK, this);

        event.Veto();
    }

private:
    wxRadioBox *m_radio;

    DECLARE_EVENT_TABLE()
};
```

The fourth and last page, wxValidationPage, overrides TransferDataFromWindow to do a validation check on the state of the check box. TransferDataFromWindow is called whenever the *Back* or *Next* buttons are clicked, and if the validation or data transfer fails, the page is not changed. As with all dialogs, instead of overriding TransferDataFromWindow, you can use validators for the page controls. This page also demonstrates the use of an image for a particular page, overriding the image passed to the wizard constructor. Here's the code for wxValidationPage:

```
// This shows how to simply control the validity of the user input
// by just overriding TransferDataFromWindow() - of course, in a
// real program, the check wouldn't be so trivial and the data
// will be saved somewhere too.
//
```

```
// It also shows how to use a different bitmap for one of the pages.
// PAGE 4
class wxValidationPage : public wxWizardPageSimple
{
public:
    wxValidationPage(wxWizard *parent) : wxWizardPageSimple(parent)
    {
        m_bitmap = wxBitmap(wiztest2_xpm);

        m_checkbox = new wxCheckBox(this, wxID_ANY,
                            wxT("&Check me"));

        wxBoxSizer *mainSizer = new wxBoxSizer(wxVERTICAL);
        mainSizer->Add(
            new wxStaticText(this, wxID_ANY,
                    wxT("You need to check the checkbox\n")
                    wxT("below before going to the next page\n")),
            0,
            wxALL,
            5
        );

        mainSizer->Add(
            m_checkbox,
            0, // No stretching
            wxALL,
            5 // Border
        );
        SetSizer(mainSizer);
        mainSizer->Fit(this);
    }

    virtual bool TransferDataFromWindow()
    {
        if ( !m_checkbox->GetValue() )
        {
            wxMessageBox(wxT("Check the checkbox first!"),
                        wxT("No way"),
                        wxICON_WARNING | wxOK, this);

            return false;
        }
        return true;
    }

private:
    wxCheckBox *m_checkbox;
};
```

The code that puts all the pages together and starts the wizard looks like this:

```
void MyFrame::OnRunWizard(wxCommandEvent& event)
{
    wxWizard *wizard = new wxWizard(this, wxID_ANY,
                    wxT("Absolutely Useless Wizard"),
                    wxBitmap(wiztest_xpm),
                    wxDefaultPosition,
                    wxDEFAULT_DIALOG_STYLE | wxRESIZE_BORDER);
```

```
        // a wizard page may be either an object of a predefined class
        wxWizardPageSimple *page1 = new wxWizardPageSimple(wizard);
        wxStaticText *text = new wxStaticText(page1, wxID_ANY,
            wxT("This wizard doesn't help you\nto do anything at all.\n")
            wxT("\n")
            wxT("The next pages will present you\nwith more useless
controls."),
            wxPoint(5,5)
            );

        // ... or a derived class
        wxRadioboxPage *page3 = new wxRadioboxPage(wizard);
        wxValidationPage *page4 = new wxValidationPage(wizard);

        // set the page order using a convenience function - could
        // also use SetNext/Prev directly as below
        wxWizardPageSimple::Chain(page3, page4);

        // this page is not a wxWizardPageSimple, so we use SetNext/Prev
        // to insert it into the chain of pages
        wxCheckboxPage *page2 = new wxCheckboxPage(wizard, page1, page3);
        page1->SetNext(page2);
        page3->SetPrev(page2);

        // allow the wizard to size itself around the pages
        wizard->GetPageAreaSizer()->Add(page1);

        if ( wizard->RunWizard(page1) )
        {
            wxMessageBox(wxT("The wizard successfully completed"),
              wxT("That's all"), wxICON_INFORMATION | wxOK);
        }

        wizard->Destroy();
}
```

When the wizard is finished or canceled, MyFrame intercepts the events and, in this example, reports them on the frame's status bar. You could equally intercept these events in a class derived from wxWizard.

The full listing of the sample can be found in Appendix J, "Code Listings," and the code can be found in examples/chap12 on the CD-ROM.

wxHtmlWindow

wxHtmlWindow is used by wxWidgets' built-in help system, and it is also a great control to use in your applications whenever you need to display formatted text and graphics, such as reports. It can display a useful subset of HTML, including tables, but not frames. Features include animated GIFs, highlighted links, fonts, background color, nested lists, centering, right-alignment, horizontal rules, character encoding support, and more. It doesn't support style sheets, but you can normally achieve the effects you want by writing or generating the appropriate tags. HTML text is selectable and can be copied to the clipboard or returned to the application as plain text.

Figure 12-4 shows the wxHtmlWindow demo program that you can compile and run in samples/html/test.

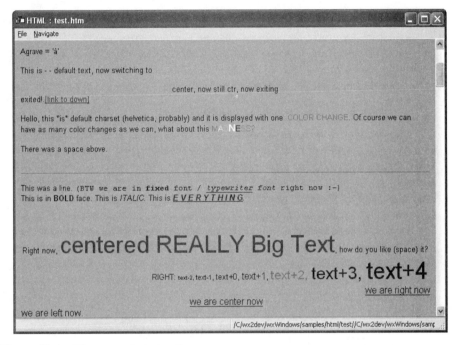

Figure 12-4   The wxHtmlWindow demo program

Because wxHtmlWindow is small and fast (unlike a full web browser), you can use it liberally in your application. Figure 12-5 shows an example of wxHtmlWindow in an "About" box.

Figure 12-5   wxHtmlWindow in an About box

The code to create this dialog is shown in Listing 12-1. In this example, the HTML control is sized to fit the HTML that has been loaded, and then the dialog sizers set the dialog to fit around the wxHtmlWindow.

Listing 12-1   Code to Create an HTML About Box

```
#include "wx/html/htmlwin.h"

void MyFrame::OnAbout(wxCommandEvent& WXUNUSED(event))
{
    wxBoxSizer *topsizer;
    wxHtmlWindow *html;
    wxDialog dlg(this, wxID_ANY, wxString(_("About")));

    topsizer = new wxBoxSizer(wxVERTICAL);

    html = new wxHtmlWindow(&dlg, wxID_ANY, wxDefaultPosition,
            wxSize(380, 160), wxHW_SCROLLBAR_NEVER);

    html->SetBorders(0);

    html->LoadPage(wxT("data/about.htm"));

    // Fit the HTML window to the size of its contents
    html->SetSize(html->GetInternalRepresentation()->GetWidth(),
                  html->GetInternalRepresentation()->GetHeight());

    topsizer->Add(html, 1, wxALL, 10);

    topsizer->Add(new wxStaticLine(&dlg, wxID_ANY), 0, wxEXPAND ¦ wxLEFT ¦
wxRIGHT, 10);

    wxButton *but = new wxButton(&dlg, wxID_OK, _("OK"));
    but->SetDefault();

    topsizer->Add(but, 0, wxALL ¦ wxALIGN_RIGHT, 15);

    dlg.SetSizer(topsizer);
    topsizer->Fit(&dlg);

    dlg.ShowModal();
}
```

Listing 12-2 shows the HTML that displays as in the sample screenshot.

Listing 12-2   HTML for the About Box Sample

```
<html>
<body bgcolor="#FFFFFF">
<table cellspacing=3 cellpadding=4 width="100%">
```

(continues)

Listing 12-2 *(continued)*
```html
  <tr>
    <td bgcolor="#101010">
    <center>
    <font size=+2 color="#FFFFFF"><b><br>wxHTML Library Sample
0.2.0<br></b>
    </font>
    </center>
    </td>
  </tr>
  <tr>
    <td bgcolor="#73A183">
    <b><font size=+1>Copyright (C) 1999 Vaclav Slavik</font></b><p>
    <font size=-1>
      <table cellpadding=0 cellspacing=0 width="100%">
        <tr>
          <td width="65%">
            Vaclav Slavik<p>
          </td>
          <td valign=top>
            <img src="logo.png">
          </td>
        </tr>
      </table>
    <font size=1>
    Licenced under wxWindows Library Licence, Version 3.
    </font>
    </font>
    </td>
  </tr>
</table>
</body>
</html>
```

See also the `wxHtmlListBox` class as described in the section "`wxListBox` and `wxCheckListBox`" in Chapter 4, "Window Basics."

wxHtmlWindow Styles

Table 12-8 lists the styles you can pass to the `wxHtmlWindow` constructor or `Create` function. Also refer to the available styles for `wxWindow` in Table 4-1.

Table 12-8   `wxHtmlWindow` Window Styles

`wxHW_SCROLLBAR_NEVER`	Never displays scrollbars.
`wxHW_SCROLLBAR_AUTO`	Displays scrollbars only if the page size exceeds the window size.
`wxHW_NO_SELECTION`	Prevents the user from selecting text. Normally, text can be selected.

wxHtmlWindow Member Functions

These are the main member functions for wxHtmlWindow.

GetInternalRepresentation returns the top-level wxHtmlContainerCell object, whose size you can query with GetWidth and GetHeight to get the overall size of the HTML.

LoadFile loads HTML from a file and displays it. LoadPage takes a location, which may be a URL. Examples of locations include:

```
http://www.wxwindows.org/front.htm   # A URL
file:myapp.zip#zip:html/index.htm    # Gets index.htm from myapp.zip
```

SetPage sets the page using an HTML string rather than a file name or location.

OnCellClicked is called when there was a mouse click inside a cell. It takes a wxHtmlCell pointer, x and y coordinates, and a wxMouseEvent reference. The default behavior is to call OnLinkClicked if the cell contains a hyperlink.

OnLinkClicked takes a wxHtmlLinkInfo reference, and its default behavior is to load the linked page with LoadPage. You can override this behavior, for example to show the application's home page in the default browser when the user clicks on the link in your "About" box.

You can also override OnOpeningURL, which is called when a URL is being opened, and OnCellMouseHover, called when the mouse moves over an HTML cell.

ReadCustomization and WriteCustomization are used to preserve fonts and borders, and they take a wxConfig* argument and optional path to use in the configuration object.

You can select text with the functions SelectAll, SelectLine, and SelectWord. SelectionToText returns a string with the plain text in the selection. ToText returns the entire page as plain text.

Call SetBorders to set the space around the HTML. SetFonts enables you to set the faces for normal and fixed fonts, and optionally you can pass an array of seven integers specifying the point sizes of the seven font sizes.

AppendToPage can be used to add HTML to the current page and refresh the window.

You can write a custom wxHtmlFilter to read special files, and you can call AddFilter to register it with wxHtmlWindow. For example, you might write a filter to decrypt an encrypted HTML e-book.

GetOpenedAnchor, GetOpenedPage, and GetOpenedPageTitle return information about the currently loaded page.

wxHtmlWindow has a history mechanism, which you can access with HistoryBack, HistoryForward, HistoryCanBack, HistoryCanForward, and HistoryClear.

Embedding Windows in HTML Pages

You can also add windows, including your own custom controls, to an HTML page, as Figure 12-6 shows. This is done by writing a custom "tag handler," which parses the HTML fragment for a specified tag name and creates and inserts a window.

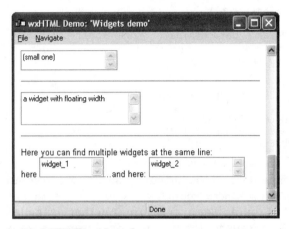

Figure 12-6   Embedded HTML widget demo

This is part of the HTML page shown in the screenshot:

```
<mybind name="(small one)" x=150 y=30>
<hr>
<mybind name="a widget with floating width" float=y x="50" y=50>
<hr>
Here you can find multiple widgets at the same line:<br>
 here
<mybind name="widget_1" x="100" y=30>
...and here:
<mybind name="widget_2" x="150" y=30>
```

The code to implement the custom HTML tag `mybind` looks like this:

```
#include "wx/html/m_templ.h"

TAG_HANDLER_BEGIN(MYBIND, "MYBIND")

TAG_HANDLER_PROC(tag)
{
    wxWindow *wnd;
    int ax, ay;
    int fl = 0;
```

```
    tag.ScanParam(wxT("X"), wxT("%i"), &ax);
    tag.ScanParam(wxT("Y"), wxT("%i"), &ay);

    if (tag.HasParam(wxT("FLOAT"))) fl = ax;

    wnd = new wxTextCtrl(m_WParser->GetWindow(), wxID_ANY,
tag.GetParam(wxT("NAME")),
        wxPoint(0,0), wxSize(ax, ay), wxTE_MULTILINE);

    wnd->Show(true);

    m_WParser->GetContainer()->InsertCell(new wxHtmlWidgetCell(wnd, fl));

    return false;
}

TAG_HANDLER_END(MYBIND)

TAGS_MODULE_BEGIN(MyBind)
    TAGS_MODULE_ADD(MYBIND)
TAGS_MODULE_END(MyBind)
```

This technique might be useful if you wanted to create a whole user interface around wxHtmlWindow, possibly using scripts to generate the HTML and respond to input, like a web form. Another example is a registration dialog, with text controls for the user to enter his or her details and a *Register* button that sends the details to your organization. Or you might want to generate a report with items that can be selected and viewed in more detail by toggling a check box next to each item.

For more details of how to write your own tag handlers, see samples/ html/widget and the wxWidgets reference manual.

HTML Printing

It's likely that if you use wxHtmlWindow extensively within your application, you'll want to print HTML files, too. wxWidgets provides a class to make this easy, appropriately called wxHtmlEasyPrinting. Create one instance of this class for the lifetime of your application and then call PreviewFile and PrintFile with the name of the local HTML file to print. You can also call PageSetup to show the page setup dialog, and you can retrieve the print and page setup settings using GetPrintData and GetPageSetupData. Customize the header and footer of the printout with SetHeader and SetFooter, which can contain the keywords @PAGENUM@ (the current page) and @PAGESCNT@ (the total number of pages).

This fragment from the sample in samples/html/printing demonstrates the basic principles and shows how to change the font sizes.

```
#include "wx/html/htmlwin.h"
#include "wx/html/htmprint.h"
```

```
MyFrame::MyFrame(const wxString& title,
                const wxPoint& pos, const wxSize& size)
       : wxFrame((wxFrame *)NULL, wxID_ANY, title, pos, size)
{
    ...

    m_Name = wxT("testfile.htm");

    m_Prn = new wxHtmlEasyPrinting(_("Easy Printing Demo"), this);
    m_Prn->SetHeader(m_Name + wxT("(@PAGENUM@/@PAGESCNT@)<hr>"),
                     wxPAGE_ALL);
}

MyFrame::~MyFrame()
{
    delete m_Prn;
}

void MyFrame::OnPageSetup(wxCommandEvent& event)
{
    m_Prn->PageSetup();
}


void MyFrame::OnPrint(wxCommandEvent& event)
{
    m_Prn->PrintFile(m_Name);
}


void MyFrame::OnPreview(wxCommandEvent& event)
{
    m_Prn->PreviewFile(m_Name);
}

void MyFrame::OnPrintSmall(wxCommandEvent& event)
{
    int fontsizes[] = { 4, 6, 8, 10, 12, 20, 24 };
    m_Prn->SetFonts(wxEmptyString, wxEmptyString, fontsizes);
}

void MyFrame::OnPrintNormal(wxCommandEvent& event)
{
    m_Prn->SetFonts(wxEmptyString, wxEmptyString, 0);
}

void MyFrame::OnPrintHuge(wxCommandEvent& event)
{
    int fontsizes[] = { 20, 26, 28, 30, 32, 40, 44 };
    m_Prn->SetFonts(wxEmptyString, wxEmptyString, fontsizes);
}
```

For examples of all the preceding wxHTML topics, see the samples under samples/html in your wxWidgets distribution.

wxGRID

wxGrid is a versatile and somewhat complex class for presenting information in a tabular form. You could make a property sheet out of a grid with name and value columns, create a general-purpose spreadsheet by adding your own formula evaluation code, show a table from a database, or display statistical data generated by your application. In some situations, you might consider wxGrid as an alternative to wxListCtrl in report mode, particularly if you need to display images or arbitrary graphics in cells.

A grid can display optional row and column headers, drawn in a similar way to the headers in a spreadsheet application. The user can drag column and row dividers, select one or more cells, and click a cell to edit it. Each cell in a grid has its own attributes for font, color, and alignment and also may have its own specialized renderer (for drawing the data) and editor (for editing the data). You can write your own renderers and editors: see include/wx/generic/grid.h and src/generic/grid.cpp in your wxWidgets distribution for guidance. By default, a grid cell will use a simple string renderer and editor. If you have complex requirements for cell formatting, then rather than set attributes for each cell, you can create an "attribute provider" class that dynamically returns attributes for each cell when needed.

You can also create a potentially enormous "virtual" grid where storage is provided by the application, not by wxGrid. To do this, you derive a class from wxGridTableBase and override functions including GetValue, GetNumberRows, and GetNumberCols. These functions will reflect data stored in your application or perhaps in a database. Then plug the table into a grid using SetTable, and the grid will use your data. These more advanced techniques are demonstrated in samples/grid in your wxWidgets distribution, as shown in Figure 12-7.

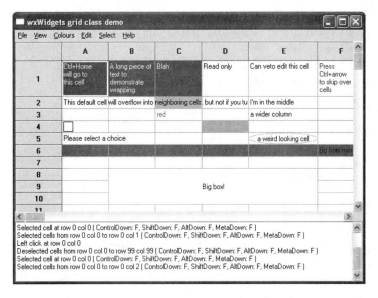

Figure 12-7 `wxGrid`

Listing 12-3 shows an example of creating a simple grid with eight rows and ten columns.

Listing 12-3 Simple Use of *wxGrid*

```
#include "wx/grid.h"

// Create a wxGrid object
wxGrid* grid = new wxGrid(frame, wxID_ANY,
                          wxDefaultPosition, wxSize(400, 300));
// Then we call CreateGrid to set the dimensions of the grid
// (8 rows and 10 columns in this example)
grid->CreateGrid(8, 10);

// We can set the sizes of individual rows and columns
// in pixels
grid->SetRowSize(0, 60);
grid->SetColSize(0, 120 );

// And set grid cell contents as strings
grid->SetCellValue(0, 0, wxT("wxGrid is good"));

// We can specify that some cells are read-only
grid->SetCellValue(0, 3, wxT("This is read-only"));
grid->SetReadOnly(0, 3);

// Colors can be specified for grid cell contents
grid->SetCellValue(3, 3, wxT("green on grey"));
grid->SetCellTextColour(3, 3, *wxGREEN);
grid->SetCellBackgroundColour(3, 3, *wxLIGHT_GREY);
```

(continues)

Listing 12-3   *(continued)*
```
// We can specify that some cells will store numeric
// values rather than strings. Here we set grid column 5
// to hold floating point values displayed with width of 6
// and precision of 2
grid->SetColFormatFloat(5, 6, 2);
grid->SetCellValue(0, 6, wxT("3.1415"));

// Set the grid size to the minimum required to show the content
grid->Fit();

// Set the parent frame client size to fit the grid
frame->SetClientSize(grid->GetSize());
```

The *wxGrid* System of Classes

As you have probably gathered by now, wxGrid is not really a single class—it's a set of interacting classes. Table 12-9 clarifies what's available and how the classes relate to each other.

Table 12-9   wxGrid Classes

wxGrid	The main grid window class, containing further windows that manage cells, rows, and columns.
wxGridTableBase	A base class enabling an application to provide data to a virtual grid. An instance of a derived class plugs into wxGrid with SetTable.
wxGridCellAttr	Holds visual attributes used to render a cell. You can implicitly change attributes using convenience functions such as SetCellTextColour. You can set attributes for a cell with SetAttr or for a whole row or column with SetRowAttr and SetColAttr. You can provide a GetAttr function in your table class to return attributes for a given cell.
wxGridCellRenderer	This class is responsible for actually drawing the cell in the grid. You can pass it to wxGridCellAttr (or use wxGrid::SetCellRenderer) to change the format of one cell, or you can pass it to wxGrid::SetDefaultRenderer to change the appearance of all cells. This is an abstract class, and you will normally use one of the predefined derived classes or derive your own class from it. Examples include wxGridCellStringRenderer, wxGridCellNumberRenderer, wxGridCellFloatRenderer, and wxGridCellBoolRenderer.

wxGridCellEditor	This class is responsible for providing and manipulating the in-place edit controls for the grid. Instances of classes derived from wxGridCellEditor can be associated with the cell attributes for individual cells, rows, columns, or even for the entire grid. For example, use wxGrid::SetCellEditor to set an editor for one cell. Examples of editors include wxGridCellTextEditor, wxGridCellFloatEditor, wxGridCellBoolEditor, wxGridCellNumberEditor, and wxGridCellChoiceEditor.
wxGridEvent	Contains information about various grid events, such as mouse clicks on cells, data changing in a cell, a cell being selected, and a cell editor being shown or hidden.
wxGridRangeSelectEvent	This event is sent when the user selects a range of cells.
wxGridSizeEvent	This event class contains information about a row/column resize event.
wxGridEditorCreatedEvent	This event is sent when an editor is created.
wxGridCellCoords	A class representing a cell in the grid. Use GetRow and GetCol to retrieve its position.
wxGridCellCoordsArray	An array of wxGridCellCoords objects. This object is returned by the functions GetSelectedCell, GetSelectionBlockTopLeft, and GetSelectionBlockBottomRight.

wxGrid Events

Table 12-10 lists the major grid events you can catch. Note that each EVT_GRID_... macro also has a form EVT_GRID_CMD_... that takes an identifier and can be used by an ancestor of the grid to avoid the need for deriving a new class.

Table 12-10 wxGrid Events

EVT_GRID_CELL_LEFT_CLICK(func)	The user clicked a cell with the left mouse button.
EVT_GRID_CELL_RIGHT_CLICK(func)	The user clicked a cell with the right mouse button.
EVT_GRID_CELL_LEFT_DCLICK(func)	The user double-clicked a cell with the left mouse button.

(continues)

Table 12-10 wxGrid Events *(Continued)*

EVT_GRID_CELL_RIGHT_DCLICK(func)	The user double-clicked a cell with the right mouse button.
EVT_GRID_LABEL_LEFT_CLICK(func)	The user clicked a label with the left mouse button.
EVT_GRID_LABEL_RIGHT_CLICK(func)	The user clicked a label with the right mouse button.
EVT_GRID_LABEL_LEFT_DCLICK(func)	The user double-clicked a label with the left mouse button.
EVT_GRID_LABEL_RIGHT_DCLICK(func)	The user double-clicked a label with the right mouse button.
EVT_GRID_CELL_CHANGE(func)	The user changed the data in a cell.
EVT_GRID_SELECT_CELL(func)	The user moved to and selected a cell.
EVT_GRID_EDITOR_HIDDEN(func)	The editor for a cell was hidden.
EVT_GRID_EDITOR_SHOWN(func)	The editor for a cell was shown.
EVT_GRID_COL_SIZE(func)	The user resized a column by dragging it.
EVT_GRID_ROW_SIZE(func)	The user resized a row by dragging it.
EVT_GRID_RANGE_SELECT(func)	The user selected a group of contiguous cells.
EVT_GRID_EDITOR_CREATED(func)	The editor for a cell was created.

wxGrid Member Functions

The following is a selection of the most significant wxGrid functions, grouped by functionality. For a complete reference, and for the members of other related classes, please refer to the reference manual.

Functions for Creation, Deletion, and Data Retrieval

These functions relate to creation and deletion of the grid and its cells and interaction with the data in its table.

AppendCols and AppendRows append columns and rows, respectively, to the right or bottom of the grid. You can also use InsertCols and InsertRows to insert them at a given position. If you are using a table, you need to override similarly named functions in your table class.

Use GetNumberCols and GetNumberRows to return the number of columns or rows in the grid table associated with the grid.

CreateGrid creates a grid with the specified initial number of rows and columns. Call this directly after the grid constructor. When you use this function, wxGrid will create and manage a simple table of string values for you. All of the grid data will be stored in memory. For applications with more complex data types or relationships, or for dealing with very large datasets, you should derive your own grid table class and pass a table object to the grid with wxGrid::SetTable.

ClearGrid clears all data in the underlying grid table and repaints the grid. The table is not deleted by this function. If you are using a derived table class, then you need to override wxGridTableBase::Clear for this function to have any effect. ClearSelection deselects all cells that are currently selected.

Use DeleteCols and DeleteRows to delete columns and rows, respectively.

GetColLabelValue returns the specified column label. The default grid table class provides column labels of the form A, B...Z, AA, AB...ZZ, AAA... If you are using a custom grid table, you can override wxGridTableBase:: GetColLabelValue to provide your own labels. Similarly, GetRowLabelValue returns the specified row label. The default grid table class provides numeric row labels. If you are using a custom grid table, you can override wxGridTable Base::GetRowLabelValue to provide your own labels. Use SetColLabelValue and SetRowLabelValue to the set the label for a given column or row.

GetCellValue returns the string contained in the cell at the specified location. For simple applications where a grid object automatically uses a default grid table of string values, you use this function together with SetCellValue to access cell values. For more complex applications where you have derived your own grid table class, you only use this function for cells that contain string values.

Presentation Functions

These functions relate to the way the grid is displayed.

Use BeginBatch and EndBatch to suppress painting between these calls. Painting will only be done when GetBatchCount returns zero.

EnableGridLines turns the drawing of grid lines on or off. Call GridLinesEnabled to determine if they are on or off.

ForceRefresh causes immediate repainting of the grid. Use this instead of the usual wxWindow::Refresh.

Call Fit to fit the grid window to the smallest size required, given the current number of rows and columns.

GetCellAlignment gets the arguments to the horizontal and vertical text alignment values for the grid cell at the specified location. GetColLabel Alignment gets the current column label alignment, and GetRowLabelAlignment gets the current row label alignment. GetDefaultCellAlignment gets the default alignment for a cell. These functions have corresponding setters. Horizontal alignment will be one of wxALIGN_LEFT, wxALIGN_CENTRE (wxALIGN_CENTER), or wxALIGN_RIGHT. Vertical alignment will be one of wxALIGN_TOP, wxALIGN_CENTRE (wxALIGN_CENTER), or wxALIGN_BOTTOM.

GetCellBackgroundColour returns the background color of the cell at the specified location. GetDefaultCellBackgroundColour returns the default background color for the grid. Get the label background color with GetLabel BackgroundColour. These functions have corresponding setters.

GetCellFont gets the font for text in the grid cell at the specified location, and GetDefaultCellFont gets the default font. GetLabelFont gets the font used for row and column labels. These functions have corresponding setters.

GetCellTextColour returns the text color for the grid cell at the specified location. Use GetDefaultCellTextColour to get the default cell text color and GetLabelTextColour to get the label text color. Corresponding setters are provided.

Change and get the color used for grid lines with SetGridLineColour and GetGridLineColour.

SetColAttr and SetRowAttr set the cell attributes for all cells in the given column or row.

To set the format used for a particular column, use SetColFormatBool, SetColFormatNumber, SetColFormatFloat, and SetColFormatCustom.

Functions for Setting and Getting *wxGrid* Metrics

The following functions use pixel dimensions.

AutoSize automatically sets the height and width of all rows and columns to fit their contents. You can also use AutoSizeColumn, AutoSizeColumns, AutoSizeRow, and AutoSizeRows.

CellToRect returns the rectangle corresponding to the grid cell's size and position.

Use SetColMinimalWidth and SetRowMinimalHeight to set the column and row minimum dimensions, and retrieve them with GetColMinimalWidth and GetRowMinimalHeight.

Use these functions for getting a variety of dimensions in pixels: GetColLabelSize, GetDefaultColLabelSize, GetDefaultColSize, GetColSize, GetDefaultRowLabelSize, GetRowSize, GetDefaultRowSize, and GetRowLabelSize. There are corresponding setters.

If you need extra space around the grid, call SetMargins.

If you need to find the column or row for a given x or y pixel position, use XToCol and YToRow. To find the column whose right edge is closest to a given x position, use XToEdgeOfCol. To find the row whose bottom edge is close to the given y position, use YToEdgeOfRow.

Selection and Cursor Functions

These functions let you control the grid cursor (current focus position) and selection.

GetGridCursorCol and GetGridCursorRow return the current column and row positions of the cursor. Set the cursor position with SetGridCursor.

You can move the cursor one row or column at a time with MoveCursorDown, MoveCursorLeft, MoveCursorRight, and MoveCursorUp. To do the same thing but to skip to the next non-empty cell in the row or column, use MoveCursorDownBlock, MoveCursorLeftBlock, MoveCursorRightBlock, and MoveCursorUpBlock.

Move a page at a time with MovePageDown and MovePageUp, where a page is determined by the size of the grid window.

GetSelectionMode returns one of wxGrid::wxGridSelectCells (the default mode where individual cells are selected), wxGrid::wxGridSelectRows (selections consist of whole rows), and wxGrid::wxGridSelectColumns (selections consist of whole columns). Set the selection mode with SetSelectionMode.

You can retrieve all selected cells with GetSelectedCells, which returns a wxGridCellCoordsArray object containing the cells GetSelectedCols and GetSelectedRows. Because a user can select several non-contiguous blocks of cells, both GetSelectionBlockTopLeft and GetSelectionBlockBottomRight return a wxGridCellCoordsArray. You can identify the blocks by iterating through these arrays.

Call IsInSelection with with a row and column or wxGridCellCoords object to determine whether the cell is within the selection. IsSelection returns true if there are any selections in the grid.

Select everything in the grid with SelectAll, select a whole column with SelectCol, and select a whole row with SelectRow. You can select a rectangular block with SelectBlock, passing the top-left and bottom-right cell coordinates as either four integers or two wxGridCellCoords objects.

Miscellaneous *wxGrid* Functions

These functions deal with various other types of wxGrid functionality.

GetTable retrieves the table associated with the grid, holding the actual data displayed by the grid. If you use CreateGrid, wxGrid creates a table of string data itself. Alternatively, you can use SetTable to set your own table object.

GetCellEditor and SetCellEditor get and set a pointer to the editor for the cell at the specified location. Call GetDefaultEditor and SetDefaultEditor to get and set the default editor used for all cells.

GetCellRenderer and SetCellRenderer get and set a pointer to the renderer for the grid cell at the specified location. Call GetDefaultRenderer and SetDefaultRenderer to get and set the default renderer used for all cells.

ShowCellEditControl and HideCellEditControl show and hide the edit control for the cell at the current cursor position. This is normally done automatically when the user clicks on a cell to edit it or presses Enter or Escape (or clicks on another window) to finish editing. SaveEditControlValue transfers the value of the in-place edit control to the cell—you may want to call this before closing a grid or retrieving values from a grid to make sure the grid reflects the latest edits.

EnableCellEditControl enables or disables in-place editing of grid cell data. The grid will issue either a wxEVT_GRID_EDITOR_SHOWN or wxEVT_GRID_EDITOR_HIDDEN event when this function is called. Call IsCellEditControl Enabled to determine if the cell can be edited. IsCurrentCellReadOnly returns true if the current cell is read-only.

EnableDragColSize enables or disables column sizing by dragging with the mouse. EnableDragGridSize enables or disables row and column resizing by dragging gridlines with the mouse. EnableDragRowSize enables or disables row sizing by dragging with the mouse.

EnableEditing sets the whole grid as read-only if the argument is false. If the argument is true, the grid is set to the default state where cells may be edited. In the default state, you can set single grid cells and whole rows and columns to be editable or read-only via wxGridCellAttribute::SetReadOnly. For single cells, you can also use the convenience function wxGrid::SetReadOnly. Call IsEditable to determine whether the grid is editable.

You can make a cell read-only with SetReadOnly and retrieve its read-only status with IsReadOnly.

IsVisible returns true if the cell is wholly or partially visible in the grid window. You can make sure a cell is visible by calling MakeCellVisible.

wxTaskBarIcon

This class installs an icon on the system tray (Windows, Gnome, or KDE) or dock (Mac OS X). Clicking on the icon will pop up a menu that the application supplies, and an optional tooltip can be shown when the mouse hovers over the icon. This technique gives quick access to important application functionality without having to use the regular application user interface. The application can display status information by switching icons, as per the battery and connection indicators in Windows.

Figure 12-8 shows the result of running the wxTaskBarIcon sample on Windows (see samples/taskbar). The wxWidgets icon is installed, and hovering the mouse pointer over the icon shows the tooltip text "wxTaskBarIconSample." Right-clicking on the icon shows the menu with three options. *Selecting Set New Icon* sets the icon to a smiley face and also resets the tooltip text to a new string.

Figure 12-8   wxTaskBarIcon on Windows

The implementation of a `wxTaskBarIcon`-derived class can be very simple, as Listing 12-4 shows (taken from the `wxTaskBarIcon` sample). The derived class `MyTaskBarIcon` overrides `CreatePopupMenu` and implements event handlers to intercept a left double-click and three menu commands.

Listing 12-4   Deriving from *wxTaskBarIcon*

```
class MyTaskBarIcon: public wxTaskBarIcon
{
public:
    MyTaskBarIcon() {};

    void OnLeftButtonDClick(wxTaskBarIconEvent&);
    void OnMenuRestore(wxCommandEvent&);
    void OnMenuExit(wxCommandEvent&);
    void OnMenuSetNewIcon(wxCommandEvent&);

    virtual wxMenu *CreatePopupMenu();

DECLARE_EVENT_TABLE()
};

enum {
    PU_RESTORE = 10001,
    PU_NEW_ICON,
    PU_EXIT,
};

BEGIN_EVENT_TABLE(MyTaskBarIcon, wxTaskBarIcon)
    EVT_MENU(PU_RESTORE, MyTaskBarIcon::OnMenuRestore)
    EVT_MENU(PU_EXIT,    MyTaskBarIcon::OnMenuExit)
    EVT_MENU(PU_NEW_ICON,MyTaskBarIcon::OnMenuSetNewIcon)
    EVT_TASKBAR_LEFT_DCLICK  (MyTaskBarIcon::OnLeftButtonDClick)
END_EVENT_TABLE()

void MyTaskBarIcon::OnMenuRestore(wxCommandEvent& )
{
    dialog->Show(true);
}

void MyTaskBarIcon::OnMenuExit(wxCommandEvent& )
{
    dialog->Close(true);
}

void MyTaskBarIcon::OnMenuSetNewIcon(wxCommandEvent&)
{
    wxIcon icon(smile_xpm);

    if (!SetIcon(icon, wxT("wxTaskBarIcon Sample - a different icon")))
        wxMessageBox(wxT("Could not set new icon."));
}
```

(continues)

Listing 12-4   *(continued)*

```
// Overridables
wxMenu *MyTaskBarIcon::CreatePopupMenu()
{
    wxMenu *menu = new wxMenu;

    menu->Append(PU_RESTORE, wxT("&Restore TBTest"));
    menu->Append(PU_NEW_ICON,wxT("&Set New Icon"));
    menu->Append(PU_EXIT,    wxT("E&xit"));

    return menu;
}

void MyTaskBarIcon::OnLeftButtonDClick(wxTaskBarIconEvent&)
{
    dialog->Show(true);
}
```

The rest of the code to show a dialog and install the initial icon is equally straightforward, as Listing 12-5 shows.

Listing 12-5   Showing a Taskbar Icon

```
#include "wx/wx.h"
#include "wx/taskbar.h"

// Define a new application
class MyApp: public wxApp
{
public:
    bool OnInit(void);
};

class MyDialog: public wxDialog
{
public:
    MyDialog(wxWindow* parent, const wxWindowID id, const wxString& title,
        const wxPoint& pos, const wxSize& size, const long windowStyle =
wxDEFAULT_DIALOG_STYLE);
    ~MyDialog();

    void OnOK(wxCommandEvent& event);
    void OnExit(wxCommandEvent& event);
    void OnCloseWindow(wxCloseEvent& event);
    void Init(void);

protected:
    MyTaskBarIcon    *m_taskBarIcon;

DECLARE_EVENT_TABLE()
};

#include "../sample.xpm"
```

(continues)

Listing 12-5

```
#include "smile.xpm"

MyDialog    *dialog = NULL;

IMPLEMENT_APP(MyApp)

bool MyApp::OnInit(void)
{
    // Create the main frame window
    dialog = new MyDialog(NULL, wxID_ANY, wxT("wxTaskBarIcon Test
Dialog"), wxDefaultPosition, wxSize(365, 290));

    dialog->Show(true);

    return true;
}

BEGIN_EVENT_TABLE(MyDialog, wxDialog)
    EVT_BUTTON(wxID_OK, MyDialog::OnOK)
    EVT_BUTTON(wxID_EXIT, MyDialog::OnExit)
    EVT_CLOSE(MyDialog::OnCloseWindow)
END_EVENT_TABLE()

MyDialog::MyDialog(wxWindow* parent, const wxWindowID id, const wxString&
title,
    const wxPoint& pos, const wxSize& size, const long windowStyle):
  wxDialog(parent, id, title, pos, size, windowStyle)
{
    Init();
}

MyDialog::~MyDialog()
{
    delete m_taskBarIcon;
}

void MyDialog::OnOK(wxCommandEvent& WXUNUSED(event))
{
    Show(false);
}

void MyDialog::OnExit(wxCommandEvent& WXUNUSED(event))
{
    Close(true);
}

void MyDialog::OnCloseWindow(wxCloseEvent& WXUNUSED(event))
{
    Destroy();
}

void MyDialog::Init(void)
{
    (void)new wxStaticText(this, wxID_ANY, wxT("Press 'Hide me' to hide me,
Exit to quit."),
                          wxPoint(10, 20));
```

(continues)

Listing 12-5   *(continued)*
```
(void)new wxStaticText(this, wxID_ANY, wxT("Double-click on the taskbar
icon to show me again."),
                              wxPoint(10, 40));

(void)new wxButton(this, wxID_EXIT, wxT("Exit"), wxPoint(185, 230),
wxSize(80, 25));
(new wxButton(this, wxID_OK, wxT("Hide me"), wxPoint(100, 230),
wxSize(80, 25)))->SetDefault();
Centre(wxBOTH);

m_taskBarIcon = new MyTaskBarIcon();
if (!m_taskBarIcon->SetIcon(wxIcon(sample_xpm), wxT("wxTaskBarIcon
Sample")))
        wxMessageBox(wxT("Could not set icon."));
}
```

wxTaskBarIcon Events

To process events from a taskbar icon, use the event handler macros listed in Table 12-11 to direct input to member functions that take a wxTaskBarIcon Event argument. Note that not all ports are required to send these events, and so you should override CreatePopupMenu if you want to show a popup menu in reaction to a mouse click. Note also that wxTaskBarIconEvent doesn't pass any mouse status information such as position.

Table 12-11   wxTaskBarIcon Events

EVT_TASKBAR_MOVE(func)	The mouse moved over the icon.
EVT_TASKBAR_LEFT_DOWN(func)	The left mouse button was pressed down.
EVT_TASKBAR_LEFT_UP(func)	The left mouse button was released.
EVT_TASKBAR_RIGHT_DOWN(func)	The right mouse button was pressed down.
EVT_TASKBAR_RIGHT_UP(func)	The right mouse button was released.
EVT_TASKBAR_LEFT_DCLICK(func)	The left mouse button was double-clicked.
EVT_TASKBAR_RIGHT_DCLICK(func)	The right mouse button was double-clicked.

wxTaskBarIcon Member Functions

The wxTaskBarIcon API is very simple. These are all the member functions for this class.

CreatePopupMenu is a virtual function that should be overridden by the derived class to return a new wxMenu when called by wxWidgets in response to a wxEVT_TASKBAR_RIGHT_DOWN event (this event is simulated on Mac OS X). wxWidgets will also delete the menu when it is dismissed.

IsIconInstalled returns true if SetIcon was successfully called.

IsOk returns true if the wxTaskBarIcon object initialized successfully.

PopupMenu shows a menu at the current position. It's not recommended to call this directly; instead, override CreatePopupMenu and let wxWidgets show the menu for you.

RemoveIcon removes the icon previously set with SetIcon.

SetIcon sets an icon (wxIcon) and optional tooltip text. You can call this multiple times.

WRITING YOUR OWN CONTROLS

This section discusses how you can create your own controls in wxWidgets. wxWidgets does not have the concept of a "custom control" in the sense of a binary, drop-in component to which Windows programmers might be accustomed. Third-party controls are usually supplied as source code and follow the same pattern as generic controls within wxWidgets, such as wxCalendarCtrl and wxGrid. We're using the term "control" loosely here because controls do not have to be derived from wxControl; you might want to use wxScrolledWindow as a base class, for example.

Ten major tasks are involved in writing a new control:

1. Write a class declaration that has a default constructor, a constructor that creates the window, a Create function, and preferably an Init function to do shared initialization.

2. Add a function DoGetBestSize that returns the best minimal size appropriate to this control (based on a label size, for example).

3. Add a new event class for the control to generate, if existing event classes in wxWidgets are inadequate. A new type of push button might just use wxCommandEvent, but more complex controls will need a new event class. Also add event handler macros to use with the event class.

4. Write the code to display the information in the control.

5. Write the code to handle low-level mouse and keyboard events in the control, and generate appropriate high-level command events that the application can handle.

6. Write any default event handlers that the control might have—for example, handling wxID_COPY or wxID_UNDO commands or UI update commands.

7. Optionally, write a validator class that an application can use with the control (to make it easy to transfer data to and from the control) and validate its contents.

8. Optionally, write a resource handler class so that your control can be used with the XRC resource system.

9. Test the control on the platforms you want to support.

10. Write the documentation!

Let's take the simple example we used in Chapter 3, "Event Handling," when discussing custom events: wxFontSelectorCtrl, which you can find in examples/chap03 on the CD-ROM. This class shows a font preview on which the user can click to change the font using the standard font selector dialog. Changing the font causes a wxFontSelectorCtrlEvent to be sent, which can be caught by providing an event handler for EVT_FONT_SELECTION_CHANGED(id, func).

The control is illustrated in Figure 12-9 and is shown with a static text control above it.

Figure 12-9   wxFontSelectorCtrl

The Custom Control Declaration

The following code is the class declaration for wxFontSelectorCtrl. DoGetBestSize returns a fairly arbitrary size, 200×40 pixels, which will be used if no minimum size is passed to the constructor.

```
/*!
 * A control for displaying a font preview.
 */

class wxFontSelectorCtrl: public wxControl
{
    DECLARE_DYNAMIC_CLASS(wxFontSelectorCtrl)
    DECLARE_EVENT_TABLE()

public:

    // Constructors
    wxFontSelectorCtrl() { Init(); }

    wxFontSelectorCtrl(wxWindow* parent, wxWindowID id,
```

```
                const wxPoint& pos = wxDefaultPosition,
                const wxSize& size = wxDefaultSize,
                long style = wxSUNKEN_BORDER,
                const wxValidator& validator = wxDefaultValidator)
        {
            Init();
            Create(parent, id, pos, size, style, validator);
        }

        // Creation
        bool Create(wxWindow* parent, wxWindowID id,
            const wxPoint& pos = wxDefaultPosition,
            const wxSize& size = wxDefaultSize,
            long style = wxSUNKEN_BORDER,
            const wxValidator& validator = wxDefaultValidator);

        // Common initialization
        void Init() { m_sampleText = wxT("abcdeABCDE"); }

        // Overrides
        wxSize DoGetBestSize() const { return wxSize(200, 40); }

        // Event handlers
        void OnPaint(wxPaintEvent& event);
        void OnMouseEvent(wxMouseEvent& event);

        // Accessors
        void SetFontData(const wxFontData& fontData) { m_fontData = fontData;
    };
        const wxFontData& GetFontData() const { return m_fontData; };
        wxFontData& GetFontData() { return m_fontData; };

        void SetSampleText(const wxString& sample);
        const wxString& GetSampleText() const { return m_sampleText; };

protected:
    wxFontData  m_fontData;
    wxString    m_sampleText;
};
```

To store the font information associated with the control, we are using a wxFontData object, as used by wxFontDialog, so that we can store a color selection along with the font.

The control's RTTI event table macros and creation code look like this:

```
BEGIN_EVENT_TABLE(wxFontSelectorCtrl, wxControl)
    EVT_PAINT(wxFontSelectorCtrl::OnPaint)
    EVT_MOUSE_EVENTS(wxFontSelectorCtrl::OnMouseEvent)
END_EVENT_TABLE()

IMPLEMENT_DYNAMIC_CLASS(wxFontSelectorCtrl, wxControl)

bool wxFontSelectorCtrl::Create(wxWindow* parent, wxWindowID id,
            const wxPoint& pos, const wxSize& size, long style,
            const wxValidator& validator)
{
    if (!wxControl::Create(parent, id, pos, size, style, validator))
```

```
        return false;

    SetBackgroundColour(wxSystemSettings::GetColour(
                                    wxSYS_COLOUR_WINDOW));
    m_fontData.SetInitialFont(GetFont());
    m_fontData.SetChosenFont(GetFont());
    m_fontData.SetColour(GetForegroundColour());

    // Tell the sizers to use the given or best size
    SetBestFittingSize(size);

    return true;
}
```

The call to SetBestFittingSize tells the sizer layout algorithm to use either the initial size or the "best" size returned from DoGetBestSize as the minimal control size. The control can stretch to be bigger than this size, according to the flags passed when the control is added to a sizer.

Adding *DoGetBestSize*

Implementing DoGetBestSize lets wxWidgets know the optimal minimal size of the control. Providing this information means that a control can be created with default size (wxDefaultSize) and it will size itself sensibly. We've chosen a somewhat arbitrary but reasonable size of 200×40 pixels, which will normally be overridden by application code. A control such as a label or button has a natural default size, but other controls don't, such as a scrolled window with no child windows. If your control falls into this category, your DoGetBestSize can call wxWindow::DoGetBestSize, or you can omit the function altogether. You will need to rely on the application passing a non-default size to the control's constructor or the control being sized appropriately by a parent sizer.

If your control can have child windows of arbitrary size, and you want your control to size itself according to these child windows, you can find each child's size using GetAdjustedBestSize, and you can return a size that fits around these. For example, say we're implementing a window that contains two child windows, arranged horizontally. We might have this implementation:

```
wxSize ContainerCtrl::DoGetBestSize() const
{
    // Get best sizes of subwindows
    wxSize size1, size2;
    if ( m_windowOne )
        size1 = m_windowOne->GetAdjustedBestSize();
    if ( m_windowTwo )
        size2 = m_windowTwo->GetAdjustedBestSize();
```

```
    // The windows are laid out horizontally. Find
    // the total window size.
    wxSize bestSize;
    bestSize.x = size1.x + size2.x;
    bestSize.y = wxMax(size1.y, size2.y);

    return bestSize;
}
```

Defining a New Event Class

We covered the topic of creating a new event class (wxFontSelectorCtrlEvent) and event table macro (EVT_FONT_SELECTION_CHANGED) in Chapter 3. An application that uses the font selector control doesn't have to catch this event at all because data transfer is handled separately. In a more complex control, the event class would have specific functions; we could have provided information about the font in the event class, for example, so that handlers could retrieve the selected font with wxFontSelectorCtrlEvent::GetFont.

Displaying Information on the Control

Our control has a very simple paint event handler, centering the sample text on the control as follows:

```
void wxFontSelectorCtrl::OnPaint(wxPaintEvent& event)
{
    wxPaintDC dc(this);

    wxRect rect = GetClientRect();

    int topMargin = 2;
    int leftMargin = 2;

    dc.SetFont(m_fontData.GetChosenFont());
    wxCoord width, height;
    dc.GetTextExtent(m_sampleText, & width, & height);

    int x = wxMax(leftMargin, ((rect.GetWidth() - width) / 2)) ;
    int y = wxMax(topMargin, ((rect.GetHeight() - height) / 2)) ;

    dc.SetBackgroundMode(wxTRANSPARENT);
    dc.SetTextForeground(m_fontData.GetColour());
    dc.DrawText(m_sampleText, x, y);
    dc.SetFont(wxNullFont);
}
```

For drawing standard elements, such as a splitter sash or a border, consider using wxNativeRenderer (please see the reference manual for more details).

Handling Input

Our control detects a left-click and shows a font dialog. If the user confirmed the choice, the font data is retrieved from the font dialog, and an event is sent to the control using ProcessEvent. This event can be processed by a function in a class derived from wxFontSelectorCtrl or a function in the dialog (or other window) containing the control.

```
void wxFontSelectorCtrl::OnMouseEvent(wxMouseEvent& event)
{
    if (event.LeftDown())
    {
        // Get a parent for the font dialog
        wxWindow* parent = GetParent();
        while (parent != NULL &&
                !parent->IsKindOf(CLASSINFO(wxDialog)) &&
                !parent->IsKindOf(CLASSINFO(wxFrame)))
            parent = parent->GetParent();

        wxFontDialog dialog(parent, m_fontData);
        dialog.SetTitle(_("Please choose a font"));

        if (dialog.ShowModal() == wxID_OK)
        {
            m_fontData = dialog.GetFontData();
            m_fontData.SetInitialFont(
                        dialog.GetFontData().GetChosenFont());

            Refresh();

            wxFontSelectorCtrlEvent event(
                wxEVT_COMMAND_FONT_SELECTION_CHANGED, GetId());
            event.SetEventObject(this);
            GetEventHandler()->ProcessEvent(event);
        }
    }
}
```

This class has no keyboard handling, but you could interpret an Enter key press to do the same as left-click. You could also draw a focus rectangle to indicate that the control has the focus, using wxWindow::FindFocus to determine whether this is the focused window. You would need to intercept focus events with EVT_SET_FOCUS and EVT_KILL_FOCUS to refresh the control so that the correct focus graphic is drawn.

Defining Default Event Handlers

If you look at implementations of wxTextCtrl, for example src/msw/textctrl.cpp, you will find that standard identifiers such as wxID_COPY, wxID_PASTE, wxID_UNDO, and wxID_REDO have default command event and UI update event handlers. This means that if your application is set up to direct events to the focused control (see Chapter 20, "Perfecting Your Application"), your standard menu items and toolbar buttons will respond correctly according to the state of the control. Our example control is not complex enough to warrant these handlers, but if you implement undo/redo or clipboard operations, you should provide them. For example:

```
BEGIN_EVENT_TABLE(wxTextCtrl, wxControl)
    ...
    EVT_MENU(wxID_COPY, wxTextCtrl::OnCopy)
    EVT_MENU(wxID_PASTE, wxTextCtrl::OnPaste)
    EVT_MENU(wxID_SELECTALL, wxTextCtrl::OnSelectAll)

    EVT_UPDATE_UI(wxID_COPY, wxTextCtrl::OnUpdateCopy)
    EVT_UPDATE_UI(wxID_PASTE, wxTextCtrl::OnUpdatePaste)
    EVT_UPDATE_UI(wxID_SELECTALL, wxTextCtrl::OnUpdateSelectAll)
    ...
END_EVENT_TABLE()

void wxTextCtrl::OnCopy(wxCommandEvent& event)
{
    Copy();
}

void wxTextCtrl::OnPaste(wxCommandEvent& event)
{
    Paste();
}

void wxTextCtrl::OnSelectAll(wxCommandEvent& event)
{
    SetSelection(-1, -1);
}

void wxTextCtrl::OnUpdateCopy(wxUpdateUIEvent& event)
{
    event.Enable( CanCopy() );
}

void wxTextCtrl::OnUpdatePaste(wxUpdateUIEvent& event)
{
    event.Enable( CanPaste() );
}

void wxTextCtrl::OnUpdateSelectAll(wxUpdateUIEvent& event)
{
    event.Enable( GetLastPosition() > 0 );
}
```

Implementing Validators

As we saw in Chapter 9, "Creating Custom Dialogs," validators are a very convenient way to specify how data is validated and transferred between variables and associated controls. When you write a new control class, you can provide a special validator class to use with it.

wxFontSelectorValidator is a validator you can use with wxFontSelector
Ctrl. You can pass font and color pointers or a pointer to a wxFontData object.
These variables are usually declared in the dialog class so that they persist
and can be retrieved when the dialog has been dismissed. Note that the validator is passed as an object, *not* using the new operator, and the object is
copied by SetValidator before it goes out of scope and is deleted.

For example:

```
wxFontSelectorCtrl* fontCtrl =
    new wxFontSelectorCtrl( this, ID_FONTCTRL,
                wxDefaultPosition, wxSize(100, 40), wxSIMPLE_BORDER );

// Either a pointer to a wxFont and optional wxColour...
fontCtrl->SetValidator( wxFontSelectorValidator(& m_font,
                                            & m_fontColor) );

// ...or a pointer to a wxFontData
fontCtrl->SetValidator( wxFontSelectorValidator(& m_fontData) );
```

The m_font and m_fontColor variables (or m_fontData variable) will reflect any
changes to the font preview made by the user. This transfer of data happens
when the dialog's TransferDataFromWindow function is called (which it is by
default, from wxWidgets' standard wxID_OK handler).

You must implement a default constructor, further constructors that take
pointers to variables, and a Clone function to duplicate the object. The Validate
function should be implemented to check that the data in the control is valid,
showing a message and returning false if not. TransferToWindow and
TransferFromWindow must be implemented to copy the data to and from the control, respectively.

Here's the declaration of wxFontSelectorValidator:

```
/*!
 * Validator for wxFontSelectorCtrl
 */

class wxFontSelectorValidator: public wxValidator
{
DECLARE_DYNAMIC_CLASS(wxFontSelectorValidator)
public:

    // Constructors
    wxFontSelectorValidator(wxFontData *val = NULL);
    wxFontSelectorValidator(wxFont *fontVal,
                            wxColour* colourVal = NULL);
    wxFontSelectorValidator(const wxFontSelectorValidator& val);

    // Destructor
    ~wxFontSelectorValidator();

    // Make a clone of this validator
    virtual wxObject *Clone() const
    { return new wxFontSelectorValidator(*this); }
```

```
    // Copies val to this object
    bool Copy(const wxFontSelectorValidator& val);

    // Called when the value in the window must be validated.
    // This function can pop up an error message.
    virtual bool Validate(wxWindow *parent);

    // Called to transfer data to the window
    virtual bool TransferToWindow();

    // Called to transfer data to the window
    virtual bool TransferFromWindow();

    wxFontData* GetFontData() { return m_fontDataValue; }

DECLARE_EVENT_TABLE()

protected:
    wxFontData*     m_fontDataValue;
    wxFont*         m_fontValue;
    wxColour*       m_colourValue;

    // Checks that the validator is set up correctly
    bool CheckValidator() const;
};
```

We will leave you to peruse the source in fontctrl.cpp to find out how the class is implemented.

Implementing Resource Handlers

If your class is to be used with XRC files, it is convenient to provide a suitable resource handler to use with the control. This is not illustrated in our example, but refer to the discussion of the XRC system in Chapter 9, and refer also to the existing handlers in the directories include/wx/xrc and src/xrc in your wxWidgets distribution.

After the handler is registered by an application, XRC files containing objects with your control's properties will be loaded just like any file containing standard wxWidgets controls. Writing the XRC file is another matter, though, because design tools cannot currently be made aware of new resource handlers. However, with DialogBlocks' simple "custom control definition" facility, you can set up the name and properties for a custom control, and the correct XRC definition will be written, even if it can only display an approximation of the control while editing.

Determining Control Appearance

When writing your own control, you need to give wxWidgets a few hints about the control's appearance. Bear in mind that wxWidgets tries to use the system colors and fonts wherever possible, but also enables an application to customize these attributes where permitted by the native platform. wxWidgets also lets the application and the control choose whether or not child windows inherit their attributes from parents. The system for controlling these attributes is a little involved, but developers won't have to know about these unless they heavily customize control colors (which is not recommended) or implement their own controls.

If explicitly provided by an application, foreground colors and fonts for a parent window are normally inherited by its children (which may include your custom control). However, this may be overridden—if the application has called SetOwnFont for the parent, the child controls will not inherit the font, and similarly for SetOwnForegroundColour. Also, your control can specify whether it can inherit its parent's foreground color by returning true from ShouldInheritColours (the default for wxControl, but not for wxWindow). Background colors are not explicitly inherited; preferably, your control should use the same background as the parent by not painting outside the visible part of the control.

In order to implement attribute inheritance, your control should call InheritAttributes from its constructor after window creation. Depending on platform, you can do this when you call wxControl::Create from within your constructor.

Some classes implement the static function GetClassDefaultAttributes, returning a wxVisualAttributes object with background color, foreground color, and font members. It takes a wxWindowVariant argument used only on Mac OS X. This function specifies the default attributes for objects of that class and will be used by functions such as GetBackgroundColour in the absence of specific settings provided by the application. If you don't want the default values to be returned, you can implement it in your class. You will also need to override the virtual function GetDefaultAttributes, calling GetClassDefaultAttributes, to allow the correct attributes to be returned for a given object. If your control has similar attributes to a standard control, you could use its attributes, for example:

```
// The static function, for global access
static wxVisualAttributes GetClassDefaultAttributes(
            wxWindowVariant variant = wxWINDOW_VARIANT_NORMAL)
{
    return wxListBox::GetClassDefaultAttributes(variant);
}

// The virtual function, for object access
virtual wxVisualAttributes GetDefaultAttributes() const
{
    return GetClassDefaultAttributes(GetWindowVariant());
}
```

The wxVisualAttributes structure is defined as follows:

```
// struct containing all the visual attributes of a control
struct wxVisualAttributes
{
    // the font used for the control's label or text inside it
    wxFont font;

    // the foreground color
    wxColour colFg;

    // the background color; may be wxNullColour if the
    // control's background color is not solid
    wxColour colBg;
};
```

If your control should have a transparent background—for example, if it's a static control such as a label—then provide the function HasTransparent Background as a hint to wxWidgets (currently on Windows only).

Finally, sometimes your control may need to delay certain operations until the final size or some other property is known. You can use idle time processing for this, as described in "Alternatives to Multithreading" in Chapter 17, "Writing Multithreaded Aplications."

A More Complex Example: *wxThumbnailCtrl*

The example we looked at previously, wxFontSelectorCtrl, was simple enough that we could briefly demonstrate the basics of creating new control, event, and validator classes. However, it's a bit thin on interesting display and input code. For a more complex example, take a look at wxThumbnailCtrl in examples/chap12/thumbnail on the CD-ROM. This control displays a scrolling page of thumbnails (little images) and can be used in any application that deals with images. (In fact, it's not limited to images; you can define your own classes derived from wxThumbnailItem to display thumbnails for other file types, or for images within archives, for example.)

Figure 12-10 shows the control being used with a wxGenericDirCtrl inside an image selection dialog (wxThumbnailBrowserDialog). The supplied sample comes with a selection of images in the images subdirectory for demonstration purposes.

The class illustrates the following topics, among others:

☞ **Mouse input:** Items can be selected with left-click or multiply selected by holding down the Control key.

☞ **Keyboard input**: The thumbnail grid can be navigated and scrolled with the arrow keys, and items can be selected by holding down the Shift key.

☞ **Focus handling:** "Set" and "kill" focus events are used to update the currently focused item when the control itself receives or loses the focus.

☞ **Optimized drawing:** Painting uses `wxBufferedPaintDC` for flicker-free updates and also checks the update region to eliminate unnecessary drawing.

☞ **Scrolling:** The control derives from `wxScrolledWindow` and adjusts its scrollbars according to the number of items in the control.

☞ **Custom events:** `wxThumbnailEvent` is generated with several event types including selection, deselection, and right-click.

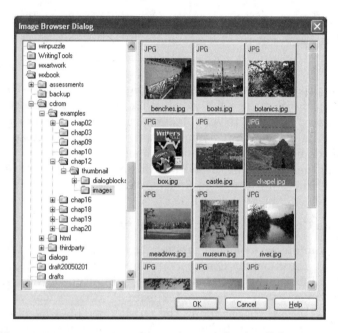

Figure 12-10   `wxThumbnailCtrl` used in an image selection dialog

`wxThumbnailCtrl` doesn't load a directory full of images itself; for flexibility, `wxThumbnailItem` objects are explicitly added, as the following code shows:

```
// Create a multiple-selection thumbnail control
wxThumbnailCtrl* imageBrowser =
   new wxThumbnailCtrl(parent, wxID_ANY,
        wxDefaultPosition, wxSize(300, 400),
        wxSUNKEN_BORDER|wxHSCROLL|wxVSCROLL|wxTH_TEXT_LABEL|
        wxTH_IMAGE_LABEL|wxTH_EXTENSION_LABEL|wxTH_MULTIPLE_SELECT);

// Set a nice big thumbnail size
imageBrowser->SetThumbnailImageSize(wxSize(200, 200));

// Don't paint while filling the control
imageBrowser->Freeze();
```

```
// Set some bright colors
imageBrowser->SetUnselectedThumbnailBackgroundColour(*wxRED);
imageBrowser->SetSelectedThumbnailBackgroundColour(*wxGREEN);

// Add images from directory 'path'
wxDir dir;
if (dir.Open(path))
{
    wxString filename;

    bool cont = dir.GetFirst(&filename, wxT("*.*"), wxDIR_FILES);
    while ( cont )
    {
        wxString file = path + wxFILE_SEP_PATH + filename;
        if (wxFileExists(file) && DetermineImageType(file) != -1)
        {
            imageBrowser->Append(new wxImageThumbnailItem(file));
        }

        cont = dir.GetNext(&filename);
    }
}

// Sort by name
imageBrowser->Sort(wxTHUMBNAIL_SORT_NAME_DOWN);

// Tag and select the first thumbnail
imageBrowser->Tag(0);
imageBrowser->Select(0);

// Delete the second thumbnail
imageBrowser->Delete(1);

// Now display the images
imageBrowser->Thaw();
```

If you look through the source code in thumbnailctrl.h and thumbnail.cpp, you should get plenty of ideas for implementing your own controls. Feel free to use wxThumbnailCtrl in your own applications, too.

SUMMARY

This chapter has covered visual classes that you probably won't use in your first explorations of wxWidgets, but you'll almost certainly want to consider them as your applications become more sophisticated. Their source also gives you plenty of tips for learning how to write your own controls, as described in the final part of this chapter.

Refer also to Appendix D, "Other Features in wxWidgets," for other advanced controls distributed with wxWidgets, and Appendix E, "Third-Party Tools for wxWidgets," for third-party controls.

Next, we'll have a look at the data structure classes available in wxWidgets.

CHAPTER 13

Data Structure Classes

Storing and processing data is an essential part of any application. From simple classes that store information about size and position to complex types such as arrays and hash maps, wxWidgets provides a comprehensive selection of data structures. This chapter presents many of wxWidgets' data structures, highlighting the frequently used methods of each structure. Less frequently used structures and features can be found by reading the complete APIs in the wxWidgets documentation.

Note that data structure theories and implementations are not covered in this book. However, anyone should be able to use the data structure classes, even without understanding their internals.

WHY NOT STL?

First, let's deal with a question commonly asked about wxWidgets data structure classes: "Why doesn't wxWidgets just use the Standard Template Library (STL)?" The main reason is historical: wxWidgets has existed since 1992, long before STL could reliably be used across different platforms and compilers. As wxWidgets has evolved, many of the data structure classes have gravitated towards an STL-like API, and it is expected that eventually STL equivalents will replace some wxWidgets classes.

Meanwhile, you can still use STL functionality in your wxWidgets applications by setting wxUSE_STL to 1 in setup.h (or by passing −enable-stl when configuring) to base wxString and other containers on the STL equivalents. Be warned that using STL with wxWidgets can increase both the library size and compilation time, especially when using GCC.

STRINGS

The benefits of working with a string class instead of standard character pointers are well established. wxWidgets includes its own string class, wxString, used both internally and for passing and returning information. wxString has all the standard operations you expect to find in a string class: dynamic memory management, construction from other strings, C strings, and characters, assignment operators, access to individual characters, string concatenation and comparison, substring extraction, case conversion, trimming and padding (with spaces), searching and replacing, C-like printf, stream-like insertion functions, and more.

Beyond being just another string class, wxString has other useful features. wxString fully supports Unicode, including methods for converting to and from ANSI and Unicode regardless of your build configuration. Using wxString gives you the ability to pass strings to the library or receive them back without any conversion process. Lastly, wxString implements 90% of the STL std::string methods, meaning that anyone familiar with std::string can use wxString without any learning curve.

Using *wxString*

Using wxString in your application is very straightforward. Wherever you would normally use std::string or your favorite string implementation, use wxString instead. All functions taking string arguments should take const wxString& (which makes assignment to the strings inside the function faster because of reference counting), and all functions returning strings should return wxString, which makes it safe to return local variables.

Because C and C++ programmers are familiar with most string methods, a long and detailed API reference for wxString has been omitted. Please consult the wxWidgets documentation for wxString, which provides a comprehensive list of all its methods.

You may notice that wxString sometimes has two or more functions that do the same thing. For example, Length, Len, and length all return the length of the string. In all cases of such duplication, the usage of std::string-compatible methods is strongly advised. It will make your code more familiar to other C++ programmers and will let you reuse the same code in both wxWidgets and other programs, where you can typedef wxString as std::string. Also, wxWidgets might start using std::string at some point in the future, so using these methods will make your programs more forward-compatible (although the wxString methods would be supported for some time for backwards compatibility).

wxString, Characters, and String Literals

wxWidgets has a wxChar type which maps either to char or wchar_t depending on the application build configuration (Unicode or ANSI). As already mentioned, there is no need for a separate type for char or wchar_t strings because wxString stores strings using the appropriate underlying C type. Whenever you work directly with strings that you intend to use with a wxWidgets class, use wxChar instead of char or wchar_t directly. Doing so ensures compatibility with both ANSI and Unicode build configuration without complicated preprocessor conditions.

When using wxWidgets with Unicode enabled, standard string literals are not the correct type: an unmodified string literal is always of type char*. In order for a string literal to be used in Unicode mode, it must be a wide character constant, usually marked with an L. wxWidgets provides the wxT macro (identical to _T) to wrap string literals for use with or without Unicode. When Unicode is not enabled, _T is an empty macro, but with Unicode enabled, it adds the necessary L for the string literal to become a wide character string constant. For example:

```
wxChar ch = wxT('*');
wxString s = wxT("Hello, world!");
wxChar* pChar = wxT("My string");
wxString s2 = pChar;
```

For more details about using Unicode in your applications, please see Chapter 16, "Writing International Applications."

Basic *wxString* to C Pointer Conversions

Because there may be times when you need to access a wxString's data as a C type for low-level processing, wxWidgets provides several accessors:

- ☞ mb_str returns a C string representation of the string, a const char*, regardless of whether Unicode is enabled. In Unicode mode, the string is converted, and data may be lost.
- ☞ wc_str returns a wide character representation of the string, a wchar_t*, regardless of whether Unicode is enabled. In ANSI mode, the string is converted to Unicode.
- ☞ c_str returns a pointer to the string data (const char* in ANSI mode, const wchar_t* in Unicode mode). No conversion takes place.

You can convert between std::string and wxString by means of c_str, as follows:

```
std::string str1 = wxT("hello");
wxString str2 = str1.c_str();
std::string str3 = str2.c_str();
```

One trap when using wxString is the implicit conversion operator to const char
*. It is advised that you use c_str to indicate clearly when the conversion is
done. The danger of this implicit conversion may be seen in the following code
fragment:

```
// converts the input string to uppercase, outputs it to the
// screen, and returns the result (buggy)
const char *SayHELLO(const wxString& input)
{
    wxString output = input.Upper();

    printf("Hello, %s!\n", output);

    return output;
}
```

There are two nasty bugs in these four lines. The first is in the call to the
printf function. The implicit conversion to a C string is automatically applied
by the compiler in the case of functions like puts because the argument of puts
is known to be of the type const char *. However, this is not done for printf,
which is a function with a variable number of arguments whose types are
unknown. Such a call to printf might do anything at all (including displaying
the correct string on screen), although the most likely result is a program
crash. The solution is to use c_str:

```
printf(wxT("Hello, %s!\n"), output.c_str());
```

The second bug is that returning the variable named output doesn't work. The
implicit cast is used again, so the code compiles, but it returns a pointer to a
buffer belonging to a local variable that is deleted as soon as the function exits.
The solution to this problem is also easy: have the function return a wxString
instead of a C string. The corrected code looks like this:

```
// converts the input string to uppercase, outputs it to the
// screen, and returns the result (corrected)
wxString SayHELLO(const wxString& input)
{
    wxString output = input.Upper();

    printf(wxT("Hello, %s!\n"), output.c_str());

    return output;
}
```

Standard C String Functions

Because most programs use character strings, the standard C library provides
quite a few functions to work with them. Unfortunately, some of them have

rather counterintuitive behavior (like `strncpy`, which doesn't always terminate the resulting string with a NULL) or are considered unsafe with possible buffer overflows. Moreover, some very useful functions are not standard at all. This is why in addition to all `wxString` functions, there are a few global string functions that try to correct these problems: `wxIsEmpty` verifies whether the string is empty (returning `true` for NULL pointers), `wxStrlen` handles NULLs correctly and returns 0 for them, and `wxStricmp` is a platform-independent version of the case-insensitive string comparison function known either as `stricmp` or `strcasecmp` on different platforms.

The "`wx/string.h`" header also defines `wxSnprintf` and `wxVsnprintf` functions that should be used instead of the inherently dangerous standard `sprintf`. The "n" functions use `snprintf`, which does buffer size checks whenever possible. You may also use `wxString::Printf` without worrying about the vulnerabilities typically found in `printf`.

Converting to and from Numbers

Programmers often need to convert between string and numeric representations of numbers, such as when processing user input or displaying the results of a calculation.

`ToLong(long* val, int base=10)` attempts to convert the string to a signed integer in base `base`. It returns `true` on success, in which case the number is stored in the location pointed to by `val`, or `false` if the string does not represent a valid number in the given base. The value of `base` must be between 2 and 36, inclusive, or a special value 0, which means that the usual rules of C numbers are applied: if the number starts with 0x, it is considered to be in base 16; if it starts with 0-, it is considered to be in base 8, and in base 10 otherwise.

`ToULong(unsigned long* val, int base=10)` works identically to `ToLong`, except that the string is converted to an unsigned integer.

`ToDouble(double* val)` attempts to convert the string to a floating point number. It returns `true` on success (the number is stored in the location pointed to by `val`) or `false` if the string does not represent such a number.

`Printf(const wxChar* pszFormat, ...)` is similar to the C standard function `sprintf`, enabling you to put information into a `wxString` using standard C string formatting. The number of characters written is returned.

`static Format(const wxChar* pszFormat, ...)` returns a `wxString` containing the results of calling `Printf` with the passed parameters. The advantage of `Format` over `Printf` is that `Format` can be used to add to an existing string:

```
int n = 10;
wxString s = "Some Stuff";
s += wxString::Format(wxT("%d"),n );
```

`operator<<` can be used to append an int, a float, or a double to a `wxString`.

wxStringTokenizer

wxStringTokenizer helps you to break a string into a number of tokens, replacing and expanding the C function strtok. To use it, create a wxStringTokenizer object and give it the string to tokenize and the delimiters that separate the tokens. By default, white space characters will be used. Then call GetNextToken repeatedly until HasMoreTokens returns false.

```
wxStringTokenizer tkz(wxT("first:second:third:fourth"), wxT(":"));
while ( tkz.HasMoreTokens() )
{
    wxString token = tkz.GetNextToken();
    // process token here
}
```

By default, wxStringTokenizer will behave in the same way as strtok if the delimiters string contains only white space characters. Unlike the standard functions, however, it will return empty tokens if appropriate for other non-white space delimiters. This is helpful for parsing strictly formatted data where the number of fields is fixed but some of them may be empty, as in the case of tab- or comma-delimited text files.

wxStringTokenizer's behavior is governed by the last constructor parameter, which may be one of the following:

- ☞ wxTOKEN_DEFAULT: Default behavior as described previously; same as wxTOKEN_STRTOK if the delimiter string contains only white space, and same as wxTOKEN_RET_EMPTY otherwise.
- ☞ wxTOKEN_RET_EMPTY: In this mode, the empty tokens in the middle of the string will be returned. So a::b: will be tokenized into three tokens a, "", and b.
- ☞ wxTOKEN_RET_EMPTY_ALL: In this mode, empty trailing tokens (after the last delimiter character) will be returned as well. a::b: will contain four tokens: the same as wxTOKEN_RET_EMPTY and another empty one as the last one.
- ☞ wxTOKEN_RET_DELIMS: In this mode, the delimiter character after the end of the current token is appended to the token (except for the last token, which has no trailing delimiter). Otherwise, it is the same mode as wxTOKEN_RET_EMPTY.
- ☞ wxTOKEN_STRTOK: In this mode, the class behaves exactly like the standard strtok function. Empty tokens are never returned.

wxStringTokenizer has two other useful accessors:

- ☞ CountTokens returns the number of remaining tokens in the string, returning 0 when there are no more tokens.
- ☞ GetPosition returns the current position of the tokenizer in the original string.

wxRegEx

wxRegEx represents a regular expression. This class provides support for regular expression matching and replacement. wxRegEx is either built on top of the system library (if it is available and has support for POSIX regular expressions, which is the case for most modern Unix variants, including Linux and Mac OS X) or uses the built-in library by Henry Spencer. Regular expressions, as defined by POSIX, come in two variations: extended and basic. The built-in library also adds an advanced mode, which is not available when using the system library.

On platforms where a system library is available, the default is to use the built-in library for Unicode builds, and the system library otherwise. Bear in mind that Unicode is fully supported only by the built-in library. It is possible to override the default when building wxWidgets. When using the system library in Unicode mode, the expressions and data are translated to the default 8-bit encoding before being passed to the library.

Use wxRegEx as you would use any POSIX regular expression processor. Due to the advanced nature and specialized uses of regular expressions, please see the wxWidgets documentation for a complete discussion and API reference.

WXARRAY

wxWidgets provides a dynamic array structure using wxArray, similar to C arrays in that the member access time is constant. However, these arrays are dynamic in the sense that they will automatically allocate more memory if there is not enough of it for adding a new element. Adding items to the arrays is also implemented in more or less constant time—but the price is pre-allocating the memory in advance. wxArray also provides range checking, asserting in debug builds or silently returning in release builds (though your program might get an unexpected value from array operations).

Array Types

wxWidgets has three different kinds of arrays. All derive from wxBaseArray, which works with untyped data and cannot be used directly. The macros WX_DEFINE_ARRAY, WX_DEFINE_SORTED_ARRAY, and WX_DEFINE_OBJARRAY are used to define a new class deriving from it. The classes are referred to as wxArray, wxSortedArray, and wxObjArray, but you should keep in mind that no classes with such names actually exist.

wxArray is suitable for storing integer types and pointers, which it does not treat as objects in any way—that is, the element referred to by the pointer is not deleted when the element is removed from the array. It should be noted that all of wxArray's functions are inline, so it costs nothing to define as many array types as you want (either in terms of the executable size or speed). This class has one serious limitation: it can only be used for storing integral types (bool, char, short, int, long, and their unsigned variants) or pointers (of any kind). Data of type float or double should not be stored in a wxArray.

wxSortedArray is a wxArray variant that should be used when you will be searching the array frequently. wxSortedArray requires you to define an additional function for comparing two elements of the array element type and always stores its items in the sorted order (according to the sort function). Assuming that you search the array far less frequently than you add to it, wxSortedArray may lead to huge performance improvements compared to wxArray. It should be noted that wxSortedArray shares wxArray's type restriction and should only be used for storing integral types or pointers.

wxObjArray class treats its elements like objects. It can delete them when they are removed from the array (invoking the correct destructor), and it copies them using the object's copy constructor. The definition of the wxObjArray arrays is split into two parts. First, you should declare the new wxObjArray class using the WX_DECLARE_OBJARRAY macro. Second, you must include the file defining the implementation of template type <wx/arrimpl.cpp> and define the array class with the WX_DEFINE_OBJARRAY macro from a point where the full declaration of the array elements class is in scope. This technique will be demonstrated in the array sample code presented later in this chapter.

wxArrayString

wxArrayString is an efficient container for storing wxString objects and has the same features as the other wxArray classes. It is also very compact and doesn't take more space than a C array wxString[] type (wxArrayString uses its knowledge of internals of wxString class to achieve this). All of the methods available in the other wxArray types are also available in wxArrayString.

This class is used in the same way as other dynamic arrays, except that no WX_DEFINE_ARRAY declaration is needed for it—you can use wxArrayString directly. When a string is added or inserted in the array, a copy of the string is created, so the original string may be safely deleted. In general, there is no need to worry about string memory management when using this class—it will always free the memory it uses.

The references returned by Item, Last, or operator[] are not constant, so the array elements may be modified in place:

```
array.Last().MakeUpper();
```

There is also a variant of wxArrayString called wxSortedArrayString that has exactly the same methods as wxArrayString, but always keeps its strings in alphabetical order. wxSortedArrayString uses binary search in its Index, which makes it much more efficient if you rarely add strings to the array but search for them often. The Insert and Sort methods should not be used with wxSortedArrayString because they are likely to break the order of items.

Array Construction, Destruction, and Memory Management

Array classes are C++ objects and as such have the appropriate copy constructors and assignment operators. Copying a wxArray copies the elements, but copying a wxObjArray copies the array's items. However, for the sake of memory efficiency, neither of these classes has a virtual destructor. It is not very important for wxArray, which has a trivial destructor, but it does mean that you should avoid deleting wxObjArray through a wxBaseArray pointer and that you should not derive your own classes from the array classes.

Automatic array memory management is quite trivial: the array starts by pre-allocating some minimal amount of memory (defined by WX_ARRAY_DEFAULT_INITIAL_SIZE). When further new items exhaust previously allocated memory, the array reallocates itself, adding 50% of the currently allocated amount, but no more than ARRAY_MAXSIZE_INCREMENT. The Shrink method deallocates any extra memory. The Alloc method can be quite useful if you know in advance how many items you are going to put in the array, and using it will prevent the array code from reallocating the memory more often than needed.

Array Sample Code

The array sample presented here shows the most complex case, using a wxObjArray to store custom objects. Using a wxArray for primitive types or pointers would work identically in terms of syntax and semantics, but the wxArray would never take ownership of the objects.

```
// Our data class to store in the array
class Customer
{
public:
    int CustID;
    wxString CustName;
};

// this part might be in a header or source (.cpp) file
// declare our array class:
// this macro declares and partly implements CustomerArray class
// (which derives from wxArrayBase)
WX_DECLARE_OBJARRAY(Customer, CustomerArray);

// the only requirement for the rest is to be AFTER the full
// declaration of Customer (for WX_DECLARE_OBJARRAY forward
// declaration is enough), but usually it will be found in the
// source file and not in the header
#include <wx/arrimpl.cpp>
WX_DEFINE_OBJARRAY(CustomerArray);
```

```
// Used when sorting to compare objects
int arraycompare(Customer** arg1, Customer** arg2)
{
    return ((*arg1)->CustID < (*arg2)->CustID);
}

// Show Array operations
void ArrayTest()
{
    // Declare an instance of our array
    CustomerArray MyArray;

    bool IsEmpty = MyArray.IsEmpty(); // will be true

    // Create some customers
    Customer CustA;
    CustA.CustID = 10;
    CustA.CustName = wxT("Bob");

    Customer CustB;
    CustB.CustID = 20;
    CustB.CustName = wxT("Sally");

    Customer* CustC = new Customer();
    CustC->CustID = 5;
    CustC->CustName = wxT("Dmitri");

    // Append two customers to the array
    MyArray.Add(CustA);
    MyArray.Add(CustB);

    // Insert last customer into arbitrary place in the array
    // The array will not own this CustC object, it will own a copy
    MyArray.Insert(*CustC, (size_t)0);

    int Count = MyArray.GetCount(); // will be 3

    // If not found, wxNOT_FOUND is returned
    int Index = MyArray.Index(CustB); // will be 2

    // Process each customer in the array
    for (unsigned int i = 0; i < MyArray.GetCount(); i++)
    {
        Customer Cust = MyArray[i]; // or MyArray.Item(i);

        // Process Customer
    }

    // Sort the customers according to the sort function
    MyArray.Sort(arraycompare);

    // Remove Customer A from the array, but do not delete
    Customer* pCustA = MyArray.Detach(1);
    // We must deallocate the object ourself if using Detach
    delete pCustA;

    // Remove will also delete the Customer object
    MyArray.RemoveAt(1);

    // Clears the array, deleting all objects
```

```
        MyArray.Clear();

        // The array never owned this object
        delete CustC;
}
```

*WX**L**IST* AND *WX**N**ODE*

The wxList class is a doubly linked list that can store data of an arbitrary type. wxWidgets requires that you explicitly define a new list type for each type of list data, providing strong type checking for the list's data type. The wxList class also allows you to optionally specify a key type for primitive lookups (see the wxHashMap section if you need a structure with fast random access).

The wxList class makes use of an abstract wxNode class. When you define a new list, a new node type deriving from wxNodeBase is also created, providing type-safe node operations. The most important methods of the node class are the self-explanatory GetNext, GetPrevious, and GetData, which provide access to the next node, the previous node, and the current node's data.

The only remarkable operation for a wxList is data deletion. By default, removing a node does *not* delete the data being stored by that node. The DeleteContents method allows you to change this behavior and set the data itself to be deleted along with the nodes. If you want to empty a list of all data *and* delete the data, be sure to call DeleteContents with true before calling Clear.

Rather than rehash the contents of the manual, a small but comprehensive code example shows the wxList methods as well as how to create and use your custom list type. Note that the WX_DECLARE_LIST macro would typically appear in a header file, while the WX_DEFINE_LIST macro would almost always appear in a source file.

```
// Our data class to store in the list
class Customer
{
public:
    int CustID;
    wxString CustName;
};

// this part might be in a header or source file
// declare our list class:
// this macro declares and partly implements CustomerList class
// (which derives from wxListBase)
WX_DECLARE_LIST(Customer, CustomerList);

// the only requirement for the rest is to be AFTER the full
// declaration of Customer (for WX_DECLARE_LIST forward declaration
// is enough), but usually it will be found in the source file and
// not in the header
```

```cpp
#include <wx/listimpl.cpp>
WX_DEFINE_LIST(CustomerList);

// Used for sorting to compare objects
int listcompare(const Customer** arg1, const Customer** arg2)
{
    return ((*arg1)->CustID < (*arg2)->CustID);
}

// Show List operations
void ListTest()
{
    // Declare an instance of our list
    CustomerList* MyList = new CustomerList();

    bool IsEmpty = MyList->IsEmpty(); // will be true

    // Create some customers
    Customer* CustA = new Customer;
    CustA->CustID = 10;
    CustA->CustName = wxT("Bob");

    Customer* CustB = new Customer;
    CustB->CustID = 20;
    CustB->CustName = wxT("Sally");

    Customer* CustC = new Customer;
    CustC->CustID = 5;
    CustC->CustName = wxT("Dmitri");

    // Append two customers to the list
    MyList->Append(CustA);
    MyList->Append(CustB);

    // Insert last customer into arbitrary place in the list
    MyList->Insert((size_t)0, CustC);

    int Count = MyList->GetCount(); // will be 3

    // If not found, wxNOT_FOUND is returned
    int index = MyList->IndexOf(CustB); // will be 2

    // Customized node holds our customized data
    CustomerList::Node* node = MyList->GetFirst();

    // Traverse the nodes and process the customers
    while (node)
    {
        Customer* Cust = node->GetData();

        // Process Customer

        node = node->GetNext();
    }

    // Returns the node at the specified position
    node = MyList->Item(0);

    // Sort the customers according to the sort function
    MyList->Sort(listcompare);
```

```
        // Remove Customer A node from the list
        MyList->DeleteObject(CustA);
        // CustA object is NOT deleted by removing the node
        delete CustA;

        // Returns the node whose client data is the object
        node = MyList->Find(CustB);

        // Specifies that data should be deleted when node is deleted
        MyList->DeleteContents(true);

        // Removes node from the list and deletes that node's
        // data (CustB)
        MyList->DeleteNode(node);

        // Clears the list, and deletes all stored data
        // (DeleteContents is true)
        MyList->Clear();

        delete MyList;
}
```

wxHashMap

The wxHashMap class is a simple, type-safe, and reasonably efficient hash map class, with an interface that is a subset of the interface of STL containers. In particular, the interface is modeled after std::map and the non-standard std::hash_map. By using macros to create hash maps, you can choose from several combinations of keys and values, including int, wxString, or void* (arbitrary class).

There are three macros for declaring a hash map. To declare a hash map class named CLASSNAME with wxString keys and VALUE_T values:

```
WX_DECLARE_STRING_HASH_MAP(VALUE_T, CLASSNAME);
```

To declare a hash map class named CLASSNAME with void* keys and VALUE_T values:

```
WX_DECLARE_VOIDPTR_HASH_MAP(VALUE_T, CLASSNAME);
```

To declare a hash map class named CLASSNAME with arbitrary keys or values:

```
WX_DECLARE_HASH_MAP(KEY_T, VALUE_T, HASH_T, KEY_EQ_T, CLASSNAME);
```

HASH_T and KEY_EQ_T are the types used for the hashing function and key comparison. wxWidgets provides three predefined hashing functions: wxInteger Hash for integer types (int, long, short, and their unsigned counterparts), wxStringHash for strings (wxString, wxChar*, char*), and wxPointerHash for any kind of pointer. Similarly, three equality predicates are provided: wxInteger Equal, wxStringEqual, and wxPointerEqual.

The following code example shows the wxHashMap methods as well as how to create and use your custom hash type.

```cpp
// Our data class to store in the hash
class Customer
{
    public:
        int CustID;
        wxString CustName;
};

// Declare our hash map class
// This macro declares and implements CustomerList as a hash map
WX_DECLARE_HASH_MAP(int, Customer*, wxIntegerHash,
                    wxIntegerEqual, CustomerHash);

void HashTest()
{
    // Declare an instance of our list
    CustomerHash MyHash;

    bool IsEmpty = MyHash.empty(); // will be true

    // Create some customers
    Customer* CustA = new Customer;
    CustA->CustID = 10;
    CustA->CustName = wxT("Bob");

    Customer* CustB = new Customer;
    CustB->CustID = 20;
    CustB->CustName = wxT("Sally");

    Customer* CustC = new Customer;
    CustC->CustID = 5;
    CustC->CustName = wxT("Dmitri");

    // Add the customers to the hash
    MyHash[CustA->CustID] = CustA;
    MyHash[CustB->CustID] = CustB;
    MyHash[CustC->CustID] = CustC;

    int Size = MyHash.size(); // will be 3

    // count returns 0 or 1, i.e. is 20 in the hash?
    int Present = MyHash.count(20); // will be 1

    // Customized iterator for our hash map
    CustomerHash::iterator i = MyHash.begin();

    // End represents one past the last element
    while (i != MyHash.end())
    {
```

```
        // first is the key, second is the value
        int CustID = i->first;
        Customer* Cust = i->second;

        // Process Customer

        // Advance to the next element in the hash
        i++;
    }

    // Remove Customer A from the hash
    MyHash.erase(10);
    // CustA object is NOT deleted by removing from hash
    delete CustA;

    // Return an iterator to the node with the specified key
    CustomerHash::iterator i2 = MyHash.find(21);

    // Find returns hash::end if the key was not found
    bool NotFound = (i2 == MyHash.end()); // will be true

    // This time the find will be successful
    i2 = MyHash.find(20);

    // Removing an element using the iterator
    MyHash.erase(i2);
    delete CustB;

    // Side-effect: A NULL value is inserted in the hash for key 30
    Customer* Cust = MyHash[30]; // Cust will be NULL

    // Empties the hash map of all elements
    MyHash.clear();

    delete CustC;
}
```

STORING AND PROCESSING DATES AND TIMES

wxWidgets provides a comprehensive wxDateTime class for representing date and time information with many operations such as formatting, time zones, date and time arithmetic, and more. Static functions provide information such as the current date and time, as well as queries such as whether a given year is a leap year. Note that the wxDateTime class is the appropriate class to use even when you need to store only date *or* time information. Helper classes wxTimeSpan and wxDateSpan provide convenient ways for modifying an existing wxDateTime object.

wxDateTime

The `wxDateTime` class has too many methods to include in a concise discussion; the complete API reference is available in the wxWidgets documentation. What is presented here is an overview of the most frequently used `wxDateTime` methods and operations.

Note that although time is always stored internally in Greenwich Mean Time (GMT), you will usually work in the local time zone. Because of this, all `wxDateTime` constructors and modifiers that compose a date or time from components (for example hours, minutes, and seconds) assume that these values are for the local time zone. All methods returning date or time components (month, day, hour, minute, second, and so on) will also return the correct values for the local time zone by default; no effort is required to get correct results for your time zone. If you want to manipulate time zones, please refer to the documentation.

wxDateTime Constructors and Modifiers

`wxDateTime` objects can be constructed from Unix timestamps, time-only information, date-only information, or complete date and time information. For each constructor, there is a corresponding `Set` method that modifies an existing object to have the specified date or time. There are also individual modifiers such as `SetMonth` or `SetHour` that change just one component of the date or time.

`wxDateTime(time_t)` constructs an object with the date and time set according to the specified Unix timestamp.

`wxDateTime(const struct tm&)` constructs an object using the data from the C standard `tm` structure.

`wxDateTime(wxDateTime_t hour, wxDateTime_t minute = 0, wxDateTime_t second = 0, wxDateTime_t millisec = 0)` constructs an object based on the specified time information.

`wxDateTime(wxDateTime_t day, Month month = Inv_Month, int year = Inv_Year, wxDateTime_t hour = 0, wxDateTime_t minute = 0, wxDateTime_t second = 0, wxDateTime_t millisec = 0)` constructs an object with the specified date and time information.

wxDateTime Accessors

The accessors for `wxDateTime` are mostly self-explanatory: `GetYear`, `GetMonth`, `GetDay`, `GetWeekDay`, `GetHour`, `GetMinute`, `GetSecond`, `GetMillisecond`, `GetDayOfYear`, `GetWeekOfYear`, `GetWeekOfMonth`, and `GetYearDay`. `wxDateTime` also provides the following:

- ☞ `GetTicks` returns the date and time in Unix timestamp format (seconds since January 1, 1970 at midnight).
- ☞ `IsValid` returns whether or not the object is in a valid state (the object could have been constructed but never given a date or time).

Getting the Current Time

wxDateTime provides two static methods for retrieving the current time:

- ☞ wxDateTime::Now creates a wxDateTime object with the current time, accurate to up the second.
- ☞ wxDateTime::UNow creates a wxDateTime object with the current time, including milliseconds.

Parsing and Formatting Dates

The functions in this section convert wxDateTime objects to and from text. The conversions to text are mostly trivial: you can use the default date and time representations for the current locale (FormatDate and FormatTime), use the international standard representation defined by ISO 8601 (FormatISODate and FormatISOTime), or specify any format at all by using Format directly.

The conversions from text are more interesting because there are many more possibilities. The simplest cases can be taken care of with ParseFormat, which can parse any date in a specified (rigid) format. ParseRfc822Date parses dates using the format from RFC 822 that defines the format of email messages on the Internet.

The most interesting functions are ParseTime, ParseDate, and ParseDateTime, which try to parse the date and/or time in "free" format, allowing them to be specified in a variety of ways. These functions can be used to parse user input that is not bound by any predefined format. As an example, ParseDateTime can parse strings such as "tomorrow", "March first", and even "next Sunday".

Date Comparisons

Two wxDateTime objects can easily be compared using one of many available comparison functions. All of these methods return true or false.

The following methods all make comparisons to one other wxDateTime object: IsEqualTo, IsEarlierThan, IsLaterThan, IsSameDate, and IsSameTime.

The following methods all make comparisons using two other wxDateTime objects: IsStrictlyBetween and IsBetween. The difference between these two is that IsStrictlyBetween would return false if the wxDateObject in question exactly equaled one of the range extremes, whereas IsBetween would return true.

Date Arithmetic

wxWidgets provides two very robust classes for performing arithmetic on wxDateTime objects: wxTimeSpan and wxDateSpan. wxTimeSpan is simply a difference in milliseconds and always gives fast, predictable results. On the other hand, time has larger meaningful units, such as weeks or months. wxDateSpan handles these operations in the most natural way possible, but note that manipulating intervals of this kind is not always well-defined. For example, Jan 31 plus one month will give Feb 28 (or 29), the last day of February, and not the non-existent Feb 31. Of course, this is what is usually wanted, but you still might be surprised that subtracting back the same interval from Feb 28 will result in Jan 28 (not the January 31 that we started with).

Many different operations may be performed with the dates, but not all combinations of them make sense. For example, multiplying a date by a number is an invalid operation, even though multiplying either of the time span classes by a number is perfectly valid.

☞ **Addition**: A wxTimeSpan or wxDateSpan can be added to wxDateTime resulting in a new wxDateTime object. Also, two objects of the same span class can be added together, resulting in another object of the same class.

☞ **Subtraction**: The same operations as addition are valid for subtraction. Additionally, a difference between two wxDateTime objects can be taken and will return a wxTimeSpan object.

☞ **Multiplication**: A wxTimeSpan or wxDateSpan object can be multiplied by an integer number, resulting in an object of the same type.

☞ **Unary minus**: A wxTimeSpan or wxDateSpan object may be negated, resulting in an interval of the same magnitude but in the opposite time direction.

The following small code example demonstrates how to use wxDateSpan and wxTimeSpan to change the time stored in a wxDateTime object. See the wxWidgets manual for a complete list of available methods.

```
void TimeTests()
{
    // Get the current day and time
    wxDateTime DT1 = wxDateTime::Now();

    // A span of 2 weeks and 1 day, or 15 days
    wxDateSpan Span1(0, 0, 2, 1);

    // Substract 15 days from today
    wxDateTime DT2 = DT1 - Span1;

    // Static creation of a one-day difference
    wxDateSpan Span2 = wxDateSpan::Day();

    // Span 3 will now be 14 days
    wxDateSpan Span3 = Span1 - Span2;

    // 0 days (the span is defined as 2 weeks)
    int Days = Span3.GetDays();

    // 14 days (2 weeks)
    int TotalDays = Span3.GetTotalDays();

    // 2 weeks into the past
    wxDateSpan Span4 = -Span3;
```

```
    // A span of 3 months
    wxDateSpan Span5 = wxDateSpan::Month() * 3;

    // 10 hours, 5 minutes and 6 seconds
    wxTimeSpan Span6(10, 5, 6, 0);

    // Add the specified amount of time to DT2
    wxDateTime DT3 = DT2 + Span6;

    // Span7 is 3 times longer than Span6, but in the past
    wxTimeSpan Span7 = (-Span6) * 3;

    // SpanNeg will be true, the span is negative (in the past)
    bool SpanNeg = Span7.IsNegative();

    // Static creation of a span of one hour
    wxTimeSpan Span8 = wxTimeSpan::Hour();

    // One hour is not longer than 30+ hours (uses absolutes)
    bool Longer = Span8.IsLongerThan(Span7);
}
```

HELPER DATA STRUCTURES

wxWidgets makes use of several data structures internally and as parameters and return types in public library methods. Application programmers are encouraged to use the wxWidgets helper data structures in their projects.

wxObject

The wxObject class is the base class of all wxWidgets classes, providing runtime type information, reference counting, virtual destructor declaration, and optional debugging versions of new and delete. The wxClassInfo class is used to store meta-data about classes and is used by some of the wxObject methods.

```
MyWindow* window = wxDynamicCast(FindWindow(ID_MYWINDOW), MyWindow);
```

IsKindOf takes a wxClassInfo pointer and returns true if the object is of the specified type. For example:

```
bool tmp = obj->IsKindOf(CLASSINFO(wxFrame));
```

Ref takes a const wxObject& and replaces the current object's data with a reference to the passed object's data. The reference count of the current object is decremented, possibly freeing its data, and the reference count of the passed object is incremented.

UnRef decrements the reference count of the associated data and deletes the data if the reference count has fallen to 0.

wxLongLong

The wxLongLong class represents a 64-bit long number. A native 64-bit type is always used when available, and emulation code is used when the native type is unavailable. You would usually use this type in exactly the same manner as any other (built-in) arithmetic type. Note that wxLongLong is a signed type; if you want unsigned values, use wxULongLong, which has exactly the same API as wxLongLong except for some logical exceptions (such as the absolute value method). All of the usual mathematical operations are defined, as well as several convenient accessors:

☞ Abs returns the absolute value of the value as a wxLongLong, either as a copy if used on a constant reference or modifying it in place if mutable.

☞ ToLong returns a long representation of the stored value, triggering a debug assertion if any precision was lost.

☞ ToString returns the string representation of the stored value in a wxString.

wxPoint and wxRealPoint

wxPoint is used throughout wxWidgets for specifying integer screen or window locations. As the names imply, the point classes store coordinate pairs as x and y values. The data members are declared as public and can be accessed directly as x and y. wxPoint provides + and – – operators that allow you to add or subtract by wxPoint or wxSize. wxRealPoint stores coordinates as double rather than int and provides + and – – operators accepting only other wxRealPoint objects.

Constructing a wxPoint is very straightforward:

```
wxPoint myPoint(50, 60);
```

wxRect

Used for manipulating rectangle information, the wxRect class is used by wxWidgets mostly with drawing or widget classes, such as wxDC or wxTreeCtrl. The wxRect class stores an x, y coordinate pair, as well as width and height, all of which are public. Rectangles can be added and subtracted from each other, and there are some other calculation methods as well.

GetRight returns the x position of the right edge of the rectangle.

GetBottom returns the y position of the bottom edge of the rectangle.

GetSize returns the size of the rectangle (the height and width) in a wxSize object.

Inflate increases the size of the rectangle by the specified values, either uniformly (one parameter) or differently in each direction (two parameters).

Inside determines whether a given point is inside the rectangle. The point can be specified as separate x and y coordinates or as a wxPoint.

Intersects takes another wxRect object and determines whether the two rectangles overlap.

Offset moves the rectangle by the specified offset. The offset can be specified as separate x and y coordinates or as a wxPoint.

A wxRect object can be constructed with data in three different ways. The following three objects would all represent the exact same rectangle:

```
wxRect myRect1(50, 60, 100, 200);
wxRect myRect2(wxPoint(50, 60), wxPoint(150, 260));
wxRect myRect3(wxPoint(50, 60), wxSize(100, 200));
```

wxRegion

A wxRegion represents a simple or complex region on a device context or window. It uses reference counting, so copying and assignment operations are fast. The primary use for wxRegion is to define or query clipping or update regions.

Contains returns true if the given coordinate pair, wxPoint, rectangle, or wxRect is within the region.

GetBox returns a wxRect representing the area of the region.

Intersect returns true if the given rectangle, wxRect, or wxRegion intersects the current region.

Offset moves the region by the specified offset. The offset is specified as separate x and y coordinates.

Subtract, Union, and Xor change the region in a variety of ways, offering ten overloads among the three methods. All these methods have overloads that take a wxRegion or a wxPoint parameter; see the wxWidgets documentation for a complete list of all available methods.

The following are the four most common ways to create a wxRegion; all these examples would create an object representing the same region:

```
wxRegion myRegion1(50, 60, 100, 200);
wxRegion myRegion2(wxPoint(50, 60), wxPoint(150, 260));
wxRect myRect(50, 60, 100, 200);
wxRegion myRegion3(myRect);
wxRegion myRegion4(myRegion1);
```

You can use the wxRegionIterator class to iterate through the rectangles in a region, for example to repaint "damaged" areas in a paint event handler, as in the following example:

```
// Called when the window needs to be repainted
void MyWindow::OnPaint(wxPaintEvent& event)
{
    wxPaintDC dc(this);

    wxRegionIterator upd(GetUpdateRegion());
    while (upd)
    {
        wxRect rect(upd.GetRect());

        // Repaint this rectangle
        ...some code...

        upd ++ ;
    }
}
```

wxSize

wxSize is used throughout wxWidgets for specifying integer sizes for windows, controls, canvas objects, and so on. A wxSize object is also frequently returned when using methods that would return size information.

GetHeight and GetWidth return the height or width.

SetHeight and SetWidth take integer parameters for setting a new height or width.

Set takes both a height and a width parameter to update the current size.

A wxSize object is very simply created by specifying a height and a width:

```
wxSize mySize(100, 200);
```

wxVariant

The wxVariant class represents a container for any type. A variant's value can be changed at runtime, possibly to a different type of value. This class is useful for reducing the programming for certain tasks, such as an editor for different data types, or a remote procedure call protocol.

wxVariant can store values of type bool, char, double, long, wxString, wxArrayString, wxList, wxDateTime, void pointer, and list of variants. However, an application can extend wxVariant's capabilities by deriving from the class wxVariantData and using the wxVariantData form of the wxVariant constructor or assignment operator to assign this data to a variant. Actual values for user-defined types will need to be accessed via the wxVariantData object, unlike basic data types, for which convenience functions such as GetLong can be used.

Bear in mind that not all types can be converted automatically to all other types; for example, it doesn't make much sense to convert a boolean into a wxDateTime object or to convert an integer to a wxArrayString. Use common sense to decide which conversions are appropriate, and remember that you can always get the current type using GetType. Here is a small example using wxVariant:

```
wxVariant Var;

// Store a wxDateTime, get a wxString
Var = wxDateTime::Now();
wxString DateAsString = Var.GetString();

// Store a wxString, get a double
Var = wxT("10.25");
double StringAsDouble = Var.GetDouble();

// Type will be "string"
wxString Type = Var.GetType();

// This is not a valid conversion, a string can't become a character
// so c will be 0 due to being unable to convert
char c = Var.GetChar();
```

SUMMARY

The data structures provided by wxWidgets allow you to easily pass and receive structured data to and from wxWidgets and within your own applications. By providing powerful data processing methods and classes such as wxRegEx, wxStringTokenizer, wxDateTime, and wxVariant, almost any data storage and processing needs can be met by wxWidgets without having to use third-party libraries.

Next, we'll look at what wxWidgets offers for reading and writing data using files and streams.

CHAPTER 14

Files and Streams

In this chapter, we'll look at the classes that wxWidgets provides for low-level file access and streaming. wxWidgets' stream classes not only protect your application from the idiosyncrasies of different standard C++ libraries but also provide a complete set of classes including compression, writing to zip archives, and even socket streaming. We'll also describe wxWidgets' *virtual file system* facility, which lets your application easily take data from sources other than normal disk files.

FILE CLASSES AND FUNCTIONS

wxWidgets provides a range of functionality for platform-independent file handling. We'll introduce the major classes before summarizing the file functions.

wxFile and wxFFile

wxFile may be used for low-level input/output. It contains all the usual functions to work with integer file descriptors (opening/closing, reading/writing, seeking, and so on), but unlike the standard C functions, it reports errors via wxLog and closes the file automatically in the destructor. wxFFile brings similar benefits but uses buffered input/output and contains a pointer to a FILE handle.

You can create a wxFile object by using the default constructor followed by Create or Open, or you can use the constructor that takes a file name and open mode (wxFile::read, wxFile::write, or wxFile::read_write). You can also create a wxFile from an existing file descriptor, passed to the constructor or Attach function. A wxFile can be closed with Close, which is called automatically (if necessary) when the object is destroyed.

You can get data from the object with Read, passing a void* buffer and the number of bytes to read. Read will return the actual number of bytes read, or wxInvalidOffset if there was an error. Use Write to write a void* buffer or wxString to the file, calling Flush if you need the data to be written to the file immediately.

To test for the end of the file, use Eof, which will return true if the file pointer is at the end of the file. (In contrast, wxFFile's Eof will return true only if an attempt has been made to read *past* the end of the file.) You can determine the length of the file with Length.

Seek and SeekEnd seek to a position in the file, taking an offset specified as starting from the beginning or end of the file, respectively. Tell returns the current offset from the start of the file as a wxFileOffset (a 64-bit integer if the platform supports it, or else a 32-bit integer).

Call the static Access function to determine whether a file can be opened in a given mode. Exists is another static function that tests the existence of the given file.

The following code fragment uses wxFile to open a data file and read all the data into an array.

```
#include "wx/file.h"

if (!wxFile::Exists(wxT("data.dat")))
    return false;

wxFile file(wxT("data.dat"));

if ( !file.IsOpened() )
    return false;

// get the file size
wxFileOffset nSize = file.Length();
if ( nSize == wxInvalidOffset )
    return false;

// read the whole file into memory
wxUint* data = new wxUint8[nSize];

if ( file.Read(data, (size_t) nSize) != nSize )
{
    delete[] data;
    return false;
}

file.Close();
```

To illustrate file writing, here's a function that will dump the contents of a text control to a file.

```
bool WriteTextCtrlContents(wxTextCtrl* textCtrl,
                           const wxString& filename)
{
    wxFile file;
    if (!file.Open(filename, wxFile::write))
        return false

    int nLines = textCtrl->GetNumberOfLines();
    bool ok = true;

    for ( int nLine = 0; ok && nLine < nLines; nLine++ )
    {
        ok = file.Write(textCtrl->GetLineText(nLine) +
                        wxTextFile::GetEOL());
    }

    file.Close();
    return ok;
}
```

wxTextFile

wxTextFile provides a very straightforward way to read and write small files
and process them line-by-line.

Use Open to read a file into memory and split it into lines, and use Write
to save it. You can use GetLine or the array operator to retrieve a specified line,
or you can iterate through the file with GetFirstLine, GetNextLine, and
GetPrevLine. Add lines to the file with AddLine or InsertLine, and remove lines
by passing the line number to RemoveLine. You can clear the whole file with
Clear.

In the following example, each line of a file is prepended with a given
string before being written back to the same file.

```
#include "wx/textfile.h"

void FilePrepend(const wxString& filename, const wxString& text)
{
    wxTextFile file;
    if (file.Open(filename))
    {
        size_t i;
        for (i = 0; i < file.GetLineCount(); i++)
        {
            file[i] = text + file[i];
        }
        file.Write(filename);
    }
}
```

wxTempFile

wxTempFile is derived from wxFile and uses a temporary file to write data, not writing to the actual file until Commit is called. When you write a user's data, it's a good idea to write to a temporary file because if an error occurs during the save operation (such as a power failure, program bug, or other cataclysm), this error will not corrupt the current file on disk.

Note

The document/view framework does *not* write to a temporary file when creating an output stream and calling SaveObject, so you may want to override DoSaveDocument and construct a wxFileOutputStream from a wxTempFile object. After writing data, call Sync on the stream followed by Commit on the temporary file object.

---

wxDir

wxDir is a portable equivalent of the Unix open/read/closedir functions, which support enumeration of the files in a directory. wxDir supports enumeration of files as well as directories. It also provides a flexible way to enumerate files recursively using Traverse or the simpler GetAllFiles function.

After opening a file with Open (or by passing a path to the constructor), call GetFirst passing a pointer to a string to receive the found file name. You can also pass a file specification (defaulting to the empty string to match all files) and optional flags. Then call GetNext until there are no more matching files and the function returns false. The file specification can contain wildcards, such as "*" (match any number of characters) and "?" (match one character). For the flags argument, pass a bit-list of wxDIR_FILES (match files), wxDIR_DIRS (match directories), wxDIR_HIDDEN (match hidden files), and wxDIR_DOTDOT (match "." and ".."). The default is to match everything except "." and "..".

Here's an example of its use:

```
#include "wx/dir.h"

wxDir dir(wxGetCwd());

if ( !dir.IsOpened() )
{
    // Deal with the error here - wxDir already logs an error message
    // explaining the exact reason of the failure
    return;
}

puts("Enumerating object files in current directory:");

wxString filename;
wxString filespec = wxT("*.*");
int flags = wxDIR_FILES|wxDIR_DIRS;
```

```
bool cont = dir.GetFirst(&filename, filespec, flags);
while ( cont )
{
    wxLogMessage(wxT("%s\n"), filename.c_str());

    cont = dir.GetNext(&filename);
}
```

Note that if there is a problem when enumerating files—for example, if the directory does not exist—wxDir will generate a log message. To suppress this behavior, use the wxLogNull object to temporarily disable logging:

```
// Create scope for logNull
{
    wxLogNull logNull;

    wxDir dir(badDir);
    if ( !dir.IsOpened() )
    {
        return;
    }
}
```

wxFileName

wxFileName models the name of a file; it can parse and reconstitute the components of a file name, and it also provides a variety of file operations, some of which are static functions. Here are some examples of what you can do with this class. Please see the reference manual for the many other operations.

```
#include "wx/filename.h"

// Create a filename from a string
wxFileName fname(wxT("MyFile.txt"));

// Normalize, including making sure the filename is in its long form
// on Windows
fname.Normalize(wxPATH_NORM_LONG|wxPATH_NORM_DOTS|wxPATH_NORM_TILDE|
                wxPATH_NORM_ABSOLUTE);

// Get the full path as a string
wxString filename = fname.GetFullPath();

// Make it relative to the current path
fname.MakeRelativeTo(wxFileName::GetCwd());

// Does the file exist?
bool exists = fname.FileExists();

// Does a different file exist?
bool exists2 = wxFileName::FileExists(wxT("c:\\temp.txt"));

// Return the name part
```

```
wxString name = fname.GetName();

// Return the path part
wxString path = fname.GetPath();

// Return the short version on Windows, or identity
// on other systems
wxString shortForm = fname.GetShortPath();

// Makes a directory
bool ok = wxFileName::Mkdir(wxT("c:\\thing"));
```

File Functions

The most commonly used file functions are listed in Table 14-1, and are
defined in wx/filefn.h. See also the wxFileName class, especially the static functions you can use without constructing a wxFileName object, such as
wxFileName::FileExists.

wxWidgets also wraps many of the standard C file functions, such as
wxFopen, wxFputc, and wxSscanf. These are not currently documented, but their
definitions may be found in include/wx/wxchar.h in your wxWidgets distribution.

Table 14-1   File Functions

wxDirExists(dir)	Tests whether the directory exists. See also wxFileName::DirExists.
wxConcatFiles(f1, f2, f3)	Concatenates f1 and f2 to f3, returning true on success.
wxCopyFile(f1, f2, overwrite)	Copies f1 to f2, optionally overwriting f2. Returns true on success.
wxFileExists(file)	Tests whether the file exists. See also wxFileName::FileExists.
wxFileModificationTime(file)	Returns the time (as a time_t) of the last file modification. See also wxFileName::GetModificationTime, which returns a wxDateTime.
wxFileNameFromPath(file)	Returns the file name part of the path. The recommended method is to use wxFileName::SplitPath.
wxGetCwd()	Returns the current working directory. See also wxFileName::GetCwd.
wxGetDiskSpace (path, total, free)	Returns available disk space on the disk containing the given path, returning total space and free space in the wxLongLong pointer arguments.

wxIsAbsolutePath(path)	Tests whether the given path is absolute or relative.
wxMkdir(dir, permission=777)	Creates the given directory, optionally specifying an access mask. The parent directory must exist. Returns true on success.
wxPathOnly(path)	Returns the directory part of the given path.
wxRemoveFile(file)	Removes the file, returning true on success.
wxRenameFile(file1, file2)	Renames the file, returning true on success. This may return false if the files are on different volumes, for example, in which case a file copy is required.
wxRmdir(file)	Removes the directory, returning true on success.
wxSetWorkingDirectory(file)	Sets the current working directory, returning true on success.

It's also useful to know about the wxFILE_SEP_PATH symbol, which is the appropriate path separator for the platform on which the application is running (for example, backslash on Windows and forward slash on Unix-based systems).

STREAM CLASSES

Streams offer a higher-level model of reading and writing data than files; you can write code that doesn't care whether the stream uses a file, memory, or even sockets (see Chapter 18, "Programming with *wxSocket*," for an example of using sockets with streams). Some wxWidgets classes that support file input/output also support stream input/output, such as wxImage.

wxStreamBase is the base class for streams, declaring functions such as OnSysRead and OnSysWrite to be implemented by derived classes. The derived classes wxInputStream and wxOutputStream provide the foundation for further classes for reading and writing, respectively, such as wxFileInputStream and wxFileOutputStream. Let's look at the stream classes provided by wxWidgets.

File Streams

wxFileInputStream and wxFileOutputStream are based on the wxFile class and can be initialized from a file name, a wxFile object, or an integer file descriptor. Here's an example of using wxFileInputStream to read in some data, seek to the beginning of the stream, and retrieve the current position.

```
#include "wx/wfstream.h"

// The constructor initializes the stream buffer and opens the
// file descriptor associated with the name of the file.
// wxFileInputStream will close the file descriptor on destruction.
```

```
wxFileInputStream inStream(filename);

// Read some bytes
int byteCount = 100;
char data[100];

if (inStream.Read((void*) data, byteCount).
            LastError() != wxSTREAM_NOERROR)
{
    // Something bad happened.
    // For a complete list, see the wxStreamBase documentation.
}

// You can also get the last number of bytes really read.
size_t reallyRead = inStream.LastRead();

// Moves to the beginning of the stream. SeekI returns the last position
// in the stream counted from the beginning.
off_t oldPosition = inStream.SeekI(0, wxFromBeginning);

// What is my current position?
off_t position = inStream.TellI();
```

Using wxFileOutputStream is similarly straightforward. The following code uses a wxFileInputStream and wxFileOutputStream to make a copy of a file, writing in 1024-byte chunks for efficiency. Error checking has been omitted for the sake of brevity.

```
// Copy a fixed size of data from an input stream to an
// output stream, using a buffer to speed it up.
void BufferedCopy(wxInputStream& inStream, wxOutputStream& outStream,
                  size_t size)
{
    static unsigned char buf[1024];
    size_t bytesLeft = size;

    while (bytesLeft > 0)
    {
        size_t bytesToRead = wxMin((size_t) sizeof(buf), bytesLeft);

        inStream.Read((void*) buf, bytesToRead);
        outStream.Write((void*) buf, bytesToRead);

        bytesLeft -= bytesToRead;
    }
}

void CopyFile(const wxString& from, const wxString& to)
{
    wxFileInputStream inStream(from);
    wxFileOutputStream outStream(to);

    BufferedCopy(inStream, outStream, inStream.GetSize());
}
```

wxFFileInputStream and wxFFileOutputStream are identical to wxFileInputStream and wxFileOutputStream, except that they are based on the wxFFile class instead of wxFile. They can therefore be initialized from a FILE pointer or wxFFile object. The behavior of end-of-file handling also differs: wxFileInputStream will report wxSTREAM_EOF after having read the last byte, whereas wxFFileInputStream will report wxSTREAM_EOF after trying to read past the last byte.

Memory and String Streams

wxMemoryInputStream and wxMemoryOutputStream use an internal buffer for streaming data. The constructors for both of these classes take a char* buffer and size, which can be omitted to let the class allocate space dynamically. We'll see a memory stream being used shortly.

wxStringInputStream takes a wxString reference from which data is to be read. wxStringOutputStream takes an optional wxString pointer to which to stream the data; if this is omitted, an internal string is created that can be accessed with GetString.

Reading and Writing Data Types

So far, we've described stream classes that access raw bytes, which must be converted to something useful by the application. To help with this process, you can use four classes to read and write data at a higher level: wxTextInputStream, wxTextOutputStream, wxDataInputStream, and wxDataOutput Stream. Objects of these classes are constructed by referring to existing streams, and they provide insertion and extraction operators for use with a variety of C++ types.

wxTextInputStream reads data from a human-readable text file. If you're scanning through a file using wxTextInputStream, you should check for end of file before reading the next item. You should be prepared, however, to receive an empty item (such as an empty string or zero number) at the end of the file. This issue is unavoidable because most files end with white space, usually a newline. Here's an example of using a wxTextInputStream in conjunction with wxFileInputStream:

```
wxFileInputStream input( wxT("mytext.txt") );
wxTextInputStream text( input );
wxUint8 i1;
float f2;
wxString line;
text >> i1;        // read an 8 bit integer.
text >> i1 >> f2;  // read an 8 bit integer followed by float.
text >> line;      // read a text line
```

wxTextOutputStream writes text data to an output stream, using the native line-ending format by default. The following example writes to the standard error stream.

```
#include "wx/wfstream.h"
#include "wx/txtstrm.h"

wxFFileOutputStream output( stderr );
wxTextOutputStream cout( output );

cout << wxT("This is a text line") << endl;
cout << 1234;
cout << 1.23456;
```

wxDataInputStream and wxDataOutputStream are similar but write binary data. The data is streamed in a portable way so that the same data files can be read and written, regardless of platform. Here's an example of reading from a data file.

```
#include "wx/wfstream.h"
#include "wx/datstrm.h"

wxFileInputStream input( wxT("mytext.dat") );
wxDataInputStream store( input );
wxUint8 i1;
float f2;
wxString line;

store >> i1;        // read an 8 bit integer
store >> i1 >> f2;  // read an 8 bit integer followed by float
store >> line;      // read a text line
```

And to write the data:

```
#include "wx/wfstream.h"
#include "wx/datstrm.h"

wxFileOutputStream output(wxT("mytext.dat") );
wxDataOutputStream store( output );

store << 2 << 8 << 1.2;
store << wxT("This is a text line") ;
```

Socket Streams

wxSocketOutputStream and wxSocketInputStream are initialized from a wxSocket object; see Chapter 18 for more details.

Filter Streams

wxFilterInputStream and wxFilterOutputStream are base classes for streams
that can be placed on top of other streams. wxZlibInputStream is an example. If
you pass an input stream that has been created from a zlib or glib file, you can
read data from the wxZlibInputStream without worrying about the mechanics
of decompression. Similarly, you can create a wxZlibOutputStream passing an
output stream such as wxFileOutputStream—writing data to the wxZlibOutput
Stream will cause it to be compressed and sent to the wxFileOutputStream.

The following example compresses a string of data (buf) into a memory
stream and then copies the compressed data to a permanent storage area
(data).

```
#include "wx/mstream.h"
#include "wx/zstream.h"

const char* buf =
    "012345678901234567890123456789012345678901234567890123456789";

// Create a zlib output stream writing to a memory stream
wxMemoryOutputStream memStreamOut;
wxZlibOutputStream zStreamOut(memStreamOut);

// Write the contents of 'buf' to memory via the zlib stream
zStreamOut.Write(buf, strlen(buf));

// Get the size of the memory stream buffer
int sz = memStreamOut.GetSize();

// Create storage big enough for the compressed data, and
// copy the data out of the memory stream
unsigned char* data = new unsigned char[sz];
memStreamOut.CopyTo(data, sz);
```

Zip Streams

wxZipInputStream is a more complex kind of stream, working on an archive, not
just a linear stream of data. In fact, archives are handled by a comprehensive
suite of classes including wxArchiveClassFactory and wxArchiveEntry, but you
can read and write zip files without using these directly. To use
wxZipInputStream, you can create the stream either from a wxInputStream,
which has itself opened the archive, or by explicitly specifying the archive file
name plus the file name within the archive. Both methods are illustrated in
the following example, where string data is read from one or more files in the
archive (first example) or a single specified file (second example).

```
#include "wx/wfstream.h"
#include "wx/zipstrm.h"
```

```
#include "wx/txtstrm.h"

// Method 1: create the zip input stream in two steps

wxZipEntry* entry;

wxFFileInputStream in(wxT("test.zip"));
wxZipInputStream zip(in);
wxTextInputStream txt(zip);
wxString data;

while (entry = zip.GetNextEntry())
{
    wxString name = entry->GetName();      // access meta-data
    txt >> data;                           // access data
    delete entry;
}

// Method 2: specify the archived file in the constructor

wxZipInputStream in(wxT("test.zip"), wxT("text.txt"));
wxTextInputStream txt(zip);

wxString data;
txt >> data;                               // access data
```

wxZipOutputStream is the class for writing to zip files. PutNextEntry or
PutNextDirEntry is used to create a new entry in the zip file, and then the
entry's data can be written. For example:

```
#include "wx/wfstream.h"
#include "wx/zipstrm.h"
#include "wx/txtstrm.h"

wxFFileOutputStream out(wxT("test.zip"));
wxZipOutputStream zip(out);
wxTextOutputStream txt(zip);

zip.PutNextEntry(wxT("entry1.txt"));
txt << wxT("Some text for entry1\n");

zip.PutNextEntry(wxT("entry2.txt"));
txt << wxT("Some text for entry2\n");
```

Virtual File Systems

wxWidgets provides a virtual file system capability that enables an application to read data from a variety of sources as if it were dealing with ordinary
files. It supports reading from a zip file, from memory, and from HTTP and
FTP locations. Although it can't be used for storing editable documents
because it's mainly a read-only mechanism, you could, for example, use it for
accessing resources in a single zip archive. wxHtmlWindow, the wxWidgets

HTML help controller, and the XRC resource system recognize virtual file system locations. Virtual file systems can be more convenient to work with than
the archive classes mentioned in the last section, but the latter have the
advantage of being able to write to archives. Although both systems use
streams, they are otherwise unrelated.

The different virtual file systems are implemented by classes derived
from wxFileSystemHandler, and instances of these classes need to be added via
wxFileSystem::AddHandler (usually in the application's OnInit function) before
the file systems can be used. Usually all interaction with the file system happens through a wxFileSystem object, but occasionally a handler provides functions that can be used directly by the application, such as wxMemoryFSHandler's
AddFile and RemoveFile.

Before getting into the details of how an application can interact with the
file system API in C++, let's look at a couple of ways that we can use virtual
file systems implicitly through other wxWidgets subsystems. Here's an example of a URL that can be used in an HTML file displayed by wxHtmlWindow:

```
<img src="file:myapp.bin#zip:images/logo.png">
```

The part before the hash (#) is the name of the archive, and the part after the
hash is the name of the file system protocol followed by the location of the file
within the zip archive.

Similarly, we can specify a virtual file location in an XRC file:

```
<object class="wxBitmapButton">
    <bitmap>file:myapp.bin#zip:images/fuzzy.gif</bitmap>
</object>
```

In these examples, the code to use the virtual file system is hidden in the
wxHtmlWindow and XRC implementations. To use virtual file systems directly,
you use the wxFileSystem and wxFSFile classes. In the following snippet, a
wxBitmap is loaded from an image in a zip archive. When the application initializes, the wxZipFSHandler is registered with wxFileSystem. An instance of
wxFileSystem, which can be temporary or can last the lifetime of the application, is used to open the file logo.png from within the myapp.bin archive. The
wxFSFile object returned is queried for the associated stream, which is used to
read in the image (because wxImage is stream-aware). The image is converted
to a wxBitmap, and the wxFSFile and wxFileSystem objects are deleted.

```
#include "wx/fs_zip.h"
#include "wx/filesys.h"
#include "wx/wfstream.h"

// This should be done once, in app initialization
wxFileSystem::AddHandler(new wxZipFSHandler);

wxFileSystem* fileSystem = new wxFileSystem;
```

```
wxString archive = wxT("file:///c:/myapp/myapp.bin");
wxString filename = wxT("images/logo.png");

wxFSFile* file = fileSystem->OpenFile(
             archive + wxString(wxT("#zip:")) + filename);
if (file)
{
    wxInputStream* stream = file->GetStream();

    wxImage image(* stream, bitmapType);
    wxBitmap bitmap = wxBitmap(image);

    delete file;
}
delete fileSystem;
```

Note that you must pass a URL, *not* a regular file name, to wxFileSystem::
OpenFile. When specifying an absolute file location on the left side of a
URL, you should use the form file:/<hostname>//<file>, and if there is
no hostname, three slashes should still be used. You can convert from a
file name to a URL using wxFileSystem::FileNameToURL and back again with
wxFileSystem::URLToFileName.

As a further demonstration of using zip archives, LoadTextResource (as
shown in the following example) loads an ASCII text file (such as an HTML
file) into the variable text, given an archive file name and the name of the text
file within the archive.

```
// Load a text resource from zip file
bool LoadTextResource(wxString& text, const wxString& archive,
                      const wxString& filename)
{
    wxString archiveURL(wxFileSystem::FileNameToURL(archive));
    wxFileSystem* fileSystem = new wxFileSystem;

    wxFSFile* file = fileSystem->OpenFile(
                archiveURL + wxString(wxT("#zip:")) + filename);
    if (file)
    {
        wxInputStream* stream = file->GetStream();
        size_t sz = stream->GetSize();
        char* buf = new char[sz + 1];
        stream->Read((void*) buf, sz);
        buf[sz] = 0;

        text = wxString::FromAscii(buf);

        delete[] buf;

        delete file;
        delete fileSystem;
        return true;
    }
    else
        return false;
}
```

The wxMemoryFSHandler allows you to store data in the application's memory and uses the memory protocol name. Obviously your application has to be careful not to store enormous amounts of data in memory, but it can be very handy when writing to actual disk files is not appropriate or efficient. For example, when previewing XRC dialogs, DialogBlocks adds to memory the bitmaps shown when a user-defined bitmap is not available. These bitmaps don't exist anywhere on disk, but they can still be referenced by the XRC as if they were files:

```
<object class="wxBitmapButton">
    <bitmap>memory:default.png</bitmap>
</object>
```

wxMemoryFSHandler has an overloaded AddFile function that takes a file name argument and a wxImage, wxBitmap, wxString, or void* data argument. When you no longer need that data in memory, you can remove it with RemoveFile. For example:

```
#include "wx/fs_mem.h"
#include "wx/filesys.h"
#include "wx/wfstream.h"
#include "csquery.xpm"

wxFileSystem::AddHandler(new wxMemoryFSHandler);

wxBitmap bitmap(csquery_xpm);
wxMemoryFSHandler::AddFile(wxT("csquery.xpm"), bitmap,
                           wxBITMAP_TYPE_XPM);
...
wxMemoryFSHandler::RemoveFile(wxT("csquery.xpm"));
```

The third and final virtual file system handler supported by wxWidgets is wxInternetFSHandler, which handles the FTP and HTTP protocols.

SUMMARY

This chapter has given an overview of the classes that wxWidgets offers to let your application work with files and streams in a portable way. We've also touched on the virtual file system facility that makes it easy to get data from compressed archives, data in memory, and Internet files.

Next, we'll tackle issues that are not directly related to what your users see on their screens but are nevertheless crucial: memory management, debugging, and error checking.

CHAPTER 15

Memory Management, Debugging, and Error Checking

Tracking down errors is an essential, if unglamorous, part of developing an application. This chapter describes the facilities that wxWidgets provides to detect memory problems and also to encourage "defensive programming"—checking for problems as early as possible—which makes for much more reliable and easily debugged software. We also explain when you should create objects on the heap and when to create them on the stack, and we discuss how to use the run-time type information facilities, the module mechanism, and wxWidgets C++ exception support. We finish with some general debugging tips.

MEMORY MANAGEMENT BASICS

As in all C++ programming, you will create objects either on the stack, or on the heap using new. An object created on the stack is only available until it goes out of scope, at which time its destructor is called and it no longer exists. An object created on the heap, on the other hand, will stay around until either it is explicitly deleted using the delete operator or the program exits.

Creating and Deleting Window Objects

As a general rule, you will create window objects such as wxFrame and wxButton on the heap using new. Window objects normally have to exist for an indeterminate amount of time—that is, until the user decides the window will be closed. Note that wxWidgets will destroy child objects automatically when the parent is destroyed. Thus, you don't have to destroy a dialog's controls explicitly: just delete the dialog with Destroy. Similarly, upon deletion, a frame automatically deletes any children contained within it. However, if you create a top-level window (such as a frame) as a child of another top-level window (such as another frame), the parent frame does not destroy the child frame. An exception to this is MDI (Multiple Document Interface), where the child frames are not independent windows and are therefore destroyed by the parent.

You can create dialogs on the stack, but they must be modal dialogs: call ShowModal to enter an event loop so that all required interaction can happen before the dialog object goes out of scope and is deleted.

The mechanics of closing and deleting frames and dialogs can be a source of confusion. To destroy a frame or modeless dialog, the application should use Destroy, which delays deletion until the event queue is empty to avoid events being sent to non-existent windows. However, for a modal dialog, EndModal should first be called to exit the event loop. Event handlers (for example, for an *OK* button) should not normally destroy the dialog because if the modal dialog is created on the stack, it will be destroyed twice: once by the event handler, and again when the dialog object goes out of scope. When the user closes a modal dialog, the wxEVT_CLOSE_WINDOW event is triggered, and the corresponding event handler should call EndModal (but should not destroy the dialog). The default "close" behavior when clicking on the close button in the title bar is to emulate a wxID_CANCEL command event, whose handler will normally close the dialog. The dialog is then deleted when it goes out of scope. This is how standard dialogs such as wxFileDialog and wxColourDialog work, allowing you to retrieve values from the dialog object when the event loop returns. You can design modal dialogs that destroy the dialog from event handlers, but then you will not be able to create such a dialog on the stack or retrieve values from the dialog object when the user has dismissed it.

Here are two ways of using a wxMessageDialog.

```
// 1) Creating the dialog on the stack: no explicit destruction
wxMessageDialog dialog(NULL, _("Press OK"), _("App"), wxOK¦wxCANCEL);
if (dialog.ShowModal() == wxID_OK)
{
    // 2) Creating the dialog on the heap: must delete with Destroy()
    wxMessageDialog* dialog = new wxMessageDialog(NULL,
        _("Thank you! "), _("App"), wxOK);
    dialog->ShowModal();
    dialog->Destroy();
}
```

Modeless dialogs and frames will usually need to destroy themselves when closed, either from a control or from the standard window close button or menu. They cannot be created on the stack because they would immediately go out of scope and be destroyed.

If you maintain pointers to windows, be sure to reset them to NULL when the corresponding windows have been destroyed. Code to reset the pointer can be written in the window destructor or close handler. For example:

```
void MyFindReplaceDialog::OnCloseWindow(wxCloseEvent& event)
{
    wxGetApp().SetFindReplaceDialog(NULL);
    Destroy();
}
```

Creating and Copying Drawing Objects

Drawing objects, such as wxBrush, wxPen, wxColour, wxBitmap, and wxImage, can be created on the stack or on the heap. Drawing code will often create such temporary objects on the stack. These objects are reference-counted, which means that you can use these objects (not pointers to them) with very little overhead: when you assign a brush object to another brush variable, only a reference to the internal data is copied, not all the data itself. This behavior can have slightly unexpected side effects, though, when altering one object also alters another. To avoid such an association between objects, create the copy using a suitable constructor and explicitly assign the properties of the source object to the copy. Here are some examples of reference-counted and "genuine" copying.

```
// Reference-counted copy
wxBitmap newBitmap = oldBitmap;

// Genuine copy
wxBitmap newBitmap = oldBitmap.GetSubBitmap(
    wxRect(0, 0, oldBitmap.GetWidth(), oldBitmap.GetHeight()));

// Reference-counted copy
wxFont newFont = oldFont;

// Genuine copy
wxFont newFont(oldFont.GetPointSize(), oldFont.GetFamily(),
    oldFont.GetStyle(), oldFont.GetWeight(),
    oldFont.GetUnderlined(), oldFont.GetFaceName());
```

Initializing Your Application Object

Because your application object may be created before wxWidgets has initialized all its internal objects, such as its color database and default fonts, take care not to rely on such wxWidgets objects within your application constructor. Instead, let these data members take a default value in the constructor and initialize them in OnInit. For example:

```
MyApp::MyApp()
{
    // Do not set at this point
    // m_font = *wxNORMAL_FONT;
}

bool MyApp::OnInit()
{
    m_font = *wxNORMAL_FONT;
    ...
    return true;
}
```

Cleaning Up Your Application

You can override wxApp::OnExit and place much of your cleanup code here. This function is called after all application windows have been destroyed but just before wxWidgets cleans up its own objects. However, some cleanup may need to be done in your main window's close handler, such as killing a process that might try to write to a window.

DETECTING MEMORY LEAKS AND OTHER ERRORS

Ideally, when your application exits, all objects will be cleaned up either by your application or by wxWidgets itself, and no allocated memory will be left for the operating system to clean up automatically. Although it may be tempting simply not to bother with some cleanup, you really should take care to clean everything up yourself. Often such memory leaks are symptomatic of a problem with your code that could lead to large amounts of memory being wasted during a session. It's much harder to go back and figure out where leaks are coming from after you have moved on to another aspect of your application, so try to have zero tolerance for leaks.

So how do you know whether your application is leaking memory? Various third-party memory-checking tools are available to do this and more, and wxWidgets has a simple built-in memory checker. To use this checker for your debug configuration, you need to set some switches in setup.h (Windows) or configure (other platforms or GCC on Windows).

On Windows, these are:

```
#define wxUSE_DEBUG_CONTEXT 1
#define wxUSE_MEMORY_TRACING 1
#define wxUSE_GLOBAL_MEMORY_OPERATORS 1
#define wxUSE_DEBUG_NEW_ALWAYS 1
```

For configure, pass these switches:

```
--enable-debug --enable-mem_tracing --enable-debug_cntxt
```

There are some restrictions to this system: it doesn't work for MinGW or Cygwin (at the time of writing), and you cannot use wxUSE_DEBUG_NEW_ALWAYS if you are using STL in your application or the CodeWarrior compiler.

If wxUSE_DEBUG_NEW_ALWAYS is on, then all instances of the new operator in wxWidgets and your code will be defined to be new(__TFILE__,__LINE__), which has been reimplemented to use custom memory allocation and deletion routines. To use this version of new explicitly, without defining new, use WXDEBUG_NEW where you would normally write new.

The easiest way to use the memory checking system is to do nothing special at all: just run your application in the debugger, quit the application, and see if any memory leaks are reported. Here's an example of a report:

```
There were memory leaks.

— —- Memory dump — —-
.\memcheck.cpp(89): wxBrush at 0xBE44B8, size 12
..\..\src\msw\brush.cpp(233): non-object data at 0xBE55A8, size 44
.\memcheck.cpp(90): wxBitmap at 0xBE5088, size 12
..\..\src\msw\bitmap.cpp(524): non-object data at 0xBE6FB8, size 52
.\memcheck.cpp(93): non-object data at 0xBB8410, size 1000
.\memcheck.cpp(95): non-object data at 0xBE6F58, size 4
.\memcheck.cpp(98): non-object data at 0xBE6EF8, size 8


— —- Memory statistics — —-
1 objects of class wxBitmap, total size 12
5 objects of class nonobject, total size 1108
1 objects of class wxBrush, total size 12

Number of object items: 2
Number of non-object items: 5
Total allocated size: 1132
```

This example tells us that a wxBrush and a wxBitmap were allocated but not freed, along with some other objects whose class is unknown because they do not have wxWidgets type information. In some IDEs, you can double-click on the line with the error and see the source line at which the object was allocated. This functionality is a very good first step in tracking down the cause of the memory leak. For best results, add run-time type information (RTTI) to any classes that are descendants of wxObject. Add DECLARE_CLASS(class) in your class declaration and IMPLEMENT_CLASS(class, parentClass) somewhere in your implementation file.

The memory checking system also tries to catch memory overwrite and double-deletion bugs. The allocation routines write a special signature for a "good" block of memory and another signature for deleted memory. If the application tries to delete a block without the signature, the problem will be reported, as will a deletion that occurs when the block has already been deleted. This will make it easier to catch the kind of memory bugs that only cause problems some time after the real error has occurred.

Using static members of the wxDebugContext class, you can get a listing of the current objects in the system with PrintClasses or show a count of objects and non-objects (those without wxWidgets RTTI information) with PrintStatistics. Using SetCheckpoint, you can tell wxDebugContext to only show statistics from the checkpoint onwards, ignoring memory allocations done prior to this point. For more details, see samples/memcheck and the reference for wxDebugContext.

Instead of using the basic system in wxWidgets, you may want to use a commercial tool such as BoundsChecker, Purify, or AQtime, or a free alternative such as StackWalker, ValGrind, Electric Fence, or MMGR from Fluid Studios. If you are using Visual C++, wxWidgets uses the compiler's standard leak detection, which doesn't report class names but gives you the line numbers. For best results, make sure wxUSE_DEBUG_NEW_ALWAYS is set to 1 in setup.h. Because it redefines new, you might need to disable it if it causes problems with other libraries.

FACILITIES FOR DEFENSIVE PROGRAMMING

Often a bug will only surface some time after the logic error actually occurs. If an inconsistent or invalid value isn't detected early, the program can execute thousands of lines of code before it crashes or you get mysterious results. You can spend a lot of time trying to figure out the real cause of the error. However, if you add regular checks to your code—for example, to detect bad values passed to functions—your code will end up being much more robust, and you will save yourself (and your users) a potentially huge amount of trouble. This technique is called *defensive programming*, and your classes and functions can defend themselves both against improper use by other code and against internal logic errors. Because most of these checks are compiled out in release builds, there is no overhead.

As you would expect, wxWidgets does a lot of error checking internally, and you can use the same macros and functions in your own code. There are three main families of macros: variations of wxASSERT, wxFAIL, and wxCHECK. wxASSERT macros show an error message if the argument doesn't evaluate to true; the checks only occur in debug builds. wxFAIL will always generate an error message and is equivalent to wxASSERT(false). These checks are also removed in the release build. wxCHECK checks that the condition is true and returns a given value if not. Unlike the others, occurrences of wxCHECK remain (but do not display a message) in release builds. These macros have variations that let you display a custom error message in the assertion message box.

Here are some examples of using these macros.

```
// Add two positive numbers under 100
int AddPositive(int a, int b)
{
    // Check if a is positive
    wxASSERT(a > 0);

    // Check if b is positive, with custom error message
    wxASSERT_MSG(b > 0, wxT("The second number must be positive!"));

    int c = a + b;
```

```
    // Return -1 if the result was not positive
    wxCHECK_MSG(c > 0, -1, wxT("Result must be positive!"));

    return c;
}
```

You can also use wxCHECK2 and wxCHECK2_MSG to execute an arbitrary operation if the check failed instead of just returning a value. wxCHECK_RET can be used in void functions and returns no value. For less frequently used macros, such as wxCOMPILE_TIME_ASSERT and wxASSERT_MIN_BITSIZE, please refer to the reference manual.

Figure 15-1 shows the assertion dialog that appears when an assertion condition has evaluated to false. The user can stop the program (*Yes*), ignore the warning (*No*), or ignore all further warnings (*Cancel*). If the program is running under a debugger, stopping the program will cause a break in the debugger, and you can navigate the call stack to see exactly where the problem was and the values of variables at that point.

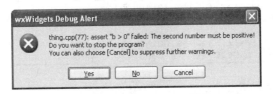

Figure 15-1   Assertion alert

ERROR REPORTING

Sometimes you need to display messages on the console or in a dialog to help with debugging, or when an error occurs that would not normally be detected by application code. wxWidgets provides a range of logging functions for the different ways in which you might want to use logging. For example, if allocation fails when trying to create a very large wxBitmap, an error will be reported in a dialog box using wxLogError (see Figure 15-2). Or if you simply want to print the values of a function's arguments on the debugger window, you can use wxLogDebug. Where the error actually appears (in a dialog, on the debugger window, or on the standard error stream) depends on the name of the logging function used and also on the wxLog "target" that is currently active, as described later.

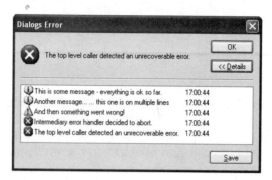

Figure 15-2   Log dialog

All logging functions have the same syntax as `printf` or `vprintf`—that is, they take the format string as the first argument and a variable number of arguments or a variable argument list pointer. For example:

```
wxString name(wxT("Calculation"));
int nGoes = 3;

wxLogError(wxT("%s does not compute! You have %d more goes."),
           name.c_str(), nGoes);
```

The logging functions are as follows.

`wxLogError` is the function to use for error messages that must be shown to the user. The default behavior is to pop up a message box to inform the user about the error. Why not just use `wxMessageBox`? Well, messages that come from `wxLogError` can be suppressed by creating an object of `wxLogNull` and log errors are also queued up and shown in idle time in a single dialog. So if a series of errors happens, the user won't have to click on *OK* for each and every error.

`wxLogFatalError` is like `wxLogError`, but it also terminates the program with exit code 3 (using the standard `abort` function). Unlike all the other logging functions, this function can't be overridden by changing the log target.

`wxLogWarning` is like `wxLogError`, but the information is presented as a warning, not an error.

`wxLogMessage` is for all normal, informational messages. They also appear in a message box by default.

`wxLogVerbose` is for verbose output. Normally, the messages are suppressed, but they can be activated by calling `wxLog::SetVerbose` if the user wants to know more details about the program's progress.

`wxLogStatus` is for status messages, which will be displayed in the status bar of the active or specified `wxFrame`, if it has one.

wxLogSysError is mostly used by wxWidgets itself. It logs the specified message text as well as the last system error code (errno or the result of GetLastError depending on the platform) and the corresponding error message. The second form of this function takes the error code explicitly as the first argument.

wxLogDebug is the function to use for debug output. It only displays the message in debug mode (when the preprocessor symbol __WXDEBUG__ is defined) and expands to nothing in release mode. Under Windows, you must either run the program under a debugger or use a third-party program such as DebugView from http://www.sysinternals.com to actually see the debug output.

wxLogTrace only does anything in debug builds, like wxLogDebug. The reason for making it a separate function is that usually there are a lot of trace messages, so it makes sense to separate them from other debug messages. Moreover, the second version of this function takes a trace mask as the first argument, which enables you to further restrict the number of messages generated. For example, wxWidgets uses the mousecapture mask internally. If you add this string to the trace masks via wxLog::AddTraceMask, you will see trace messages when the mouse is captured.

```
void wxWindowBase::CaptureMouse()
{
    wxLogTrace(wxT("mousecapture"), wxT("CaptureMouse(%p) "), this);
...
}

void MyApp::OnInit()
{
    // Add mousecapture to the list of trace masks
    wxLog::AddTraceMask(wxT("mousecapture"));
    ...
}
```

You may be wondering, why not use C standard input/output functions or C++ streams? The short answer is that they're good generic mechanisms, but they are not really adapted for wxWidgets, whereas the log classes are. There are three main advantages.

First, wxLog is portable. It is a common practice to use printf statements or cout and cerr C++ streams for writing information. Although this works just fine under Unix, these messages go nowhere under Windows, where the stdout of graphical applications is not assigned to anything. Thus, you might view wxLogMessage as a simple substitute for printf.

You can also redirect logging calls to cout by writing:

```
wxLog *logger=new wxLogStream(&cout);
wxLog::SetActiveTarget(logger);
```

There is also the possibility to redirect the output sent to cout to a wxTextCtrl by using the wxStreamToTextRedirector class.

Second, wxLog is more flexible. The output of wxLog functions can be redirected or suppressed entirely based on their importance, which is either impossible or difficult to do with traditional methods. For example, only error messages or only error messages and warnings might be logged, filtering out all informational messages.

Third, wxLog is more complete. Usually, an error message should be presented to the user when some operation fails. Let's take the simple but common case of a file error: suppose that you're writing your data file on disk and there is not enough space. The actual error might have been detected inside wxWidgets code (say, in wxFile::Write), so the calling function doesn't really know the exact reason of the failure; it only knows that the data file couldn't be written to the disk. However, as wxWidgets uses wxLogError in this situation, the exact error code and the corresponding error message will be given to the user.

Now we'll describe how logging works, in case you need to use more than the default behavior.

wxWidgets has the notion of a log target: it is just a class derived from wxLog. It implements the virtual functions of the base class, which are called when a message is logged. Only one log target is active at any moment—the one used by logging functions. The normal usage of a log object is to install it as the active target with a call to wxLog::SetActiveTarget, and it will be used automatically by all subsequent calls to logging functions.

To create a new log target class, you only need to derive it from wxLog and implement one (or both) of DoLog and DoLogString. Implementing DoLogString is enough if you're happy with the standard wxLog message formatting (prepending Error: or Warning: and time-stamping) but just want to send the messages somewhere else. You can override DoLog to do whatever you want, but you have to distinguish between the different message types yourself. See src/common/log.cpp for how wxWidgets does it.

There are some predefined classes deriving from wxLog that you can use without change, and looking at these classes might be helpful to show you how to create a new log target class.

wxLogStderr logs messages to the file pointer argument (FILE*), using stderr if no argument was supplied.

wxLogStream has the same functionality as wxLogStderr but uses ostream and cerr instead of FILE* and stderr.

wxLogGui is the standard log target for wxWidgets applications and is used by default. It provides the most reasonable handling of all types of messages for a given platform.

wxLogWindow provides a "log console," which collects all messages generated by the application and also passes them to the previously active log target. The log window frame has a menu that lets the user clear the log, close it completely, or save all messages to a file.

wxLogNull may be used to temporarily suppress output of the logging functions. As an example, trying to open a non-existent file will usually provoke an error message, but if for some reason this is unwanted, just create an instance of wxLogNull on the stack. While the object is in scope, no errors will be reported. You can use an extra pair of braces to create the appropriate scope. For example:

```
wxFile file;

// wxFile.Open() normally complains if file can't be opened;
// we don't want it to
{
    wxLogNull logNo;
    if ( !file.Open("bar") )
      ... process error ourselves ...
} // ~wxLogNull called, old log target restored

wxLogMessage("..."); // ok
```

Log targets can also be combined: for example, you might want to redirect the messages somewhere else (perhaps to a file) but also to process them as usual. For this, you can use wxLogChain and wxLogPassThrough. For example:

```
// This implicitly sets the active log target
wxLogChain *logChain = new wxLogChain(new wxLogStderr);

// all the log messages are sent to stderr and also processed
// as usual

// don't delete logChain directly as this would leave a dangling
// pointer as active log target; use SetActiveTarget instead
delete wxLog::SetActiveTarget(new wxLogGui);
```

wxMessageOutput Versus *wxLog*

Sometimes, wxLog is not the most appropriate class to use, with its higher-level functionality such as time-stamping and delayed log messages. The wxMessageOutput class and its derivatives offer a low-level printf replacement that you can use in console and GUI applications. Use wxMessageOutput::Printf where you would normally use printf; for example, to write to standard error:

```
#include "wx/msgout.h"

wxMessageOutputStderr err;
err.Printf(wxT("Error in app %s.\n"), appName.c_str());
```

You can also use wxMessageOutputDebug to write to the debugger's console or standard error, depending on platform and whether the program is being run in the debugger. Unlike wxLogDebug, these calls are not stripped out in release mode. GUI applications can use wxMessageOutputMessageBox to immediately show the message in a dialog, not collating and delaying the messages as wxLog does. There is also a wxMessageOutputLog class, which passes messages to wxLogMessage.

As with wxLog, wxMessageOutput has the concept of a current target, set with wxMessageOutput::Set and retrieved with wxMessageOutput::Get. This target is set with an appropriate object when wxWidgets initializes: an instance of wxMessageOutputStderr for console applications, and a wxMessageOutputMessageBox for GUI applications. wxWidgets makes use of this object internally, for example in wxCmdLineParser, as follows:

```
wxMessageOutput* msgOut = wxMessageOutput::Get();
if ( msgOut )
{
    wxString usage = GetUsageString();

    msgOut->Printf( wxT("%s%s"), usage.c_str(), errorMsg.c_str() );
}
else
{
    wxFAIL_MSG( _T("no wxMessageOutput object?") );
}
```

PROVIDING RUN-TIME TYPE INFORMATION

In common with most frameworks, wxWidgets provides methods to define more RTTI than C++'s own RTTI. This is useful for making run-time decisions based on an object's type and for error reporting as we have seen in the last section, and it also enables you to create objects dynamically simply by providing a string containing the name of the class. Only classes that have wxObject as an ancestor class can have wxWidgets RTTI.

If you don't need the dynamic creation ability, use the macro DECLARE_CLASS(class) in the class declaration and IMPLEMENT_CLASS(class, base Class) in the class implementation file. If you need dynamic creation, use DECLARE_DYNAMIC_CLASS(class) in the class declaration and IMPLEMENT_DYNAMIC_ CLASS(class, baseClass) in the class implementation file. In the dynamic case, you will also need to make sure there is a default constructor for the class; otherwise the compiler will complain when it comes across the function that wxWidgets generates to create an object of this class.

Here's an example of using RTTI to allow dynamic creation of objects.

```
class MyRecord: public wxObject
{
DECLARE_DYNAMIC_CLASS(MyRecord)
public:
```

```
      MyRecord() {}
      MyRecord(const wxString& name) { m_name = name; }

      void SetName(const wxString& name) { m_name = name; }
      const wxString& GetName() const { return m_name; }
private:
      wxString m_name;
};

IMPLEMENT_DYNAMIC_CLASS(MyRecord, wxObject)

MyRecord* CreateMyRecord(const wxString& name)
{
      MyRecord* rec = wxDynamicCast(wxCreateDynamicObject(wxT("MyRecord")),
MyRecord);
      if (rec)
          rec->SetName(name);
      return rec;
}
```

When code calls `CreateMyRecord` with the name to be set, `wxCreateDynamicObject` creates the object, and `wxDynamicCast` confirms that it really is an object of type `MyRecord`—it will return `NULL` if not. Although it might not appear useful at first sight, dynamic object creation is very handy when loading a complex file containing objects of different types. An object's data can be stored along with the name of its class, and when the file is read back, a new instance of the class can be created and then the object can read in its data.

There are other RTTI macros you can use, as follows.

`CLASSINFO(class)` returns a pointer to the `wxClassInfo` object associated with a class. You can use it with `wxObject::IsKindOf` to test the type of a class:

```
if (obj->IsKindOf(CLASSINFO(MyRecord)))
{
    ...
}
```

Use `DECLARE_ABSTRACT_CLASS(class)` and `IMPLEMENT_ABSTRACT_CLASS(class, baseClass)` with abstract classes.

Use `DECLARE_CLASS2(class)` and `IMPLEMENT_CLASS2(class, baseClass1, baseClass2)` where there are two base classes.

Use `DECLARE_APP(class)` and `IMPLEMENT_APP(class)` to make the application class known to wxWidgets.

`wxConstCast(ptr, class)` is a macro that expands into `const_cast<class *>(ptr)` if the compiler supports `const_cast` or into an old, C-style cast otherwise.

`wxDynamicCastThis(class)` is equivalent to `wxDynamicCast(this, class)`, but the latter provokes spurious compilation warnings from some compilers (because it tests whether this pointer is non-`NULL`, which is always `true`), so this macro should be used to avoid them.

wxStaticCast(ptr, class) checks that the cast is valid in debug mode (an assert failure will result if wxDynamicCast(ptr, class) == NULL) and then returns the result of executing an equivalent of static_cast<class*>(ptr).

wx_const_cast(T, x) is the same as const_cast<T>(x) if the compiler supports const cast or (T)x for old compilers. Unlike wxConstCast, this casts it to the type T, not to T*, and also the order of arguments is the same as for the standard cast.

wx_reinterpret_cast(T, x) is the same as reinterpret_cast<T>(x) if the compiler supports reinterpret cast or (T)x for old compilers.

wx_static_cast(T, x) is the same as static_cast<T>(x) if the compiler supports static cast or (T)x for old compilers. Unlike wxStaticCast, no checks are done, and the meaning of the macro arguments is exactly the same as for the standard static cast—that is, T is the full type name and a * is not appended to it.

USING *wxMODULE*

The module system is a very simple mechanism to allow applications (and parts of wxWidgets itself) to define initialization and cleanup functions that are automatically called on wxWidgets startup and exit. It can save an application from having to call a lot of initialization and cleanup code in its OnInit and OnExit functions, depending on the features that it uses.

To define a new kind of module, derive a class from wxModule, override the OnInit and OnExit functions, and add the DECLARE_DYNAMIC_CLASS and IMPLEMENT_DYNAMIC_CLASS to the class and implementation (which can be in the same file). On initialization, wxWidgets will find all classes derived from wxModule, create an instance of each, and call each OnInit function. On exit, wxWidgets will call the OnExit function for each module instance.

For example:

```
// A module to allow DDE initialization/cleanup
class wxDDEModule: public wxModule
{
DECLARE_DYNAMIC_CLASS(wxDDEModule)
public:
    wxDDEModule() {}
    bool OnInit() { wxDDEInitialize(); return true; };
    void OnExit() { wxDDECleanUp(); };
};

IMPLEMENT_DYNAMIC_CLASS(wxDDEModule, wxModule)
```

LOADING DYNAMIC LIBRARIES

If you need to run functions in dynamic libraries, you can use the
wxDynamicLibrary class. Pass the name of the dynamic library to the constructor or Load, and pass wxDL_VERBATIM if you don't want wxWidgets to append an
appropriate extension, such as .dll on Windows or .so on Linux. If the library
was loaded successfully, you can load functions by name using GetSymbol.
Here's an example that loads and initializes the common controls library on
Windows:

```
#include "wx/dynlib.h"

INITCOMMONCONTROLSEX icex;
icex.dwSize = sizeof(icex);
icex.dwICC = ICC_DATE_CLASSES;

// Load comctl32.dll
wxDynamicLibrary dllComCtl32(wxT("comctl32.dll"), wxDL_VERBATIM);

// Define the ICCEx_t type
typedef BOOL (WINAPI *ICCEx_t)(INITCOMMONCONTROLSEX *);

// Get the InitCommonControlsEx symbol
ICCEx_t pfnInitCommonControlsEx =
    (ICCEx_t) dllComCtrl32.GetSymbol(wxT("InitCommonControlsEx"));

// Call the function to initialize the common controls library
if ( pfnInitCommonControlsEx )
{
    (*pfnInitCommonControlsEx)(&icex);
}
```

You could also write the GetSymbol line more succinctly using the
wxDYNLIB_FUNCTION macro:

```
wxDYNLIB_FUNCTION( ICCEx_t, InitCommonControlsEx, dllComCtl32 );
```

wxDYNLIB_FUNCTION allows you to specify the type only once, as the first parameter, and creates a variable of this type named after the function but with a pfn
prefix.

If the library was loaded successfully in the constructor or Load, the function Unload will be called automatically in the destructor to unload the library
from memory. Call Detach if you want to keep a handle to the library after the
wxDynamicLibrary object has been destroyed.

EXCEPTION HANDLING

wxWidgets was created long before exceptions were introduced in C++ and has had to work with compilers with varying levels of exception support, so exceptions are not used throughout the framework. However, it safe to use exceptions in application code, and the library tries to help you.

There are several choices for using exceptions in wxWidgets programs. First, you can avoid using them at all. The library doesn't throw any exceptions by itself, so you don't have to worry about exceptions at all unless your own code throws them. This is the simplest solution, but it may be not the best one to deal with all possible errors.

Another strategy is to use exceptions only to signal truly fatal errors. In this case, you probably don't expect to recover from them, and the default behavior—to simply terminate the program—may be appropriate. If it is not, you can override OnUnhandledException in your wxApp-derived class to perform any cleanup tasks. Note that any information about the exact exception type is lost when this function is called, so if you need this information, you should override OnRun and add a try/catch clause around the call of the base class version. This would enable you to catch any exceptions generated during the execution of the main event loop. To deal with exceptions that may arise during the program startup and shutdown, you should insert try/catch clauses in OnInit and OnExit.

Finally, you might also want the application to continue running even when certain exceptions occur. If all your exceptions can happen only in the event handlers of a single class (or only in the classes derived from it), you can centralize your exception handling code in the ProcessEvent method of this class. If this is impractical, you might also consider overriding the wxApp::HandleEvent, which allows you to handle all the exceptions thrown by any event handler.

To enable exception support in wxWidgets, you need to build it with wxUSE_EXCEPTIONS set to 1. This should be the case by default, but if it isn't, you should edit include/wx/msw/setup.h under Windows or run configure with --enable-exceptions under Unix. If you do not plan to use exceptions, setting this flag to 0 or using --disable-exceptions results in a leaner and slightly faster library. Also, if you have Visual C++ and want a user-defined wxApp::OnFatalException function to be called instead of a GPF occurring, set wxUSE_ON_FATAL_EXCEPTION to 1 in your setup.h. Conversely, if you would rather be dropped into the debugger when an error in your program occurs, set this to 0.

Please look at samples/except for examples of using exceptions with wxWidgets.

DEBUGGING TIPS

Defensive programming, error reporting, and other coding techniques can only go so far—you also need a debugger that lets you step through your code examining variables and tells you exactly where your program is misbehaving or has crashed. So, you will need to maintain at least two configurations of your application—a debug version and a release version. The debug version will contain more error checking, will have compiler optimizations switched off, and will contain the source file, line, and other debug information that the debugger needs. The preprocessor symbol __WXDEBUG__ will always be defined in debug mode, and you can test for this when you need to write debug-only code. Some functions, such as wxLogDebug, will be removed in release mode anyway, reducing the need to test for this symbol.

A surprising number of users will try to get away without using a debugger, but the effort expended in getting to know your tools will pay off. On Windows, Visual C++ comes with a very good debugger; if using GCC on Windows or Unix, you can use the basic GDB package (from a command line or editor), and there is a selection of IDEs that use GDB but present a more friendly GUI to the debugger. For information on these, see Appendix E, "Third-Party Tools for wxWidgets."

wxWidgets allows multiple configurations to be used simultaneously. On Windows, you can pass BUILD=debug or BUILD=release to the wxWidgets library makefile, or when using configure, you configure and build in two or more separate directories, passing --enable-debug or --disable-debug. Some IDEs don't allow multiple configurations of your application to be maintained simultaneously without changing settings and recompiling in debug mode and then changing the settings back and recompiling in release mode—for obvious reasons, avoid such tools!

Debugging X11 Errors

Rarely, your wxGTK application might crash with X11 errors, and the program will immediately exit without giving you a stack trace. This makes it very hard to find where the error occurred. In this case, you need to set an error handler, as the following code shows.

```
#if defined(__WXGTK__)
#include <X11/Xlib.h>

typedef int (*XErrorHandlerFunc)(Display *, XErrorEvent *);

XErrorHandlerFunc gs_pfnXErrorHandler = 0;

int wxXErrorHandler(Display *display, XErrorEvent *error)
{
    if (error->error_code)
    {
        char buf[64];
```

```
          XGetErrorText (display, error->error_code, buf, 63);

          printf ("** X11 error in wxWidgets for GTK+: %s\n  serial %ld
error_code %d request_code %d minor_code %d\n",
          buf,
          error->serial,
          error->error_code,
          error->request_code,
              error->minor_code);
     }

     // Uncomment to forward to the default error handler
#if 0
     if (gs_pfnXErrorHandler)
        return gs_pfnXErrorHandler(display, error);
#endif
     return 0;
}
#endif
  // __WXGTK__

bool MyApp::OnInit(void)
{
#if defined(__WXGTK__)
     // install the X error handler
     gs_pfnXErrorHandler = XSetErrorHandler( wxXErrorHandler );
#endif
     ...
     return true;
}
```

Now the application will give a segmentation fault when an X11 error occurs, and if you have passed -sync to the application when running it, the crash should occur reasonably close to where the bad value was passed to an X11 function.

Simplify the Problem

If you have a bug that seems intractable, a good strategy is to try to reproduce the problem in the smallest possible application. You might take one of the wxWidgets samples and add code that demonstrates the problem. Or you could take a copy of the application source and strip it down to a bare minimum so that you can identify the code change that reveals or cures the bug. If you think the problem is in wxWidgets, then adding a small change to one of the samples will help you or the wxWidgets developers reproduce the problem and hopefully fix it.

Debugging a Release Build

Occasionally your application may work in debug mode but not in release mode, and this might be due to slight differences in the run-time library used by the compiler. If you are using Visual C++, you can create a new configuration that's identical to a debugging configuration but that defines NDEBUG, which means that all your application and wxWidgets debug symbols will be present, but the application will use the release version of the run-time library. This will enable you at least to eliminate the possibility of differences due to the run-time library version.

Normally you distribute your application in release mode with all debug information stripped, but if your customers are experiencing crashes that you find hard to reproduce, you might want to send them a debugging version of the application (on Windows, you might need to configure wxWidgets to link statically to the run-time library to avoid legal issues with the distribution of the debugging run-time DLL). You can compile your application with symbols that are used by an application called Dr. Watson that runs on your customer's PC and saves information about a crash. See your compiler information and the web for how to use the files that Dr. Watson writes to track down the cause of the crash.

If you are using MinGW, you can use a tool called Dr. MinGW that can catch exceptions such as segmentation faults and print a useful backtrace, if debugging is enabled in the code (-g has been specified). You can download it from http://www.mingw.org. If you have patient and cooperative customers, you can supply this tool for them to install on their computers and ask them to send you the reports.

On Unix, a debugging executable will produce a core file (depending on how the user has his or her system set up; see the documentation for the Unix command ulimit). You can place the core in the same file as your debugging executable, and the debugger will show where in your source files the crash occurred. However, core files can be very big, so your customer might not be very willing to send you the core dump.

Alternatively, your application can write log files that give status information at important parts of your application's execution. See also the documentation in the wxWidgets reference manual for the wxDebugReport class, which writes a report suitable for emailing to the application vendor. Similar functionality can be found in wxCrashPrint at http://wxcode.sf.net (for Linux) and BlackBox at http://www.codeproject.com/tools/blackbox.asp (for Windows).

SUMMARY

In this chapter, we've covered various aspects of memory management and error checking. You now know when to use new and when to create objects on the stack, how your application should clean itself up, how to identify memory leaks, and how to use macros for "defensive programming." You've seen how to write code that creates objects dynamically, and you should be able to decide when to use wxLogDebug and when to use wxLogError. You have also seen how to use C++ exceptions with wxWidgets, and we have presented some tips to help you debug your application. Next, we'll show how you can make your application work in many languages.

CHAPTER 16

Writing International Applications

If you target multiple languages as well as multiple platforms, you have the potential to reach a huge audience, which greatly increases your application's chances of success. This chapter covers what you need to do to make your application amenable to internationalization, which is sometimes abbreviated to "i18n" (an "i" followed by "18" characters followed by "n").

INTRODUCTION TO INTERNATIONALIZATION

When taking your application to an international market, the first thing that comes to mind is *translation*. You will need to provide a set of translations for all the strings your application presents in each foreign language that it supports. In wxWidgets, you do this by providing *message catalogs* and loading them through the wxLocale class. This technique may differ from how you are used to implementing translations if you currently use string tables. Instead of referring to each string by an identifier and switching tables, message catalogs work by translating a string using an appropriate catalog. (Alternatively, you can use your own system for handling translations if you prefer, but be aware that messages in the wxWidgets library itself rely on catalogs.)

Without message catalogs, the untranslated strings in the source code will be used to display text in menus, buttons, and so on. If your own language contains non-ASCII characters, such as accents, you will need a separate "translation" (message catalog) for it because source code should only contain ASCII.

Representing text in a different language can also involve different *character encodings*, which means that the same byte value might represent different characters when displayed on-screen. You need to make sure that your application can correctly set up the character encodings used by your GUI elements and in your data files. You need to be aware of the specific encoding used in each case and how to translate between encodings.

Another aspect of internationalization is formatting for numbers, date, and time. Note that formatting can be different even for the same language. For example, the number represented in English by 1,234.56 is represented as 1.234,56 in Germany and as 1'234.56 in the German-speaking part of Switzerland. In the USA, the 10th of November is represented as 11/10, whereas the same date for a reader in the UK means the 11th of October. We'll see shortly how wxWidgets can help here.

Translated strings are longer than their English counterpart, which means that the window layout must adapt to different sizes. Sizers are best suited to solve this part and are explained in Chapter 7, "Window Layout Using Sizers." Another layout problem is that for Western languages, the flow of reading goes from left to right, but other languages such as Arabic and Hebrew are read from right to left (called RTL), which means that the entire layout must change orientation. There is currently no specific mechanism for implementing RTL layout in wxWidgets.

The last group of elements to be adapted to a different language or culture consists of images and sounds. For example, if you are writing a phone directory application, you might have a feature that speaks the numbers, which will be language-dependent, and you might want to display different images depending on the country.

PROVIDING TRANSLATIONS

wxWidgets provides facilities for message translation using the wxLocale class and is itself fully translated into several languages. Please consult the wxWidgets home page for the most up-to-date translations.

The wxWidgets approach to internationalization closely follows the GNU gettext package. wxWidgets uses message catalogs, which are binary compatible with gettext catalogs allowing you to use all the gettext tools. No additional libraries are needed during runtime because wxWidgets is able to read message catalogs.

During program development, you will need the gettext package for working with message catalogs (or poEdit; see the next section). There are two kinds of message catalog: source catalogs, which are text files with extension .po, and binary catalog which are created from the source files with the msgfmt program (part of the gettext package) and have the extension .mo. Only the binary files are needed during program execution. For each language you support, you need one message catalog.

poEdit

You don't have to use command-line tools for maintaining your message catalogs. Vaclav Slavik has written poEdit, a graphical front-end to the gettext package available from http://www.poedit.org. poEdit, shown in Figure 16-1, helps you to maintain message catalogs, generate .mo files, and merge in changes to strings in your application code as your application changes and grows.

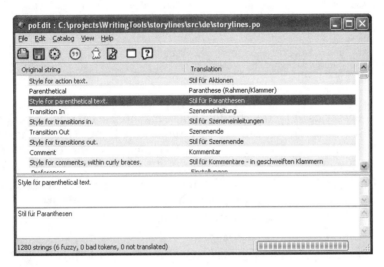

Figure 16-1   poEdit

Step-by-Step Guide to Using Message Catalogs

These are the steps you need to follow to create and use message catalogs:

1. Wrap literal strings in the program text that should be translated with wxGetTranslation or equivalently with the _() macro. Strings that will not be translated should be wrapped in wxT() or the alias _T() to make them Unicode-compatible.

2. Extract the strings to be translated from the program into a .po file. Fortunately, you don't have to do this by hand; you can use the xgettext program or, more easily, poEdit. If you use xgettext, you can use the -k option to recognize wxGetTranslation as well as _(). poEdit can also be configured to recognize wxGetTranslation via the catalog settings dialog.

3. Translate the strings extracted in the previous step to another language by editing the .po file or using poEdit (one .po file per language). You must also indicate the character set you are using for the translated strings.

   If you do not use poEdit, you will have to do it by hand, using your favorite text editor. The header of your .po file will look something this:

```
# SOME DESCRIPTIVE TITLE.
# Copyright (C) YEAR Free Software Foundation, Inc.
# FIRST AUTHOR <EMAIL@ADDRESS>, YEAR.
```

```
#
msgid ""
msgstr ""
"Project-Id-Version: PACKAGE VERSION\n"
"POT-Creation-Date: 1999-02-19 16:03+0100\n"
"PO-Revision-Date: YEAR-MO-DA HO:MI+ZONE\n"
"Last-Translator: FULL NAME <EMAIL@ADDRESS>\n"
"Language-Team: LANGUAGE <LL@li.org>\n"
"MIME-Version: 1.0\n"
"Content-Type: text/plain; charset=iso8859-1\n"
"Content-Transfer-Encoding: 8bit\n"
```

Note the `charset` property in the second to last line, specifying the character set used by the catalog. All strings in the catalog are encoded using this character set. This is very important if non-Unicode encodings are used because otherwise the GUI elements cannot correctly display all characters.

4. Compile the `.po` file into the binary `.mo` file to be used by the program. You can do this within poEdit, or you might want to add it as a step in your distribution script, for example using:

```
msgfmt -o myapp.mo myapp.po
```

5. Set the appropriate locale in your program to use the strings for the given language (see the next section, "Using `wxLocale`").

Under Mac OS X, you'll need to make one modification to the `Info.plist` file, which describes the contents of the "application bundle." This file (an XML text file encoded in UTF-8) should have a `CFBundleDevelopmentRegion` entry describing the language of the developer—such as English—and Mac OS X will query the bundle for the presence of certain resource directories to find out which languages are supported. For example, for German, this might be the directory `German.lproj`. Because wxWidgets applications do not use these directories for storing resource information, instead storing the translation in `.mo` files, the application needs to be told explicitly which languages are supported. You do this by adding a `CFBundleLocalizations` entry to `Info.plist`. It might look like this:

```
<key>CFBundleDevelopmentRegion</key>
<string>English</string>
<key>CFBundleLocalizations</key>
<array>
        <string>en</string>
        <string>de</string>
        <string>fr</string>
</array>
```

Using *wxLocale*

The wxLocale class encapsulates all language-dependent settings and is a generalization of the C locale concept. Normally you add a wxLocale member variable to your application class, say m_locale, and in your application OnInit function, you initialize the locale as follows:

```
if (m_locale.Init(wxLANGUAGE_DEFAULT,
                  wxLOCALE_LOAD_DEFAULT | wxLOCALE_CONV_ENCODING))
{
    m_locale.AddCatalog(wxT("myapp"));
}
```

Note that wxLocale::Init will try to find and add the wxstd.mo catalog, containing wxWidgets' own translations. The parameter wxLANGUAGE_DEFAULT means use the system language, and you can also force a certain language using the correct wxLANGUAGE_xxx code.

When you tell the wxLocale class to load a message catalog, the catalog is converted to the character set used by the user's operating system. This is the default behavior of the wxLocale class; you can disable it by not passing wxLOCALE_CONV_ENCODING to wxLocale::Init as the second parameter.

Where does wxWidgets find its message catalogs? For each directory <DIR> in its internal list, wxWidgets looks in:

☞ <DIR>/<LANG>/LC_MESSAGES

☞ <DIR>/<LANG>

☞ <DIR>

The rules about which directories are taken into account are different on each platform:

☞ On all platforms, the value of the LC_PATH environment variable is searched.

☞ On Unix and Mac OS X, the wxWidgets installation directory is searched, and also /share/locale, /usr/share/locale, /usr/lib/locale, /usr/locale /share/locale, and the current directory.

☞ On Windows, the application directory is also searched.

You can add further search directories using the function wxLocale::AddCatalogLookupPathPrefix. For example:

```
wxString resDir = GetAppDir() + wxFILE_SEP_PATH + wxT("resources");
m_locale.AddCatalogLookupPathPrefix(resDir);

// If resDir is c:\MyApp\resources, AddCatalog will now look for the
// French catalog in these places as well as the standard dirs:
//
// c:\MyApp\resources\fr\LC_MESSAGES\myapp.mo
// c:\MyApp\resources\fr\myapp.mo
```

```
// c:\MyApp\resources\myapp.mo

m_locale.AddCatalog(wxT("myapp"));
```

The usual method for distributing message catalogs is to create a subdirectory for each language, using the standard canonical name, containing <appname>.mo in each directory. For example, the wxWidgets internat sample has directories fr and de representing French and German using ISO 639 language codes.

CHARACTER ENCODINGS AND UNICODE

There are more characters around on Earth than can fit into the 256 possible byte values that the classical 8-bit character represents. In order to be able to display more than 256 different glyphs, another layer of indirection has been added: the character encoding or character set. (The "new and improved" solution, Unicode, will be presented later in this section.)

Thus, what is represented by the byte value 161 is determined by the character set. In the ISO 8859-1 (Latin-1) character set, this is ¡—an inverted exclamation mark. In ISO 8859-2 (Latin-2), it represents a ¥ (Aogonek).

When you are drawing text on a window, the system must know about the encoding used. This is called the "font encoding," although it is just an indication of a character set. Creating a font without indicating the character set means "use the default encoding." This is fine in most situations because the user is normally using the system in his or her language.

But if you know that something is in a different encoding, such as ISO 8859-2, then you need to create the appropriate font. For example:

```
wxFont myFont(10, wxFONTFAMILY_DEFAULT, wxNORMAL, wxNORMAL,
              false, wxT("Arial"), wxFONTENCODING_ISO8859_2);
```

Otherwise, it will not be displayed properly on a western system, such as ISO 8859-1.

Note that there may be situations where an optimal encoding is not available. In these cases, you can try to use an alternative encoding, and if one is available, you must convert the text into this encoding. The following snippet shows this sequence: a string text in the encoding enc should be shown in the font facename. The use of wxCSConv will be explained shortly.

```
// We have a string in an encoding 'enc' which we want to
// display in a font called 'facename'.
//
// First we must find out whether there is a font available for
// rendering this encoding

wxString text; // Contains the text in encoding 'enc'
```

```
if (!wxFontMapper::Get()->IsEncodingAvailable(enc, facename))
{
    // We don't have an encoding 'enc' available in this font.
    // What alternative encodings are available?

    wxFontEncoding alternative;
    if (wxFontMapper::Get()->GetAltForEncoding(enc, &alternative,
                                              facename, false))
    {
        // We do have a font in an 'alternative' encoding,
        // so we must convert our string into that alternative.

        wxCSConv convFrom(wxFontMapper::GetEncodingName(enc));
        wxCSConv convTo(wxFontMapper::GetEncodingName(alternative));
        text = wxString(text.wc_str(convFrom), convTo) ;

        // Create font with the encoding alternative

        wxFont myFont(10, wxFONTFAMILY_DEFAULT, wxNORMAL, wxNORMAL,
                false, facename , alternative);
        dc.SetFont(myFont);
    }
    else
    {
        // Unable to convert; attempt a lossy conversion to
        // ISO 8859-1 (7-bit ASCII)

        wxFont myFont(10, wxFONTFAMILY_DEFAULT, wxNORMAL, wxNORMAL,
                false, facename, wxFONTENCODING_ISO8859_1);
        dc.SetFont(myFont);
    }
}
else
{
    // The font with that encoding exists, no problem.

    wxFont myFont(10, wxFONTFAMILY_DEFAULT, wxNORMAL, wxNORMAL,
            false, facename, enc);
    dc.SetFont(myFont);
}

// Finally, draw the text with the font we've selected.

dc.DrawText(text, 100, 100);
```

Converting Data

The previous code example needs a chain of bytes to be converted from one encoding to another. There are two ways to achieve this. The first, using wxEncodingConverter, is deprecated and should not be used in new code. Unless your compiler cannot handle wchar_t, you should use the character set converters (wxCSConv, base class wxMBConv).

wxEncodingConverter

This class supports only a limited subset of encodings, but if your compiler doesn't recognize wchar_t, it is the only solution you have. For example:

```
wxEncodingConverter converter(enc, alternative, wxCONVERT_SUBSTITUTE);
text = converter.Convert(text);
```

wxCONVERT_SUBSTITUTE indicates that it should try some lossy substitutions if it cannot convert a character strictly. This means that, for example, acute capitals might be replaced by ordinary capitals and en dashes and em dashes might be replaced by "-", and so on.

wxCSConv (wxMBConv)

Unicode solves the ambiguity problem mentioned earlier by using 16 or even 32 bits in a wide character (wchar_t) to store all characters in a "global encoding." This means that you don't have to deal with encodings unless you need to read or write data in an 8-bit format, which as we know does not have enough information and needs an indication of its encoding.

Even when you don't compile wxWidgets in Unicode mode (where wchar_t is used internally to store the characters in a string), you can use these wide characters for conversions, if available. You convert from one encoding into wide character strings and then back to a different encoding. This is also used in the wxString class to offer you convenient conversions. Just bear in mind that in non-Unicode builds, wxString itself uses 8-bit characters and does not know how this string is encoded.

To transfer a wxString into a wide character array, you use the wxString::wc_str function, which takes a multi-byte converter class as its parameter. This parameter tells a non-Unicode build which encoding the string is in, but it is ignored by the Unicode build because the string is already using wide characters internally.

In a Unicode build, we can then build a string directly from these characters, but in a non-Unicode build, we must indicate which character set this should be converted to. So in the line below, convTo is ignored in Unicode builds.

```
text = wxString(text.wc_str(convFrom), convTo);
```

The character set encoding offers more possibilities than font encodings, so you'd have to convert from font encoding to character set encoding using

```
wxFontMapper::GetEncodingName(fontencoding);
```

This means that our previous task would be written as follows using character set encoding:

```
wxCSConv convFrom(wxFontMapper::GetEncodingName(enc));
wxCSConv convTo(wxFontMapper::GetEncodingName(alternative));
text = wxString(text.wc_str(convFrom) , convTo) ;
```

There are situations where you output 8-bit data directly instead of a wxString, and this can be done using a wxCharBuffer instance. So the last line would read as follows:

```
wxCharBuffer output = convTo.cWC2MB(text.wc_str(convFrom));
```

And if your input data is not a string but rather 8-bit data as well (a wxCharBuffer named input below), then you can write:

```
wxCharBuffer output = convTo.cWC2MB(convFrom.cMB2WC(input));
```

A few global converter objects are available; for example, wxConvISO8859_1 is an object, and wxConvCurrent is a pointer to a converter that uses the C library locale. There are also subclasses of wxMBConv that are optimized for certain encoding tasks, namely wxMBConvUTF7, wxMBConvUTF8, wxMBConvUTF16LE/BE, and wxMBConvUTF32LE/BE. The latter two are typedefed to wxMBConvUFT16/32 using the byte order native to the machine. For more information, see the topic "wxMBConv Classes Overview" in the wxWidgets reference manual.

Converting Outside of a Temporary Buffer

As just discussed, the conversion classes allow you to easily convert from one string encoding to another. However, most conversions return either a newly created wxString or a *temporary* buffer. There are instances where we might need to perform a conversion and then hold the result for later processing. This is done by copying the results of a conversion into separate storage.

Consider the case of sending strings between computers, such as over a socket. We should agree on a protocol for what type of string encoding to use; otherwise, platforms with different default encodings would garble received strings. The sender could convert to UTF-8, and the receiver could then convert from UTF-8 into its default encoding.

The following short example demonstrates how to use a combination of techniques to convert a string of any encoding into UTF-8, store the result in a char* for sending over the socket, and then later convert that raw UTF-8 data back into a wxString.

```
// Convert the string to UTF-8
const wxCharBuffer ConvertToUTF8(wxString anyString)
```

```
{
    return wxConvUTF8.cWC2MB( anyString.wc_str(*wxConvCurrent) ) ;
}

// Use the raw UTF-8 data passed to build a wxString
wxString ConvertFromUTF8(const char* rawUTF8)
{
    return wxString(wxConvUTF8.cMB2WC(rawUTF8), *wxConvCurrent);
}

// Test our wxString<->UTF-8 conversion
void StringConversionTest(wxString anyString)
{
    // Convert to UTF-8, keep the char buffer around
    const wxCharBuffer bUTF8 = ConvertToUTF8(anyString);

    // wxCharBuffer has an implicit conversion operator for char *
    const char *cUTF8 = bUTF8 ;

    // Rebuild the string
    wxString stringCopy = ConvertFromUTF8(cUTF8);

    // The two strings should be equal
    wxASSERT(anyString == stringCopy);
}
```

Help Files

You will want to distribute a separate help file for each supported language. Your help controller initialization will select the appropriate help file name according to the current locale, perhaps using wxLocale::GetName to form the file name, or simply using _() to translate to the appropriate file name. For example:

```
m_helpController->Initialize(_("help_english"));
```

If you are using wxHtmlHelpController, you need to make sure that all the HTML files contain the META tag, for example:

```
<meta http-equiv="Content-Type" content="text/html; charset=iso8859 //2">
```

You also need to make sure that the project file (extension HHP) contains one additional line in the OPTIONS section:

```
Charset=iso8859-2
```

This additional entry tells the HTML help controller what encoding is used in contents and index tables.

NUMBERS AND DATES

The current locale is also used for formatting numbers and dates. The printf-based formatting in wxString takes care of this automatically. Consider this snippet:

```
wxString::Format(wxT("%.1f") , myDouble);
```

Here, Format uses the correct decimal separator. And for date formatting:

```
wxDateTime t = wxDateTime::Now();
wxString str = t.Format();
```

Format presents the current date and time in the correct language and format. Have a look at the API documentation to see all the possibilities for passing a format description to the Format call—just don't forget that you will probably have to translate this format string as well for using it in a different language because the sequence for different parts of the date can differ among languages.

If you want to add the correct thousands separator or just want to know the correct character for the decimal point, you can ask the locale object for the corresponding strings using the GetInfo method:

```
wxString info = m_locale.GetInfo(wxLOCALE_THOUSANDS_SEP,
                                 wxLOCALE_CAT_NUMBER) ;
```

OTHER MEDIA

You can also load other data such as images and sounds depending on the locale. You can use the same mechanism as for text, for example:

```
wxBitmap bitmap(_("flag.png"));
```

This code will cause flag.png to appear on your list of strings to translate, so you just translate the string flag.png into the appropriate file name for your platform, for example de/flag.png. Make sure that the translated versions are also available as true files in your application, or you can load them from a compressed archive (refer to Chapter 14, "Files and Streams").

A SIMPLE SAMPLE

To illustrate some of the concepts that we've covered, you can find a little sample in `examples/chap16` on the CD-ROM. It shows some strings and a flag graphic for three languages: English, French, and German. You can change the language from the File menu, which will change the menu strings, the `wxStaticText` strings, and the flag graphic to suit the newly selected language. To demonstrate the different behavior of `_()` and `wxT()`, the menu help in the status line remains in English.

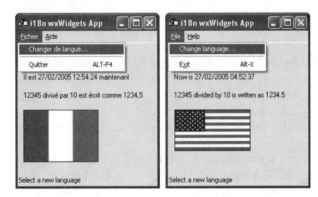

Figure 16-2   The internationalization samples

The sample's application class contains a `wxLocale` pointer and a function `SelectLanguage` that will re-create the locale object with the appropriate language. This is the application class declaration and implementation:

```
class MyApp : public wxApp
{
public:
    ~MyApp() ;

    // Initialize the application
    virtual bool OnInit();

    // Recreates m_locale according to lang
    void SelectLanguage(int lang);

private:
    wxLocale* m_locale; // 'our' locale
};

IMPLEMENT_APP(MyApp)

bool MyApp::OnInit()
{
    wxImage::AddHandler( new wxPNGHandler );
```

```
    m_locale = NULL;
    SelectLanguage( wxLANGUAGE_DEFAULT );

    MyFrame *frame = new MyFrame(_("i18n wxWidgets App"));

    frame->Show(true);
    return true;
}

void MyApp::SelectLanguage(int lang)
{
    delete m_locale;
    m_locale = new wxLocale( lang );
    m_locale->AddCatalog( wxT("i18n") );
}

MyApp::~MyApp()
{
    delete m_locale;
}
```

There are two functions of particular interest in the frame class: SetupStrings
and OnChangeLanguage. SetupStrings sets the labels and re-creates the menu
bar, using translations for all the strings apart from the menu help strings, as
follows:

```
void MyFrame::SetupStrings()
{
    m_helloString->SetLabel(_("Welcome to International Sample"));
    m_todayString->SetLabel( wxString::Format(_("Now is %s") ,
wxDateTime::Now().Format().c_str() ) );
    m_thousandString->SetLabel( wxString::Format(_("12345 divided by 10
is written as %.1f") , 1234.5 ) );
    m_flag->SetBitmap(wxBitmap( _("flag.png") , wxBITMAP_TYPE_PNG ));

    // create a menu bar
    wxMenu *menuFile = new wxMenu;

    // the "About" item should be in the help menu
    wxMenu *helpMenu = new wxMenu;
    helpMenu->Append(wxID_ABOUT, _("&About...\tF1"),
                     wxT("Show about dialog"));

    menuFile->Append(wxID_NEW, _("Change language..."),
                     wxT("Select a new language"));
    menuFile->AppendSeparator();
    menuFile->Append(wxID_EXIT, _("E&xit\tAlt-X"),
                     wxT("Quit this program"));

    wxMenuBar *menuBar = new wxMenuBar();
    menuBar->Append(menuFile, _("&File"));
    menuBar->Append(helpMenu, _("&Help"));

    wxMenuBar* formerMenuBar = GetMenuBar();
```

```
        SetMenuBar(menuBar);
        delete formerMenuBar;

        SetStatusText(_("Welcome to wxWidgets!"));
}
```

OnChangeLanguage is called when the user wants to specify a new language, and it maps the user's selection into a locale identifier such as wxLANGUAGE_GERMAN. This identifier is passed to MyApp::SelectLanguage before SetupStrings is called to change the labels and flag bitmap. Here is the implementation of OnChangeLanguage:

```
void MyFrame::OnChangeLanguage(wxCommandEvent& event)
{
    wxArrayInt languageCodes;
    wxArrayString languageNames;

    languageCodes.Add(wxLANGUAGE_GERMAN);
    languageNames.Add(_("German"));

    languageCodes.Add(wxLANGUAGE_FRENCH);
    languageNames.Add(_("French"));

    languageCodes.Add(wxLANGUAGE_ENGLISH);
    languageNames.Add(_("English"));

    int lang = wxGetSingleChoiceIndex( _("Select language:"),
                          _("Language"), languageNames );

    if ( lang != -1 )
    {
        wxGetApp().SelectLanguage(languageCodes[lang]);
        SetupStrings();
    }
}
```

SUMMARY

We've discussed the variety of ways in which wxWidgets helps you handle translations as well as formatting issues related to time and date, currency, and so on. You should work with someone familiar with the target languages or locales who will be able to find differences that you might have missed.

For another example of a translated application, see samples/internat in your wxWidgets distribution. It demonstrates translation of strings in menu items and dialogs for ten languages.

Next, we'll take a look at how you can make your applications perform several tasks at once with multithreading.

CHAPTER 17

Writing Multithreaded Applications

Most of the time, the event-driven nature of GUI programming maintains a good illusion of handling multiple tasks simultaneously. Redrawing a window usually takes a tiny fraction of a second, and user input can be handled rapidly. However, there are times when a task cannot easily be broken down into small chunks handled by a single thread, and this is where multithreaded programming becomes useful. This chapter shows you how threads can be controlled in wxWidgets, and it ends with some alternatives to using threads.

WHEN TO USE THREADS, AND WHEN NOT TO

A thread is basically a path of execution through a program. Threads are sometimes called lightweight processes, but the fundamental difference between threads and processes is that the memory spaces of different processes are separate, whereas all threads in the same process share the same address space. Although this makes it much easier to share common data between several threads, multithreading also makes it easier to shoot oneself in the proverbial foot by accessing the same data simultaneously, so careful use of synchronization objects such as mutexes and critical sections is recommended.

When used properly, multithreading enables the programmer to simplify the application architecture by decoupling the user interface from the "real work." Note that this won't result in faster applications unless the computer has multiple processors, but the user interface will be more responsive.

wxWidgets provides both a thread class and the necessary synchronization objects (mutexes and critical sections with conditions). The threading API in wxWidgets resembles the POSIX threading API (pthreads), although several functions have different names, and some features inspired by the Win32 thread API are also available.

These classes make writing multithreaded applications easier, and they also provide some extra error checking compared with the native thread API. However, using threads is still a non-trivial undertaking, especially for large projects. Before starting a multithreaded application or adding multithreaded features to an existing one, it is worth considering alternatives to threads to implement the same functionality. In some situations, threads are the only reasonable choice, such as an FTP server application that launches a new thread for each new client. However, using an extra thread to show a progress dialog during a long computation would be overkill. In this case, you could do the calculations in an idle handler and call wxWindow::Update periodically to update the screen. For more details, see "Alternatives to Multithreading" toward the end of this chapter.

If you decide to use threads in your application, it is strongly recommended that only the main thread call GUI functions. The wxWidgets thread sample shows that it is possible for many different threads to call GUI functions at once, but in general, it is a very poor design choice. A design that uses one GUI thread and several worker threads that communicate with the main one using events is much more robust and will undoubtedly save you countless problems. For example, under Win32, a thread can only access GDI objects such as pens, brushes, and so on, created by itself, not those created by other threads.

For communication between threads, you can use wxEvtHandler::Add PendingEvent or its short version, wxPostEvent. These functions have thread-safe implementations so that they can be used for sending events between threads.

USING *wxThread*

If you want to implement functionality using threads, you write a class that derives from wxThread and implements at least the virtual Entry method, which is where the work of the thread takes place. Let's say you wanted to use a separate thread to count the number of colors in an image. Here's the declaration of the thread class:

```
class MyThread : public wxThread
{
public:
    MyThread(wxImage* image, int* count):
        m_image(image), m_count(count) {}
    virtual void *Entry();
private:
    wxImage* m_image;
    int*     m_count;
};

// An identifier to notify the application when the
// work is done
#define ID_COUNTED_COLORS    100
```

The `Entry` function does the calculation and returns an exit code that will be returned by `Wait` (for joinable threads only). Here's the implementation for `Entry`:

```
void *MyThread::Entry()
{
    (* m_count) = m_image->CountColours();

    // Use an existing event to notify the application
    // when the count is done
    wxCommandEvent event(wxEVT_COMMAND_MENU_SELECTED,
                         ID_COUNTED_COLORS);
    wxGetApp().AddPendingEvent(event);

    return NULL;
}
```

For simplicity, we're using an existing event class to send a notification to the application when the color count is done.

Creation

Threads are created in two steps. First the object is instantiated, and then the `Create` method is called:

```
MyThread *thread = new MyThread();
if ( thread->Create() != wxTHREAD_NO_ERROR )
{
    wxLogError(wxT("Can't create thread!"));
}
```

There are two different types of threads: the ones that you start and then forget about and the ones from which you are awaiting a result. The former are called *detached* threads, and the latter are *joinable* threads. Thread type is indicated by passing `wxTHREAD_DETACHED` (the default) or `wxTHREAD_JOINABLE` to the constructor of a `wxThread`. The result of a joinable thread is returned by the `Wait` function. You cannot wait for a detached thread.

You shouldn't necessarily create all threads as joinable, however, because joinable threads have a disadvantage; you must wait for the thread using `wxThread::Wait` or else the system resources that it uses will never be freed, and you must delete the corresponding `wxThread` object yourself (once used, it cannot be reused). In contrast, detached threads are of the "fire-and-forget" kind. You only have to start a detached thread, and it will terminate and destroy itself.

This means, of course, that all detached threads must be created on the heap because the thread will call `delete this` upon termination. Joinable threads may be created on the stack, although usually they will be created on the heap as well. Don't create global thread objects because they allocate memory in their constructor, which will cause problems for the memory checking system.

Specifying Stack Size

You can indicate the desired stack size for the thread as a parameter for Create. Passing zero tells wxWidgets to use the platform default.

Specifying Priority

Some operating systems let the application supply a hint about how much execution time a thread needs. Call wxThread::SetPriority with a number between 0 and 100, where 0 is the minimum and 100 is the maximum. The symbols WXTHREAD_MIN_PRIORITY, wxTHREAD_DEFAULT_PRIORITY, and wxTHREAD_MAX_PRIORITY are predefined, with values 0, 50, and 100, respectively. You should call SetPriority after calling Create but before calling Run.

Starting the Thread

After calling Create, the thread is not yet running. You need to call wxThread::Run to start the thread, and wxWidgets will call the thread's Entry function.

How to Pause a Thread or Wait for an External Condition

If a thread needs to wait for something to happen, you should avoid both polling and idling in a loop that keeps the processor busy doing nothing ("busy waiting").

If you just want to wait a few seconds, then send the thread to sleep using wxThread::Sleep.

If you are waiting for something else to happen, you should use a call that blocks execution of the thread until you are notified of a change. For example, if you are using sockets in a thread, you should use blocking socket calls, which will simply pause or "hang" until data is available so that no cycles are wasted. Or if you are waiting for data in a queue and are using a joinable thread, you should block on the Wait method.

You might be tempted to use the Pause and Resume functions to temporarily put your thread to sleep. However, there are a couple of problems with this approach. First, because Pause may be emulated on some operating systems (notably POSIX systems), the thread must periodically call TestDestroy and terminate as soon as possible if it returns true. Secondly, it is very difficult to get right. An operating system may suspend you at any moment, which could easily lead to an application deadlock because you might lock a mutex at that moment.

So in most cases, it is not really a sound design to use Pause and Resume. You should try to transform your code to wait for synchronization objects (see the following section, "Synchronization Objects").

Termination

As we have mentioned, detached threads are automatically destroyed after completion. For a joinable thread, you can simply call wxThread::Wait immediately, or in a GUI application, you can poll wxThread::IsAlive from an idle handler in the main thread and only call Wait if IsAlive returns false. Calling Wait permits thread resources to be freed. Of course, a neater alternative is to simply use a detached thread and post an event when it's done.

You can use wxThread::Delete to request that a thread be deleted. For this to work, the thread must periodically call TestDestroy.

SYNCHRONIZATION OBJECTS

In almost any use of threads, data is shared between different threads. When two threads attempt to access the same data, whether it is an object or a resource, then the access has to be synchronized to avoid data being accessed or modified by more than one thread at the same time. There are almost always so-called *invariants* in a program—assumptions about related elements of data, such as having a correct first element pointer in a list and having each element point to the next element and a NULL pointer in the last element. During insertion of a new element, there is a moment when this invariant is broken. If this list is used from two threads, then you must guard against this moment so that no other client of the list is using it in this intermediate state.

It is the programmer's responsibility to make sure that shared data is not just grabbed by any thread but rather is accessed in a controlled manner. This section describes the classes you can use to achieve this protection.

wxMutex

The name comes from *mutual exclusion* and is the easiest synchronization element to use. It makes sure that only one thread is accessing a particular piece of data. To gain access to the data, the application calls wxMutex::Lock, which blocks (halts execution) until the resource is free. wxMutex::Unlock frees the resource again. Although you can use wxMutex's Lock and Unlock functions directly, by using the wxMutexLocker class, you can be sure that the mutex is always released correctly when the instance is destroyed, even if an exception occurred in your code.

In the following example, we assume that the MyApp class contains an m_mutex member of type wxMutex.

```
void MyApp::DoSomething()
{
    wxMutexLocker lock(m_mutex);
    if (lock.IsOk())
```

```
    {
        ... do something
    }
    else
    {
        ... we have not been able to
        ... acquire the mutex, fatal error
    }
}
```

There are three important rules for using mutexes:

1. A thread cannot generally lock a mutex that is already locked (no mutex recursion). Although there are systems that allow this, it is not portable across all operating systems.

2. A thread cannot unlock a mutex that a different thread has locked. If you need such a construct, you must use semaphores (discussed later).

3. If you are in a thread that is able to do other work if it cannot lock the mutex, you should call wxMutex::TryLock. It returns immediately and indicates whether it was able to lock the mutex (wxMUTEX_NO_ERROR) or not (wxMUTEX_DEAD_LOCK or wxMUTEX_BUSY). This is especially important for the main (GUI) thread, which should never be blocked because your application would become unresponsive to user input.

Deadlocks

A deadlock occurs if two threads are waiting for resources that the other thread has already acquired. So supposing that thread A has already acquired mutex 1 and thread B has already acquired mutex 2, if thread B is now waiting for mutex 1 and thread A is waiting for mutex 2, the wait would go on forever. Some systems will be able to indicate this by returning the special error code wxMUTEX_DEAD_LOCK from Lock, Unlock, or TryLock. On other systems, the application will just hang until the user kills it.

There are two common solutions to this problem:

☞ **Fixed order.** A consistent hierarchy is imposed for acquiring multiple locks on objects. In the previous example, every thread must always acquire mutex 1 first and then mutex 2 so that deadlock cannot occur.

☞ **Try lock.** Acquire the first lock and then call TryLock on any subsequent mutex. If this fails, release all locks and start again. This is a more costly approach, but you might use it when a fixed order solution is not flexible enough and would result in complicated code.

wxCriticalSection

A critical section is used for guarding a certain section of code rather than data, but in practice, it is very similar to a mutex. It is only different on those platforms where a mutex is visible outside an application and can be shared between processes, whereas a critical section is only visible within the application. This makes a critical section slightly more efficient—at least on the platforms that have a native implementation. Because of this origin, the terminology is also slightly different—a mutex may be locked (or acquired) and unlocked (or released), whereas a critical section is entered and left by the program.

You should try to use the wxCriticalSectionLocker class whenever possible instead of directly using wxCriticalSection for the same reasons that wxMutexLocker is preferable to wxMutex.

wxCondition

A condition variable is used for waiting on some change of state on shared data. For example, you could have a condition indicating that a queue has data available. The shared data itself—the queue in this example—is usually protected by a mutex.

You could try to solve the entire problem with a loop that locks a mutex, tests the amount of available data, and releases the lock again if there is no data. However, this is very inefficient because the loop is running all the time, just waiting for the right moment to grab the mutex. Such situations are more efficiently solved using conditions because the thread can block until another thread indicates a change of state.

Multiple threads may be waiting on the same condition, in which case you have two choices to wake up one or more of the threads. You can call Signal to wake one waiting thread, or you can call Broadcast to wake up all of the threads waiting on the same condition. If several predicates are signaled through the same wxCondition, then Broadcast must be used; otherwise a thread might be awakened and be unable to run because it waits for the "wrong" predicate to become true.

wxCondition Example

Let's suppose we have two threads:

- ☞ A producing thread, which puts ten elements onto the queue and then signals "queue full" and waits for "queue empty" before it starts filling the queue again.
- ☞ A consuming thread, which has to wait for "queue full" before removing items.

We need one mutex, m_mutex, guarding the queue and two condition variables, m_isFull and m_isEmpty. These are constructed passing the m_mutex variable as parameter. It is important that you always explicitly test the predicate because a condition might have been signaled before you were waiting on it.

In pseudo-code, this is the Entry code for the producing thread:

```
while ( notDone )
{
    wxMutexLocker lock(m_mutex) ;
    while( m_queue.GetCount() > 0 )
    {
        m_isEmpty.Wait() ;
    }
    for ( int i = 0 ; i < 10 ; ++i )
    {
        m_queue.Append( wxString::Format(wxT("Element %d"),i) ) ;
    }
    m_isFull.Signal();
}
```

Here's the code for the consuming thread:

```
while ( notDone )
{
    wxMutexLocker lock(m_mutex) ;
    while( m_queue.GetCount() == 0 )
    {
        m_isFull.Wait() ;
    }
    for ( int i = queue.GetCount() ; i > 0 ; —i )
    {
        m_queue.RemoveAt( i ) ;
    }
    m_isEmpty.Signal();
}
```

The Wait method unlocks the mutex and then waits for the condition to be signaled. When it returns, it has locked the mutex again, leading to a clean synchronization.

It is important to test the predicate not only before entering but also when Wait returns because something else might have been going on between the signaling and the awakening of our thread so that the predicate is not true anymore; there are even systems that produce spurious wakeups.

Note that a call to Signal might happen before the other thread calls Wait and, just as with pthread conditions, the signal is lost. So if you want to be sure that you don't miss a signal, you must keep the mutex associated with the condition initially locked and lock it again before calling Signal. This means that this call is going to block until Wait is called by another thread.

The following example shows how a main thread can launch a worker thread, which starts running and then waits until the main thread signals it to continue:

```
class MySignallingThread : public wxThread
{
public:
    MySignallingThread(wxMutex *mutex, wxCondition *condition)
    {
        m_mutex = mutex;
        m_condition = condition;

        Create();
    }

    virtual ExitCode Entry()
    {
        ... do our job ...

        // tell the other(s) thread(s) that we're about to
        // terminate: we must lock the mutex first or we might
        // signal the condition before the waiting threads start
        // waiting on it!
        wxMutexLocker lock(m_mutex);
        m_condition.Broadcast(); // same as Signal() here -
                                 // one waiter only

        return 0;
    }

private:
    wxCondition *m_condition;
    wxMutex *m_mutex;
};

void TestThread()
{
    wxMutex mutex;
    wxCondition condition(mutex);

    // the mutex should be initially locked
    mutex.Lock();

    // create and run the thread but notice that it won't be able to
    // exit (and signal its exit) before we unlock the mutex below
    MySignallingThread *thread =
        new MySignallingThread(&mutex, &condition);

    thread->Run();

    // wait for the thread termination: Wait() atomically unlocks
    // the mutex which allows the thread to continue and starts
    // waiting
    condition.Wait();

    // now we can exit
}
```

Of course, here it would be much better to simply use a joinable thread and call wxThread::Wait on it, but this example does illustrate the importance of properly locking the mutex when using wxCondition.

wxSemaphore

Semaphores are a kind of universal combination of mutex and counter. The most important difference from a mutex is that they can be signaled from any thread, not just the owning one, so you can think of a semaphore as a counter without an owner.

A thread calling `Wait` on a semaphore has to wait for the counter to become positive, and then the thread decrements the counter and returns. A thread calling `Post` on a semaphore increments the counter and returns.

There is one additional feature of a semaphore in wxWidgets—you can indicate a maximum value at construction time, 0 being the default (representing "unlimited"). If you have given a non-zero maximum value, and a thread calls `Post` at the wrong moment, leading to a counter value higher the maximum, you will get a `wxSEMA_OVERFLOW` error. To illustrate this concept, let's look at the "universal mutex" described earlier:

☞ A mutex that can be locked and unlocked from different threads would be implemented using a semaphore with an initial count of 1. The `mutex.Lock` would be implemented using `semaphore.Wait` and `mutex.Unlock` using `semaphore.Post`.

☞ The first thread calling `Lock` (that is, `Wait`) finds a positive value in the semaphore, decrements it, and continues immediately.

☞ The next thread calling `Lock` sees a zero value and has to wait until someone (not necessarily the first thread) calls `Unlock` (that is, `Post`).

THE WXWIDGETS THREADS SAMPLE

You can find a working example of many of the features we have described in `samples/thread` in your wxWidgets distribution (see Figure 17-1). In this example, you can start, stop, pause, and resume threads. It demonstrates a "worker thread" that periodically posts events to the main thread with `wxPostEvent`, indicated by a progress dialog that cancels the thread when it reaches the end of its range.

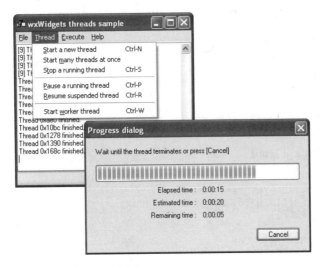

Figure 17-1 wxWidgets Threads Sample

ALTERNATIVES TO MULTITHREADING

If you find threads daunting, you may well be able to get away with a simpler approach, using timers, idle time processing, or both.

Using *wxTimer*

The wxTimer class lets your application receive periodic notification, either as a "single shot" or repeatedly. You can use wxTimer as an alternative to threads if you can break your task up into small chunks that are performed every few milliseconds, giving enough time for the application to respond to user interface events.

You can choose how your code will be notified. If you prefer to use a virtual function, derive a class from wxTimer and override the Notify function. If you prefer to receive a wxTimerEvent event, pass a wxEvtHandler pointer to the timer object (in the constructor or using SetOwner), and use EVT_TIMER(id, func) to connect the timer to an event handler function.

Optionally, you can pass an identifier that you passed to the constructor or SetOwner to uniquely identify the timer object and then pass that identifier to EVT_TIMER. This technique is useful if you have several timer objects to handle.

Start the timer by calling Start, passing a time interval in milliseconds and wxTIMER_ONE_SHOT if only a single notification is required. Calling Stop stops the timer, and IsRunning can be used to determine whether the timer is running.

The following example shows the event handler approach.

```
#define TIMER_ID 1000

class MyFrame : public wxFrame
{
public:
    ...
    void OnTimer(wxTimerEvent& event);

private:
    wxTimer m_timer;
};

BEGIN_EVENT_TABLE(MyFrame, wxFrame)
    EVT_TIMER(TIMER_ID, MyFrame::OnTimer)
END_EVENT_TABLE()

MyFrame::MyFrame()
        : m_timer(this, TIMER_ID)
{
    // 1 second interval
    m_timer.Start(1000);
}

void MyFrame::OnTimer(wxTimerEvent& event)
{
    // Do whatever you want to do every second here
}
```

Note that your event handler is not guaranteed to be called exactly every n milliseconds; the actual interval depends on what other processing was happening before the timer event was processed.

While we're on the subject of marking time, wxStopWatch is a useful class for measuring time intervals. The constructor starts the timer; you can pause and resume it and get the elapsed time in milliseconds. For example:

```
wxStopWatch sw;

SlowBoringFunction();

// Stop the watch
sw.Pause();

wxLogMessage("The slow boring function took %ldms to execute",
             sw.Time());

// Resume the watch
sw.Resume();

SlowBoringFunction();

wxLogMessage("And calling it twice took %ldms in all", sw.Time());
```

Idle Time Processing

Another way your application can be notified periodically is by implementing idle event handlers. The application object and all windows are sent idle events when other event processing is finished. If an idle event handler calls `wxIdleEvent::RequestMore`, then idle events will be generated again; otherwise, no more idle events will be sent until after the next batch of user interface events has been found and processed. You should usually call `wxIdleEvent::Skip` so that base class idle handlers can be called.

In this example, a hypothetical function `FinishedIdleTask` does portions of a task, and when it's finished, it returns `true`.

```
class MyFrame : public wxFrame
{
public:
    ...
    void OnIdle(wxIdleEvent& event);

    // Do a little bit of work, return true if
    // task finished
    bool FinishedIdleTask();
};

BEGIN_EVENT_TABLE(MyFrame, wxFrame)
    EVT_IDLE(MyFrame::OnIdle)
END_EVENT_TABLE()

void MyFrame::OnIdle(wxIdleEvent& event)
{
    // Do idle processing, ask for more idle
    // processing if we haven't finished the task

    if (!FinishedIdleTask())
        event.RequestMore();

    event.Skip();
}
```

Although we used a frame in this example, idle event processing is not limited to top-level windows; any window can intercept idle events. For example, you might implement an image display custom control that only resizes its image to fit its window size in idle time to avoid aggressive flicker as the window is resized. To be sure that the application's idle events don't accidentally interfere with the control's implementation, you can override the virtual function `OnInternalIdle` in your control. Call the base class's `OnInternalIdle` from your overridden function. The image control might use code that looks like this:

```
void wxImageCtrl::OnInternalIdle()
{
    wxControl::OnInternalIdle();
```

```
    if (m_needResize)
    {
        m_needResize = false;
        SizeContent();
    }
}

void wxImageCtrl::OnSize(wxSizeEvent& event)
{
    m_needResize = true;
}
```

Sometimes you might want to force idle event processing, even when there are no other pending events to force idle event processing to happen. You can kick-start idle event processing with the function wxWakeUpIdle. Another method is to start a wxTimer that performs no work; because it sends timer events, it will also cause idle event processing to happen every so often. To process all idle events immediately, call wxApp::ProcessIdle, but note that this might affect internal idle updating, depending on platform (on GTK+, window painting is done in idle time).

User interface update handling, covered previously in Chapter 9, "Creating Custom Dialogs," is a form of idle event processing that enables controls to update themselves by handling wxUpdateUIEvent.

Yielding

When an application is busy doing a lengthy task and the user interface locks up, you might get away with calling wxApp::Yield (or its synonym wxYield) periodically to process pending events. This technique should be used sparingly because it can lead to unwanted side effects, such as reentrancy. For example, Yield might process user command events, leading to the task being executed again, even while it's still in progress. The function wxSafeYield disables all windows, yields, and then enables the windows again to guard against user interaction calling reentrancy. If you pass true to wxApp::Yield, it will only yield if it's not already in a yield, which is another way to mitigate reentrancy problems.

If you're trying to update a specify display periodically, try calling wxWindow::Update instead. This processes just the pending paint events for this window.

SUMMARY

Just as giving a cashier two lines to process instead of one won't make her process more customers per hour, multithreading won't make your application go faster (at least without special hardware). However, it can seem faster to the user because the user interface is more responsive, and like a cashier waiting for credit-card clearance on one of the lines while processing the other, multithreading can use available resources more efficiently. It can also be a good way to solve certain problems more elegantly than would be possible if using only a single thread. In this chapter, we've also touched briefly on avoiding multithreading by using timers, idle event processing, and yielding.

There is more to multithreaded programming than this chapter can cover. For further reading, we recommend *Programming with POSIX Threads* by David R. Butenhof.

Our next chapter looks at using programming with sockets to pass data between processes.

CHAPTER 18

Programming with *wxSocket*

A socket is a conduit for data. A socket doesn't care what kind of data passes through it, where the data is going, or where the data is coming from; its goal is to transport data from point A to point B. Sockets are used every time you surf the web, check your email, or sign on to an instant messenger. One of the neatest aspects of sockets is that they can be used to connect any two devices that support sockets, even if one of them is a computer and the other is a refrigerator!

The socket API was originally a part of the BSD Unix operating system, and because that socket API originated from only one source, it has become the standard. All modern operating systems offer a socket layer, providing the ability to send data over a network (such as the Internet) using common protocols such as TCP or UDP. Using wxWidgets' wxSocket classes, you can reliably communicate any amount of data from one computer to another. This chapter assumes some basic socket terminology knowledge, but socket operations are generally straightforward.

Even though the basic socket features and functions are very similar on Windows, Linux, and Mac OS X, each socket API implementation has its own nuances, usually necessitating platform-specific tweaks. More importantly, event-based sockets have very different APIs from one platform to the next, often making it a significant challenge to use them. wxWidgets provides socket classes that make it easy to use sockets in advanced applications without having to worry about platform-specific implementations or quirks.

Please note that wxWidgets does not, at the time of this writing, support sending and receiving datagrams using the UDP protocol. Future releases of wxWidgets might add UDP capabilities.

SOCKET CLASSES AND FUNCTIONALITY OVERVIEW

At the core of socket operations is `wxSocketBase`, which provides the basic socket functionality for sending and receiving data, closing, error reporting, and so on. Establishing a listening socket or connecting to a server requires `wxSocketServer` or `wxSocketClient`, respectively. `wxSocketEvent` is used to notify the application of an event that has occurred on a socket. The abstract class `wxSocketBase` and its children such as `wxIPV4address` enable you to specify remote hosts and ports. Lastly, stream classes such as `wxSocketInputStream` and `wxSocketOutputStream` can be coupled with other streams to move and transform data over a socket. Streams were discussed in Chapter 14, "Files and Streams."

Sockets in wxWidgets can operate in different ways, as discussed later in the "Socket Flags" section. The traditional threaded socket approach is handled by disabling the socket events and using blocking socket calls. On the other hand, you can enable socket events and eliminate the need for a separate thread; wxWidgets will send an event to your application when processing is required on a socket. By letting the data arrive in the background and processing data only when it is present, you avoid blocking the GUI, and you avoid the complexity of putting each socket in its own thread.

This chapter provides examples of both methods as well as a thorough explanation of the API for `wxSocket` and related classes. The examples and reference can be read and used independently, although the examples are intended to preface the explanation of the APIs.

INTRODUCTION TO SOCKETS AND BASIC SOCKET PROCESSING

As an introduction to socket programming with wxWidgets, let's jump right in to an event-based client/server example. The code is fairly readable with just a basic background in socket programming. For brevity, the GUI elements of the program are omitted, and we focus only on the socket functions; the complete application is available on the CD-ROM in `examples/chap18`. The detailed socket API reference follows the order of the code in the example.

The program performs a very simple task. The server listens for connections, and when a connection is made, the server reads ten characters from the client and then sends those same ten characters back to the client. Likewise, the client creates a connection, sends ten characters, and then receives ten characters in return. The string sent by the client is hard-coded in the example to `0123456789`. The server and client programs are illustrated in Figure 18-1.

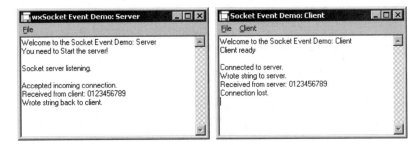

Figure 18-1 Socket server and client programs

The Client

This is the code for the client program.

```
BEGIN_EVENT_TABLE(MyFrame, wxFrame)
    EVT_MENU(CLIENT_CONNECT, MyFrame::OnConnectToServer)
    EVT_SOCKET(SOCKET_ID,    MyFrame::OnSocketEvent)
END_EVENT_TABLE()

void MyFrame::OnConnectToServer(wxCommandEvent& WXUNUSED(event))
{
    wxIPV4address addr;
    addr.Hostname(wxT("localhost"));
    addr.Service(3000);

    // Create the socket
    wxSocketClient* Socket = new wxSocketClient();

    // Set up the event handler and subscribe to most events
    Socket->SetEventHandler(*this, SOCKET_ID);
    Socket->SetNotify(wxSOCKET_CONNECTION_FLAG |
                                    wxSOCKET_INPUT_FLAG |
                                    wxSOCKET_LOST_FLAG);

    Socket->Notify(true);

    // Wait for the connection event
    Socket->Connect(addr, false);
}

void MyFrame::OnSocketEvent(wxSocketEvent& event)
{
    // The socket that had the event
    wxSocketBase* sock = event.GetSocket();

    // Common buffer shared by the events
    char buf[10];

    switch(event.GetSocketEvent())
    {
        case wxSOCKET_CONNECTION:
        {
```

```
                    // Fill the arry with the numbers 0 through 9
                    // as characters
                    char mychar = '0';
                    for (int i = 0; i < 10; i++)
                    {
                        buf[i] = mychar++;
                    }

                    // Send the characters to the server
                    sock->Write(buf, sizeof(buf));

                    break;
                }
                case wxSOCKET_INPUT:
                {
                    sock->Read(buf, sizeof(buf));

                    break;
                }

                // The server hangs up after sending the data
                case wxSOCKET_LOST:
                {
                    sock->Destroy();

                    break;
                }
        }
}
```

The Server

This is the code for the server program.

```
BEGIN_EVENT_TABLE(MyFrame, wxFrame)
    EVT_MENU(SERVER_START, MyFrame::OnServerStart)
    EVT_SOCKET(SERVER_ID,  MyFrame::OnServerEvent)
    EVT_SOCKET(SOCKET_ID,  MyFrame::OnSocketEvent)
END_EVENT_TABLE()

void MyFrame::OnServerStart(wxCommandEvent& WXUNUSED(event))
{
    // Create the address - defaults to localhost:0 initially
    wxIPV4address addr;
    addr.Service(3000);

    // Create the socket. We maintain a class pointer so we can
    // shut it down
    m_server = new wxSocketServer(addr);

    // We use Ok() here to see if the server is really listening
    if (! m_server->Ok())
    {
        return;
    }
```

```
        // Set up the event handler and subscribe to connection events
        m_server->SetEventHandler(*this, SERVER_ID);
        m_server->SetNotify(wxSOCKET_CONNECTION_FLAG);
        m_server->Notify(true);
}

void MyFrame::OnServerEvent(wxSocketEvent& WXUNUSED(event))
{
        // Accept the new connection and get the socket pointer
        wxSocketBase* sock = m_server->Accept(false);

        // Tell the new socket how and where to process its events
        sock->SetEventHandler(*this, SOCKET_ID);
        sock->SetNotify(wxSOCKET_INPUT_FLAG | wxSOCKET_LOST_FLAG);
        sock->Notify(true);
}

void MyFrame::OnSocketEvent(wxSocketEvent& event)
{
    wxSocketBase *sock = event.GetSocket();

    // Process the event
    switch(event.GetSocketEvent())
    {
        case wxSOCKET_INPUT:
        {
            char buf[10];

            // Read the data
            sock->Read(buf, sizeof(buf));

            // Write it back
            sock->Write(buf, sizeof(buf));

            // We are done with the socket, destroy it
            sock->Destroy();

            break;
        }
        case wxSOCKET_LOST:
        {
            sock->Destroy();
            break;
        }
    }
}
```

Connecting to a Server

This section explains how to initiate a client connection to a server using the wxSockAddress and wxSocketClient classes.

Socket Addresses

All socket address classes derive from the abstract base class wxSockAddress, providing a common parameter type for socket methods regardless of the address protocol being used. The wxIPV4address class provides all of the methods necessary for specifying a remote host using the current standard Internet address scheme, IPv4. A wxIPV6address class is partially implemented and will certainly be completed when IPv6 is more widely available.

Note: When representing addresses as unsigned longs, network order is expected, and network order is always returned. Network order corresponds to big endian (Intel or AMD x86 architecture is little endian; Apple's architecture is big endian). Depending on how the unsigned long addresses are stored or entered, you can probably use the byte-order macro wxINT32_SWAP_ON_LE, which will swap the byte order only on little endian platforms. For example:

```
IPV4addr.Hostname(wxINT32_SWAP_ON_LE(longAddress));
```

Hostname takes either a wxString for a string address (for example, www. wxwidgets.org) or an IP address in 4-byte unsigned long format (in big endian, as noted previously). Without any parameters, Hostname returns the name of the currently specified host.

Service sets the remote port, using either a wxString description for a well-known port or an unsigned short for any port. Without any parameters, Service returns the port number currently chosen.

IPAddress provides a dotted-decimal notation representation in a wxString of the remote host.

AnyAddress sets the address to any of the addresses of the current machine. This is the same as setting an address to INADDR_ANY.

Socket Clients

The wxSocketClient class derives from wxSocketBase and inherits all of the common socket methods. The only methods added to the client class are those necessary to initiate and establish a connection to a remote server.

Connect takes a wxSockAddress parameter telling the socket client the address and port for the connection. As mentioned earlier, you would use a class such as wxIPV4address rather than wxSockAddress directly. The second parameter, a boolean, defaults to true, indicating that the call to Connect should block until the connection is established. If this is done from the main GUI thread, the GUI will block while connecting.

WaitOnConnect can be used after a call to Connect if Connect was told *not* to block. The first parameter is the number of seconds to wait, and the second parameter is the number of milliseconds to wait. If the connection succeeds or definitively fails (for example, if the host does not exist), true is returned. If a timeout occurs, `false` is returned. Passing `-1` for the number of seconds specifies the default timeout value, which is 10 minutes unless overridden with a call to `SetTimeout`.

Socket Events

All socket events are filtered through one event, `EVT_SOCKET`.

`EVT_SOCKET(identifier, function)` sends socket events for the socket identifier to the specified function. The function should take a `wxSocketEvent` parameter.

The `wxSocketEvent` class is by itself very simple, but by providing both the event type *and* the socket for which the event was generated, the need to manually store socket pointers is reduced.

Socket Event Types

Table 18-1 lists the event types that are returned from `GetSocketEvent`.

Table 18-1   Socket Event Types

wxSOCKET_INPUT	Issued whenever there is data available for reading. This will be the case if the input queue was empty and new data arrives, or if the application has read some data but there is still more data available.
wxSOCKET_OUTPUT	Issued when a socket is first connected with `Connect` or accepted with `Accept`. After that, new events will be generated only after an output operation fails and buffer space becomes available again.
wxSOCKET_CONNECTION	Issued when a delayed connection request completes successfully (client) or when a new connection arrives at the incoming queue (server).
wxSOCKET_LOST	Issued when a close indication is received for the socket. This means that the connection broke down or that the peer closed it. This event will also be issued if a connection request fails.

wxSocketEvent Major Member Functions

`wxSocketEvent` is used as a parameter to socket event handlers.

`GetSocket` returns a `wxSocketBase` pointer to the socket that generated this event.

`GetSocketEvent` returns the event type of this socket event, as per Table 18-1.

Using Socket Events

In order to use socket events, you must provide an event handler and specify which events you want to receive for processing. The wxSocketBase class gives you several methods for using events, which you can see being used in the server example program after the socket listener is created. Note that the event handling parameters affect *only the socket on which they are set*, so you need to specify the events you want to receive for each socket.

SetEventHandler takes a reference to an event handler and an event identifier. The event identifier should correspond to an entry in the event table for the event handler class.

SetNotify takes a bit-list of the socket events for which you want to be notified. For example, wxSOCKET_INPUT_FLAG ¦ wxSOCKET_LOST_FLAG would send an event when there is data to read on the socket or when the socket is closed.

Notify takes a boolean indicating whether you want to receive events. This allows you to enable or disable events as needed without reconfiguring the events that you want to receive.

Socket Status and Error Notifications

Before discussing sending and receiving data, we describe the auxiliary methods for status and error notification so that we can refer to them from the data methods' descriptions.

Close shuts down the socket, disabling further data transmission. The peer is explicitly notified that you have closed the socket. Note that events might have been queued already when you close the socket, *so you must be prepared to continue receiving socket events even after closing the socket*.

Destroy is used instead of the delete operator because events might reach the socket after it has been deleted if delete were used. Destroy closes the socket and adds the socket to the list of objects to be deleted on idle time, after all events have been processed.

Error returns true if an error occurred in the last operation.

GetPeer returns a wxSockAddress reference containing information about the peer side of the connection, such as IP address and port.

IsConnected returns true if the socket is connected and false otherwise.

LastCount returns the number of bytes read or written by the last I/O call.

LastError returns the last error. Note that a successful operation does *not* update the error code, so Error must be used first to determine whether an error occurred. Table 18-2 lists the error code values.

Table 18-2 Socket Error Codes

wxSOCKET_INVOP	Invalid operation, such as using an invalid address type.
wxSOCKET_IOERR	I/O error, such as being unable to initialize a socket.
wxSOCKET_INVADDR	Invalid address, which will occur when trying to connect without specifying an address or when the address is malformed.
wxSOCKET_INVSOCK	A socket was used in an invalid way or wasn't properly initialized.
wxSOCKET_NOHOST	The specified address does not exist.
wxSOCKET_INVPORT	An invalid port was specified.
wxSOCKET_WOULDBLOCK	The socket is non-blocking, and the operation would block (see the discussion of socket modes).
wxSOCKET_TIMEDOUT	The socket operation exceeded the timeout.
wxSOCKET_MEMERR	Memory could not be allocated for the socket operation.

Ok returns true for a socket client only when the client is connected to server, and it only returns true for a socket server if the socket could bind to the port and is listening.

SetTimeout specifies how long to wait, in seconds, before a blocking socket operation times out. The default value is 10 minutes.

Sending and Receiving Socket Data

wxSocketBase provides a variety of basic and advanced methods for reading and writing socket data. All of the read and write operations store the results of the operation and enable you to access the number of bytes read with LastCount and the last error with LastError.

Reading

Discard deletes all incoming data from the socket buffer.

Peek enables you to copy data from the socket buffer without removing the data from the buffer. You must provide a buffer for the data and the maximum number of bytes to peek.

Read pulls data from the socket buffer and copies it to the specified buffer, up to the maximum size specified.

ReadMsg reads data sent by WriteMsg into the specified buffer, up to the maximum size specified. If the buffer becomes full, the rest of the data is discarded. ReadMsg always waits for the full message sent with WriteMsg to arrive unless an error occurs.

Unread copies data from the data buffer back into the socket buffer. You must also specify how many bytes to put back.

Writing

Write sends data over the socket connection; you must specify a pointer to the data and the number of bytes to send.

WriteMsg is similar to Write, except that WriteMsg adds a header to the data being sent so that the call to ReadMsg on the other end will know exactly how much data to read. Note that data sent with WriteMsg should always be read by a call to ReadMsg.

Creating a Server

The wxSocketServer class adds only a few methods to the wxSocketBase class for creating a listener and accepting connections. In order to create a server, you must specify what port to listen on for incoming connections. wxSocketServer uses the same wxIPV4address class used by wxSocketClient, except without specifying a remote host. In most cases, you should call Ok after creating a socket server to verify that the socket is bound and listening.

wxSocketServer Major Member Functions

wxSocketServer accepts an address object specifying the listen port, and optional socket flags (see the "Socket Flags" section later in this chapter).

Accept returns a new socket connection if one is available, optionally waiting for the connection to be made or returning NULL immediately if no connections are pending. If the wait flag is specified, the GUI will block.

AcceptWith works just like Accept, but you must pass in an already existing wxSocketBase object (by reference), and a boolean is returned indicating whether a connection was accepted.

WaitForAccept takes a seconds parameter and a milliseconds parameter for how long to wait for a connection, returning true when a connection is available, or false if the time period elapses without a connection arriving.

Handling a New Connection Event

When the listening socket detects an incoming connection, a connection event is sent for processing. From the event handler, you can accept the connection and perform any necessary immediate processing. Assuming that the connection has some longevity and isn't immediately closed, you also need to specify an event handler for the new socket. Remember that a listening socket continues to listen until closed, and new sockets are created for each new connection. In the lifetime of a server program, the same listening socket can spawn thousands of new sockets.

Socket Event Recap

From the programmer's standpoint, event-based sockets are a boon for easily processing socket data, eliminating the need for creating and shutting down threads. The example program doesn't use threads, but the GUI will never block waiting for data. Because read commands are not issued until there is data to read, calls to read will immediately succeed and return the available data. If larger amounts of data need to be read, the data can be read in pieces and added to a buffer. Alternatively, a call can be made to Peek to determine how much data is available, and if not enough data has arrived, the application can simply wait for the next input event to arrive.

Next, we will look at how to use different socket flags to change a socket's behavior.

SOCKET FLAGS

The behaviors of a socket when using the socket classes can be quite different depending on which socket flags are set. The socket flags and their meanings are described in Table 18-3 and in more detail below.

Table 18-3   Socket Flags

wxSOCKET_NONE	Normal functionality (the behavior of the underlying send and recv functions).
wxSOCKET_NOWAIT	Read or write as much data as possible and return immediately.
wxSOCKET_WAITALL	Wait for all required data to be read or written unless an error occurs.
wxSOCKET_BLOCK	Block the GUI while reading or writing data.

If no flag is specified (the same as wxSOCKET_NONE), I/O calls will return after some data has been read or written, even when the transfer might not be complete. This is the same as issuing exactly one blocking low-level call to recv or send. Note that blocking here refers to when the function returns, not whether the GUI blocks during this time.

If wxSOCKET_NOWAIT is specified, I/O calls will return immediately. Read operations will retrieve only the available data, and write operations will write as much data as possible, depending on how much space is available in the output buffer. This is the same as issuing exactly one non-blocking low-level call to recv or send. Note that *non-blocking* here refers to when the function returns, not whether the GUI blocks during this time.

If `wxSOCKET_WAITALL` is specified, I/O calls won't return until *all* the data has been read or written (or until an error occurs), blocking if necessary and issuing several low-level calls if needed. This is the same as having a loop that makes as many blocking low-level calls to `recv` or `send` as needed to transfer all the data. Again, *blocking* here refers to when the function returns, not whether the GUI blocks during this time. Note that `ReadMsg` and `WriteMsg` will implicitly use `wxSOCKET_WAITALL` and ignore `wxSOCKET_NONE` and `wxSOCKET_NOWAIT`.

The `wxSOCKET_BLOCK` flag controls whether the GUI blocks during I/O operations. If this flag is specified, the socket will not yield during I/O calls, so the GUI will remain blocked until the operation completes. If it is not used, then the application must take extra care to avoid unwanted re-entrance.

To summarize:

☞ `wxSOCKET_NONE` will try to read at least *some* data, no matter how much.

☞ `wxSOCKET_NOWAIT` will always return immediately, even if it cannot read or write *any* data.

☞ `wxSOCKET_WAITALL` will only return when it has read or written *all* the data.

☞ `wxSOCKET_BLOCK` has nothing to do with the previous flags; it controls whether the GUI blocks during socket operations.

Blocking and Non-Blocking Sockets in wxWidgets

The term *blocking* has a dual meaning in wxWidgets. In standard socket programming, blocking means that the current thread hangs (blocks) on the `recv` function until a timeout occurs or the full amount of data is read. If that thread happens to be the main thread, then the GUI blocks as well.

Under wxWidgets, however, blocking can refer to two different types of blocking: socket blocking and GUI blocking. The purpose of the `wxSOCKET_BLOCK` flag is to specify whether the GUI will block if the socket call blocks. How is it possible that the socket call can block but the GUI does not? This is possible because events can continue to be processed through calls to `wxYield` while the socket operation is incomplete. `wxYield` will process pending events in the event queue, including GUI events. As long as the socket operation has not completed, your code is blocked on the socket function, but events are continuously processed.

To the wxWidgets newcomer, this appears to be a panacea for socket applications. The first time you work with sockets on wxWidgets, it's easy to believe that you will never need another thread to process sockets. You might think that you could simply use socket events and set all sockets to use `wxSOCKET_WAITALL` without `wxSOCKET_BLOCK`. Unfortunately, attempting this can have a deadly side effect, and it produces a warning message that can be a source of confusion.

Consider the case of a server with two active connections, each connection with wxSOCKET_WAITALL as the active socket flag. Furthermore, imagine that a large amount of data is being received over a slow connection. Socket 1 has no data in the read buffer, so it calls wxYield. There is still a pending event on Socket 2, so wxWidgets attempts to process that event. However, that event cannot complete, and it also calls wxYield. This will cause the infamous "wxYield called recursively" message to appear. Eventually the stack would fill up with recursive calls to wxYield as long as all the data has not yet arrived and the call stack cannot unwind. Many users immediately assume that this error message indicates a flaw in wxWidgets, when the truth is that it represents a problem in the application code. Simply stated, applications should be programmed so that this situation does not occur; the error is present to reveal a problem *in the application code* so that it can be fixed.

That aside, there is still another side effect of allowing socket calls to block without blocking the GUI—your application will consume as much CPU time as has been allocated to it. The reason for this is that events must be immediately processed for the application to remain responsive, but the socket must also be monitored for data so that it can return immediately when data is available. The only way to do this is in a busy loop, constantly calling a non-blocking select on the socked followed by a call to wxYield.

The Impossible Socket Combination

Just to reiterate, do not be fooled into thinking that wxWidgets has created miraculous socket processing. You cannot simultaneously have all of the following, no matter how much it appears at first glance that you can:

- ☞ wxSOCKET_WAITALL
- ☞ No GUI blocking
- ☞ Less than 100% CPU usage
- ☞ A single thread

You *can* specify wxSOCKET_WAITALL without blocking the GUI, but it will cause 100% CPU usage. You *can* use wxSOCKET_WAITALL and have 0% CPU usage if you also block the GUI with wxSOCKET_BLOCK. You *can* use wxSOCKET_WAITALL without blocking the GUI or using 100% CPU if you use secondary threads. You *can* use sockets in a single thread without 100% CPU usage or blocking the GUI, but you have to use wxSOCKET_NOWAIT. You can have any three of these things simultaneously, just not all four.

How Flags Affect Socket Behavior

Given that wxSOCKET_NONE, wxSOCKET_NOWAIT, and wxSOCKET_WAITALL are mutually exclusive, and that wxSOCKET_BLOCK makes no sense combined with wxSOCKET_NOWAIT (if the function returns immediately, how can the GUI ever block?), there are five meaningful flag combinations:

☞ wxSOCKET_NONE | wxSOCKET_BLOCK: Behaves like standard blocking socket calls (calls to recv and send).

☞ wxSOCKET_NOWAIT: Behaves like standard non-blocking socket calls.

☞ wxSOCKET_WAITALL ¦ wxSOCKET_BLOCK: Behaves like standard blocking socket calls, except that the underlying send or recv will be called repeatedly until all data is sent or received.

☞ wxSOCKET_NONE: Behaves like standard socket calls except that the GUI will not block because of continuous calls to wxYield while the socket operation is incomplete (for example, not all data has been read).

☞ wxSOCKET_WAITALL: Behaves like wxSOCKET_WAITALL ¦ wxSOCKET_BLOCK except that the GUI will not block.

Only the last two can lead to the recursive wxYield problem, although they are also the most useful when using socket events in the primary thread (because they are socket blocking but not GUI blocking). Extreme caution should be exercised while using these two options. Although they are very powerful, they are also the source of many problems and frustrations because they are so frequently misunderstood.

Using *wxSocket* as a Standard Socket

Using sockets with wxSOCKET_NONE ¦ wxSOCKET_BLOCK or wxSOCKET_NOWAIT in wxWidgets is no different from using C sockets, except that you use wxSocket methods instead of C functions. The wxSocket class still provides many advantages over using the C API directly, including an object-oriented interface, hiding a lot of the bulky platform-dependent initialization code, providing consistent behavior from one platform to the next (especially with regards to error codes, which differ widely from platform to platform), and some higher-level functions like WriteMsg and ReadMsg. As we'll see next, using wxSocket also lets us take advantage of socket streams.

USING SOCKET STREAMS

Using wxWidgets' streams, it is easy to move and transform large amounts of data with only a few lines of code. Consider the task of sending a file over a socket. One approach would be to open the file, read the entire file into memory, and then send the memory block to the socket. This approach is fine for small files, but reading a large multi-megabyte file into memory might not be very speedy on a slower, low-memory computer. Furthermore, what if you were required to also compress the file as you send it to reduce network traffic? Reading a large file into memory, compressing it all at once, and then writing it to a socket simply would not be efficient or practical.

A second approach might be to read the file in small pieces, such as several kilobytes, compress the pieces, and then output these pieces over the socket. Unfortunately, compressing the individual pieces is not going to be as efficient as compressing the whole file at once. A refinement might be to maintain stateful compression streams from one piece to the next (where the compression of one frame can use compression information from the previous, most notably avoiding the need for each frame to have its own header), but you're already looking at dozens of lines of code and the delicate synchronization of reading from the file, compressing, and sending. With wxWidgets, there is a better way.

Because wxWidgets provides both `wxSocketInputStream` and `wxSocketOutputStream` classes, it is very easy to stream data in and out of sockets through other streams. Consider that wxWidgets provides streams for files, strings, text, memory, and Zlib compression, and some very interesting possibilities become apparent for using sockets in unique and powerful ways. If we revisit the file sending with compression problem with streams on our tool belt, a new solution is available. To send a file, we can stream data from the file to the Zlib compression to the socket, and suddenly we have stateful file compression, resulting in a completely compressed file being sent without reading more than a few kilobytes at a time. On the receiving end, we can stream the data from the socket through the Zlib decompression, and finally into the output file. All this can be done in only a few lines of code.

We will do our file streaming in a thread so that we can block on the socket operations and not worry about blocking the GUI or running into the 100% CPU usage issue detailed earlier, which is quite possible if we were to send large multi-megabyte files.

The complete socket stream sources can be found on the accompanying CD-ROM in `examples/chap18`.

File Sending Thread

The sending thread demonstrates using streams allocated dynamically on the heap. `FileSendThread` derives from `wxThread`.

```
FileSendThread::FileSendThread(wxString Filename,
                               wxSocketBase* Socket)
{
    m_Filename = Filename;
    m_Socket = Socket;

    Create();
    Run();
}

void* FileSendThread::Entry()
{
    // If we can't write anything for 10 seconds, assume a timeout
    m_Socket->SetTimeout(10);

    // Wait for all the data to write, blocking on the socket calls
    m_Socket->SetFlags(wxSOCKET_WAITALL | wxSOCKET_BLOCK);
```

```
    // Read from the specified file
    wxFileInputStream* FileInputStream =
        new wxFileInputStream(m_Filename);

    // An output stream writing to the socket
    wxSocketOutputStream* SocketOutputStream =
        new wxSocketOutputStream(*m_Socket);

    // The results of the compression will be written to the
    // socket stream
    wxZlibOutputStream* ZlibOutputStream =
        new wxZlibOutputStream(*SocketOutputStream);

    // Write the results of the zlib decompression to the file stream
    ZlibOutputStream->Write(*FileInputStream);

    // Write all data
    ZlibOutputStream->Sync();

    // Destroying will send Zlib compression EOF
    delete ZlibOutputStream;

    // Clean up
    delete SocketOutputStream;
    delete FileInputStream;

    return NULL;
}
```

File Receiving Thread

The receiving thread demonstrates using streams allocated on the stack.
FileReceiveThread derives from wxThread.

```
FileReceiveThread::FileReceiveThread(wxString Filename,
                                     wxSocketBase* Socket)
{
    m_Filename = Filename;
    m_Socket = Socket;

    Create();
    Run();
}
```

```
void* FileReceiveThread::Entry()
{
    // If we don't receive anything for 10 seconds, assume a timeout
    m_Socket->SetTimeout(10);

    // Wait for some data to come in, or for an error
    // and block on the socket calls
    m_Socket->SetFlags(wxSOCKET_WAITALL | wxSOCKET_BLOCK);

    // Output to the specified file
    wxFileOutputStream FileOutputStream(m_Filename);
```

```
    // Stream data in from the socket
    wxSocketInputStream SocketInputStream(*m_Socket);

    // The zlib decompression will decompress data from the
    // socket stream
    wxZlibInputStream ZlibInputStream(SocketInputStream);

    // Write to the file stream the results of reading from the
    // zlib input stream
    FileOutputStream.Write(ZlibInputStream);

    return NULL;
}
```

ALTERNATIVES TO *wxSocket*

Although wxSocket provides a lot of flexibility and is nicely integrated into wxWidgets, it's not the only method you can use to communicate with other processes. If you just want to perform FTP or HTTP operations, you can use wxFTP or wxHTTP, which use wxSocket. However, these classes are incomplete, and you may be better off using CURL, a popular library that gives you a very straightforward API for transferring files using a variety of common Internet protocols. There is even a wxWidgets wrapper for CURL available, called wxCURL.

wxWidgets also provides a high-level interprocess communication facility that uses the classes wxServer, wxClient, and wxConnection and an API based on Microsoft's DDE (Dynamic Data Exchange) protocol. In fact, on Windows, these classes use DDE, and on other platforms, sockets. The main advantage of using this higher-level API is its ease of use compared with using wxSocket. Another advantage is that on Windows, your applications can be DDE-aware, and other applications (not necessarily written with wxWidgets) can access it. A disadvantage is that on platforms other than Windows, it is not a recognized protocol to which non-wxWidgets applications can easily conform. However, if you just need to communicate between two wxWidgets applications, it can fit the bill. We show a very simple example in the section "Single Instance or Multiple Instances?" in Chapter 20, "Perfecting Your Application."

For more information, please refer to the topic "Interprocess Communication Overview" in the reference manual and the source in samples/ipc in your wxWidgets distribution. You can also see these classes in action in the standalone help viewer in utils/helpview/src, again in the wxWidgets distribution.

Summary

We've seen how the wxSocket class provides wxWidgets integration and numerous enhancements to the underlying C sockets layer. To make socket programming even easier, wxWidgets also gives you socket stream classes that can stream data through a variety of classes. As long as you carefully consider the socket flags discussion, you will get consistent and reliable socket operations across Windows, Linux, and Mac OS X when using wxSocket and its related classes.

Next, we'll look at how your application design and implementation can be simplified by using the wxWidgets document/view framework.

Working with Documents and Views

This chapter discusses how the document/view framework provided by wxWidgets can dramatically reduce the amount of code you need to write for a document-based application. It also discusses the related topic of providing undo and redo in your application, a seemingly miraculous facility that users now take for granted.

DOCUMENT/VIEW BASICS

The document/view system is found in most application frameworks because it can greatly simplify the code required to build many kinds of applications.

The idea is that you can model your application primarily in terms of documents, which store data and provide GUI-independent operations upon it, and views, which display and manipulate the data. It's similar to the Model-View-Controller model (MVC), but here the concept of controller is not separate from the view.

wxWidgets can provide many user interface elements and behaviors based on this architecture. After you have defined your own classes and the relationships between them, the framework takes care of showing file selectors, opening and closing files, asking the user to save modifications, routing menu commands to appropriate code, and even some default print and print preview functionality and support for command undo and redo. The framework is highly modular, enabling the application to override and replace functionality and objects to achieve more than the default behavior.

These are the main steps involved in creating an application based on the document/view framework, once you've decided that this model is appropriate for your application. The ordering is to some extent arbitrary: for example, you may choose to write your document class before thinking about how a document will be presented in the application.

1. Decide what style of interface you will use: Microsoft's MDI (multiple document child frames surrounded by an overall frame), SDI (a separate, unconstrained frame for each document), or single-window (one document open at a time, as in Windows Write).

2. Use the appropriate parent and child frame classes, based on the previous decision, such as `wxDocParentFrame` and `wxDocChildFrame`. Construct an instance of the parent frame class in your `wxApp::OnInit`, and a child frame class (if not single-window) when you initialize a view. Create menus using standard menu identifiers such as `wxID_OPEN` and `wxID_PRINT`.

3. Define your own document and view classes, overriding a minimal set of member functions for input/output, drawing, and initialization. If you need undo/redo, implement it as early as possible, instead of trying to retrofit your application with it later.

4. Define any subwindows (such as a scrolled window) that are needed for the view(s). You may need to route some events to views or documents; for example, your paint handler needs to be routed to `wxView::OnDraw`.

5. Construct a single `wxDocManager` instance at the beginning of your `wxApp::OnInit` and then as many `wxDocTemplate` instances as necessary to define relationships between documents and views. For a simple application, there will be just one `wxDocTemplate`.

We will illustrate these steps using a little application called Doodle (see Figure 19-1). As its name suggests, it supports freehand drawing in a window, with the ability to save and load your doodles. It also supports simple undo and redo.

Figure 19-1   Doodle in action

Step 1: Choose an Interface Style

Traditionally, multi-document applications on Windows have used MDI, as described in the section "wxMDIParentFrame" in Chapter 4, "Window Basics." A parent frame manages and encloses a series of document child frames, with the menu bar reflecting the commands available in either the active child frame or the parent frame if there are no child frames.

An alternative to MDI is to dispense with the concept of a "main" window and show each document in a new frame that can be moved around the desktop without constraint. This is the usual style on Mac OS, although on Mac OS, only one menu bar is shown at a time (that of the active window). Another twist on Mac OS is that unlike on other platforms, the user does not expect the application to exit when the last window is closed: there is normally an application menu bar with a reduced set of commands that shows without a window being visible. Currently, to achieve this behavior in wxWidgets, you must create an off-screen frame, whose menu bar will automatically be shown if all visible windows have been destroyed.

A variation of this technique is to show a main window in addition to separate document frames. However, it is quite rare for this to be a useful model. Yet another variation is to only show document windows, but when the last document is closed, the window remains open to let the user open or create documents. This model is employed by recent versions of Microsoft Word and is similar to the Mac OS model, except that on Mac OS where there are no documents open, there is no visible frame, only a menu bar.

Perhaps the simplest model is to have one main window, no separate child frames, and only one document open at a time: an example is Windows WordPad. This is the style chosen for our Doodle application.

Finally, you can create your own style, perhaps combining different elements of the others. DialogBlocks is an example of an application that mixes styles to give the user different ways of working. The most common way of working with DialogBlocks is to show one view at a time. When you select a document in the project tree, the current view is hidden, and the new view is shown. Optionally, you can enable tabs for quick switching between the set of the documents you're most interested in. In addition, you can drag the view's title bar to the desktop to undock the view and see multiple documents simultaneously. Internally, DialogBlocks manages the relationships between documents, views, and windows differently from the standard wxWidgets document/view management. Obviously, creating your own document management system is time-consuming, so you will probably want to choose one of the standard methods.

Step 2: Create and Use Frame Classes

For an MDI application, you will use `wxDocMDIParentFrame` and `wxDocMDIChildFrame`. For an application with one main frame and multiple separate document frames, use `wxDocParentFrame` and `wxDocChildFrame`. If you have a main frame and only one document shown at a time, use `wxDocParentFrame`.

If your application does not have a main frame, just multiple document frames, use either wxDocParentFrame or wxDocChildFrame. However, if using wxDocParentFrame, intercept the window close event handler (EVT_CLOSE) and delete all the views for the associated document because the default behavior is to delete all views known to the document manager (which will close all documents).

Here's our frame class definition. We store a pointer to the doodle canvas and a pointer to the edit menu that will be associated with the document command processor so the system can update the *Undo* and *Redo* menu items.

```
// Define a new frame
class DoodleFrame: public wxDocParentFrame
{
    DECLARE_CLASS(DoodleFrame)
    DECLARE_EVENT_TABLE()
public:
    DoodleFrame(wxDocManager *manager, wxFrame *frame, wxWindowID id,
        const wxString& title, const wxPoint& pos,
        const wxSize& size, long type);

    /// Show About box
    void OnAbout(wxCommandEvent& event);

    /// Get edit menu
    wxMenu* GetEditMenu() const { return m_editMenu; }

    /// Get canvas
    DoodleCanvas* GetCanvas() const { return m_canvas; }

private:
    wxMenu *        m_editMenu;
    DoodleCanvas*   m_canvas;
};
```

The implementation of DoodleFrame is shown next. The constructor creates a menu bar and a DoodleCanvas object with a pencil cursor. The file menu is passed to the manager object to be used for displaying recently used files.

```
IMPLEMENT_CLASS(DoodleFrame, wxDocParentFrame)

BEGIN_EVENT_TABLE(DoodleFrame, wxDocParentFrame)
    EVT_MENU(DOCVIEW_ABOUT, DoodleFrame::OnAbout)
END_EVENT_TABLE()

DoodleFrame::DoodleFrame(wxDocManager *manager, wxFrame *parent,
                wxWindowID id, const wxString& title,
                const wxPoint& pos, const wxSize& size, long type):
wxDocParentFrame(manager, parent, id, title, pos, size, type)
{
    m_editMenu = NULL;

    m_canvas = new DoodleCanvas(this,
                    wxDefaultPosition, wxDefaultSize, 0);
```

```
    m_canvas->SetCursor(wxCursor(wxCURSOR_PENCIL));

    // Give it scrollbars
    m_canvas->SetScrollbars(20, 20, 50, 50);
    m_canvas->SetBackgroundColour(*wxWHITE);
    m_canvas->ClearBackground();

    // Give it an icon
    SetIcon(wxIcon(doodle_xpm));

    // Make a menu bar
    wxMenu *fileMenu = new wxMenu;
    wxMenu *editMenu = (wxMenu *) NULL;

    fileMenu->Append(wxID_NEW, wxT("&New..."));
    fileMenu->Append(wxID_OPEN, wxT("&Open..."));

    fileMenu->Append(wxID_CLOSE, wxT("&Close"));
    fileMenu->Append(wxID_SAVE, wxT("&Save"));
    fileMenu->Append(wxID_SAVEAS, wxT("Save &As..."));
    fileMenu->AppendSeparator();
    fileMenu->Append(wxID_PRINT, wxT("&Print..."));
    fileMenu->Append(wxID_PRINT_SETUP, wxT("Print &Setup..."));
    fileMenu->Append(wxID_PREVIEW, wxT("Print Pre&view"));

    editMenu = new wxMenu;
    editMenu->Append(wxID_UNDO, wxT("&Undo"));
    editMenu->Append(wxID_REDO, wxT("&Redo"));
    editMenu->AppendSeparator();
    editMenu->Append(DOCVIEW_CUT, wxT("&Cut last segment"));

    m_editMenu = editMenu;

    fileMenu->AppendSeparator();
    fileMenu->Append(wxID_EXIT, wxT("E&xit"));

    wxMenu *helpMenu = new wxMenu;
    helpMenu->Append(DOCVIEW_ABOUT, wxT("&About"));

    wxMenuBar *menuBar = new wxMenuBar;

    menuBar->Append(fileMenu, wxT("&File"));
    menuBar->Append(editMenu, wxT("&Edit"));
    menuBar->Append(helpMenu, wxT("&Help"));

    // Associate the menu bar with the frame
    SetMenuBar(menuBar);

    // A nice touch: a history of files visited. Use this menu.
    manager->FileHistoryUseMenu(fileMenu);
}

void DoodleFrame::OnAbout(wxCommandEvent& WXUNUSED(event) )
{
    (void)wxMessageBox(wxT("Doodle Sample\n(c) 2004, Julian Smart"),
                       wxT("About Doodle"));
}
```

Step 3: Define Your Document and View Classes

Your document class should have a default constructor, and you should use the DECLARE_DYNAMIC_CLASS and IMPLEMENT_DYNAMIC_CLASS to enable the framework to create document objects on demand. (If you don't supply these, you should instead override wxDocTemplate::CreateDocument.)

You also need to tell the framework how the object will be saved and loaded. You can override SaveObject and LoadObject if you will be using wxWidgets streams, as in our example. Or if you want to implement file handling yourself, override DoSaveDocument and DoOpenDocument, which take a file name argument instead of a stream. wxWidgets streams are described in Chapter 14, "Files and Streams."

Note

The framework does not use temporary files when saving data. This is a good reason for overriding DoSaveDocument and making a stream out of a wxTempFile, as described in Chapter 14.

Here's our DoodleDocument declaration:

```
/*
 * Represents a doodle document
 */

class DoodleDocument: public wxDocument
{
    DECLARE_DYNAMIC_CLASS(DoodleDocument)
public:
    DoodleDocument() {};
    ~DoodleDocument();

    /// Saves the document
    wxOutputStream& SaveObject(wxOutputStream& stream);

    /// Loads the document
    wxInputStream& LoadObject(wxInputStream& stream);

    inline wxList& GetDoodleSegments() { return m_doodleSegments; };

private:
    wxList m_doodleSegments;
};
```

Your document class will also contain the data that's appropriate to the document type. In our case, we have a list of doodle segments, each representing the lines drawn in a single gesture while the mouse button was down. The segment class knows how to stream itself, which makes it simpler to implement the document's streaming functions. Here are the declarations for segments and lines.

```
/*
 * Defines a line from one point to the other
 */

class DoodleLine: public wxObject
{
public:
    DoodleLine(wxInt32 x1 = 0, wxInt32 y1 = 0,
               wxInt32 x2 = 0, wxInt32 y2 = 0)
    { m_x1 = x1; m_y1 = y1; m_x2 = x2; m_y2 = y2; }

    wxInt32 m_x1;
    wxInt32 m_y1;
    wxInt32 m_x2;
    wxInt32 m_y2;
};

/*
 * Contains a list of lines: represents a mouse-down doodle
 */

class DoodleSegment: public wxObject
{
public:
    DoodleSegment(){};
    DoodleSegment(DoodleSegment& seg);
    ~DoodleSegment();

    void Draw(wxDC *dc);

    /// Saves the segment
    wxOutputStream& SaveObject(wxOutputStream& stream);

    /// Loads the segment
    wxInputStream& LoadObject(wxInputStream& stream);

    /// Gets the lines
    wxList& GetLines() { return m_lines; }

private:
    wxList m_lines;
};
```

The `DoodleSegment` class knows how to render an instance of itself to a device context by virtue of its `Draw` function. This will help when implementing the doodle drawing code.

Here's the implementation of these classes.

```
/*
 * DoodleDocument
 */

IMPLEMENT_DYNAMIC_CLASS(DoodleDocument, wxDocument)

DoodleDocument::~DoodleDocument()
```

```
    {
        WX_CLEAR_LIST(wxList, m_doodleSegments);
    }

wxOutputStream& DoodleDocument::SaveObject(wxOutputStream& stream)
{
    wxDocument::SaveObject(stream);

    wxTextOutputStream textStream( stream );

    wxInt32 n = m_doodleSegments.GetCount();
    textStream << n << wxT('\n');

    wxList::compatibility_iterator node = m_doodleSegments.GetFirst();
    while (node)
    {
        DoodleSegment *segment = (DoodleSegment *)node->GetData();
        segment->SaveObject(stream);
        textStream << wxT('\n');

        node = node->GetNext();
    }

    return stream;
}

wxInputStream& DoodleDocument::LoadObject(wxInputStream& stream)
{
    wxDocument::LoadObject(stream);

    wxTextInputStream textStream( stream );

    wxInt32 n = 0;
    textStream >> n;

    for (int i = 0; i < n; i++)
    {
        DoodleSegment *segment = new DoodleSegment;
        segment->LoadObject(stream);
        m_doodleSegments.Append(segment);
    }

    return stream;
}

/*
 * DoodleSegment
 */

DoodleSegment::DoodleSegment(DoodleSegment& seg)
{
    wxList::compatibility_iterator node = seg.GetLines().GetFirst();
    while (node)
    {
        DoodleLine *line = (DoodleLine *)node->GetData();
        DoodleLine *newLine = new DoodleLine(line->m_x1, line->m_y1,
line->m_x2, line->m_y2);
```

```
            GetLines().Append(newLine);

            node = node->GetNext();
        }
    }

    DoodleSegment::~DoodleSegment()
    {
        WX_CLEAR_LIST(wxList, m_lines);
    }

    wxOutputStream &DoodleSegment::SaveObject(wxOutputStream& stream)
    {
        wxTextOutputStream textStream( stream );

        wxInt32 n = GetLines().GetCount();
        textStream << n << wxT('\n');

        wxList::compatibility_iterator node = GetLines().GetFirst();
        while (node)
        {
            DoodleLine *line = (DoodleLine *)node->GetData();
            textStream
                << line->m_x1 << wxT(" ")
                << line->m_y1 << wxT(" ")
                << line->m_x2 << wxT(" ")
                << line->m_y2 << wxT("\n");
            node = node->GetNext();
        }

        return stream;
    }

    wxInputStream &DoodleSegment::LoadObject(wxInputStream& stream)
    {
        wxTextInputStream textStream( stream );

        wxInt32 n = 0;
        textStream >> n;

        for (int i = 0; i < n; i++)
        {
            DoodleLine *line = new DoodleLine;
            textStream
                >> line->m_x1
                >> line->m_y1
                >> line->m_x2
                >> line->m_y2;
            GetLines().Append(line);
        }

        return stream;
    }

    void DoodleSegment::Draw(wxDC *dc)
    {
        wxList::compatibility_iterator node = GetLines().GetFirst();
        while (node)
        {
```

```
        DoodleLine *line = (DoodleLine *)node->GetData();
        dc->DrawLine(line->m_x1, line->m_y1, line->m_x2, line->m_y2);
        node = node->GetNext();
    }
}
```

So far, we haven't touched on how doodle segments actually get added to the document, except by loading them from a file. We can model the commands that will modify the document independently of the code that interprets mouse or keyboard input, and this is the key to implementing undo and redo. DoodleCommand is a class deriving from wxCommand: it implements the Do and Undo virtual functions that will be called by the framework at the appropriate point. So instead of directly modifying the document, the input event handlers will create a DoodleCommand with the appropriate information and submit it to the document's command processor (an instance of wxCommandProcessor). The command processor stores the command on an undo/redo stack before calling Do for the first time. The command processor is automatically created when the framework initializes the document, which is why you don't see it being created explicitly in this example.

Here is DoodleCommand's declaration:

```
/*
 * A doodle command
 */

class DoodleCommand: public wxCommand
{
public:
    DoodleCommand(const wxString& name, int cmd, DoodleDocument *doc,
DoodleSegment *seg);
    ~DoodleCommand();

    /// Overrides
    virtual bool Do();
    virtual bool Undo();

    /// Combine do/undo code since the commands are symmetric
    bool DoOrUndo(int cmd);

protected:
    DoodleSegment*   m_segment;
    DoodleDocument*  m_doc;
    int              m_cmd;
};

/*
 * Doodle command identifiers
 */

#define DOODLE_CUT         1
#define DOODLE_ADD         2
```

We define two commands, DOODLE_ADD and DOODLE_CUT. The user can delete the last segment or add a segment by drawing. Here, the two commands are both represented by the same command class, but this doesn't have to be the case. Each command object stores a pointer to the document, a segment object, and the command identifier. The implementation for DoodleCommand is:

```
/*
 * DoodleCommand
 */

DoodleCommand::DoodleCommand(const wxString& name, int command,
                             DoodleDocument *doc, DoodleSegment *seg):
    wxCommand(true, name)
{
    m_doc = doc;
    m_segment = seg;
    m_cmd = command;
}

DoodleCommand::~DoodleCommand()
{
    if (m_segment)
        delete m_segment;
}

bool DoodleCommand::Do()
{
    return DoOrUndo(m_cmd);
}

bool DoodleCommand::Undo()
{
    switch (m_cmd)
    {
    case DOODLE_ADD:
        {
            return DoOrUndo(DOODLE_CUT);
        }
    case DOODLE_CUT:
        {
            return DoOrUndo(DOODLE_ADD);
        }
    }
    return true;
}

bool DoodleCommand::DoOrUndo(int cmd)
{
    switch (cmd)
    {
    case DOODLE_ADD:
        {
            wxASSERT( m_segment != NULL );
```

```
            if (m_segment)
                m_doc->GetDoodleSegments().Append(m_segment);

            m_segment = NULL;

            m_doc->Modify(true);
            m_doc->UpdateAllViews();
            break;
        }
    case DOODLE_CUT:
        {
            wxASSERT( m_segment == NULL );

            // Cut the last segment
            if (m_doc->GetDoodleSegments().GetCount() > 0)
            {
                wxList::compatibility_iterator node = m_doc-
>GetDoodleSegments().GetLast();

                m_segment = (DoodleSegment *)node->GetData();
                m_doc->GetDoodleSegments().Erase(node);

                m_doc->Modify(true);
                m_doc->UpdateAllViews();
            }
            break;
        }
    }
    return true;
}
```

Because Do and Undo share code in our example, we have factored it out into the function DoOrUndo. So to get an undo of a DOODLE_ADD, we use the code for doing DOODLE_CUT. To get the undo of a DOODLE_CUT, we use the code for doing a DOODLE_ADD.

When a segment is added (or a cut command is undone), DoOrUndo simply adds the segment to the document's segment list and clears the pointer to it in the command object so that it doesn't get deleted when the command object is destroyed. A cut (or undo for an add command) removes the last segment from the document's list but keeps a pointer to it in case the command needs to be reversed. DoOrUndo also marks the document as modified (so that closing the application will cause a save prompt) and tells the document to update all of its views.

To define your view class, derive from wxView and again use the dynamic object creation macros. Override at least OnCreate, OnDraw, OnUpdate, and OnClose.

OnCreate is called by the framework when the view and document objects have just been created: at this point, you may need to create a frame and associate it with the view using SetFrame.

OnDraw takes a pointer to a wxDC object and implements drawing. In fact, this doesn't have to be implemented, but if drawing is implemented another way, the default print/preview behavior will not work.

OnUpdate is called with a pointer to the view that caused the update and an optional hint object to help the view optimize painting, and it notifies the view that it should be updated. OnUpdate is typically called when a command has changed the document contents and all views need to be redrawn appropriately. The application can request an update with wxDocument::UpdateAllViews.

OnClose is called when the view is about to be deleted. The default implementation calls wxDocument::OnClose to close the associated document.

Here is the declaration of our DoodleView class. As well as overriding the functions mentioned previously, it handles the DOODLE_CUT command via OnCut. The reason why DOODLE_ADD is not represented in the view's event table is that a segment is added with a mouse gesture, and mouse events are handled by DoodleCanvas, as we'll see shortly.

```
/*
 * DoodleView mediates between documents and windows
 */

class DoodleView: public wxView
{
    DECLARE_DYNAMIC_CLASS(DoodleView)
    DECLARE_EVENT_TABLE()
public:
    DoodleView() { m_frame = NULL; }
    ~DoodleView() {};

    /// Called when the document is created
    virtual bool OnCreate(wxDocument *doc, long flags);

    /// Called to draw the document
    virtual void OnDraw(wxDC *dc);

    /// Called when the view needs to be updated
    virtual void OnUpdate(wxView *sender, wxObject *hint = NULL);

    /// Called when the view is closed
    virtual bool OnClose(bool deleteWindow = true);

    /// Processes the cut command
    void OnCut(wxCommandEvent& event);

private:
    DoodleFrame*    m_frame;
};
```

The following is the implementation of DoodleView.

```
IMPLEMENT_DYNAMIC_CLASS(DoodleView, wxView)

BEGIN_EVENT_TABLE(DoodleView, wxView)
    EVT_MENU(DOODLE_CUT, DoodleView::OnCut)
END_EVENT_TABLE()
```

```cpp
// What to do when a view is created.
bool DoodleView::OnCreate(wxDocument *doc, long WXUNUSED(flags))
{
    // Associate the appropriate frame with this view.
    m_frame = GetMainFrame();
    SetFrame(m_frame);
    m_frame->GetCanvas()->SetView(this);

    // Make sure the document manager knows that this is the
    // current view.
    Activate(true);

    // Initialize the edit menu Undo and Redo items
    doc->GetCommandProcessor()->SetEditMenu(m_frame->GetEditMenu());
    doc->GetCommandProcessor()->Initialize();

    return true;
}

// This function is used for default print/preview
// as well as drawing on the screen.
void DoodleView::OnDraw(wxDC *dc)
{
    dc->SetFont(*wxNORMAL_FONT);
    dc->SetPen(*wxBLACK_PEN);

    wxList::compatibility_iterator node = ((DoodleDocument
*)GetDocument())->GetDoodleSegments().GetFirst();
    while (node)
    {
        DoodleSegment *seg = (DoodleSegment *)node->GetData();
        seg->Draw(dc);
        node = node->GetNext();
    }
}

void DoodleView::OnUpdate(wxView *WXUNUSED(sender), wxObject
*WXUNUSED(hint))
{
    if (m_frame && m_frame->GetCanvas())
        m_frame->GetCanvas()->Refresh();
}

// Clean up windows used for displaying the view.
bool DoodleView::OnClose(bool WXUNUSED(deleteWindow))
{
    if (!GetDocument()->Close())
        return false;

    // Clear the canvas
    m_frame->GetCanvas()->ClearBackground();
    m_frame->GetCanvas()->SetView(NULL);

    if (m_frame)
        m_frame->SetTitle(wxTheApp->GetAppName());

    SetFrame(NULL);
```

```
    // Tell the document manager to stop routing events to the view
    Activate(false);

    return true;
}

void DoodleView::OnCut(wxCommandEvent& WXUNUSED(event))
{
    DoodleDocument *doc = (DoodleDocument *)GetDocument();
    doc->GetCommandProcessor()->Submit(
        new DoodleCommand(wxT("Cut Last Segment"), DOODLE_CUT, doc,
NULL));
}
```

Step 4: Define Your Window Classes

You will probably need to create specialized editing windows for manipulating
the data in your views. In the Doodle example, DoodleCanvas is used for displaying the data, and to intercept the relevant events, the wxWidgets event
system requires us to create a derived class. The DoodleCanvas class declaration looks like this:

```
/*
 * DoodleCanvas is the window that displays the doodle document
 */

class DoodleView;
class DoodleCanvas: public wxScrolledWindow
{
    DECLARE_EVENT_TABLE()
public:
    DoodleCanvas(wxWindow *parent, const wxPoint& pos,
                 const wxSize& size, const long style);

    /// Draws the document contents
    virtual void OnDraw(wxDC& dc);

    /// Processes mouse events
    void OnMouseEvent(wxMouseEvent& event);

    /// Set/get view
    void SetView(DoodleView* view) { m_view = view; }
    DoodleView* GetView() const { return m_view; }

protected:
    DoodleView *m_view;
};
```

DoodleCanvas contains a pointer to the view (initialized by DoodleView::OnCreate) and handles drawing and mouse events. Here's the implementation of the class.

```
/*
 * Doodle canvas implementation
 */

BEGIN_EVENT_TABLE(DoodleCanvas, wxScrolledWindow)
    EVT_MOUSE_EVENTS(DoodleCanvas::OnMouseEvent)
END_EVENT_TABLE()

// Define a constructor
DoodleCanvas::DoodleCanvas(wxWindow *parent, const wxPoint& pos,
                           const wxSize& size, const long style):
    wxScrolledWindow(parent, wxID_ANY, pos, size, style)
{
    m_view = NULL;
}

// Define the repainting behavior
void DoodleCanvas::OnDraw(wxDC& dc)
{
    if (m_view)
        m_view->OnDraw(& dc);
}

// This implements doodling behavior. Drag the mouse using
// the left button.
void DoodleCanvas::OnMouseEvent(wxMouseEvent& event)
{
    // The last position
    static int xpos = -1;
    static int ypos = -1;
    static DoodleSegment *currentSegment = NULL;

    if (!m_view)
        return;

    wxClientDC dc(this);
    DoPrepareDC(dc);

    dc.SetPen(*wxBLACK_PEN);

    // Take into account scrolling
    wxPoint pt(event.GetLogicalPosition(dc));

    if (currentSegment && event.LeftUp())
    {
        if (currentSegment->GetLines().GetCount() == 0)
        {
            delete currentSegment;
            currentSegment = NULL;
        }
        else
        {
```

```
            // We've got a valid segment on mouse left up, so store it.
            DoodleDocument *doc = (DoodleDocument *) GetView()-
>GetDocument();

            doc->GetCommandProcessor()->Submit(
                new DoodleCommand(wxT("Add Segment"), DOODLE_ADD, doc,
currentSegment));

            GetView()->GetDocument()->Modify(true);
            currentSegment = NULL;
        }
    }

    if (xpos > -1 && ypos > -1 && event.Dragging())
    {
        if (!currentSegment)
            currentSegment = new DoodleSegment;

        DoodleLine *newLine = new DoodleLine;
        newLine->m_x1 = xpos;
        newLine->m_y1 = ypos;
        newLine->m_x2 = pt.x;
        newLine->m_y2 = pt.y;
        currentSegment->GetLines().Append(newLine);

        dc.DrawLine(xpos, ypos, pt.x, pt.y);
    }
    xpos = pt.x;
    ypos = pt.y;
}
```

As you can see, when the mouse handling code detects that user has drawn a segment, a DOODLE_ADD command is submitted to the document, where it is stored in case the user wants to undo (and perhaps later redo) the command. In the process, the segment is added to the document's segment list.

Step 5: Use *wxDocManager* and *wxDocTemplate*

You will need to create an instance of wxDocManager that exists for the lifetime of the application. wxDocManager has overall responsibility for handling documents and views.

You will also need at least one wxDocTemplate object. This class is used to model the relationship between a document class and a view class. The application creates a document template object for each document/view pair, and the list of document templates managed by the wxDocManager instance is used to create documents and views. Each document template knows what file filters and default extension are appropriate for a document/view combination and how to create a document or view.

For example, if there were two views of the data in a Doodle document—a graphical view and a list of segments—then we would create two view classes (DoodleGraphicView and DoodleListView). We would also need two document templates, one for the graphical view and another for the list view. You would pass the same document class and default file extension to both document templates, but each would be passed a different view class. When the user clicks on the *Open* menu item, the file selector is displayed with a list of possible file filters, one for each wxDocTemplate. Selecting the filter selects the wxDocTemplate, and when a file is selected, that template will be used for creating a document and view. Similarly, when the user selects *New*, wxWidgets will offer a choice of templates if there is more than one. In our Doodle example, where there is only one document type and one view type, a single document template is constructed, and dialogs will be appropriately simplified.

You can store a pointer to a wxDocManager in your application class, but there's usually no need to store a pointer to the template objects because these are managed by wxDocManager. Here's the DoodleApp class declaration:

```
/*
 * Declare an application class
 */

class DoodleApp: public wxApp
{
public:
    DoodleApp();

    /// Called on app initialization
    virtual bool OnInit();

    /// Called on app exit
    virtual int OnExit();

private:
    wxDocManager* m_docManager;
};

DECLARE_APP(DoodleApp)
```

In the DoodleApp implementation, the wxDocManager object is created in OnInit, along with a document template object associating the DoodleDocument and DoodleView classes. We pass to the template object the document manager, a template description, a file filter to use in file dialogs, a default directory to use in file dialogs (here it's empty), a default extension for the document (drw), unique type names for the document and view classes, and finally the class information for document and view classes. The DoodleApp class implementation is shown in the following.

```
IMPLEMENT_APP(DoodleApp)

DoodleApp::DoodleApp()
```

```
{
    m_docManager = NULL;
}

bool DoodleApp::OnInit()
{
    // Create a document manager
    m_docManager = new wxDocManager;

    // Create a template relating drawing documents to their views
    (void) new wxDocTemplate(m_docManager, wxT("Doodle"), wxT("*.drw"),
wxT(""), wxT("drw"), wxT("Doodle Doc"), wxT("Doodle View"),
        CLASSINFO(DoodleDocument), CLASSINFO(DoodleView));

    // Register the drawing document type on Mac
#ifdef __WXMAC__
    wxFileName::MacRegisterDefaultTypeAndCreator( wxT("drw") , 'WXMB' ,
'WXMA' ) ;
#endif

    // If we have only got one window, we only get to edit
    // one document at a time.
    m_docManager->SetMaxDocsOpen(1);

    // Create the main frame window
    DoodleFrame* frame = new DoodleFrame(m_docManager, NULL, wxID_ANY,
wxT("Doodle Sample"), wxPoint(0, 0), wxSize(500, 400),
wxDEFAULT_FRAME_STYLE);

    frame->Centre(wxBOTH);
    frame->Show(true);

    SetTopWindow(frame);
    return true;
}

int DoodleApp::OnExit()
{
    delete m_docManager;
    return 0;
}
```

Because we only show one document at a time, we need to tell the document manager this by calling SetMaxDocsOpen with a value of 1. To cater for Mac OS, we also add the MacRegisterDefaultTypeAndCreator call to tell Mac OS about this document type. The function takes the file extension, a document type identifier, and a creator identifier. (It is customary to choose four-letter identifiers for the document type and the application that creates it. You can optionally register them on the Apple web site to avoid potential clashes.)

For the complete Doodle application, please see examples/chap19/doodle.

OTHER DOCUMENT/VIEW CAPABILITIES

We've shown a simple example that demonstrates the essential steps you need to follow for a complete document-centric application. This section presents further tips on using the document/view framework.

Standard Identifiers

The document/view system has default behavior for the following standard identifiers: wxID_OPEN, wxID_CLOSE, wxID_CLOSE_ALL, wxID_REVERT, wxID_NEW, wxID_SAVE, wxID_SAVEAS, wxID_UNDO, wxID_REDO, wxID_PRINT, and wxID_PREVIEW. Use these identifiers in your menu bars and toolbars to take full advantage of the framework. The functions that handle these identifiers are mostly implemented in wxDocManager: for example, OnFileOpen, OnFileClose, and OnUndo. These handlers then call appropriate functions in the currently active document. If you want, you can override these commands in your frame class or in a class derived from wxDocManager, but this is not usually necessary.

Printing and Previewing

By default, wxID_PRINT and wxID_PREVIEW use the standard wxDocPrintout class to implement printing and print preview, taking advantage of wxView::OnDraw if implemented. However, this has very limited functionality—it only copes with a single-page document—so you're likely to want to create your own wxPrintout class and override the standard handlers for wxID_PRINT and wxID_PREVIEW. The quickest method is to use the wxHtmlEasyPrinting class, as described in "HTML Printing" in Chapter 12, "Advanced Window Classes."

File History

When your application initializes, you can load the file history shown at the bottom of the *File* menu from a wxConfig object with wxDocManager::File HistoryLoad and save it in your application cleanup with wxDocManager::FileHistorySave. For example, to load the file history, type the following:

```
// Load the file history
wxConfig config(wxT("MyApp"), wxT("MyCompany"));
config.SetPath(wxT("FileHistory"));
m_docManager->FileHistoryLoad(config);
config.SetPath(wxT("/"));
```

If you load the file history before you create your main frame and its menu bar, you will need to explicitly call wxDocManager::FileHistoryAddFilesToMenu.

If you want, you can use the wxFileHistory class independently of the other document/view classes, or to implement file history in a different way (for example, if your application requires a separate file history for each document frame).

Explicit Document Creation

Sometimes you may want to create a document explicitly in your document—for example, if you are opening the last document that was viewed. You can open an existing document like this:

```
wxDocument* doc = m_docManager->CreateDocument(filename,
                                               wxDOC_SILENT);
```

Or create a new document like this:

```
wxDocument* doc = m_docManager->CreateDocument(wxEmptyString,
                                               wxDOC_NEW);
```

In both cases, a view will be created automatically.

STRATEGIES FOR IMPLEMENTING UNDO/REDO

The way that undo/redo is implemented in your application will be determined by the nature of the document data and how the user manipulates that data. In our simple Doodle example, we only operate on one piece of data at a time, and our operations are very simple. In many applications, however, the user can apply operations to multiple objects. In this case, it's useful to introduce a further level of command granularity, perhaps called CommandState, holding the information for a particular object in the document. Your command class should maintain a list of these states and accept a list of them in the command class constructor. Do and Undo will iterate through the state list and apply the current command to each state.

One key to implementing undo/redo is noting that the user can only traverse the command history one step at a time. Therefore, your undo/redo implementation is free to take snapshots of the document state for later restoration, with the knowledge that the stored state will always be correct no matter how many times the user has gone backward or forward in the command history. All your code has to know is how to switch between "done" and "undone" states.

A common strategy is to store a copy of each document object within the command state object and also a pointer to the actual object. Do and Undo simply swap the current and stored states. Let's say the object is a shape, and the user changes the color from red to blue. The application creates a new state identical to the existing red object, but it sets the internal color attribute to blue. When the command is first executed, Do takes a copy of the current object state, applies the new command state (including the blue color) to the visible state, and repaints the object. Undo simply does the same thing. It takes a copy of the current object state, applies the current state (including red), and repaints. So code for Do and Undo is actually identical in this case. Not only that, it can be reused for other operations as well as color changes because the state of the entire object is copied. You can make this process straightforward by implementing an assignment operator and copy constructor for each class that represents an object that the user can edit.

Let's make this idea more concrete. Say we have a document of shapes, and the user can change the color of all selected shapes. We might have a command handler called ShapeView::OnChangeColor, as in the following, where a new state is created for each selected object, before being applied to the document.

```
// Changes the color of the selected shape(s)
void ShapeView::OnChangeColor(wxCommandEvent& event)
{
    wxColour col = GetSelectedColor();

    ShapeCommand* cmd = new ShapeCommand(wxT("Change color"));

    ShapeArray arrShape;
    for (size_t i = 0; i < GetSelectedShapes().GetCount(); i++)
    {
        Shape* oldShape = GetSelectedShapes()[i];
        Shape* newShape = new Shape(*oldShape);
        newShape->SetColor(col);
        ShapeState* state = new ShapeState(SHAPE_COLOR, newShape,
oldShape);
        cmd->AddState(state);
    }
    GetDocument()->GetCommandProcessor()->SubmitCommand(cmd);
}
```

Because the implementation for this kind of state change is the same for both Do and Undo, we have a single DoAndUndo function in the ShapeState class, where we do state swapping:

```
// Incomplete implementation of the state's DoAndRedo:
// for some commands, do and undo share the same code
void ShapeState::DoAndUndo(bool undo)
{
    switch (m_cmd)
    {
    case SHAPE_COLOR:
    case SHAPE_TEXT:
    case SHAPE_SIZE:
        {
            Shape* tmp = new Shape(m_actualShape);
            (* m_actualShape) = (* m_storedShape);
            (* m_storedShape) = (* tmp);
            delete tmp;

            // Do redraw here
            ...
            break;
        }
    }
}
```

In this code, we have not shown the `ShapeCommand::Do` and `ShapeCommand::Redo` functions, which iterate through all the states for this command.

SUMMARY

We've seen how taking advantage of the document/view model can simplify an application's implementation, letting wxWidgets handle much of the house-keeping such as showing file dialogs and creating document and view objects. You should now also have an understanding of how to implement undo/redo in wxWidgets—a facility that should be built in at an early stage because trying to bolt it on afterwards will involve a considerable amount of rewriting.

In our final chapter, we discuss a number of ways in which you can refine your application.

CHAPTER 20

Perfecting Your Application

There's a world of difference between an application that does its job adequately and an application that's intuitive and enjoyable to use. For internal use, a basic, no-frills application may be adequate, but if you're planning on distributing your brainchild to a wide audience, you'll want it to be as compelling and easy to use as applications from the biggest software publishers. You'll need to conform to some fundamental expectations and standards, such as the provision of configuration dialogs and online help. In this final chapter, we'll cover the following topics to help you polish your application:

- ☞ **Single instance or multiple instances?** How you can prevent "clones" of your application from proliferating.
- ☞ **Modifying event handling.** How to change the order in which events are processed.
- ☞ **Reducing flicker.** How to improve the visual quality of your application by cutting down on annoying flicker.
- ☞ **Implementing online help.** Suggestions for providing a variety of help for your users.
- ☞ **Parsing the command line.** Give your users more control over your application with command-line options and switches.
- ☞ **Storing application resources.** Ways to package files needed by your application.
- ☞ **Invoking other applications.** From simple program execution to capturing another process's input and output.
- ☞ **Managing application settings.** The use of wxConfig to save and load settings, and tips for presenting settings.
- ☞ **Application installation.** Suggestions for how users can easily install your application on the three major platforms.
- ☞ **Following UI design guidelines.** Some observations about conforming to the design recommendations on each platform.

SINGLE INSTANCE OR MULTIPLE INSTANCES?

Depending on the nature of your application, you might either want to allow users to keep invoking multiple instances of the application, or reuse the existing instance when the user tries to relaunch the application or open more than one document from the system's file manager. It's quite common to give users the option of running the application in single-instance or multiple-instance mode, depending on their working habits. One problem with allowing multiple instances is that the order in which the instances write their configuration data (usually when the application exits) is undefined, so user settings might be lost. It might also confuse novice users who don't realize they are launching new instances of the application. The behavior of allowing multiple applications to be launched is the default on all platforms (except when launching applications and opening documents via the Finder on Mac OS), so you will need to write additional code if you want to disable multiple instances.

On Mac OS (only), opening multiple documents using the same instance is easy. Override the `MacOpenFile` function, taking a `wxString` file name argument, which will be called when a document associated with this application is opened from the Finder. If the application is not already running, Mac OS will run it first before calling `MacOpenFile` (unlike on other platforms, it does not pass the file name in the command-line arguments). If you are using document/view, you might not need to provide this function because the default implementation on Mac OS X is as follows:

```
void wxApp::MacOpenFile(const wxString& fileName)
{
    wxDocManager* dm = wxDocManager::GetDocumentManager() ;
    if ( dm )
        dm->CreateDocument(fileName, wxDOC_SILENT) ;
}
```

However, even on Mac OS, this will not prevent the user from running the application multiple times if launching the executable directly, as opposed to opening an associated document. One way in which you can detect and forbid more than one instance from being run is by using the `wxSingleInstanceChecker` class. Create an object of this class that persists for the lifetime of the instance, and in your `OnInit`, call `IsAnotherRunning`. If this returns `true`, you can quit immediately, perhaps after alerting the user. For example:

```
bool MyApp::OnInit()
{
    const wxString name = wxString::Format(wxT("MyApp-%s"),
                            wxGetUserId().c_str());
    m_checker = new wxSingleInstanceChecker(name);
    if ( m_checker->IsAnotherRunning() )
```

```
                  {
                      wxLogError(_("Program already running, aborting."));
                      return false;
                  }

                  ... more initializations ...

                  return true;
          }
          int MyApp::OnExit()
          {
                  delete m_checker;

                  return 0;
          }
```

But what if you want to bring the existing instance to the front or open a file that was passed to the second instance in the first instance? In general, this requires the instances to be able to communicate with each other. We can use wxWidgets' high-level interprocess communication classes to do this.

In the following example, we'll set up communication between instances of the sample application and allow secondary instances to ask the first instance to either open a file or raise itself to indicate that the user has requested the application to open. The following declares a connection class for use by both instances, a server class for the original instance to listen for connections from other instances, and a client class that is used by subsequent instances for communicating with the original instance.

```
#include "wx/ipc.h"

// Server class, for listening to connection requests

class stServer: public wxServer
{
public:
    wxConnectionBase *OnAcceptConnection(const wxString& topic);
};

// Client class, to be used by subsequent instances in OnInit

class stClient: public wxClient
{
public:
    stClient() {};
    wxConnectionBase *OnMakeConnection() { return new stConnection; }
};

// Connection class, for use by both communicating instances

class stConnection : public wxConnection
{
public:
    stConnection() {}
```

```
    ~stConnection() {}

    bool OnExecute(const wxString& topic, wxChar*data, int size,
                   wxIPCFormat format);
};
```

OnAcceptConnection is called within the original (server) instance when the client tries to make the connection. We need to check that there are no modal dialogs running in this instance because when a modal dialog is open, there should be no other activity in the application that might require a user's attention.

```
// Accepts a connection from another instance

wxConnectionBase *stServer::OnAcceptConnection(const wxString& topic)
{
    if (topic.Lower() == wxT("myapp"))
    {
        // Check that there are no modal dialogs active
        wxWindowList::Node* node = wxTopLevelWindows.GetFirst();
        while (node)
        {
            wxDialog* dialog = wxDynamicCast(node->GetData(), wxDialog);
            if (dialog && dialog->IsModal())
            {
                return false;
            }

            node = node->GetNext();
        }
        return new stConnection();
    }
    else
        return NULL;
}
```

OnExecute is called when the client application calls Execute on its connection object. OnExecute can have an empty data argument, in which case the application should just raise its main window. Otherwise, the application should determine whether the file is already open and raise the associated window if so, or open the document if not.

```
// Opens a file passed from another instance

bool stConnection::OnExecute(const wxString& WXUNUSED(topic),
                             wxChar *data,
                             int WXUNUSED(size),
                             wxIPCFormat WXUNUSED(format))
{
    stMainFrame* frame = wxDynamicCast(wxGetApp().GetTopWindow(),
stMainFrame);
    wxString filename(data);
    if (filename.IsEmpty())
```

```
    {
        // Just raise the main window
        if (frame)
            frame->Raise();
    }
    else
    {
        // Check if the filename is already open,
        // and raise that instead.
        wxNode* node = wxGetApp().GetDocManager()-
>GetDocuments().GetFirst();
        while (node)
        {
            MyDocument* doc = wxDynamicCast(node->GetData(),MyDocument);
            if (doc && doc->GetFilename() == filename)
            {
                if (doc->GetFrame())
                    doc->GetFrame()->Raise();
                return true;
            }
            node = node->GetNext();
        }
        wxGetApp().GetDocManager()->CreateDocument(
                                    filename, wxDOC_SILENT);
    }

    return true;
}
```

In OnInit, the application will check for multiple instances using wxSingleInstanceChecker as usual. If no other instances are found, the instance can set itself up as a server, waiting for requests from future instances. If another instance *was* found, a connection is made to the other instance, and the second instance asks the first to open a file or raise its main window before exiting. Here's the code to do this:

```
bool MyApp::OnInit()
{
    wxString cmdFilename; // code to initialize this omitted

    ...

    m_singleInstanceChecker = new wxSingleInstanceChecker(wxT("MyApp"));

    // If using a single instance, use IPC to
    // communicate with the other instance
    if (!m_singleInstanceChecker->IsAnotherRunning())
    {
        // Create a new server
        m_server = new stServer;

        if ( !m_server->Create(wxT("myapp")) )
        {
            wxLogDebug(wxT("Failed to create an IPC service."));
        }
    }
```

```
        else
        {
            wxLogNull logNull;

            // OK, there IS another one running, so try to connect to it
            // and send it any filename before exiting.
            stClient* client = new stClient;

            // ignored under DDE, host name in TCP/IP based classes
            wxString hostName = wxT("localhost");

            // Create the connection
            wxConnectionBase* connection =
                        client->MakeConnection(hostName,
                                    wxT("myapp"), wxT("MyApp"));

            if (connection)
            {
                // Ask the other instance to open a file or raise itself
                connection->Execute(cmdFilename);
                connection->Disconnect();
                delete connection;
            }
            else
            {
                wxMessageBox(wxT("Sorry, the existing instance may be
                too busy too respond.\nPlease close any open dialogs and
retry."),
                        wxT("My application"), wxICON_INFORMATION¦wxOK);
            }
            delete client;
            return false;
        }

        ...

        return true;
}
```

If you want to find out more about the interprocess communication classes
used here, another example is provided by the standalone wxWidgets Help
Viewer, which you can find in utils/helpview/src in your wxWidgets distribution. This application responds to requests by an application to view a help
file. See also samples/ipc and the wxWidgets class reference for wxServer,
wxClient, and wxConnection.

MODIFYING EVENT HANDLING

Normally, wxWidgets sends an event to the window (or other event handler)
that generated it. If it's a command event, it might work its way up the window hierarchy before being processed (see Appendix H, "How wxWidgets
Processes Events," for details). For example, clicking on a copy toolbar button
will cause the toolbar event table to be searched, then the frame that contains it,

and then the application object. Although this may work fine if you support only one kind of copy command, there is a problem if you also want the copy command to apply both to your main editing window (say a drawing application) and to any focused text controls in the main window, for example. The text controls will never get copy commands from the toolbar button (or menu item) because it is wired to a custom event handler. In this case, it would be more appropriate to send the command to the *focused* control first. Then, if the focused control implements this command (such as wxID_COPY), it will be processed. If it doesn't, then the command will rise up the window hierarchy until it gets to the custom wxID_COPY event handler. The end result will be a more natural way of working, with commands applying to the data that the user is currently editing.

We can override the main frame's ProcessEvent function to catch command events and redirect them to the focused control (if any), as follows:

```
bool MainFrame::ProcessEvent(wxEvent& event)
{
    static wxEvent* s_lastEvent = NULL;

    // Check for infinite recursion
    if (& event == s_lastEvent)
        return false;

    if (event.IsCommandEvent() &&
        !event.IsKindOf(CLASSINFO(wxChildFocusEvent)) &&
        !event.IsKindOf(CLASSINFO(wxContextMenuEvent)))
    {
        s_lastEvent = & event;

        wxControl *focusWin = wxDynamicCast(FindFocus(), wxControl);
        bool success = false;

        if (focusWin)
            success = focusWin->GetEventHandler()
                                ->ProcessEvent(event);
        if (!success)
            success = wxFrame::ProcessEvent(event);

        s_lastEvent = NULL;
        return success;
    }
    else
    {
        return wxFrame::ProcessEvent(event);
    }
}
```

Currently, this is most useful when the focused control is a wxTextCtrl because for this control (on most platforms), wxWidgets supplies standard UI update and command handlers for common commands, including wxID_COPY, wxID_CUT, wxID_PASTE, wxID_UNDO, and wxID_REDO. However, you can always implement these handlers for arbitrary controls in your application or subclasses of existing wxWidgets controls such as wxStyledTextCtrl (see examples/chap20/pipedprocess for a wxStyledTextCtrl implementation enhanced in this way).

REDUCING FLICKER

Flicker is a perennial annoyance in GUI programming. Often an application will need some tweaking to reduce it; here are some tips that might help.

On Windows, if your window is using the wxFULL_REPAINT_ON_RESIZE style, try removing it. This will cause the repaint area to be restricted to only the parts of the window "damaged" by resizing, so less erasing and redrawing is done. Otherwise, even if the window was resized a tiny amount, the whole window will be refreshed, causing flicker. However, this will not work if the appearance of your window contents depends on the size because the whole window will require updating.

You may sometimes need to use the wxCLIP_CHILDREN style on Windows to prevent a window refresh from affecting its children. The style has no effect on other platforms.

When you are drawing in a scrolled window, you can do quite a lot to improve refresh speed and reduce flicker. First, optimize the way you find the appropriate data to draw: you need a way to gather just the information that is in the current view (see wxWindow::GetViewStart and wxWindow::GetClientSize), and in your paint handler, you should also be able to eliminate the graphics that are not in the update region (wxWindow::GetUpdateRegion). You need data structures that can get you to the start of the view quickly before you start drawing. You may be able to calculate that position from your graphics (rather than search), for example if you have columns with constant width. A linked list or array should be fairly fast to search. If it's time-consuming to calculate the current position, then perhaps you can use a caching mechanism to store the current list position for the last set of data displayed, and then you can simply scan back or forward to find the data at the start of the current scroll position. You can keep a tally of the window position for each piece of data so that you don't have to recalculate the whole thing from the start to find where the data should be drawn.

When implementing scrolling graphics, you can use wxWindow::ScrollWindow to physically move the pixels on the window, and this will mean that only the remaining "dirty" area of the window will need refreshing, which will further reduce flickering. (wxScrolledWindow already does this for you, by default.) GetUpdateRegion will reflect the smaller amount of screen that you need to update.

As mentioned in Chapter 5, "Drawing And, Printing," you may want to define your own erase background handler and leave it empty to stop the framework from clearing the background itself. Then you can draw the whole graphic (including as much of the background as necessary) on top of the old one without the flashing caused by clearing the entire background before drawing the content. Use `wxWindow::SetBackgroundStyle` with `wxBG_STYLE_CUSTOM` to tell wxWidgets not to automatically erase the background. Chapter 5 also discusses use of `wxBufferedDC` and `wxBufferedPaintDC`, which you can use in combination with the other techniques mentioned here.

Another problem is inefficiency and flicker caused by doing many updates to a window in quick succession. wxWidgets provides `wxWindow::Freeze` and `wxWindow::Thaw` to switch off updates while code is executed between these function calls. For example, you might want to use this when adding a lot of lines to a text control one by one or appending many items to a list box. When `Thaw` is called, the window will normally be completely refreshed. `Freeze` and `Thaw` are implemented on Windows and Mac OS X for `wxWindow` and on GTK+ for `wxTextCtrl`. You can also implement it for your own window classes to avoid doing unnecessary processing and updating (our `wxThumbnailCtrl` example from Chapter 12, "Advanced Window Classes," does this; see `examples/chap12/thumbnail`).

IMPLEMENTING ONLINE HELP

Although you should make your application as intuitive as possible so that the user rarely has to resort to the manual, it's important to supply online help for all but the simplest application. You could supply it as a PDF file or even an HTML file to be viewed by the user's favorite browser, but it will make a much better impression if you use a special-purpose help system and link to appropriate topics from all your dialogs and from your main window.

wxWidgets has the concept of *help controller*, a class that your application uses to load help files and show topics. Several help controller classes are supported:

☞ `wxWinHelpController`, for controlling RTF-based WinHelp files on Windows (extension `hlp`). This format is deprecated, and new applications should use `wxCHMHelpController`.

☞ `wxCHMHelpController`, for controlling MS HTML Help files on Windows (extension `chm`).

☞ `wxWinceHelpController`, for controlling Windows CE Help files (extension `htm`).

☞ `wxHtmlHelpController`, for controlling wxWidgets HTML Help files on all platforms (extension `htb`).

`wxHtmlHelpController` is different from the others in that instead of merely being a wrapper for an external help viewer, it is part of an entire help system implementation, and the help window resides in the same process as the application. If you want to use the wxWidgets HTML Help viewer as a separate process, compile HelpView in `utils/src/helpview` in your wxWidgets distribution. The files `remhelp.h` and `remhelp.cpp` implement a remote help controller (wxRemoteHtmlHelpController) that you can link with your application to control the HelpView instance.

Note that at the time of writing, there is no special help controller class for Mac OS X help files. You can use wxWidgets HTML Help files on this platform.

Figure 20-1 and Figure 20-2 show the same topic displayed in MS HTML Help and wxWidgets HTML Help viewers under Windows. The two provide similar functionality: HTML content on the right, and on the left, a hierarchy of topics, an index of topic names, and a keyword search facility. In addition, wxWidgets HTML Help can load multiple help files.

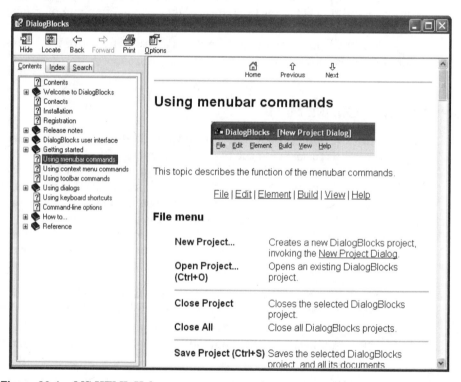

Figure 20-1   MS HTML Help

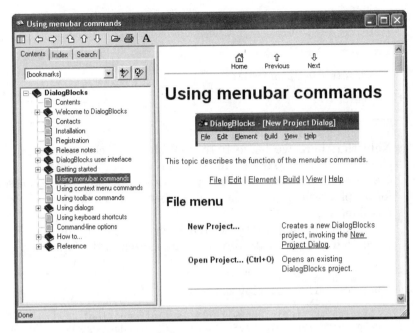

Figure 20-2   wxWidgets HTML Help

Using a Help Controller

Normally you will create a help controller object that will last the lifetime of the application instance, probably as a pointer member of your application class (create the object in `OnInit` and delete it in `OnExit`). Make it a pointer so that you can delete it fully in `OnExit` because some help controller implementations rely on a dynamic library loading class that is not available when the application object is being deleted. Then call `Initialize` with the name of the help file. You can omit the file extension, and wxWidgets will supply the relevant one for the current platform. For example:

```
#include "wx/help.h"
#include "wx/fs_zip.h"

bool MyApp::OnInit()
{
    ...

    // Required for wxWidgets HTML help
    wxFileSystem::AddHandler(new wxZipFSHandler);

    m_helpController = new wxHelpController;
    m_helpController->Initialize(helpFilePath);

    ...
```

```
    return true;
}

int MyApp::OnExit()
{
    delete m_helpController;
    ...
    return 0;
}
```

Note that here we leave it to wxWidgets to choose the appropriate help class: wxHelpController is an alias for wxCHMHelpController on Windows and wxHtmlHelpController on other platforms. You can use wxHtmlHelpController for all platforms if you want, but it's better to use a native help viewer when possible.

When the help controller has been successfully initialized, you can show the help to the user with functions illustrated in the following:

```
// Show the contents
m_helpController->DisplayContents();

// Display the topic whose title is "Introduction"
m_helpController->DisplaySection(wxT("Introduction"));

// Display the given HTML topic within the help file
m_helpController->DisplaySection(wxT("wx.html"));

// Display the given topic by ID (WinHelp, MS HTML Help only)
m_helpController->DisplaySection(500);

// Search for a keyword
m_helpController->KeywordSearch(wxT("Getting started"));
```

Typically, you'll want to call DisplayContents from the event handler for a menu item *Help Contents* in the application's *Help* menu. You might have other important topics listed on the *Help* menu, and you can display them via DisplaySection. If you want to use the topic title with DisplaySection, all the topic titles in the help file must be unique.

You also might want to add a *Help* button to all non-trivial custom dialogs in your application to show an explanation of the current dialog and its controls. However, there is a catch here: showing help from a modal dialog does not work on all platforms. Where the help viewer is an external application (for example, when using wxCHMHelpController on Windows), you can display help from a modal dialog. But when the help controller shows a modeless window that is part of the same program, as with wxHtmlHelpController, you have to be careful because in general, you cannot display a modeless window (such as a frame) from within a modal dialog. By definition, a modal dialog won't enable you to switch to another arbitrary window except for another modal dialog. If you use wxGTK, there is a workaround that allows this to work for `wxHtmlHelpController`, but on Mac OS X, you need to either use an external help viewer (such as HelpView as mentioned earlier) or show the help in a modal dialog. The latter method is described in the next section.

Extended wxWidgets HTML Help

The wxWidgets HTML Help system is great, but it does have a couple of limitations. Firstly, it can only display help in its own frame, so it can't be used for embedded help, such as in a tab on your main window. Secondly, as a result of the previous limitation, it doesn't address the problem of displaying a modeless help window from a modal dialog.

To overcome these limitations, there is a variant of wxWidgets HTML Help that implements the help viewer as a window that can be shown as a child of any window. You can copy it from `examples/chap20/htmlctrlex` on the CD-ROM or download it from `ftp://biolpc22.york.ac.uk/pub/contrib/helpctrlex`.

If you compile it with your application, you can embed `wxHtmlHelp WindowEx` in your application and control it with `wxHtmlHelpControllerEx` before using the usual controller functions for displaying help. Here's an example of embedding:

```cpp
#include "helpwinex.h"
#include "helpctrlex.h"

bool MyApp::OnInit()
{
    ...

    m_embeddedHelpController = new wxHtmlHelpControllerEx;
    m_embeddedHelpWindow = new wxHtmlHelpWindowEx;
    m_embeddedHelpWindow->SetController(m_embeddedHelpController);
    m_embeddedHelpController->SetHelpWindow(m_embeddedHelpWindow);
    m_embeddedHelpController->UseConfig(config, wxT("EmbeddedHelp"));

    m_embeddedHelpWindow->Create(parentWindow,
        wxID_ANY, wxDefaultPosition, wxSize(200, 100),
        wxTAB_TRAVERSAL|wxNO_BORDER, wxHF_DEFAULT_STYLE);

    m_embeddedHelpController->AddBook(wxT("book1.htb"));
    m_embeddedHelpController->AddBook(wxT("book2.htb"));

    return true;
}

int MyApp::OnExit(void)
{
    if (m_embeddedHelpController)
    {
        m_embeddedHelpController->SetHelpWindow(NULL);
        delete m_embeddedHelpController;
    }
    ...
    return 0;
}
```

To solve the modal dialog problem, you can use the wxModalHelp class to show a topic in a modal dialog. When the user has finished browsing the help, clicking on the *Close* button takes control back to the previous dialog. The following code is all that's needed to show a topic:

```
wxModalHelp help(parentWindow, helpFile, topic);
```

It would be inconvenient to make a distinction between modal help and normal help throughout your application, so here's a function that you can use to make life easier:

```
// Shows help using normal help controller or
// modal help controller if modalParent is non-NULL
void MyApp::ShowHelp(const wxString& topic, wxWindow* modalParent)
{
#if USE_MODAL_HELP
    if (modalParent)
    {
        wxString helpFile(wxGetApp().GetFullAppPath(wxT("myapp")));
        wxModalHelp help(modalParent, helpFile, topic);
    }
    else
#endif
    {
        if (topic.IsEmpty())
            m_helpController->DisplayContents();
        else
            m_helpController->DisplaySection(topic);
    }
}
```

The symbol USE_MODAL_HELP should be defined for those platforms that use wxHtmlHelpController. When you want to show help from a modal dialog, pass a pointer to the dialog to ShowHelp, and if necessary, it will be shown in its own modal dialog. When help isn't shown from a modal dialog, just pass NULL as the second argument of ShowHelp.

Authoring Help

Most help files nowadays are based on HTML. To make it even easier to author help on multiple platforms, wxWidgets HTML Help uses the same project, contents, and keyword files as the input to a MS HTML Help file. This way, you only have to deal with one set of files for all platforms. These are the files you'll need to create your help file:

☞ A set of HTML files, one per topic.

☞ A contents file (extension hhc) with an XML description of the topic hierarchy.

☞ An optional keyword file (extension hhk) that maps words and phrases to HTML topics.

☞ A project file (extension hhp) that describes all the other files in the project and specifies project options.

You then compile the project file into an MS HTML Help file (extension chm) or a wxWidgets HTML Help file (extension htb). For the former, use Microsoft's HTML Help Workshop, which can be invoked either from the command line or as a GUI application. For the latter, simply use your favorite zip utility to make a zip archive, renaming it with an htb extension.

Although you could write your help file by hand, it's much more convenient to use a tool. You can use a tool intended for MS HTML Help file creation, but be aware that it may output HTML that wxWidgets HTML Help cannot recognize. Anthemion Software's HelpBlocks is the only tool that specifically targets both MS HTML Help and wxWidgets HTML Help and assists you with writing HTML and organizing keywords.

To get a feel for a good help file structure, look at the help in other applications. You might consider including the following topics: *Contents*, *Welcome*, *Contacts*, *Installation*, *Registration*, *Release notes*, *Tutorial*, *Using menu commands*, *Using toolbar commands*, *Using dialogs* (with descriptions of all dialogs as subtopics), *Using keyboard shortcuts*, *Command-line options*, and *Troubleshooting*.

Remember that topics you show from the application should be designed to be standalone. Other topics, such as a tutorial, read better in a more linear fashion.

Other Ways to Provide Help

You might think of other ways to offer the user online help, perhaps using the HTML classes that wxWidgets provides. For example, Anthemion Software's Writer's Café has a modal welcome dialog with a small number of suggested options, implemented using a wxHtmlWindow. These include showing a Quick Tour consisting of a number of HTML screens to quickly give the user an idea of what the product can do (see Figure 20-3). The advantage of doing it this way is immediacy. Novice users are guided along a fairly narrow path initially, and they do not have to find their way around a full help system with ample opportunities for getting lost and confused.

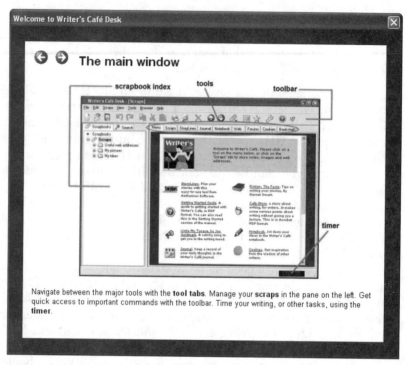

Figure 20-3   Quick Tour dialog in Writer's Café

Another popular method for providing online help is the opening tip. This is great for educating the user about the product's functionality in palatable chunks. As mentioned in Chapter 8, "Using Standard Dialogs," wxWidgets has a function `wxShowTip` that takes a parent window, a `wxTipProvider` pointer to tell wxWidgets where to find the tips, and a boolean for the initial value of a *Show Tips at Startup* check box. For example:

```
#include "wx/tipdlg.h"
...
m_tipProvider = wxCreateFileTipProvider(tipFilename, currentTip);
wxShowTip(parent, m_tipProvider, showAtStart);
```

Context-Sensitive Help and Tooltips

If possible, an application should provide context-sensitive help and the option of tooltips for controls. A tooltip is a little descriptive window that pops up over a control as the mouse pointer hovers over it. Context-sensitive help is similar, but the descriptive window is invoked by the user clicking on a button or menu item to initiate the help and then clicking on the window of interest. These topics are discussed in more detail in Chapter 9, "Creating Custom Dialogs," in the context of help for dialogs, but you can equally set context-sensitive help for arbitrary windows. For example, applications often have a *What's This?* item on the *Help* menu and toolbar, which enables the user to click on a window or control in the main window for further details. You don't have to restrict yourself to the way help is displayed by default: you can derive your own class from wxHelpProvider and implement ShowHelp yourself.

Some help controllers are able to display the context-sensitive help in a more "native" way than the default behavior. If you are using wxCHMHelpController, let wxWidgets use this help controller's context-sensitive help implementation, in the following way:

```
#include "wx/cshelp.h"

m_helpController = new wxCHMHelpController;
wxHelpProvider::Set(
        new wxHelpControllerHelpProvider(m_helpController));
```

The wxHelpControllerHelpProvider instance will use the help controller's DisplayTextPopup function to display context-sensitive help.

Note that context-sensitive help is not in the Mac OS X style guide, and so should be omitted on this platform.

Menu Help

When you append items to a menu, you have the option of specifying a help string. If the menu is part of a menu bar, and the menu bar's frame has a status bar, an item's help string will be displayed in the status bar when the mouse is over that item. You can set the status pane in which the help will be displayed using wxFrame::SetStatusBarPane (a value of -1 will disable it). The behavior is implemented in wxFrame using a default wxMenuEvent handler for EVT_MENU_HIGHLIGHT_ALL, so you can reimplement it to do something different, such as showing the help in a different window.

PARSING THE COMMAND LINE

Passing commands to the application to be read on initialization is often useful, and if the application is document-oriented, you should allow files to be loaded in this way. You also might want to let the application be run from the operating system command line, for example to automate tasks from a makefile, in which case command-line options can be used to tell the application that it should be run without a user interface. Although most configuration of an application will be done via the user interface, command-line configuration options can be appropriate in some cases, such as turning on a debug mode.

wxWidgets provides the wxCmdLineParser class to make this programming task quite easy, avoiding the need to process wxApp::argc and wxApp::argv directly. The class looks for switches (such as -verbose), options (such as -debug:1), and parameters (such as "myfile.txt"). It can recognize both short and long forms of switches and options, and each item can have a help string, which will be used by Usage when writing help text to the current log target.

Here's an example, showing how to parse switches, options, and parameters:

```
#include "wx/cmdline.h"

static const wxCmdLineEntryDesc g_cmdLineDesc[] =
{
    { wxCMD_LINE_SWITCH, wxT("h"), wxT("help"),    wxT("displays help on
the command line parameters") },
    { wxCMD_LINE_SWITCH, wxT("v"), wxT("version"), wxT("print version") },
    { wxCMD_LINE_OPTION, wxT("d"), wxT("debug"), wxT("specify a debug
level") },

    { wxCMD_LINE_PARAM,  NULL, NULL, wxT("input file"),
wxCMD_LINE_VAL_STRING, wxCMD_LINE_PARAM_OPTIONAL },

    { wxCMD_LINE_NONE }
};

bool MyApp::OnInit()
{
    // Parse command line
    wxString cmdFilename;
    wxCmdLineParser cmdParser(g_cmdLineDesc, argc, argv);
    int res;
    {
        wxLogNull log;
        // Pass false to suppress auto Usage() message
        res = cmdParser.Parse(false);
    }

    // Check if the user asked for command-line help
    if (res == -1 || res > 0 || cmdParser.Found(wxT("h")))
    {
        cmdParser.Usage();
        return false;
    }

    // Check if the user asked for the version
    if (cmdParser.Found(wxT("v")))
    {
#ifndef __WXMSW__
        wxLog::SetActiveTarget(new wxLogStderr);
#endif
        wxString msg;
        wxString date(wxString::FromAscii(__DATE__));
        msg.Printf(wxT("Anthemion DialogBlocks, (c) Julian Smart, 2005
Version %.2f, %s"), wbVERSION_NUMBER, (const wxChar*) date);
```

```
            wxLogMessage(msg);
            return false;
    }

    // Check for debug level
    long debugLevel = 0;
    if (cmdParser.Found(wxT("d"), & debugLevel))
    {
    }

    // Check for a project filename
    if (cmdParser.GetParamCount() > 0)
    {
        cmdFilename = cmdParser.GetParam(0);

        // Under Windows when invoking via a document
        // in Explorer, we are passed the short form.
        // So normalize and make the long form.
        wxFileName fName(cmdFilename);
        fName.Normalize(wxPATH_NORM_LONG|wxPATH_NORM_DOTS|
                        wxPATH_NORM_TILDE|wxPATH_NORM_ABSOLUTE);
        cmdFilename = fName.GetFullPath();
    }

    ...

    return true;
}
```

The use of wxFileName for normalizing the file name is necessary because Windows sometimes passes the short form when the application is invoked from the command line.

As we noted earlier in the chapter, Mac OS X doesn't use the command line when running an application by opening an associated document; instead, wxApp::MacOpenFile is called after the application has initialized. However, the command-line method is used by other operating systems. If you intend to write a document-based application for Mac OS X and other operating systems, you should allow for both methods.

STORING APPLICATION RESOURCES

A simple application might consist of no more than an executable, but more realistically, you'll have a help file, maybe HTML files and images, and application-specific data files. Where do these things go?

Reducing the Number of Data Files

You can do several things to create a more tidy installation. Firstly, you can include XPM images in your C++ files (with #include) instead of loading them from disk. Secondly, if you are using XRC files, you can compile them into C++ using the wxrc utility in utils/wxrc in your wxWidgets distribution:

```
wxrc resources.xrc --verbose --cpp-code --output resources.cpp
```

You can then call the InitXmlResource function defined in the generated C++ file to load the resources.

Thirdly, you can archive your data files into a standard zip file and extract them using streams and virtual file systems, as explained in for data files. Include "wx/fileloc.h" and then call the class's static functions, including GetConfigDir, GetInstallDir, GetDataDir, GetLocalDataDir, and GetUserConfig Data. Refer to the wxWidgets manual for details of these functions' return values on each platform.

On Mac OS X, you'll need to create an application bundle: a file hierarchy with standard locations for the executable, data files, and so on. See later in the chapter for information on creating a bundle.

Finding the Application Path

A common request from wxWidgets developers is a function to find the path of the currently executing application to enable the application to load data that is in the same directory. There is no such function in wxWidgets, partly because it's difficult to achieve this reliably on all platforms, and partly to encourage the installation of data into standard locations (particularly on Linux). However, it can be convenient to put all the application's files in the same folder, so in examples/chap20/findapppath, you can find code for a function wxFindAppPath:

```
// Find the absolute path the application has been run from.

wxString wxFindAppPath(const wxString& argv0, const wxString& cwd,
                const wxString& appVariableName = wxEmptyString,
              .   const wxString& appName = wxEmptyString);
```

argv0 is the value of wxApp::argv[0], which on some platforms gives the full pathname for the application.

cwd is the current working directory (obtained with wxGetCwd), which is a hint that can be used on some platforms.

appVariableName is the name of an environment variable, such as MYAPPDIR, that may have been set externally to indicate the application's location.

appName is the prefix used in a bundle to allow the function to check the bundle contents for application location. For example, in the case of DialogBlocks, the argument is DialogBlocks, and on Mac OS X, the function will try to return <currentdir>/DialogBlocks.app/Content/MacOS for the executable location.

Here's an example of using wxFindAppPath:

```
bool MyApp::OnInit()
{
    wxString currentDir = wxGetCwd();
    m_appDir = wxFindAppPath(argv[0], currentDir, wxT("MYAPPDIR"),
                             wxT("MyApp"));

    ...
    return true;
}
```

On Windows and Mac OS X, this reliably locates the executable path. On Unix, it works only if you run the application with the current directory set to the application directory, or if you set MYAPPDIR before running the application. To make it more reliable, the installer can itself create a wrapper script that sets MYAPPDIR and then runs the application. The user can be offered a choice of where to install the wrapper script, or it can be installed into a standard location, such as /usr/local/bin.

INVOKING OTHER APPLICATIONS

Sometimes you may want to run other applications from your own application, whether it's an external browser or another of your own applications. wxExecute is a versatile function that can be used to run a program with or without command-line arguments, synchronously or asynchronously, optionally collecting output from the launched process, or even redirecting input to and output from the process to enable the current application to interact with it.

Running an Application

Here are some simple examples of using wxExecute:

```
// Executes asychronously by default (returns immediately)
wxExecute(wxT("c:\\windows\\notepad.exe"));

// Does not return until the user has quit Notepad
wxExecute(wxT("c:\\windows\\notepad.exe c:\\temp\\temp.txt"),
          wxEXEC_SYNC);
```

Note that you can optionally enclose parameters and the executable in quotation marks, which is useful if there are spaces in the names.

Launching Documents

If you want to run an application to open an associated document, you can use the wxMimeTypesManager class on Windows and Linux. You can find out the file type associated with the extension and then use it to get the required command to pass to wxExecute. For example, to view an HTML file:

```
wxString url = wxT("c:\\home\\index.html");
bool ok = false;
wxFileType *ft = wxTheMimeTypesManager->
                    GetFileTypeFromExtension(wxT("html"));
if ( ft )
{
    wxString cmd;
    ok = ft->GetOpenCommand(&cmd,
              wxFileType::MessageParameters(url, wxEmptyString));
    delete ft;

    if (ok)
    {
        ok = (wxExecute(cmd, wxEXEC_ASYNC) != 0);
    }
}
```

Unfortunately, this doesn't work under Mac OS X because OS X uses a completely different way of associating document types with applications. For arbitrary documents, it's better to ask the Finder to open a document, and for HTML files, it's better to use the special Mac OS X function, ICLaunchURL. wxExecute is not always the best solution under Windows either, where ShellExecute may be a more effective function to use for HTML files. Even on Unix, there may be specific fallback scripts you want to use if an associated application is not found, such as htmlview.

To work around these problems, we include the files launch.h and launch.cpp in examples/chap20/launch. This implements the functions wxLaunchFile, wxViewHTMLFile, wxViewPDFFile, and wxPlaySoundFile that work on Windows, Linux, and Mac OS X.

wxLaunchFile is a general-purpose document launcher. Pass a document file name or an executable file name with or without arguments and an optional error message string that can be presented to the user if the operation fails. If an HTML file is passed, wxLaunchFile will call wxViewHTMLFile. On Mac OS X, it will use the finder to launch a document, and on other platforms, wxMimeTypesManager will be used. Note that on Mac OS X, applications will sometimes be launched such that their window is behind the current application's window. A workaround is to use the osascript command-line tool to bring the window to the front. If the application you have just launched is AcmeApp, you can call

```
wxExecute(wxT("osascript -e \"tell application \\\"AcmeApp\\\"\" -e
\"activate\" -e \"end tell\""));
```

For Linux, wxViewHTMLFile, wxViewPDFFile, and wxPlaySoundFile include fallbacks for when an associated application is not found. You may want to adjust the fallbacks to your own requirements. wxPlaySoundFile is intended for playing large audio files in a separate application; for small sound effects in your application, use wxSound instead.

Redirecting Process Input and Output

There may be times when you want to "capture" another process and allow your application (and/or its user) to control it. This can be preferable to rewriting an entire complex program just to have the functionality integrated in your application. wxExecute can help you integrate another console-based process by letting you redirect its input and output.

To do this, you pass an instance of a class derived from wxProcess to wxExecute. The instance's OnTerminate function will be called when the process terminates, and the process object can be used to extract output from or send input to the process.

You can see various examples of wxExecute usage in samples/exec in your wxWidgets distribution. We also provide an example of embedding the GDB debugger in examples/chap20/pipedprocess. We don't provide the toolbar bitmaps or compilable application, but otherwise it's complete and will work on Windows, Linux, and Mac OS X if GDB is available.

debugger.h and debugger.cpp implement a piped process and a window containing a toolbar and a text control, used for displaying debugger output and getting input from the user to send to the debugger.

textctrlex.h and textctrlex.cpp implement a control derived from wxStyledTextCtrl but with some wxTextCtrl compatibility functions and standard event handlers for copy, cut, paste, undo, and redo.

processapp.h and processapp.cpp implement an application class that can handle input from several processes in idle time.

The debugger is started with

```
DebuggerProcess *process = new DebuggerProcess (this);
m_pid = wxExecute(cmd, wxEXEC_ASYNC, process);
```

It can be killed with

```
wxKill(m_pid, wxSIGKILL, NULL, wxKILL_CHILDREN);
```

To send a command to the debugger, an internal variable is set to let the input to the process to be picked up in idle time:

```
// Send a command to the debugger
bool DebuggerWindow::SendDebugCommand(const wxString& cmd,
                                      bool needEcho)
{
    if (m_process && m_process->GetOutputStream())
    {
        wxString c = cmd;
```

```
            c += wxT("\n");

        if (needEcho)
            AddLine(cmd);

        // This simple sets m_input to be processed
        // by HasInput in OnIdle time
        m_process->SendInput(c);
        return true;
    }
    return false;
}
```

HasInput is called periodically by the application object from its idle handler
and is responsible for sending input to the process and reading output from
the standard error and standard output streams:

```
bool DebuggerProcess::HasInput()
{
    bool hasInput = false;
    static wxChar buffer[4096];

    if ( !m_input.IsEmpty() )
    {
        wxTextOutputStream os(*GetOutputStream());
        os.WriteString(m_input);
        m_input.Empty();

        hasInput = true;
    }

    if ( IsErrorAvailable() )
    {
        buffer[GetErrorStream()->Read(buffer, WXSIZEOF(buffer) -
1).LastRead()] = _T('\0');
        wxString msg(buffer);

        m_debugWindow->ReadDebuggerOutput(msg, true);

        hasInput = true;
    }

    if ( IsInputAvailable() )
    {
        buffer[GetInputStream()->Read(buffer, WXSIZEOF(buffer) -
1).LastRead()] = _T('\0');
        wxString msg(buffer);

        m_debugWindow->ReadDebuggerOutput(buffer, false);

        hasInput = true;
    }

    return hasInput;
}
```

Note a crucial difference from the code in the wxWidgets exec sample, which assumes that it can read a line at a time. This will cause a hang if a carriage return is not output by the process. The previous code uses a buffer to keep reading as much input as possible, which is safer.

The ProcessApp class can be used as a base class for your own application class, or you can copy the functions into your class. It maintains a list of processes, registered with the application instance with RegisterProcess and UnregisterProcess, and handles process input in idle time, as follows:

```
// Handle any pending input, in idle time
bool ProcessApp::HandleProcessInput()
{
    if (!HasProcesses())
        return false;

    bool hasInput = false;

    wxNode* node = m_processes.GetFirst();
    while (node)
    {
        PipedProcess* process = wxDynamicCast(node->GetData(),
PipedProcess);
        if (process && process->HasInput())
            hasInput = true;
        node = node->GetNext();
    }
    return hasInput;
}

void ProcessApp::OnIdle(wxIdleEvent& event)
{
    if (HandleProcessInput())
        event.RequestMore();
    event.Skip();
}
```

MANAGING APPLICATION SETTINGS

Most applications have options to let the user to change the program's behavior, such as toggling tooltips on and off, changing text fonts, or suppressing a splash screen. The developer must make choices about how these settings will be stored and displayed. For storage, the usual solution is to use the wxConfig family of classes, which is especially intended to store typed application settings. The choice of user interface is much more varied, and we'll explore some possibilities shortly.

Storing Settings

The configuration classes that wxWidgets provides are derived from wxConfigBase, which is where you'll find the documentation in the reference manual. On each platform, wxConfig is an alias for an appropriate class: on Windows it's wxRegConfig (using the Windows Registry), and on all other platforms it's wxFileConfig (using text files). wxIniConfig is available, using Windows 3.1-style .ini files, but this is rarely needed. wxFileConfig is available on all platforms.

wxConfig provides the overloaded functions Read and Write to read and store items of type wxString, long, double, and bool. Each item is referenced by a name comprising a list of slash-separated paths—for example, "/General/UseTooltips". By using wxConfig::SetPath, you can set the current position in the hierarchy, and subsequent references will be relative to that position if they do not have a leading slash. You can use paths to group your settings.

wxConfig constructors take an application name and vendor name, which are used to determine the location of the settings. For example:

```
#include "wx/config.h"

wxConfig config(wxT("MyApp"), wxT("Acme"));
```

wxRegConfig constructs a location from the vendor name and application name, and in the previous example, the settings will be stored under HKEY_CURRENT_USER/Software/Acme/MyApp in the Registry. Using wxFileConfig on Unix, the settings are stored by default in a file called ~/.MyApp. On Mac OS X, they are stored in ~/Library/Preferences/MyApp Preferences. This location can be changed by passing a third parameter to the wxConfig constructor.

Here are some examples of wxConfig usage:

```
// Read some values
wxString str;
if (config.Read(wxT("General/DataPath"), & str))
{
    ...
}
bool useToolTips = false;
config.Read(wxT("General/ToolTips"), & useToolTips));
long usageCount = 0;
config.Read(wxT("General/Usage"), & usageCount));

// Write some values
config.Write(wxT("General/DataPath"), str))
config.Write(wxT("General/ToolTips"), useToolTips));
config.Write(wxT("General/Usage"), usageCount));
```

You can also iterate through groups and entries, query whether a group or entry exists, and delete an entry or group, among other operations.

wxConfig can be used as a temporary way of reading and writing data that you store elsewhere in your application, or you can create an instance of wxConfig that is not deleted until the application exits. wxWidgets has the concept of a default wxConfig object, which you can set with wxConfig::Set. If present, the default wxConfig object may be used internally—for example, by the wxFontMapper class and the generic wxFileDialog implementation.

Editing Settings

If you only have a few settings to edit, an ordinary dialog may be sufficient. For a more complex application, you will need to use a number of dialogs or panels, and the most common method is to use a wxNotebook on a modal dialog, with *OK*, *Cancel*, and *Help* buttons underneath the notebook. The handler for the *Help* button will query the notebook for the current page in order to determine the appropriate help topic to display. wxWidgets provides wxPropertySheetDialog for this purpose, as illustrated in samples/dialogs in your wxWidgets distribution. On Pocket PC, the notebook in this dialog is displayed as a standard property sheet with tabs along the bottom.

You might want to use wxListbook or wxChoicebook instead of wxNotebook, which are alternative methods of controlling pages. In particular, wxListbook has an identical API to wxNotebook but makes use of a wxListCtrl, so you can use icons and labels instead of tabs. This makes sense if you have a lot of pages, particularly because on Mac OS X, notebook tabs don't scroll as they do on other platforms, and therefore the number of tabs is limited by the width of the settings dialog. You can download a third-party class called awxOutbarDialog, which implements an Outlook-like settings dialog using icons to switch pages.

You can also create your own paged settings dialog using a wxTreeCtrl, for example, so that your pages can be grouped in a hierarchy. To implement this, keep a list of panels, each associated with a path name, and when the user clicks on a tree item, hide the current panel and show the new panel. Another solution is to use Jorgen Bodde's wxTreeMultiCtrl, which manages a hierarchy of controls—a more direct method than separating out the tree control from the settings controls.

You might also consider using a property list: a scrolling list of items with a label on the left and editable value on the right. An advantage of this concise approach is that it's very easy to add or remove settings because the layout is not dependent on the number of settings. A disadvantage is that it's harder to edit larger multi-line text or a list of items, although you can arrange for specialized editors to be shown when you double-click the item. You can write your own implementation, perhaps using wxGrid, or you could look at third-party implementations such as Jaakko Salli's wxPropertyGrid.

Some applications mix a paged settings dialog approach with property lists, for example the Configuration panel in the DialogBlocks Settings dialog.

It is recommended that you don't use scrolling panels or dialogs if you are running out of space, because this can be confusing and awkward to navigate.

Consider storing all your application settings in a separate class and implementing a copy constructor, equality operator, and assignment operator. This way, you can easily make a temporary copy of your global settings object, pass it to the Settings dialog, and only copy the modified settings back to the global object if the dialog was dismissed using the *OK* button.

If you're not storing the settings separately, you need a way for the user to modify these settings directly. See `examples/chap20/valconfig` for a class `wxConfigValidator` that you can use with commonly used controls. The validator takes the setting path, the setting type, and a pointer to the `wxConfig` object. The type can be `wxVAL_BOOL`, `wxVAL_STRING`, or `wxVAL_LONG`. For example:

```
void MyDialog::SetValidators(wxConfig* config)
{
    FindWindow( ID_LOAD_LAST_DOCUMENT )->SetValidator(
        wxConfigValidator(wxT("LoadLastDoc"), wxVAL_BOOL, config));

    FindWindow( ID_LAST_DOCUMENT )->SetValidator(
        wxConfigValidator(wxT("LastDoc"), wxVAL_STRING, config));

    FindWindow( ID_MAX_DOCUMENTS)->SetValidator(
        wxConfigValidator(wxT("MaxDocs"), wxVAL_LONG, config));
}
```

You can find more on validators in Chapter 9. The third-party classes mentioned in this section are listed in Appendix E, "Third-Party Tools for wxWidgets."

APPLICATION INSTALLATION

A trouble-free installation goes a long way to reassure the user about your product before the application is even running. We'll deal with installation on Windows, Linux, and Mac OS X in turn. Information about where to get the third-party tools mentioned in this section is provided in Appendix E.

Installation on Windows

On Windows, an installer is pretty much necessary, both because users expect it and because of the way file associations and shortcuts need to be set up.

Because it's such a specialized area, wxWidgets doesn't attempt to provide an installation utility for your applications. Several installer creators are available, such as NSIS and InstallShield; a favorite with many developers is Inno Setup, a very capable, free installer that can be driven via a simple script or tailored using Pascal. Several third-party applications are listed on the Inno Setup web site for graphically creating a script that can be used to create an installer.

If you release your application frequently, you will probably want to automate the installer creation via a release script. In examples/chap20/install, we have provided example scripts for you to adapt for your own needs. Because they are Unix shell scripts, you will need MinGW's MSYS package, which is also supplied on the CD-ROM. Given a directory of files, makeinno.sh creates a portion of the Inno Setup script listing the subdirectories and files. It requires you to supply the hand-tailored top and bottom parts of the script specifying other details. You can invoke makeinno.sh with a command like this:

```
sh makeinno.sh c:/temp/imagedir innotop.txt innobott.txt myapps.iss
```

This will create the Inno Setup script myapp.iss from the files in c:/temp/imagedir.

You can adapt the release script makesetup.sh for building your own application's Windows installer. makesetup.sh copies required files into an "image" directory, which is used to build the installer script before invoking Inno Setup, creating the setup.exe file. This script uses variables specified in the file setup.var. You can add your own release functions, from building the application to copying files to your FTP site using the Curl utility.

When you distribute an application, don't forget to include a Windows XP "manifest" file with your application. The manifest is an XML file that tells Windows XP to apply theming to your application. You can include the manifest simply by including the wxWidgets standard resource file in your own .rc file:

```
aardvarkpro ICON aardvarkpro.ico
#include "wx/msw/wx.rc"
```

This includes a standard manifest file. If you want to include your own instead, define the wxUSE_NO_MANIFEST symbol before including wx.rc, and specify your own, as follows:

```
aardvarkpro ICON aardvarkpro.ico

#define wxUSE_NO_MANIFEST 1
#include "wx/msw/wx.rc"

1 24 "aardvark.manifest"
```

You may also simply include the manifest file alongside the application. For more information on the manifest syntax, see the file docs/msw/winxp.txt in your wxWidgets distribution.

Installation on Linux

On Linux, you can use a graphical installer, a custom shell script, or a distribution-specific package such as RPM for Red Hat-based distributions, or Debian packages for Debian distributions. You can also simply supply the distribution as a tarred, compressed archive (.tar.gz or .tar.bz2) with instructions on unarchiving into a suitable directory.

Tools for creating GUI installations for Linux include Loki Setup (free), Zero G's InstallAnywhere, and InstallShield.

A wxWidgets for GTK+ application is desktop-agnostic: there are no dependencies on either GNOME or KDE, so it can run under either desktop environment. Most KDE distributions also contain GTK+ libraries. However, because they use a different theming engine, GTK+ applications can look a little out of place on a KDE desktop, so consider recommending to your users that they install a Qt theming engine for GNOME such as GTK-Qt (but test it first with your application).

You may want to provide a desktop icon so the user can launch the application easily. To add an icon to the KDE desktop, you need to copy a suitable APP.desktop file to PREFIX/share/applications, where APP is the name of your application and PREFIX is typically /usr, /usr/local, or the value of the KDEDIR environment variable. Here's a sample desktop file for an application called Acme, assuming Acme was installed into /opt/Acme:

```
[Desktop Entry]
BinaryPattern=Acme;
MimeType=
Name=Acme
Exec=/opt/Acme/acme
Icon=/opt/Acme/acme32x32.png
Type=Application
Terminal=0
```

To add an icon to the GNOME desktop, the file follows a similar syntax but should be copied to ~/.gnome-desktop (for a single user). For more information on desktop configuration specification for KDE and GNOME, see http://www.freedesktop.org/wiki/Standards_2fdesktop_2dentry_2dspec.

Information about RPM, including a free online book, can be found at http://www.rpm.org, and instructions for creating Debian packages are at http://www.debian.org. Packaging your applications using these methods allows the system to resolve dependencies and makes it easier for the user to view and manage installed applications. For a tool that can help create RPM, .deb, and other package formats, you could try EPM.

A sample shell script installer for Linux, called installacme, is included in examples/chap20/install. It takes the user through installing the application and also creates a shell script called acme, which sets a location variable before running the actual executable. The advantage of this approach is that the application can be run without either adding a directory to the user's PATH variable or installing the actual application into an existing bin directory. In this scheme, all data files and the executable are kept in the same location, which makes it easy to uninstall the application. You may want to adapt the script to copy data files to standard Linux locations instead.

Also in examples/chap20/install is maketarball.sh, a release script that creates a distribution tarball, itself containing the installacme script and a further tarball of data files. You can alter maketarball.sh to suit your own needs.

Shared Library Issues on Linux

Because there is no standard GUI on Linux, added to the fact that there are many Linux distributions and versions of those distributions, you may find that on some systems, your application complains about missing libraries. There's a strong temptation to statically link everything with your application, but this can lead to problems, too. Although you shouldn't link GTK+ statically to your application, you can statically link wxWidgets by specifying --disable-shared when you configure wxWidgets. You can also consider bundling wxWidgets and/or GTK+ shared libraries with your application.

Compile on a Linux distribution that's not too old (very old versions of libraries won't be distributed with newer distributions) and not too new (the required libraries will be too new to appear on older distributions). Also consider prepending -lsupc++ to your linker flags so that the application statically links with some basic C++ library support without requiring the full shared library to be available, removing another potential complication. (However, be aware there are licensing issues to consider when statically linking GPL'ed code with your application.)

Ultimately, you may need to distribute different versions of your applications for different distributions. If you don't want to reboot every time you switch Linux versions, consider using a tool such as the excellent VMware that can run multiple virtual machines simultaneously.

Installation on Mac OS X

On Mac OS X, all you really need to do is make sure your bundle directory structure is correct and then make it into a suitable disk image, which we'll cover shortly. A Mac OS X application can be installed simply by dragging the folder to an appropriate location on the disk, with no "setup" application required.

We'll describe bundles briefly in the following, and you can find more information about them on the Apple web site at http://developer.apple.com/documentation/MacOSX/Conceptual/SystemOverview/Bundles/chapter_4_section_3.html.

A bundle consists of a standard hierarchy and an Info.plist file that describes key files and properties.

A minimal bundle hierarchy looks something like this:

```
DialogBlocks.app/                              ; top-level directory
    Contents/
        Info.plist                             ; the property list file
        MacOS/
            DialogBlocks                       ; the executable
        Resources/
            dialogblocks-app.icns              ; the app icon
            dialogblocks-doc.icns              ; the document icon(s)
```

Here's an example `Info.plist` file, for DialogBlocks:

```xml
<?xml version="1.0" encoding="UTF-8"?>
<!DOCTYPE plist SYSTEM
"file://localhost/System/Library/DTDs/PropertyList.dtd">
<plist version="0.9">
<dict>
        <key>CFBundleInfoDictionaryVersion</key>
        <string>6.0</string>
        <key>CFBundleIdentifier</key>
        <string>uk.co.anthemion.dialogblocks</string>
        <key>CFBundleDevelopmentRegion</key>
        <string>English</string>
        <key>CFBundleDocumentTypes</key>
        <array>
                <dict>
                        <key>CFBundleTypeExtensions</key>
                        <array>
                                <string>pjd</string>
                        </array>
                        <key>CFBundleTypeIconFile</key>
                        <string>dialogblocks-doc.icns</string>
                        <key>CFBundleTypeName</key>
                        <string>pjdfile</string>
                        <key>CFBundleTypeRole</key>
                        <string>Editor</string>
                </dict>
        </array>
        <key>CFBundleExecutable</key>
        <string>DialogBlocks</string>
        <key>CFBundleIconFile</key>
        <string>dialogblocks-app.icns</string>
        <key>CFBundleName</key>
        <string>DialogBlocks</string>
        <key>CFBundlePackageType</key>
        <string>APPL</string>
        <key>CFBundleSignature</key>
        <string>PJDA</string>
        <key>CFBundleVersion</key>
        <string>1.50</string>
        <key>CFBundleShortVersionString</key>
        <string>1.50</string>
        <key>CFBundleGetInfoString</key>
        <string>DialogBlocks version 1.50, (c) 2004 Anthemion Software
Ltd.</string>
        <key>CFBundleLongVersionString</key>
```

```
        <string>DialogBlocks version 1.50, (c) 2004 Anthemion Software
Ltd.</string>
        <key>NSHumanReadableCopyright</key>
        <string>Copyright 2004 Anthemion Software Ltd.</string>
        <key>LSRequiresCarbon</key>
          <true/>
        <key>CSResourcesFileMapped</key>
        <true/>
</dict>
</plist>
```

The icons for the application and its document types are specified with the CFBundleIconFile and CFBundleTypeIconFile properties. As mentioned in Chapter 10, "Programming with Images," if you are working mainly on Windows or Linux, you might like to create a number of different icons in 16×16, 32×32, 48×48, and 128×128 resolutions. Save them as transparent PNGs, copy them to the Mac, and then open each file with the Finder and copy and paste them into the appropriate locations in Apple's icon editor before saving as an icns file.

The maketarball.sh release script mentioned in the previous section for Linux can also create a Mac OS X disk image, such as AcmeApp-1.50.dmg. It copies a pre-existing AcmeApp.app bundle hierarchy to the release directory, copies the Mac OS X binary and data files into the bundle, and then creates an Internet-enabled disk image with the following code:

```
    echo Making a disk image...
    hdiutil create AcmeApp-$VERSION.dmg -volname AcmeApp-$VERSION -type
UDIF -megabytes 50 -fs HFS+

    echo Mounting the disk image...
    MYDEV=`hdiutil attach AcmeApp-$VERSION.dmg ¦ tail -n 1 ¦ awk '{print
$1'}`
    echo Device is $MYDEV

    echo Copying AcmeApp to the disk image...
    ditto --rsrc AcmeApp-$VERSION /Volumes/AcmeApp-$VERSION/AcmeApp-
$VERSION

    echo Unmounting the disk image...
    hdiutil detach $MYDEV

    echo Compressing the disk image...
    hdiutil convert AcmeApp-$VERSION.dmg -format UDZO -o AcmeApp-$VERSION-
compressed.dmg

    echo Internet enabling the disk image...
    hdiutil internet-enable AcmeApp-$VERSION-compressed.dmg

    echo Renaming compressed image...
    rm -f AcmeApp-$VERSION.dmg
    mv AcmeApp-$VERSION-compressed.dmg AcmeApp-$VERSION.dmg
```

The disk image file can then be copied to your FTP site or CD-ROM. When the Mac OS X user clicks on the file from within a web browser, the file will be downloaded, uninstalled, and mounted as a virtual disk without further user intervention. It then remains for the user to drag the application folder to an appropriate disk location to complete the installation.

FOLLOWING UI DESIGN GUIDELINES

It's worth researching the style guidelines for each platform. Much of the time, wxWidgets handles the differences, but there are some aspects that cannot be automated. For example, button layout differs between platforms. Apple is particularly strict about standard button ordering and spacing on Mac OS X. Here are just a few of the points to be aware of, both platform-specific rules and general observations. Also play with existing programs on different platforms for inspiration and to help you come up with an application design that is adaptable to your target platforms.

Standard Buttons

On Windows and Linux, groups of standard buttons can be centered or right justified, often in the order *OK*, *Cancel*, *Help*. On Mac OS X, however, the *Help* button (shown automatically as a question mark when using wxID_HELP) should be left justified, and the other standard buttons should be right justified with the default command as the right-most button: for example, *?*, *space*, *Cancel*, *OK*.

Use the standard wxWidgets control identifiers whenever possible (such as wxID_OK, wxID_CLOSE, wxID_APPLY) because some ports (notably wxGTK) can map them to special buttons with appropriate graphics.

Refer to the section on "Platform-Adaptive Layouts" in Chapter 7, "Window Layout Using Sizers," for information about the wxStdDialogButton Sizer class, which can be used to position standard buttons appropriately on each platform.

Menus

A menu bar should have no "empty" menus. Careful attention should be paid to label capitalization—each significant word normally has a capital first letter—and providing mnemonics (such as &File) and shortcuts (such as Ctrl+O). Common commands should be supported where appropriate (such as *Copy*, *Paste*, *Undo*, and so on), and there should be neither a small number of very long menus, nor a very large number of smaller menus (nine or ten menus is probably the maximum reasonable number). Instead of supplying lots of separate menu items for different configuration operations, consider merging them into one command that invokes a tabbed dialog.

As with standard buttons, use standard identifiers where possible: in particular, use wxID_ABOUT, wxID_PREFERENCES, and wxID_EXIT so that Mac OS X can move them to the application menu. You will need to design your menus so that removal of these items doesn't cause problems such as an empty *Help* menu or two consecutive separators.

Icons

Icons in your toolbar, frames, and other elements give a very strong impression of the quality of your application. Neglecting these can really let your application down. This is particularly true on Mac OS X, where there is a high standard of aesthetics. Consider having icons specially created, or a much cheaper alternative is to purchase packs of stock icons, perhaps getting the remaining non-standard icons designed for you in the same style. The investment will normally be well worth it, and your application will gain a stronger sense of identity. You can also find some icons on the web—for example, the L-GPL'ed Ximian collection at http://www.novell.com/coolsolutions/feature/ 1637.html.

Fonts and Colors

Don't be tempted to use a lot of different fonts and colors for your dialogs. As well as looking garish, using non-default fonts and colors makes it hard for wxWidgets to adapt to the current settings and themes to give a "native" look and feel. However, you can still allow the user to customize fonts for specific windows that present a lot of textual information, such as a report window. Refer to the platform guidelines on use of color. wxWidgets will do some adaptation here, but you may need to make further adaptations on custom windows that you implement.

Application Termination Behavior

On most platforms, document-based applications that aren't using MDI or a similar UI will show one frame per document. When the last frame closes, the application terminates. However, on Mac OS X, as we've mentioned in Chapter 19, "Working with Documents and Views," when there are no documents shown, the application should not terminate, and there should still be a menu bar from which the user can create or open documents or close the application. This can be implemented for wxWidgets applications by using an off-screen, hidden main frame, achieved with a small amount of code specific to this platform.

On embedded operating systems such as Pocket PC, applications stay in memory when their main window is closed, and the user does not usually have the opportunity to quit them. You will need to make a choice between conforming to the guidelines and permitting the user to quit the application to make room for others. On Pocket PC, wxWidgets sets the standard accelerator for quitting an application, Ctrl+Q, which sends a `wxID_EXIT` command event.

Further Reading

Listed below are useful guideline documents for the main platforms supported by wxWidgets, and books giving general advice on UI design.

- ☞ Apple Human Interface Guidelines: `http://developer.apple.com/documentation/ UserExperience/Conceptual/OSXHIGuidelines/index.html`
- ☞ Key differences between Mac OS X and Windows UIs: `http://developer. apple.com/ue/switch/windows.html`
- ☞ Microsoft Official Guidelines for UI Developers: `http://msdn.microsoft.com/ library/default.asp?url=/library/en us/dnwue/html/welcome.asp`
- ☞ GNOME Human Interface Guidelines: `http://developer.gnome.org/ projects/gup/hig`
- ☞ *GUI Bloopers: Don'ts and Do's for Software Developers and Web Designers*, by Jeff Johnson (Academic Press). ISBN 1-55860-582-7
- ☞ *User Interface Design for Programmers*, by Joel Spolsky (Apress). ISBN 1-893115-94-1
- ☞ *Software for Use: A Practical Guide to the Models and Methods of Usage-Centered Design,* by Larry L. Constantine and Lucy A.D. Lockwood (ACM Press). ISBN 0-201-92478-1

SUMMARY

This chapter covered a variety of topics for applying finishing touches to your application, and presented code to plug a few gaps left by wxWidgets. We've finished off with some tips and further reading to improve your awareness of UI design issues.

We hope that having read this book, you will agree with us that by adopting wxWidgets, you get a very powerful set of tools bringing you highly compelling benefits, including these:

- ☞ Your applications will have a *native* look and feel.
- ☞ The rich variety of classes, including simple and advanced controls, lightweight HTML functionality, wizards, online help, multithreading, interprocess communication, streams, virtual file systems, and so on, makes programming in wxWidgets highly productive and enjoyable.
- ☞ You save money by using the same code on all platforms.

☞ You can easily port your applications to platforms you might not have considered before, such as Pocket PC and Mac OS X, gaining market share in the process.

☞ By using rapid application development tools such as DialogBlocks, and the powerful sizer mechanism, you can quickly create complex, attractive, resizable and (above all) portable dialogs and other windows.

☞ wxWidgets' open source nature lets you modify the library and understand its workings.

☞ You get the advantages of the large wxWidgets community for quickly resolving problems and answering questions, plus the many third-party contributions (see Appendix E for a list of controls and tools).

We do hope that you've enjoyed reading the book and browsing the samples and tools on the CD-ROM and are now eager to apply what you've learned to your own cross-platform applications! Good luck, and we look forward to seeing you soon on the wxWidgets mailing lists and forum.

Installing wxWidgets

The process of installing wxWidgets has been made as simple as possible by using tools and techniques native to each platform. This appendix introduces the different methods for installing wxWidgets on various platforms with different compilers and discusses some of the main configuration options available. Only the most popular compilers and environments are covered in this appendix; Digital Mars C++, OpenWatcom C++, and Cygwin are all supported by wxWidgets but are not described here. However, you can find instructions for these compilers in the wxWidgets documentation under docs/msw.

If you want, you can download and unpack wxWidgets and then go straight to Appendix C, "Creating Applications with DialogBlocks," and use DialogBlocks to compile both wxWidgets and your application.

CHOOSING YOUR DEVELOPMENT TOOLS

Before we discuss wxWidgets installation, let's briefly look at choices in compiler tools to use with wxWidgets. Note that although cross-compilation is possible (compiling on one platform to run on another), you will generally need to compile, debug, and test on each platform that you support. However, you probably have a favorite platform you prefer to develop on, just compiling and testing on the others. If you only have one machine for Windows and Linux development, consider using a tool such as the excellent VMware virtual machine software to run several operating systems simultaneously.

Tools on Windows

Microsoft's Visual Studio (see the section "Windows—Microsoft Visual Studio") has a very good IDE, which makes debugging productive, and the compiler is good at optimizing executables for space and speed. It's also reasonably fast to run (though slower than Borland C++). This compiler is highly recommended for wxWidgets work, and it is the tool of choice for most wxWidgets developers on Windows.

Borland C++ (BC++) is a fast compiler, but the linker has trouble with wxWidgets executable sizes, and the compiler is not actively supported by Borland. In addition, there is no good free debugger for BC++. You can download Borland C++ from `http://www.borland.com/products/downloads/download_cbuilder.html`.

GCC is available in two forms on Windows: MinGW and Cygwin. MinGW makes use of the Windows run-time libraries and so is a better choice for "native" Windows applications. MinGW has an accompanying Unix-like shell, MSYS, which you will need if you want to use the `configure` method of compiling. MinGW can also compile wxWidgets and applications from the Windows command prompt using its own make tool and `makefile.gcc` makefiles. MinGW can be used on its own or with an IDE such as Dev-C++ or DialogBlocks. Download it from `http://www.mingw.org` or install it from the CD-ROM. Unfortunately, GCC is a slow compiler that creates huge libraries and executables, and its GDB debugger (or IDE equivalents) cannot compare with the convenience of VC++'s debugger.

Digital Mars C++ also works with wxWidgets and is quite fast; the IDE and debugger need to be purchased. Download Digital Mars C++ from `http://www.digitalmars.com` or copy it from the CD-ROM.

OpenWatcom C++ does not implement all C++ standards, but it works with wxWidgets and can be downloaded from `http://www.openwatcom.org` or copied from the CD-ROM.

CodeWarrior will also work with wxWidgets and provide a consistent environment for those using CodeWarrior on MacOS.

See also Appendix E, "Third-Party Tools for wxWidgets," for other IDEs and tools.

All the compilers mentioned here can be "driven" by DialogBlocks (on the accompanying CD-ROM), so you can design your dialogs and other user interface elements in addition to building and running your application. See Appendix C for more on DialogBlocks.

Tools on Linux and Mac OS X

On Linux, GCC is usually installed by default. However, you can use it in a number of different ways. You can use command-line tools (`configure`, `make`, and GDB for debugging), or you can use an IDE such as KDevelop, as described in this chapter (though you'll still compile the wxWidgets libraries from the command line). You also can use the command line to compile and then use GDB within Emacs to step through your application, or you can use the graphical debugger DDD.

On Mac OS X, you can download the GCC-based development tools from Apple's web site after registering as an Apple Developer Connection (ADC) member. You can use `configure` and `make` in exactly the same way as on Linux, but you can also use Apple's Xcode IDE to compile applications, again described later in this chapter. If you prefer, you can use CodeWarrior; however, you may find it harder to automate wxWidgets and application builds with CodeWarrior.

On both Linux and Mac OS X, you can also use DialogBlocks (on the CD-ROM), enabling you to create dialogs and other user interface elements easily in addition to generating makefiles and building your application with GCC. See Appendix C for more on DialogBlocks.

You may want to start off compiling wxWidgets and its samples with the command-line tools and then graduate to an IDE for new applications when you understand the basics.

DOWNLOADING AND UNPACKING WXWIDGETS

The latest version of wxWidgets can be downloaded from the wxWidgets web site, or you can use the version included on the CD-ROM. After you have downloaded the library source or copied it from the CD-ROM, you will need to extract the files to a location of your choice. Windows users also have the option of a self-extracting installer.

After you have unpacked wxWidgets, you may want to familiarize yourself with the organization of the files. The structure is similar to other open source projects, with separate directories for include files (include), source files (src), compiled library objects (lib), documentation (docs), sample programs (samples), and build information (build). Within some directories, there are further classifications of files based on which operating system(s) they are for:

- ☞ common: Used by all platforms, such as strings, streams, and database connectivity.
- ☞ expat: An XML parser library.
- ☞ generic: Widgets and dialogs implemented by wxWidgets for use where native versions are not available.
- ☞ gtk: For GTK+.
- ☞ html: For the HTML controls designed for wxWidgets.
- ☞ iodbc: The iODBClibrary for platforms without native ODBC support.
- ☞ jpeg: The JPEG library for platforms without native JPEG support.
- ☞ mac: For the Mac, further subdivided into classic (OS 9), carbon (OS 9 and OS X), and corefoundation (OS X).
- ☞ msw: For Microsoft Windows.
- ☞ png: The PNG image library for platforms without native PNG support.
- ☞ regex: A regular expression processor for platforms without native regular expression processing (or when Unicode is enabled).
- ☞ tiff: The TIFF image library for platforms without native TIFF support.
- ☞ unix: Used by all Unix-based platforms, including Linux and Mac OS X.

☞ xrc: wxWidgets' XML resource library.

☞ xml: A C++ wrapper around the XML parser Expat.

☞ zlib: The zlib compression library for platforms without native zlib support.

CONFIGURATION/BUILD OPTIONS

wxWidgets can be built using almost countless permutations of configuration options. However, four main options are available on all platforms:

☞ **Release versus Debug**: Debug builds include debug information and extra checking code, whereas release builds omit debug information and enable some level of optimization. It is strongly recommended that you develop your application using a debug version of the library to benefit from the debug assertions that can help locate bugs and other problems.

☞ **Unicode versus non-Unicode**: As discussed in Chapter 16, "Writing International Applications," Unicode facilitates the display of non-ASCII characters such as Cyrillic, Greek, Korean, Japanese, and so on. wxWidgets natively supports Unicode; there is no penalty for using Unicode in terms of available features (with the exception of wxODBC on Unix), nor is any additional coding required. Windows 95, 98, and ME do not have built-in Unicode support, but wxWidgets can be configured to use the add-on MSLU library for these operating systems.

☞ **Static versus Shared**: A static version of the library is linked with the application at compile time, whereas a shared version is linked at runtime. Using a static library results in a larger application but also relieves the end user of the need for installing shared libraries on his or her computer. On Linux and Mac OS X, static libraries end in .a, and on Windows, they end in .lib. On Linux and Mac OS X, shared libraries end in .so, and on Windows, they end in .dll. Note that there are certain memory and performance implications of static and shared libraries that are not specific to wxWidgets; they are beyond the scope of this book.

☞ **Multi-lib versus Monolithic**: The entire wxWidgets library is made up of modules that separate the GUI functionality from the non-GUI functionality as well as separate advanced features that are not frequently needed. This separation enables you to use wxWidgets modules selectively depending on your specific needs. Alternatively, you can build wxWidgets into one "monolithic" library that contains all of the wxWidgets modules in one library file.

You can build and simultaneously use more than one version and/or configuration of wxWidgets. The way you access the different builds depends on your platform, but all library files are created using a standard naming convention:

wx`<library><version><u><d>` where u and d indicate Unicode and debug, respectively. For example, the file `wxbase26ud.lib` is the Unicode debug base library for wxWidgets 2.6, and `wxmsw26u_core` contains the core GUI elements for a Unicode release build on Windows.

After building wxWidgets, you can confirm that the library is built correctly by compiling and running one of the samples. The samples are located in the `samples` folder of the main wxWidgets directory, with each sample in its own subfolder. You might try `samples/minimal` first because it's the simplest. For each compiler, directions for building one of the samples are included in `docs/<platform>/install.txt`. There are also more complete applications in the `demos` directory, and though they are not discussed here, they are built almost identically to the samples in most cases.

It is important to note that you can build wxWidgets with makefiles on any platform but still use an IDE to develop your projects. For example, you can use the Microsoft Visual C++ command-line compiler to build wxWidgets but still use Microsoft Visual Studio to create your applications.

WINDOWS—MICROSOFT VISUAL STUDIO

Many IDEs and compilers are available for Windows. The dominant IDE on Windows is Microsoft Visual Studio; wxWidgets requires at least Visual Studio 5. Microsoft has released Visual Studio 2005 Express for home enthusiasts and students, and it features all of the common Visual Studio tools, omitting only the high-powered tools typically used in large projects or a corporate environment. Although it is a free beta download at the time of writing, it will cost around $50 once it is officially released. See `http://lab.msdn.microsoft.com/vs2005/`.

You must have the Windows Platform SDK installed in order to build wxWidgets, which is a free download from `http://www.microsoft.com/msdowload/platformsdk/sdkupdate`.

When using the Platform SDK and the free compiler, install both the Core and Internet modules, and build wxWidgets with the run-time library linked statically (pass `RUNTIME_LIBS=static` to `make` or set *Runtime Linking* to *Static* in your DialogBlocks configurations). If using a project file, you will need to modify this setting manually, both in the wxWidgets and application project files. You may also need to remove the library `odbc32.lib` from the linker settings because the Platform SDK does not contain this library.

The SDK is already included with any of the professional versions of Visual Studio.

Regardless of which version of Visual Studio you are using, the process for building wxWidgets is the same. From your wxWidgets installation, open the `wx.dsw` workspace from the `build\msw` directory. If you are using a version later than 6.0, you may be prompted that the sub-projects must be converted to the current Visual C++ project format. Allow Visual Studio to proceed with the conversion; if you need the files in their original format, you can always extract the originals again. After all the projects in the workspace have been opened, you can browse the sources and classes.

If you are using Visual C++ version 7 or 8 (.NET or 2005), build wxWidgets by selecting *Build Solution* from the *Build* menu. Different solutions are used to build different library configurations, selectable from the Configuration Manager from the *Build* menu. Simply select which configuration you want to use, such as Debug, Unicode Release, or DLL Unicode Debug.

If you are using Visual Studio 5 or 6, build wxWidgets by selecting *Batch Build* from the *Build* menu and checking the desired library configurations. The wxWidgets project is set up to allow building release and debug versions of both Unicode and non-Unicode libraries, both static and shared (DLL). Ensure that you are building all of the sub-projects for the configurations that you want to use.

Most developers only need to build the release and debug libraries, or if you have a need for Unicode, the Unicode release and Unicode debug libraries. As a rule, using the static (non-DLL) libraries makes it easy to distribute a single-file application rather than needing to also distribute (or otherwise require) the correct wxWidgets DLL. Using the DLL builds can also result in quirks relating to application startup, so they should be used only when needed and only if you have a thorough understanding of how DLLs are utilized by both wxWidgets and Windows.

The compiled library files are placed into the `lib` directory under your wxWidgets directory. Two directories are created: `vc_dll` and `vc_lib`, for the shared and static builds, respectively.

If the process of building via project files seems fiddly (the number of configurations in the project file can be confusing!), consider using the command-line alternative as described in the section "Windows—Microsoft Visual C++ Command Line," or build wxWidgets via DialogBlocks.

Compiling a wxWidgets Sample Program

Workspace and project files are included for every wxWidgets sample. Use Visual Studio to open a workspace for one of the samples (in the `samples` directory within your wxWidgets installation), and then select a configuration matching any of the wxWidgets library builds that you compiled. For example, if you have built the Unicode debug library, compile the sample using the Unicode debug build. The samples are created to look within the wxWidgets tree for the include and library files in their default locations. As long as the library built successfully and the structure of the source tree hasn't been altered, the samples will build successfully as well.

> **Note**
>
> If you built wxWidgets and a sample from the command line, as described in the next section, trying to run and debug the sample in Visual Studio may result in a question about rebuilding libraries. Answer *No* to this question to continue running the sample.

WINDOWS—MICROSOFT VISUAL C++ COMMAND LINE

Microsoft's C++ compiler is part of any Visual C++ installation (or can be downloaded free from Microsoft) and can be used from the command line. The Microsoft compiler makefile is in the build\msw directory. From there, invoke the Microsoft compiler using a command such as the following ones, which demonstrate how to toggle all of the major configuration options:

```
nmake -f makefile.vc UNICODE=0 SHARED=0 BUILD=release MONOLITHIC=0
nmake -f makefile.vc UNICODE=0 SHARED=0 BUILD=debug MONOLITHIC=0
```

The compiled library files are placed into the lib directory under your wxWidgets directory. Two directories are created: vc_dll and vc_lib, for the shared and static builds, respectively.

If you need ODBC or OpenGL functionality, set wxUSE_ODBC or wxUSE_GLCANVAS to 1 in include\wx\msw\setup.h before compiling, and also pass USE_ODBC=1 or USE_OPENGL=1 on the nmake command line.

To remove the object files and libraries, append the target clean to the same command line. However, be aware that this won't clean up the copy of setup.h that is placed under the vc_lib and vc_dll directories, so if you make any edits to include\wx\msw\setup.h, delete the vc_lib or vc_dll directories yourself before recompiling.

Compiling a wxWidgets Sample Program

If you change into one of the sample program directories, you will see a makefile for Microsoft's compiler called makefile.vc. The sample programs are built using the same command and switches as the library itself, and they are designed to look within the wxWidgets tree for the include and library files in their default locations. Be sure that you specify flags for a configuration of the library that has been built, or the sample will fail to link. That is, if you have only built a Unicode static release version of wxWidgets, use the same build options for the sample. For example:

```
cd samples\widgets
nmake -f makefile.vc UNICODE=1 SHARED=0 BUILD=release MONOLITHIC=0
vc_mswd\widgets.exe
```

As with the library makefile, you can clean a sample by appending the clean
target, for example:

```
nmake -f makefile.vc UNICODE=0 SHARED=0 BUILD=debug clean
```

WINDOWS—BORLAND C++

Borland's command-line C++ compiler (BC++) is a free download, but it is
also part of Borland's professional C++Builder IDE. Building wxWidgets
with BC++ is done from the command line, using flags to the compiler to
specify the library build configuration. The BC++ makefile is in the `build\msw`
directory. From there, invoke the BC++ compiler using a command such as
the following, which demonstrates how to toggle all of the major build
options:

```
make -f makefile.bcc UNICODE=0 SHARED=0 BUILD=release MONOLITHIC=0
```

The compiled library files are placed into the `lib` directory under your
wxWidgets directory. Two directories are created: `bcc_dll` and `bcc_lib`, for the
shared and static builds, respectively.

To remove the object files and libraries, append the target `clean` to the
same command line. However, be aware that this won't clean up the copy of
`setup.h` that is placed under the `bcc_lib` and `bcc_dll` directories, so if you
make any edits to `include\wx\msw\setup.h`, delete the `bcc_lib` or `bcc_dll` directories yourself before recompiling.

Compiling a wxWidgets Sample Program

If you change into one of the sample program directories, you will see a
makefile for BC++ called `makefile.bcc`. The sample programs are built using
the same command and switches as the library itself and are designed to look
within the wxWidgets tree for the include and library files in their default
locations. Be sure that you specify flags for a configuration of the library that
has been built, or the sample will fail to link. That is, if you have only built a
Unicode static release version of wxWidgets, use the same build options for
the sample. For example:

```
cd samples\widgets
make -f makefile.bcc UNICODE=1 SHARED=0 BUILD=release MONOLITHIC=0
bcc_mswd\widgets.exe
```

As with the library makefile, you can clean a sample by appending the clean target, for example:

```
make -f makefile.bcc UNICODE=0 SHARED=0 BUILD=debug clean
```

WINDOWS—MINGW WITH MSYS

MinGW is a GNU toolset that includes Windows headers and import libraries for building Windows applications. MSYS provides an environment closely resembling a Linux or Unix shell in which to use MinGW. The process for using MinGW is very similar to the process described later for GCC.

It is recommended that you create a subdirectory within the wxWidgets directory for each configuration that you want to build. Most developers create directories using the same naming conventions as wxWidgets; if you want to compile the library in Unicode debug mode, you might create a directory named `buildud` or `build26ud` depending on how many different configurations you want to have.

After you have created your build directory, change into the build directory. The `configure` script, now located one directory up, takes many different parameters, the most important ones being those that control the main build options. For example, you could run

```
../configure --enable-unicode --disable-debug --disable-shared --disable-
monolithic
```

The `configure` script will analyze the build environment and then generate the makefiles for use with MinGW. When `configure` has finished, it will display a summary of the library build configuration.

```
Configured wxWidgets 2.6.0 for `i686-pc-mingw32'

  Which GUI toolkit should wxWidgets use?              msw
  Should wxWidgets be compiled into single library?    no
  Should wxWidgets be compiled in debug mode?          no
  Should wxWidgets be linked as a shared library?      no
  Should wxWidgets be compiled in Unicode mode?        yes
  What level of wxWidgets compatibility should be enabled?
                                 wxWidgets 2.2         no
                                 wxWidgets 2.4         yes
  Which libraries should wxWidgets use?
                                 jpeg                  builtin
                                 png                   builtin
                                 regex                 builtin
                                 tiff                  builtin
```

zlib	builtin
odbc	no
expat	builtin
libmspack	no
sdl	no

Many other individual features can be enabled or disabled using the `configure` script, a list of which can be found in the wxWidgets documentation or by passing `--help` to the `configure` script. After `configure` has generated the makefiles, build the library by running `make` in the same directory as the one in which you ran `configure`. The compiled library files are placed in the `lib` subdirectory of the directory used for the build, *not* the `lib` directory at the root of the wxWidgets tree. You may optionally use `make install` as root after the build has completed, to copy the library and the necessary headers into `/usr/local` so that all users may have access to compile, build, and run wxWidgets programs.

Compiling a wxWidgets Sample Program

The `configure` script creates a `samples` directory in your build directory, with further subdirectories for each sample. If you change into one of the sample program directories, you will see a makefile, which has been generated for your build directory and build configuration. Run `make` to build the sample. For example:

```
cd /c/wx/build26ud/samples/minimal
make
./minimal
```

WINDOWS—MINGW WITHOUT MSYS

MinGW can also be used from Microsoft's command line (`cmd.exe` or `command.com`). You can control your build style by using flags to the compiler. The MinGW makefile is in the `build\msw` directory. From there, invoke MinGW using a command such as the following, which demonstrates how to toggle all of the major build options:

```
mingw32-make -f makefile.gcc UNICODE=1 SHARED=0 BUILD=release \
    MONOLITHIC=0
```

(The backslash is only there to denote that the command should be typed all on one line.)

The compiled library files are placed into the lib directory under your wxWidgets directory. Two directories are created: `gcc_dll` and `gcc_lib`, for the shared and static builds, respectively.

To remove the object files and libraries, append the target `clean` to the same command line. However, be aware that this won't clean up the copy of `setup.h` that is placed under the `gcc_lib` and `gcc_dll` directories, so if you make any edits to `include\wx\msw\setup.h`, delete the `gcc_lib` or `gcc_dll` directories yourself before recompiling.

Note

If you are using MinGW **without** MSYS but have MSYS installed, the MSYS directories should not be in your path; otherwise, the wrong version of make could be used. If the wrong version of make is used, you will get cryptic error messages for processes that are otherwise correct. This conflict occurs because MinGW and MSYS share common file names for non-identical files that are not interchangeable.

Compiling a wxWidgets Sample Program

If you change into one of these sample program directories, you will see a makefile for MinGW called `makefile.gcc`. The sample programs are built using the same command and switches as the library itself and are designed to look within the wxWidgets tree for the include and library files in their default locations. Be sure that you specify flags for a configuration of the library that has been built, or the sample will fail to link. That is, if you have only built a Unicode static release version of wxWidgets, use the same build options for the sample. For example:

```
cd c:\wx\samples\minimal
mingw32-make -f makefile.gcc UNICODE=1 SHARED=0 BUILD=release \
    MONOLITHIC=0
minimal.exe
```

(The backslash is only there to denote that the command should be typed all on one line.)

To clean the sample, append `clean` to the `make` command.

LINUX, UNIX, AND MAC OS X—GCC

GCC is the *de facto* standard compiler on Linux and many Unix platforms, including Darwin, the BSD foundation for Mac OS X. Building wxWidgets with GCC simply requires following the typical `configure` and `make` routine common on Unix and Unix-like environments.

It is recommended that you create a subdirectory within the wxWidgets directory for each different configuration that you want to build. Most developers create directories using the same naming conventions as wxWidgets; if you want to compile the library in Unicode debug mode, you might create a directory named `buildud`, `build26ud`, or even `buildGTK26ud` depending on how many different configurations you want to have.

After you have created your build directory, change into the build directory. The `configure` script, now located one directory up, takes many different parameters, the most important ones being those that control the main build options. For example, you could run

```
../configure --enable-unicode --disable-debug --disable-shared \
    --disable-monolithic
```

(The backslash is only there to denote that the command should be typed all on one line.)

The `configure` script will analyze the build environment and then generate the makefiles for use with GCC. When `configure` has finished, it will display a summary of the library build configuration. The previous `configure` options would produce the following summary on Linux:

```
Configured wxWidgets 2.6.0 for `i686-pc-linux-gnu'

    Which GUI toolkit should wxWidgets use?              GTK+ 2
    Should wxWidgets be compiled into single library?    no
    Should wxWidgets be compiled in debug mode?          no
    Should wxWidgets be linked as a shared library?      no
    Should wxWidgets be compiled in Unicode mode?        yes
    What level of wxWidgets compatibility should be enabled?
                                        wxWidgets 2.2    no
                                        wxWidgets 2.4    yes
    Which libraries should wxWidgets use?
                                        jpeg             sys
                                        png              sys
                                        regex            builtin
                                        tiff             sys
                                        zlib             sys
                                        odbc             no
                                        expat            sys
                                        libmspack        no
                                        sdl              no
```

Many other individual features can be enabled or disabled using the `configure` script, a list of which can be found in the wxWidgets documentation or by passing `--help` to the `configure` script. Most significantly, you can also choose to override the default GUI toolkit (GTK+ 2) with GTK+, Motif, or X11.

After `configure` has generated the makefiles, build the library by running `make` in the same directory as you ran `configure`. The compiled library files are placed in the `lib` subdirectory of the directory used for the build, not the `lib` directory at the root of the wxWidgets tree. You may optionally use `make install` as root after the make has completed to copy the library and the necessary headers into `/usr/local` so that all users may have access to compile, build, and run wxWidgets programs.

Compiling a wxWidgets Sample Program

The configure script creates a `samples` directory in your build directory, with further subdirectories for each sample. If you change into one of the sample program directories, you will see a makefile, which has been generated for your build directory and build configuration. Run `make` to build the sample. For example:

```
cd ~/wx/buildGTK26ud/samples/minimal
make
./minimal
```

MODIFYING *SETUP.H* FOR FURTHER CUSTOMIZATIONS

If you want to further customize your wxWidgets library by enabling or disabling certain features, all of the configuration options are centralized into a file called `setup.h`. A separate `setup.h` file is automatically created from the default `setup.h` file for each library build and is placed in the `lib` directory of that build. The exact subdirectory depends on the compiler. For compilers using `configure` and `make`, `setup.h` is in `lib/wx/include/<configname>/wx` from the build directory. For other compilers, `setup.h` is in `lib/<compiler>_lib/<configname>/wx`.

`setup.h` mostly contains a long list of `wxUSE_...` defines. For example, `#define wxUSE_THREADS 1` indicates to build the library with support for threads using the `wxThread` class. If you change the 1 to a 0, `wxThread` will no longer be compiled into the library, and you will be unable to build programs that use `wxThread`. By enabling only the features that you need, you can build your own smaller, customized library. Most features are enabled by default, but some specialized features, such as ODBC, must be enabled if you want to use them. The `setup.h` file is heavily commented, pointing out possible side effects of enabling or disabling certain key features. Note that a change to `setup.h` requires recompiling the entire library because `setup.h` is at the very top of the wxWidgets include chain. On Windows, you may also need to pass extra options to the command line, such as `USE_OPENGL=1` or `USE_ODBC=1`.

On Windows, there is a common `setup.h` in `include/wx/msw` that is copied, the first time the library is built, to the library configuration's build directory. Changing the `setup.h` in `include/wx/msw` will result in changes for all configurations, whereas changing the `setup.h` in the `lib/XX_lib` directory will only change that one configuration. This does not apply if you are using configure and make under MinGW/MSYS, which creates the `setup.h` file as part of the configure process.

REBUILDING AFTER UPDATING WXWIDGETS FILES

Changes to Source or Header Files

There may be times that you change the wxWidgets sources, perhaps to apply some code that fixes a bug or adds a new feature that you need. If you change only source files, you can simply rebuild the library using the same commands used to build it originally. However, if you are rebuilding after changing header files, you may need to do some additional cleaning in order for wxWidgets to build correctly due to precompiled headers that may not be automatically updated to reflect the latest changes to the header files.

☞ **Microsoft Visual Studio**: After changing header files, you will want to rebuild the library rather than just build it, forcing any precompiled headers to be discarded and re-created.

☞ **GCC or MinGW using configure**: Remove the .deps directory before rebuilding. This one is easy to miss because the ls command does not list the directory by default.

If you continue to receive errors that indicate that an old header file is being used (for example, the compiler can't find a function that was just added and that did not exist the first time you built wxWidgets), you may need to completely remove the build directory and rebuild the library. The build directories should not contain anything besides object files and compiled library files, so you won't lose any data related to your projects.

Changes to *setup.h* on Windows

Whenever you change the common setup.h (in include/wx/msw), it is very important that it be properly copied to its installed location in the lib subdirectory. If the setup.h being used to build your applications is out of sync with the setup.h used to compile the library, you will almost certainly receive link errors due to missing symbols. Although not hard to do, it is an easy step to overlook. If you are using configure and make under MSYS or MinGW, you can re-run configure. Otherwise, you will need to delete all of the setup.h files for each library build configuration in the lib subdirectory. Because the whole library needs to be rebuilt anyway, it is just as easy to delete the entire XX_lib or XX_dll directory.

USING CONTRIB LIBRARIES

Included with wxWidgets is a variety of contributed libraries, found in the `contrib` subdirectory of your wxWidgets distribution. These are libraries that are distributed with wxWidgets but are not part of the core toolkit. Although they are not officially supported and may not be actively maintained by the core wxWidgets developers, they can still be very useful. It's easy to build the contrib libraries and use them in your projects.

You can build one or all of the contrib libraries using the same process as building the samples, discussed briefly with each compiler earlier. For Windows compilers, the libraries are compiled from within the `contrib/ build/<name>` subdirectories. Compiled libraries are automatically placed alongside the main wxWidgets library files, eliminating the need to add any additional directories to the link path. You do, however, need to add `contrib/include` to your include path.

For descriptions of the more important contrib libraries, such as `wxStyledTextCtrl`, see Appendix D, "Other Features in wxWidgets."

Building Your Own wxWidgets Applications

This appendix shows you how to use Visual Studio for Windows, KDevelop for Linux, and Xcode for Mac OS X to create your own projects in an IDE. There is also a basic discussion of makefiles that applies to any compiler on any platform, a description of the Bakefile makefile-generation system, information on using the `wx-config` command, and a list of wxWidgets preprocessor symbols you will find useful when writing your applications.

If you're new to wxWidgets, we recommend that you initially skip this chapter and use DialogBlocks to get started with compiling your own application, as detailed in Appendix C, "Creating Applications with DialogBlocks."

If your favorite compiler or IDE is not detailed here, or if you just want the quick overview, there are essentially three major sets of files required to build a project using wxWidgets:

1. **Include files**. The wxWidgets headers must be available to the compiler when compiling your project; otherwise, none of the wxWidgets classes are declared.
2. **Library files**. The wxWidgets compiled library must be available to link with your compiled program.
3. **System files**. Whatever system libraries are needed to link for the platform must be linked in with your program.

Important: You must have compiled and built at least one configuration of the wxWidgets library, as covered in Appendix A, "Installing wxWidgets," prior to proceeding with creating your own wxWidgets projects.

WINDOWS—MICROSOFT VISUAL STUDIO

Before covering the step-by-step directions for creating wxWidgets projects with Visual Studio, it should be noted that there are alternatives for generating Visual Studio project files using third-party tools. Although not covered here, utilities like DialogBlocks, wxHatch, wxWinWizard, and wxVisualSetup can be used to generate project files that can be loaded and used in Visual Studio. If you want detailed control over your project or need to make specific modifications, however, it may be necessary to have an understanding of the individual settings.

Microsoft Visual Studio enables you to quickly and easily build wxWidgets projects by adding just a few wxWidgets directories and files into your project settings. Although the exact location for each setting is slightly different in each version of Visual Studio, the options are named roughly the same; please look at nearby options or consider alternate wordings if the setting isn't listed exactly as specified here.

1. Create a new Win32 Project or Solution. Choose the most minimal options available.

2. Open the *Project Settings / Properties* dialog.

3. Find the *Preprocessor Definitions* under the C/C++ Settings. You will want to be sure that all of the following are defined: WIN32, __WXMSW__, _WINDOWS. If you are using a debug version of wxWidgets to build your project, you will also need to define _DEBUG, __WXDEBUG__. Note that some versions of Visual Studio will not show the C/C++ options until a C or C++ source file has been added to the project.

4. Find the *Additional Include Directories* under the C/C++ settings and enter both the core include directory (such as c:\wxWidgets\include) and the include directory for the library configuration that you are using (such as c:\wxWidgets\lib\vc_lib\mswu). This configuration-specific include directory must be included for the compiler to find the setup.h that specifies what features are enabled for that build.

5. Find the *Additional Libraries Directories* under the *Link Settings* and enter the directory where the compiled wxWidgets library files are located (such as c:\wxWidgets\lib\vc_lib).

6. Find the *Additional Dependencies* or *Object Modules* setting to specify additional libraries to link with your application. The wxWidgets library names will vary depending on your build configuration but will follow the library naming conventions outlined in the installation appendix. For example, for the debug build, you would need to link at least wxmsw26d_core.lib and wxbase26d.lib. Depending on which wxWidgets features you are using, you may need to link with more of the libraries: wxbase26d_net.lib, wxbase26d_odbc.lib, wxexpatd.lib, wxjpegd.lib, wxmsw26d_adv.lib, wxmsw26d_grid.lib, wxmsw26_gl.lib, wxmsw26d_html.lib, wxmsw26d_xrc.lib, wxmsw26d_xml, wxpngd.lib, wxregexd.lib, wxtiffd.lib, and wxzlibd.lib. Again, remember the build configuration postfixes for the build you are using. You can always look at the compiled library files for a complete list of libraries.

7. The Win32 libraries that you need to link, depending on your build configuration and what features you have enabled, could include some or all of the following: `kernel32.lib`, `user32.lib`, `gdi32.lib`, `winspool.lib`, `comdlg32.lib`, `advapi32.lib`, `shell32.lib`, `ole32.lib`, `oleaut32.lib`, `uuid.lib`, `odbc32.lib`, `odbccp32.lib`, `winmm.lib`, `comctl32.lib`, `rpcrt4.lib`, and `wsock32.lib`. Visual Studio usually adds some or all of these libraries when the project is created. Not all libraries are always needed; for example, if you do not use sockets, you would not need to link `wsock32.lib`.

8. Find the *Run-time Library* selection from the *C/C++ Code Generation* settings and select either *Multithread DLL* or *Multithread Debug DLL*. You will not be able to link your program using the single-thread libraries or the non-DLL libraries. If you see a handful of linking errors about Windows symbols already being defined, you probably did not select a DLL run-time library.

9. You can now add your source files to the project, if you have not already done so, and build your wxWidgets application.

Troubleshooting

If you receive any compile or link errors when building, double-check that you carefully followed all of the steps in the previous section to specify the include directories, the library directories, the wxWidgets and Win32 libraries, and the correct run-time library. You can also compare the project settings in any of the samples to the settings in your own project, looking for any discrepancies. Some developers start with a sample application's project file so that most of the settings are already defined correctly.

Some common error messages and solutions include the following:

☞ `Cannot open include file: 'wx/wx.h': No such file or directory`—This happens in two situations. One, the library itself hasn't been compiled yet; see Appendix A. Two, the library's include directory cannot be found (for example, `c:\wxWidgets\lib\vc_lib\mswd`); check that it is listed in the additional include directories.

☞ `Cannot open include file: 'wx/setup.h': No such file or directory`—The library's include directory cannot be found (such as `c:\wxWidgets\lib\vc_lib\mswd`); check that it is listed in the additional include directories.

☞ `Cannot open file wxmswXXXX`—Either the libraries haven't been compiled or the wxWidgets libraries cannot be found because the directories have not been added to the additional library paths. Ensure that the library directory containing your compiled wxWidgets library has been added to the additional libraries.

☞ **Unresolved symbols to wxWidgets classes**—Some or all of the necessary wxWidgets library modules could not be found. Examine the symbols listed to determine the missing libraries, check the previous list of libraries, and add any missing library modules.

☞ **Unresolved symbols to Windows functions**—The linker could not find the Windows symbols needed to link your application. Ensure that the Windows libraries are included in the list of modules to be linked.

Using Multiple Configurations

Visual Studio creates two project configurations, debug and release, when you create a new project. Most wxWidgets developers test their applications using a debug build of wxWidgets to benefit from the debug information and the run-time assertions that may indicate certain problems. You will need to re-enter most of the settings for each different project configuration that you use keeping in mind which wxWidgets build the project configuration will be using. To save some time, you can copy one configuration rather than manually re-creating all of the settings each time.

The sample applications have over a dozen project configurations if you want to see how the settings may differ for each configuration.

Linux—KDevelop

KDevelop, a subproject of the KDE desktop environment, is arguably the most robust, mature, and stable IDE for developing applications on Linux. Not only does KDevelop provide a powerful editor, but it also generates and updates your makefiles for you, saving you a considerable amount of work. You only need to add a few settings to KDevelop's project settings for it to compile your wxWidgets application.

1. Create a *New Project* (from the *Project* menu).
2. Expand *C++* and choose *Simple Hello World Program* or some other minimal project setting. Some newer versions of KDevelop have a wxWidgets project option, but it is not as reliable or as flexible as setting up the project yourself. Finish creating the project in a place of your choosing.
3. Delete any source files created by KDevelop, most likely a simple source file with a `main` and little else.
4. Open the *Project Options* from the *Project* menu and select *Configure Options* from the pane of options on the left. You should see several tabs, including *General*, *C*, and *C++*.
5. Click on the *C++* tab. Paste the results of using `wx-config --cxxflags` from the command line (see the later section "Using wx-config"), clearing any options that may already be present. These flags are the necessary header includes and defines to build your wxWidgets application.

6. Click on the *General* tab. Paste the results of using wx-config --libs from the command line. These are the necessary libraries for linking wxWidgets as well as linking the necessary X11, GTK+, and other system libraries.

7. After clicking *OK* to close the project options dialog, KDevelop will prompt you to re-run configure for this build configuration. Although this is a necessary step later, do not run configure yet.

8. You can now add your wxWidgets source files to the project. You will need to add at least one source file to the project before proceeding to the next step. You can add sources by using the *Automake Manager* tab. If you haven't written any code yet, begin your application and then come back to these steps, even if you only write a skeletal program that has a wxApp class and little else.

9. Run automake by selecting *Run Automake & Friends* from the *Build* menu.

10. Run configure by selecting *Run Configure* from the *Build* menu.

11. You can now build your wxWidgets application. As your application grows, simply add the new files using the Automake Manager, and KDevelop will automatically update the makefiles.

KDevelop allows you to create multiple build configurations. By default, configurations named "debug" and "optimized" are created. If you want to be able to create both debug and release versions of your application, you can place the wx-config flags specifying the different library configurations into separate KDevelop configurations, giving you the flexibility of choosing to build a debug or a release simply by switching your configuration from within KDevelop.

Mac OS X—Xcode

Apple makes it easy for developers to create Mac OS X applications by providing Xcode, a free IDE and front-end for GCC. Xcode is a rich IDE, and this short guide is not intended to replace books or other resources on all of Xcode's features and options. Fortunately, it takes only a few steps to create an Xcode project and add the necessary build flags for wxWidgets.

1. Create a *New Project* (*File* menu).

2. From the *New Project Assistant*, select *Empty Project* for the project type.

3. Select the location for your project files.

4. From the *Project* menu, select *New Target* and choose *Carbon/Application*. This will tell Xcode that you are creating an application. You will be asked to provide a name for the target. The *Target Info* window will then appear, allowing you to change the configuration for the new target.

5. From the *Settings* drop-down menu, choose *Language* under *GNU C/C++ Compiler*, and find the *Other C++ Flags* option. This is where you will paste the results of using `wx-config --cxxflags` from the command line (see the later section "Using wx-config"). These flags are the necessary header includes and defines to build your wxWidgets application.

6. From the settings drop-down menu, choose *Linking* under *General*, and find the *Other Linker Flags* option. This is where you will paste the results of using `wx-config --libs` from the command line. The libs are the necessary libraries for linking wxWidgets as well as linking the necessary Mac OS X system files.

7. You can now add your wxWidgets source files to the project by selecting *Add to Project* from the *Project* menu. Because you have provided Xcode with the necessary flags from `wx-config`, your wxWidgets programs will compile and link right from within Xcode.

Your Xcode project will also contain a file matching your project's name, ending in `.plist`. This is an XML file that contains information about your application and is included in your application bundle. On Mac OS X, every application is actually an application bundle, a complete directory with a hierarchy of files that are part of the application. This allows Mac OS X programs to be easily copied and moved as a single icon from Finder while still giving developers a chance to include any needed auxiliary files. For example, interface translations can be a part of the application bundle, so the application can be shown in the user's native language without downloading any additional files.

Xcode allows you to specify multiple targets and multiple build styles for each target. For example, Xcode automatically creates deployment and development build styles for each target. If you want to be able to create both debug and release versions of your application, you could place the `wx-config` flags specifying the different library configurations into the build styles rather than the target, giving you the flexibility of choosing to build a debug or a release simply by switching your build style.

ANY PLATFORM—MAKEFILES

Makefiles are available when building with almost any compiler and are largely standardized. Makefile syntax is beyond the scope of this book, but to get started quickly with makefiles, you can create a DialogBlocks project, add suitable configurations and some source files, and select *Generate Makefile* from the *Build* menu. Invoke the resulting makefile from the command line with `CONFIG=<config>` where `<config>` is one of the configurations listed when you invoke the makefile with the `help` target.

If you built wxWidgets with `configure`, your application makefile is likely to contain references to `wx-config` to supply the correct flags (see the later section "Using wx-config"). For example:

```
CC = gcc

minimal: minimal.o
        $(CC) -o minimal minimal.o `wx-config —libs`

minimal.o: minimal.cpp mondrian.xpm
        $(CC) `wx-config —cxxflags` -c minimal.cpp -o minimal.o

clean:
        rm -f *.o minimal
```

Modifying makefiles by hand can quickly become tedious as your project grows. The next section describes how to use Bakefile to generate makefiles for all platforms.

CROSS-PLATFORM BUILDS USING BAKEFILE

Maintaining a large number of different project files and formats can quickly become overwhelming. To simplify the maintenance of these formats, Vaclav Slavik created Bakefile, an XML-based makefile wrapper that generates all the native project files for wxWidgets. So now, even though wxWidgets supports all these formats, wxWidgets developers need only update one file—the bakefile—and Bakefile handles the rest. Fortunately, Bakefile isn't specific to wxWidgets in any way—you can use Bakefile for your own projects.

Note that this tutorial assumes that you are familiar with how to build software using one of the supported makefile systems, that you have some basic familiarity with how makefiles work, and that you are capable of setting environment variables on your platform. Also note that the terms "Unix" and "Unix-based" refer to all operating systems that share a Unix heritage, including FreeBSD, Linux, Mac OS X, and various other operating systems.

Getting Started

First, you'll need to install Bakefile. You can always find the latest version for download at Bakefile's web site: `http://bakefile.sf.net`.

It is also available on the CD-ROM included with this book. A binary installer is provided for Windows users, whereas users of Unix-based operating systems will need to unpack the tarball and run

```
configure && make && make install
```

Packages for some distributions are also available; check the web site for details.

Setting Up Your wxWidgets Build Environment

Before you can build wxWidgets software using Bakefile or any other build system, you need to make sure that wxWidgets is built and that wxWidgets projects can find the wxWidgets includes and library files. wxWidgets build instructions can be found by going to the docs subfolder, then looking for the subfolder that corresponds to your platform (such as msw, gtk, mac) and reading install.txt there. After you've done that, the following sections provide some extra steps you should take to make sure your Bakefile projects work with wxWidgets.

On Windows

After you've built wxWidgets, you should create an environment variable named WXWIN and set it to the home folder of your wxWidgets source tree. (If you use the command line to build, you can also set or override WXWIN at build time by passing it in as an option to your makefile.)

On Unix and Mac OS X

In a standard install, you need not do anything as long as wx-config is on your PATH. wx-config is all you need; see "Using wx-config" later in this appendix.

A Sample wxWidgets Project Bakefile

Now that everything is set up, it's time to take Bakefile for a test run. It is recommended that you use the wxWidgets sample bakefile to get started. It can be found in the build/bakefiles/wxpresets/sample directory in the wxWidgets source tree. Here is the minimal.bkl bakefile used in the sample:

```
<?xml version="1.0" ?>
<!— $Id: minimal.bkl,v 1.1 2005/01/27 22:47:37 VS Exp $ —>

<makefile>

    <include file="presets/wx.bkl"/>

    <exe id="minimal" template="wx">
        <app-type>gui</app-type>
        <debug-info>on</debug-info>
        <runtime-libs>dynamic</runtime-libs>

        <sources>minimal.cpp</sources>
```

```
        <wx-lib>core</wx-lib>
        <wx-lib>base</wx-lib>
    </exe>

</makefile>
```

It's a complete sample ready to be baked, so go into the directory mentioned previously and run the following command.

On Windows:

```
bakefile -f msvc -I.. minimal.bkl
```

On UNIX:

```
bakefile -f gnu -I.. minimal.bkl
```

It should generate a makefile (`makefile.vc` or `GNUmakefile`, respectively), which you can use to build the software. You can then build the software using the command `nmake -f makefile.vc` or `make -f GNUmakefile` respectively. Now let's take a look at some of the basic Bakefile concepts that you'll need to know to move on from here.

Project Types

As mentioned earlier, Bakefile builds makefiles for many different development environments. The `-f` option accepts a list of formats that you would like to build, separated by commas. Valid values are shown in Table B-1.

Table B-1   Bakefile Project Types

autoconf	GNU autoconf Makefile.in files
borland	Borland C/C++ makefiles
cbuilderx	C++ Builder X project files
dmars	Digital Mars makefiles
dmars_smake	Digital Mars makefiles for SMAKE
gnu	GNU toolchain makefiles (Unix)
mingw	MinGW makefiles (mingw32-make)
msevc4prj	MS Embedded Visual C++ 4 project files
msvc	MS Visual C++ nmake makefiles
msvc6prj	MS Visual C++ 6.0 project files
watcom	OpenWatcom makefiles

autoconf Project Type

You may notice that in the sample folder, there is also a file called `configure.in`. That file is the input for `autoconf`, which creates the `configure` scripts that you often see when you build software from source on Unix-based platforms. People use configure scripts because they make your Unix makefiles more portable by automatically detecting the right libraries and commands to use on the user's operating system. This is necessary because there are many Unix-based operating systems and they are all slightly different.

Bakefile does not generate a `configure` or `configure.in` script, so if you want to use these scripts with your Unix-based software, you will need to learn how to use `autoconf`. Unfortunately, this topic deserves its own a book and is beyond the scope of this tutorial, but a free book on the subject can be found online at: `http://sources.redhat.com/autobook/`.

Note that you do not need to use `automake` when you are using Bakefile, just `autoconf`, as Bakefile essentially does the same thing as `automake`.

Targets

Every project needs to have a target or targets, specifying what is to be built. With Bakefile, you specify the target by creating a tag named with the target type. The possible names for targets are shown in Table B-2.

Table B-2   Bakefile Targets

`exe`	Create an executable file.
`dll`	Create a shared library.
`lib`	Create a static library.
`module`	Create a library that is loaded at runtime (a plugin).

Note that the previous sample is an "exe" target. After you create the target, all the build settings, including flags and linker options, should be placed inside the target tag as they are in the `minimal.bkl` sample.

Adding Sources and Includes

Obviously, you need to be able to add source and include files to your project. You add sources using the `<sources>` tag (as shown previously), and you add include directories using the `<include>` tag. You can add multiple `<sources>` and `<include>` tags to add multiple source files, or you can add multiple sources and includes into one tag by separating them with a space, like this:

```
<sources>minimal.cpp minimal2.cpp minimal3.cpp</sources>
```

If your sources are in a subfolder of your Bakefile, you use the slash character to denote directories, even on Windows. (For example, `src/minimal.cpp`.) For more options and flags, please consult the Bakefile documentation in the `doc` subfolder of Bakefile or on the Bakefile web site.

Build Options

What if you want to offer a debug and a release build? Or separate Unicode and ANSI builds? You can do this in Bakefile by creating options. To create an option, use the `<option>` tag. A typical option has three important parts: a name, a default value, and a comma-separated list of values. For example, here is how to create a `DEBUG` option that builds debug by default:

```
<option name="DEBUG">
     <default-value>1</default-value>
     <values>0 1</values>
</option>
```

You can then test the value of this option and conditionally set build settings, flags, and so on. For more information on both options and conditional statements, please refer to the Bakefile documentation.

Bakefile Presets/Templates and Includes

Most projects will reuse certain settings, or options, in their makefiles, such as `DEBUG` or static/dynamic library options. Also it is common to have to use settings from another project; for example, any project that uses wxWidgets will need to build using the same flags and options used to build wxWidgets. Bakefile makes these things easier by letting users create Bakefile templates, where you can store common settings.

Bakefile ships with a couple of templates, found in the `presets` subfolder of your Bakefile installation. The `simple.bkl` template adds a `DEBUG` option to makefiles so that you can build in release or debug mode. To add this template to your project, simply add the tag `<include file="presets/simple.bkl"/>` to the top of your bakefile. Then, when creating your target, add the `template="simple"` attribute to it. Now, when you have built the makefile, your users can write commands like

```
nmake -f makefile.vc DEBUG=1
```

or

```
make -f GNUmakefile DEBUG=1
```

in order to build the software in debug mode.

To simplify the building of wxWidgets-based projects, wxWidgets contains a set of bakefiles that automatically configure your build system to be compatible with wxWidgets. As you'll notice in the previous sample, the sample project uses the wx template. After you've included the template, your software will now build with wxWidgets support.

Because the wxWidgets presets don't exist in the Bakefile presets subfolder, Bakefile needs to know where to find these presets. The -I command adds the wxpresets folder to Bakefile's search path.

If you regularly include Bakefile presets in places other than the Bakefile presets folder, then you can set the BAKEFILE_PATHS environment variable so that Bakefile can find these Bakefiles and include them in your project. This way you no longer need to specify the -I flag each time you build.

Lastly, it's important to note that the Win32 wx project bakefiles come with some common build options that users can use when building the software. These options are shown in Table B-3.

Table B-3   Bakefile Build Options

Option	Values	Description
WX_SHARED	0 (default), 1	Specify static or dynamic wxWidgets libs.
WX_UNICODE	0 (default), 1	Use ANSI or Unicode wxWidgets libs.
WX_DEBUG	0, 1 (default)	Use release or debug wxWidgets libs.
WX_VERSION	25 and higher (default is 26)	Specify version of wxWidgets libs.

Note that these options are not needed under Unix because wx-config can be used to specify these options.

bakefile_gen — Automated Bakefile Scripts

If you have a large project, you can imagine that the calls to Bakefile would get more and more complex and unwieldy. For this reason, a script called bakefile_gen was created, which reads in a .bkgen file that provides all the commands needed to build all the makefiles your project supports. A discussion of how to use bakefile_gen is beyond the scope of this tutorial, but it deserves a mention because it can be invaluable to large projects. Documentation on bakefile_gen can be found in the Bakefile distribution.

Conclusion

This concludes our basic tutorial of the cross-platform Bakefile build system management tool. From here, please be sure to take a good look at the Bakefile documentation to see what else it is capable of. Please post questions to the Bakefile mailing list, or if you have questions specific to the wxWidgets template Bakefile, send an email to the wxWidgets mailing list. See the Bakefile and wxWidgets web sites for information on how to subscribe to these lists.

Enjoy using Bakefile!

USING *WX-CONFIG*

When you build wxWidgets using `configure` and `make`, wxWidgets creates a special script called `wx-config`, which produces the necessary compiler flags for compiling and linking wxWidgets programs, and manages returning the correct flags when you have multiple versions of the wxWidgets libraries installed in the same location (such as `/usr/local`). You can use `wx-config` from makefiles or run it by hand to see what flags you need to insert into your IDE settings. If you're using Visual Studio, BC++, or MinGW without MSYS, you won't use `wx-config`.

If you look in your wxWidgets build directory, you will see `wx-config` there, and also in `/usr/local/bin` if you ran `make install`.

The flags that produce the necessary compile and link settings are `--cxxflags` and `--libs`, respectively. For example, on Mac OS X, the output of each could be

```
$ wx-config --cxxflags
-I/usr/local/lib/wx/include/mac-unicode-release-static-2.6
-I/usr/local/include/wx-2.6 -D__WXMAC__  -D_FILE_OFFSET_BITS=64
-D_LARGE_FILES -DWX_PRECOMP -DNO_GCC_PRAGMA

$ wx-config --libs
-L/usr/local/lib   -framework QuickTime -framework IOKit -framework Carbon
-framework Cocoa -framework System  /usr/local/lib/libwx_macu_xrc-2.6.a
/usr/local/lib/libwx_macu_html-2.6.a /usr/local/lib/libwx_macu_adv-2.6.a
/usr/local/lib/libwx_macu_core-2.6.a
/usr/local/lib/libwx_base_carbonu_xml-2.6.a
/usr/local/lib/libwx_base_carbonu_net-2.6.a
/usr/local/lib/libwx_base_carbonu-2.6.a -framework WebKit -lexpat -lz
-lpthread -liconv -lwxregexu-2.6 -lwxtiff-2.6 -lwxjpeg-2.6-lwxpng-2.6
```

Without passing these flags to the compiler and linker when building your own applications, you are likely to receive hundreds of errors because the compiler won't know anything about the wxWidgets classes that your program is using.

Using *wx-config* from the Build Directory

If you did not install the wxWidgets files into `/usr/local`, you will need to use `wx-config` "in-place," meaning that it will produce absolute paths to that build's files right from the build directory. This should be done by passing the `--inplace` flag to `wx-config` with whatever flags you are requesting. Even if you did run `make install`, nothing prevents you from using the in-place flag with a particular build of wxWidgets. When running in-place, you do not need to pass any build configuration parameters because an in-place wx-config knows only about one build, the build from which you are running wx-config in-place.

Using *wx-config* from */usr/local* and Choosing Your Configuration

When you have built and installed multiple configurations of wxWidgets, you can specify to wx-config which configuration's build flags you would like returned. For example, if you are creating both debug and release builds of your project, you should be sure to get the correct flags for each configuration from wx-config, for example:

```
wx-config --debug=no
```

or

```
wx-config --debug=yes
```

Many options are available to choose specific build configurations. The most commonly used flags are

```
wx-config [--inplace] [--unicode[=yes¦no]] [--debug[=yes¦no]] [--
version[=VERSION]] [--release] [--static]
```

You can also retrieve a list of available configurations using wx-config –list. A full list of flags is available by using wx-config --help.

wxWIDGETS SYMBOLS AND HEADERS

Although wxWidgets defines a lot of symbols, there is only a handful that you are likely to need to use in your projects. Sometimes, it may be necessary to execute certain code only on certain platforms or under certain conditions, such as the following:

```
#ifdef __WXMAC__
// Do something Mac-only
#endif
```

For your convenience, Table B-4 lists the common symbols and when they are defined. Additional symbols may be defined by the ports not covered in this book (such OS/2, Palm, and Cocoa).

Table B-4   Platform and Toolkit Symbols

Platform and Toolkit Symbols	
__WXMSW__	Microsoft Windows
__WXWINCE__	Microsoft Windows CE
__WXMAC__	Mac OS X
__WXGTK__	Using the GTK library, version 1 or 2
__WXGTK20__	Using the GTK library, version 2
__UNIX__	Unix-based platform (for example, Linux, Mac OS X, HP-UX)
__DARWIN__	Open-source BSD variant used by Mac OS X
__LINUX__	Any Linux-based platform
Library / Build Options	
wxUSE_UNICODE	Enable string Unicode support.
__WXDEBUG__	Library compiled with debugging support.
WX_PRECOMP	Use pre-compiled headers.

The use of defined symbols ties in very closely to wxWidgets' directory structure, as discussed in Appendix A. Consider for a moment that you can include a single file, regardless of the target platform, and yet wxWidgets always uses the correct platform information. Nearly all of the header files in include/wx have a block like the following (taken from combobox.h):

```
#if defined(__WXUNIVERSAL__)
    #include "wx/univ/combobox.h"
#elif defined(__WXMSW__)
    #include "wx/msw/combobox.h"
#elif defined(__WXMOTIF__)
    #include "wx/motif/combobox.h"
#elif defined(__WXGTK__)
    #include "wx/gtk/combobox.h"
#elif defined(__WXMAC__)
    #include "wx/mac/combobox.h"
#elif defined(__WXCOCOA__)
    #include "wx/cocoa/combobox.h"
#elif defined(__WXPM__)
    #include "wx/os2/combobox.h"
#endif
```

By using the symbols defined for various platforms or toolkits, one common header file can include the correct platform-specific header without you needing to perform these tedious checks yourself. Simply include the correct header in include/wx, and wxWidgets does the rest. For example, you would only need to use one line to add the necessary headers to support combo boxes:

```
#include "wx/combobox.h"
```

However, it would still be very tedious to add the headers for all of the wxWidgets classes that you use in each source file. wxWidgets provides include/wx/wx.h, which itself includes many of the commonly used class headers. There is also include/wx/wxprec.h, which you need to include when using precompiled headers on supported platforms. For example:

```
// For compilers that support precompilation, includes "wx.h".
#include <wx/wxprec.h>

#ifndef WX_PRECOMP
// Include your minimal set of headers here, or wx.h
#include <wx/wx.h>
#endif

... now your other include files ...
```

If your code must work across different versions of wxWidgets, it's useful to know about the macro wxCHECK_VERSION(major, minor, release). It succeeds if the version that the source is being compiled against is at least the version specified. For example:

```
#if wxCHECK_VERSION(2,5,5)
    // Anything for wxWidgets 2.5.5 and above
#else
    // Anything for wxWidgets 2.5.4 and below
#endif
```

Creating Applications with DialogBlocks

As we noted in Chapter 9, "Creating Custom Dialogs," when creating your own dialogs, you really need a resource editor to take the pain out of tasks such as laying out the controls and maintaining event tables. DialogBlocks from Anthemion Software is one such tool, and you'll find a special version of DialogBlocks on the accompanying CD-ROM to accelerate your wxWidgets learning and development on Windows, Linux, or Mac OS X. This appendix describes the tool and how you can use it to create, compile, and run your own applications. If you use DialogBlocks, you can avoid manually performing most of the procedures detailed in the previous two appendices because the tool can compile both wxWidgets and your own application.

WHAT IS DIALOGBLOCKS?

DialogBlocks is a Rapid Application Development (RAD) tool that can generate XRC or C++ code for your dialogs and frames. It can also generate a skeleton application and makefile and even compile your code using a range of popular compilers. DialogBlocks can invoke the GDB debugger for simple debugging with the GCC compiler, but it's recommended that you use a more sophisticated debugger for intensive use.

When DialogBlocks generates code, it inserts special comments, and it is free to replace code between these comments. You can edit the file outside these blocks, either using the DialogBlocks source editor or in an external editor or IDE. When you switch back to DialogBlocks from another application, DialogBlocks will prompt you to reload changed files as appropriate.

Unlike other dialog editor tools you may be used to, DialogBlocks doesn't support drag and drop for placing elements. Instead, you place elements inside sizers, which know how to lay out their children. So to lay out three buttons in a row, for example, you create a horizontal box sizer and insert three buttons. You build up a hierarchy of sizers and controls, and this provides the portability, adaptation to translations, and resizing ability described in Chapter 7, "Window Layout Using Sizers." If it feels a little odd at first, persevere—after a short while, it will "click," and then you'll find it a very powerful and easy way to build complex and attractive dialogs.

DialogBlocks Personal Edition has the following restrictions: wizards are limited to four pages, only one "custom control definition" can be created, there is the occasional nag screen, Windows RC file import is disabled, and the tool is for personal rather than commercial use. The full version of DialogBlocks can be purchased from http://www.anthemion.co.uk/dialogblocks.

INSTALLING DIALOGBLOCKS

Windows

Just run the setup program in the DialogBlocks directory on the CD-ROM (or via the CD-ROM's HTML interface) and follow the prompts. Run DialogBlocks from its menu group or the desktop icon. To uninstall, use the *Uninstall DialogBlocks* icon in the DialogBlocks program group, or you can uninstall via the Control Panel.

Linux

Unarchive the tarred, gzipped file to a suitable location in your file system. A directory of the form DialogBlocks-x.xx (where x.xx is the version number) will be created.

Add the location to your PATH variable and run the dialogblocks command. You will need to set the environment variable DIALOGBLOCKSDIR so that DialogBlocks can find its data files.

For example:

```
% cd ~
% tar xvfz DialogBlocks-1.90.tar.gz
% export DIALOGBLOCKSDIR=`pwd`/DialogBlocks-1.90
% export PATH=$PATH:$DIALOGBLOCKSDIR
% dialogblocks
```

If you don't want to change your PATH, you could place a script in a location already on your path, such as /usr/local/bin. For example:

```
#!/bin/sh
# Invokes DialogBlocks
export DIALOGBLOCKSDIR=/home/mydir/DialogBlocks-1.90
$DIALOGBLOCKSDIR/dialogblocks $*
```

To uninstall, delete the DialogBlocks folder.

Mac OS X

Clicking on the dmg file will mount the virtual disk containing the DialogBlocks folder. To install, simply drag this folder to a suitable location on your hard disk. To uninstall, drag the folder to the trash can.

Upgrading DialogBlocks

You can get bug fixes for DialogBlocks Personal Edition simply by uninstalling DialogBlocks and reinstalling the latest download from the DialogBlocks web site. The registration information is not removed when uninstalling, so a newer version will still run in Personal Edition mode. You need to install from the CD-ROM and run DialogBlocks once to make sure the registration information is available for subsequent upgrades.

THE DIALOGBLOCKS INTERFACE

When you run DialogBlocks, you see a project tree on the left, various content windows on the right including the dialog editor itself, and at the bottom, an optional output window to show the results of compiling an application. Figure C-1 shows a typical session. The dialog editor is available when you have clicked on a dialog element in the project tree, and it shows a visual representation of the dialog on the left with the selected element's properties on the right.

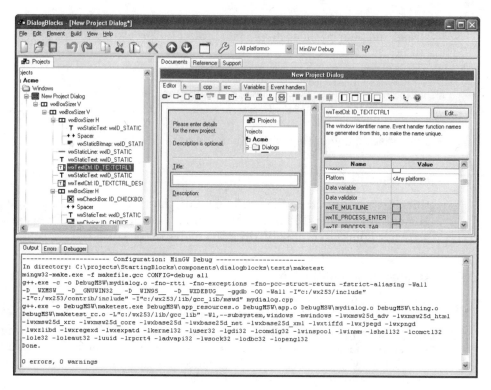

Figure C-1   The DialogBlocks main window

New controls and sizers can be selected from drop-down menus attached to the dialog editor's toolbar buttons (above the property editor). The toolbar also gives shortcuts to various sizer properties such as alignment, stretch factor, and spacing.

There are also tabs to view the C++ and XRC code generated for the current element, and further tabs let you define variables and event handlers for the selected element.

You can view the wxWidgets reference by clicking on the *Reference* tab (pressing F1 goes to the appropriate topic for the selected element). The *Support* page lists useful links for the wxWidgets developer, which on Windows can be browsed from within DialogBlocks.

THE DIALOGBLOCKS SAMPLE PROJECT

If you open the sample "Acme" project, you can get a feel for how DialogBlocks works by navigating through the project. There are several top-level elements, including dialogs, a frame, and an application object. The latter generates the wxApp-derived class that is necessary for a wxWidgets application to compile and run. It's not essential to have this element in DialogBlocks if you are writing your application class by hand and are just using DialogBlocks to create visual elements.

If you click on a dialog element, the dialog editor will be shown, and you can click on either the dialog editor or the project tree to select controls and sizers within the dialog. A selected element is shown with a red outline, and its parent with a blue outline, to allow you to see the context of the element. Try double-clicking on a control: normally you will be shown an editor for the default property, for example a button label. Other properties can be edited via the property editor: scroll down and single-click on the value of the property you're interested in, or double-click to invoke a specialized editor such as a multiline text editor or color selector.

COMPILING THE SAMPLE

You can compile your project from within DialogBlocks for a range of popular compilers including Visual C++, Borland C++, GCC, MinGW, and Digital Mars C++. DialogBlocks lets you to add as many *configurations* as you want, each based on a particular compiler. You will typically have debug and release configurations for each compiler you use. You could have separate configurations for different versions of wxWidgets, too.

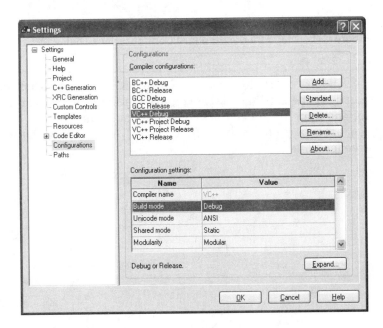

Figure C-2   DialogBlocks configurations dialog

The Acme sample has several configurations, one of which you can select via the second drop-down list on the toolbar. You can add more by clicking on the *Configuration* panel on the settings dialog (Figure C-2) and clicking on *Add*. Or, to quickly add standard Debug and Release configurations, click on *Standard*, and choose a compiler (Figure C-3). Configuration properties can be edited in the scrolling property panel: changing a high-level property (such as *Build Mode*) can change the default value for a low-level property (such as *Preprocessor Flags*).

Figure C-3   DialogBlocks Standard Configurations Dialog

Before compiling, you'll need to set up some paths: click on the *Paths* panel on the settings dialog (Figure C-4) and browse for the top-level path for the appropriate compiler variable, such as MINGWDIR or MSVCDIR. (This is not necessary on Linux or Mac OS X.) Also specify the wxWidgets source tree for WXWIN.

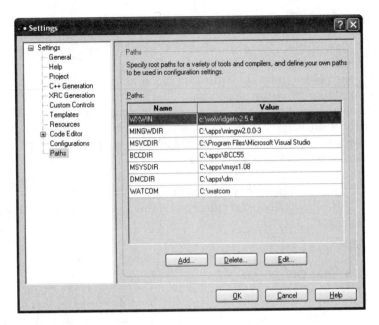

Figure C-4   DialogBlocks paths dialog

When you've selected the appropriate configuration in the main DialogBlocks toolbar, you can choose *Build wxWidgets* on the *Build* menu to first make libraries that are consistent with the project configuration. This will take some time. On Windows, the build will be done in build\msw in the wxWidgets tree, and on Linux and Mac OS X, it will be done in a build directory under the wxWidgets tree. (If you need to stop a GCC build of wxWidgets, you can restart it manually by changing directory to the build directory—for example, GCCDebugGTK2—and typing make.)

Then click on the *Build Project* menu item (or F8) to build the Acme project. If all went well, you can click on *Run Project* (or F9) to run the application.

When run, the Acme project shows one of its dialogs by virtue of the *Main Window* property of the AcmeApp element. You can try changing this property to ID_FRAME and rebuilding to show the frame as the main window instead.

CREATING A NEW PROJECT

The New Project Wizard (invoked from the *New Project* menu item or toolbar button) leads you through a series of pages. In the first page, enter the full path of the new DialogBlocks file, and optionally your name and a copyright string to be inserted into generated files. The second page gives you the opportunity to decide to generate C++ code that uses XRC files instead of creating all elements in C++ code (you can change this option later). The third page lets you tailor the name of application class that DialogBlocks will generate (if any). Clear the check box if you don't want DialogBlocks to generate the application class. Finally, you will be asked if you want to create some default debug and release configurations for a selected compiler.

After you've created the project, you can add dialogs and other elements as required.

CREATING A DIALOG

Create a new dialog either using the drop-down menu on the *New Top-Level Element* toolbar button or from the *Element* menu. Fill in the title, class name, and C++ file names for this dialog. A dialog starts out with a default vertical box sizer, but you can delete this and replace it with a different sizer.

Select the top-level sizer and add a wxButton by clicking on the left-most button in the dialog editor toolbar (just above the property editor). Now add a single-line wxTextCtrl. It appears beneath the button because the containing sizer is a vertical box sizer. Now try adding a horizontal box sizer, then several buttons. The horizontal box sizer will stretch to fit the new buttons, expanding the dialog (Figure C-5).

Figure C-5   A simple dialog with two sizers

The first button you created is now centered in the horizontal axis because this is the default. You can experiment with different alignments using the yellow toolbar buttons.

Now select the wxTextCtrl you created earlier and add a wxListBox. It's created just after the text control with a default size; you can make it stretch to fit the available horizontal space by clicking on the *Expand Horizontally* button. Try previewing the dialog with F5 and resizing it. You'll notice that there's a lot of empty space if you make the dialog big (Figure C-6).

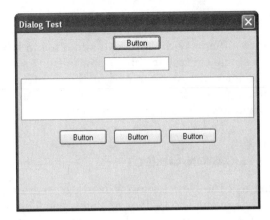

Figure C-6 Wasted space when resizing

Close the preview, click on the list box, and click on the double-headed arrow ("the stretch factor"). Now resizing the dialog makes the list box grow to take up available space (Figure C-7).

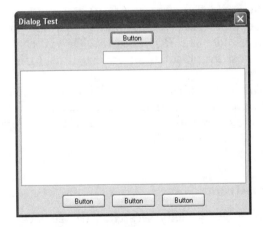

Figure C-7 Stretching a control to fit available space

By default, DialogBlocks creates a dialog with the *Fit to Content* property on so that the dialog will wrap around the content. If you want the dialog to show at a predetermined size initially and have the content stretch appropriately, switch this property off and provide suitable *Width* and *Height* property values for the dialog.

CREATING A FRAME

A frame starts off empty, and you can add a menu bar, a toolbar, a status bar, and either a single control or subwindow to fill the client area or a single top-level sizer under which you can add further controls and/or subwindows. You can't add multiple windows directly under the frame, but you can use a sizer or a parent window to contain further windows.

CREATING AN APPLICATION OBJECT

If you didn't ask the New Project Wizard to create an application object, you can still add one from the toolbar or menu bar. This will create the class and OnInit function, which you can edit as required. Select a window identifier in the *Main Window* property to have DialogBlocks generate the code to create the main window object.

DEBUGGING YOUR APPLICATION

If you are using GCC on any platform, you can use the *Debug Project* command on the *Build* menu to show GDB in a window, with a toolbar to accelerate common debugging commands. A manual for GDB is supplied with DialogBlocks under the *Reference* tab. Or you can use GDB standalone via Emacs or via a graphical front-end such as Insight, DDD, or KDbg (KDE only).

On Windows, you can use the debugger that comes with your compiler. In particular, to use the Visual Studio debugger, create a configuration for VC++ Project, select this configuration in the DialogBlocks toolbar, generate the project file, and open it in Visual Studio.

FURTHER INFORMATION

This introduction has only scratched the surface of what you can do with DialogBlocks. Please refer to the online help for further information, in particular the "How To..." section. See also the DialogBlocks web site and mailing list at http://www.anthemion.co.uk/dialogblocks.

Other Features in wxWidgets

wxWidgets is a large system, and we couldn't cover all its features in depth. Here we present a sampler of other aspects that may be useful to you; details on most of them can be found in the wxWidgets reference manual. See also Appendix E, "Third-Party Tools for wxWidgets," for third-party classes.

FURTHER WINDOW CLASSES

wxGenericDirCtrl shows a hierarchy of directories, and optionally files; it can be used to build browsers.

wxCalendarCtrl (see Figure D-1) is an attractive way for the user to enter date information. This control can be customized in various ways, including highlighting special dates and starting the week with either Monday or Sunday. wxCalendarCtrl is in the core wxWidgets library, and the sample is in samples/calendar.

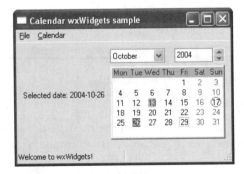

Figure D-1 wxCalendarCtrl

wxDatePickerCtrl is a more compact control than wxCalendarCtrl that allows the user to select a date. On Windows, it uses a native Win32 control, and on other platforms, a generic wxWidgets version is used.

wxTipWindow is a kind of wxPopupWindow that can be used for showing tooltips, and it is used by wxSimpleHelpProvider to show popup help. The tooltip text is provided in the constructor itself.

wxStyledTextCtrl is a wrapper around Scintilla, a highly capable code editor with highlighting, wrapping, and many other features. With minimal code, your application can support editing text files for a large number of different file formats and programming languages. The Scintilla project can be found at www.scintilla.org, and wxStyledTextCtrl can be found in the contrib hierarchy of your wxWidgets distribution. Check out the demo in contrib/samples/stc (see Figure D-2); documentation is available at http://www.yellowbrain.com/stc.

Figure D-2   wxStyledTextCtrl example

wxStaticPicture shows an arbitrary, possibly scaled image, working around a restriction in wxStaticBitmap image size on Windows. See contrib/src/gizmos.

wxLEDNumberCtrl (see Figure D-3) is a simulation of an LED display for showing a numeric string. See contrib/src/gizmos.

Figure D-3   LED control

wxEditableListBox shows a list of strings with controls to add, delete, and move items.

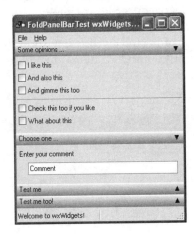

Figure D-4   Folding panel

wxFoldPanelBar (see Figure D-4) is an alternative to tabs as a way of showing multiple panels of controls economically. The titles of "folded" panels stack up along the bottom when not in use, and unlike with a tabbed interface, you can choose any combination of panels to be shown simultaneously. See contrib/src/foldbar.

wxGIFAnimationCtrl can be used for simple, small animations (see Figure D-5). It uses a generic set of classes for flipbook-style animation, and these classes can be extended to use sources of animation data other than GIF. Note that wxHtmlWindow can also display animated GIFs, using its own method. See contrib/src/animate.

Figure D-5   GIF animation control

wxSplashScreen shows a window with a thin border, displaying a bitmap describing your application. Show it in application initialization and then either explicitly destroy it or let it time-out.

OGL (Object Graphics Library) provides a way to display diagrams consisting of shapes connected by lines, with optional arrows and labels. Figure D-6 shows the wxPython OGL demo displaying a variety of shape types. See contrib/src/ogl.

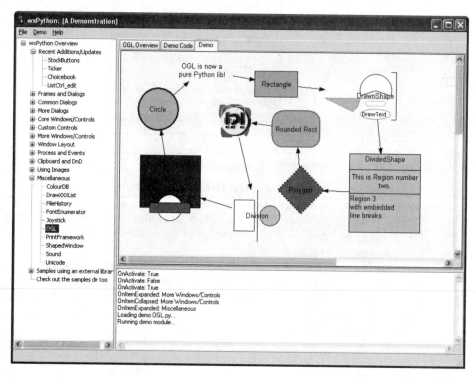

Figure D-6   wxPython running the OGL demo

FL (Frame Layout) manages the layout for windows that can be moved around a frame and "undocked." This will soon be superceded by an improved solution. See `contrib/src/fl`.

ODBC CLASSES

ODBC is a cross-platform standard for accessing databases, so it's natural for wxWidgets to provide support for it. Using wxODBC, you can access a wide variety of databases including DB2, DBase, Firebird, INFORMIX, Interbase, MS SQL Server, MS Access, MySQL, Oracle, Pervasive SQL, PostgreSQL, Sybase, XBase, Sequiter, and VIRTUOSO. The main wxODBC classes are `wxDb` and `wxDbTable`. For more information, see "Database Classes Overview" in the wxWidgets reference manual. See also `samples/db` and `demos/dbbrowse` (see Figure D-7). You may also be interested in reusing the generic tab and page controls that are part of this demo.

For other wxWidgets database access wrappers, see wxOTL and wxSQLite in Appendix E.

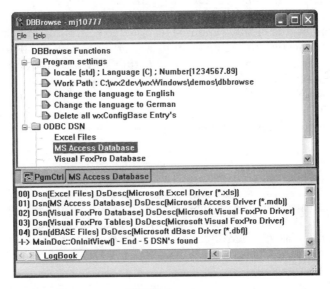

Figure D-7   wxWidgets `dbbrowse` ODBC demo

MIME TYPES MANAGER

The wxMimeTypesManager class enables an application to retrieve information about all known MIME types from a system-specific location, including the file extension for each MIME type. An application uses a global instance of it, called wxTheMimeTypesManager.

NETWORK FUNCTIONALITY

wxWidgets provides more than just the wxSocket class for working with networks. These are some of the network-related wxSocket classes that you can find more about from the manual.

wxURI can be used to extract information from a URI (Uniform Resource Identifier). A URL is a subset of a URI, so the wxURL class (for parsing and streaming from URLs) is derived from wxURI.

wxIPV4address is used to represent a standard Internet address.

wxFTP and wxHTTP can be used for performing FTP and HTTP operations. However, for a fuller implementation, consider using the CURL library instead (see Appendix E for wxCURL and wxCurlDAV).

wxDialUpManager encapsulates functions dealing with verifying the connection status of the computer (connected to the Internet via a direct connection, connected through a modem, or not connected at all) and to establish this connection if required. The application can also request notification about changes in the connection status. This class is currently only supported on Windows.

The wxEmail class in contrib/src/net can be used to send mail via SMAPI on Windows or the sendmail program on Linux.

MULTIMEDIA CLASSES

You can use the wxSound class on all platforms to load and play short sound files. On Windows, wxSound uses wave files (.wav). On Linux, the Open Sound System is used where available, and so it supports the formats handled by OSS. On Mac OS X, wxSound uses Apple's QuickTime to play wave and other formats.

From wxWidgets 2.5.4, the wxMediaCtrl class is available on Windows, Mac OS X, and Linux. wxMediaCtrl can play sound and video files, and it uses DirectShow on Windows, QuickTime on Mac OS X, and GStreamer on Linux.

EMBEDDED WEB BROWSERS

Although `wxHtmlWindow` is a fantastic lightweight HTML viewer, sometimes you need full web facilities in your application. Eventually wxWidgets will provide a single class to embed an appropriate browser on each platform, but for now there are different classes to achieve this.

On Mac OS X, wxWidgets comes with `wxWebKitCtrl`, which you need to enable by passing `--enable-webkit` to configure when building wxWidgets.

On Linux, you can download `wxMozilla` (see Appendix E). Be warned that your application distribution will swell by many megabytes if embedding Mozilla.

On Windows, you can download `wxIE` (see Appendix E) to embed Internet Explorer in your application. You can also consider using `wxMozilla` on Windows.

ACCESSIBILITY

Because wxWidgets uses native widgets wherever possible, applications built with it are already quite accessible and tend to be friendly towards screen-reading applications. However, there is a `wxAccessible` class that can be used to make an application more accessible on Windows by deriving from the class, providing implementations of virtual classes, and associating an instance of it with the appropriate window instance. The class should be enabled with `wxUSE_ACCESSIBILITY` to `1` in `setup.h`. Currently, only Microsoft Active Accessibility is supported.

OLE AUTOMATION

The `wxAutomationObject` class represents an OLE automation object containing a single data member, an `IDispatch` pointer. It contains a number of functions that make it easy to perform automation operations and set and get properties. The class makes heavy use of the `wxVariant` class and is only available under Windows.

The usage of these classes is quite close to OLE automation usage in Visual Basic. The API is high-level, and the application can specify multiple properties in a single string. The following example gets the current Excel instance, and if it exists, makes the active cell bold:

```
wxAutomationObject excelObject;
if (excelObject.GetInstance("Excel.Application"))
    excelObject.PutProperty("ActiveCell.Font.Bold", true);
```

RENDERER CLASSES

The `wxRendererNative` class and derivatives abstract high-level drawing operations for widgets or parts of widgets, such as buttons, splitter bars, and so on. This allows windows that are drawn "generically" using wxWidgets to use native or at least consistent components. For more information, please see the documentation for `wxRendererNative`.

EVENT LOOPS

The event loop is modeled with the `wxEventLoop` class. Start the loop by calling `Run`, test whether the loop is running with `IsRunning`, and exit the loop with `Exit`. This class is used for the main loop of the application, and you can also use it for subordinate event loops, as used when showing a modal dialog.

Third-Party Tools for wxWidgets

This appendix lists a selection of libraries and tools you can use with wxWidgets. More can be found on the wxWidgets web site, particularly in the Resources and Contributions sections, and also on `http://wxcode.sf.net`.

LANGUAGE BINDINGS

C++ is not the only language you can use for wxWidgets programming: the following projects integrate wxWidgets with other languages. Some are more fully developed than others, and not all work on all major platforms. wxPython is the most mature and popular of all bindings, and it works on Windows, Linux, and Mac.

wxPython combines wxWidgets and the Python language to create a powerful and popular tool for rapid GUI programming. Figure E-1 shows wxPython running its demo program—even if you won't be using the Python language, it's worth installing it and trying out the demo because it covers a lot of wxWidgets functionality. wxPython is on the accompanying CD-ROM and is also available from `http://www.wxpython.org`.

wxPerl adds wxWidgets GUI programming to the Perl language. It's available from `http://wxperl.sourceforge.net`.

wxBasic is a combination of wxWidgets and a variant of the BASIC language. It's available from `http://wxbasic.sourceforge.net`.

wxLua binds the lightweight Lua language to wxWidgets and is easy to integrate into applications as a GUI-enabled extension language. It's available from `http://www.luascript.thersgb.net`.

wxJavaScript integrates wxWidgets with JavaScript. It's available from `http://wxjs.sourceforge.net`.

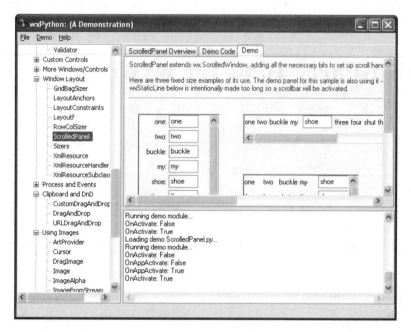

Figure E-1   The wxPython demo

wx4j is a binding of Java to wxWidgets. It's available from `http://www.wx4j.org`.

wxRuby combines wxWidgets and the Ruby language. It's available from `http://wxruby.rubyforge.org`.

wxEiffel combines wxWidgets and the Eiffel language. It's available from `http://elj.sourceforge.net`.

wx.NET is a C# binding for .NET and Mono. It's available from `http://wxnet.sourceforge.net`.

wxHaskell is a Haskell binding for wxWidgets. It's available from `http://wxhaskell.sourceforge.net`.

wxEuphoria is a Euphoria binding for wxWidgets. It's available from `http://wxeuphoria.sourceforge.net`.

TOOLS

These are tools that are either specifically designed to help you with your wxWidgets application development or are generally useful for application development.

wxDesigner is a commercial dialog editor and RAD tool and can write C++, Python, Perl, and C# code directly. Its interface lets anyone somewhat familiar with wxWidgets to create aesthetically pleasant cross-platform dialogs in a matter of minutes. Features such as supporting copy/cut/paste, infinite undo/redo, and previewing make testing easy and safe. It's available for Windows, Linux, and Mac OS X from `http://www.roebling.de`.

DialogBlocks is a sizer-based resource editor that creates professional-looking dialogs, wizards, and frames for deployment on any supported wxWidgets platform. DialogBlocks also generates makefiles and project files for a range of compilers. It's available for Windows, Linux, and Mac OS X from `http://www.anthemion.co.uk/dialogblocks`.

poEdit is a gettext catalog (`.po` file) editor. Unlike other catalogs editors, poEdit shows data in very compact way. Entries are arranged in a list so that you can easily navigate large catalogs and immediately get an idea about how much of the catalog is already translated, what needs translating, and which parts are only translated in a "fuzzy" way. It's available for Windows, Linux, and Mac OS X from `http://poedit.sourceforge.net`.

Bakefile generates makefiles for multiple platforms. Originally designed for the wxWidgets project, it can also be applied to your own applications and libraries. It's available for Windows, Linux, and Mac OS X from `http://bakefile.sourceforge.net`.

HelpBlocks is an authoring tool for MS HTML Help and wxWidgets HTML Help files, available on Windows, Linux, and Mac (beta) from `http://www.helpblocks.com`.

wxVisualSetup integrates wxWidgets help with Microsoft Visual Studio and includes a wxWidgets project wizard, Intellisense support, dynamic help, and tips and tricks. It's available from `http://www.litwindow.com/wxVisualSetup`.

wxGlade is a GUI designer built with wxPython, generating Python, C++, and XRC code. It's available from `http://wxglade.sourceforge.net`.

wxDev-CPP is a wxWidgets form designer plugin for the Dev-C++ IDE. It's available from `http://wxdsgn.sourceforge.net`.

wxHatch is a free RAD tool for wxWidgets. It's available from `http://biolpc22.york.ac.uk/wx/wxhatch`.

XRCed is a wxWidgets and wxPython development tool written in wxPython. It's available from `http://xrced.sourceforge.net`.

wxWinWiz is a Visual C++ wizard for creating wxWidgets projects. It's available from `http://www.koansoftware.com/en/prd_svil_wxdownload.htm`.

wxCRP is a tool to generate snippets of code from templates. It's available from `http://www.xs4all.nl/~jorgb/wxcrp`.

Chinook Developer Studio is a multi-platform C/C++ integrated development environment. It's available for Windows and Linux from `http://www.degarrah.com`.

MinGW Developer Studio is an IDE written in, and for, developing programs with wxWidgets and MinGW. It's available for Windows and Linux from `http://www.parinyasoft.com`.

CodeBlocks is an IDE written with wxWidgets, available for Windows and Linux from `http://www.codeblocks.org`.

KDevelop is a capable, free IDE for Linux. It's available from
`http://www.kdevelop.org`.

Curl is a command-line utility for transferring files by FTP and other
protocols; it's useful for uploading your finished application. It's available from
`http://curl.haxx.se`.

VMware is machine virtualization software that lets you run multiple
operating systems simultaneously. Several wxWidgets developers
use it, and they find it an indispensable resource. It's available from
`http://www.vmware.com`.

Inno Setup is an excellent and widely used Windows installer creator. It's
available from `http://www.jrsoftware.org/isinfo.php`.

NSIS (Nullsoft Scriptable Install System) is a free, highly customizable
Windows installer creator. It's available from `http://nsis.sourceforge.net`.

Loki Setup is an installer utility for Linux. It's available from
`http://www.lokigames.com/development/setup.php3`.

InstallAnywhere by Zero G is a multi-platform installer creator. It's available from `http://www.zerog.com/products_ia.shtml`.

InstallShield has a range of installers for most operating systems:
`http://www.installshield.com`.

EPM is a tool that can help create RPM, `.deb`, and other package forms.
It's available from `http://www.easysw.com/epm`.

Doxygen is a popular tool that helps automate your code documentation.
It's available from `http://www.doxygen.org`.

GTK-Qt is a theming engine that can make wxGTK applications look
more at home under KDE. It's available from `http://www.kde-apps.org/`
`content/show.php?content=20042`.

ADD-ON LIBRARIES

This section presents a selection of add-on libraries for wxWidgets available at
the time of writing. These tend to be distributed as source code, which you
must compile, and there is currently no standard way of doing this. With some,
you can simply add the source files to your own make or project file; others
come with their own make or project file or even use a configure script, creating
libraries for you to link against. Please see the individual packages for build
instructions. A package manager and standards for third-party code are being
developed to make this easier in the future.

wxMozilla is a project to develop a wxWindows component for embedding
the Mozilla browser into any wxWidgets application. It's available from
`http://wxmozilla.sourceforge.net`.

wxIndustrialControls provides a set of widgets for showing digital and
analog values. Includes Angular Meter, Linear Meter, Angular Regulator,
Linear Regulator, Bitmap Switcher, Bitmap Check Box, LCD Display, and

LCD Clock. It's available from `http://www.koansoftware.com/en/prd_svil_` `wxindctrl.htm`.

wxCURL is a simplified and integrated interface between LibCURL and wxWidgets. wxCURL provides several classes for simplified interfaces to HTTP, WebDAV, FTP, and Telnet-based resources. It's available from `http://sourceforge.net/projects/wxcurl`.

wxCurlDAV is a C++ class designed for people using wxWidgets to simply and easily add WebDAV functionality to their application. It's available from `http://homepage.mac.com/codonnell/wxcurldav`.

ToasterBox is a cross-platform library to make the creation of MSN style "Toaster" popups easier (message windows that slide up and down). It's available from `http://toasterbox.sourceforge.net`.

wxVTK enables the 3D graphics library VTK to render to and interact with wxWidgets. It's available from `http://wxvtk.sourceforge.net`.

wxDockIt is a docking library by Mark McCormack. It's available from `http://sourceforge.net/projects/wxextended`.

wxIFM (Interface Management System) is a docking library based on a plug-in architecture. It's available from `http://www.snakesoft.net/wxifm`.

wxMathPlot is a framework for mathematical graph plotting in wxWidgets. It's available from `http://wxmathplot.sourceforge.net`.

wxTreeMultiCtrl enables you to add any `wxWindow`-derived class to a tree shaped structure similar to a `wxTreeCtrl`. It is well suited for a scrollable property sheet. It's available from `http://www.solidsteel.nl/jorg/components/` `treemultictrl/wxTreeMultiCtrl.php`.

wxVirtualDirTreeCtrl is a very handy component for quickly creating project browsers, repository views, and smart directory selectors based upon event handlers, which can be overridden to make it look even more flexible. It is based upon a `wxTreeCtrl` component and designed in such a way that the native functionality of this class can still be used. It's available from `http://www.solidsteel.nl/jorg/components/virtualdirtreectrl/wxVirtualDir` `TreeCtrl.php`.

wxPropertyGrid is a specialized two-column grid for editing properties such as strings, numbers, flagsets, string arrays, and colors. It's available from `http://www.geocities.com/jmsalli/propertygrid/index.html`.

wxSMTP is a an email framework including an SMTP class. See also `contrib/src/net` in the wxWidgets distribution for simple email-sending functionality. wxSMTP is available from `http://www.frank-buss.de/` `wxwindows/wino.html`.

wxResizeableControl provides a user interface for child windows placed within other windows. The user can drag them around and resize them using eight marks drawn on the edges and corners of the control. This class sends notification events to its parent when the window is created, resized, moved, or deleted. It's available from `http://de.geocities.com/markusgreither/` `resizec.htm`.

wxOTL is an alternative database connectivity library for wxWidgets based on the Oracle, ODBC, and DB2-CLI Template Library from S. Kuchin. It's available from `http://home.tiscali.be/t.bogaert/wxOTL`.

wxReportWriter allows you to create table-based reports for all kinds of data. It's available from `http://www.daily.de/RepWrt`.

wxHyperlinkCtrl is a hyperlink control providing the ability to intercept mouse click events to perform your own custom event handling and the ability to open a link in a new or current browser window. It's available from `http://www.spaceblue.com/codedetail.php?CodeID=7`.

wxSQLite is a wrapper for the SQLite database engine. It's available from `http://wxsqlite.sourceforge.net`.

wxIE allows you to embed Internet Explorer in your wxWidgets for Windows applications. Incorporates the `wxActiveX` class for embedding ActiveX controls in a `wxWindow`. It's available from `http://sourceforge.net/projects/wxactivex`.

wxCTB is a serial communications package for Windows and Linux. It's available from `http://www.iftools.com/download.en.html`. A fully featured terminal program called wxTerm that makes use of wxCTB can also be downloaded from this site.

AWX is a library of add-on classes. It includes `awxOutlookDialog` (a settings dialog using icons to switch pages), `awxButton` (an enhanced bitmap button), `awxToolbar` (a `wxToolBar`-like class with enhanced deactivated button support), and `awxLed` (an LED simulator with red, yellow, and green states). It's available from `http://www.iftools.com/awx.en.html`.

wxSpellChecker is a generic spell-check framework that can use different engines. It's available from `http://www-personal.umich.edu/~jblough/wxspellchecker`.

wxArt2D is a library for advanced 2D graphical programming, with SVG and CVG support. It's available from `http://wxart2d.sourceforge.net`.

wxImprola is a GUI framework for the Improla image processing library. It's available from `http://improla.sourceforge.net`.

Extended wxHTML Help lets you invoke modal wxHTML Help dialogs from other modal dialogs, and it also allows you to embed wxHTML Help within your application. It's available from `ftp://biolpc22.york.ac.uk/pub/contrib/helpctrlex`.

wxStEdit is a library and sample program for `wxStyledTextCtrl` that is a wrapper around the Scintilla text editor widget. It is meant to be used as a component of a larger program, and although it tries to manage as much as possible, it's fairly extensible as well. It's available from `http://www.lehigh.edu/~jrl1/wxwindows/wxStEdit`.

wxLCDWindow displays numbers like a liquid crystal display. It's available from `ftp://biolpc22.york.ac.uk/pub/contrib/lcdwindow`.

mmwx is a class library containing the following classes: `mmMultiButton`, `mmNavigator`, `mmMonthCtrl`, `mmDropMonth`, `mmDropMenu`, `mmDropWindow`, `mmHyperText`, `mmHyperBitmap`, `mmTextStretch`, and `mmLogonDialog`. It's available from `http://mindmatters.no/mmwx`.

LitWindow Library is a system for specifying dialog behavior using constraint rules. It's available from `http://www.litwindow.com/Library/`.

Keybinder is a generic system to let your users bind one or more shortcut keys to commands, and includes a user interface for editing shortcuts. It's available from `http://wxcode.sourceforge.net`.

wxBetterDialog is a collection of dialogs, including an enhanced color selection dialog. It's available from `http://wxcode.sourceforge.net`.

wxBZipStream contains Bzip compression and decompression stream classes. It's available from `http://wxcode.sourceforge.net`.

wxCrashReport formats and prints a report in case the application crashes on Linux. Also included is support for BlackBox.dll, which does the same on Windows. It's available from `http://wxcode.sourceforge.net`.

wxHTTPServer is a HTTP 1.0-compliant web server class that uses wxWidgets for events and sockets. It's available from `http://wxcode.sourceforge.net`.

wxHyperLink contains a static text element that links to an URL. Clicking on the URL activates the standard browser and opens the URL. It's available from `http://wxcode.sourceforge.net`.

wxListCtrlEx is a subclass of `wxListCtrl` with advanced features such as column sorting (which can sort both text and numbers) and a simplified virtual data interface. It also can correctly resize your columns (maintaining their original proportions) when you resize it. It's available from `http://wxcode.sourceforge.net`.

wxRarInputStream implements RAR file extraction. It's available from `http://wxcode.sourceforge.net`.

wxSheet is a rewrite of the `wxGrid` widget, with more control for intercepting events and extending functionality. It's available from `http://wxcode.sourceforge.net`.

wxStreamMerger is a class for obtaining the difference between two streams. It's available from `http://wxcode.sourceforge.net`.

wxWidgets Application Showcase

There are hundreds, if not thousands, of applications using wxWidgets. All of the applications in this selection are mature, usable programs that are actively developed and supported. See also the "Tools" section in Appendix E, which also contains good examples of wxWidgets applications. In addition, there are some small but complete applications in the demos directory of the wxWidgets distribution, including a card game, a poetry viewer, a cellular automaton toy, and a fractal mountain generator.

AOL Communicator is a convenient way for AOL members to manage their email, address book, and much more. Communicator integrates email (including multiple email addresses), spam filtering, AIM instant messaging, and news in one interface. It's available for Windows and Mac OS X from http://communicator.aol.com.

Audacity is a free audio editor that can record and play sounds, import and export WAV, AIFF, Ogg Vorbis, and MP3 files, and more. It also has a built-in amplitude envelope editor, a customizable spectrogram mode, and a frequency analysis window for audio analysis applications. It's available for Windows, Linux, and Mac OS X (see Figure F-1) from http://audacity.sourceforge.net.

AVG Antivirus is a comprehensive antivirus program. The unique combination of detection methods (heuristic analysis, generic detection, scanning, and integrity checking) ensures maximum protection on multiple levels. There are versions for workstations, networks, email servers, and file servers. It's available for Windows and Linux from http://www.grisoft.com.

BitWise IM is an instant messenger with text, file transfer/sharing, whiteboard, and voice capability. All data sent between clients is automatically encrypted for privacy. The cross-platform interoperability of all features is unmatched by any other instant messenger. A free Personal and a paid Professional version are available for Windows, Linux, and Mac OS X (see Figure F-2) from http://www.bitwiseim.com.

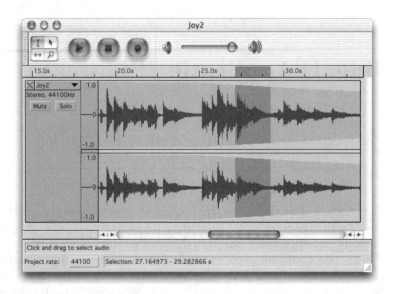

Figure F-1   Audacity running on MacOS X

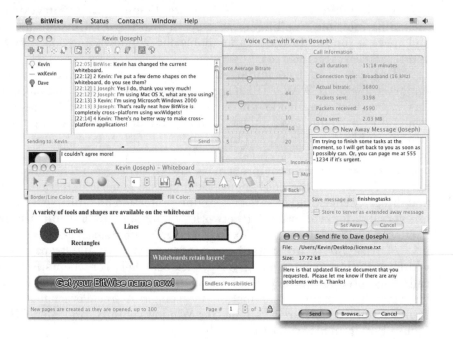

Figure F-2   BitWise on Mac OS X

Chess Commander is a chess game featuring legal move display, realistic voices, an orchestral soundtrack, and board annotation. Play chess against the computer as well as against email and network opponents with one interface. It's available for Windows (see Figure F-3) from http://www.chesscommander.com.

Cn3D is an application for viewing 3D structures from the National Center for Biotechnology Information's Entrez retrieval service. Cn3D runs on Windows (see Figure F-4), Mac, and Unix. Cn3D simultaneously displays structure, sequence, and alignment. It's available from http://www.ncbi.nlm.nih.gov/Structure/CN3D/cn3d.shtml.

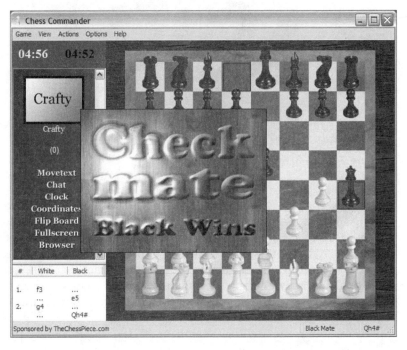

Figure F-3   Chess Commander

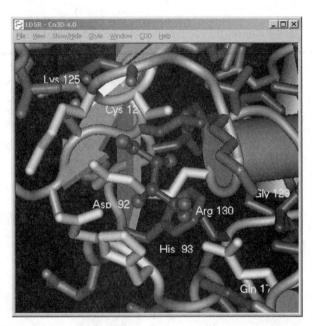

Figure F-4   Cn3D

Documancer is a programmer's documentation reader for Unix and Windows that has very fast full-text searching. It is written in wxPython using Mozilla as the rendering engine. It's available for Windows and Linux from http://documancer.sourceforge.net.

EarthVision is software for 3D model building and visualization that makes accurate well positioning, reservoir characterization, and environmental analysis easy. EarthVision's multitude of visualization tools, including integrated seismic display and interactive well design, improve and simplify quality control, well planning, and communication to management, investors, partners, and the diverse members of the asset team. It's available for Windows and Linux from http://www.dgi.com/earthvision.

Forte Agent is the top-rated UseNet newsreader on the Internet and is also a POP email client. Agent provides basic newsreader functionality, along with threaded discussions, off-line newsgroup datastore, automatic multi-part binary combining, yEnc encoding and decoding, kill and watch lists, cross-post management, and more. It's available for Windows from http://www.forteinc.com/agent/index.php.

KICAD is an open source (GPL) application for designing electronic schematic diagrams and printed circuit board artwork. Figure F-5 shows 2D and 3D views of different KICAD designs. It's available for Windows and Linux from http://www.lis.inpg.fr/realise_au_lis/kicad.

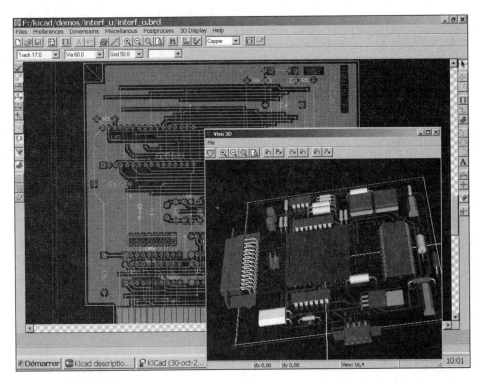

Figure F-5 KICAD

Kirix Strata is a dynamic database application for Windows (see Figure F-6) and Linux. With Strata, users can integrate data from diverse systems, create instant calculations across millions of records, and manipulate data interactively in a flexible graphical environment. Kirix Strata won the LinuxWorld 2005 Product Excellence Award for Best Desktop/Productivity/ Business Application. It's available from http://www.kirix.com.

Mahogany Mail is an open source mail and news client, focusing on IMAP4 support. Everything within Mahogany is configurable, and Mahogany also includes Python scripting, built-in filters, multiple identities, calendars, a powerful address book, Palm synchronization, fax capability, and much more. It's available for Windows, Linux (see Figure F-7), and Mac OS X from http://mahogany.sourceforge.net.

Mojoworld is a 3D world generator, with a procedural fractal engine that creates pixel-level detail at any resolution, distance, or field of view. It's available for Windows and Mac OS X from http://www.pandromeda.com.

pgAdmin III is a powerful administration and development platform for the PostgreSQL database, free for any use. The graphical interface supports all PostgreSQL features and makes administration easy. pgAdmin also includes a query builder, an SQL editor, a server-side code editor, and much more. It's available for Windows and Linux from http://www.pgadmin.org.

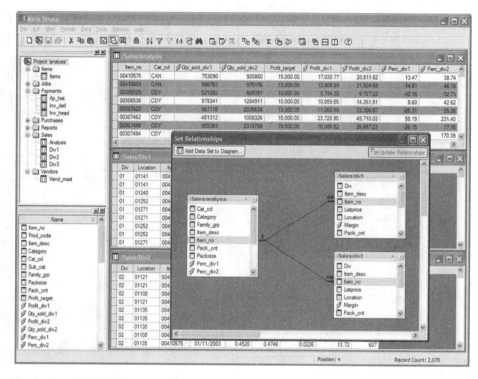

Figure F-6   KIRIX Strata

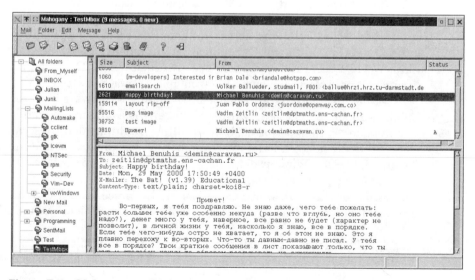

Figure F-7   Mahogany on Linux

SILO is a production-quality commercial 3D modeling application, employing advanced polygonal modeling tools and integrated subdivision surfaces. Silo is being used for video games, architectural design, film animation, and more. It's available for Windows and Mac OS X from `http://nevercenter.com`.

Tortoise CVS is a CVS version control interface that integrates with Windows Explorer. It enables direct check out, update, commit, and diffs by right-clicking on files and folders within Explorer. It shows a file's state on top of the normal icons within Explorer. It even works from within the File Open dialog. It's available for Windows from `http://www.tortoisecvs.org`.

Transcribe! is an assistant for people who sometimes want to work out a piece of music from a recording in order to write it out or play it themselves, or both. Transcribe! is not an editor. It reads, plays, and records audio files but does not modify them. It's available for Windows, Linux, and Mac OS X (see Figure F-8) from `http://www.seventhstring.com/xscribe/overview.html`.

VLC (VideoLAN client) is a highly portable multimedia player for various audio and video formats (such as MPEG-1, MPEG-2, MPEG-4, DivX, MP3, and OGG) as well as DVDs, VCDs, and various streaming protocols. It can also be used as a server to stream in unicast or multicast in IPv4 or IPv6 on a high-bandwidth network. It's available for Windows, Linux, and Mac OS X from `http://www.videolan.org/vlc`.

Writer's Café is a software toolkit for all fiction writers, whether experienced or just starting out. The heart of Writer's Café is StoryLines, a powerful but simple-to-use story development tool that dramatically accelerates the creation and structuring of your novel or screenplay. It's available for Windows (see Figure F-9), Linux, and Mac OS X (beta) from `http://www.writerscafe.co.uk`.

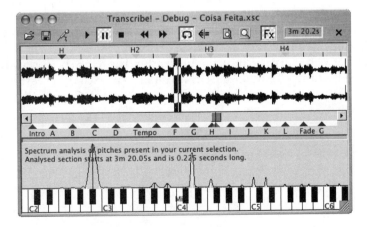

Figure F-8 Transcribe! running on Mac OS X

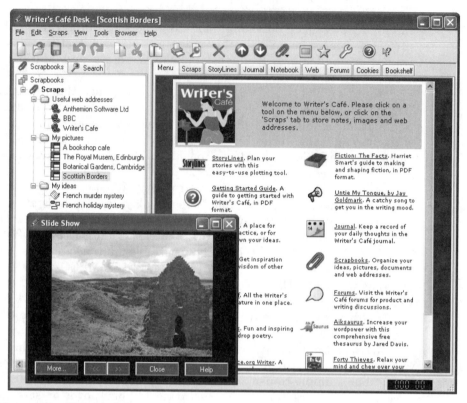

Figure F-9   Writer's Café

xCHM is a viewer for chm files (Microsoft Compiled HTML Help Files). It can show the contents tree if one is available; print the displayed page; change fonts, faces, and size; work with bookmarks; do the usual history stunts (forward, back, home); and search for text in the whole book. wxHtmlWindow is used to render the HTML. It's available for Linux (see Figure F-10) and Mac OS X from http://xchm.sourceforge.net.

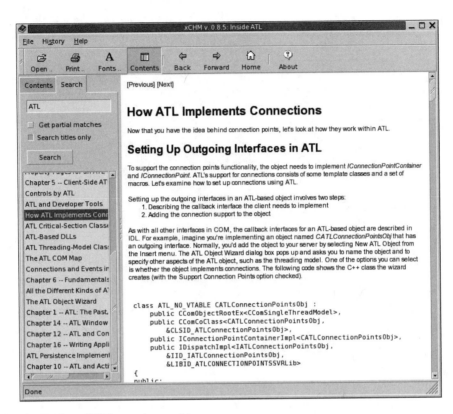

Figure F-10   xCHM running on Linux

Using the CD-ROM

BROWSING THE CD-ROM

The CD-ROM can be read under Windows, Mac OS X, and Linux (and other UNIX systems). The HTML contents should open automatically when you insert the CD-ROM under Windows and Linux. Otherwise, please open the file BrowseMe.htm with your preferred web browser.

THE CD-ROM CONTENTS

Here's what's on the disk:

☞ **Code examples.** Paste snippets into your own application, or compile the examples with your preferred compiler. In addition to the examples covered in this book, we include a bonus sample, "Riffle." This little image browser comes complete with source, installation scripts, and binaries for four platforms.

☞ **wxWidgets 2.6.** wxWidgets supports Windows (for desktop and Pocket PC), Unix/Linux, Mac OS X, and other platforms not covered by this book. Refer to Appendix A, "Installing wxWidgets," for installation details for the three major platforms.

☞ **DialogBlocks Personal Edition.** A version of the commercial DialogBlocks dialog editor/RAD tool for personal use. DialogBlocks runs on Windows, Linux, and Mac OS X with powerful sizer-based layout tools and the ability to compile your source using popular compilers. See Appendix C, "Creating Applications with DialogBlocks," to find out how to install and use DialogBlocks.

☞ **Compilers.** For Windows, we supply MinGW, Digital Mars C++, and OpenWatcom C++. (For Linux, GCC can be installed from your distribution, and for Mac OS X, the Apple Developer Tools are available from the Apple web site.)

☞ **poEdit.** poEdit is an essential tool to help you create message catalogs for your internationalized application.

☞ **wxPython.** wxPython is a powerful blend of wxWidgets and the Python language.

For updates, please see http://www.wxwidgets.org/book.

How wxWidgets Processes Events

This appendix takes a closer look at how wxWidgets processes events, going into details omitted from the simplified view we've seen so far.

When an event is received from the windowing system, wxWidgets calls `wxEvtHandler::ProcessEvent` on the first event handler object belonging to the window generating the event.

Figure H-1 summarizes the order of event table searching by `ProcessEvent`. Here's how it works:

1. If the object is disabled (via a call to `wxEvtHandler::SetEvtHandlerEnabled`), the function skips to Step 6.

2. If the object is a `wxWindow`, `ProcessEvent` is recursively called on the window's `wxValidator`. If this returns `true`, the function exits.

3. `SearchEventTable` is called for this event handler. If this fails, the base class table is tried, the next base class table is tried, and so on, until no more tables exist or an appropriate function is found, in which case the function exits.

4. The search is applied down the entire chain of event handlers. (Usually the chain has a length of one.) If this succeeds, the function exits.

5. If the object is a `wxWindow` and the event is set to propagate (only `wxCommandEvent` objects are normally set to propagate), `ProcessEvent` is recursively applied to the parent window's event handler. If this returns `true`, the function exits.

6. Finally, `ProcessEvent` is called on the `wxApp` object.

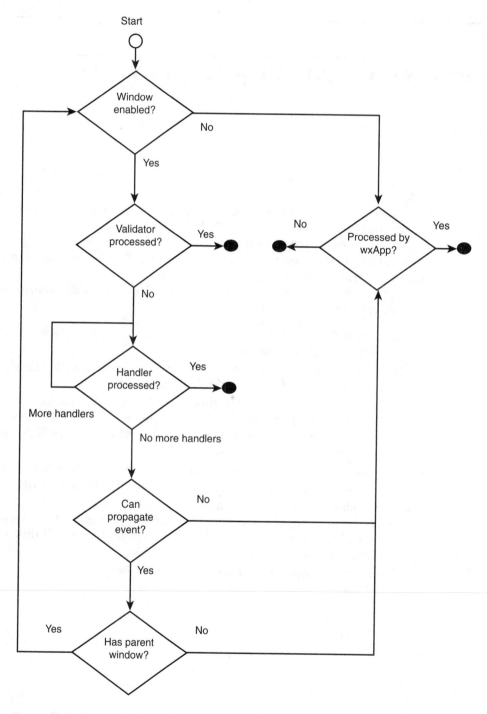

Figure H-1   Event processing flow

Pay close attention to Step 5. People often overlook or get confused by this powerful feature of the wxWidgets event processing system. To put it a different way, events set to propagate (most likely derived either directly or indirectly from `wxCommandEvent`) will travel up the containment hierarchy from child to parent until the maximal propagation level is reached or an event handler is found that doesn't call `Skip`.

When propagating command events upwards to the parent window, event propagation stops when it reaches the parent dialog, if any. This means that you don't risk getting unexpected events from dialog controls (which might be left unprocessed by the dialog itself because it doesn't care about them) when a modal dialog is popped up. The events do propagate beyond frames, however. The rationale for this choice is that a typical application has only a few frames, and their parent-child relationships are well understood by the programmer, whereas in a complex program, it may be very difficult, if not impossible, to track down all the dialogs that may be popped up (remember that some are created automatically by wxWidgets). If you need to specify a different behavior for some reason, you can use `SetExtraStyle(wxWS_EX_BLOCK_EVENTS)` explicitly to prevent events from being propagated beyond the given window, or you can unset this flag for dialogs, which have it set by default.

Fundamental window events (size, motion, paint, mouse, keyboard, and so on) are sent only to the window. Events that have a higher level of meaning or that are generated by the window itself—for example, button clicks, menu selection, tree expansion, and so on—are command events and are sent up to the parent to see if it is interested in the event.

Note that you might want your application to override `ProcessEvent` to redirect processing of events. This is done in the document-view framework, for example, to enable event handlers to be defined in the document or view. To test for command events (which will probably be the only events you want to redirect), you can use `wxEvent::IsCommandEvent` for efficiency instead of using the slower run-time type system.

Event Classes and Macros

In the wxWidgets reference, the documentation for specific event macros is organized by their event classes (such as wxCommandEvent), which are themselves referenced by the control class documentation (such as wxButton). You can refer to these sections for details, but it's useful to summarize the most commonly used event classes and macros, as shown in Table I-1.

Table I-1   Commonly Used Event Macros

Class: *wxActivateEvent*	
EVT_ACTIVATE(func)	Sent when a user activates or deactivates a top-level window.
EVT_ACTIVATE_APP(func)	Sent when a user activates or deactivates the window of a different application.
Class: *wxCommandEvent*	
EVT_COMMAND(id, event, func)	The same as EVT_CUSTOM, but expects a member function with a wxCommandEvent argument.
EVT_COMMAND_RANGE (id1, id2, event, func)	The same as EVT_CUSTOM_RANGE, but expects a member function with a wxCommandEvent argument.
EVT_BUTTON(id, func)	Processes a wxEVT_COMMAND_BUTTON_CLICKED event, generated when the user left-clicks on a wxButton.
EVT_CHECKBOX(id, func)	Processes a wxEVT_COMMAND_CHECBOX_CLICKED event, generated when the user checks or unchecks a wxCheckBox control.
EVT_CHECKLISTBOX(id, func)	Processes a wxEVT_COMMAND_CHECKLISTBOX_ TOGGLED event, generated by a wxCheckListBox control when the user checks or unchecks an item.

(continues)

Table I-1   Commonly Used Event Macros (*Continued*)

`EVT_CHOICE(id, func)`	Processes a `wxEVT_COMMAND_CHOICE_SELECTED` event, generated by a `wxChoice` control when the user selects an item in the list.
`EVT_COMBOBOX(id, func)`	Processes a `wxEVT_COMMAND_COMBOBOX_SELECTED` event, generated by a `wxComboBox` control when the user selects an item in the list.
`EVT_LISTBOX(id, func)`	Processes a `wxEVT_COMMAND_LISTBOX_SELECTED` event, generated by a `wxListBox` control when the user selects an item in the list.
`EVT_LISTBOX_DCLICK(id, func)`	Processes a `wxEVT_COMMAND_LISTBOX_DOUBLECLICKED` event, generated by a `wxListBox` control when the user double-clicks on an item in the list.
`EVT_TEXT(id, func)`	Processes a `wxEVT_COMMAND_TEXT_UPDATED` event, generated by a `wxTextCtrl`, `wxComboBox`, or `wxSpinCtrl` control when the text is edited.
`EVT_TEXT_ENTER(id, func)`	Processes a `wxEVT_COMMAND_TEXT_ENTER` event, generated by a `wxTextCtrl` control when the user presses the Enter key. Note that you must use `wxTE_PROCESS_ENTER` style when creating the control if you want it to generate such events.
`EVT_TEXT_MAXLEN(id, func)`	Processes a `wxEVT_COMMAND_TEXT_MAXLEN` event, generated by a `wxTextCtrl` control when the user tries to enter more characters into it than the limit previously set with `SetMaxLength`. Windows and GTK+ only.
`EVT_TOGGLEBUTTON(id, func)`	Processes a `wxEVT_COMMAND_TOGGLEBUTTON_CLICKED` event, generated when the user clicks the button.
`EVT_MENU(id, func)`	Processes a `wxEVT_COMMAND_MENU_SELECTED` event, generated by a menu item.
`EVT_MENU_RANGE(id1, id2, func)`	Processes a `wxEVT_COMMAND_MENU_RANGE` event, generated by a range of menu items.
`EVT_SLIDER(id, func)`	Processes a `wxEVT_COMMAND_SLIDER_UPDATED` event, generated by a `wxSlider` control when the user moves the slider.
`EVT_RADIOBOX(id, func)`	Processes a `wxEVT_COMMAND_RADIOBOX_SELECTED` event, generated by a `wxRadioBox` control when the user clicks on a radio button.

EVT_RADIOBUTTON(id, func)	Processes a wxEVT_COMMAND_RADIOBUTTON_ SELECTED event, generated by a wxRadioButton control when a user clicks on it.
EVT_SCROLLBAR(id, func)	Processes a wxEVT_COMMAND_SCROLLBAR_ UPDATED event, generated by a wxScrollBar control when any scroll event occurs. For more specific scrollbar event macros, see the documentation for wxScrollEvent.
EVT_TOOL(id, func)	Processes a wxEVT_COMMAND_TOOL_CLICKED event (a synonym for wxEVT_COMMAND_MENU_ SELECTED), generated when the user clicks on a toolbar tool. Pass the identifier of the tool.
EVT_TOOL_RANGE(id1, id2, func)	Processes a wxEVT_COMMAND_TOOL_CLICKED event for a range of identifiers. Pass the identifier of the tools.
EVT_TOOL_RCLICKED(id, func)	Processes a wxEVT_COMMAND_TOOL_RCLICKED event, generated when the user right-clicks on a control. Pass the identifier of the tool.
EVT_TOOL_RCLICKED_RANGE (id1, id2, func)	Processes a wxEVT_COMMAND_TOOL_RCLICKED event for a range of identifiers. Pass the identifiers of the tools.
EVT_TOOL_ENTER(id, func)	Processes a wxEVT_COMMAND_TOOL_ENTER event, generated when the mouse pointer moves into or out of a tool. Pass the identifier of the toolbar itself. The value of wxCommand Event::GetSelection is the tool identifier, or -1 if the pointer has moved off a tool.
Class: *wxCloseEvent*	
EVT_CLOSE(func)	Processes a wxEVT_CLOSE_WINDOW event, generated when the user closes a window via the window manager. This event applies to wxFrame and wxDialog classes. The event can be vetoed if CanVeto returns true.
EVT_QUERY_END_SESSION(func)	Processes a wxEVT_QUERY_END_SESSION event, generated when the session is about to end but can be vetoed by the user. This event applies to wxApp only. Windows only.
EVT_END_SESSION(func)	Processes a wxEVT_END_SESSION event, generated when the session is about to end. This event applies to wxApp only. Windows only.

(continues)

Table I-1   Commonly Used Event Macros (*Continued*)

Class: *wxContextMenuEvent*	
EVT_CONTEXT_MENU(id, func)	Processes the event generated when the user has requested a popup menu to appear by pressing a special keyboard key (under Windows) or by right-clicking the mouse.
EVT_COMMAND_CONTEXT_MENU (id, func)	The same as EVT_CONTEXT_MENU, but takes a window identifier.
Class: *wxEraseEvent*	
EVT_ERASE_BACKGROUND(func)	Processes a wxEVT_ERASE_BACKGROUND event, generated when a window's background needs to be repainted.
Class: *wxEvent*	
EVT_CUSTOM(event, id, func)	Allows you to add a custom event table entry by specifying the event identifier (such as wxEVT_SIZE), the window identifier, and a member function to call.
EVT_CUSTOM_RANGE (event, id1, id2, func)	The same as EVT_CUSTOM, but responds to a range of window identifiers.
Class: *wxFocusEvent*	
EVT_SET_FOCUS(func)	Processes a wxEVT_SET_FOCUS event, when a window gains the keyboard focus.
EVT_KILL_FOCUS(func)	Processes a wxEVT_KILL_FOCUS event, when a window loses the keyboard focus.
Class: *wxIdleEvent*	
EVT_IDLE(func)	Handles a wxEVT_IDLE event, passed to Windows and the application object in idle time (when all other events have been processed).
Class: *wxInitDialogEvent*	
EVT_INIT_DIALOG(func)	Handles a wxEVT_INIT_DIALOG event, sent when a dialog is initialized.
Class: *wxKeyEvent*	
EVT_CHAR(func)	Handles a wxEVT_CHAR event, generated when the user presses a key. Provides a translated keycode value
EVT_KEY_DOWN(func)	Handles a wxEVT_KEY_DOWN event, generated when the user presses a key. Provides an untranslated keycode value.
EVT_KEY_UP(func)	Handles a wxEVT_KEY_UP event, generated when a key has been released. Provides an untranslated keycode value.

Class: *wxMenuEvent*	
EVT_MENU_OPEN(func)	Handles a wxEVT_MENU_OPEN event, sent when a menu is about to be opened. On Windows, this is only sent once for each navigation of the menu bar.
EVT_MENU_CLOSE(func)	Handles a wxEVT_MENU_CLOSE event, sent when a menu has just been closed.
EVT_MENU_HIGHLIGHT(id, func)	Handles a wxEVT_MENU_HIGHLIGHT event, sent when the menu item with the specified id has been highlighted. This is used to show help prompts in a frame's status bar.
EVT_MENU_HIGHLIGHT_ALL(func)	Handles a wxEVT_MENU_HIGHLIGHT event for any menu identifier.
Class: *wxMouseEvent*	
EVT_LEFT_DOWN(func)	Handles a wxEVT_LEFT_DOWN event, generated when the left mouse button changes to the "down" state.
EVT_LEFT_UP(func)	Handles a wxEVT_LEFT_UP event, generated when the left mouse button changes to the "up" state.
EVT_LEFT_DCLICK(func)	Handles a wxEVT_LEFT_DCLICK event, generated when the left mouse button is double-clicked.
EVT_MIDDLE_DOWN(func)	Handles a wxEVT_MIDDLE_DOWN event, generated when the middle mouse button changes to the "down" state.
EVT_MIDDLE_UP(func)	Handles a wxEVT_MIDDLE_DCLICK event, generated when the middle mouse button is double-clicked.
EVT_MIDDLE_DCLICK(func)	Handles a wxEVT_MIDDLE_DCLICK event, generated when the middle mouse button is double-clicked.
EVT_RIGHT_DOWN(func)	Handles a wxEVT_RIGHT_DOWN event, generated when the right mouse button changes to the "down" states.
EVT_RIGHT_UP(func)	Handles a wxEVT_RIGHT_UP event, generated when the right mouse button changes to the "up" states.
EVT_RIGHT_DCLICK(func)	Handles a wxEVT_RIGHT_DCLICK event, generated when the right mouse button is double-clicked.

(continues)

Table I-1   Commonly Used Event Macros (*Continued*)

EVT_MOTION(func)	Handles a wxEVT_MOTION event, generated when the mouse moves.
EVT_ENTER_WINDOW(func)	Handles a wxEVT_ENTER_WINDOW event, generated when the mouse enters the window.
EVT_LEAVE_WINDOW(func)	Handles a wxEVT_LEAVE_WINDOW event, generated when the mouse leaves the window.
EVT_MOUSEWHEEL(func)	Handles a wxEVT_MOUSEWHEEL event, generated when the mouse wheel moves.
EVT_MOUSE_EVENTS(func)	Handles all mouse events.
Class: *wxMoveEvent*	
EVT_MOVE(func)	Handles a wxEVT_MOVE event, generated when a window is moved.
Class: *wxNotebookEvent*	
EVT_NOTEBOOK_PAGE_CHANGED (id, func)	The page selection has changed.
EVT_NOTEBOOK_PAGE_CHANGING (id, func)	The selection is about to change. You can veto the selection change with Veto.
Class: *wxPaintEvent*	
EVT_PAINT(func)	Handles a wxEVT_PAINT event, generated when an area of a window needs to be repainted.
Class: *wxScrollEvent* [1]	
EVT_SCROLL(func)	Handles all scroll events.
EVT_SCROLL_TOP(func)	Handles wxEVT_SCROLL_TOP scroll-to-top events (minimum position).
EVT_SCROLL_BOTTOM(func)	Handles wxEVT_SCROLL_TOP scroll-to-bottom events (maximum position).
EVT_SCROLL_LINEUP(func)	Handles wxEVT_SCROLL_LINEUP line up events.
EVT_SCROLL_LINEDOWN(func)	Handles wxEVT_SCROLL_LINEDOWN line down events.
EVT_SCROLL_PAGEUP(func)	Handles wxEVT_SCROLL_PAGEUP page up events.
EVT_SCROLL_PAGEDOWN(func)	Handles wxEVT_SCROLL_PAGEDOWN page down events.
EVT_SCROLL_THUMBTRACK(func)	Handles wxEVT_SCROLL_THUMBTRACK thumb track events (frequent events sent as the user drags the thumbtrack).
EVT_SCROLL_THUMBRELEASE(func)	Handles wxEVT_SCROLL_THUMBRELEASE thumb release events.
EVT_SCROLL_ENDSCROLL(func)	Handles wxEVT_SCROLL_ENDSCROLL end of scrolling events (Windows only).
EVT_COMMAND_SCROLL(id, func)	Handles all scroll events.

1. These macros are used to handle scroll events from wxScrollBar, wxSlider, and wxSpinButton. See wxScrollWinEvent for wxScrolledWindow events.

EVT_COMMAND_SCROLL_TOP (id, func)	Handles wxEVT_SCROLL_TOP scroll-to-top events (minimum position).
EVT_COMMAND_SCROLL_BOTTOM (id, func)	Handles wxEVT_SCROLL_TOP scroll-to-bottom events (maximum position).
EVT_COMMAND_SCROLL_LINEUP (id, func)	Handles wxEVT_SCROLL_LINEUP line up events.
EVT_COMMAND_SCROLL_LINEDOWN (id, func)	Handles wxEVT_SCROLL_LINEDOWN line down events.
EVT_COMMAND_SCROLL_PAGEUP (id, func)	Handles wxEVT_SCROLL_PAGEUP page up events.
EVT_COMMAND_SCROLL_PAGEDOWN (id, func)	Handles wxEVT_SCROLL_PAGEDOWN page down events.
EVT_COMMAND_SCROLL_THUMBTRACK (id, func)	Handles wxEVT_SCROLL_THUMBTRACK thumb track events (frequent events sent as the user drags the thumbtrack).
EVT_COMMAND_SCROLL_THUMBRELEASE (id, func)	Handles wxEVT_SCROLL_THUMBRELEASE thumb release events.
EVT_COMMAND_SCROLL_ENDSCROLL (id, func)	Handles wxEVT_SCROLL_ENDSCROLL end of scrolling events (Windows only).
Class: _wxScrollWinEvent_ [2]	
EVT_SCROLLWIN(func)	Handles all scroll events.
EVT_SCROLLWIN_TOP(func)	Handles wxEVT_SCROLLWIN_TOP scroll-to-top events.
EVT_SCROLLWIN_BOTTOM(func)	Handles wxEVT_SCROLLWIN_TOP scroll-to-bottom events.
EVT_SCROLLWIN_LINEUP(func)	Handles wxEVT_SCROLLWIN_LINEUP line up events.
EVT_SCROLLWIN_LINEDOWN(func)	Handles wxEVT_SCROLLWIN_LINEDOWN line down events.
EVT_SCROLLWIN_PAGEUP(func)	Handles wxEVT_SCROLLWIN_PAGEUP page up events.
EVT_SCROLLWIN_PAGEDOWN(func)	Handles wxEVT_SCROLLWIN_PAGEDOWN page down events.
EVT_SCROLLWIN_THUMBTRACK(func)	Handles wxEVT_SCROLLWIN_THUMBTRACK thumbtrack events (frequent events sent as the user drags the thumbtrack).
EVT_SCROLLWIN_THUMBRELEASE (func)	Handles wxEVT_SCROLLWIN_THUMBRELEASE thumb release events.

(continues)

2. These macros are used to handle scroll events from scrolling windows. See also wxScrollEvent earlier.

Table I-1   Commonly Used Event Macros (*Continued*)

Class: *wxSizeEvent*	
`EVT_SIZE(func)`	Handles a `wxEVT_SIZE` event, generated when the window is resized.
Class: *wxSpinEvent*	
`EVT_SPIN(id, func)`	Handles a `wxEVT_SCROLL_THUMBTRACK` event, generated for a `wxSpinButton` or `wxSpinCtrl` whenever the up or down arrows are clicked.
`EVT_SPIN_UP(id, func)`	Handles a `wxEVT_SCROLL_LINEUP` event, generated for a `wxSpinButton` or `wxSpinCtrl` when the up arrow is clicked.
`EVT_SPIN_DOWN(id, func)`	Handles a `wxEVT_SCROLL_LINEDOWN` event, generated for a `wxSpinButton` or `wxSpinCtrl` when the down arrow is clicked.
`EVT_SPINCTRL(id, func)`	Handles all events generated for a `wxSpinCtrl`.
Class: *wxSplitterEvent*	
`EVT_SPLITTER_SASH_POS_CHANGING(id, func)`	Processes a `wxEVT_COMMAND_SPLITTER_SASH_POS_CHANGING` event, generated when the sash position is in the process of being changed.
`EVT_SPLITTER_SASH_POS_CHANGED (id, func)`	Processes a `wxEVT_COMMAND_SPLITTER_SASH_POS_CHANGED` event, generated when the sash position is changed. May be used to modify the sash position before it is set, or to prevent the change from taking place.
`EVT_SPLITTER_UNSPLIT(id, func)`	Processes a `wxEVT_COMMAND_SPLITTER_UNSPLIT` event, generated when the splitter is unsplit.
`EVT_SPLITTER_DCLICK(id, func)`	Processes a `wxEVT_COMMAND_SPLITTER_DOUBLECLICKED` event, generated when the sash is double-clicked.
Class: *wxSysColourChangeEvent*	
`EVT_SYS_COLOUR_CHANGED event, (func)`	Processes a `wxEVT_SYS_COLOUR_CHANGED` generated when the user changed a color in the control panel (Windows only).
Class: *wxUpdateUIEvent*	
`EVT_UPDATE_UI(id, func)`	The `EVT_UPDATE_UI` macro is used to handle user interface update pseudo-events, which are generated to give the application the chance to update the visual state of menus, toolbars, and controls (see Chapter 9, "Creating Custom Dialogs"). Processes a `wxEVT_UPDATE_UI` event.
`EVT_UPDATE_UI_RANGE (id1, id2, func)`	Processes a `wxEVT_UPDATE_UI` event for a range of identifiers.

Class: *wxWindowCreateEvent*	
`EVT_WINDOW_CREATE(func)`	Processes a `wxEVT_CREATE` propagating event, generated when the underlying window has just been created.
Class: *wxWindowDestroyEvent*	
`EVT_WINDOW_DESTROY(func)`	Processes a `wxEVT_DELETE` propagating event, generated when the window is about to be destroyed.
`EVT_MIDDLE_DCLICK(func)`	Handles a `wxEVT_MIDDLE_DCLICK` event, generated when the middle mouse button is double-clicked.
`EVT_RIGHT_DOWN(func)`	Handles a `wxEVT_RIGHT_DOWN` event, generated when the right mouse button changes to the "down" states.
`EVT_RIGHT_UP(func)`	Handles a `wxEVT_RIGHT_UP` event, generated when the right mouse button changes to the "up" states.

Code Listings

CUSTOM DIALOG CLASS IMPLEMENTATION

These are the header and implementation files for the `PersonalRecordDialog` class described in Chapter 9, "Creating Custom Dialogs." It can be found in `examples/chap09` on the CD-ROM.

Listing J-1   Header File for *PersonalRecordDialog*

```
////////////////////////////////////////////////////////////////////
// Name:       personalrecord.h
// Purpose:    Dialog to get name, age, sex, and voting preference
// Author:     Julian Smart
// Created:    02/28/04 06:52:49
// Copyright:  (c) 2004, Julian Smart
// Licence:    wxWindows license
////////////////////////////////////////////////////////////////////

#ifndef _PERSONALRECORD_H_
#define _PERSONALRECORD_H_

#ifdef __GNUG__
#pragma interface "personalrecord.cpp"
#endif

/*!
 * Includes
 */

#include "wx/spinctrl.h"
#include "wx/statline.h"

/*!
 * Control identifiers
 */
```

(continues)

Listing J-1   (*Continued*)

```
enum {
    ID_PERSONAL_RECORD = 10000,
    ID_NAME = 10001,
    ID_AGE = 10002,
    ID_SEX = 10003,
    ID_VOTE = 10006,
    ID_RESET = 10004
};

/*!
 * PersonalRecordDialog class declaration
 */

class PersonalRecordDialog: public wxDialog
{
    DECLARE_CLASS( PersonalRecordDialog )
    DECLARE_EVENT_TABLE()

public:

//// Constructors

    PersonalRecordDialog( );

    PersonalRecordDialog( wxWindow* parent,
      wxWindowID id = ID_PERSONAL_RECORD,
      const wxString& caption = wxT("Personal Record"),
      const wxPoint& pos = wxDefaultPosition,
      const wxSize& size = wxDefaultSize,
      long style = wxCAPTION|wxRESIZE_BORDER|wxSYSTEM_MENU );

    /// Member initialization
    void Init();

    /// Creation
    bool Create( wxWindow* parent,
      wxWindowID id = ID_PERSONAL_RECORD,
      const wxString& caption = wxT("Personal Record"),
      const wxPoint& pos = wxDefaultPosition,
      const wxSize& size = wxDefaultSize,
      long style = wxCAPTION|wxRESIZE_BORDER|wxSYSTEM_MENU );

    /// Creates the controls and sizers
    void CreateControls();

    /// Sets the validators for the dialog controls
    void SetDialogValidators();

    /// Sets the help text for the dialog controls
    void SetDialogHelp();

    /// Name accessors
    void SetName(const wxString& name) { m_name = name; }
    wxString GetName() const { return m_name; }

    /// Age accessors
    void SetAge(int age) { m_age = age; }
    int GetAge() const { return m_age; }
```

```
    /// Sex accessors (male = false, female = true)
    void SetSex(bool sex) { sex ? m_sex = 1 : m_sex = 0; }
    bool GetSex() const { return m_sex == 1; }

    /// Does the person vote?
    void SetVote(bool vote) { m_vote = vote; }
    bool GetVote() const { return m_vote; }

//// PersonalRecordDialog event handler declarations

    /// wxEVT_UPDATE_UI event handler for ID_VOTE
    void OnVoteUpdate( wxUpdateUIEvent& event );

    /// wxEVT_COMMAND_BUTTON_CLICKED event handler for ID_RESET
    void OnResetClick( wxCommandEvent& event );

    /// wxEVT_COMMAND_BUTTON_CLICKED event handler for wxID_HELP
    void OnHelpClick( wxCommandEvent& event );

//// PersonalRecordDialog member variables

    /// Data members
    wxString    m_name;
    int         m_age;
    int         m_sex;
    bool        m_vote;
};

#endif

    // _PERSONALRECORD_H_
```

Listing J-2 Implementation File for *PersonalRecordDialog*

```
///////////////////////////////////////////////////////////////
// Name:        personalrecord.cpp
// Purpose:     Dialog to get name, age, sex, and voting preference
// Author:      Julian Smart
// Created:     02/28/04 06:52:49
// Copyright:   (c) 2004, Julian Smart
// Licence:     wxWindows license
///////////////////////////////////////////////////////////////

#ifdef __GNUG__
#pragma implementation "personalrecord.h"
#endif

// For compilers that support precompilation, includes "wx/wx.h".
#include "wx/wxprec.h"

#ifdef __BORLANDC__
#pragma hdrstop
#endif

#include "wx/valtext.h"
#include "wx/valgen.h"
```

(continues)

Listing J-2   (*Continued*)

```
#include "personalrecord.h"

/*!
 * PersonalRecordDialog type definition
 */

IMPLEMENT_CLASS( PersonalRecordDialog, wxDialog )

/*!
 * PersonalRecordDialog event table definition
 */

BEGIN_EVENT_TABLE( PersonalRecordDialog, wxDialog )
    EVT_UPDATE_UI( ID_VOTE, PersonalRecordDialog::OnVoteUpdate )
    EVT_BUTTON( ID_RESET, PersonalRecordDialog::OnResetClick )
    EVT_BUTTON( wxID_HELP, PersonalRecordDialog::OnHelpClick )
END_EVENT_TABLE()

/*!
 * PersonalRecordDialog constructors
 */

PersonalRecordDialog::PersonalRecordDialog( )
{
    Init();
}

PersonalRecordDialog::PersonalRecordDialog( wxWindow* parent,
  wxWindowID id, const wxString& caption,
  const wxPoint& pos, const wxSize& size, long style )
{
    Init();

    Create(parent, id, caption, pos, size, style);
}

/// Initialization
void PersonalRecordDialog::Init( )
{
    m_name = wxEmptyString;
    m_age = 25;
    m_sex = false;
    m_vote = false;
}

/*!
 * PersonalRecord creator
 */

bool PersonalRecordDialog::Create( wxWindow* parent,
  wxWindowID id, const wxString& caption,
  const wxPoint& pos, const wxSize& size, long style )
{
    // We have to set extra styles before creating the
    // dialog

    SetExtraStyle(wxWS_EX_BLOCK_EVENTS¦wxDIALOG_EX_CONTEXTHELP);
```

```
        if (!wxDialog::Create( parent, id, caption, pos, size, style ))
            return false;

        CreateControls();
        SetDialogHelp();
        SetDialogValidators();

        // This fits the dialog to the minimum size dictated by
        // the sizers

        GetSizer()->Fit(this);

        // This ensures that the dialog cannot be sized smaller
        // than the minimum size

        GetSizer()->SetSizeHints(this);

        // Centre the dialog on the parent or (if none) screen

        Centre();

        return true;
    }

    /*!
     * Control creation for PersonalRecordDialog
     */

    void PersonalRecordDialog::CreateControls()
    {
        // A top-level sizer

        wxBoxSizer* topSizer = new wxBoxSizer(wxVERTICAL);
        this->SetSizer(topSizer);

        // A second box sizer to give more space around the controls

        wxBoxSizer* boxSizer = new wxBoxSizer(wxVERTICAL);
        topSizer->Add(boxSizer, 0, wxALIGN_CENTER_HORIZONTAL¦wxALL, 5);

        // A friendly message

        wxStaticText* descr = new wxStaticText( this, wxID_STATIC,
            wxT("Please enter your name, age and sex, and specify whether you
    wish to\nvote in a general election."), wxDefaultPosition, wxDefaultSize,
    0 );
        boxSizer->Add(descr, 0, wxALIGN_LEFT¦wxALL, 5);

        // Spacer

        boxSizer->Add(5, 5, 0, wxALIGN_CENTER_HORIZONTAL¦wxALL, 5);

        // Label for the name text control

        wxStaticText* nameLabel = new wxStaticText ( this, wxID_STATIC,
            wxT("&Name:"), wxDefaultPosition, wxDefaultSize, 0 );
        boxSizer->Add(nameLabel, 0, wxALIGN_LEFT¦wxALL, 5);

        // A text control for the user's name
```

(continues)

```
    wxTextCtrl* nameCtrl = new wxTextCtrl ( this, ID_NAME, wxT("Emma"),
wxDefaultPosition, wxDefaultSize, 0 );
    boxSizer->Add(nameCtrl, 0, wxGROW|wxALL, 5);


    // A horizontal box sizer to contain age, sex and vote

    wxBoxSizer* ageSexVoteBox = new wxBoxSizer(wxHORIZONTAL);
    boxSizer->Add(ageSexVoteBox, 0, wxGROW|wxALL, 5);

    // Label for the age control

    wxStaticText* ageLabel = new wxStaticText ( this, wxID_STATIC,
        wxT("&Age:"), wxDefaultPosition, wxDefaultSize, 0 );
    ageSexVoteBox->Add(ageLabel, 0, wxALIGN_CENTER_VERTICAL|wxALL, 5);

    // A spin control for the user's age

    wxSpinCtrl* ageSpin = new wxSpinCtrl ( this, ID_AGE,
        wxEmptyString, wxDefaultPosition, wxSize(60, -1),
        wxSP_ARROW_KEYS, 0, 120, 25 );
    ageSexVoteBox->Add(ageSpin, 0, wxALIGN_CENTER_VERTICAL|wxALL, 5);

    // Label for the sex control

    wxStaticText* sexLabel = new wxStaticText ( this, wxID_STATIC,
        wxT("&Sex:"), wxDefaultPosition, wxDefaultSize, 0 );
    ageSexVoteBox->Add(sexLabel, 0, wxALIGN_CENTER_VERTICAL|wxALL, 5);

    // Create the sex choice control

    wxString sexStrings[] = {
        wxT("Male"),
        wxT("Female")
    };

    wxChoice* sexChoice = new wxChoice ( this, ID_SEX,
        wxDefaultPosition, wxSize(80, -1), WXSIZEOF(sexStrings),
            sexStrings, 0 );
    sexChoice->SetStringSelection(wxT("Female"));
    ageSexVoteBox->Add(sexChoice, 0, wxALIGN_CENTER_VERTICAL|wxALL, 5);

    // Add a spacer that stretches to push the Vote control
    // to the right

    ageSexVoteBox->Add(5, 5, 1, wxALIGN_CENTER_VERTICAL|wxALL, 5);

    wxCheckBox* voteCheckBox = new wxCheckBox( this, ID_VOTE,
        wxT("&Vote"), wxDefaultPosition, wxDefaultSize, 0 );
    voteCheckBox ->SetValue(true);
    ageSexVoteBox->Add(voteCheckBox, 0,
        wxALIGN_CENTER_VERTICAL|wxALL, 5);

    // A dividing line before the OK and Cancel buttons

    wxStaticLine* line = new wxStaticLine ( this, wxID_STATIC,
        wxDefaultPosition, wxDefaultSize, wxLI_HORIZONTAL );
    boxSizer->Add(line, 0, wxGROW|wxALL, 5);
```

```
        // A horizontal box sizer to contain Reset, OK, Cancel and Help

        wxBoxSizer* okCancelBox = new wxBoxSizer(wxHORIZONTAL);
        boxSizer->Add(okCancelBox, 0, wxALIGN_CENTER_HORIZONTAL|wxALL, 5);

        // The Reset button

        wxButton* reset = new wxButton( this, ID_RESET, wxT("&Reset"),
            wxDefaultPosition, wxDefaultSize, 0 );
        okCancelBox->Add(reset, 0, wxALIGN_CENTER_VERTICAL|wxALL, 5);

        // The OK button

        wxButton* ok = new wxButton ( this, wxID_OK, wxT("&OK"),
            wxDefaultPosition, wxDefaultSize, 0 );
        okCancelBox->Add(ok, 0, wxALIGN_CENTER_VERTICAL|wxALL, 5);

        // The Cancel button

        wxButton* cancel = new wxButton ( this, wxID_CANCEL,
            wxT("&Cancel"), wxDefaultPosition, wxDefaultSize, 0 );
        okCancelBox->Add(cancel, 0, wxALIGN_CENTER_VERTICAL|wxALL, 5);

        // The Help button

        wxButton* help = new wxButton( this, wxID_HELP, wxT("&Help"),
            wxDefaultPosition, wxDefaultSize, 0 );
        okCancelBox->Add(help, 0, wxALIGN_CENTER_VERTICAL|wxALL, 5);
}

// Set the validators for the dialog controls
void PersonalRecordDialog::SetDialogValidators()
{
    FindWindow(ID_NAME)->SetValidator(
        wxTextValidator(wxFILTER_ALPHA, & m_name));
    FindWindow(ID_AGE)->SetValidator(
        wxGenericValidator(& m_age));
    FindWindow(ID_SEX)->SetValidator(
        wxGenericValidator(& m_sex));
    FindWindow(ID_VOTE)->SetValidator(
        wxGenericValidator(& m_vote));
}

// Sets the help text for the dialog controls
void PersonalRecordDialog::SetDialogHelp()
{
    wxString nameHelp = wxT("Enter your full name.");
    wxString ageHelp = wxT("Specify your age.");
    wxString sexHelp = wxT("Specify your gender, male or female.");
    wxString voteHelp = wxT("Check this if you wish to vote.");

    FindWindow(ID_NAME)->SetHelpText(nameHelp);
    FindWindow(ID_NAME)->SetToolTip(nameHelp);

    FindWindow(ID_AGE)->SetHelpText(ageHelp);
    FindWindow(ID_AGE)->SetToolTip(ageHelp);

    FindWindow(ID_SEX)->SetHelpText(sexHelp);
    FindWindow(ID_SEX)->SetToolTip(sexHelp);
```

(continues)

Listing J-2   (*Continued*)

```
    FindWindow(ID_VOTE)->SetHelpText(voteHelp);
    FindWindow(ID_VOTE)->SetToolTip(voteHelp);
}

/*!
 * wxEVT_UPDATE_UI event handler for ID_CHECKBOX
 */

void PersonalRecordDialog::OnVoteUpdate( wxUpdateUIEvent& event )
{
    wxSpinCtrl* ageCtrl = (wxSpinCtrl*) FindWindow(ID_AGE);
    if (ageCtrl->GetValue() < 18)
    {
        event.Enable(false)
        event.Check(false);
    }
    else
        event.Enable(true);
}

/*!
 * wxEVT_COMMAND_BUTTON_CLICKED event handler for ID_RESET
 */

void PersonalRecordDialog::OnResetClick( wxCommandEvent& event )
{
    Init();
    TransferDataToWindow();
}

/*!
 * wxEVT_COMMAND_BUTTON_CLICKED event handler for wxID_HELP
 */

void PersonalRecordDialog::OnHelpClick( wxCommandEvent& event )
{
    // Normally we would wish to display proper online help.
    // For this example, we're just using a message box.
    /*
    wxGetApp().GetHelpController().DisplaySection(wxT("Personal record
dialog"));
     */

    wxString helpText =
      wxT("Please enter your full name, age and gender.\n")
      wxT("Also indicate your willingness to vote in general
elections.\n\n")
      wxT("No non-alphabetical characters are allowed in the name
field.\n")
      wxT("Try to be honest about your age.");

    wxMessageBox(helpText,
      wxT("Personal Record Dialog Help"),
      wxOK¦wxICON_INFORMATION, this);

}
```

WXWIZARD SAMPLE CODE

This code is the full listing for the wxWizard example as described in Chapter 12, "Advanced Window Classes." It can be found in examples/chap12 on the CD-ROM.

Listing J-3   Wizard Sample Code

```cpp
/////////////////////////////////////////////////////////////////
// Name:          wizard.cpp
// Purpose:       wxWidgets sample demonstrating wxWizard control
// Author:        Vadim Zeitlin
// Licence:       wxWindows licence
/////////////////////////////////////////////////////////////////

// headers

#include "wx/wx.h"
#include "wx/wizard.h"

#include "wiztest.xpm"
#include "wiztest2.xpm"

// constants

// ids for menu items
enum
{
    Wizard_Quit = 100,
    Wizard_Run,
    Wizard_About = 1000
};

// private classes

class MyApp : public wxApp
{
public:
    // override base class virtuals
    virtual bool OnInit();
};

class MyFrame : public wxFrame
{
public:
    // ctor(s)
    MyFrame(const wxString& title);

    // event handlers
    void OnQuit(wxCommandEvent& event);
    void OnAbout(wxCommandEvent& event);
    void OnRunWizard(wxCommandEvent& event);
    void OnWizardCancel(wxWizardEvent& event);
    void OnWizardFinished(wxWizardEvent& event);

private:
    DECLARE_EVENT_TABLE()
};
```

(continues)

Listing J-3   *(Continued)*

```cpp
// some pages for our wizard
// this shows how to simply control the validity of the user input
// by just overriding TransferDataFromWindow() - of course, in a
// real program, the check wouldn't be so trivial and the data
// will be probably saved somewhere too
//
// it also shows how to use a different bitmap for one of the pages
class wxValidationPage : public wxWizardPageSimple
{
public:
    wxValidationPage(wxWizard *parent) : wxWizardPageSimple(parent)
    {
        m_bitmap = wxBitmap(wiztest2_xpm);

        m_checkbox = new wxCheckBox(this, wxID_ANY,
                        wxT("&Check me"));

        wxBoxSizer *mainSizer = new wxBoxSizer(wxVERTICAL);
        mainSizer->Add(
            new wxStaticText(this, wxID_ANY,
                    wxT("You need to check the checkbox\n")
                    wxT("below before going to the next page\n")),
            0,
            wxALL,
            5
        );

        mainSizer->Add(
            m_checkbox,
            0, // No stretching
            wxALL,
            5 // Border
        );
        SetSizer(mainSizer);
        mainSizer->Fit(this);
    }

    virtual bool TransferDataFromWindow()
    {
        if ( !m_checkbox->GetValue() )
        {
            wxMessageBox(wxT("Check the checkbox first!"),
                        wxT("No way"),
                        wxICON_WARNING | wxOK, this);

            return false;
        }
        return true;
    }

private:
    wxCheckBox *m_checkbox;
};

// This is a more complicated example of validity checking:
// using events we may allow the user to return to the previous
// page, but not to proceed. It also demonstrates how to
// intercept a Cancel button press.
class wxRadioboxPage : public wxWizardPageSimple
```

```
{
public:
    // directions in which we allow the user to proceed from this page
    enum
    {
        Forward, Backward, Both, Neither
    };

    wxRadioboxPage(wxWizard *parent) : wxWizardPageSimple(parent)
    {
        // should correspond to the enum above
        static wxString choices[] = { wxT("forward"), wxT("backward"),
wxT("both"), wxT("neither") };

        m_radio = new wxRadioBox(this, wxID_ANY, wxT("Allow to proceed:"),
                                 wxDefaultPosition, wxDefaultSize,
                                 WXSIZEOF(choices), choices,
                                 1, wxRA_SPECIFY_COLS);
        m_radio->SetSelection(Both);

        wxBoxSizer *mainSizer = new wxBoxSizer(wxVERTICAL);
        mainSizer->Add(
            m_radio,
            0, // No stretching
            wxALL,
            5 // Border
        );
        SetSizer(mainSizer);
        mainSizer->Fit(this);
    }

    // wizard event handlers
    void OnWizardCancel(wxWizardEvent& event)
    {
        if ( wxMessageBox(wxT("Do you really want to cancel?"),
wxT("Question"),
                          wxICON_QUESTION | wxYES_NO, this) != wxYES )
        {
            // not confirmed
            event.Veto();
        }
    }

    void OnWizardPageChanging(wxWizardEvent& event)
    {
        int sel = m_radio->GetSelection();

        if ( sel == Both )
            return;

        if ( event.GetDirection() && sel == Forward )
            return;

        if ( !event.GetDirection() && sel == Backward )
            return;

        wxMessageBox(wxT("You can't go there"), wxT("Not allowed"),
                     wxICON_WARNING | wxOK, this);
```

(continues)

Listing J-3   (*Continued*)

```
            event.Veto();
    }

private:
    wxRadioBox *m_radio;

    DECLARE_EVENT_TABLE()
};

// this shows how to dynamically (i.e. during run-time) arrange
// the page order
class wxCheckboxPage : public wxWizardPage
{
public:
    wxCheckboxPage(wxWizard *parent,
                   wxWizardPage *prev,
                   wxWizardPage *next)
        : wxWizardPage(parent)
    {
        m_prev = prev;
        m_next = next;

        wxBoxSizer *mainSizer = new wxBoxSizer(wxVERTICAL);

        mainSizer->Add(
            new wxStaticText(this, wxID_ANY, wxT("Try checking the box
below and\n")
                                        wxT("then going back and clearing it")),
            0, // No vertical stretching
            wxALL,
            5 // Border width
        );

        m_checkbox = new wxCheckBox(this, wxID_ANY,
                        wxT("&Skip the next page"));
        mainSizer->Add(
            m_checkbox,
            0, // No vertical stretching
            wxALL,
            5 // Border width
        );

        SetSizer(mainSizer);
        mainSizer->Fit(this);
    }

    // implement wxWizardPage functions
    virtual wxWizardPage *GetPrev() const { return m_prev; }
    virtual wxWizardPage *GetNext() const
    {
        return m_checkbox->GetValue() ? m_next->GetNext() : m_next;
    }

private:
    wxWizardPage *m_prev,
                 *m_next;

    wxCheckBox *m_checkbox;
```

```
    };

    // implementation

    // event tables and such

    BEGIN_EVENT_TABLE(MyFrame, wxFrame)
        EVT_MENU(Wizard_Quit,   MyFrame::OnQuit)
        EVT_MENU(Wizard_About,  MyFrame::OnAbout)
        EVT_MENU(Wizard_Run,    MyFrame::OnRunWizard)

        EVT_WIZARD_CANCEL(wxID_ANY, MyFrame::OnWizardCancel)
        EVT_WIZARD_FINISHED(wxID_ANY, MyFrame::OnWizardFinished)
    END_EVENT_TABLE()

    BEGIN_EVENT_TABLE(wxRadioboxPage, wxWizardPageSimple)
        EVT_WIZARD_PAGE_CHANGING(wxID_ANY,
    wxRadioboxPage::OnWizardPageChanging)
        EVT_WIZARD_CANCEL(wxID_ANY, wxRadioboxPage::OnWizardCancel)
    END_EVENT_TABLE()

    IMPLEMENT_APP(MyApp)

    // the application class

    bool MyApp::OnInit()
    {
        MyFrame *frame = new MyFrame(wxT("wxWizard Sample"));

        frame->Show(true);

        // we're done
        return true;
    }

    // MyFrame

    MyFrame::MyFrame(const wxString& title)
            : wxFrame((wxFrame *)NULL, wxID_ANY, title,
                      wxDefaultPosition, wxSize(250, 150))  // small frame
    {
        wxMenu *fileMenu = new wxMenu;
        fileMenu->Append(Wizard_Run, wxT("&Run wizard...\tCtrl-R"));
        fileMenu->AppendSeparator();
        fileMenu->Append(Wizard_Quit, wxT("E&xit\tAlt-X"), wxT("Quit this
    program"));

        wxMenu *helpMenu = new wxMenu;
        helpMenu->Append(Wizard_About, wxT("&About...\tF1"), wxT("Show about
    dialog"));

        // now append the freshly created menu to the menu bar...
        wxMenuBar *menuBar = new wxMenuBar();
        menuBar->Append(fileMenu, wxT("&File"));
        menuBar->Append(helpMenu, wxT("&Help"));

        // ... and attach this menu bar to the frame
        SetMenuBar(menuBar);
```

(continues)

Listing J-3   (*Continued*)

```
    // also create status bar which we use in OnWizardCancel
    CreateStatusBar();
}

void MyFrame::OnQuit(wxCommandEvent& WXUNUSED(event))
{

    // true is to force the frame to close
    Close(true);
}

void MyFrame::OnAbout(wxCommandEvent& WXUNUSED(event))
{
    wxMessageBox(wxT("Demo of wxWizard class\n")
                 wxT("(c) 1999, 2000 Vadim Zeitlin"),
                 wxT("About wxWizard sample"), wxOK | wxICON_INFORMA-
TION, this);
}

void MyFrame::OnRunWizard(wxCommandEvent& WXUNUSED(event))
{
    wxWizard *wizard = new wxWizard(this, wxID_ANY,
                 wxT("Absolutely Useless Wizard"),
                 wxBitmap(wiztest_xpm),
                 wxDefaultPosition,
                 wxDEFAULT_DIALOG_STYLE | wxRESIZE_BORDER);

    // a wizard page may be either an object of predefined class
    wxWizardPageSimple *page1 = new wxWizardPageSimple(wizard);
    wxStaticText *text = new wxStaticText(page1, wxID_ANY,
        wxT("This wizard doesn't help you\nto do anything at all.\n")
        wxT("\n")
        wxT("The next pages will present you\nwith more useless con-
trols."),
        wxPoint(5,5)
        );

    // ... or a derived class
    wxRadioboxPage *page3 = new wxRadioboxPage(wizard);
    wxValidationPage *page4 = new wxValidationPage(wizard);

    // set the page order using a convenience function - could
    // also use SetNext/Prev directly as below
    wxWizardPageSimple::Chain(page3, page4);

    // this page is not a wxWizardPageSimple, so we use SetNext/Prev
    // to insert it into the chain of pages
    wxCheckboxPage *page2 = new wxCheckboxPage(wizard, page1, page3);
    page1->SetNext(page2);
    page3->SetPrev(page2);

    // allow the wizard to size itself around the pages
    wizard->GetPageAreaSizer()->Add(page1);

    if ( wizard->RunWizard(page1) )
    {
```

```
            wxMessageBox(wxT("The wizard successfully completed"),
                wxT("That's all"), wxICON_INFORMATION ¦ wxOK);
    }

    wizard->Destroy();
}

void MyFrame::OnWizardFinished(wxWizardEvent& WXUNUSED(event))
{
    wxLogStatus(this, wxT("The wizard finished successfully."));
}

void MyFrame::OnWizardCancel(wxWizardEvent& WXUNUSED(event))
{
    wxLogStatus(this, wxT("The wizard was cancelled."));

}
```

Porting from MFC

There are thousands of applications and millions of lines of code written in MFC, and it's increasingly common for organizations and individuals to migrate from MFC to wxWidgets to take advantage of other platforms and markets. Porting is easier than you might think because the wxWidgets API has many concepts and constructs that are similar to those in MFC. This appendix gives you an idea of what's involved, provides comparisons for particular features, and suggests some porting strategies.

GENERAL OBSERVATIONS

The processes of programming with MFC and programming with wxWidgets are fairly similar. In each, you write application, window, and other classes; create dialogs using suitable tools; define how user interaction relates to code; and compile and link the code with the GUI library. You can continue to use (say) Visual Studio to edit, compile, and debug your wxWidgets applications, using external tools such as DialogBlocks to create your dialogs. Or, you can use an open source IDE such as Dev-C++ or Eclipse; you can even switch to Linux or Mac as your main platform.

On Windows, you can combine MFC and wxWidgets code into a single executable: see samples/mfc in wxWidgets. So if you really need to, you may be able to delay porting parts of your code as long as you only need it on Windows. However, the complexity and space overhead of combining two frameworks means that a clean break from MFC is a better strategy.

FEATURE COMPARISON

We continue with a selection of topics to show how MFC constructs can be ported to wxWidgets.

Application Initialization

Like MFC, a wxWidgets application is driven by an application class: wxApp instead of CWinApp. The CWinApp::InitInstance override is replaced by wxApp::OnInit, which returns a boolean value to indicate that the event loop should be started. Application cleanup is done in wxApp::OnExit instead of CWinApp::ExitInstance.

wxWidgets applications require the IMPLEMENT_APP declaration to be placed in the application class implementation file, for example:

```
IMPLEMENT_APP(MyApp)
```

MFC applications access the command line with the m_lpCmdLine string member of CWinApp (or GetCommandLine), whereas in wxWidgets, you access the argc and argv members of wxApp, which are in the same format as the parameters of the traditional C main function. To help convert your existing command-line parsing code, use the wxCmdLineParser class explained in Chapter 20, "Perfecting Your Application."

Message Maps

Where MFC has message maps, wxWidgets uses event tables. (wxWidgets can also route events dynamically, using a different syntax.) The principle of event tables should be immediately familiar to MFC programmers. Although message handler functions can have an arbitrary number of parameters, wxWidgets event handlers always take a single event argument, through which information can be passed in and out of the event handler. As with MFC, event tables can be placed in a window or in the application class, and in document and view classes when using the document/view framework. Let's compare an MFC message map with a wxWidgets event table. Here's the application class and message map in MFC (note that the class declaration and message map would normally be in separate files):

```
//
// MFC message map
//

class CDemoApp: public CWinApp
{
public:
    CDemoApp();

    // Overrides
    virtual BOOL InitInstance();

// Implementation

    afx_msg void OnAppAbout();
    afx_msg void OnFileSave();
```

```
        afx_msg void OnStretchMode();
        afx_msg void OnUpdateStretchMode(CCmdUI* pCmdUI);

// Attributes
private:

    int        m_stretchMode;
    MyFrame *m_mainFrame;

    DECLARE_MESSAGE_MAP()
};

BEGIN_MESSAGE_MAP(CDemoApp, CWinApp)
        ON_COMMAND(ID_APP_ABOUT, CDemoApp::OnAppAbout)
        ON_COMMAND(ID_FILE_SAVE, CDemoApp::OnFileSave)
        ON_COMMAND(ID_STRETCH_MODE, CDemoApp::OnUpdateStretchMode)
        ON_UPDATE_COMMAND_UI(ID_STRETCH_MODE, OnUpdateStretchMode)
END_MESSAGE_MAP()

void CDemoApp::OnAppAbout()
{
    m_mainFrame->MessageBox(_T("Demo App (c) 2005"), _T("About Demo
App"));
}

void CDemoApp::OnFileSave()
{
    CFileDialog fileDialog(false, _T("txt"), NULL, NULL,
OFN_OVERWRITEPROMPT,
        _T("Text files (*.txt)¦*.txt"), m_mainFrame);

    if (fileDialog.DoModal() == IDOK)
    {
        CString fullPath = fileDialog.GetPathName();
        ...
    }
}

void CDemoApp::OnStretchMode()
{
    m_stretchMode = !m_stretchMode;
}

void CDemoApp::OnUpdateStretchMode(CCmdUI* pCmdUI)
{
    pCmdUI->SetCheck(m_stretchMode);
    pCmdUI->Enable(true);
}
```

In wxWidgets, the equivalent class declaration and event table are as follows:

```
//
// wxWidgets event table
//

class CDemoApp: public wxApp
{
public:
```

```
    wxApp();

    // Overrides
    virtual bool OnInit();

// Implementation

    void OnAppAbout(wxCommandEvent& event);
    void OnFileSave(wxCommandEvent& event);
    void OnStretchMode(wxCommandEvent& event);
    void OnUpdateStretchMode(wxUpdateUIEvent& event);

// Attributes
private:
    int        m_stretchMode;
    MyFrame *m_mainFrame;

    DECLARE_EVENT_TABLE()
};

BEGIN_EVENT_TABLE(CDemoApp, wxApp)
        EVT_MENU(ID_APP_ABOUT, CDemoApp::OnAppAbout)
        EVT_MENU(CDemoApp::OnFileSave)
        EVT_MENU(CDemoApp::OnUpdateStretchMode)
        EVT_UPDATE_UI(ID_STRETCH_MODE, CDemoApp::OnUpdateStretchMode)
END_EVENT_TABLE()

void CDemoApp::OnAppAbout(wxCommandEvent& event)
{
    wxMessageBox(wxT("Demo App (c) 2005"), wxT("About Demo App"));
}

void CDemoApp::OnFileSave(wxCommandEvent& event)
{
    wxFileDialog fileDialog(m_mainFrame, wxT("Choose a file"),
        wxEmptyString, wxEmptyString, wxT("Text files (*.txt)|*.txt")),
        wxSAVE|wxOVERWRITE_PROMPT);

    if (fileDialog.DoModal() == IDOK)
    {
        wxString fullPath = fileDialog.GetPath();
        ...
    }
}

void CDemoApp::OnStretchMode(wxCommandEvent& event)
{
    m_stretchMode = !m_stretchMode;
}

void CDemoApp::OnUpdateStretchMode(wxUpdateUIEvent& event)
{
    event.Check(m_stretchMode);
    event.Enable(true);
}
```

As you can see, wxWidgets has an equivalent of MFC's user-interface updating, discussed in Chapter 9, "Creating Custom Dialogs."

Converting Dialogs and Other Resources

Resource Files

wxWidgets uses Windows RC files to include only a small number of essential resources, not for an application's dialogs and menus. Instead, wxWidgets has the XRC resource system, whose files can be written by a variety of commercial and open source dialog designers (refer to Appendix C, "Creating Applications with DialogBlocks," and Appendix E, "Third-Party Tools for wxWidgets"). You can also choose to have a designer tool generate C++ code to create the dialogs and menus.

With Windows resource files, most of an application's resources are bound with the executable (by linking the binary RES file). If you use wxWidgets' XRC files, you can load resources dynamically, or you can use the wxrc utility to convert your XRC files into a zip file, or C++ code that can be compiled into the application. However, bitmap files are not included in this process. You can consider converting small bitmaps to XPM files, which are supported on all platforms, or putting them in a zip archive with any other application files (refer to Chapter 20).

A wxWidgets application's RC file typically looks like this:

```
aaaaaa ICON "myapp.ico"

#include "wx/msw/wx.rc"
```

The only purpose of the "aaaaaa" icon is to ensure that Windows shows the correct application icon in the Explorer, desktop, or Start menu. The name reflects the fact that the alphabetically first icon is used. The icon in your Windows resources is not generally used for setting a frame icon in wxWidgets application code. Instead, an icon is provided by loading XPM images into a wxIconBundle object and associating it with the window. You may want to edit icons in a bitmap editor capable of saving PNG files with transparency information and convert these files to XPM using an application such as Anthemion Software's ImageBlocks. For creating the application icon (myapp.ico), you can paste images into an icon editor, such as *PC Magazine*'s IconEdit32.

Re-Creating the Dialogs

Faced with the task of converting many MFC dialogs, there is bad news, and there is good news. The bad news is that there is no way to fully automate the conversion. The good news is that there are tools to help make the task much easier, and the similarities between the wxWidgets API and the MFC API make conversions straightforward.

With a dialog editor (or RAD tool), you can rapidly re-create and surpass your MFC dialogs: your dialogs will be resizable, they will adapt to changes in label lengths due to translation, and they will adapt to controls of different sizes on different platforms. In addition, DialogBlocks has a resource import function that can do a first-pass conversion of RC-based dialogs into wxWidgets dialogs. Because these still use absolute positioning, it's recommended that you use the resulting dialogs only for reference and that you copy and paste the controls to a sizer-based dialog.

One possible strategy for converting your dialogs is to first re-create the dialogs visually, getting the UI appearance and resize behavior working and adding event handler "stubs." Then refer back to the MFC code and see how the existing message handlers can be adapted to the event handlers. The code will need to be changed, but in many cases, not by much.

Another strategy is to first rework your MFC code so that the user interface is separated from the functionality as far as possible. Write new classes encapsulating the desired functionality that are independent from toolkit-specific classes and invoke the new functions from the UI code, which should now be much simpler. Test that it works under MFC and then reuse the new classes inside your wxWidgets code. This method can work especially well if you have a period of transition where the MFC application must be maintained in parallel with the new wxWidgets port. Some #ifdef-ing will probably be required to deal with differences in data structure classes between the two toolkits.

Dialog Data Exchange and Validation

MFC employs a function DoDataExchange, a class CDataExchange, and DDX (dialog data exchange) functions such as DDX_Check to connect a data variable and the control. DDV (dialog data validation) functions are used to do validation. wxWidgets provides the virtual functions TransferDataToWindow and TransferDataFromWindow, but you don't normally need to implement these directly. You can use the more elegant concept embodied by the wxValidator class. To associate a variable with a control, you associate a validator with the control, for example:

```
FindWindow(ID_TEXT)->SetValidator(wxTextValidator(& m_strText));
```

Now when the TransferDataToWindow function is called (automatically from the default window initialization event handler), all controls call a function in the validator to transfer the data to the control. Similarly, when TransferDataFromWindow is called (from the default wxID_OK event handler, for example), another validator function is called to transfer the data back from the control. A similar process happens for validation (checking for valid values), which is initiated by wxWindow::Validate.

So, use validators instead of `DoDataExchange`. Most of the time, the two built-in validators, `wxTextValidator` and `wxGenericValidator`, will suffice, but for special validation and transfer needs, you can write your own `wxValidator`-derived class or implement it within overridden `TransferDataToWindow` and `TransferDataFromWindow` functions.

Documents and Views

Broadly, the MFC and wxWidgets document/view mechanisms are very similar. These are some of the key differences:

☞ **Document manager**: In wxWidgets, you need to create a `wxDocManager` object in your application initialization before you can start creating template objects. There is no equivalent in MFC.

☞ **Serialization**: In MFC, documents may be loaded and saved by implementing the `Serialize` function. In wxWidgets, you can implement `LoadObject` and `SaveObject`, which take `wxInputStream` and `wxOutputStream` arguments. Just as with MFC, you can override `OnOpenDocument` and `OnSaveDocument` with file name arguments if you want to avoid using streams.

☞ **Views**: In MFC, `CView` and its derivatives are window classes. In wxWidgets, `wxView` derives from `wxEvtHandler`, and you provide a window object separately. The view class manages the window object.

☞ **Command processing**: Each `wxDocument` can contain a `wxCommandProcessor` object, which together with the `wxCommand` class helps an application implement undo/redo. MFC has no equivalent. This facility is optional.

Please refer to Chapter 19, "Working with Documents and Views," for more information.

Printing

In MFC, printing is tied to the `CView` class, and the application overrides functions in this class such as `OnPrint`, `OnPreparePrinting`, `OnPrepareDC`, `OnBeginPrinting`, and `OnEndPrinting`. In wxWidgets, printing is separated out from the document/view framework, and you derive from the `wxPrintout` class. Objects of this class are passed to the `wxPrinter` class to initiate printing or `wxPrintPreview` to initiate previewing. Override `wxPrintout` functions such as `GetPageInfo`, `HasPage`, `OnBeginDocument`, `OnPreparePrinting`, `OnPrintPage` and so on.

`wxHtmlPrintout` is a useful predefined printout class, controlled by the `wxHtmlEasyPrinting` class. This family of classes makes it straightforward to print simple HTML documents without requiring specific printing code to be added to an application.

String Handling and Translation

Replacing CString with wxString will work for most code, but if you find that too much conversion to wxString syntax is required, you could derive a class CString from wxString and emulate some of the missing functions.

Literal strings and characters that are enclosed in the _T macro don't have to be changed, but you have the option of using the synonym wxT.

A translated MFC application will normally have a different string table for each language. wxWidgets doesn't have string tables and instead uses *message catalogs*. A message catalog provides a mapping between the strings in the application and the strings in the target language. You can either implement your own system to store and load string tables, or you can convert your code to use message catalogs. If the latter, you could put quotation marks around the identifiers and use them as indexes into the message catalogs, or you could put the strings back into the application, such that no message catalog is required for the native language. Here are examples of two ways to use message catalogs:

```
// Original MFC code to access IDS_WELCOME="Welcome!"
CString str;
str.LoadString(IDS_WELCOME);

// wxWidgets solution (1)
// "IDS_WELCOME" is replaced by a value in the message catalog
wxString str(_("IDS_WELCOME"));

// wxWidgets solution (2)
// "Welcome!" is replaced by a value in the message catalog
wxString str(_("Welcome!"));
```

Database Access

If you currently use Data Access Objects (DAO), you might consider using the Windows-only wxDao library from Koan Software, which can be downloaded from http://www.koansoftware.com/it/prd_svil_wxdownload.htm.

You can also use ODBC directly or by using wxWidgets' wxODBC classes.

Configurable Control Bars

wxWidgets doesn't natively support toolbars and menu bars that can be repositioned and undocked, but you can use the third-party wxDockIt library (refer to Appendix E, "Third-Party Tools for wxWidgets") or the unsupported Frame Layout library in contrib/src/fl in your wxWidgets distribution. Other solutions are under development, so please see the Contributions page of the wxWidgets web site for the latest information.

EQUIVALENT FUNCTIONALITY

The following tables compare MFC and wxWidgets constructs, grouped by macros and classes.

Equivalent Macros in MFC and wxWidgets

Table K-1 lists some important MFC macros and their wxWidgets equivalents.

Table K-1   MFC and wxWidgets Macros

MFC Version	wxWidgets Version
BEGIN_MESSAGE_MAP	BEGIN_EVENT_TABLE
END_MESSAGE_MAP	END_EVENT_TABLE
DECLARE_DYNAMIC	DECLARE_CLASS
DECLARE_DYNCREATE	DECLARE_DYMAMIC_CLASS
IMPLEMENT_DYNAMIC	IMPLEMENT_CLASS
IMPLEMENT_DYNCREATE	IMPLEMENT_DYNAMIC_CLASS
IsKindOf(RUNTIME_CLASS(CWindow))	IsKindOf(CLASSINFO(wxWindow))

Equivalent Classes in wxWidgets

Table K-2 lists the main MFC classes and their wxWidgets equivalents. MFC classes not present in the table have no direct equivalent.

Table K-2   MFC and wxWidgets Classes

Miscellaneous Classes	
MFC Version	**wxWidgets Version**
CWinApp	wxApp
CObject	wxObject
CCmdTarget	wxEvtHandler
CCommandLineInfo	wxCmdLineParser
CMenu	wxMenu, wMenuBar, wxMenuItem
CWaitCursor	wxBusyCursor
CDataExchange	wxValidator
Window Classes	
MFC Version	**wxWidgets Version**
CFrameWnd	wxFrame
CMDIFrameWnd	wxMDIParentFrame
CMDIChildWnd	wxMDIChildFrame
CSplitterWnd	wxSplitterWindow

(continues)

Table K-2   MFC and wxWidgets Classes (*Continued*)

Window Classes	
MFC Version	**wxWidgets Version**
CToolBar	wxToolBar
CStatusBar	wxStatusBar
CReBar	None, but see contrib/src/fl and wxDockIt (Appendix E)
CPropertyPage	wxPanel
CPropertySheet	wxNotebook, wxPropertySheetDialog
Dialog Classes	
MFC Version	**wxWidgets Version**
CDialog	wxDialog
CColorDialog	wxColourDialog
CFileDialog	wxFileDialog
CFindReplaceDialog	wxFindReplaceDialog
CFontDialog	wxFontDialog
CPageSetupDialog	wxPageSetupDialog
CPrintDialog	wxPrintDialog
Control Classes	
MFC Version	**wxWidgets Version**
CAnimateCtrl	wxMediaCtrl, wxAnimationCtrl
CButton	wxButton
CBitmapButton	wxBitmapButton
CComboBox	wxComboBox, wxChoice
CDateTimeCtrl	wxDatePickerCtrl
CEdit	wxTextCtrl
CHotKeyCtrl	None, but see Keybinder (Appendix E)
CListBox, CDragListBox	wxListBox
CCheckListBox	wxCheckListBox
CListCtrl	wxListCtrl, wxListView
CMonthCalCtrl	wxCalendarCtrl
CProgressCtrl	wxGauge
CReBarCtrl	None, but see contrib/src/fl and wxDockIt (Appendix E)
CRichEditCtrl	wxTextCtrl has limited rich edit functionality
CScrollBar	wxScrollBar
CSliderCtrl	wxSlider
CSpinButtonCtrl	wxSpinButton, wxSpinCtrl
CStatic	wxStaticText, wxStaticLine, wxStaticBox, wxStaticBitmap

CStatusBarCtrl	wxStatusBar
CTabCtrl	wxTabCtrl (some platforms only; use wxNotebook instead)
CToolBarCtrl	wxToolBar
CToolTipCtrl	wxToolTip
CTreeCtrl	wxTreeCtrl

Graphics Classes

MFC Version	wxWidgets Version
CBitmap	wxBitmap, wxImage, wxIcon, wxCursor
CBrush	wxBrush
CPen	wxPen
CFont	wxFont
CImageList	wxImageList, wxIconBundle
CPalette	wxPalette
CRgn	wxRegion
CClientDC	wxClientDC
CMetaFileDC	wxMetaFileDC (Windows and Mac OS X only)
CPaintDC	wxPaintDC
CWindowDC	wxWindowDC
CDC	wxMemoryDC

Data Structure Classes

MFC Version	wxWidgets Version
CArray, CObArray, CPtrArray	wxArray
CStringArray	wxArrayString
CDWordArray, CByteArray, CUIntArray	wxArrayInt
CList, CPtrList, CObList	wxList
CStringList	wxArrayString, wxStringList
CMap... classes	wxHashMap
CString	wxString
CPoint	wxPoint
CRect	wxRect
CSize	wxSize
CTime	wxDateTime
CTimeSpan	wxTimeSpan, wxDateSpan
COleVariant	wxVariant

(continues)

Table K-2   MFC and wxWidgets Classes (*Continued*)

Internet Classes	
MFC Version	**wxWidgets Version**
CSocket	wxSocket
CFtpConnection	wxFTP
CHttpConnection	wxHTTP
Document/View Classes	
MFC Version	**wxWidgets Version**
CDocument	wxDocument
CView	wxView
CDocTemplate, CSingleDocTemplate, CMultiDocTemplate	wxDocTemplate
Drag and Drop	
MFC Version	**wxWidgets Version**
COleDataSource	wxDataObject
COleDropSource	wxDropSource
COleDropTarget	wxDropTarget
File Classes	
MFC Version	**wxWidgets Version**
CFile	wxFile, wxFFile, wxTextFile
CMemFile	wxMemoryInputStream, wxMemoryOutputStream
CSocketFile	wxSocketInputStream, wxSocketOutputStream
CRecentFileList	wxFileHistory
Multithreading Classes	
MFC Version	**wxWidgets Version**
CWinThread	wxThread
CCriticalSection	wxCriticalSection
CMutex	wxMutex
CSemaphore	wxSemaphore

The following classes have no equivalent in wxWidgets: CDialogBar, all classes prefixed COle, all C...View classes, all C...Exception classes, CHeaderCtrl, and CIPAddressCtrl.

FURTHER INFORMATION

A useful article on this subject is *Porting MFC Applications to Linux*, by Markus Neifer, found at `http://www-106.ibm.com/developerworks/library/l-mfc/?n-l-4182`.

This includes full source code for a wxWidgets document/view sample application, together with the original MFC application.

accelerator A key combination, such as Control-S, that allows selection of menu items, buttons, and other controls using the keyboard.

accessibility An accessible application is one that can be used by people with impaired vision or other disabilities.

ANSI An acronym for American National Standards Institute, an organization that defined a standard character set. wxWidgets distinguishes between compilation in ANSI and Unicode mode. In ANSI mode, character encodings must be used to switch between languages, but this is not necessary with Unicode. In this context, ANSI and ASCII are interchangeable, as the differences are slight.

alpha channel Extra information in a bitmap that can be used to draw the bitmap with translucency. Each pixel in the bitmap has an 8-bit alpha value indicating the pixel's intensity.

API Application Programming Interface, the published set of classes and functions that a library offers to an application.

assertion A test supplied in debug mode that causes an error message to be shown if the test fails.

bakefile A makefile generation system used within wxWidgets that can also be used for other libraries and applications.

bit-list An integer containing flags that are combined with the binary OR operator ("|")—for example, wxSUNKEN_BORDER¦wxTAB_TRAVERSAL. The presence of a flag can be tested by using the binary AND operator ("&").

block Describes the suspension of a function's execution while waiting for something, such as for a modal dialog to be dismissed or data to become available on a socket.

bundle A Mac OS X application is packaged in a bundle, which has a specific directory structure and is described by an XML file.

Carbon The Apple API supplied for compatibility with both Mac OS 9 and Mac OS X, used by the wxMac port to implement GUI functionality.

client area   The area in which an application can draw or place child windows. For example, the client area of a frame with a menu bar is the portion below the menu bar.

client data   Arbitrary user data that can be associated with a window or its items. In some cases, it is deleted automatically by the window, and in others cases, it is the application's responsibility.

Cocoa   Mac OS X's native API for GUI functionality, used by the wxCocoa port.

control   A window that displays a value that can usually be changed by the user. It is also known as a "widget". There is no absolute distinction between a control and a window, but you might use "control" to distinguish between a control on a dialog, such as a button or list box, and a window that manages other windows, such as a splitter window.

character encoding   A specification that maps raw values to actual characters. Because ASCII cannot encompass all languages, there are many encodings for different languages. Using Unicode eliminates the need for separate encodings because it allows multiple bytes per character.

cross-platform programming   Programming for more than one platform.

default   The value or behavior that is assumed to be present if no other specification has been made.

device context   An object on which an application can draw. For example, a wxClientDC object can be used to draw on a window.

dialog   A window that is shown to convey information or present choices.

double-buffering   A flicker-reduction technique whereby graphics are drawn offscreen on a bitmap before being transferred to a window.

dynamic event handler   A handler that has been installed during the running of the program, rather than by "static" event table entries that are built into the program at compile time.

cache   A data structure used to speed up an operation by storing results from previous operations.

embedded system   Refers to a small or industrial device, in contrast with a desktop system—for example, a mobile phone, PDA, or wireless terminal. wxWidgets supports embedded systems via wxWinCE, wxGTK, wxMGL, and wxX11.

event   In wxWidgets, an action taken by the user (such as a button press), the operating system (such as a color change event), or the framework (such as a dialog initialization event).

event loop   Code that waits for events and dispatches them to suitable event handlers that can handle them. There is a "main" event loop, and showing a modal dialog causes a further event loop to be entered until the dialog is dismissed.

event table   A mapping that tells wxWidgets how to route events to handler functions by specifying an event type and identifier that should match.

focus   The window that has the focus can accept keyboard input.

frame   A "top-level" window used to contain other windows, menu bars, toolbars, and so on.

framework   A set of classes for handling a set of related problems, providing default functionality that can be replaced. wxWidgets is a *GUI* framework.

generic   Used to describe classes that are implemented by wxWidgets itself, where there is no "native" equivalent.

GTK+   The widget set used by applications that are designed for the GNOME desktop environment, which is popular on Linux.

GUI   Graphical User Interface, a term applied to programs and operating systems that support a windowing environment and pointing device.

IDE   Integrated Development Environment, a tool that handles many aspects of the development process, such as editing, compiling, and debugging.

identifier   An integer used for identifying windows and other objects and mapping commands to event handler functions. wxWidgets provides standard identifiers such as `wxID_OK`.

idle event   An event sent to each window of an application after normal events have all been processed to allow low-priority tasks to be performed.

image   Any bitmap (pixel-based) graphic; image classes in wxWidgets include `wxImage`, `wxBitmap`, `wxCursor`, and `wxIcon`.

internationalization   The process of converting an application to display and handle information in more than one language. Also known informally as "i18n" ("i" followed by 18 characters, followed by "n").

locale   The representation of a geopolitical location that has potentially distinct properties for date and currency formats, character sets, and so on. This is represented in wxWidgets by `wxLocale`.

makefile   A file that defines how a set of source files is used to create an executable, processed by a program called "make." Some development tools (such as DialogBlocks) generate and invoke makefiles.

manifest   Under Windows, refers to an XML file that must accompany an executable (or be compiled into its resources) for the application to take advantage of XP themes.

mask   A monochrome (1-bit) bitmap that specifies the visible parts of another bitmap. A bitmap may have a mask, an alpha channel, or neither.

MDI   Multiple Document Interface, from the Windows user interface style where the main window fully contains any document windows.

MFC   Microsoft Foundation Classes, a framework for building Windows applications.

MGL   A low-level 2D graphics API by SciTech Software Inc. for Linux, DOS, and embedded systems, supported by the wxMGL port.

mnemonic   An assigned character in a user interface element such as a button that gives a keyboard equivalent to mouse input.

modifier key   A key, such as Control or Shift, that generally needs another key to be pressed to generate input.

modal   A modal dialog "blocks" program flow when shown, disabling other windows, and therefore puts the application in a particular mode. A modeless dialog does not usually interrupt program flow or disable other windows.

monolithic   wxWidgets can be compiled as one large library ("monolithic") or as a collection of separate libraries ("multilib").

Motif   A widget set layered on top of X11 and supported by wxWidgets.

multi-platform application   An application that can be compiled to run on several platforms without significant changes to the source code.

multilib   Used to distinguish between a build of wxWidgets that splits it into several libraries, compared with a "monolithic" build, where there is only one wxWidgets library file.

native   A widget is said to be "native" if it uses an implementation supplied by the vendor of the underlying toolkit or operating system. Examples include wxButton on Windows, GTK+, and Mac OS X.

OpenGL   A popular 3D graphics language available on most platforms, supported in wxWidgets through the wxGLCanvas class.

platform   Denotes a particular combination of hardware, operating system, windowing environment, and underlying widget set. For example, GTK+ on i386 Linux, Motif on i386 Linux, Windows, and Mac OS X represent distinct platforms. Depending on context, platform may also refer only to a distinct operating system or a family of operating systems, such as "the Microsoft Windows Mobile platform."

port   An implementation of the wxWidgets API for a particular operating system and widget set. For example, the Windows port is wxMSW, and the GTK+ port is wxGTK.

PNG   Portable Network Graphics, a popular file format for images, invented to replace the GIF format.

propagating event   An event that can be handled by an ancestor of the object that generated the event; for example, if a button is on a panel in a frame, the button click event may be handled by the button itself, the panel, or the frame containing the panel.

quantization   The process of reducing the number of unique colors in an image without severely degrading it.

RAD   Rapid Application Development, used to describe tools such as DialogBlocks and wxDesigner that boost productivity.

reentrant   Code that is executed recursively (entered multiple times), possibly with harmful consequences.

resource   An overloaded term that means different things in different contexts. A wxWidgets resource is generally an element in an XRC resource file. A bitmap resource may refer to binary data added to a Windows application's executable by the Windows resource compiler, or it may refer simply to extra files required by an application.

resource handler   A class whose instance is plugged into the wxWidgets resource system in order to interpret values specified in an XRC file and apply them to a new resource.

RGB   The Red, Green, and Blue values that form a color specification.

RTTI   Run-time type information, whereby a class is annotated so that applications can query aspects of the class, such as its name and base class.

static control   A control that is for display only and that does not support user input.

sizer   A container for laying out windows or further sizers in a hierarchy.

stock   Refers to an object or identifier that is provided by wxWidgets or by the underlying toolkit, for convenience or to promote standardization. Stock cursors, stock colors, and stock buttons are examples of this usage.

stream   An instance of a class that handles sequential input or output for a particular data source. It is a higher-level construct than the file, being applicable to arbitrary data sources, and wxWidgets defines its own set of stream classes.

theme   Some desktop environments let the user select a different look and feel, varying the way windows are drawn, colors used, and so on. wxWidgets will use the current theme for its widgets where possible.

transparency   Usually refers to the 1-bit "mask" that can be associated with bitmaps to determine which parts of the image should be visible, in contrast with an alpha channel, which enables "translucency" (the blending of an image with the graphic underneath).

transient window   A window that shows for a short time and normally has very little decoration. Examples are menus and tooltips.

UI update event   A user interface event generated by wxWidgets in idle time to give the application a chance to update the state of a window.

Unicode   A specification that eliminates the need for separate encodings by allowing multiple byes per character.

universal widget set   A term used to describe the widget set (wxUniversal) that wxWidgets uses where there are no "native" widgets. Used in wxX11 and wxMGL.

validator   An object that can be associated with a window that checks whether the user has entered valid data. It can also transfer data to and from the window, for example at dialog initialization and when a dialog is dismissed, respectively.

virtual file system   A set of classes that enables data sources other than ordinary files to be used. This facility in wxWidgets allows data to be streamed from files within compressed archives, for example.

widget   A window with specific display and input functionality, such as a `wxButton`.

widget set   A widget set consists of the widgets (or "controls") that wxWidgets uses to implement its API. Examples are Win32, GTK+, Motif, and wxUniversal (a set of widgets implemented using wxWidgets itself).

Win32   The API for writing GUI applications on Windows, supported by the wxMSW port.

window decorations   The buttons, border, caption bar, and other elements of a top-level window, normally drawn by the window manager.

window manager   The part of the desktop environment that provides decoration for and behavior of top-level application windows. Under X11, the desktop environment such as GNOME or KDE provides window management. Under Windows and Mac OS X, there is no choice of window manager: this function is performed by the operating system.

Windows   The family of operating systems from Microsoft. The use of "Windows" in this book usually denotes the desktop variants, including Windows 2000 and Windows XP.

Windows CE   The family of embedded operating systems from Microsoft, also known as Windows Mobile. It includes the variations Pocket PC, Smartphone, Portable Media Center, and Windows CE .NET.

wxBase   A build of the wxWidgets library with no GUI functionality that can be used to build command-line applications.

X11   The windowing system, and its communication protocol, used on most Unix systems.

XPM   X11 Pixmap, a file format for small images that can be included in C++ source files.

Symbols

3D graphics, wxGLCanvas, 168-169

A

accelerators, 180-181
accessibility, 591
accessing screens with wxScreenDC, 139
accessors, wxDateTime, 388
Acme, 534
adapting dialogs for small devices, 254-255
ADC (Apple Developer Connection), 544
add-on libraries, 596-599
AddFile, 411
adding
    help, creating custom dialogs, 251-253
    icons
        to GNOME desktop, 534
        to KDE desktop, 534
    source and includes, Bakefile, 568-569
addition, 390
AddRoot, 321
aesthetics, designing dialogs, 257
alignment, sizers, 191
alternatives
    to dialogs, 257
    to wxNotebook, 76
    to wxSocket, 479
    to wxSplitterWindow, 85
Anthemion Software, DialogBlocks.
    See **DialogBlocks**
AOL Communicator, 601

Apple Developer Connection (ADC), 544
application class, 16-17
application objects
    creating with DialogBlocks, 584
    initializing, 415
application paths, finding, 524-525
application resources, storing
    finding application paths, 524-525
    reducing data files, 523
    standard locations, 524
application settings
    editing, 531-532
    storing, 529-530
application termination behavior, UI design guidelines, 539
applications
    associating with icons, 274-275
    cleaning up, 416
    creating
        with Bakefile. See Bakefile
        with KDevelop, 562-563
        with Makefiles, 564
        with Microsoft Visual Studio. See
            Microsoft Visual Studio
        with Xcode, 563
    debugging with DialogBlocks, 584
    Doodle. *See* Doodle
    installing. *See* installing
    running wxExecute, 525
arbitrary areas, filling, 159
architecture of wxWidgets, 8
    internal organization, 12-13
    wxCocoa, 10
    wxGTK, 8
    wxMac, 10

S

THIS BOOK IS SAFARI ENABLED

INCLUDES FREE 45-DAY ACCESS TO THE ONLINE EDITION

The Safari® Enabled icon on the cover of your favorite technology book means the book is available through Safari Bookshelf. When you buy this book, you get free access to the online edition for 45 days.

Safari Bookshelf is an electronic reference library that lets you easily search thousands of technical books, find code samples, download chapters, and access technical information whenever and wherever you need it.

TO GAIN 45-DAY SAFARI ENABLED ACCESS TO THIS BOOK:

- Go to **http://www.phptr.com/safarienabled**

- Complete the brief registration form

- Enter the coupon code found in the front of this book on the "Copyright" page

If you have difficulty registering on Safari Bookshelf or accessing the online edition, please e-mail customer-service@safaribooksonline.com.

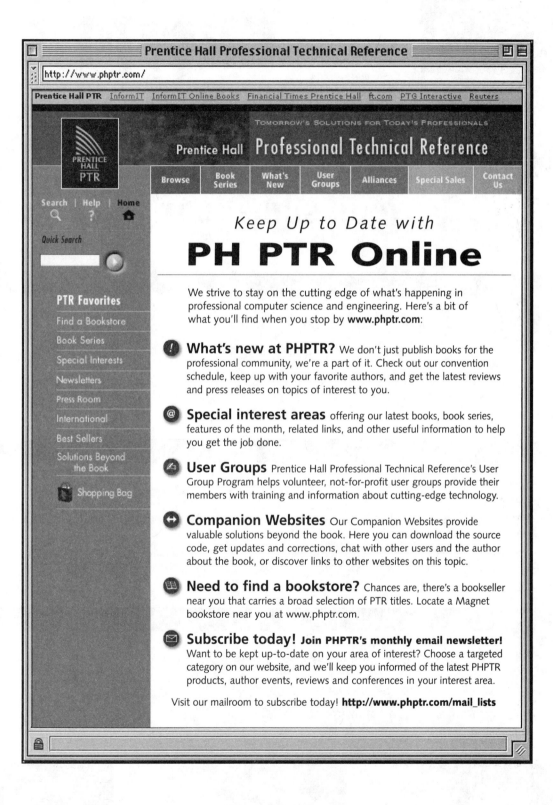